MULTIVARIATE TECHNIQUES IN HUMAN COMMUNICATION RESEARCH

HUMAN COMMUNICATION RESEARCH SERIES

PETER R. MONGE, Editor

Monge and Cappella:
MULTIVARIATE TECHNIQUES IN
HUMAN COMMUNICATION RESEARCH 1980

Cushman and McPhee:
MESSAGE-ATTITUDE-BEHAVIOR
RELATIONSHIP 1980

Woelfel and Fink:
MEASUREMENT OF COMMUNICATION
PROCESSES 1980

MULTIVARIATE TECHNIQUES IN HUMAN COMMUNICATION RESEARCH

Edited by
Peter R. Monge
Department of Communication
Michigan State University
East Lansing, Michigan

Joseph N. Cappella
Department of Communication Arts
University of Wisconsin
Madison, Wisconsin

 1980

ACADEMIC PRESS

A Subsidiary of Harcourt Brace Jovanovich, Publishers
New York   London   Toronto   Sydney   San Francisco

ACADEMIC PRESS, INC.
111 Fifth Avenue, New York, New York 10003

United Kingdom Edition published by
ACADEMIC PRESS, INC. (LONDON) LTD.
24/28 Oval Road, London NW1 7DX

Library of Congress Cataloging in Publication Data
Main entry under title:

Multivariate techniques in human communication research.

Includes index.
1. Communication——Statistical methods.
2. Communications research. I. Monge, Peter R.
II. Cappella, Joseph N.
P93.7.M84   001.51'07'2   79–28430
ISBN 0–12–504450–X

PRINTED IN THE UNITED STATES OF AMERICA

80 81 82 83   9 8 7 6 5 4 3 2 1

To those scientists who are seeking to understand and explain
the intricate processes of human communication

CONTENTS

LIST OF CONTRIBUTORS

Numbers in parentheses indicate the pages on which the authors' contributions begin.

Arthur P. Bochner (143), Department of Speech, Temple University, Philadelphia, Pennsylvania 19122

Joseph N. Cappella (1, 57), Department of Communication Arts, University of Wisconsin, Madison, Wisconsin 53706

Lawrence J. Chase (205), Communication Studies Department, California State University, Sacramento, California 95819

Jeffrey E. Danes (333), Department of Business Administration, Virginia Polytechnic Institute and State University, Blacksburg, Virginia 24061

Dennis K. Davis (429), Department of Communication, Cleveland State University, Cleveland, Ohio 44115

Richard V. Farace (365), Department of Communication, Michigan State University, East Lansing, Michigan 48824

Edward L. Fink (111), Department of Communication, Michigan State University, East Lansing, Michigan 48824

Mary Anne Fitzpatrick (143), Department of Communication Arts, University of Wisconsin, Madison, Wisconsin 53706

Dean Hewes (393), Department of Communication Arts, University of Wisconsin, Madison, Wisconsin 53706

Kook Ching Huber (529), Client Services Department, Information Sciences Division, Blue Cross and Blue Shield of Indiana, Indianapolis, Indiana

John E. Hunter (229), Department of Psychology, Michigan State University, East Lansing, Michigan 48824

Klaus Krippendorff (259), The Annenberg School of Communications, University of Pennsylvania, Philadelphia, Pennsylvania 19174

Jae-Won Lee (429), Department of Communication, Cleveland State University, Cleveland, Ohio 44115

Timothy Mabee* (365), Department of Communication, Michigan State University, East Lansing, Michigan 48824

Margaret L. McLaughlin (175), Division of Speech Communication, Texas Tech University, Lubbock, Texas

*Present Address: Office of Institutional Research, Michigan State University, East Lansing, Michigan.

Peter R. Monge (1, 13), Department of Communication, Michigan State University, East Lansing, Michigan 48824

Robert W. Norton (309), Department of Communication, Purdue University, West Lafayette, Indiana

William D. Richards, Jr. (455), Department of Communication, Simon Fraser University, Burnaby, V5A 1S6 British Columbia, Canada

Raymond K. Tucker (205), School of Speech Communication, Bowling Green State University, Bowling Green, Ohio 43403

John W. Tukey (489), Department of Statistics, Princeton University, Princeton, New Jersey 08540 and Bell Laboratories, Princeton, New Jersey, Murray Hill, New Jersey

Joseph Woelfel (333), Department of Rhetoric and Communication, State University of New York at Albany, Albany, New York

FOREWORD

If there was one overriding quality that emerged in the Conference on Multivariate Analysis in Communication Research, which led to this book, it was that discussions progressively took on a practical quality. Whereas proponents of research strategies often pursue them with near religious zeal, the papers in this volume reflect the leveling effect of the didactic interchanges with the brilliant John Tukey, the many pragmatic questions of application raised by the observers, and perhaps most of all the often delightful exchanges among the participants, ranging from substantive arguments over a particular analysis to tweaking at one another's technical parochialism.

Another quality of this volume is that it is certainly a benchmark in the progress of serious research into human communication. Conceptualizations of human communication have evolved a great distance from simple message $\rightarrow$ effect models loosely based on stimulus–response psychology or the Shannon diagram of an electronic communication system which sired so many source–message–effect models over the years. Today's views of human communication are distinctly multivariate. Conceptualizations often attempt to account simultaneously for interactions of encoder and decoder characteristics, message phenomena, coorientations, and the like. The bias is away from often studying only usage of a single communications medium, and is now on the communication user as a dynamic information seeker and processor. Such a multivariate view has both raised the need for and no doubt prompted the rapid increase of the use of multivariate statistics in our human communications field.

Slightly over a decade ago when I was preparing my little volume, *Reasoning with Statistics* (designed primarily for the person with absolutely no background in statistics but who needed an orientation sufficient to read journal articles), I included only those techniques that were particularly prevalent in the journal literature. Except for the emergence of semantic differential studies in those years, the appearance of multivariate techniques in journals was relatively rare. In a recent publisher's survey of adopters, conducted to facilitate my revision of this text, some 48 of 52 questionnaires contained suggestions for the inclusion of multivariate techniques! There is no doubt that the communication researcher of today and the near tomorrow will have to have a practical understanding of such techniques not only to pursue research but even to be sufficiently literate to comprehend journal literature. The present volume and others like it must certainly occupy a key place in our contemporary curriculum in communications research.

Somewhat fortuitously, but probably also causally, the rise of the electronic computer has certainly contributed to the feasibility of undertaking multi-variate statistical analyses. To those of us whose statistical training dates back to Pearson correlation worksheets or one week take-home problems in a centroid analysis, the analytic power, speed, and economy of the modern computer is almost dazzling. There is a simple but most utilitarian dividend in the inextricable relation between the computer and the multivariate tech-niques in the sense that any researcher with sufficient savvy to adapt the software for multivariate analysis has, in a very literal sense, an operational definition at hand. There is a negative side, however, since this ready availability of inexpensive and powerful software prompts users to sometimes become technique rather than problem oriented.

In reflecting upon this problem a number of the more practical of us at the conference argued for the primacy of a problem orientation in dealing with multivariate techniques lest the stress in evaluating such techniques become overly focused on the elegancies of statistical architecture rather than on research application. Is there a danger that quantitative strategies become themselves more complex than the phenomena that we are trying to under-stand?

Along this utilitarian line, an informal discussion topic among the ob-servers at this conference, and one not found frequently on the pages of this volume, was the distinction between employing multivariate techniques in a tightly reasoned hypothesis testing strategy as against their application in data reduction, or a more or less "sorting out" function. As might be expected, there were more discussions of hazards than of benefits. Probably most interesting were discussions about the use of factor analysis, where extremes ranged among comments such as "testing a Piper Cub hypothesis in a rotated 747 matrix," "whether varimax rotation is better than reading tea leaves," and the popular "garbage in–garbage out" observation.

Another vein of practical discussion was the considerable utility of multi-variate analysis techniques as applied to data from field studies. Adding to the trend of multivariate approaches to the study of communication has no doubt been the renewed interest in the field study or the quasi-experimental design conducted in the field. Such studies have always lagged behind their laboratory counterparts because of the low level of generalization possible from simple cross-tabulation analyses, or those two-by-two tables which I chide my Michigan State colleagues as having made nearly immortal. Multi-variate techniques have given us powerful and efficient means for combining variables in field study data so as to characterize and eventually to test much more scientifically interesting generalizations than heretofore obtained. The practical reader of this volume will probably sense more application of the techniques discussed here to studies in the field as against those in the laboratory.

There is one final somewhat intangible quality to the conference which may or may not be evident to a reader of this volume, but which may be evident in the next decade of communication research. The study of communication in and of itself is still a fledgling field. So often when communication researchers assemble, some energy is given off toward that on-going discussion of what we think we are about. In this conference, however, "dues paying" discussions of mutual assurance that we do have a field were almost nonexistent. The participants, to a person, were intent on thorough and vigorous interaction on the strengths and weaknesses of early drafts of the papers which appear in this volume. The results were three days of sharpening, leveling, and an intellectual momentum that may serve the field for years to come.

The Annenberg School of Communications   FREDERICK WILLIAMS
University of Southern California

PREFACE

The number and sophistication of statistical techniques that are currently being used by social scientists for the analysis of data have increased rapidly in recent years. Along with other social scientists, communication researchers are finding that these analytic techniques are very useful for generating scientific knowledge about the processes of human communication; they provide greater flexibility and variety in the data that can be examined, and give greater depth and breadth to the knowledge claims that can be made.

Like other technological developments, however, greater power often carries greater risk. Consequently, it is essential that anyone who employs multivariate techniques for data analysis does so with a clear understanding of the procedures and with reasonable insight as to their proper use. The purposes of this book, then, are (1) to present the family of analytic techniques loosely labeled multivariate statistics, (2) to demonstrate the range of its applicability to the problems encountered by researchers in the area of human communication, and (3) to focus attention on the limitations associated with its use.

Although the number of textbooks available on multivariate statistics is not large, there are several, some of which are excellent. (The latter are included in our bibliography.) It is not our intent to duplicate the material already available in those works. Anyone who has seriously studied multivariate statistics probably has already adopted a "favorite textbook," or more likely, has learned to shift from one book to another as various problems in particular topics are explored. Instead, we provide an introduction to the basic ideas of multivariate analysis, explore the wide variety of topics included under this rubric, and finally demonstrate and extensively illustrate both the applications and limitations of multivariate techniques in communication research.

The book had a rather idyllic beginning. In early April 1977 the authors, after agreeing nearly a year earlier to prepare papers for a conference on multivariate analysis, convened for four days at the Asilomar Conference Grounds located amid the pines, sand, and surf of the Monterey, California coastline. Each day, three or four authors presented their papers and engaged in extensive discussion with the entire assembled group. Also during each day, authors whose papers covered related topics met in smaller groups to discuss and criticize each other's work. Throughout the session, Professor John Tukey, the guest critic for the conference, offered extensive commentary, suggestions for revision, and constructive criticism. His formal address to the conferees focused on critical issues and opportunities in multivariate analysis. In the final sessions of the conference, the authors openly discussed the modifications required in each paper to give it consistency and continuity with the other book chapters. With comments from the editors, Professor Tukey, and the other authors, the conferees returned to their campuses to prepare final chapter versions. This volume is the end product of that process.

In preparing the book, it was necessary to make a number of decisions regarding the book's primary audience. Foremost, we wanted the book to be useful to graduate students preparing for careers in research, and it is to them that the book is primarily tailored. We also assumed that the reader would be knowledgeable in matrix algebra, or if not, sufficiently motivated to remedy the deficiency. The literature on multivariate analysis is so heavily dependent upon matrix algebra that it is the sine qua non for competent use of the various techniques. For those who wish a companion volume which presents a comprehensive treatment of the necessary mathematical tools for multivariate analysis (including matrix algebra), the recent work by Green and Carroll (1976) is highly recommended.

Some chapters are more mathematical than others. The reader should not assume however that those chapters that contain more abstract formulations represent more difficult topics. Virtually all the topics could be handled on greater or lesser levels of mathematical abstraction. The authors attempted to keep the level of abstraction to a minimum, but one author's minimum varies considerably from another's.

Since practical experience in analyzing data with a particular multivariate technique is probably the best way to learn it, and since most multivariate analysis depends heavily on computerized analysis routines, a chapter has been included that reviews currently available computer programs. It is hoped that this will enable the reader to identify those computer programs which are appropriate to the analysis of interest and to make wise selections among software alternatives when they are available.

Throughout the book the authors and the editors attempted to compose each chapter so that it would mesh well with the others in the volume and could also be studied as a self-contained treatment of the topic. This will, it is hoped, enable the volume to be used both as a reference to specific topics as well as a textbook which reviews the major multivariate topics. Throughout the text, the examples and illustrations come from the area of communication research.

The reader will not become an expert in multivariate analysis from the study of this work; to gain expertise is a lifelong process to which the study of this volume can only make a partial contribution. To achieve its fullest potential, the book should be used in conjunction with reference to the rapidly expanding journal literature and to other works on multivariate methods. The review of multivariate textbooks by Monge and Day (1976) may help the reader select alternative treatments for any given topic.

PETER R. MONGE
JOSEPH N. CAPPELLA

REFERENCES

Green, P. E., & Carroll, J. D. *Mathematical tools for applied multivariate analysis*. New York: Academic Press, 1976.
Monge, P. R., & Day, P. D. Multivariate analysis in communication research. *Human Communication Research*, 1976, **2**, 207–220.

ACKNOWLEDGMENTS

The completion of a major, intricate task such as preparing the present volume requires the efforts of many people. Not often enough in life does one have the pleasure of acknowledging publicly the contributions made by others. In the present case, we are delighted to be able to indicate the people and institutions that contributed to the final manuscript.

Initially, the most important assistance came from the institutions that provided funds and resources for the Conference on Multivariate Analysis in Communication Research held at Asilomar. These institutions are the National Aeronautics and Space Administration's Ames Research Center, The Office of Naval Research, through a contract with the Smithsonian Institution, and San Jose State University. Without their support, the conference would not have convened. We also wish to express our appreciation to the members of these organizations who provided us with many and varied kinds of assistance in organizing the project. These are C. A. Syvertson and Cynthia Smith of Ames Research Center, Drs. John Nagey and Gene Gloye of ONR, and Drs. James Sawrey and Gerald Wheeler, Deans of the School of Social Science at San Jose State University.

We wish also to express our appreciation to several people who directly contributed to the preparation of the book. The Department of Speech-Communication at SJSU and its chair, Dr. Marie Carr, provided time for Professor Monge's editorial work on the manuscripts. Dr. Bradley S. Greenberg, chair of the Department of Communication at Michigan State University, also provided time during Professor Monge's visiting faculty appointment to complete the editing of the manuscripts.

Also, our thanks go to the people who handled so many of the detailed tasks associated with completion of the final manuscript; to Jennifer Shelby of Michigan State University and Robert Smart of San Jose State University for their assistance in coordination of several aspects of the project; to Jane A. Edwards, University of California, Berkeley, for proofreading many of the initial manuscripts; to Kathryn Green, San Jose State University, for initial typing of many of the manuscripts; to the many unnamed secretaries in the institutions of contributing authors who typed individual manuscripts; to Janet Hoel and the marvelous secretarial staff of the Department of

Communication, Michigan State University, for converting revised manuscripts with illegible scrawl into clean, readable final copy; and finally, to Eric Eisenberg, Michigan State University, for compiling a detailed and functional index.

We wish particularly to acknowledge the willingness of Academic Press to venture into publishing graduate-level material in the relatively young and emerging scientific discipline of human communication. We applaud their foresight and appreciate their continued support.

Finally, all of the contributors to this book wish to join the editors in expressing our deepest appreciation to Professor John Tukey, Department of Statistics, Princeton University, whose intellectual guidance and editorial assistance were invaluable to the success and completion of this book. If new insights are presented, it is partly in response to his ability to challenge accepted notions and propose unique alternatives. If old procedures are presented more sharply, it is in part due to his skill at honing. And if errors remain, it is not due to want of a heroic effort on his part to excise them.

Chapter 1

INTRODUCTION

PETER R. MONGE
Department of Communication
Michigan State University
East Lansing, Michigan

JOSEPH N. CAPPELLA
Department of Communication Arts
University of Wisconsin
Madison, Wisconsin

I. INTRODUCTION

Several years ago Cattell (1966) began one of the earliest books on multivariate data analysis with the rather remarkable assertion "that the most revolutionary transitions in sciences have usually occurred through methodological innovation rather than grand and bookish theories. A new direction and power is given by devices . . . by the light of which all can see emerging new theories [p. viii]." While the history of science certainly contains counterexamples to this position, it seems sufficiently accurate to warrant repeating at the outset of a new book on multivariate data analysis.

Cattell and his colleagues founded the Society for Multivariate Experimental Psychology partly in the hope that the widespread adoption of multivariate statistical techniques would materially assist the development of theory and research in the social and behavioral sciences. Since the diffusion of multivariate techniques has not been completed, it is not yet possible to test Cattell's assertion. In fact, even casual acquaintance with the prominent periodicals in the social sciences shows that the primary methodologies employed by practicing researchers are typically univariate, involving either a single criterion variable and one or more predictors, or worse, several criterion variables treated as if there were several separate instances of a single

MULTIVARIATE TECHNIQUES
IN HUMAN COMMUNICATION RESEARCH

criterion. It is only recently that multivariate techniques have begun to be widely employed in published research. The present volume seeks to further the diffusion and adoption of multivariate techniques in the social and behavioral sciences in general, and in the emerging area of communication research in particular. The techniques are presented primarily because they are better designed to evaluate the theories and answer the research questions which are currently being proposed in communication research. If, additionally, as Cattell asserts, the techniques enable us to pose new questions, develop new theories, and generate new substantive knowledge, all the more has been gained.

II. WHY MULTIVARIATE ANALYSIS?

By multivariate data analysis one typically means the application of descriptive and inferential statistical procedures to data arrays consisting of multiple elementary responses across several observational units. These multiple elementary responses may be parallel items on a test, observed types of behaviors in a group, multiple dependent variables of an experiment, or in general any set of responses from the observational units where the set is greater than or equal to two. The requirement that the number of elementary responses be greater than or equal to two immediately restricts the class of multivariate analysis techniques to situations where at least two responses (or two criterion variables or two dependent variables) per observation unit are available. Consequently, we consider regression with a large number of predictors but only one criterion variable to be a univariate rather than a multivariate technique; similarly for an N-factor analysis of variance with one response per observation unit (i.e., one dependent variable). The final data display may consist of a large number of predictor or manipulated variables but if there is only a single elementary response obtained from each observation unit, the data are considered univariate and appropriate objects for the more well-known univariate statistical procedures such as multiple regression and analysis of variance. Univariate procedures are not discussed in the subsequent chapters except as special cases.

Our definition makes it difficult to deny that multivariate data abound in research and theory. Even the early commentators, who like Berlo (1960) asserted that communication be studied as a process, invariably insisted that communication phenomena could not be understood unless the complex dependencies and interdependencies among variables could be unraveled. The influence which Berlo's view has had on more recent inquiries has been traced in Cappella (1977). The pervasive effect of Berlo's assumptions places at the heart of most approaches to communication an orientation toward multiple variable dependencies and, therefore, a demand for methodologies to unravel them. Simply put, the process conception of communication requires data on a multiplicity of interdependent variables and the tools to unearth the structure of their interrelation.

On a more concrete level, there are several reasons that justify the widespread adoption and use of multivariate techniques by communication researchers. First, current communication research questions and research practices produce multiple response data which in turn demand methods appropriate to their analysis. For example, as researchers attempt to review and summarize research in a substantive area (e.g., Siebold, 1975), seldom do they examine the relationship between a single predictor and a single criterion. Rather, these important literature reviews frequently produce *sets* of predictors *and sets* of criterion measures, which are further proposed to be conceptually related to other criterion measures, which in turn are often related among themselves. Most social scientists have long abandoned the single predictor–single criterion relationship (and even the multiple predictor–single criterion relationship) in their conceptualizations of social and behavioral processes; it is also time that they abandoned such univariate analytical techniques in the testing of their conceptualizations. As the theorems of Fisher and Ando (1971) show, if one arbitrarily breaks apart a system of variables for a study of the parts separately, one risks drawing invalid conclusions on the short term behavior and possibly the long term behavior of the system.

Second, another research practice which produces multiple response data is the use of multiple operationalizations of some variable of interest. This practice is, of course, standard in test construction and development but may also be prompted by theoretical considerations (as for example in obtaining affective, connotative, and behavioral measures of attitude) or by "open-textured" concepts requiring several operationalizations in exploratory work. Whatever the motivation behind obtaining multiple responses, their multiplicity raises questions about whether combinations should be taken, and, if so, how and what would constitute a consistent or inconsistent pattern across the multiple responses. Certain multivariate techniques take direct aim at these questions.

The presence of multiple response data raises a third reason for adding multivariate analysis procedures to one's statistical armamentarium. Whenever the researcher is carrying out significance testing on a set of criterion measures the question of the experimentwise error rate must be raised. The multiple comparison issue is simply put. Conventional significance tests usually establish an error rate such that $\alpha \times 100\%$ of the time a relationship will be found statistically significant even though the relationship is actually nonexistent. As the *number* of such tests increases due to the multiple responses, the chances of finding one or more relationships *by chance alone* when none actually exists also increases. The researcher is placed in a difficult position since the requirements of theory and sound research practice often demand multiple responses but these same data cannot be treated as if they were mere repetitions of univariate hypotheses without potentially serious bias. Several of the techniques discussed subsequently are designed to correct for simultaneous significance testing with multiple response data. Professor Tukey's essay also comments on this matter in more general terms.

It is our opinion that the above reasons offer strong justification for the modern communication scientist's attention to multivariate analysis procedures. While statistical procedures alone can never provide substantive insight, neither can substantive insights be validated with methods inappropriate to the research task.

III. THE GENERAL LINEAR MODEL AND COMMUNICATION RESEARCH

In the introduction to a widely read article, Cohen (1968) observed that few psychologists were (at that time) aware of the equivalence of multiple regression and the fixed-effects-model analysis of variance, that is, that both are variants of the general linear model, which comprises the general theory of relationships among data, both univariate and multivariate. The reason for this, he suggested, was that two major forms of psychological inquiry developed simultaneously though independently: the study of *natural* variation, which uses the techniques developed at the turn of the century by Galton, Pearson, and Yule, and the study of *artificial* or experimentally manipulated variation, which uses the techniques pioneered by R. A. Fisher in the 1920s and 1930s.

A similar observation could be made about the communication discipline. Much of the early research in communication, e.g., persuasion processes, interpersonal communication, small group discussion processes, etc., were judged amenable to experimental variation, were studied under laboratory conditions, and were analyzed by means of analysis of variance techniques. Other communication processes, such as mass communication, organizational communication, and attitude and opinion assessment, seemed to fit the natural variation mode, were studied in the field, and were analyzed by multiple regression techniques. Only recently have communication researchers begun to understand that the two forms of analysis are equivalent under quite general conditions.

Today, many communication scientists conduct their research in both settings, attempting in the one case to gain additional control over their findings regarding natural variation by manipulating it in the laboratory and attempting in the other case to extend their findings from artificial manipulation in the laboratory to the naturally occurring variation in the field setting. While we would not argue that there are no differences between the two settings, either in terms of interpretation of results or in terms of conditions for hypothesis testing and estimation, we would urge that for the most part the multivariate statistics discussed in this book are equally appropriate for either setting. After all, the statistical procedures do not know from which setting the data come. Consequently, in the chapters that follow, we have attempted to give relatively equal treatment to both research settings.

Furthermore, most, though not all, of the techniques discussed in this book can be viewed as special cases of the general linear model. Where possible, the authors have attempted to show how their techniques are related to the general linear model, and in some cases, how they are related to other techniques that comprise other parts of the model. The advantage of such a perspective is that the reader can see how each technique is a variation on a theme rather than a new composition. It is this unification into a coherent whole of what is often presented as separate unrelated statistical tools that constitutes the beauty and elegance of the general linear model. The reader is encouraged to actively pursue an understanding of the various techniques at this level.

It is well known that inferential (rather than descriptive) statistics contains two major divisions: parameter estimation and hypothesis testing. This division applies equally well to the general linear model. Parameter estimation is the process of obtaining the best possible value for the magnitude of a population parameter based upon the limited information provided by the sample statistic. Hypothesis testing is the process of determining whether the estimated magnitude of the parameter is large enough to be considered a true characteristic of the population or so small as to be attributable to the random fluctuations associated with drawing the sample.

While both procedures are important, each has tended to be associated with different traditions in communication research: hypothesis testing with laboratory experimentation and parameter estimation with field research. Within the laboratory tradition, tests for differences among means either through F-tests, t-tests, or planned comparisons, has been the primary analytical tool; little attention has been placed upon the problem of estimation of parameters in the laboratory setting. In the case of field studies, emphasis has been placed upon estimation of regression parameters with little attention paid to the testing of significance of those estimates.

Our concern here is not to criticize previous research; rather we are interested in encouraging researchers to utilize *both* processes in their analysis of data. As an example, consider Finn's (1974) discussion of how the initial estimates of means obtained from an analysis of variance design in which *some* of the variables are not significant may be incorrect. He states:

> Only effects that are nonzero in the population should be maintained in the model. The common research procedure is to test the significance of all terms in the model that may contribute to criterion variation (all main effects and interactions that the design permits). Those that are not significant may be omitted, and best estimates may be obtained of those remaining. This procedure usually requires two passes with most computer programs, one for significance testing and another for estimation [p. 327].

Sometimes (e.g., in the case of regression analysis) obtaining the final estimates of the model after the process of hypothesis testing is called reestimation (see Chapter 2). In the chapters that follow, the authors have, in general, attempted to give equal emphasis to explication of parameter estimation and hypothesis testing procedures.

IV. THE STRUCTURE OF MULTIVARIATE DATA

The data appropriate to multivariate analytic techniques is best described in terms of the standard rectangular data array usually input to computer software packages:

$$
\begin{array}{c}
\qquad\qquad\qquad\text{Variables} \\
\begin{array}{cccc}
X_{11} & X_{12} & \cdots & X_{1P} \\
X_{21} & X_{22} & \cdots & X_{2P} \\
\vdots & \vdots & \cdots & \vdots \\
X_{N1} & X_{N2} & \cdots & X_{NP}
\end{array}
\end{array}
$$

(Observation units)

The rows of this array refer to observation units: individuals, dyads, groups, television networks, societies, or a time sequence of observations. The columns represent scores on the P variables of interest. These variables may be categorical, ordinal, interval, or ratio and conceptually may be manipulated variables, predictors, criterion scores, or any other variable classification. Any row represents P numbers or responses on each of the variables for that observation unit. The array is defined to be multivariate when two or more of the columns are specified a priori to be criterion variables. Criterion variables are those whose variation is to be explained rather than those which are explanatory. If only one column is so identified, the data array is defined to be univariate. All the columns may be criterion variables.

In general there is no requirement that the criterion variables meet any standards of level of measurement. For example, the criterion variables may be categorical as would be the case in discriminant analysis. Similarly there is no general requirement that the observations (rows) be independent of one another. For example. the N observation units might be sequential time samples on the same person which are usually dependent upon one another. Furthermore, with time-series observations the column variables might be the lagged versions of other column variables. The standard rectangular data array may be used to display any type and level of data.

The standard data array can be useful as a framework for describing various multivariate techniques. However, the reader should not be led to conclude that the data structure available determines statistical technique; quite the contrary, one's research questions should determine what analysis techniques are appropriate. Some generalized orientation to the relationship among various multivariate techniques can be gleaned from studying alternative forms of the data matrix.

Since we presume that there are at least two criterion variables, the first split between the various multivariate techniques is over the question: Are there any predictor variables? If no observed variables are so classified, then all variables are "criterion" variables and analysis techniques are basically concerned with discovering the structure within this set. The structure finding procedures discussed in this volume include cluster analysis, factor analysis, multidimensional scaling, smallest space analysis, and network analysis. Their common concern is to array the set of variables in some spatial arrangement so that variables close on some measure of association (e.g., Pearson **r**) or distance (e.g., generalized Euclidean distance) are also close in the output spatial arrangement.

If one or more of the variables is identified as a predictor variable, then the data array can be divided vertically into a set of η predictors and $P - \eta$ criterion variables. It is matrix operations within and between these two data arrays which constitute predictor–criterion multivariate procedures. Those discussed here include multivariate multiple regression (MMR), multivariate analysis of variance (MANOVA), structural equation modeling (SEM), canonical correlation (CANCOR), and multiple discriminant analysis (DIS-CRIM). Each of these procedures seeks to establish estimates of the degree of relationship between predictor and criterion sets while taking into account the dependencies among the criterion variables, including conceptual or observed variational dependency. The goal is to offer an accounting of the size, direction, and significance of the statistical relationship between the explanatory and explained variables which utilizes rather than ignores the information on the variation among criterion variables.

A number of other distinctions among multivariate techniques can be made which will offer some insight into their differences and similarities. Useful comparative descriptions are available in Harris (1975), Van der Geer (1971), Green and Carroll (1976), and Monge and Day (1976). Inevitably these distinctions break down as the type of data shade together, techniques are combined, odd varieties of one technique look suspiciously familiar, and so on. The basic distinction into criterion-only and predictor–criterion variables made above should be sufficient for a gross separation of multivariate techniques. With this separation in mind we turn to a brief chapter-by-chapter overview of the multivariate techniques discussed in this book.

Chapters 2–4 are extensions of well-known regression techniques. In Chapter 2 Monge's presentation of multivariate multiple regression begins with a review of the classical linear regression model. The extension is then made to regression systems which contain multiple dependent variables. Monge discusses alternative techniques for estimating parameters and appropriate procedures for testing both the multiple dependent variables (step-down techniques) and multiple independent variables (stepwise techniques). Emphasis is placed on a priori model specification to protect significance tests and on reestimating the coefficients of the reduced model.

Chapter 3, by Cappella, discusses structural equation modeling. It focuses on the use of regression techniques for examining systems of relations among variables, with particular attention given to drawing casual inferences from cross-sectional data. Two types of systems are distinguished in detail: recursive, which admit only one-way causal relations, and nonrecursive, which incorporate feedback loops into the system. Estimation, hypothesis-testing, and model-fitting procedures are discussed at length as is the important issue of identification of equations. The chapter concludes with a discussion of structural equation procedures for modeling time dependent processes.

Chapter 4 presents structural equation modeling with unobserved variables. In it Fink differentiates between theoretical variables, which are defined as true unobserved variables, and observed variables, which are actually measured. This distinction enables researchers to explicitly incorporate measurement models into the theoretical model and to evaluate both theoretical and measurement models simultaneously. Fink discusses the identification problem when structural models include measurement models and gives extensive attention to full information, maximum likelihood methods of estimation, as well as chi-square tests of the entire model.

Chapters 5 and 6 deal with extensions of the univariate analysis of variance problem. In Chapter 5, Bochner and Fitzpatrick's discussion of multivariate analysis of variance closely parallels the presentation of multivariate multiple regression, but does so with the restriction to categorical independent variables. Emphasis is placed on specification of the correct formal model, construction of the design matrix, and associated hypothesis testing and estimation techniques. An important contribution of this chapter is the discussion of nonorthogonal (unbalanced) designs and three methods for estimating effects: the regression method, the classical experimental-design approach, and the hierarchical method.

In Chapter 6 by McLaughlin discriminant analysis may be viewed as a companion technique to MANOVA or as a technique useful in its own right. The chapter includes descriptions of both classification and hypothesis testing techniques. The chapter describes how to use a set of variables to maximally separate or distinguish between two or more different groups of subjects.

Chapter 7 on canonical correlation by Tucker and Chase is a transition chapter. Canonical correlation includes aspects of relating two sets of variables like the six chapters which precede it and aspects of data reduction like several of the chapters which follow it. Canonical correlation may be viewed as a procedure for finding the best linear combination of variables in each set which will maximally correlate. Tucker and Chase describe the procedures for calculating the canonical variates and the canonical correlation and distinguish between the canonical weights and canonical loadings.

Chapters 8–11 all focus on techniques for data reduction. In Chapter 8 Hunter reviews the two major approaches to factor analysis: principal components (which he calls dust bowl empiricism) and principal axes (sometimes called principal factors, which he refers to as classical trait theory). He then contrasts these two procedures with cluster analysis and arrives at the rather startling conclusion that cluster analysis comes much closer to providing the information that factor analysts have said they seek than do the actual methods of factor analysis.

Chapter 9 is an explication of cluster analysis. In his presentation of the standard agglomerative and divisive techniques Krippendorff makes an interesting argument: that many multivariate techniques are inherently biordinal (i.e., based upon bivariate relations) whereas clustering procedures can be used to assess multiordinal relations; his arguments and line of reasoning merit careful consideration. Careful attention is given to the dendrogram and other forms of data presentation as well as the relation between clustering and other forms of multivariate analysis (such as factor analysis). The chapter also includes an exploration of properties of emerging clusters. The discussion of computation algorithms for cluster analysis will be of interest to those who wish to understand the techniques in some depth or to develop their own computer programs.

Chapters 10 and 11 discuss the techniques of multidimensional scaling. They are complementary in that the chapter by Norton discusses the recently developed nonmetric approaches to multidimensional scaling (he primarily discusses one of the nonmetric techniques called smallest space analysis) while Woelfel and Danes discuss the classical metric model. There are an interesting point and counterpoint (or counterpoint and point!) that run through the two chapters. Norton's position is that many communication data are inherently weak (at best at the ordinal level of measurement), and hence we need to utilize analytic techniques which do not make stronger assumptions about the quality of the data. Woelfel and Danes argue that better techniques need to be developed to provide ratio level data which can be used with the stronger analytic technique of metric scaling. Two important aspects of the Woelfel and Danes paper are the discussion of the comparison of multidimensional spaces and the discussion of the theory describing the role of messages in cognitive systems. Readers should be alerted to the fact that the equations developed by Woelfel and Danes utilize tensor notation and not the traditional matrix algebra utilized in the rest of the book.

Chapter 12 on network analysis by Farace and Mabee provides a broad overview of the large family of network analysis techniques. They review the major network properties which have been utilized in research and discuss the major clique detection procedures. The chapter usefully compares the available alternatives and ends with a discussion of major problems still to be resolved in network analysis.

Chapters 13–15 all deal with models in which time plays an important part. In Chapter 13 on stochastic modeling, Hewes builds a strong argument for developing communication models which describe how the entire probability distributions of variables change over time rather than their mean value. Hewes then distinguishes between continuous and discrete state models and develops a rationale for why discrete state models are better for particular types of communication theories. The procedures are explicated and illustrated with reference to the research literature. Careful attention is given to assumptions of the model and procedures for testing them.

Chapter 14 on time-series analysis by Davis and Lee examines the analysis of single and multiple variables gathered at many points in time. The authors present the two standard models for dealing with time dependent data: autoregressive and moving averages. They also discuss the Box and Jenkins regression procedures and spectrum analysis. A brief discussion of structural equation models is also included.

Chapter 15 on simulation techniques by Richards reviews a variety of simulation techniques but focuses largely on computer analysis. A useful distinction is made between a model and the procedures used to simulate the model. A brief discussion is also provided about the processes of testing and validating simulations.

Chapter 16 by Tukey addresses a number of issues raised at various points throughout the book. It is the product of his careful reviewing and prodding and probing into areas that are both provocative and problematic. It points to problems of disagreement, to places where there is superficial or inadequate treatment, and/or to places where no one has yet ventured to tread. Ironically (and perhaps intentionally!), it raises more questions than it answers. There are scattered throughout its pages a number of insightful gems which future scholars will want to mine and explore in greater depth.

Chapter 17 by Huber is a brief overview of the major computer software packages currently available for performing various multivariate analyses. It serves as a handy reference for those who would like to acquire a package which will permit utilization of one or more of the particular techniques discussed in this book.

V. CAVEATS

A. A Note about Notation

A comment about the notation in the present volume seems in order. A story is occasionally told (undoubtedly by now much embellished) about a famous but aging statistics professor who systematically and deliberately changed the notation system he used in his first-term graduate statistics course. By the end of the first week his new students amusedly thought him highly prone to error, by the end of the second week they generously thought him quietly slipping into senility, but by the end of the third week their frustration led them to hypothesize that he secretly delighted in their torture. It was only then that he indicated to the students that the purpose behind his apparent madness was to force them to focus on the concepts represented by the symbols and not the symbols themselves. Consistency was important, he maintained, so he never used the same symbol to stand for different concepts. But he likewise asserted that flexibility was also valuable, so he frequently used several different symbols to stand for the same concept.

The reader who wishes to test the efficacy of this position will find the present volume an excellent testing ground. In the chapters that follow we have employed this approach, though more from the exigencies of the matter than pedagogical principle. While each chapter employs a notation which is internally consistent and constant, the notational system changes somewhat from chapter to chapter, requiring some flexibility on the part of the reader. The editors attempted to standardize the notation as much as possible, but some differences between chapters still remain. For example, Monge uses Greek letters to refer to population values (or estimates thereof) and Cappella and Fink use Greek letters to refer to theoretical (as opposed to observed) variables. Readers should also be aware that the notation utilized by Woelfel and Danes is tensor analysis and not the standard matrix algebra employed in the other chapters of the book.

B. A Precautionary Comment

The chapters which you are about to read each take a cautious approach to their subject matter. This caution exhibits itself in what is a typically careful exposition of the assumptions under which a particular technique operates. Of course the function of these assumptions is primarily to permit mathematical deductions relevant to estimation, hypothesis testing, and their properties in the formal mathematical system in which the method is embedded. The assumptions may or may not be met in a particular sample, and the consequences of violating assumptions may have serious or only slight effects on estimators and significance tests. For example, with univariate ANOVA, evidence from simulation studies suggests that the significance tests are rather robust under violations of the variance homogeneity assumption.

In the case of most multivariate techniques evidence on the robustness of the output (whether point estimates or spatial configurations) under various types and degrees of violation is not as yet settled. As these procedures become more widely adopted, simulation evidence and data handling experience on the effects of violations will accumulate, and we may find the methods to be robust or to be inflexible to violations. In the interim the researcher should be clearly aware of the conditions under which we know the methods to produce useful conclusions. If we must err in order to use these methods, then let our error be on the side of conservatism.

References

Berlo, D. *The process of communication.* New York: Holt, 1960.

Cappella, J. N. Communication research methodology: Review and commentary. In B. Ruben (Ed.), *Communication yearbook I.* New Brunswick, New Jersey: Transaction, 1977. pp. 37–53.

Cattell, R. (Ed.) Preface. *Handbook of multivariate experimental psychology.* Chicago, Illinois: Rand-McNally, 1966.

Cohen, J. Multiple regression as a general data-analytic system. *Psychological Bulletin*, 1968, **70**, 426–443.

Finn, J. D. *A general model for multivariate analysis*. New York: Holt, 1974.

Fisher, F. M., and Ando, A. Two theorems on *ceteris paribus* in the analysis of dynamic systems. In H. M. Blalock (Ed.), *Causal models in the social sciences*. Chicago, Illinois: Aldine-Atherton, 1971.

Green, P. E., and Carroll, J. D. *Mathematical tools for applied multivariate analysis*. New York: Academic Press, 1976.

Harris, R. J. *A primer of multivariate statistics*. New York: Academic Press, 1975.

Monge, P. R., and Day, P. D. Multivariate analysis in communication research. *Human Communication Research*, 1976, **2**, 207–220.

Seibold, D. R. Communication research and the attitude–verbal report–overt behavior relationship: A critque and theoretic reformulation. *Human Communication Research*, 1975, **2**, 3–32.

Van der Geer, J. P. *Introduction to multivariate analysis for the social sciences*. San Francisco, California: Freeman, 1971.

Chapter 2

MULTIVARIATE MULTIPLE REGRESSION

PETER R. MONGE

Department of Communication
Michigan State University
East Lansing, Michigan

Far better an *approximate* answer to the *right* question, which is often vague, than an *exact* answer to the *wrong* question, which can always be made precise [Tukey, 1962, p. 13].

I. INTRODUCTION

The scientific study of human communication, like any other science, is fundamentally concerned with establishing laws of relations among the variables that constitute its subject matter. While formulating laws is, of course, a theoretical endeavor, establishing them is an empirical enterprise. When communication scientists undertake research to establish a candidate to grow into a law, they must choose a statistical technique from among the large repertoire available which in their judgment is the one best suited to enable them to derive meaningful conclusions. This paper will present one alternative, multivariate multiple regression (MMR) and its univariate counterpart, which in my opinion are often ideally suited to this task. In fact, as Blalock (1964) says, "It is the regression coefficients which give us the laws of science" [p. 51].

It is not my intention, however, to argue for the superiority of MMR over other analytic techniques. Rather, it seems important that communication researchers understand the technique *and its assumptions* so that, as with all statistical procedures, they will have a rational basis for selecting it when it is best suited to their needs. In this regard, the assumptions are most critical, for here is where researchers must compare the nature and assumptions of the theory being tested (i.e., the proposed law) with the assumptions of the analytic technique. Should the theoretical and analytic assumptions fail to correspond, then the analysis under one set of assumptions of data gathered under the other set is bound to be in error.

The purpose of this paper, then, is to examine the multivariate multiple regression model and to explore its applicability to the domain of communication inquiry. We will begin with a prelude on partitioning a data matrix as a heuristic device for distinguishing among alternative regression models. In the second section we will discuss the major aspects of univariate multiple regression: (a) the form of the model, (b) using the model for descriptive purposes, (c) estimators and their properties, (d) assumptions of the model, (e) procedures for parameter estimation, (f) hypothesis testing procedures, (g) interpretation of regression coefficients, and (h) reestimation. The third section will provide a parallel presentation for multivariate multiple regression. The fourth section will present a worked example with communication data. In the final section, we shall turn to several additional topics. These will include (a) tests of assumptions, (b) coping with failed assumptions, (c) the relation of MMR to other multivariate procedures, and (d) the advantages and disadvantages of MMR.

A. Notation

In terms of notation it may be helpful at the outset to make the conventions we shall utilize explicit. For parameters, i.e., characteristics of populations, we shall use upper- and lower-case Greek letters, e.g., Σ, σ^2, β, μ. For estimators of parameters from sample data, we shall use the same Greek letters as the corresponding parameter augmented by a caret above each symbol, e.g., $\hat{\beta}$ as an estimator of β. For statistics, i.e., characteristics of samples, and for computational forms, we shall use English equivalents (or alternatives, if necessary) to the Greek symbols, e.g., **S** for Σ, **b** for β, etc. Vectors will be identified by lower-case letters, matrices by upper case, and both will always be boldfaced to distinguish them from scalars and other data representations; thus, β is a single regression coefficient, $\boldsymbol{\beta}$ is a vector of coefficients, and **B** is a matrix of coefficients.

B. Partitioning the Data Matrix for Regression

Virtually every communication researcher has gathered data for several different variables on some number of subjects. The most traditional way to prepare these data for analysis is to arrange them into a subjects-by-variables data matrix. In fact, virtually all standard computerized statistical packages require that data be prepared in this way. Here the deck of punched cards may be considered the data matrix, where each card corresponds to the set of observations (scores or measurements) on a single subject, i.e., a row of the data matrix. Since this format is generally familiar to researchers, let us examine various partitionings of this matrix in order to provide an overview of alternative linear regression models.

Suppose that we have a data matrix, $\mathbf{A}_{N \times M}$, which consists of measurements for N subjects ($i = 1, 2, \ldots, N$) on M variables ($j = 1, 2, \ldots, M$). Our matrix is then of order $N \times M$. Let us assume that we are interested in how the values of some variables *can be determined* (usually approximately) from knowledge about the values of other variables; regression analysis is appropriate for examining this kind of dependency. Some variables in the matrix will be identified as predictor variables and others as criterion variables. We can partition the data matrix into two submatrices, one for predictor variables and one for criterion variables, and examine the interrelations among the two submatrices.

According to convention, we shall label the predictor variables the **X** variables and the criterion variables the **Y** variables. We shall label our criterion submatrix, $\mathbf{Y}_{N \times P}$, and our predictor submatrix, $\mathbf{X}_{N \times K}$. It is possible to have one or more of each kind of variable, i.e., one or more criterion variables *and* one or more predictor variables, which provide four possible combinations or regression models. The first situation occurs if we have a data matrix with only two variables. Then we would partition $\mathbf{A}_{N \times M}$ ($M = 2$)

as follows (where $M = P + K = 1 + 1 = 2$)

$$\underset{N \times 2}{\mathbf{A}} = \left[\begin{array}{c:c} \underset{N \times P}{\mathbf{Y}} & \underset{N \times K}{\mathbf{X}} \end{array} \right] = \left[\begin{array}{c:c} \underset{N \times 1}{\mathbf{Y}} & \underset{N \times 1}{\mathbf{X}} \end{array} \right] = \left[\begin{array}{c:c} \underset{N \times 1}{\mathbf{y}} & \underset{N \times 1}{\mathbf{x}} \end{array} \right] \qquad (1)$$

With one criterion variable and one predictor variable we have the data partition for *univariate simple regression*. Note that since there is only one criterion and one predictor variable, that the submatrices are really vectors (and $\mathbf{A}_{N \times M}$ is $N \times 2$).

Now assume that M is greater than two. We must decide how to partition the matrix. If we choose *one* variable (the first, for convenience) as the criterion variable, so that $P = 1$, and treat *all* the remaining variables as predictor variables ($K \geqslant 2$), then we would partition $\mathbf{A}_{N \times M}$ ($M \geqslant 3$) as follows

$$\underset{N \times M}{\mathbf{A}} = \left[\begin{array}{c:c} \underset{N \times P}{\mathbf{Y}} & \underset{N \times K}{\mathbf{X}} \end{array} \right] = \left[\begin{array}{c:c} \underset{N \times 1}{\mathbf{y}} & \underset{N \times K}{\mathbf{X}} \end{array} \right] \qquad (2)$$

and call it the data partition for *univariate multiple regression*. There is a single vector of criterion scores but a matrix of two or more predictor scores (one score for each subject on each predictor variable).

Now consider what would happen if we were to partition $\mathbf{A}_{N \times M}$ so that there were two or more criterion variables ($P \geqslant 2$) but only one predictor variable ($K = 1$). $\mathbf{A}_{N \times M}$ would look like

$$\underset{N \times M}{\mathbf{A}} = \left[\begin{array}{c:c} \underset{N \times P}{\mathbf{Y}} & \underset{N \times 1}{\mathbf{x}} \end{array} \right] \qquad (M = P + K = P + 1 \geqslant 3) \qquad (3)$$

This data partition can still be treated as a regression problem. Since there are several criterion variables but only one predictor variable it would be the appropriate data display for a *multivariate simple regression* analysis.

Finally, assume that the researcher is interested in examining the regression of two or more criterion variables ($p \geqslant 2$) on two or more predictor variables ($K \geqslant 2$). Then,

$$\underset{N \times M}{\mathbf{A}} = \left[\begin{array}{c:c} \underset{N \times P}{\mathbf{Y}} & \underset{N \times k}{\mathbf{X}} \end{array} \right] \qquad (M = P + k \geqslant 4) \qquad (4)$$

This partitioning of the data matrix into two submatrices is appropriate for analysis under the *multivariate multiple regression* model.

During the remainder of this paper we will work with the criterion and predictor submatrices, $\mathbf{Y}_{N \times P}$ and $\mathbf{X}_{N \times K}$, rather than the full data matrix, $\mathbf{A}_{N \times M}$. Since it is helpful in sorting out the differences from the various forms of analysis, the results of this section are summarized in Table I. This data partitioning will also be useful when it comes to comparing the regression procedures with related techniques.

TABLE I

Partition of a Data Matrix $A_{N \times M}{}^a$

	Criterion variable(s)	
Predictor variable(s)	Univariate $(P = 1)$	Multivariate $(P \geqslant 2)$
Simple $(K = 1)$:	(1) $\underset{N \times M}{A} = \begin{bmatrix} \underset{N \times 1}{y} & \vdots & \underset{N \times 1}{x} \end{bmatrix}$	(3) $\underset{N \times M}{A} = \begin{bmatrix} \underset{N \times P}{Y} & \vdots & \underset{N \times 1}{x} \end{bmatrix}$
Multiple $(K \geqslant 2)$:	(2) $\underset{N \times M}{A} = \begin{bmatrix} \underset{N \times 1}{y} & \vdots & \underset{N \times K}{X} \end{bmatrix}$	(4) $\underset{N \times M}{A} = \begin{bmatrix} \underset{N \times P}{Y} & \vdots & \underset{N \times K}{X} \end{bmatrix}$

^{a}Partitioning is into four possible combinations of predictor variables, $X_{N \times K}$, and criterion variables, $Y_{N \times P}$, submatrices, $M = P + K$. The four cells provide the data partitions for (1) univariate simple regression, (2) univariate multiple regression, (3) multivariate simple regression, and (4) multivariate multiple regression.

While we shall assume at the outset that the reader is familiar with standard simple and multiple regression techniques, a presentation of the univariate model will help to set the stage for our discussion of the multivariate case. To that task we will now turn.

II. UNIVARIATE MULTIPLE REGRESSION

A. The Univariate Multiple Regression Model

The classical univariate linear multiple regression model can be given by

$$Y_i = \beta_0 + \beta_1 X_{i1} + \cdots + \beta_k X_{ik} + \varepsilon_i \qquad (5)$$

which shows the relationship between two or more (k) predictor or independent variables (X) and a criterion or dependent variable (Y) all measured simultaneously on the ith subject. The model is called linear (or linear in the parameters) because the effects of the various predictor variables are treated as additive, i.e., Y_i is composed of a linear combination of regression parameters. The regression parameters ($\beta_0, \ldots, \beta_k$) are the population partial regression coefficients or weights which are determined from the sample data and used to optimally predict Y_i. β_0 is a scaling constant which absorbs the differences in the scales used to measure the Y and X variables. The ε_i represents the error term, i.e., the extent to which the model fails to predict the criterion scores, Y_i. This can be seen by rewriting (5) as,

$$\varepsilon_i = Y_i - (\beta_0 + \beta_1 X_{i1} + \cdots + \beta_k X_{ik}) \qquad (6)$$

Since data are gathered on each subject ($i = 1, \ldots, N$) in the sample, there are N equations of the form depicted in Eq. (5), one for each subject.

$$
\begin{aligned}
y_1 &= (1)\beta_0 + \beta_1 X_{11} + \beta_2 X_{12} + \cdots + \beta_k X_{1k} + \varepsilon_1 \\
y_2 &= (1)\beta_0 + \beta_1 X_{21} + \beta_2 X_{22} + \cdots + \beta_k X_{2k} + \varepsilon_2 \\
&\vdots \\
y_N &= (1)\beta_0 + \beta_1 X_{N1} + \beta_2 X_{N2} + \cdots + \beta_k X_{Nk} + \varepsilon_N
\end{aligned}
\tag{7}
$$

These equations may be represented in matrix form as

$$
\begin{bmatrix} y_1 \\ y_2 \\ \vdots \\ y_N \end{bmatrix} = \begin{bmatrix} 1 & X_{11} & X_{12} & \cdots & X_{1k} \\ 1 & X_{21} & X_{22} & \cdots & X_{2k} \\ \vdots & \vdots & \vdots & & \vdots \\ 1 & X_{N1} & X_{N2} & \cdots & X_{Nk} \end{bmatrix} \begin{bmatrix} \beta_0 \\ \beta_1 \\ \vdots \\ \beta_k \end{bmatrix} + \begin{bmatrix} \varepsilon_1 \\ \varepsilon_2 \\ \vdots \\ \varepsilon_N \end{bmatrix}
\tag{8}
$$

or, more compactly, as

$$
\underset{N \times 1}{\mathbf{y}} = \underset{N \times q}{\mathbf{X}} \; \underset{q \times 1}{\boldsymbol{\beta}} + \underset{N \times 1}{\boldsymbol{\varepsilon}}
\tag{9}
$$

$\mathbf{y}$ is the $N \times 1$ vector of criterion or dependent scores, with one criterion score for each subject in the sample. $\mathbf{X}$ is the $N \times q$ *model matrix* which contains an initial vector of unities and the data for the k predictor or independent variables ($q = 1 + k$). $\boldsymbol{\beta}$ is the $q \times 1$ vector of partial regression coefficients and $\boldsymbol{\varepsilon}$ is the $N \times 1$ vector of error terms.

The model given in (9) is often called the raw or raw score form of the linear regression of y on x. Two other forms of the model are also possible and frequently encountered in regression work. One alternative, following Timm (1975, p. 270), is called the *reparameterized* or *deviation* model. In this model all predictor scores are measured as deviations about their respective means. Thus, the regression equation would be

$$
y_i = \beta_0 + \sum_{j=1}^{k} \beta_j \bar{X}_j + \sum_{j=1}^{k} \beta_j \left(X_{ij} - \bar{X}_j \right) + \varepsilon_i
\tag{10}
$$

which can be represented in matrix notation as

$$
\underset{N \times 1}{\mathbf{y}} = \underset{N \times q}{\mathbf{X}_{\mathrm{d}}} \; \underset{q \times 1}{\boldsymbol{\eta}} + \underset{N \times 1}{\boldsymbol{\varepsilon}}
\tag{11}
$$

where $q = k + 1$, and $\mathbf{X}_{\mathrm{d}}$ is the model matrix of the deviation scores $(X_{ij} - \bar{X}_j)$, and $\boldsymbol{\eta}$ (i.e., eta) is the vector of regression coefficients for the reparameterized model.

The other alternative is to *standardize* the elements of both $\mathbf{y}$ and $\mathbf{X}$, which is accomplished by dividing each deviation score by the standard deviation of that variable. The standardized regression model is

$$
\begin{bmatrix} y_{1z} \\ y_{1z} \\ \vdots \\ y_{Nz} \end{bmatrix} = \begin{bmatrix} Z_{11} & Z_{12} & \cdots & Z_{1k} \\ Z_{21} & Z_{22} & \cdots & Z_{2k} \\ \vdots & \vdots & & \vdots \\ Z_{N1} & Z_{N2} & \cdots & Z_{Nk} \end{bmatrix} \begin{bmatrix} \gamma_1 \\ \gamma_2 \\ \vdots \\ \gamma_k \end{bmatrix} + \begin{bmatrix} \varepsilon_1 \\ \varepsilon_2 \\ \vdots \\ \varepsilon_N \end{bmatrix} \tag{12}
$$

or

$$
\underset{N \times 1}{\mathbf{y}_z} = \underset{N \times k}{\mathbf{Z}} \underset{k \times 1}{\boldsymbol{\gamma}} + \underset{N \times 1}{\boldsymbol{\varepsilon}} \tag{13}
$$

Note that the orders of the data matrix $\mathbf{Z}$ and the regression vector $\boldsymbol{\gamma}$ in Eq. (13) are k rather than $q = k + 1$. Since all variables are standardized to the same scale, there is no longer the necessity for a scaling term; hence, there is no initial vector of unities in $\mathbf{Z}$, and no γ_0 in $\boldsymbol{\gamma}$. It is also worth noting that some authors do not use different symbols for these two models; rather, they simply define the data matrix to be deviation or standardized scores.

B. Description

Suppose that a communication researcher wishes simply to *describe* the relations among variables in a set of data. Multiple regression procedures may be used straightforwardly in this case as a descriptive device. The data will be divided into a criterion variable and one or more predictor variables. Using English letters to indicate that regression coefficients are to be calculated from sample data for descriptive purposes only, the regression equation specifying the relation among the variables is given by

$$
\underset{N \times 1}{\mathbf{y}} = \underset{N \times q}{\mathbf{X}} \underset{q \times 1}{\mathbf{b}} + \underset{N \times 1}{\mathbf{e}} \tag{14}
$$

where $\mathbf{y}$ is an $N \times 1$ column vector of observations on the criterion score (sometimes called the regressand), $\mathbf{X}$ is the $N \times q$ ($q = 1 + k$) data matrix of observed predictor variables (sometimes called regressors) augmented by an initial column vector of unities, $\mathbf{b}$ is the unknown $q \times 1$ vector of regression coefficients, and $\mathbf{e}$ is the unknown $N \times 1$ vector of errors. The problem is one of determining the unknown regression coefficients and calculating the error components of the equation.

By manipulation of Eq. (14) we can create an equation which will give us a solution for the regression parameters. In order to obtain the *best* possible solution, we would like our regression coefficients when multiplying the $\mathbf{X}$ scores to reproduce the $\mathbf{y}$ scores as exactly as possible. Another way to state this is that the error component of the model, the difference between observed and calculated Y scores, or more precisely the error sum of squares, will be at a minimum. First we calculate the error sum of squares, $\mathbf{e}'\mathbf{e}$.

$$\mathbf{e} = \mathbf{y} - \mathbf{Xb} \qquad\qquad \text{rearranging Eq. (14)}$$

$$\mathbf{e}'\mathbf{e} = (\mathbf{y} - \mathbf{Xb})'(\mathbf{y} - \mathbf{Xb}) \qquad \text{multiplying} \qquad\qquad (15)$$

$$= \mathbf{y}'\mathbf{y} - \mathbf{y}\mathbf{Xb} - \mathbf{b}'\mathbf{X}'\mathbf{y} + \mathbf{b}'\mathbf{X}'\mathbf{Xb} \qquad \text{collecting terms}$$

$$= \mathbf{y}'\mathbf{y} - 2\mathbf{b}'\mathbf{X}'\mathbf{y} + \mathbf{b}'\mathbf{X}'\mathbf{Xb}$$

Draper and Smith (1966) explain this last step by noting that "$\mathbf{b}'\mathbf{X}'\mathbf{y}$ is a 1×1 matrix, or a scalar, whose transpose $(\mathbf{b}'\mathbf{X}'\mathbf{y})' = \mathbf{y}'\mathbf{Xb}$ must have the same value" [p. 58]. Since we are interested in finding the $\mathbf{b}$ which gives the smallest error sum of squares, we differentiate this error sum of squares with respect to $\mathbf{b}$

$$\frac{\partial(\mathbf{e}'\mathbf{e})}{\partial \mathbf{b}} = -2\mathbf{X}'\mathbf{y} + 2\mathbf{X}'\mathbf{Xb} \qquad\qquad (16)$$

This solution to $\partial(\mathbf{e}'\mathbf{e})/\partial\mathbf{b}$, when set equal to 0, gives the "normal equations"

$$\mathbf{X}'\mathbf{Xb} = \mathbf{X}'\mathbf{y} \qquad\qquad (17)$$

Here $\mathbf{X}'\mathbf{X}$ is the sum of squares and cross products for the predictors, $\mathbf{b}$ is the vector of regression coefficients, and $\mathbf{X}'\mathbf{y}$ is the sum of squares and cross products for the predictor and criterion variables.

Simple algebraic manipulation of Eq. (17) gives us the solution for the regression coefficients we seek.

$$\mathbf{b} = (\mathbf{X}'\mathbf{X})^{-1}\mathbf{X}'\mathbf{y} \qquad\qquad (18)$$

For those familiar with the calculation of simple regression coefficients in summation notation it might be useful to point out that in the bivariate case Eq. (18) is equivalent to

$$b_{yx} = \frac{\sum xy}{\sum x^2} \qquad\qquad (19)$$

which is the ratio of variation between x and y to variation in x alone.

Having now obtained $\mathbf{b}$ it is possible to insert the values of $\mathbf{b}$ into the equation to *calculate* or *predict* the values of $\mathbf{y}$. Since we already possess the observed predictor scores, $\mathbf{X}$, the calculated scores, $\tilde{\mathbf{y}}$, are

$$\tilde{\mathbf{y}} = \mathbf{Xb} \qquad\qquad (20)$$

If we now compare our calculated criterion values, $\tilde{\mathbf{y}}$, with the observed criterion values, $\mathbf{y}$, we shall discover the extent to which our predictor variables, $\mathbf{X}$, when multiplied by the best possible regression coefficients, $\mathbf{b}$, accurately reproduce the observed scores, $\mathbf{y}$. As a measure of our *failure* to correctly reproduce the observed scores from our predictor variables and the regression coefficients we construct an equation for "residuals."

$$\mathbf{e} = \mathbf{y} - \mathbf{Xb} = \mathbf{y} - \tilde{\mathbf{y}} \qquad \text{since} \quad \tilde{\mathbf{y}} = \mathbf{Xb} \qquad (21)$$

where $\mathbf{e}$ is the vector of residuals obtained by comparing the observed $\mathbf{y}$ scores with the calculated or predicted scores, $\tilde{\mathbf{y}}$.

Having obtained our best weights for the set of predictors it is useful to determine how well the prediction model, $\mathbf{Xb}$, "fits" the observation vector, $\mathbf{y}$. The procedure, following Goldberger (1964, p. 159), is to partition or decompose the variance of $\mathbf{y}$ into its component parts. The parts of the decomposition can then be developed into a measure of the goodness of fit, R^2. First, we obtain the sum of squares *for residuals*.

$$\mathbf{e'e} = (\mathbf{y} - \mathbf{Xb})'(\mathbf{y} - \mathbf{Xb}) \qquad \text{from Eq. (21)}$$
$$= \mathbf{y'y} - \mathbf{y'Xb} - \mathbf{b'X'y} + \mathbf{b'X'Xb} \qquad \text{multiplying}$$
$$= \mathbf{y'y} - 2\mathbf{b'X'y} + \mathbf{b'X'X(X'X)}^{-1}\mathbf{X'y} \qquad \begin{array}{l}\text{combining terms and}\\ \text{from Eq. (18)}\end{array} \qquad (22)$$
$$\mathbf{e'e} = \mathbf{y'y} - \mathbf{b'X'y} \qquad \text{since } \mathbf{X'X(X'X)}^{-1} = \mathbf{I}$$
$$= \mathbf{y'y} - \mathbf{b'X'Xb} \qquad \begin{array}{l}\text{an alternative form, see}\\ \text{Kmenta (1971, p. 365)}\end{array}$$

Also, from Eq. (20) we can obtain the sum of squares for the calculated scores, $\tilde{\mathbf{y}}$.

$$\tilde{\mathbf{y}}'\tilde{\mathbf{y}} = (\mathbf{Xb})'(\mathbf{Xb}) \qquad \text{squaring Eq. (20)}$$
$$= \mathbf{b'X'Xb} \qquad \text{rearranging} \qquad (23)$$
$$= \mathbf{b'X'y} \qquad \text{or equivalently, see Kmenta, (1971, p. 365)}$$

By substituting (23) in (22) and rearranging terms, we obtain sum of squares total for the observed $\mathbf{y}$ scores.

$$\mathbf{y'y} = \tilde{\mathbf{y}}'\tilde{\mathbf{y}} + \mathbf{e'e} \qquad (24)$$

This provides the fundamental partition for linear regression. The partition states that total variation in observed $\mathbf{y}$ can be decomposed into two components: (1) sum of squares for predicted $\mathbf{y}$, also called sum of squares for regression, SS_R, and (2) sum of squares error, SS_E. If we treat the sum of squares as deviations from their respective means, we then have

$$SS_T = SS_R + SS_E \qquad (25)$$

As a measure of the "goodness of fit," the sample coefficient of multiple determination, R^2, is calculated.

$$R^2 = 1 - \frac{SS_E}{SS_T} = 1 - \frac{\Sigma e^2}{\Sigma(y - \bar{y})^2} = \frac{SS_R}{SS_T} \qquad (26)$$

which varies between 0 and 1. As Goldberger (1964) says, "When the fit is perfect, the least squares plane passes through every observed y, every $e = 0$, so $R^2 = 1$. At the other extreme $b_1 = \cdots = b_k = 0$, $b_0 = \bar{y}$, the plane is horizontal at $\bar{y}$, every $e = y - \bar{y}$, so $R^2 = 0$" [p. 160]. R, the square root of R^2, is called the sample multiple correlation coefficient.

The results of this section indicate that regression analysis may be used for purely descriptive purposes. Regression coefficients may be obtained and the adequacy of the predictor variables may be determined as proportions of variance accounted for or as goodness of fit between observed and predicted scores.

Communication researchers are rarely interested in simple description. Typically, we draw samples and wish to make inferences back to the population from which the sample came. In regression analysis, this inference will typically encompass two different but related processes: (1) estimation of population parameters (regression coefficients) from sample data, and (2) hypothesis tests regarding the parameters.

C. Parameter Estimation

The process of making an inference about the value of a population parameter, θ, from a sample statistic is called estimation. An estimator, $\hat{\theta}$, is a function or formula which tells how to combine sample observations in order to make the estimate about the parameter. An estimate is the value (scalar) obtained for any given sample from an estimator formula. According to Kmenta (1971, p. 9) characteristics of estimators are derived by examining their sampling distributions. The parameters typically estimated in regression analysis are the regression coefficients, $\beta_0, \ldots, \beta_k$, i.e., the intercept and slope values of the regression equation.

It is useful to distinguish between finite (sometimes called small sample) and asymptotic (sometimes called large sample) properties of estimators. By finite is meant that the properties will hold for samples of any fixed size, even small samples. Asymptotic sample properties, on the other hand, are assumed to hold only as sample sizes approach infinity. In practice, small sample refers to samples of less than 100 (and often less than 30), while asymptotic properties are invoked only for samples in the hundreds and thousands. We shall briefly discuss small sample properties before turning our attention to asymptotic properties.

As many econometricians point out (e.g., Kmenta, 1971; Goldberger, 1964) it is important that estimators possess certain properties. There are three desirable properties of finite sample estimators: unbiasedness, efficiency, and BLUE.

(1) $\hat{\theta}$ is defined as an unbiased estimator of θ if the mean of the sampling distribution of the estimator equals the parameter. This property is typically symbolized as $E(\hat{\theta}) = \theta$, which indicates that *on the average*, an unbiased estimator will equal the true population parameter. It should be pointed out that an estimator is not necessarily good just because it is unbiased. As Kmenta (1971) indicates, unbiasedness "implies nothing about the *dispersion*

of the distribution of the estimator. An estimator which is unbiased, but one which has a large variance, will frequently lead to estimates that are quite far off the mark. On the other hand, an estimator which has a very small variance but is biased—and the extent of bias is unknown—is even less useful" [p. 158]. The sample mean is an unbiased estimator of the population mean.

(2) $\hat{\theta}$ is an efficient estimator of θ if it is unbiased and if it has minimum variance. Efficiency then refers only to the class of estimators that are unbiased and implies a comparison among them. If two or more unbiased estimators are compared, the one with the smallest variance is the most efficient. Another desirable property of estimators that is often mentioned separately is sufficiency. A sufficient estimator is one that uses all of the available information in a sample in making the estimation to the population. For example, since the median uses only rank ordering information and not interval information out of a set of scores, it is not a sufficient estimator; the mean, on the other hand uses both ordering and interval information and is a sufficient estimator. Sufficiency is mentioned here under the heading of efficiency because as Kmenta (1971) points out, "sufficiency is a necessary condition for efficiency" [p. 162].

(3) $\hat{\theta}$ is a best linear unbiased estimator of θ if the estimator is a linear combination of the observations in the sample, it is unbiased, and it is efficient. This is often referred to as the BLUE property. The sample mean is a BLUE of the population mean because it is a linear combination of the sample observations, it is unbiased, and it has a minimum variance as an estimator.

There are three desirable properties of asymptotic sample estimators: asymptotic unbiasedness, consistency, and asymptotic efficiency.

(1) The property of asymptotic unbiasedness states that as sample size gets large and approaches infinity, the estimator will become unbiased. Though infinity is, of course, the limit of the argument, in practice this implies that as sample size gets larger (say into the hundreds) the estimator with this property will become unbiased. The sample variance is an estimator that is biased (though only slightly) for finite samples but is asymptotically unbiased.

(2) The property of consistency states that as sample size increases the variance of the estimator gets smaller and at infinity the estimate equals the parameter. In a sense, this is a focusing property, in that samples of larger size will have less variance and on the average be closer to the parameter than samples of smaller size.

(3) An estimator that is asymptotically efficient is one that, like its finite counterpart, will have a smaller variance than other estimators for samples of given large size. Also required are that the estimator have a finite mean and variance and that the estimator be consistent.

Although it will not be proved in this chapter, it should not come as a surprise to many readers that the least squares procedures, which were discussed earlier for determining regression coefficients for descriptive purposes, turn out to be, under certain circumstances, BLUE of population parameters. We now turn to those assumptions.

D. Assumptions of the Linear Regression Model

In order to make parameter estimates on the basis of sample data it is necessary to make a number of assumptions about the population. If these assumptions are warranted, then statistical theory regarding sampling distributions and properties of estimators can be used to formulate inferences about the parameters.

The assumptions of the *classical linear* regression model can be summarized by several equations which will be briefly discussed in this section.

Assumption (1) is

$$\mathbf{y} = \mathbf{X}\boldsymbol{\beta} + \boldsymbol{\varepsilon} \tag{27}$$

which specifies the functional form of the relationship in the population. It states that the observed scores, the y_i, are linearly dependent upon the X_{ij} scores and the disturbance or error terms, ε_i.

Assumption (2) is

$$E(\boldsymbol{\varepsilon}) = \mathbf{0} \qquad \text{or, alternatively} \qquad E(\mathbf{y}) = \mathbf{X}\boldsymbol{\beta} \tag{28}$$

This assumption states that each disturbance term has an expected value of zero. The two forms of the assumption are equivalent because if $\mathbf{y} = \mathbf{X}\boldsymbol{\beta} + \boldsymbol{\varepsilon}$ and $E(\mathbf{y}) = \mathbf{X}\boldsymbol{\beta}$, then it must follow that $E(\boldsymbol{\varepsilon}) = \mathbf{0}$.

Assumption (3) also may be written in two forms:

$$V(\boldsymbol{\varepsilon}) = E(\boldsymbol{\varepsilon}'\boldsymbol{\varepsilon}) = \sigma^2 \mathbf{I} \qquad \text{or} \qquad V(\mathbf{y}) = \sigma^2 \mathbf{I} \tag{29}$$

The variance of ε equals the variance of $\mathbf{y}$ because ε and $\mathbf{y}$ are separated only by a constant, which does not affect the variance. This equation states that the expected value for the sum of squares for the disturbances will equal a constant variance times the identity matrix. This really encompasses two assumptions. First, assumption (3) specifies that for all values, X_{ij}, of any given predictor variable, X_j, the variances will be constant; i.e., they will be *homoskedastic*. The assumption of homoskedasticity is sometimes written as

$$E(\varepsilon_i^2) = \sigma^2 \tag{29a}$$

Violation of the assumption, i.e., $E(\varepsilon_i^2) \neq \sigma^2$, is referred to as heteroskedasticity. Second, since an identity matrix has zeros in the off-diagonal position, assumption (3) implies that the errors are uncorrelated, which can also be written as

$$E(\varepsilon_i \varepsilon_j) = 0 \qquad \text{for all} \quad i \neq j \tag{29b}$$

This assumption is often referred to as nonautoregression or nonautoregressive disturbances.

Assumption (4) stipulates that

$$\mathbf{X} \text{ is an } N \times q \text{ matrix that is fixed in repeated samples} \qquad (30)$$

This assumption implies a nonstochastic X which further implies that $\mathbf{X}$ and $\boldsymbol{\varepsilon}$ are independent.

Assumption (5) is that the

$$\text{Rank of } \mathbf{X} = q \leqslant N \qquad (31)$$

which indicates that there are more subjects than variables and that no exact linear combinations exist among the predictor variables. This latter statement, that there is no exact correlation among the predictors, is often referred to as lack of multicollinearity. In practice we are often more concerned with high degrees of multicollinearity than with perfect multicollinearity.

If we add one additional assumption, (6), that the ε_i are normally distributed, to the previous five, the model becomes the *classical normal linear regression model*. Assumptions (1)–(3) and (6) may be compactly summarized for this model as

$$\mathbf{y} \sim N(\mathbf{X}\boldsymbol{\beta}, \sigma^2 \mathbf{I}) \quad \text{or, alternately} \quad \boldsymbol{\varepsilon} \sim N(\mathbf{0}, \boldsymbol{\Sigma}), \quad \text{where} \quad \boldsymbol{\Sigma} = \sigma^2 \mathbf{I}$$
$$(32)$$

This format for synthesizing assumptions (1)–(3) and normality may be read as "Y is a normally distributed random variable with expectation (mean) equal to $\mathbf{X}\boldsymbol{\beta}$, and variance equal to $\sigma^2 \mathbf{I}$," or alternatively, "the errors are normally distributed with zero mean and equal variance, $\boldsymbol{\Sigma}$." It is also often assumed that the X_{ij} scores are measured on scales that have at least ordinal properties, but that is not required by either model.

E. Estimating Univariate Regression Parameters

Having stated a model of the form

$$\mathbf{y} = \mathbf{X}\boldsymbol{\beta} + \boldsymbol{\varepsilon}$$

and specified a number of assumptions about that model, how can we obtain BLUE estimates of the regression parameters? *If the assumptions are valid*, it turns out that the least squares procedures that were utilized for descriptive purposes, may also be used for inferential purposes. Using the caret (read "hat") to indicate that sample data are being used to *estimate* the population regression parameters, Eq. (9) is rewritten as

$$\underset{N \times 1}{\mathbf{y}} = \underset{N \times q}{\mathbf{X}} \underset{q \times 1}{\hat{\boldsymbol{\beta}}} + \underset{N \times 1}{\boldsymbol{\varepsilon}} \qquad (33)$$

where the details of the vectors and matrices are as previously specified. Equation (33) may be manipulated in identical fashion to the way Eq. (18)

was derived from Eq. (14). These operations lead to the least squares *estimate* of the population regression coefficients (see Finn (1974, p. 97), for a demonstration without using calculus that $\hat{\beta}$ is a minimum sum of squared errors estimate of β).

$$\hat{\beta} = (\mathbf{X}\mathbf{X})^{-1}\mathbf{X}\mathbf{y} \tag{34}$$

$\hat{\beta}$ is an unbiased estimator of β because $E(\hat{\beta}) = \beta$. This can be shown fairly easily.

$$
\begin{aligned}
E(\hat{\beta}) &= E(\mathbf{X}'\mathbf{X})^{-1}\mathbf{X}'\mathbf{y} &&\text{taking expectations of Eq. (34)} \\
&= (\mathbf{X}'\mathbf{X})^{-1}\mathbf{X}E(\mathbf{y}) &&\text{since } \mathbf{X} \text{ is constant} \\
&= (\mathbf{X}'\mathbf{X})^{-1}\mathbf{X}'\mathbf{X}\beta &&\text{from assumption (2) } E(\mathbf{y}) = \mathbf{X}\beta \\
&= \beta &&\text{since } (\mathbf{X}'\mathbf{X})^{-1}\mathbf{X}'\mathbf{X} = \mathbf{I}
\end{aligned}
\tag{35}
$$

$\hat{\beta}$ is also efficient, i.e., minimum variance. (See Finn (1974, p. 99), for proof.) And in general, $\hat{\beta}$ is a BLUE of β (see Kmenta, 1971, pp. 209–216).

Since an estimate, though unbiased, will be correct only on the average [i.e., $E(\hat{\theta}) = \theta$], it is important to obtain an estimate of the variability of $\hat{\beta}$ over repeated samples (of the same size). This, of course, is equivalent to asking, What is the variance or standard deviation of the sampling distribution of the estimator, in this case β? The variance of β (see Johnston, 1972, pp. 125, 126) is given by

$$V(\hat{\beta}) = \sigma^2 \operatorname{diag}(\mathbf{X}'\mathbf{X})^{-1} \tag{36}$$

and the standard deviation of $\hat{\beta}$, called the standard error of estimate of $\hat{\beta}$, is given by

$$\sigma(\hat{\beta}) = \sigma \operatorname{diag}(\mathbf{X}'\mathbf{X})^{-1} \tag{37}$$

Thus, for the jth regression coefficient, $\hat{\beta}_j$, the standard error of estimate is

$$\sigma_{\hat{\beta}_j} = \sigma \operatorname{diag}(\mathbf{X}'\mathbf{X})_{jj}^{-1} \tag{38}$$

Both the variance of $\hat{\beta}$ and the standard error of estimate can be found on the diagonals of their respective matrices.

The conventions regarding reporting of regression results in economics might usefully be incorporated into communication research. As Kmenta (1971) indicates, "It has become customary to present all these results by writing out the estimated regression equation with the estimated standard errors in parentheses under the respective coefficients. This is followed by the value of R^2" [p. 242]. For our development we would write

$$Y_i = \hat{\beta}_0 + \hat{\beta}_1 X_i + \cdots + \hat{\beta}_k X_k + e_i, \qquad R^2 = \ldots; \qquad Z = \ldots$$
$$(\sigma_{\hat{\beta}_0}) \quad (\sigma_{\hat{\beta}_1}) \qquad \cdots \qquad (\hat{\sigma}_{\beta_k}) \tag{39}$$

The foregoing indicates that the procedures for determining regression coefficients for inferential purposes (parameter estimation) are no different from those employed for descriptive purposes. What does differ is that in the former case a number of critical assumptions are made about the population, while in the latter case, no assumptions are made. These assumptions, of course, make all the difference. Depending on the extent to which they are invalid, the researcher must either abandon ordinary least squares (OLS) techniques in favor of other alternatives (e.g., two stage least squares, instrumental variables, etc.) or be left in the unenviable position of being able only to *describe* relations in the obtained data. We shall briefly review those alternatives at a later point in this chapter. Now, having shown how to obtain parameters estimates, we shall briefly review various interpretations of regression coefficients before turning to the important topic of how to test the significance of those estimates.

F. Interpretation of Regression Coefficients

It might be helpful at this point to be explicit about the interpretation of the various regression coefficients. As already mentioned, the parameter, β_0, its estimator counterpart, $\hat{\beta}_0$, and the descriptive sample coefficient, b_0, are all scaling coefficients which are necessitated if y and X are measured on different scales, i.e., in different units of measurement. These coefficients ensure the equality of the right-hand and left-hand sides of their respective equations, which can be shown by the following simple manipulation of the standard regression equation:

$$y = \beta_0 + \beta_1 X_1 + \cdots + \beta_k X_k + \varepsilon$$

$$\beta_0 = y - (\beta_1 X_1 + \cdots + \beta_k X_k + \varepsilon)$$

(40)

If the variables are all measured on the same scale, the coefficient will equal zero. Thus, in the standardized model where all variables are converted to the same scale by Z score transformations there are no γ_0, $\hat{\gamma}_0$, or g_0 coefficients (remember, γ_0 is the standardized coefficient that corresponds to β_0); β_0, $\hat{\beta}_0$, and b_0 are defined only for the raw and deviation forms of the regression model. Each may also be considered the *intercept* of the line, plane, or hyperplane of the regression equation (depending upon whether it is a simple regression, two variable multiple regression, or greater than two variable multiple regression equation). As an intercept, it is the value of y when $X_1 = 0$ in the one predictor case, when X_1 and $X_2 = 0$ in the two predictor case or $X_1 \cdots X_k = 0$ in the greater than two predictor variable case. It should be pointed out that many texts also symbolize this coefficient as α, $\hat{\alpha}$, and a.

The other regression coefficients, $\beta_1, \ldots, \beta_k, \hat{\beta}_1, \ldots, \hat{\beta}_k$, and $b_1, \ldots, b_k$ are called partial regression coefficients. They should be interpreted as *the apparent change in y per unit change in X_j*. This quantity is typically referred to as the *slope* of the line, plane, or hyperplane of the regression of y on X_j. Alternatively, they may be thought of as weights which are used as multipliers for the X_j in order to optimally predict y. They are called partial regression coefficients because each shows the relationship between y and a given X_j partialing out (or sometimes controlling for) the influences of *all other Xs in the equation*. Though not always stated, the term regression coefficient is always understood to mean partial regression coefficient. (Even the intercept or scaling coefficient, β_0, is a partial regression coefficient on the unit vector or carrier "1," despite the fact that some authors prefer to give it an entirely different symbol, i.e., α.) As should also be clear shortly, they are sometimes referred to as *un*standardized regression coefficients, where the term "partial" is again understood. Furthermore, since *un*standardized regression coefficients are appropriately used only with the raw score or deviation forms of the regression equation, they are sometimes referred to as raw regression coefficients. Finally, some authors refer to unstandardized coefficients as metric regression coefficients.

It is important to note that changing the order of variables in the equation (e.g., exchanging the first and last variables, X_1 and X_k) will *not* alter the magnitude of any of the regression coefficients. Adding or deleting variables, on the other hand, will typically change the magnitude and/or sign of the coefficients, in some cases, quite drastically. This is so because partial regression coefficients are defined *for a given set of predictors*; change the set and the coefficients also change.

Interpretation of a partial regression coefficient by comparing it to other regression coefficients in an equation is difficult if the variables are measured on different scales. Regression coefficients will differ simply as a function of the difference in scales on which the respective X_j variables were measured in addition to any contributions they make to regression. To overcome the problem of differences in regression coefficients attributable to scaling it is customary to calculate the *standardized* partial regression coefficients $\gamma_1, \ldots, \gamma_k; \hat{\gamma}_1, \ldots, \hat{\gamma}_k;$ and $g_1, \ldots, g_k$. A standardized regression coefficient is equivalent to a raw coefficient multiplied by the standard deviation of X_j and divided by the standard deviation of y.

$$\gamma_k = \beta_k(\sigma_{X_j}/\sigma_y) \tag{41}$$

Since all variables are measured on the same scale the standardized coefficients are more directly interpretable. A unit change in y per unit change in X_j will give a regression line at $45°$ from the origin, for each X_j. Multiples and fractions of change in y per unit change in X_j are also the same for each X_j. Therefore, the comparison of the magnitudes of the various γ, $\hat{\gamma}$, and g *within* an equation is facilitated. As Blalock (1971) indicates, standardized regression coefficients are probably best suited for comparing relationships within equations while unstandardized coefficients are more appropriate for "comparing populations or stating general laws" [p. 145] (see also, Tukey, 1954, Chapter 3, Cappella, Chapter 3 of this volume).

It should be pointed out that one common convention in some social sciences is to call the standardized regression coefficient a "beta" weight and to reserve for it the symbol "β". This is *not* the convention in econometrics and many multivariate texts where Greek letters are reserved for population parameters or estimators. (Finn, 1974, in fact, reverses the convention and uses β for the unstandardized and b for the standardized coefficients. Goldberger's, 1964, usage is such that he directly warns his readers about not confusing "beta" coefficients with the elements of the population coefficient vector β.) Sorting out the variety of conventions of b and β is not always easy and it is the main reason why, following Timm (1975) and others, I have chosen to use an entirely different symbol, γ, for the standardized coefficients. The important thing to remember is not the symbol; rather, remember (1) there are (at least) two forms of the slope coefficients, standardized and unstandardized, (2) the interpretation appropriate to each, and (3) that each may be defined as a parameter, an estimator, or a descriptive statistic.

G. Hypothesis Testing

Hypothesis testing in regression analysis is the procedure whereby inferences about the significance of population regression coefficients (parameters) are made on the basis of sample regression coefficients (statistics). As Finn (1975, p. 134) indicates, this process requires two separate steps: (1) partitioning of variation and covariation in the criterion variables into components for different (sets of) predictor variables, which consists of *hypothesis sum of squares* (and cross products) and *error or residual sum of squares* (and cross products), and (2) a comparison between the *hypothesis sum of squares* and *error sum of squares* with one or more test statistics.

In a previous section we partitioned the total variance, SS_T, into sum of squares for regression, SS_R, and those for error, SS_E. Recalling Eqs. (22)–(25), let us now use $\hat{\varepsilon}$ as an estimator of ε (instead of using e for descriptive purposes) and call the SS_E, which is a scalar quantity, $Q_{\hat{\varepsilon}}$ for convenience. Thus, the sum of squares (and cross products) due to error are

$$Q_{\hat{\varepsilon}} = \hat{\varepsilon}'\hat{\varepsilon} = y'y - \hat{\beta}'X'X\hat{\beta} \quad \text{from Eq. (22)} \quad (42)$$

and the sum of squares (and cross products) for hypothesis, or as it is often called, sum of squares for regression, are

$$Q_h = \tilde{y}'\tilde{y} = \hat{\beta}'X'X\hat{\beta} \quad \text{from Eq. (23)} \quad (43)$$

We can now establish null and alternative hypotheses that will enable us to test whether *all* of the regression coefficients are jointly significant, i.e., whether the entire vector of coefficients, β, is significant. Thus,

$$H_0: \quad \beta = 0 \quad (44)$$

with the alternative

$$H_A: \quad \beta \neq 0 \quad (45)$$

To test Eq. (42) we calculate a standard F ratio of the two sums of squares divided by their degrees of freedom, i.e., a ratio of two mean squares, MS_h and MS_ε.

$$F = \frac{Q_h/(k+1)}{Q_\varepsilon/(N-k-1)} = \frac{\hat{\beta}'X'X\hat{\beta}/(k+1)}{y'y - \hat{\beta}'X'X\hat{\beta}/(N-k-1)} \qquad (46)$$

An ANOVA table (see Table II) may be constructed to summarize the information for the test with $(k+1)$ and $(N-k-1)$ degrees of freedom.

This particular test, though the most general, is of little practical utility since it tests *all* of the regression coefficients, including the intercept, $\hat{\beta}_0$. To overcome this problem, it is possible to examine the equivalent test for the standardized vector of regression coefficients, γ, which does not contain an intercept coefficient, or alternatively, to partition the vector into *two* subsets, $\hat{\beta}_0$ and $\hat{\beta}_1, \ldots, \hat{\beta}_k$, and examine only the slope coefficients (see Timm, 1975, pp. 273–274; and Goldberger, 1964, pp. 176–177).

TABLE II

ANOVA TABLE FOR TESTING $\beta = O^a$

Source	df	SS	E(MS)	F
Total regression	$k+1$	$Q_h = \hat{\beta}'X'X\hat{\beta}$	$\sigma^2 + \dfrac{\beta'X'X\beta}{k+1}$	MS_h/MS_e
Residual	$N-k-1$	$Q_\varepsilon = y'y - \hat{\beta}'X'X\hat{\beta}$	σ^2	
Total	N	$Q_T = y'y$		

^{a}From Timm, 1975, p. 273.

In the latter case, the hypothesis would be

$$H_0 : \beta = \begin{bmatrix} \beta_1 \\ \beta_2 \\ \vdots \\ \beta_k \end{bmatrix} = \begin{bmatrix} 0 \\ 0 \\ \vdots \\ 0 \end{bmatrix} \qquad (47)$$

where β_0 is omitted.

As Timm (1975) indicates, "Testing that all the (slope) coefficients $\beta_1, \ldots, \beta_k$ are equal to 0 is a special case of the more general problem of testing that some subset of the coefficients is 0, with no restrictions on the other elements" [p. 275].

The general procedure is similar to the one just described. Partition β into two subvectors

$$\beta = \begin{bmatrix} \beta_0 \\ \hline \beta_h \end{bmatrix} \qquad (48)$$

where β_0 contains the regressors *not* being tested (including the intercept) and β_h contains those that are under test by the hypothesis. Thus, the null form and the alternative are

$$H_0: \quad \beta_h = 0 \quad \text{and} \quad H_A: \quad \beta_h \neq 0 \qquad (49)$$

which hypothesize that the variables in the second set which correspond to β_h significantly contribute to the variance in y over and above the regressors in the first set, β_0.

A convenient technique for testing this hypothesis is to formulate *two separate* regression equations. The first equation contains the first m of the k predictors ($m < k$) which are known or assumed to significantly contribute to criterion variance; the second equation contains all k predictors, i.e., the first m variables not being tested plus the remaining $k - m$ variables which constitute β_h. The respective equations would be

$$\beta_0: \quad \underset{N \times 1}{y} \ = \ \underset{N \times (m+1)}{X} \ \underset{(m+1) \times 1}{\beta} \ + \ \underset{N \times 1}{\varepsilon} \qquad (50a)$$

and

$$\beta_h: \quad \underset{N \times 1}{y} \ = \ \underset{N \times q}{X} \ \underset{q \times 1}{\beta} \ + \ \underset{N \times 1}{\varepsilon} \quad \text{where} \quad q = k + 1 \qquad (50b)$$

These two equations can, of course, be represented by their respective measures of "goodness of fit," R_0^2 for the reduced set of regressors, β_0, and R_h^2 for the full set of regressors, $\beta_0 + \beta_h = \beta$. It is then possible to construct an F statistic that will enable us to determine the significance of the β_h vector over and above the β_0 vector.

$$F = \frac{R_k^2 - R_m^2}{1 - R_k^2} \cdot \frac{N - k - 1}{K - m} \qquad (51)$$

which has $(k - m)$ and $(N - k - 1)$ degrees of freedom, m equal to the number of X variables in the reduced vector β_0, and k equal to the full set of X variables in β. If F is significant at $P \leqslant \alpha$, then H_0 is rejected and it is concluded that *some* of the regressors in β_h do contribute significantly to variation in y. The squared partial multiple coefficient of determination is given by

$$R_y^2 X_{(m+1, \ldots, k)} \cdot X_{(1, \ldots, m)} = \frac{R_k^2 - R_m^2}{1 - R_m^2} \qquad (52)$$

and indicates the amount of variation in Y which remains after the first m variables have been partialed out of the regression equation.

When β_h contains only one regression coefficient so that $\beta_0 = k - 1$ (i.e., β_0 contains all but the last coefficient), Eq. (51) has a special interpretation which is of considerable importance. We can test whether an *individual* regression coefficient differs significantly from zero, and thereby contributes significantly to criterion variation. The size of $r^2_{YX_k \cdot X(1, \ldots, k-1)}$, the squared *partial correlation coefficient*, also provides a measure of the inevitably shared variation between the two variables.

The formula provided in Eq. (52) is perfectly adequate for examining the contribution to criterion variance made by the last variable in the equation. In general, however, if we examine more than the final variable we find that the regression coefficients for pairs of predictors are generally correlated. Let us suppose that we wish to obtain individual *sequential* tests for each of the final $K - m > 1$ predictors, i.e., the last variable, the next to last variable, etc., until we get back to the mth variables. Finn (1974) indicates, "A series of independent tests is facilitated by transforming the predictor variables to a new set of uncorrelated measures, in a specified order. We shall substitute for predictor X_j in **X** only the linear function or portion of X_j that is uncorrelated with preceding predictors $X_1, X_2, \ldots, X_{j-1}$. That is, we shall find the X_j values that are obtained if we 'partial out' or 'hold constant' the effects of earlier predictors in the set" [p. 137]. There are two important points to note here. The first is that each variable is orthogonalized (made to be uncorrelated) with only those variables that precede it in the equation. The second is that the process requires that the variables be arranged in a prespecified order.

The process which Finn (1974, pp. 134–144; see also Timm, 1975; Kshirsagar, 1959; and Anderson, 1958) describes produces *orthogonal estimates* of regression coefficients or *semipartial regression coefficients*. Each semipartial regression coefficient indicates the relation between Y and X_j controlling for the variance contributed by variables preceding X_j in the equation, but *not* controlling for the variance of those variables which follow it. It is important to note that the full partial regression coefficient for X_j is the same as the semipartial regression coefficient for X_j when that variable is the last one in the equation. The process of sequentially estimating the effect of each predictor variable eliminating those preceding it is called *stepwise elimination*.

In general, the r^2s between Y and each X_j will *not* add up to $R^2_{Y \cdot X_1, \ldots, k}$ because the r^2s are correlated. The *squared semipartial* correlation coefficients will, however, add to $R^2_{y \cdot X_1, \ldots, k}$ since the constraint is imposed that each sequential $r^2_{y(X_j \cdot X_1, \ldots, j-1)}$ will account only for variance not accounted for by preceding variables. Thus, as Kerlinger and Pedhazur (1973, p. 94) indicate,

$$R^2_{y \cdot X_1, \ldots, k} = r^2_{yX_1} + r^2_{y(X_2 \cdot X_1)} + r^2_{y(X_3 \cdot X_{1,2})} + \cdots + r^2_{y(X_k \cdot X_{1, \ldots, k-1})} \quad (53)$$

which is read, "The total amount of shared variance in y and **X** is given by the sum of the squared semipartial correlation coefficients, i.e., the squared correlation between Y and X_1 plus the variance between Y and X_2 removing the influence of X_1 from the relation with Y, plus . . . plus the variance between Y and X_k removing the influence of X_1 through X_{k-1} from the relation with Y."

Often a researcher is interested in whether the combined effects of two (or more) variables viewed together significantly contribute to criterion variation *over and above* the variation accounted for by the variables viewed separately. This *interaction* between (among) variables can be examined in regression analysis by the inclusion of multiplicative or cross-product terms in the prediction equation. Each interaction term is treated as a new predictor variable in the linear model. The new variable is created by cross multiplying the observed values for each subject on the original variables, e.g., $X_{ij_1}X_{ij_2}$ or $X_{ij_1}X_{ij_2}X_{ij_3}$, etc. Since the model is still linear this multiplicative term is *added* to the model and a regression parameter is estimated for the new term. For example, given two variables, X_1 and X_2, one linear model which includes the interaction term would be

$$y_i = \beta_0 + \beta_1 X_{i1} + \beta_2 X_{i2} + \beta_3 X_{i1}X_{i2} + \varepsilon_i \tag{54}$$

Another, often much more convenient linear model would be

$$y_i = \left(\beta_0 + \Sigma\beta_j \bar{X}_j\right) + \sum_i \beta_j\left(X_{ij} - \bar{X}_j\right) + \beta_3\left(X_{1j} - \bar{X}_j\right)\left(X_{2j} - \bar{X}_j\right) + \varepsilon_i \tag{55}$$

Other nonlinear interactions, such as products of powered (polynomial) terms, e.g., linear by quadratic ($X_1^1 X_1^2$, $X_1^1 X_2^2$, etc.) and quadratic by cubic ($X_1^2 X_1^3$, $X_1^2 X_2^3$, etc.) can also be added to a linear regression model (see Cohen, 1968, pp. 436–437).

To calculate interaction terms it is sometimes useful to first standardize the respective variables prior to computation of the cross-product terms. As Finn (1975) indicates, "The dominance of the interaction by one or another variable due to scaling is avoided. The interaction terms themselves need not be standardized" [p. 85]. Once this is accomplished, the OLS estimation and hypothesis testing techniques described earlier can be employed. It should be noted, however, that it is customary, and often important, to add the multiplicative terms into the equation last, thus testing them first if backward elimination techniques are employed.

Several hypotheses have been identified in this section which a researcher might profitably examine. These do not exhaust the possibilities, however. Table III presents those discussed plus several other alternatives which are worthy of consideration. Which test to use depends, of course, upon the theory guiding the research. Perhaps an example will help to illustrate this point.

Attention in communication research tends to focus almost exclusively on slope regression coefficients, i.e., β_i ($i = 1, \ldots, k$) to the exclusion of the

TABLE III.

HYPOTHESES AND TEST STATISTICS FOR TESTING REGRESSION COEFFICIENTS

Hypothesis	Test statistic	Comment
(1)　H_0:　$\hat{\beta}_k = 0$	$t = \dfrac{\hat{\beta}_k}{S_{b_k}}$	$\hat{\beta}_k$ equals zero. Can be used to test the intercept, $\hat{\beta}_0$. See Johnston (1972, p. 138).
(2)　H_0:　$\hat{\beta}_k = M_k$	$t = \dfrac{\hat{\beta}_k - M_k}{S_k}$	$\hat{\beta}_k$ equals some constant, M_k. See Kmenta (1971, p. 366).
(3)　H_0:　$\hat{\gamma} = 0$ or $\hat{\beta}_1, \ldots, \hat{\beta}_k = 0$	$F = \dfrac{SS_R/(k-1)}{SS_E/(N-k-1)}$ $= \left(\dfrac{N-k}{k-1}\right)\left(\dfrac{R^2}{1-R^2}\right)$	All coefficients except the intercept are zero. See Goldberger (1964, p. 176), and Timm (1975, p. 273).
(4)　H_0:　$\hat{\beta}_h = 0$	$F = \left(\dfrac{R_0^2 - R_h^2}{1 - R_0^2}\right)\left(\dfrac{N-k-1}{k-m}\right)$	Some subset of the coefficients (perhaps the final one) is zero. See Goldberger (1964).
(5)　H_0:　$\beta_j = \beta_k$ (for $j \neq k$)	$t = \dfrac{\hat{\beta}_j - \hat{\beta}_k}{S_{\beta_j - \beta_k}}$	One regression coefficient equals another. See Goldberger (1964, p. 175).
(6)　H_0:　$\beta_j + \beta_k = a$	$t_{N-k} = \dfrac{\hat{\beta}_j + \hat{\beta}_k - a}{S_{\beta_j - \beta_k}}$	The *sum* of two (or more $= k$) coefficients equals a constant. See Kmenta (1971, p. 372).
(7)　H_0:　$\hat{\beta} = \hat{\delta}$ ($\hat{\delta}$ is the vector of regression coefficients for a second equation)		Two regression equations are equal. See Kmenta (1971, p. 373), for the test statistics.

intercept coefficient, β_0 (or α). Unless data have been reparameterized to force the intercept to the origin (or some other level) of the coordinate system, the value of the intercept may also be of considerable theoretical interest. If we modify an example given by Kmenta (1971, pp. 204–205) we can see the importance of the intercept. Suppose that media consumption (i.e., number of hours/week spent watching television), Y, is regressed on amount of leisure time (number of hours not devoted to gainful employment or primary occupation), X, and a linear relationship of the form $Y = \beta_0 + \beta_1 X + \epsilon$ is determined. The slope coefficient, β_1, would be interpreted as the marginal propensity to watch television, i.e., the amount of increase in watching television for every unit increase in amount of leisure time. Now examine β_0. Assuming that people will consume (use) *at least some* television even if they have no leisure time, β_0 indicates the minimal or subsistence consumption of television, i.e., the amount of television exposure when the value of leisure time is zero. Hypotheses regarding the intercept coefficient could be of significant theoretical value. Refering to Table III we might utilize test (1), that H_0: $\hat{\beta}_k = 0$, for the intercept coefficient β_0. If our theory were more sophisticated we might utilize test (2), that H_0: $\hat{\beta}_0 = M_k$, for some constant, which is tantamount to asserting that we can predict "subsistence" media consumption at some number greater than zero.

H. Reestimation of Parameters

As was pointed out earlier in the paper, estimates of regression parameters are valid, under the assumptions of the model, only for a given set of regressors. If we change the set of regressors, either by adding or deleting predictor variables, the coefficients for the original equation for which the estimates were obtained will no longer be appropriate. New estimates should be obtained. It is important to emphasize that these new coefficients will estimate parameters with different meanings than the original parameters.

It should be clear that the hypothesis testing procedures described in the previous section lead, if significant, to the deletion of variables from the full set of variables included in the original equation. Or, alternatively conceived, the procedures lead to the addition of significant variables over and above those already included in the equation. (It is possible, of course, to test the entire set of variables.) Under either conceptualization, obtaining significant results in hypothesis testing is likely to lead to a different set of variables, a different regression equation, than the one with which the researcher began.

In situations where this occurs, the researcher should reestimate the parameters of the final obtained regression equation. The procedures for reestimation are identical to those for estimation. The final set of variables are estimated by OLS procedures, with the variance of the rejected variables pooled with the error variance. A final estimate of the standard error of estimate should also be obtained. The final equation which contains the final estimates of regression parameters, the final standard errors of estimate, and the recomputed final R^2 should be presented in the research report. It is equally important to describe the steps in reestimation in equivalent detail.

III. MULTIVARIATE MULTIPLE REGRESSION

In this section we will extend the findings developed for the univariate model to the multivariate case. Most of the presentation will be by analogy with univariate results.

A. The Multivariate Multiple Regression Model

Let us assume that a communication researcher has two or more variables that are considered worthy of examination as criterion variables in relation to the same set of predictor variables that we assumed in the univariate case. This is a problem for which multivariate regression analysis is appropriate.

The multivariate multiple regression model is given by

$$\underset{N \times p}{\mathbf{Y}} = \underset{N \times q}{\mathbf{X}} \underset{q \times p}{\mathbf{B}} + \underset{N \times p}{\mathbf{E}} \qquad (56)$$

which in expanded form is

$$
\begin{bmatrix}
y_{11} & y_{12} & \cdots & y_{1p} \\
y_{21} & y_{22} & \cdots & y_{2p} \\
\vdots & \vdots & \cdots & \vdots \\
y_{N1} & y_{N2} & \cdots & y_{Np}
\end{bmatrix}
=
\begin{bmatrix}
1 & X_{11} & X_{12} & \cdots & X_{1q} \\
1 & X_{21} & X_{22} & \cdots & X_{2q} \\
\vdots & \vdots & \vdots & \cdots & \vdots \\
1 & X_{N1} & X_{N2} & \cdots & X_{Nq}
\end{bmatrix}
$$

$$
\times
\begin{bmatrix}
\beta_{01} & \beta_{02} & \cdots & \beta_{0p} \\
\beta_{11} & \beta_{12} & \cdots & \beta_{1p} \\
\vdots & \vdots & \cdots & \vdots \\
\beta_{q1} & \beta_{q2} & \cdots & \beta_{qp}
\end{bmatrix}
$$

$$
+
\begin{bmatrix}
\varepsilon_{11} & \varepsilon_{12} & \cdots & \varepsilon_{1p} \\
\varepsilon_{21} & \varepsilon_{22} & \cdots & \varepsilon_{2p} \\
\vdots & \vdots & \cdots & \vdots \\
\varepsilon_{N1} & \varepsilon_{N2} & \cdots & \varepsilon_{Np}
\end{bmatrix}
$$

This equation states that a data matrix $A_{N \times M}$ has been partitioned into two submatrices, $Y_{N \times p}$ which contains two or more criterion variables and $X_{N \times q}$ which contains all the data for the predictor variables augmented by an initial column of unities. Furthermore, the scores in the Y matrix are composed of linear combinations of the X scores, each weighted by a regression coefficient, β_k, and added to the error term, ε_{ij}. That is,

$$
y_{ij} = \beta_{0j} + \beta_{ij}X_{i1} + \beta_{2j}X_{i2} + \cdots + \beta_{kj}X_{ik} + \varepsilon_{ij} \tag{57}
$$

E, then, is an $N \times p$ matrix of error terms, with one column of errors for each criterion variable. If the model is intended to be a multivariate classical linear regression model we assume

$$
E(Y) = XB \quad \text{which is equivalent to} \quad E(E) = 0 \tag{58}
$$

since the expectation of Y is XB, and

$$
V(Y) = I_N \otimes \Sigma \quad \text{which is equivalent to} \quad V(E) = I_N \otimes \Sigma \tag{59}
$$

since Y and E differ only by a constant, namely XB. The Kronecker product operator, $\otimes$, which is used to define the variance of Y, produces in this case a diagonal matrix with diagonal elements equal to Σ and off-diagonal elements 0. Thus

$$
V(Y) = V(E) = I_N \otimes \Sigma =
\begin{bmatrix}
\Sigma & 0 & \cdots & 0 \\
0 & \Sigma & \cdots & 0 \\
\vdots & \vdots & \vdots & \vdots \\
0 & 0 & \cdots & \Sigma
\end{bmatrix}
\tag{60}
$$

These assumptions may be summarized as

$$E \sim N_N(0, I \otimes \Sigma) \qquad (61)$$

which states that Y is a multivariate normal distribution, that the errors have constant variance, and that the errors are uncorrelated. It is also possible to state the model in equivalent mean deviation (reparameterized) and standardized forms. In the former case we have

$$\underset{N \times p}{Y} = \underset{N \times q}{X_d} \underset{q \times p}{H} + \underset{N \times p}{E} \qquad (62)$$

where eta (H) is the matrix of partial regression coefficients for the mean-adjusted scores, X_d. In the latter case we have

$$\underset{N \times p}{Y_z} = \underset{N \times k}{Z} \underset{k \times p}{\Gamma} + \underset{N \times p}{E} \qquad (63)$$

where gamma (Γ) is the matrix of standardized partial regression coefficients.

B. Estimation of Multivariate Regression Parameters

In order to estimate the regression parameters we proceed as in the univariate case. The process is to apply the Gauss–Markoff theorem (see Timm, 1975, pp. 185–188) to obtain the matrix B so that the sum of squared errors is minimized. The theorem states that this can be accomplished by minimizing the trace of the sum of squared errors matrix, $E'E$. Thus, let S_E be equal to the sum of squared errors to be minimized, then

$$S_E = \text{Tr}(\hat{E}'\hat{E}) \qquad \text{since Tr}(\hat{E}'\hat{E}) = \sum_{i=1}^{k} \sum_{j=1}^{p} \hat{\varepsilon}_{ij}^2$$

$$= \text{Tr}(Y - X\hat{B})'(Y - X\hat{B}) \qquad \text{rearranging Eq. (56)} \qquad (64)$$

When the partial derivatives of S_E with respect to $\hat{B}$ are set equal to zero and solved, the following normal equations are obtained

$$X'X\hat{B} = X'Y \qquad (65)$$

which can be solved for $\hat{B}$

$$\hat{B} = (X'X)^{-1}X'Y \qquad (66)$$

This equation states that under the assumptions of the model the best linear unbiased *estimates* of the matrix of regression coefficients can be obtained directly from the sums of squares and cross-products matrices of the raw data, i.e., from $X'Y$ and the inverse of $X'X$. Comparison of Eq. (66) with Eqs. (18) and (34) indicates that the multivariate solution is completely analogous to its univariate counterpart; that is, *each* regression coefficient, $\hat{\beta}_{ij}$, in the matrix of regressions, $\hat{B}$, is equivalent to $\Sigma xy / \Sigma x^2$. This can be seen from the fact that $(X'X)^{-1}XY$ does not depend upon which responses are involved.

$\hat{\mathbf{B}}$, of course, consists of a matrix of partial regression coefficients. For *each* criterion variable there are as many coefficients as there are predictor variables, plus one coefficient for the intercept. Thus, if there are two criterion variables and three predictor variables, there would be $2 \times (3 + 1) = 8$ regression coefficients. In general, using the orders of our matrices, there will be $(q \times p)$ regression coefficients (remember, $q = k$ predictor variables $+ 1$) for the raw form of the regression model. In the standardized model there would be $(p \times k)$ coefficients.

Since $\hat{\mathbf{B}}$ has been estimated from the data, it is desirable to obtain a measure of the stability of the estimate. Sampling theory specifies that upon *repeated* sampling from a given population we would obtain a distribution of **B**s for samples of a given size, N. That sampling distribution would have both an expected value and a variance (as well as higher order moments). Finn (1973) indicates that "the estimate $\hat{\mathbf{B}}$, like its univariate counterpart, is unbiased and minimum variance" [p. 113], under sufficiently strong assumptions, of course. Its expectation and variance–covariance matrix are

$$
\begin{aligned}
E(\hat{\mathbf{B}}) &= E[(\mathbf{X'X})^{-1}\mathbf{X'Y}] && \text{from Eq. (66)} \\
&= (\mathbf{X'X})^{-1}\mathbf{X'}E(\mathbf{Y}) && \text{since } \mathbf{X} \text{ is constant} \\
&= (\mathbf{X'X})^{-1}\mathbf{X'XB} && \text{by substitution from Eq. (58)} \\
&= \hat{\mathbf{B}} && \text{since } (\mathbf{X'X})^{-1}\mathbf{X'X} = \mathbf{I}
\end{aligned}
$$

(67)

and

$$
\begin{aligned}
V(\hat{\mathbf{B}}) &= V[(\mathbf{X'X})^{-1}\mathbf{X'Y}] && \text{from Eq. (66)} \\
&= (\mathbf{X'X})^{-1} \otimes \mathbf{\Sigma} && \text{see Finn (p. 114) for proof}
\end{aligned}
$$

(68)

Using Eq. (64) we can also see than an unbiased (maximum likelihood) estimate of the error variance of $\mathbf{Y}$, $\hat{\mathbf{\Sigma}}$, can be obtained directly from the observed data. Let $\mathbf{S_E}$ represent the residual or error sum of squares and cross-products matrix, and we obtain the variance–covariance estimate by dividing by the degrees of freedom scalar, $N - q$,

$$
\begin{aligned}
\hat{\mathbf{\Sigma}} &= \frac{1}{N - q}\mathbf{S_E} = \frac{1}{N - q}\mathrm{Tr}(\hat{\mathbf{E}}'\hat{\mathbf{E}}) && \text{from Eq. (64)} \\[2mm]
&= \frac{(\mathbf{Y} - \mathbf{X}\hat{\mathbf{B}})'(\mathbf{Y} - \mathbf{X}\hat{\mathbf{B}})}{N - q} && \text{substituting} \\[2mm]
&= \frac{\mathbf{Y'Y} - \hat{\mathbf{B}}'\mathbf{X'Y}}{N - q} && \text{by multiplication and canceling} \\[2mm]
&= \frac{\mathbf{Y'Y} - \hat{\mathbf{B}}'\mathbf{B'X}\hat{\mathbf{B}}}{N - q} && \text{a frequently encountered equivalent form}
\end{aligned}
$$

(69)

It should be obvious that each element of $\hat{\boldsymbol{\Sigma}}$ is an estimate of population variance (σ_j^2 on the diagonal) and covariance ($\sigma_{ij}, i \neq j$, on the off-diagonal cells).

As in the univariate case, the variance in $\mathbf{Y}_{N \times p}$ can be partitioned. Let $\mathbf{S}_Y$ represent the total sum of squares and cross products in the sample criterion scores, $\mathbf{Y}$, and $\mathbf{S}_R$ the variation in the predicted scores, $\tilde{\mathbf{Y}}'\tilde{\mathbf{Y}} = \hat{\mathbf{B}}'\mathbf{X}'\mathbf{X}\hat{\mathbf{B}}$, called the sum of squares for regression. Then the partition is

$$\mathbf{S}_Y = \mathbf{S}_R + \mathbf{S}_E \tag{70}$$

which breaks the total variation into two components: that attributable to regression and that attributable to error. If $\mathbf{S}_R$ approximates $\mathbf{S}_Y$, then $\mathbf{S}_E$ will be small and the predictor scores will predict the criterion scores quite well. If $\mathbf{S}_R$ is small compared to $\mathbf{S}_Y$, then the linear model does not fit the data well and $\mathbf{S}_E$ will be quite large.

The "goodness of fit" of the model can be determined in a way that is identical to that in univariate regression. As Press (1972) indicates, "In multivariate regression, the value of R^2 can be computed for each equation separately to study the effectiveness of each relationship in accounting for observed variation" [p. 195].

As Timm (1975) indicates, "Estimation theory, using the multivariate linear model is no different from employing p univariate models. It is not until hypothesis-testing theory is employed that the models really differ. Univariate analysis does not address itself to the dependency that exists among a set of **p** response (criterion) variables" [p. 309]. We turn now to the question of hypothesis testing.

C. Hypothesis Testing for Multivariate Regression

The logic of hypothesis testing in multivariate multiple regression is similar to that of its univariate counterpart except that multiple criterion variables can be tested simultaneously. The purpose of the simultaneous test is to maintain protection levels at a point predetermined by the researcher, i.e., at α. Were separate tests run for each dependent variable, the likelihood of obtaining a false significant value would increase in direct proportion to the number of dependent variables being tested, i.e., the power of the test decreases.

The general test for *all* coefficients of the raw form of the model is

$$H_0: \quad \mathbf{B} = \mathbf{0} \tag{71}$$

which can be examined by using a multivariate analysis of variance (MANOVA) table. To conduct the test we must obtain the sum of squares and cross-products *matrices* for both hypothesis and error, from which mean squares may be determined. These are, by extension from the univariate case

$$\mathbf{Q}_e = \mathbf{Y}'\mathbf{Y} - \hat{\mathbf{B}}'\mathbf{X}'\mathbf{X}\hat{\mathbf{B}} \quad \text{and} \quad \mathbf{Q}_h = \hat{\mathbf{B}}'\mathbf{X}'\mathbf{X}\hat{\mathbf{B}} \tag{72}$$

The MANOVA table (see Table IV) can then be constructed.

TABLE IV

MANOVA TABLE FOR TESTING $\mathbf{B} = \mathbf{0}^a$

Sources	df	SS	$E(MS)$
Total regression	$k + 1$	$\mathbf{Q_h} = \hat{\mathbf{B}}'\mathbf{X}'\mathbf{X}\hat{\mathbf{B}}$	$\mathbf{\Sigma} + \dfrac{\hat{\mathbf{B}}'\mathbf{X}'\mathbf{X}\hat{\mathbf{B}}}{k + 1}$
Residual	$N - k - 1$	$\mathbf{Q_e} = \mathbf{Y}'\mathbf{Y} - \hat{\mathbf{B}}'\mathbf{X}'\mathbf{X}\hat{\mathbf{B}}$	$\mathbf{\Sigma}$
Total	N	$\mathbf{Q_T} = \mathbf{Y}'\mathbf{Y}$	

^{a}From Timm (1975, p. 309).

Normally, of course, we are not interested in testing all of the regression equations, since we seldom test the intercept and usually are interested in testing only a subset of the slope coefficients. Hence we would partition the model into two separate regressions and develop an hypothesis which would enable us to test the subset. The partitioned model would be

$$\mathbf{Y} = \begin{bmatrix} \mathbf{X_I} & \mathbf{X_{II}} \end{bmatrix} \begin{bmatrix} \mathbf{B_I} \\ \mathbf{B_{II}} \end{bmatrix} + \mathbf{E} \tag{73}$$

with the hypothesis that

$$H_0: \quad \mathbf{B_{II}} = \mathbf{0} \tag{74}$$

Equations (73) and (74) simply assert that the first set of variables $\mathbf{X_I}$ $(I = 1, \ldots, m)$ and regression coefficients $\mathbf{B_I}(I = 0, \ldots, m)$ are *not* being tested while the remaining variables in $\mathbf{X_{II}}(II = m + 1, \ldots, k)$ and the coefficients in $\mathbf{B_{II}}(II = m + 1, \ldots, k)$ are under test. It is, of course, possible to test the final set of coefficients, $\mathbf{B_k}$, by setting the indicator m to $k - 1$. Then we would have $\mathbf{B_I}$ equal to all $k - 1$ coefficients and $\mathbf{B_{II}}$ equal to the last set of k coefficients.

There are a number of alternative procedures available to test the hypotheses stated in Eqs. (71) and (74). These all depend on solutions for the roots or eigenvalues $\lambda_1, \lambda_2, \ldots, \lambda_s$ of the characteristic equation

$$|\mathbf{Q_h} - \lambda \mathbf{Q_e}| = 0 \tag{75}$$

where the roots are ordered from largest, λ_1, to smallest, λ_s. Anderson (1958, Chapter 8) and Timm (1975, pp. 137–140, 146–149, and 308–313) describe a number of criteria which may be used to test the hypotheses. These tests are provided in Table V. Tables for each of these distributions at selected degrees of freedom are available in Timm (1975). Since most of these distributions are unfamiliar to communication researchers, Table V includes tests for multivariate hypotheses by approximations to χ^2 and F statistics which have been derived from the other distributions.

It is instructive to examine the logic of the Wilks' likelihood ratio criterion, Λ. The determinant of a variance–covariance matrix can be considered a measure of generalized variance. Wilks' Λ is the ratio of two generalized variances. The numerator contains the variance for the reduced model, $\mathbf{Q_e}$,

TABLE V

CRITERIA AND TESTS FOR MULTIVARIATE HYPOTHESES

$$H_0: \ \mathbf{B} = \mathbf{0}; \qquad H_0: \ \Gamma = \mathbf{0}; \qquad H_0: \ \mathbf{B}_{II} = \mathbf{0}$$

(1) Wilks' likelihood ratio criterion

$$\Lambda = \frac{|\mathbf{Q}_e|}{|\mathbf{Q}_e + \mathbf{Q}_h|} = \sum_{i=1}^{s} (1 + \lambda_i)^{-1} < U^{\alpha}(P, k + 1, N - k - 1)$$

(2) Roy's largest root criterion

$$\theta_s = \frac{\lambda_1}{1 + \lambda_1} > \theta^{\alpha}(s, m, n)$$

(3) Lawley–Hotelling trace criterion (or Hotelling's generalized T^2 statistic)

$$U^s = \frac{T_0^2}{N - k - 1} = \sum_{i=1}^{s} \lambda_i > U_0^{\alpha}(s, m, n)$$

(4) Pillai's trace condition

$$V^s = \sum_{i=1}^{s} \frac{\lambda_i}{1 + \lambda_i} > V^{\alpha}(s, m, n)$$

(5) Bartlett's χ_B^2-test

$$\chi_B^2 = -[(N - 1) - 1/2(P + k + 1)] \log \Lambda > \chi_{\alpha}^2(pk)$$

(6) Fisher's F-test

$$F = \frac{\nu_e}{\nu_h} \frac{1 - \Lambda}{\Lambda} > F^{\alpha}(\nu_e, \nu_h)$$

where

$$s = \min(\nu_h, p) = \min(k + 1, p), \qquad m = \frac{|u - \nu_h| - 1}{2} = \frac{|p - k - 1| - 1}{2}$$

$$n = \frac{\nu_e - u - 1}{2} = \frac{N - k - p - 2}{2}$$

ν = degrees of freedom

i.e., those variables not under test; the denominator contains the variance for the full set of predictors, i.e., those predictors not under test *plus* those that are being tested, $\mathbf{Q}_h$. Thus

$$\Lambda = \frac{|\mathbf{Q}_e|}{|\mathbf{Q}_e + \mathbf{Q}_h|} \tag{76}$$

It should be apparent that if $\mathbf{B}_{II} = 0$ then $\mathbf{Q}_h = 0$ and $\Lambda = |\mathbf{Q}_e|/|\mathbf{Q}_e| = 1$, which is the upper bound of the statistic. On the other hand, to the extent that $\mathbf{Q}_h$ (i.e., $X_{m+1}, \ldots, X_k$) adds variance over and above the reduced model, the denominator will increase and $\Lambda < 1$. Thus, the smaller Λ is, the more that $\mathbf{Q}_h$ or $\mathbf{B}$ is adding to criterion variation. The F and χ^2-tests simply transform the Λ statistic (really, the U distribution) to the more familiar F and χ^2

distributions. Most computerized MMR routines will print both Λ and either F or χ^2-test statistics.

Testing the criterion variables.   If Λ (or any other test criterion) is significant it is then possible to determine which of the criterion variables are being affected by the variables in the predictor set. Univariate F ratios may be used to accomplish this task. The univariate F that is largest is the one which shows which of the criterion variables is most affected by the predictors, and so on down to the smallest F ratio which shows the criterion variable which is least affected by predictors. However, as Finn (1975) points out, these tests are *not* independent: "there is no necessary relationship of the significance of the univariate and multivariate tests for one hypothesis. For example, one or more univariate F's may be significant and not the multivariate statistic, or vice versa" [p. 157]. Consequently, it is usually recommended that in addition to the univariate F-tests, researchers examine the simple and multiple correlations to aid in interpretation.

To deal with this problem of interdependence of multivariate and univariate tests for locating effects, it is possible to conduct a *step-down analysis* which will provide *independent* univariate tests for the criterion variables. The term *step-down* as used here and by Bock (1966) and Finn (1974, pp. 157–160) refers to the fact that the *criterion* variables rather than the predictor variables are being examined (eliminated) sequentially. The tests, which are described by Roy (1958) require that the researcher impose an a priori ordering on the *criterion* variables. If the researcher has no rational basis for such an ordering, then step-down tests will be of little value. The reason for this is, as with stepwise procedures in univariate multiple regression, the capitalization on chance by numerous (or all possible) orderings of variables, which drastically increases the alpha level for significance tests, thereby invalidating inference procedures unless compensated for by other procedures (e.g., reducing alpha to a small enough value that when multiplied by the number of different orderings examined it equals the originally desired protection levels). The procedures for conducting the tests are identical to calculating F-tests (for each of the p criterion variables) with the condition imposed that only the conditional variance in the criterion variables be analyzed. The tests proceed by regressing all the q predictor variables on y_1, on y_2 eliminating y_1, on y_3 eliminating y_1 and y_2, etc., but does so in a form of backward elimination. First, the pth criterion variable y_p is eliminated, i.e., the last one in the ordered set. Then the next to the last is eliminated y_{p-1}, etc., down to first criterion, y_1. At each step an F statistic is calculated; if F is nonsignificant, and H_0 for a particular criterion cannot be rejected, it means that the predictor *set* does not inevitably contribute significantly to variation in particular criterion variable y_j. Each time that H_0 cannot be rejected, the *step-down* procedure continues until such a time as an H_0 must be rejected in favor of the alternative H_A. At that point testing terminates since all remaining tests are nonindependent. See Bock (1966) and Finn (1974) for additional details on step-down analysis.

Testing the predictor variables.   Having determined how the set of predictor variables differentially affects the criterion variables it is often of interest, as in the univariate case, to test hypotheses regarding a subset of the predictor variables. Tests for contributions to criterion variance of individual predictors are facilitated by creating orthogonal columns of **B**, i.e., converting the partial regression coefficients to semipartial regression coefficients. Each semipartial regression coefficient accounts for variance in **Y** *not* accounted for by predictor variables that precede it in the regression equation. This orthogonalization process, of course, requires that the researcher impose an a priori order on the predictors. This a priori ordering should be based in theory or at the very least on empirical considerations such as " . . . when subjects have been tested repeatedly over time, when measures involve progressively more complex behaviors, or whenever there exists a systematic progression from one outcome measure to another" [Finn, 1975, p. 157]. When the backward sequential tests on the predictor variables encounter a variable which significantly contributes to criterion variance, the testing procedure must stop, since all subsequent tests are nonindependent. It should be apparent from this discussion that the researcher must rely heavily upon theory to specify the order of the predictor variables so that the anticipated strongest predictor is the first variable in the equation and the anticipated weakest is last. This task may be aided by cross-validation from multiple studies of the same phenomena.

D. Reestimation of Multivariate Parameters

As in the univariate case, if a researcher either adds or deletes variables from the orginal equation, it is important to reestimate the parameters of the resultant or final equation. Variance in the nonsignificant variables is pooled with error variance to make the final estimate. It should be emphasized that the interpretation of any regression coefficient is specific to the set of variables which constitute the regression equation. Addition or deletion of variables will change the set of which the equation is comprised and hence the interpretation and meaning of the individual coefficients. Discussions of reestimated parameters should include comments on how the reestimated coefficients substantially differ in interpretation from those in the original equation. Finn (1975) indicates that "under ideal circumstances, these final estimates should be obtained from a sample other than the one used for significance tests" [p. 165]. Cross-validation can provide extremely useful information in this process.

IV. A COMMUNICATION EXAMPLE

To illustrate the procedures just presented, we will utilize the data reported by Korzenny and Bauer (1979), which is an experiment designed as an initial test of Korzenny's (1978) theory of electronic propinquity. The theory attempts to account for the level of satisfaction which people experience when they participate in mediated communication such as teleconferencing. Specifically, it states that people will be more satisfied with their communication as a function of an increase in their propinquity (i.e., a decrease in their perceived psychological distance) from the other participants. Propinquity, in turn, is postulated to be a function of five antecedent variables: feedback (the amount of information exchanged in the experiment), regulation of communication interaction (the amount perceived by participants), complexity of information (the perceived number of discrepant factors in the initial message), bandwidth (the perceived information transmission capacity of the various forms of mediated communication), and perceived level of communication skills (each person evaluated by all others in the conference). The predictor variables were ordered on the basis of known relationships to criterion varibles and preliminary research. While the theory specifies a causal ordering among the variables as indicated above, the present analysis will treat propinquity and satisfaction as dependent variables only. The theory will be used to *order* these two variables, but not to imply causality.

The model to be analyzed is

$$\underset{112\times2}{\mathbf{Y}} = \underset{112\times6}{\mathbf{X}}\ \underset{6\times2}{\mathbf{B}} + \underset{112\times2}{\mathbf{E}}$$

There are two criterion variables, propinquity and communication satisfaction, in that order, and five predictor variables, in the order indicated previously. In the model matrix there is an initial column of unities to provide an estimate for the intercept term, which corresponds to the first row (with two entries, one for each equation) in the coefficients matrix. There are 112 subjects.

The hypothesis testing procedure will proceed in three steps. First the overall relation between the two sets of variables will be examined. Then the contribution of the predictor set to each of the criterion variables, in the order specified by the theory, will be explored. Finally, the individual contribution of each of the predictor variables to variance in the criterion variables will be determined. Following the tests to determine the significant relationships, the final reduced equation will be reestimated. We begin the analysis by specifying the hypotheses and showing the partitioning of the coefficients matrix:

$$H_0:\ \mathbf{B_h} = \mathbf{0}; \qquad H_A:\ \mathbf{B_h} \neq \mathbf{0}, \qquad \alpha = .05$$

$$\mathbf{B} = \begin{bmatrix} \mathbf{B_0} \\ \text{----} \\ \mathbf{B_h} \end{bmatrix}$$

containing intercept and feedback variable, x_1, not being tested.

containing the 2nd–5th predictors, being tested as a group.

Since the first predictor variable, feedback, is known to be significantly related to the criterion variables, it is not tested. Data were analyzed with the SPSS (version 7.0) MANOVA computer routine and with MULTIVARI-ANCE (version 4).

As a preliminary to undertaking the three sets of statistical tests, it is important to determine the appropriateness of proceeding with the analysis. Bartlett's sphericity test was conducted with a resultant value of 5.54, which with one degree of freedom is significant at $p = 0.01859$. Thus, we know that the data matrix contains more that just random variation. Next, we examine the value of the determinant, which equals .95. Since the determinant is not close to zero we know that there are no linear combinations among the variables and that the matrix is of full rank. We also examine the correlations among the criterion variables, adjusted for the five independent variables. The correlation is .32, which indicates that there is a fairly sizable amount of covariation among the criterion variables and that a multivariate analysis is appropriate. Had there been little or no covariation, it would have been appropriate to proceed with separate univariate analyses.

The first test examines the overall relationship between both sets of variables. SPSS MANOVA prints values for all four multivariate tests discussed earlier in this chapter. For the present data, all four are statistically significant at $p < .0001$. We report only Wilks': $\Lambda = .17881$. These tests all indicate that there is a significant relationship between the two sets of variables.

Next we examine the differential contribution of the *set* of predictor variables to each of the criterion variables by means of the Roy–Bargmann step-down tests. The two criterion variables are ordered in terms of their priority in the theory of electronic propinquity, i.e., propinquity precedes communication satisfaction. The step-down tests are printed by SPSS in this order. The appropriate procedure to interpret these tests, however, is in reverse order, from the last to the first. This procedure will indicate the extent to which the set of predictor variables contribute variation in the satisfaction measure over and above that variation that they account for in the propinqu-ity measure alone. The F-test for the variation in communication satisfication alone, controlling for variation in propinquity is $F = 32.11$, which at 5 and 105 degrees of freedom is significant at $p < .00001$. Since this test is signifi-cant, it is not correct to proceed with a step-down test of the other criterion (the first) variable(s); any further tests would be confounded with the results of this one. We would have been able to proceed with subsequent step-down tests only so long as we failed to reject the null hypothesis of no relationship.

For pedagogical reasons we make two observations. First, the step-down test for the first (in order of priority) variable, propinquity, is $F = 25.68$, which with 5 and 106 degrees of freedom is significant at $p < .00001$. Thus, both step-down F-tests are significant though as indicated in the previous paragraph, only the first may legitimately be interpreted. The value for this step-down F-test is the same as the univariate F-test *for this criterion* variable, since no other criterion variable is being controlled. The univariate F-test for the second criterion, communication satisfaction, is $F = 83.75$, which with 5 and 106 degrees of freedom is significant at $p < .00001$. Clearly, the step-down F-test (32.11) for this variable is considerably different (though still significant) from the univariate test, since the step-down test accounts for variance in communication satisfaction after partialing out the variance attributable to propinquity. Second, we examine the values in the step-down F-tests that *would have occurred* had we ordered the criterion variables in the reverse order. The step-down test for propinquity controlling for communication satisfaction is $F = 2.16$, which with 5 and 105 degrees of freedom is nonsignificant ($p = .06420$). The step-down F-test for communication satisfaction alone is highly significant: $F = 67.83$, $p < .00001$, 5 and 106 degrees of freedom. With this incorrect ordering of variables, the second variable is nonsignificant, the first is significant, and both tests may be legitimately interpreted. In the original ordering of variables both step-down F-tests were significant, but only the test for the second variable controlling for the first was legitimately interpreted since it was significant. These two pedagogical observations may help to illustrate how multivariate tests are different from their univariate counterparts when there is correlation among the criterion variables, and to demonstrate the impact that the ordering of the criterion variables has on the outcome of the statistical tests.

The final set of tests to be performed are for the contribution of each of the predictor variables to the criterion variables. The multiple hypotheses are formulated as a partitioning of the coefficients matrix:

$$H_{0_j}: \quad \mathbf{B}_{h_j} = \mathbf{0}; \qquad H_{A_j}: \quad \mathbf{B}_{h_j} \neq \mathbf{0}$$

and

$$\mathbf{B} = \begin{bmatrix} \mathbf{B}_0 \\ \hline \mathbf{B}_{h_j} \end{bmatrix}$$

constant and 1st variable feedback, not being tested

2nd–5th variables, being individually tested, i.e., $j = 1, \ldots, 4$, since 4 variables are being tested seperately

Each test is a test of two coefficients specifying the relationship between a given predictor variable and the two criterion variables, i.e., a row of the coefficients matrix. MULTIVARIANCE provides the stepwise regressions on the predictor variables, which are summarized in Table VI.

Table VI reveals that neither communication skills (the fifth variable) nor bandwidth (the fourth variable) contribute significantly to variation in either criterion variable over and above those predictors which precede them in the equations. Thus, $\mathbf{B}_{h_j} = \mathbf{B}_{h_4} = \mathbf{B}_{h_3} = \mathbf{0}$. Neither accounts for more than 1% of the variance in the criterion variables. Complexity of information (the third variable) is a significant predictor of communication satisfaction ($F = 21.98$, $p < .0001$, 1, and 108 degrees of freedom), though not a significant predictor

TABLE VI

SUMMARY OF RESULTS FOR STEPWISE TESTS OF PREDICTOR VARIABLES ON TWO CRITERION VARIABLES,
PROPINQUITY AND COMMUNICATION SATISFACTION

Source of variation	Degrees of freedom	Univariate F (% of variation)	
		Propinquity	Comm. Satis.
Feedback	1	121.88[a]	249.36[a]
		(52.56)	(69.39)
Regulation	1	2.49	25.80[a]
		(1.06)	(5.86)
Complexity	1	0.03	18.50[a]
		(0.02)	(3.62)
Bandwidth	1	1.70	3.46
		(0.72)	(0.66)
Communication Skills	1	0.97	1.43
		(0.41)	(0.27)

[a]Significant at $p < .05$.

of propinquity. Complexity contributes 3.6% of the variance in communication satisfaction over and above the two predictor variables which precede it
in the equation. Since a significant F has been obtained for the communication satisfaction variable, we do not proceed to interpret any further tests for
that criterion variable. Since we have not yet encountered a significant
predictor for propinquity, we proceed with testing predictors for that criterion
variable. The second variable, regulation of communication interaction, was
not significantly related to propinquity, though it did contribute 1.06% to
variation in that criterion variable. Thus, none of the variables being tested
were significantly related to propinquity. Though not being tested, we note
that feedback is highly related to the criterion variables, as was expected. In
summary, step-wise elimination analysis of the predictor variables has indicated (1) that propinquity is dependent upon feedback and none of the other
variables, and (2) that communication satisfaction depends upon feedback,
regulation of communication interaction, and complexity though the role of
regulation has not been identified unambiguously.

Having identified the various predictor variables which are significantly
related to and contribute significant amounts of variation in the criterion
variables, it is appropriate to reestimate the coefficients for the final equations, provide the standard errors for these reduced equations, and indicate
the respective squared multiple correlation coefficients. These are provided in
Eq. (77).

$$Y_1 = 42.00 + .78\, X_1 \qquad\qquad (R^2 = .53; \quad p < .05)$$
$$(19.39)\ \ (.071)$$
$$Y_2 = 28.33 + .62\, X_1 + .41\, X_2 + .04\, X_3 \qquad (R^2 = .789; \quad p < .0001)$$
$$(11.07)\ \ (.045)\quad (.072)\quad (.008) \tag{77}$$

Residuals should be examined for Eqs. (77) as described in the next section.

V. ISSUES AND IMPLICATIONS

In this final section of the paper we shall briefly explore several topics which are raised by or related to MMR. These should help to place the information just presented in a broader context.

A. Algorithms for Selecting Predictor Variables

There are a number of computerized algorithms which can be used to select an optimal set of predictors for a regression equation. In fact, Draper and Smith (1966) identify six different alternative procedures. Four of these are summarized in this section; for details the reader is referred to the fuller explication in Draper and Smith and also to Kerlinger and Pedhazur (1973, pp. 285–295).

The first procedure is termed all possible regressions. Here separate regression equations are calculated for all possible combinations of predictor variables: (1) each predictor variable examined separately, (2) all possible predictor pairs, (3) all possible triplets, (4) and in general, all possible k-tuples ($i = 1, \ldots, k$ predictors), where the final k-tuple contains one set of all k variables. A moment's reflection will indicate that a total of 2^k separate regressions must be computed since each variable may either be included or excluded from the equation. Within each of the k-tuple regressions (i.e., pairs, triplets, etc.), equations are ordered according to some criterion, usually the amount of variance accounted for, R^2. The researcher then selects what he considers the best equation, often by looking for "any consistent pattern of variables in the leading equations in each set" [Draper and Smith, p. 162].

The second procedure is called *backward elimination*. There are three basic steps. First, calculate a regression equation which includes all the k predictor variables. Second, calculate partial F-tests for *each* of the k variables which indicate the significance of X_k as if it were the last variable entered into the equation. Finally, select the lowest partial F value and compare it with a partial F value set equal to some predetermined level of significance, α. If the smallest partial F is *less than* F_α, then delete that variable and repeat the process for k-1 predictor variables. This sequence continues until the smallest partial F at any given step ($k - 1$ predictor variables to 1 predictor) is *greater than* F_α. The variables that remain are considered significant predictors.

The third alternative for choosing predictors is *forward selection*. In this process variables are added to the regression equation one at a time rather than deleted from the equation as was done in backward elimination. The first step is to select the largest zero order simple correlation coefficient between y and X_j. This variable is used to construct a simple regression equation. Second, an F test is calculated to determine whether the simple regression of y on the first predictor variable is significant. Assuming this test is significant, the third step is to calculate first order partial rs between y and all *other* X_j controlling for the predictor variable already in the simple regression equation. The X_j with the *highest* partial r (or squared partial r) is then selected for the construction of a multiple regression equation with two predictor variables. Fourth, as with the backward elimination procedure, partial F-tests are undertaken to determine whether the variable selected for inclusion contributes significantly to the variance in y over and above the variance accounted for by those predictors already in the equation, i.e., R^2 for the simple regression and R^2 for the two variable multiple regression. Finally, this process (calculating higher order partial rs, selecting the one of greatest magnitude, creating a new regression equation with this variable added, calculating the significance of the increase in variance contributed by this variable) continues until the partial F-test indicates that the variable selected for inclusion at the next iteration is nonsignificant. The final equation includes all variables found significant up to the point at which adding an additional predictor variable does not significantly increase the amount of variance accounted for in the criterion variable; all remaining predictors are considered nonsignificant and omitted from the equation.

The fourth procedure, which is called *stepwise regression*, is really a variation on the forward selection procedure. For any given set of variables, the magnitude of regression coefficients does *not* vary according to their *order in* a regression equation. For example, the regression coefficients for three variables, call them A, B, and C, will be the same regardless of the order in which these three variables are arranged in a three variable multiple regression equation, i.e., whether variable A is first, second, or last, whether variable B is first, second, . . . , etc. If, however, a varible, say D, is added to this equation, or one of the three variables, A, B, or C, is deleted from the equation, it is highly likely that the magnitude of all the coefficients in the new (four variable or two variable) equation will be considerably altered. The reason for this is that regression coefficients are a patterned function of a set of variables, such that they account for as much variance as possible in y or Y, given that *particular* set of predictors and that set only; in fact, the very definition of a regression coefficient depends on *which* other variables are *in* the regression equation. The amount that the regression coeffficients will change is a function of the degree to which they share variance with each other and the criterion variable(s); the more variance they share in common, the greater the coefficients will change by adding or deleting variables. It should be apparent that the three procedures identified so far all require the addition or deletion of variables. The stepwise procedure attempts to compensate for the fact that at each step *adding* a variable (remember, it is a variation on the forward selection procedure) could *reduce* the amount of variation contributed by one or more of the variables *already in the equation* to a point at which it (they) would no longer be considered significant. Thus, after each step in which a variable is selected for inclusion in the next larger multiple regression equation, a partial F test is performed on all variables in the equation to which the new variable is being added to determine whether each still significantly contributes to criterion variance. Any that fail to meet F_α are *deleted* from the regression equation and join the set of predictor variables not in the equation. Then the process is repeated: new nth order partial rs are calculated; the largest is selected for inclusion in a new regression equation; a test of the significance of this new variable is conducted; if it exceeds F_α for appropriate ν, a separate partial F is conducted for each criterion variable already in the equation; any criterion that fails the F_α is removed from the equation. The process terminates when there is no new variable that can be added to the equation and significantly increase criterion variation.

An alternative procedure, called *stagewise regression*, will not be discussed since it is not a least squares procedure. Also, it should be noted that there are some "variations on the themes" presented in these four alternatives (see Draper and Smith, 1966, pp. 172–173).

Given the four procedures just described, which one should the researcher choose? That, of course, is a judgement call, which each person will have to make depending upon his or her research needs. In general, however, all possible regressions, since it is both impractical and totally unguided by theory, should be avoided. Draper and Smith (p. 172) recommend the stepwise procedure but indicate that it too can be abused by the inexperienced. In this context, Finn (1974), makes an additional important point: "Stepwise procedures which attempt all possible orderings, or search for the best single prediction equation do not generally yield valid test statistics, and must be interpreted with caution. With a predetermined order of predictor variables, valid sequential test statistics are obtained. Using a fixed order, it is also possible to test important combinations or sets of variables"[p. 161].

B. Testing Model Assumptions

In this chapter we have stressed the importance of the assumptions of the model being employed. The only way to determine whether a given set of assumptions is viable for any given study is to test them. As Timm (1975) indicates, "Plots of residuals against the fitted values, against the independent variables, and sometimes against variables not included in the model help to determine (1) whether model assumptions are reasonable, (2) the linearity of the regression function, and (3) whether important variables have been left out of the model" [p. 269]. Another, sometimes better alternative, is to plot the residuals against $X_{i.\text{rest}}$ (i.e., X_i controlling for the other variables). Draper and Smith (1966) review these procedures in detail and Daniel and Wood (1971) give several illustrative examples; the procedures will be discussed only briefly here.

The logic of the examination is as follows: Recall that our assumptions for the classical normal linear regression model specified that the errors were normally distributed with zero mean and constant variance and that they were independent. If the assumptions are correct, the residuals (which may behave like estimates of the errors) ought to display these characteristics.

The first procedure is to undertake an overall plot of the residuals. Normality, or departure from normality, can be crudely judged by plotting the residuals on standard probability paper. Alternatively, the residuals may be transformed to "unit normal deviate" form, in which case we would expect that 95% of the residuals would fall within the $\pm 1.96\sigma$ limits. Outliers, which are residuals which lie far out in the tails of the distribution, say ± 3 or 4 standard deviations, can also be identified. Some standard regression computer packages now have subroutines which permit the plotting of residuals in unit normal deviate form.

Another procedure is to plot each residual against the predicted value which helped to generate it, i.e., $\hat{Y}_i$. Here, a horizontal band of scores lying relatively equidistant from zero would indicate that certain assumptions have been met. If the distribution of residuals shows divergence (or convergence) across the $\hat{Y}_i$ scores, the constant variance assumption is challenged. If the variance is constant, but there is an upward or downward trend in the plot, then there has probably been an error in the analysis or the constant term, β_0, has been omitted. Finally, if the plot looks curvilinear, then the assumption of linearity is questioned. Transformation on the variables (for example, by reexpressing the Y_i, see Tukey, 1977, pp. 171–175) or extra terms (square or cross products) may be required in the model. A researcher might also try plotting Y_{all} versus $X_{i.rest}$ to detect these problems.

Residuals may be plotted against the independent variables, or perhaps better, against each X_i controlling for the other X_i. As with the plot against $\hat{Y}_i$, the existence of a horizontal band of residuals is the desired form. Failure to obtain such a plot would raise similar sorts of questions as those in the previous paragraph.

Statistics are available for formally testing residuals. The reader is referred to the work by Anscombe (1961) and Anscombe and Tukey (1963) for the details. Other plots are also possible and Draper and Smith (1966) recommend that any residual plot should be made that makes sense in light of the research (e.g., plotting residuals against a variable measured on the same subjects but *not* included in the regression equation). For an example of testing assumptions in communication research see Monge *et al.* (1976), who examined the plot of the residuals for a fully recursive structural equation model of the determinants of communication structure in large organizations.

Techniques for explicitly examining multivariate residuals are still in the developmental stage. Current practice is to analyze the residuals from each of the separate univariate equations by one of the methods just discussed. While this can provide very useful information, it may not reveal some important characteristics of the residuals for the equations *taken as a set*. Gnanadesikan (1977, pp. 258–285) provides an excellent summary of the newly developed procedures for examining multivariate residuals. One technique is to investigate the entire set of residuals (p-dimensional) by means of principal components analysis. An alternative procedure, which is to examine stepdown residuals, utilizes "all the responses that have been analyzed at the preceding stages as covariates" [p. 264]. Readers are directed to Gnanadesikan for further details.

Residuals, of course, are not the only way to test assumptions. First order autoregression for static models can be ascertained by the Durbin–Watson test (for more complex situations, see Hibbs, 1974). Multicollinearity can be determined by examining the determinant of $(\mathbf{X'X})$; if it approaches zero some column of the matrix is linearly dependent upon some other column(s) of the matrix, and one or more columns (i.e., variables) must be deleted or (nonlinearly) transformed. Homoskedasticity can be examined by a homogeneity of variance test and other procedures which are discussed in most standard econometrics texts (e.g., Goldberger, 1964; Johnston, 1972; Kmenta, 1971).

In practice, since real data are never "perfect" (i.e., conform to ideal forms), some violations of assumptions are inevitable. These violations may or may not have serious implications for analysis and interpretation. The critical points which the researcher must consider are (1) the degree to which the assumptions have been violated and (2) the degree to which violations invalidate the statistical procedures. As an example of the first point, consider the problem of multicollinearity. While only perfect multicollinearity is a formal problem (since it reduces the rank of the model), "high" multicollinearity (say, correlation among two or more predictors above .70) can seriously affect the magnitude of the respective regression coefficients. At that point, the researcher should give serious consideration to deleting one or more of the highly redundant variables. The second point is one of robustness, which is a measure of the degree to which violations invalidate statistical procedures. Some assumptions are known to be highly robust, while others are less so. Bohrnstedt and Carter (1971), for example, indicated that estimation procedures for regression parameters are highly robust to violations of the assumptions of homogeneity of variance. Their review of the robustness of all of the assumptions for regression analysis is excellent, and the reader is referred to their work for further details.

The important point to remember from this section is that when communication researchers undertake a regression analysis, they should *always* test the assumptions of the model. Only when this becomes standard practice in communication research shall we be able to have confidence in research findings that employ statistical inference, and more importantly, find some of those unexpected things we need to find.

C. Comparisons with Related Techniques

Multivariate multiple regression has been presented in the context of its univariate counterpart, linear multiple regression. To provide a broader context it might be useful to examine the relationship between MMR and several other techniques. I shall briefly discuss (1) the general linear model, (2) MANOVA, (3) canonical correlation, and (4) general systems of equations.

Multivariate multiple regression has been treated as a special case of the general linear model which consists of the functional form of the model and the assumptions specified in the Gauss–Markoff theorem (set up). Many of the multivariate techniques, e.g., MANOVA and canonical correlation, are derivable from the general linear model. To understand that point provides two important insights. First, it emphasizes that many of the multivariate statistics are highly interrelated and not separate, independent techniques. Second, it emphasizes how the various techniques differ as a function of the differences in their assumptions so that modifying an assumption of the general linear model makes it appropriate to choose an alternative form of analysis (i.e., a different multivariate technique).

Comparing MMR with MANOVA helps to illustrate these two points. First, Timm (1975) demonstrates how both are special cases of the multivariate general linear model. Second, if the researcher assumes categorical rather than continuous measurement on X_j then MANOVA is the appropriate form of the model to utilize. Actually, as Bochner and Fitzpatrick illustrate in Chapter 5, a MANOVA model can be analyzed with MMR techniques by use of special (dummy, effect, or orthogonal) coding techniques (see also Kerlinger and Pedhazur, 1973; Press, 1972; Kmenta, 1971).

Canonical correlation is a technique that is appropriate when there are two sets of variables. The coefficient, R_c is the simple correlation between two random variables which are each linear *composites* of two or more variates. Each composite is defined by weights applied to its variates designed to maximize its correlation, R_c, with the other composite. As Finn (1974) indicates, when one of the "composites" consists of only one variate, R_c becomes "the multiple correlation of one measure with the other set. The weights are the partial regression coefficients" [p. 188]. MMR is the appropriate technique when the researcher is interested in explaining variation in one set of variables by variation in the other; canonical correlation is appropriate when one is interested in forming composites which maximally share variance with each other. One additional difference between the two procedures as presented in this book is that of emphasis (which is not inherit in the techniques). As presented, MMR techniques require ordering of both predictor and criterion variables in order to undertake any of the analyses beyond the omnibus multivariate test between the two sets of variables; this, presumably, requires theory. While this is one of its strengths, canonical correlation may be more appropriate to use in more exploratory situations.

Some econometrics texts treat MMR under the topic of sets of linear regression relations (see, e.g., Goldberger, 1964, pp. 201–212; Huang, 1970, pp. 183–207). This extension to sets of dependent variables from the univariate case is, as we have shown, quite straightforward. Yet always the emphasis is on explaining variance in the criterion variables by variation in the predictor variables. If, however, a researcher is interested in testing a theory which consists of a *system* of linear relations (either single equations which are part of a larger system of equations or the entire system itself), then the OLS estimation procedures described in this paper are appropriate only in the special case of a fully recursive system. Simultaneous linear structural equation systems require alternative estimation procedures; this is the topic of other chapters in this book (see Chapters 3 and 4).

D. Coping with Failed Assumptions

In this chapter considerable emphasis has been placed on the importance of the assumptions in the classical linear model. Our discussion, however, has been limited to OLS techniques; we have not examined alternative estimation procedures. Though it is beyond the scope of this paper it is important to point out that procedures have been developed to permit statistical inference in spite of violations of OLS assumptions.

One alternative which has received considerable attention from statisticians recently is that of robust and robust/resistant techniques (see Tukey, 1977b). The median, for example, is a more robust and resistant estimator of location than the mean since addition or deletion of extreme score does not seriously alter the estimate of the median but does seriously affect the estimate of the mean. Most attention has been directed at developing robust estimators for measures of location and dispersion. In fact, as Gnanadesikan (1977) indicates, "It is only very recently that robust estimation methods have been proposed for doing multiple regression analysis" [p. 136]. Furthermore, most of these efforts have been devoted to estimates for the univariate rather than the multivariate case. The reader is encouraged to pursue these and other references for further information.

Some of the other alternative techniques, such as two or three stage least squares to estimate coefficients for feedback loops and autoregressive disturbances, are simply more sophisticated applications of OLS procedures. Others, such as instrumental variables or maximum-likelihood procedures, require complete abandonment of OLS techniques. Whatever the case may be, the communication researcher is strongly encouraged to consult multivariate and econometric texts to discover the appropriate alternatives which are necessitated by violations of assumptions in his or her data.

E. Advantages and Limitations of MMR

Kerlinger and Pedhazur (1973) review in depth a number of social science studies that employed multiple regression; their comments give the reader an excellent notion of the breadth of applications that are possible with the technique (see Chapters 15 and 16). They also discuss the limitations and strengths of regression techniques (pp. 441–445) and that material, some of which has already been mentioned, will not be repeated here. Rather, I prefer to make three brief points.

First, MMR techniques lend themselves to simultaneously replicating previous research and developing new findings. This can occur by including preditors in the regression equation which have been shown to be important in earlier research. New variables may then be added and tested for significance over and above those already in the equation. If these new variables prove to be significant, the definitions of the old coefficients will change. In this way results become both cumulative and progressive and we can build communication theories of known predictors.

The second point is that regression analysis, if done correctly, virtually necessitates the formal specification of the regression equation. To my way of thinking this particularly facilitates interpretation of complex relations, particularly interaction terms. Furthermore, since traditional ANOVA and more complex MANOVA (fixed effects or Model I) designs may be analyzed via regression techniques, it is possible to develop "mixed" designs which include *both* categorical and continuous predictors.

Third, though we have only discusses cross-sectional data in this paper, all econometrics texts also discuss estimation procedures for time series data. These may vary from simple lagged variables to complex simultaneous structural equation systems. These procedures can be used to explicitly capture the processual nature of many communication phenomena.

VI. CONCLUSION

At the outset of this paper we began with a quotation from Tukey (1962), which asserts not only that our most important questions are more likely to be vague than precise but also that our best answers will often be approximate rather then exact. Asking the right questions is a theoretical endeavor; offering our best approximations to answers is a statistical undertaking.

Having shown in this chapter how analysts may expand the relations they can examine via regression techniques to include multiple criterion variables, it seems important to stress the necessity for theorists to develop formulations which will incorporate this expanded capability. To develop multivariate theories that can be studied by multivariate multiple regression should lead us a long way toward asking the right questions and obtaining regression coefficient approximations to laws of human communication.

ACKNOWLEDGMENTS

The author wishes to express his appreciation to Professors Joseph Cappella, Edward Fink, and John Tukey for helpful comments on earlier drafts of this chapter. Appreciation is also expressed to Professor Felipe Korzenny and Ms. Connie Bauer for permission to utilize their data for the communication example in the chapter and to Ms. Bauer and Mr. Jacquard Guenon for assistance in data processing.

References

Anderson, T. W. *An introduction to multivariate statistical analysis.* New York: Wiley, 1958.

Anscombe, F. J. Examination of residuals. *Proceedings of the Fourth Berkeley Symposium on Mathematics, Statistics, and Probability,* 1961, **I**, 1–36.

Anscombe, F. J., and Tukey, J. W. The examination and analysis of residuals. *Technometrics*, 1963, **5**, 141–160.

Blalock, H. M., Jr. *Causal inferences in nonexperimental research*. Chapel Hill, North Carolina: Univ. of North Carolina Press, 1964.

Blalock, H. M., Jr. (Ed.) *Causal models in the social sciences*. New York: Aldine, 1971.

Bock, R. D. Contributions of multivariate experimental designs to educational research. In R. B. Cattell (Ed.), *Handbook of multivariate experimental psychology*. Chicago, Illinois: Rand McNally, 1966.

Bock, R. D. *Multivariate statistical methods in behavioral research*. New York: McGraw-Hill, 1975.

Bohrnstedt, G. W., and Carter, T. M. Robustness in Regression Analysis. In H. L. Costner (Ed.), *Sociological methodology 1971*. San Francisco, California: Jossey-Bass, 1971.

Cohen, J. Multiple regression as a general data-analytic system, *Psychological Bulletin*, 1968, **70**, 426–443.

Cohen, J., and Cohen, P. *Applied multiple regression/correlation analysis for the behavioral sciences*. New York: Wiley, 1975.

Daniel, C., and Wood, F. S. *Fitting equations to data*. New York: Wiley, 1971.

Draper, N. R., and Smith, H. *Applied regression analysis*. New York: Wiley, 1966.

Finn, J. D. *A general model for multivariate analysis*. New York: Holt, 1974.

Gnanadesikan, R. *Methods for statistical data analysis of multivariate observations*. New York: Wiley, 1977.

Goldberger, A. S. *Econometric theory*. New York: Wiley, 1964.

Hibbs, D. A., Jr. Problems of statistical estimation and causal inference in time-series regression models. In H. L. Costner (Ed.), *Sociological methodology 1973–1974*, San Francisco, California: Jossey-Bass, 1974.

Huang, D. S. *Regression and econometric methods*. New York: Wiley, 1970.

Johnston, J. *Econometric methods* (2nd ed.). New York: McGraw-Hill, 1972.

Kerlinger, F. N., and Pedhazur, E. J. *Multiple regression in behavioral research*. New York: Holt, 1973.

Kmenta, J. *Elements of econometrics*. New York: Macmillian, 1971.

Korzenny, F. A Theory of electronic propinquity. *Communication Research*, 1978, **5**, 3–24.

Korzenny, F., and Bauer, C. *A preliminary test of the theory of electronic propinquity: Organizational teleconferencing*. Paper presented at the annual meeting of the International Communication Association, Philadelphia, Pennsylvania: May, 1979.

Kshirsagar, A. M. Bartlett decomposition and Wishart distributions. *Annals of Mathematical Statistics*, 1959, **30**, 239–241.

Monge, P. R., Boismier, J. M., Cook, A. L., Day, P. D., Edwards, J. A., Kirste, K. K. *Determinants of communication structure in large organizations*. Paper presented to the Information Systems Division of the International Communication Association, Portland, Oregon, April, 1976.

Press, S. J. *Applied multivariate analysis*. New York: Holt, 1972.

Roy, J. Step-down procedure in multivariate analysis. *Annals of Mathematical Statistics*, 1958, **29**, 1177–1187.

Timm, N. H. *Multivariate analysis with applications in education and psychology*. Monterey, California: Brooks/Cole, 1975.

Tukey, J. W. Causation, regression, and path analysis. In O. Kempthorne *et al.* (Eds.), *Statistics and Mathematics in Biology*. Ames, Iowa: Iowa State College Press, 1954.

Tukey, J. W. The future of data analysis. *Annals of Mathematical Statistics*, 1962, **33**, 1–67.

Tukey, J. W. *Exploratory data analysis*. Reading, Massachusetts: Addison-Wesley, 1977(a).

Tukey, J. W. *What modern statistical techniques might do for forecasting*. Paper presented at the Public Utilities Forecasting Conference, Browness-On-Windermere, Cumbria, England, March, 1977(b).

Chapter 3

STRUCTURAL EQUATION MODELING: AN INTRODUCTION

JOSEPH N. CAPPELLA

Department of Communication Arts
University of Wisconsin
Madison, Wisconsin

I. INTRODUCTION

Structural equation modeling (SEM) may be the modern version of alchemy, an attempt to translate "worthless" correlational information into "precious" causal information. This alchemy has been conducted under various aliases: structural equation modeling (Goldberger & Duncan, 1973), causal modeling (Blalock, 1969; Heise, 1975), path analysis (Wright, 1934; Duncan, 1975), and econometric methods (Goldberger, 1964). The task before us is to describe and evaluate structural equation modeling procedures

MULTIVARIATE TECHNIQUES
IN HUMAN COMMUNICATION RESEARCH

so that researchers in communication contemplating these techniques can be informed as to their merits and demerits.

The discussion divides easily into three major sections. Section II is concerned with the standard techniques of translating verbal propositions into a mathematical form which constitutes a structural equation. Section III considers procedures for statistical estimation, hypothesis testing, and model fitting required by various types of structural equation models. This section is restricted to error-free, cross-sectional data. Section IV treats rather circumspectly the emerging area of structural modeling of time dependent processes. This section emphasizes structural models of time-series data (theory first) in contrast to the emphasis by Davis and Lee (Chapter 14, this volume) on pure time-series data exploration (data first). Monge (Chapter 2) provides additional background on multiple regression pertinent to SEM, and Fink (Chapter 4) discusses the case of structural models with measurement error.

II. FROM VERBAL TO PICTORIAL TO MATHEMATICAL REPRESENTATIONS

Most theories in the social sciences are still cast in the verbal mode of representation (see Harris, 1976, for certain of the problems which this creates). As a result building structural equation models usually requires translation from a verbal representation. This section aims to point out certain of the requirements of this translation. Further discussion of the problem of translating verbal information into mathematical propositions is available in Cappella (1978).

A. Categories of Causal Propositions

In order to keep track of the several ways of representing causal propositions, we need to develop certain classes of propositions and some conventions for presenting them. The three modes of representing propositions are verbal, pictorial, using path diagrams, and mathematical (a representation which is isomorphic to the pictorial one). Within each mode, there are two general classes of propositions, dynamic and static. Dynamic propositions take time into account explicitly, with the effect lagged behind the cause. Static propositions do not take time into account and the cause and effect are treated as coextensive (Zetterberg, 1965, p. 70). An asymmetry between static and dynamic propositions exists such that given the dynamic proposition, one can uniquely derive the static, but the reverse is not true. On the basis of McClelland's (1975) discussion we should expect the form of representation of both dynamic and static propositions to reflect a theoretical version and an observation version of the proposition. Indeed, this is the case for all the representations, although it is of greater significance for the pictorial and mathematical ones. Thus we have a $3 \times 2 \times 2$ category scheme, three representational modes (verbal, pictorial, and mathematical) by two classes (dynamic and static) by two levels (theoretical and observational).

Let us consider a simple example of the categories. Consider only two variables: ξ, the cause, and η, the effect. Although verbal propositions relating ξ and η do not often distinguish between theoretical and observational, and static and dynamic, let us force the distinction.

The pictorial and mathematical representations of the propositions that "ξ causes η ceteris paribus" and the "the greater the ξ, the greater the η ceteris paribus" are quite straightforward (Heise, 1975, Chapters 2 and 4, offers an especially clear discussion):

(1) Pictorial (theoretical, dynamic)

$$\xi(t) \xrightarrow{\gamma} \eta(t + 1)$$

(2) Mathematical (theoretical, dynamic)

$$\eta(t + 1) = \gamma\xi(t)$$

(3) Pictorial (theoretical, static)

$$\xi(t) \xrightarrow{\gamma'} \eta(t)$$

(4) Mathematical (theoretical, static)

$$\eta(t) = \gamma'\xi(t)$$

(5) Pictorial (observational, dynamic)

$$\xi(t) \xrightarrow{\gamma} \eta(t + 1) \longleftarrow \zeta(t + 1)$$

(6) Mathematical (observational, dynamic)

$$\eta(t + 1) = \gamma\xi(t) + \zeta(t + 1)$$

(7) Pictorial (observational, static)

$$\xi(t) \xrightarrow{\gamma'} \eta(t) \longleftarrow \zeta(t)$$

(8) Mathematical (observational, static)[1]

$$\eta(t) = \gamma'\xi(t) + \zeta(t)$$

In the above examples, the arrow indicates the direction of causal flow. γ and γ' are constants, usually between -1 and 1, which indicate how much of

---

[1] In writing the structural equations we assume without loss of generality that the expected value of the variable is zero. This assumption frees us from having to worry about the constant (or intercept) in the structural equations.

a change in ξ will be transferred to η. The terms within parentheses following ξ and η are indicators of time and carry information about the statics and dynamics. The mathematical representations in examples (2), (4), (6), and (8) are direct translations of the pictorial representations immediately above them.

Two observations about these representational systems must be stressed: (a) When time of occurrence differs between variables [as in examples (1), (2), (5), and (6)], then the causal relationships are dynamic. (b) The observational and theoretical representations [(1)–(4) versus (5)–(8)] are distinguished by adding the variable ζ in examples (5)–(8). ζ is an unobserved variable whose purpose is to represent all other causal variables not explicitly included in the theoretical proposition linking ξ and η. Since it functions as a surrogate for what has been excluded, measuring its causal impact on the effect η can indicate how important the excluded factors are. Thus the effect of this surrogate is in part to check the extent of violence done by the ceteris paribus assumption by assessing the degree of sufficiency of the causal predictors.

B. Categories of Causal Systems

The key advantage of SEM of causal theories is that a *system* of causal relationships can be treated. The complexity of social and psychological processes often requires that the effects of one cause are the causes of other effects. Such interdependency requires procedures of representation and of testing which can disentangle the web of causes and effects. The systematic treatment of cause–effect relationships is certainly one of the chief drawing cards of SEM.

1. TERMINOLOGICAL CONVENTIONS

For our purposes only three types of variables need to be described in any causal system: exogenous,[2] endogenous, and disturbance. Exogenous variables are those determined completely outside the system. They function only as causes in the particular system under scrutiny. In Fig. 1 the exogenous variables are those which have no causal arrows pointing toward them. Endogenous variables are both causes of other variables and are caused by exogenous and other endogenous variables. In Fig. 1 the endogenous variables, η_1, η_2, η_3, are those which have causal arrows pointing to them. Disturbance variables are hypothetical variables which represent all the other unmeasured variables causing variation in the endogenous variables. Disturbance variables are surrogates for the omitted causal variables producing each effect.

---

[2]More generally, the class of exogenous variables would be labeled predetermined and include both exogenous variables and endogenous variables which are lagged in time (Kmenta, 1971, p. 532).

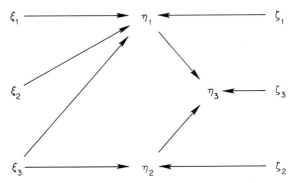

FIG. 1. A recursive causal system with three exogenous, three endogenous, and three disturbance variables.

2. TYPES OF CAUSAL LINKAGES

The types of relationships which these classes of variables produce are simply described. The *inventory of causes* is represented by

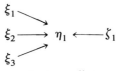

where there are several independent predictors of the endogenous variable. This is the case of simple multiple regression with three regressors. The *inventory of effects* is described as

$$\begin{array}{c} \nearrow \ \eta_1 \longleftarrow \zeta_1 \\ \xi_1 \longrightarrow \eta_2 \longleftarrow \zeta_2 \\ \searrow \ \eta_3 \longleftarrow \zeta_3 \end{array}$$

which is the case of three separate univariate regressions. The case of one-directional causal influence is illustrated by the inventory of causes, the inventory of effects, and the example of Fig. 1. In this case the flow of causal influence never "doubles back" so that an effect never directly or indirectly influences its cause. On the other hand, mutual causal relationships and causal loops do exhibit this "doubling back" character. Figure 2 shows a causal system in which the endogenous variables η_1, η_2, η_3 are related in a loop of causal influence and η_3 and η_4 are mutually causally related.

The cases of an inventory of causes and an inventory of effects are not of interest in SEM since they represent the case of multiple regressions and of several separate regressions, respectively (see Chapter 2). The issues of estimation and hypothesis testing are simply those associated with standard regression procedures. However, it is not obvious that the systems of relationships specified in the examples of Figs. 1 and 2 can be treated simply as several separate regressions. They may require special treatment since certain of the

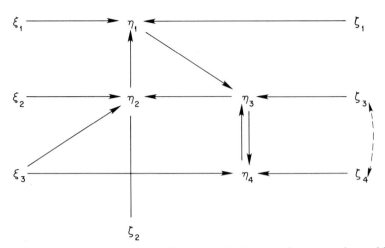

FIG. 2. A nonrecursive causal system with one feedback loop and one mutual causal loop.

variables act as both dependent and independent variables. Whether "special treatment" of the system is required or not depends on an important distinction between recursive causal systems and nonrecursive ones.

3. RECURSIVE SYSTEMS

The examples of Figs. 1 and 2 exemplify the important classes of causal systems: recursive and nonrecursive, respectively. A system of variables is said to be recursive if and only if (1) the relationships among the exogenous and endogenous variables are one directional, involving no feedback loops, and (2) each causal variable is uncorrelated with the disturbance variable affecting its consequent. Thus in Fig. 1 there are no feedback loops and it is assumed that ξ_1 and ξ_2 are uncorrelated with ζ_1, ξ_3 is uncorrelated with ζ_2, and η_1 and η_2 are uncorrelated with ζ_3. The assumed lack of correlation is displayed in Fig. 1 by the absence of *dotted* lines linking for example ξ_1 and ξ_2 with ζ_1. It is easy to show that the absence of correlation between causal antecedents and disturbance variables for each effect (1) implies that the disturbance variables are all uncorrelated with one another and (2) does *not* imply that the disturbance of a prior endogenous variable is uncorrelated with a later endogenous variable (for example, ζ_1 and ζ_2 can be correlated with η_3 in Fig. 1) (see Duncan, 1975, p. 29).

The mathematical representation of a recursive system is very simple. Following the rules described earlier for translating pictorial into mathematical representations, we have for Fig. 1

$$\eta_1 = \gamma_{11}\xi_1 + \gamma_{12}\xi_2 + \gamma_{13}\xi_3 + \zeta_1 \tag{1}$$

$$\eta_2 = \gamma_{23}\xi_3 + \zeta_2 \tag{2}$$

$$\eta_3 = \beta_{31}\eta_1 + \beta_{32}\eta_2 + \zeta_3 \tag{3}$$

These are called the *structural equations*. Putting all the endogenous variables on the left side and all the exogenous ones on the right side of the equal sign, we have

$$\eta_1 \qquad\qquad = \gamma_{11}\xi_1 + \gamma_{12}\xi_2 + \gamma_{13}\xi_3 + \zeta_1$$

$$\eta_2 \qquad = \qquad\qquad \gamma_{23}\xi_3 + \zeta_2$$

$$-\beta_{31}\eta_1 - \beta_{32}\eta_2 + \eta_3 = \qquad\qquad \zeta_3$$

which in matrix form is

$$
\begin{bmatrix} 1 & 0 & 0 \\ 0 & 1 & 0 \\ -\beta_{31} & -\beta_{32} & 1 \end{bmatrix}
\begin{bmatrix} \eta_1 \\ \eta_2 \\ \eta_3 \end{bmatrix}
=
\begin{bmatrix} \gamma_{11} & \gamma_{12} & \gamma_{13} \\ 0 & 0 & \gamma_{23} \\ 0 & 0 & 0 \end{bmatrix}
\begin{bmatrix} \xi_1 \\ \xi_2 \\ \xi_3 \end{bmatrix}
+
\begin{bmatrix} \zeta_1 \\ \zeta_2 \\ \zeta_3 \end{bmatrix}
$$

In general any recursive system of causes will have the following structure:

$$
\begin{bmatrix} 1 & 0 & 0 & \cdots & 0 \\ \beta_{21} & 1 & 0 & \cdots & 0 \\ & & 1 & & \\ \vdots & & & \ddots & \vdots \\ \beta_{m1} & \beta_{m2} & & \cdots & 1 \end{bmatrix}
\begin{bmatrix} \eta_1 \\ \eta_2 \\ \vdots \\ \eta_m \end{bmatrix}
=
\begin{bmatrix} \gamma_{11} & \gamma_{12} & \cdots & \gamma_{1n} \\ \gamma_{21} & \gamma_{22} & \cdots & \gamma_{2n} \\ \vdots & & & \vdots \\ \gamma_{m1} & \gamma_{m2} & \cdots & \gamma_{mn} \end{bmatrix}
\begin{bmatrix} \xi_1 \\ \xi_2 \\ \vdots \\ \xi_n \end{bmatrix}
+
\begin{bmatrix} \zeta_1 \\ \zeta_2 \\ \vdots \\ \zeta_m \end{bmatrix}
$$

$$(4)$$

or

$$\mathbf{B}\eta = \Gamma\xi + \zeta \qquad\qquad (5)$$

where η is an $m \times 1$ vector of endogenous variables, ξ an $n \times 1$ vector of exogenous variables, and ζ and $m \times 1$ vector of disturbance variables. $\mathbf{B}$ is the $m \times m$ matrix of structural coefficients where each coefficient indicates the impact of every endogenous variable on each endogenous variable to which a causal connection has been specified. Γ is the $m \times n$ matrix of structural coefficients indicating the impact of each exogenous variable on every endogenous variable to which a causal connection has been specified.

Interestingly, each equation of a recursive system when written separately [e.g., Eqs. (1)–(3)] appears to be structurally identical to any multiple regression equation. Why then do we talk of a recursive *system* instead of a set of separate regressions? In fact the set of equations is a system only if it is *not* recursive. It is not recursive if either (1) the matrix $\mathbf{B}$ has coefficients other than zero above the diagonal (which occurs when there are feedback loops in the system) or (2) the variance–covariance matrix among the disturbance variables is not diagonal (which occurs whenever any predictor in a structural equation is correlated with the disturbance variable in that equation). Thus, the systemic character of a set of causal propositions depends upon the structure of the $m \times m$ matrix $\mathbf{B}$ of structural coefficients and the structure of the $m \times m$ matrix of variances and covariances among the ζ_i (let us call it Ψ).

When **B** is lower triangular and Ψ is diagonal, then the "system" is actually no system at all; it is recursive and each equation can be treated separately. If **B** is not lower triangular and/or Ψ is not diagonal, the system of causal propositions is a true system. It is nonrecursive and the equations must be solved simultaneously.

4. NONRECURSIVE SYSTEMS

The example of Fig. 2 is a nonrecursive system having both feedback loops and covariation among the disturbances. The covariation among the disturbances ζ_3 and ζ_4 indicated by the dotted lines is *required* in this example because (as can easily be shown) the presence of mutual causal relationships ensures a correlation among residuals of the variables involved in the mutual causality (Duncan, 1976, pp. 67–69).

Writing the structural equations for a nonrecursive system is no different from writing the equations for a recursive system. For Fig. 2 we should write

$$
\begin{aligned}
\eta_1 &= \gamma_{11}\xi_1 & &+ \beta_{12}\eta_2 & &+ \zeta_1 \\
\eta_2 &= \gamma_{22}\xi_2 + \gamma_{23}\xi_3 + & &+ \beta_{23}\eta_3 & &+ \zeta_2 \\
\eta_3 &= & \beta_{31}\eta_1 & &+ \beta_{34}\eta_4 + \zeta_3 \\
\eta_4 &= \gamma_{43}\xi_3 & & &+ \beta_{43}\eta_3 + \zeta_4
\end{aligned}
$$

which in matrix form is

$$
\begin{bmatrix}
1 & -\beta_{12} & 0 & 0 \\
0 & 1 & -\beta_{23} & 0 \\
-\beta_{31} & 0 & 1 & -\beta_{34} \\
0 & 0 & -\beta_{43} & 1
\end{bmatrix}
\begin{bmatrix}
\eta_1 \\ \eta_2 \\ \eta_3 \\ \eta_4
\end{bmatrix}
=
\begin{bmatrix}
\gamma_{11} & 0 & 0 \\
0 & \gamma_{22} & \gamma_{23} \\
0 & 0 & 0 \\
0 & 0 & \gamma_{43}
\end{bmatrix}
\begin{bmatrix}
\xi_1 \\ \xi_2 \\ \xi_3
\end{bmatrix}
+
\begin{bmatrix}
\zeta_1 \\ \zeta_2 \\ \zeta_3 \\ \zeta_4
\end{bmatrix}
$$

$$(6)$$

The matrix Eq. (6) is an example of the general Eq. (5) where **B** is no longer lower triangular and Ψ is no longer diagonal.

Nonrecursive systems are true systems in that the equations cannot in general be separated from one another. As a result of the simultaneous character of a nonrecursive set of causal propositions, some knotty estimation procedures must be faced.

III. SINGLE EQUATION ESTIMATION IN STATIC CAUSAL SYSTEMS

Since the initial upsurge of interest in SEM, or path analysis as it was known in sociology (Duncan, 1971; Heise, 1968; Land, 1968; Blalock, 1964), several excellent introductory treatments of the procedures of SEM have appeared (Heise, 1975; Duncan, 1975; Kerlinger & Pedhazur, 1973, pp. 305–330; Namboodiri, Carter, and Blalock, 1975, pp. 439–532; Cappella, 1975, for a guide to other sources) to supplement the more advanced texts usually available in the econometrics literature (Kmenta, 1971; Wannacott & Wannacott, 1970). This section aims to summarize the key features and issues in SEM so that the reader can begin to make informed decisions during the development of theory and during the conduct of research.

The approach taken here to the variety of SEM techniques and procedures is a limited one. In particular, only the case of static SEMs that are free of measurement error is treated. The case of time-series models of causal processes is discussed later while the case of errors in the variables (measurement error) is treated in Chapter 4. Testing causal models without measurement error can be treated as a special case of the very general estimation techniques developed by Joreskog and his associates (Joreskog, 1970, 1973; Werts, Joreskog, and Linn, 1973) and discussed in Chapter 4. Thus the models discussed in this section can also be estimated using the system procedures advocated by Joreskog. We shall focus on equation-by-equation rather than the all-at-once (or system) estimation techniques advocated by Joreskog and discussed in Chapter 4.[3]

A. Terminology Related to Estimation

Just as the structure and mathematical form of the propositions are the causal *theory*, estimation is the statistical process through which the observational representation of the theory is tested. Estimation takes the empirical knowledge we have about a causal system and generates (through a set of rules) the theoretical knowledge we desire. On the basis of Eq. (5) the knowledge we have consists of the $\frac{1}{2}(m + n)(m + n + 1)$ variances and covariances among the m endogenous and n exogenous variables; the knowledge needed is the $\frac{1}{2}m(3m + 2n + 1)$ parameters in $\mathbf{B}$ and $\mathbf{\Gamma}$ and variances and covariances in $\mathbf{\Psi}$.

If possible we should like our estimates of theoretical parameters (βs and γs and unobserved variances and covariances) to have certain properties. In the best of all situations the estimates of the theoretical parameters should be *efficient*; that is, the expected value of the estimate should equal the theoretical parameter even in small samples and the dispersion of the distribution of the estimate should be as small as possible. However, it will often be the case

---

[3]There are important differences between equation-by-equation estimation and so-called system estimation techniques. As Christ (1966), Johnston (1972, p. 414), and Heise (1975, p. 181) point out, system estimation is especially useful for well-validated theory since all available information is used in making estimates of impact parameters but, at the same time, errors in parts of a theory are dispersed throughout the system rather than being tied to a single portion as they are in equation-by-equation estimation.

that the preceding properties of estimators will be true only in very large samples so that the estimator is *asymptotically efficient*. Without asymptotic efficiency estimates of theoretical parameters are useless for evaluating the theory from sample observations. In such cases, it may be necessary to settle for one-half of asymptotic efficiency, that is unbiasedness in large samples (or consistency). *Consistency* at least permits some trust in the value of a parameter although evaluating the statistical significance of the sample value is rendered problematic. We shall discuss just such a case in Section IV.C.

Fortunately, most causal systems based on cross-sectional data are not so difficult to handle.

B. Estimation in Recursive Systems

Recursive systems have some very simple and very familiar characteristics. As a result, they have a tendency to draw attention. Because they are simple, researchers and theorists seek to formulate their models as recursive. The question then which needs some attention is, when can a recursive system be assumed? The facetious but accurate answer is, when the causal process is recursive! This is really the only answer possible. Recursivity requires, first, one-way causation. An undebatable temporal priority among variables will help ensure this unidirectionality, but strict temporal priority does not rule out feedback since the temporal ordering in loops may be just as clear as that in recursive sequences. Thus, only substantive theoretical arguments can assure or deprive the modeler of one-way causation. Recursivity also requires an absence of correlation between predictors and residuals in each structural equation, thereby ensuring zero correlation among residuals. How can the modeler know that the residuals are uncorrelated if they are unobservable? Obviously such information is not available from observation. Since the assumption simplifies, why not adopt it?

Assuming that the residuals are uncorrelated is a significant substantive assumption about one's theory. Such an assumption maintains that there is no possible external variable which can act as the spurious cause of the presumed cause and effect. For example, in Fig 1, assuming that ζ_1 and ζ_3 are uncorrelated means that the theorist has seriously considered the possibility that an external variable (or complex of variables) is the common cause of η_1 and η_3 and has consciously rejected that possibility. Because the assumption of recursivity is so powerful, it must not be undertaken lightly. The critic of a recursive model always has the edge since he or she only need find that plausible, unmeasured spurious cause to call into question a specified and empirically verified link. The assumption of uncorrelated residuals points out the fundamental importance of substantive and theoretical criteria in the development of causal models.

Let us now suppose that all the theoretical work is done and the recursive causal model to be estimated is that depicted in Fig. 3, with the correspond-

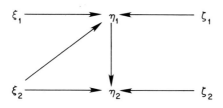

FIG. 3. A four variable recursive system.

ing structural equations

$$\eta_1 = \gamma_{11}\xi_1 + \gamma_{12}\xi_2 \qquad + \zeta_1 \qquad (7)$$

$$\eta_2 = \qquad \gamma_{22}\xi_2 + \beta_{21}\eta_1 + \zeta_2 \qquad (8)$$

The task is to estimate the γs and βs in Eqs. (7) and (8). Let us do so by treating the two equations as if they were two independent multiple regression equations. Such treatment is not implausible since in each equation the predictor variables are uncorrelated with the residual variable in the same equation. [If this were not the case in Eq. (8), then ζ_1 and ζ_2 would be correlated.] Focusing on Eq. (8) for k observations

$$
\begin{bmatrix} \eta_{21} \\ \eta_{22} \\ \vdots \\ \eta_{2k} \end{bmatrix}
=
\begin{bmatrix} \xi_{21} & \eta_{11} \\ \xi_{22} & \eta_{12} \\ \vdots & \vdots \\ \xi_{2k} & \eta_{1k} \end{bmatrix}
\begin{bmatrix} \gamma_{22} \\ \beta_{21} \end{bmatrix}
+
\begin{bmatrix} \zeta_{21} \\ \zeta_{22} \\ \vdots \\ \zeta_{2k} \end{bmatrix}
\qquad (9)
$$

Since there are two parameters to be estimated, two estimation equations are necessary. If Eq. (9) is premultiplied by the transpose of

$$
\begin{bmatrix} \xi_{21} & \eta_{11} \\ \xi_{22} & \eta_{12} \\ \vdots & \vdots \\ \xi_{2k} & \eta_{1k} \end{bmatrix}
$$

then

$$
\begin{bmatrix} \sum_{i=1}^{k} \xi_{2i}\eta_{2i} \\ \sum_{i=1}^{k} \eta_{1i}\eta_{2i} \end{bmatrix}
=
\begin{bmatrix} \sum_{i=1}^{k} \xi_{2i}^2 & \sum_{i=1}^{k} \eta_{1i}\xi_{2i} \\ \sum_{i=1}^{k} \eta_{1i}\xi_{2i} & \sum_{i=1}^{k} \eta_{1i}^2 \end{bmatrix}
\begin{bmatrix} \gamma_{22} \\ \beta_{21} \end{bmatrix}
+
\begin{bmatrix} \sum_{i=1}^{k} \xi_{2i}\zeta_{2i} \\ \sum_{i=1}^{k} \eta_{1i}\zeta_{2i} \end{bmatrix}
\qquad (10)
$$

Taking expectations (Hays, 1963, Appendix B) of Eq. (10) yields the two desired equations

$$\sigma_{\xi_2 \eta_2} = \gamma_{22} \sigma_{\xi_2 \xi_2} + \beta_{21} \sigma_{\eta_1 \xi_2} + 0 \tag{11}$$

$$\sigma_{\eta_2 \eta_1} = \gamma_{22} \sigma_{\eta_1 \xi_2} + \beta_{21} \sigma_{\eta_1 \eta_1} + 0 \tag{12}$$

where σ_{ij} is the population covariance or variance when $i = j$. The right-hand-most terms are 0, since *by assumption* the expected value of the covariance of the predictors with the disturbance term is 0.

Equations (11) and (12) can be solved directly to yield

$$\gamma_{22} = \left(\sigma_{\eta_1 \eta_1} \sigma_{\xi_2 \eta_2} - \sigma_{\eta_1 \eta_2} \sigma_{\eta_1 \xi_2} \right) / \left(\sigma_{\eta_1 \eta_1} \sigma_{\xi_2 \xi_2} - \sigma_{\eta_1 \xi_2}^2 \right) \tag{13}$$

$$\beta_{21} = \left(\sigma_{\xi_2 \xi_2} \sigma_{\eta_1 \eta_2} - \sigma_{\xi_2 \eta_2} \sigma_{\eta_1 \xi_2} \right) / \left(\sigma_{\eta_1 \eta_1} \sigma_{\xi_2 \xi_2} - \sigma_{\eta_1 \xi_2}^2 \right) \tag{14}$$

Remarkably, these estimates are identical to those derived using ordinary least squares (MR) procedures. That is, if we had treated Eq. (8) as if it were an ordinary multiple regression equation and not a part of a recursive causal system, then the same population estimates of γ_{22} and β_{21} would have been derived.

The point of this somewhat extended arithmetic is twofold: (1) The derivation of Eqs. (13) and (14) depends centrally upon the assumption of zero covariation between predictors and disturbances [hence, the zeros in Eqs. (11) and (12)]. The assumption of *nonzero* covariation produces estimation difficulties as shall be discussed below. (2) The suggestion raised by Eqs. (13) and (14) that estimation of the parameters of a recursive causal system proceeds as m separate multiple regressions (one for each endogenous variable) is not a coincidence, but rather is true in general. The m structural equations of a recursive system can be treated as if each were a separate and distinct multiple regression equation (Land, 1973; Kmenta, 1971, p. 586). Further, this profound simplification is a direct consequence of point (1) above. The independence of predictors and disturbances permits separability.

Estimation in any causal system depends upon two classes of assumptions: logical or theoretical ones and empirical ones. What differentiates the two sets is whether the validity of the assumption can be assessed on the basis of single sample observations. Theoretical assumptions cannot; empirical assumptions can. The theoretical assumptions for a recursive system include one-way causality, absence of measurement error, constancy of structural equations across the k observation units, absence of covariation between predictors and disturbance variables in the same structural equation, absence of specification error,[4] and system equilibrium (for cross-sectional data). The

---

[4]Specification error refers to inaccurate structural equations due to omission of a relevant predictor variable or to inclusion of an irrelevant predictor variable or to an incorrect mathemati-

empirical assumptions for estimation in a recursive causal system are just those for any multiple regression (see Chapter 2) and include linearity of the structural equations,[5] disturbances distributed normally with zero mean, and fixed variance for each observation (homogeneity), disturbances uncorrelated across observations, fixed predictor variables, observations in excess of predictors, and no multicollinearity (predictors must not be linearly dependent upon one another). Violations of most of these empirical assumptions[6] are detectable (Kmenta, 1971, Chapter 8 and pp. 380–391; Draper & Smith, 1966) and correctable (Kmenta, 1971, Chapter 12; Wannacott and Wannacott, 1970, Chapter 16). The theoretical or logical assumptions are not. In fact, in order to make theoretical assumptions testable (e.g., the assumption no covariation among disturbance terms), more general assumptions than those above must be made. This will be done in subsequent sections on nonrecursive systems and time-series data.

Since recursive systems can be separated into m separate regressions, all of the desirable properties of OLS estimators of the βs, γs, and disturbance variances and covariances follow; namely, the estimates are efficient. For the researcher with access to the usual MR software packages (see Chapter 17) recursive systems present no formidable difficulties. The "system" is estimated equation by equation with the usual reports of R^2, corrected R^2, unstandardized regression coefficients (the βs and γs), standard errors of the coefficients, and significance values. Interpretation of these statistics proceeds as in any multiple regression.

C. Selected Issues in Recursive Systems

Before turning to estimation in nonrecursive systems, several issues which have commonly arisen in the regression of recursive systems deserve comment:

(1) If one focuses on Eq. (8), there are two predictor variables, ξ_2 and η_1, which following the analogy of Eq. (9) give rise to two estimation (or normal) equations from which the two structural coefficients γ_{22} and β_{21} can be estimated [as in Eqs. (11)–(14)]. Since there are two equations and two

---

cal formulation of the structural equation (for example, specifying linear relationships when they should be quadratic). Other types of specification error are possible as well (see Kmenta, 1971, p. 392). The first two types of specification error are not in general disastrous to estimation when the culprit variable is uncorrelated with the included predictor variables. However, the third type of misspecification is more serious (Kmenta, 1971, pp. 391–405).

[5]Linearity is not demanded in causal models. In estimating coefficients and confidence intervals for nonlinear equations it is important to distinguish between equations which are intrinsically linear and those which are intrinsically nonlinear; the former are easier to handle than the latter (Kmenta, 1971, pp. 451–456).

[6]Bohrnstedt and Carter (1971) summarize the effect of various violations under different degrees of severity.

unknowns to be estimated, a unique estimate for each is possible (Ayres, 1962, pp. 75–79). But the variable ξ_1 is predetermined with respect to η_2 so that three independent equations

$$\sigma_{\xi_1\eta_2} = \gamma_{22}\sigma_{\xi_1\xi_2} + \beta_{21}\sigma_{\eta_1\xi_1}$$

$$\sigma_{\xi_2\eta_2} = \gamma_{22}\sigma_{\xi_2\xi_2} + \beta_{21}\sigma_{\xi_2\eta_1}$$

$$\sigma_{\eta_1\eta_2} = \gamma_{22}\sigma_{\eta_1\xi_2} + \beta_{21}\sigma_{\eta_1\eta_2}$$

are conceivably available to estimate only two unknowns (γ_{22} and β_{21}). As the early path analysts realized, the system provided an abundance of information which might be used to check the internal consistency of the results (Boudon, 1968; Costner, 1969). Simply put, if the system of recursive relations permits more than one estimate of the structural coefficients, then the consistency of these estimates might be an indicator of the logical consistency of the system. However, as Goldberger (1970) has shown, there is no optimal way to weigh the different estimates in that the combined estimate will always have a variance greater than the estimates based upon the ordinary least squares procedures of multiple regression. Hence, the ordinary least squares estimates are to be preferred.

(2) Even though a recursive system is separable into separate regressions, the system is still logically interdependent. Thus, the researcher may wish to ask how well the presumed recursive structure fits the entire data set (however, see Namboodiri *et al.*, 1975, pp. 458–59) not equation by equation, but rather the fit of the *observed* variance–covariance matrix among the variables (ηs and ξs) to the *predicted* matrix of variances and covariances. The early path analysis literature (Heise, 1968) recommended reproducing the correlation matrix and eyeballing its discrepancy from the observed correlations. In an unpublished paper Monge (1975) follows such a recommendation with reasonable success. The problems with the procedure as initially proposed were that (1) no guidelines, statistical or heuristic, were available to suggest what constituted a good or poor fit, and (2) as the system of causal relationships becomes more fully recursive (all possible one-way causes included), the system becomes artifactually more successful at reproducing the observed variances and covariances. The general data handling procedures developed by Joreskog (1970, 1973) remedy both of the above problems (1) by developing a χ^2 test of the fit between an observed and projected variance–covariance matrix for any structural system and (2) because the test is a function of the degrees of freedom available.

The degrees of freedom for such tests depend upon the number of "overidentifying restrictions" that occur in the particular causal model. In particular, the number of such restrictions in a recursive model equals the number of zeros in the Γ matrix plus the number of zeros in the lower triangular portion of the **B** matrix. As the number of parameters to be estimated, r, increases, the degrees of freedom $[=\frac{1}{2}(m + n + 1)(m + n + 1) - r]$ decreases, the critical value of chi-squared decreases, and the probability of achieving a significant difference between the observed and predicted covariance matrices increases. Do not be misled however, the hypothesis of no difference is the one which the researcher favors. Thus, as the number of overidentifying restrictions decreases, the chances of finding in favor of the null actually decreases for a fixed pair of observed and predicted covariance matrices. Research justice is served as the theorist who "takes chances" by specifying more overidentifying restrictions is not penalized. See the Chapter 4 for further introduction to these system procedures of estimation and of fitting.

The techniques of estimation advanced by Joreskog which in essence estimate all the system's parameters at the same time have certain disadvantages. In the event that one or more structural equations are seriously misspecified, that specification error will be spread throughout the set of equations when systems procedures are employed but will be restricted to a single equation when estimation procedures are used one equation at a time (see footnotes 3 and 4). Therefore it would be desirable to have an equation-by-equation procedure to test the overidentifying restrictions; that is, does the entire pattern of observed variances and covariances fit the predicted ones well enough under the assumption that certain of the βs and γs are zero ? Land (1973, p. 46) reports such a test which can easily be computed with standard output from a MR program. The test statistic is distributed as chi-squared with degrees of freedom the same as above. The statistic is obtained as follows:

(a) The sum of the squared residuals for each structural equation is obtained by performing a MR on each yielding $\hat{\sigma}_{\eta_i \eta_i}$, $i = 1, 2, \ldots, m$.

(b) The sum of squared residuals is obtained for each η_i by regressing η_i on *all* exogenous and endogenous variables which are causally prior to η_i yielding $\hat{\sigma}^*_{\eta_i \eta_i}$, $i = 1, 2, \ldots, m$.

(c) The statistic $k\sum_{i=1}^{m} \log(\hat{\sigma}^*_{\eta_i \eta_i} / \hat{\sigma}_{\eta_i \eta_i})$ is distributed as χ^2 in large samples with $\frac{1}{2}(m + n)(m + n + 1) - r$ degrees of freedom.

If the overidentifying restrictions are not useful, the statistic will be large, and if the restrictions are useful, the statistic will be nonsignificant (near one).

It should be noted that tests of fit for entire systems of relationships have not been universally welcomed. Duncan (1976, p. 98) notes that if the reproduced variances and covariances differ significantly from those observed so that the null hypothesis must be rejected, one only knows that "something is wrong, not what in particular is likely to be wrong" [p. 98]. While this is correct, one of the aims of causal modeling is or should be the rejection of inadequate causal representations (Simon, 1957, 1971). Thus, one of the advantages of overall tests of fit is to contrast the degree of fit of competing causal models which have been specified a priori. Rejection of all competing models places the researcher in the conundrum described by Duncan. But recognition of this problem should give greater impetus to a priori specification of competing alternatives.

(3) Perhaps the key theoretical assumption in making a causal system recursive is the one which insists that the predictor variables in a structural equation be uncorrelated with the disturbance variable in that equation. Since the researcher cannot assess the validity of this assumption, one would think that simulations of its effect on estimates under various conditions abound. Bohrnstedt and Carter's (1971) review of violations of assumptions in multiple regression report only their own calculations for the case of a univariate regression with single, fixed variance for the predictor and a fixed covariance between the predicted and predictor variables. They find a significant departure from the true regression coefficient even under moderate (.4 to .6) correlation between predictor and residual. These results are, however, unsatisfying since more complex situations are likely to produce results which are not quite so straightforward. The cliché that "more research is required" holds.

In the interim, the a priori stipulation that there exists no covariation among residuals seems presumptuous. Once the assumption has been made there is no longer any opportunity to test it. Also, such a presumption is strong theoretically since it implicitly maintains that no spurious unmeasured factor is causing the observed covariation between predictor and consequent variables. In essence, it make strong claims about the closure of the system to external forces. Given the naiveté of theories about communication processes, the opportunity to test claims about spurious causes should remain open.

(4) From its earliest days the path analysis literature has carried the controversy over standardized and unstandardized structural coefficients (Wright, 1971; Blalock, 1971). Recent wisdom has been that to compare different populations with potentially different distributional characteristics on the same structural coefficient requires that the structural coefficients *not* be standardized so that the inherent variability of each population is allowed to "naturally" affect its structural coefficient (Heise, 1975, p. 127; Blalock, 1972, pp. 383–385; Nie, Hull, Jenkins, Steinbrenner, & Bent, 1975, pp. 394–397). The standard wisdom has been strongly challenged by Hargens (1976) and Hotchkiss (1976). Hargen's claim is that in some research circumstances variables might be chosen which, for theoretical reasons, necessitate standardization across populations for the purposes of comparison. He especially points to cases in which an individual's score on cause and effect variables may be relative to the particular population so that invariance of the cause–effect relation between populations could only be revealed by standardizing within each population. In general, this seemingly straightforward statistical issue must be resolved on criteria which are particular to the substantive theory under investigation. Researchers are admonished, however, to employ unstandardized coefficients when comparing two or more

populations unless it can be argued that the impact of a variable ξ on a variable η depends upon the value of ξ relative to the population of scores from which ξ is sampled (Hargens, 1976, p. 252). In the latter case, the causal proposition actually relates z scores to one another, and hence, the standardized regression coefficient is the correct specification parameter.

D. Estimation in Nonrecursive Systems

From a statistical point of view the enterprise of causal modeling for the researcher competent in multiple regression necessitates nothing new when the system is recursive and has no measurement error. However, once recursivity is lost, then so is statistical simplicity. Recursivity can be lost in three ways. (1) The assumption that predictor variables in each structural equation are uncorrelated with residuals may be relaxed. In this case the modeler may not have sufficient faith in the validity of the specified causal relationships to assume that spuriousness is impossible. If the correlations among residuals can be estimated, then the researcher will have an empirical index of the presence of an external explanatory variable spuriously affecting causal relationships in the system. (2) The theory specified may involve feedback loops. Such a possibility should be the rule in self-regulating systems with internal mechanisms for adaptation to environmental changes (Cappella, 1976; Watzlawick, Beavin , and Jackson, 1967; Simon, 1969). The presence of feedback loops (length greater than 2) does not require that disturbances be correlated. (3) The theory may require mutual causal loops in which case the disturbances of the mutual causal variables are, of necessity, correlated.

In order to see what happens to ordinary least squares estimates when the system is no longer recursive, consider the example of Eqs. (7) and (8) except now assume that the residuals ζ_1 and ζ_2 are correlated as in Fig. 4. The structural equations for this figure are the same as Eqs. (7) and (8). In fact, the estimates of γ_{11} and γ_{12} remain the same since ξ_1 and ξ_2 are still uncorrelated with ζ_1 so that the predictors in structural Eq. (7) meet the assumptions required of multiple regression. Let us also treat the structural Eq. (8) as if it were an ordinary multiple regression equation. Following the same procedure employed in deriving Eq. (10), we obtain the two equations:

$$\sigma_{\xi_2 \eta_2} = \gamma_{22} \sigma_{\xi_2 \xi_2} + \beta_{21} \sigma_{\xi_2 \eta_1} \tag{15}$$

$$\sigma_{\eta_1 \eta_2} = \gamma_{22} \sigma_{\eta_1 \xi_2} + \beta_{21} \sigma_{\eta_1 \eta_1} + \sigma_{\eta_1 \zeta_2} \tag{16}$$

Notice that Eq. (16) has a term representing the correlation between η_1 and ζ_2 which will not disappear. Solving Eqs. (15) and (16) yields

$$\gamma_{22} = \frac{\sigma_{\eta_1 \eta_1} \sigma_{\xi_1 \eta_2} - \sigma_{\xi_2 \eta_1} \sigma_{\eta_1 \eta_2}}{\sigma_{\xi_2 \xi_2} \sigma_{\eta_1 \eta_1} - \sigma_{\eta_1 \xi_2}^2} + \frac{\sigma_{\xi_2 \eta_1} \sigma_{\eta_1 \zeta_2}}{\sigma_{\xi_2 \xi_2} \sigma_{\eta_1 \eta_1} - \sigma_{\eta_1 \xi_2}^2}$$

$$= \text{OLS estimate of } \gamma_{22} + \text{bias;} \quad \text{similarly for } \beta_{21}$$

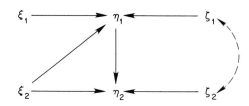

FIG. 4. A four variable system with one-way influence and correlated errors.

Thus, ordinary multiple regression under the assumption of correlated disturbances yields estimates of structural coefficients which are biased[7] (Kmenta, 1971, pp. 302–303, 534). The result holds in general. Estimation in nonrecursive cases then must turn from ordinary least squares and develop estimation techniques which *at least* provide unbiased estimates in large sample cases.

1. IDENTIFICATION STATUS

The work of econometricians over the past 25 years has been aimed at the development of just such estimation techniques. The most direct way to organize a discussion of the most common and useful of these techniques is to introduce a classification of various types of nonrecursive systems in terms of the *identification* status of the individual equations.

There are three classes of identification: under, over, and exact. The concept of identification is roughly described as the degree of availability of observed covariational information as compared to the required estimation information. In essence knowing the identification status indicates whether there is not enough information available to make unique estimates (under), just enough information available to make unique estimates (exact), or an abundance of information leading to more than one estimate per parameter (over). Two procedures are available for determining the identification status of a given structural equation. The first is not very useful but is conceptually very important in revealing the logic behind identification.

a. Identification and reduced form   Every structural equation has either exogenous and endogenous variables or only endogenous variables. It is always possible to express the endogenous variables solely as functions of the exogenous variables by substituting for those endogenous variables that are predictors their exogenous predictors.[8] In the case of Eqs. (7) and (8) of Fig.

---

[7]More specifically, the ordinary least squares estimators are inconsistent in the face of correlated disturbance so that even in very large samples the bias will not go away. This can be seen by noting that Eq. (16) is written at the level of the population and not at the level of sample statistics.

[8]With focus on matrix Eq. (5), $\mathbf{B}\eta = \Gamma\xi + \zeta$ becomes $\eta = \mathbf{B}^{-1}\Gamma\xi + \mathbf{B}^{-1}\zeta$ if $\mathbf{B}$ is nonsingular. This is known as the reduced form and is usually written $\eta = \Pi\xi + \mathbf{V}$ where $\Pi = \mathbf{B}^{-1}\Gamma$ and $\mathbf{V} = \mathbf{B}^{-1}\zeta$.

4, only Eq. (8) needs to be rewritten in terms of exogenous variables. Substituting Eq. (7) into (8) for η_1 we have

$$\eta_2 = \gamma_{22}\xi_2 + \beta_{21}(\gamma_{11}\xi_1 + \gamma_{12}\xi_2) + \zeta_2 + \beta_{21}\zeta_1$$

$$= \gamma_{11}\beta_{21}\xi_1 + (\gamma_{22} + \gamma_{12}\beta_{21})\xi_2 + \zeta_2 + \beta_{21}\zeta_1 \qquad (17)$$

which along with Eq. (7) ($\eta_1 = \gamma_{11}\xi_1 + \gamma_{12}\xi_2 + \zeta_1$) are known as the *reduced form* equations. They have a very desirable property. The predictors (which are the exogenous variables of the system) are *by assumption* always uncorrelated with the disturbance of the reduced form equation even if the residuals in the structural equations are assumed to be correlated across equations.

Since the predictors ξ_1 and ξ_2 are uncorrelated with ζ_1 and ζ_2 in Eqs. (7) and (17), regressing η_1 and η_2 on ξ_1 and ξ_2 yields unbiased estimates of

$$\gamma_{11} = \hat{a} \qquad (18)$$

$$\gamma_{12} = \hat{b} \qquad (19)$$

$$\gamma_{11}\beta_{21} = \hat{c} \qquad (20)$$

$$(\gamma_{22} + \gamma_{12}\beta_{21}) = \hat{d} \qquad (21)$$

But estimates of the structural coefficients rather than the reduced form coefficients are desired. These are obtainable if an only if the nonlinear Eqs. (18)–(21) can be inverted so that expressions for $\gamma_{11}, \gamma_{12}, \gamma_{22}, \beta_{21}$ in terms of $\hat{a}, \hat{b}, \hat{c}, \hat{d}$ can be generated. In this case the Eqs. (18)–(21) can be inverted yielding one and only one estimate for each structural coefficient:

$$\gamma_{11} = \hat{a}, \qquad \gamma_{12} = \hat{b}, \qquad \beta_{21} = \hat{c}/\hat{a}, \qquad \gamma_{22} = \hat{d} - \hat{b}\hat{c}/\hat{a} \qquad (22)$$

Whenever the reduced form coefficients yield one and only one estimate of the structural coefficients, the equation is exactly identified. When there is more than one expression for a structural coefficient in terms of the reduced form coefficients, the equation is overidentified. When the structural coefficient cannot be solved uniquely in terms of the reduced form coefficients, the equation is underidentified. The move to describe the identification status of an equation in terms of the relationship between an always estimable reduced form and a sometimes estimable structural equation is as ingenious as it is useless. For anything other than very simple systems, solving equations of the form in Eqs. (18)–(21) is very difficult. The reduced form, however, is the basis for the derivation of a very simple and useful condition for determining the identification status of an equation: the order condition.

b. Identification and the order condition The order condition is a simple counting rule which offers a necessary but not sufficient condition[9] for determining the identification status of a given equation. It may be stated as follows (see Christ, 1966, pp. 324–327 for further elaboration):

(1) Each structural equation has at a maximum m endogenous and n predetermined (exogenous plus lagged endogenous) variables.

(2) Of the n possible predetermined variables in a structural equation N of them are omitted a priori (the so-called "zero restrictions," a particular type of overidentifying restriction) and M of the enodogenous are omitted a priori. Therefore, the equation has $m - M$ endogenous and $n - N$ predetermined variables in it.

(3) The structural equation is *exactly identified* if the number of predetermined variables left out of the equation, N, just equals the number of endogenous variables in it less one, $m - M - 1$.

(4) The equation is *overidentified* if N is greater than $m - M - 1$.

(5) The equation is *underidentified* if N is less than $m - M - 1$.

The order condition is especially useful because it does not require any attention to the reduced form at all. Figure 5 illustrates all three situations in the same hypothetical causal model. η_4 is overidentified because there are two exogenous variables left out, ξ_1 and ξ_2, which is one more than the two minus one endogenous variables appearing in the equation for η_4. η_2 is underidentified because there are no exogenous variables omitted, which is one less than the two minus one endogenous variables that appear in the equation. η_1 is exactly identified since ξ_3 is omitted, which equals two endogenous variables less one.

Once the identification status of each structural equation is set (at least by the order condition), then estimation can proceed for the exactly identified and overidentified equations, one equation at a time.

2. ESTIMATING EXACTLY IDENTIFIED STRUCTURAL EQUATIONS

There are basically two procedures for estimating structural coefficients in exactly identified equations: indirect least squares (ILS) and instrumental variables (IV). They are mathematically equivalent procedures in this case. Actually we have already discussed the workings of ILS estimation in the

---

[9]The sufficient condition is known as the rank condition (Kmenta, 1971, p. 543) and basically ensures that the set of equations relating reduced form and structural coefficients are all independent. See Namboodiri *et al.* (1975, pp. 504–505) for a clear and readable discussion of the rank condition. The question of the utility of the order condition which is merely a necessary condition often arises. As both Christ (1966, p. 322) and Namboodiri *et al.* (1975, p. 505) note, (a) the rank condition will almost always be met when the order condition is and (b) since the rank condition concerns the *population* parameters, the researcher can never know if the particular sample can be applied with certainty; the actual rank will remain indeterminate. The bottom line is that the order condition is treated as if it were sufficient.

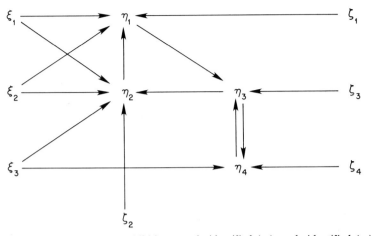

FIG. 5. A nonrecursive system exhibiting exactly identified (η_1), underidentified (η_2), and overidentified (η_3, η_4) structural equations: All disturbances assumed correlated.

example of Eq. (17) but since the procedure is seldom used in place of the equivalent but simpler IV procedure (even in econometric software packages), it will not be discussed further.

Two types of exactly identified structural equations need distinction. The first type is one in which all the predictor variables are exogenous (such as the equation for η_1 in Fig. 3). Equations of this type can be estimated using ordinary multiple regression since the exogenous variables are always assumed to be uncorrelated with the criterion variable in the equation. The second type of exactly identified structural equation is one in which there is at least one endogenous variable as a predictor which is assumed to be correlated with the disturbance variable of that equation (such as the equation for η_2 in Fig. 4). This type requires IV techniques.

In any exactly identified structural equation in a nonrecursive system with several exogenous variables and at least one endogenous variable as predictor, one cannot use the endogenous predictor to generate a usable normal equation because the endogenous predictors are in general correlated with the disturbance terms. This is what happened in Eq. (16). What is needed are other variables to generate normal equations without a covariation between the predictor and the disturbance. If there happened to be such variables available (as many as there are endogenous predictor variables in the equation) which (1) did not appear in the structural equation and (2) were uncorrelated with the disturbance in that equation, then one could multiply through the equation by these variables and take expectations [as we did in Eqs. (10)–(12)]. For an exactly identified structural equation there are always just enough of these variables in the group of exogenous variables omitted from the structural equation.

Consider the overworked example of Fig. 4. The exactly identified structural equation for η_2 is

$$\eta_2 = \gamma_{22}\xi_2 + \beta_{21}\eta_1 + \zeta_2 \tag{23}$$

To estimate γ_{22} and β_{21}, two equations with just two unknowns are required. The first equation is obtained by "multiplying through Eq. (23) by ξ_2 and taking expectations" analogously to Eq. (10) yielding

$$\sigma_{\xi_2\eta_2} = \gamma_{22}\sigma_{\xi_2\xi_2} + \beta_{21}\sigma_{\xi_2\eta_1} \tag{24}$$

In the language of instrumental variables ξ_2 serves as its own instrument in Eq. (23) to generate (24). We cannot do the same with η_1 since it is correlated with ζ_2 yielding Eq. (16) and another unknown. However, ξ_1 could serve as an instrument for η_1 since it is uncorrelated with ζ_2 yielding

$$\sigma_{\xi_1\eta_2} = \gamma_{22}\sigma_{\xi_1\xi_2} + \beta_{21}\sigma_{\eta_1\xi_1} \tag{25}$$

Equations (24) and (25) are the desired equations that can be solved to obtain consistent and (in this case) asymptotically efficient estimates of γ_{22} and β_{21}.

The IV procedure may be summarized as follows:

(1) Write out the exactly identified structural equation with its $n - N$ exogenous and $m - M - 1$ endogenous predictors.

(2) Multiply through and take expectations by each of the $n - N$ exogenous variables and each of the N *omitted exogenous* variables yielding n normal equations.

(3) Solve the normal equations for the structural parameters.

Notice that because the equation is exactly identified the number of omitted exogenous variables N will by definition be just equal to the number of endogenous predictors, $m - M - 1$. Instrumental variables techniques will yield estimates of the structural coefficients which are unbiased in large samples and, if all the other equations in the system are exactly identified, estimates with variances that are as small as can be expected (Kmenta, 1971, p. 551). Unfortunately, IV techniques are *not* computationally simple in complex structural equations and, therefore, usually require specialized software. The usual MR software cannot be deceived into producing IV estimates (but there are ways around this as we shall see below).

Finally, some controversy exists over what criteria to use in the inclusion of instrumental variables (see, for example, Wannacott & Wannacott, 1970, pp. 153, 160, as opposed to Heise, 1975, pp. 160–165). However, in the case of exactly identified equations most econometrics texts take the omitted exogenous variables (Kmenta, 1971, p. 554; Christ, 1966, p. 405) as instruments.

3. Estimating Overidentified Structural Equations

The case of overidentification can be illustrated with the following causal system which is a variant of Fig. 3:

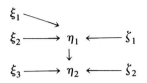

in which η_1 is exactly identified but η_2 is overidentified. The structural equation for η_2 is

$$\eta_2 = \gamma_{23}\xi_3 + \beta_{21}\eta_1 + \zeta_2 \tag{26}$$

η_2 is overidentified because there are two exogenous variables left out of Eq. (26) and only one of them is needed.

If we employ the instrumental variables technique to estimate the coefficients in Eq. (26), we see that there are three instruments ξ_1, ξ_2, and ξ_3 available. These three instruments yield three independent normal equations with only two unknowns:

$$\sigma_{\xi_1\eta_2} = \gamma_{23}\sigma_{\xi_1\xi_3} + \beta_{21}\sigma_{\eta_1\xi_1}$$

$$\sigma_{\xi_2\eta_2} = \gamma_{23}\sigma_{\xi_2\xi_3} + \beta_{21}\sigma_{\eta_1\xi_2}$$

$$\sigma_{\xi_3\eta_2} = \gamma_{23}\sigma_{\xi_3\xi_3} + \beta_{21}\sigma_{\eta_1\xi_3}$$

These three equations can be solved two at a time to yield two independent sets of estimates of the coefficients γ_{23} and β_{21}.

Thus the overidentified Eq. (26) is overidentified in the sense that more than one estimate is available for each parameter. While such a state of affairs is not undesirable, the researcher now has no clear rational basis for choice between the estimates, given the likely circumstance that they yield different values. The solution as Christ (1966, p. 411) puts it is to find a "compromise" set of estimates that exactly satisfies none of the estimates but optimizes among them on some criterion.

The commonly used optimization procedure is known as two-stage least squares (2SLS) (Christ, 1966, pp. 432–452; Duncan, 1975, Chapter 7) and works exactly as its name describes, least squares two times. Most discussions of two-stage least squares are quite foreboding due to their technical sophistication. However, the "trick" behind two-stage procedures is both simple and fascinating. In Eq. (26) what we need are just two instrumental variables which are uncorrelated with the disturbance ζ_2 in order to estimate γ_{23} and β_{21}. ξ_3 is one such instrument but η_1 is not since it is correlated with

ζ_2. However, if we write the reduced form equation for η_1

$$\eta_1 = \pi_{11}\xi_1 + \pi_{12}\xi_2 + \pi_{13}\xi_3 + \text{error terms}$$

and estimate the πs by ordinary multiple regression yielding $\hat{\pi}$s, then we can use the $\hat{\pi}$s and the observed ξs to calculate a predicted η_1, $\hat{\eta}_1$. That is,

$$\hat{\eta}_1 = \hat{\pi}_{11}\xi_1 + \hat{\pi}_{12} + \hat{\pi}_{13}\xi_3$$

The useful characteristic of $\hat{\eta}_1$ is that it is uncorrelated with ζ_2. Simply because $\hat{\eta}_1$ is a function of the exogenous variables which are themselves uncorrelated with ζ_2 by definition, $\hat{\eta}_1$ is a perfect candidate to serve as an instrument for Eq. (26). The trick works in general and may be summarized as follows (Heise, 1975, p. 169):

(1) Write the overidentified structural equation with its $n - N$ exogenous and $m - M - 1$ endogenous predictors.

(2) Regress each of the $m - M - 1$ endogenous predictors on *all* of the exogenous variables thereby generating *predicted* values for each of the $m - M - 1$ endogenous predictor variables for each observation case in the sample.

(3) Return to the structural equation and regress the original dependent variable on the $n - N$ exogenous variables and the *predicted* values of the $m - M - 1$ endogenous variables generated in (2).

(4) This second set of regression coefficients from (3) are the 2SLS estimates.

The procedure can be carried out on any multiple regression computer package as long as the predicted values for the second set of regressions are made available from the first regressions.

In the preceding example, η_2 would be estimated by 2SLS as follows:

(1) Regress η_1 on ξ_1, ξ_2, and ξ_3.

(2) Based upon the regression coefficients from 1, generate $\hat{\eta}_{1i}$ for all i cases which is the predicted value of η_1 for each i.

(3) Regress η_2 on ξ_3 and $\hat{\eta}_1$ to obtain the 2SLS coefficients.

Two-stage least squares produces estimates which are unbiased in large samples but do not necessarily have small variances in such samples primarily because the correlation among disturbances across equations has not been taken into account in the estimation procedure (Kmenta, 1971, p. 562). Thus, the usual estimates of standard errors are suspect in small samples for the purposes of significiance testing.

4. ESTIMATING UNDERIDENTIFIED STRUCTURAL EQUATIONS

When a structural equation is underidentified then there is not enough information available to generate a unique estimate of each structural coefficient. In general estimation cannot proceed. However, if the researcher had measured certain exogenous variables (or could obtain such measures) which were not a part of the initial specification of the causal system, then those variables might serve as instruments for the purposes of estimation (see, e.g., Salteil & Woelfel, 1975; Heise, 1977).

But as Fisher (1971) has pointed out, what makes a variable a good instrument involves trade-offs. A useful instrumental variable should be highly correlated with the variable for which it will be used as an instrument and essentially uncorrelated with the disturbance of that variable. As Fisher (1971) notes these two requirements may be mutually incompatible. The closer the causal link, the higher the potential of correlation with the residual. The farther removed from the variable (causally), the less likely the correlations with the residual but the lower the correlation with the dependent variable.

The problem of choosing an instrument post hoc in order to make statistical estimation possible again points to the necessity of making these choices on a priori substantive and theoretic grounds. The issues of system structure determine the possibility and even the quality of estimation. In turn system structure is determined by the quality of the theory on which it is based.

E. Summary of (Single Equation) Estimation Procedures

The previous material has presented an array of procedures necessary for estimating parameters of various classes of structural equations.[10] These procedures are summarized in Table I. This table should be used to guide choice and not to dictate choice in a particular research application. It also refers to each equation in the causal system and, hence, must be applied m times. Finally, the number of different procedures necessary for estimation in any causal system is not as large as Table I indicates. Rather, the researcher only needs to focus on OLS and 2SLS. As it turns out, if one were to apply 2SLS to an exactly identified equation in a nonrecursive system, the estimates of the structural coefficients and their variances would be identical to those provided by IV and ILS procedures. While 2SLS would not be necessary, it can more easily take the place of IV and ILS, since 2SLS software is more readily available and ordinary MR software can be used to produce 2SLS estimates as was described earlier. However, the user should be wary of employing MR programs to produce 2SLS estimates (Hout, 1977).[11]

---

[10]Actually there are other procedures which we have not considered: other single equation estimators (e.g., limited information maximum likelihood) and system estimators (e.g., full information maximum likelihood and three-stage least squares).

[11]Hout (1977) shows that applying OLS twice to obtain 2SLS estimates produces (1) incorrect estimates of the *standardized* coefficients, (2) incorrect estimates of the variances of the disturbance variables, and, hence, (3) invalid tests of significance. Hout shows that these difficulties will likely be serious but that straightforward corrections (p. 344) will produce accurate estimates.

TABLE I

A SUMMARY OF SINGLE EQUATION ESTIMATION PROCEDURES
FOR RECURSIVE AND NONRECURSIVE SYSTEMS

System type	Equation status	Estimation procedure		
		OLS	IV	2SLS
	Under	NP[a]	NP	NP
Recursive	Exact	P[a]	P	P
	Over	NA[a]	NA	NA
	Under	NP	NP	NP
Nonrecursive	Exact	NP/P[b]	P	P
	Over	NP	NP	R[a]

[a]NP = not permitted; NA = not applicable; P = permitted; R = required.

[b]Permitted if all predictor variables are exogenous.

Overall, while estimation in causal systems seems to involve procedures unfamiliar to the researcher well trained in MR techniques, the use of such procedures can be reduced to MR techniques or a variant thereof.

F. Testing Nonrecursive Models

The statistical evaluation of nonrecursive causal systems can involve three types of procedures: significance tests of the structural coefficients, overall tests of the fit of the system to observed variation and covariation, and the size of the variation in and covariation between disturbance variables. Let us consider each of these procedures in turn.

Significance testing in ordinary regression involves taking a ratio between an estimated regression coefficient and its standard error. This ratio is usually assumed to be distributed as t in small samples and, hence, is compared to that distribution (degrees of freedom appropriately noted) for the purposes of significance evaluation.

Unfortunately, in 2SLS we only know the variance of the structural coefficients in very large samples. Their character in small samples (most common in the typical communication study) is unknown. Worse, its distributional properties in small samples is therefore also unknown and significance testing is stymied.

Despite these problems researchers routinely test a structural coefficient estimated by 2SLS by taking a ratio of the estimated coefficient to the standard error and comparing the ratio to the t sampling distribution. Of course, this is technically unwarranted but accepted. Thus routine output from a 2SLS procedure should include the estimate of each coefficient, its associated standard error, and a t value.

There is some evidence, primarily from Monte Carlo studies, that treating 2SLS estimates as if their small sample properties were as just described does not do grave harm to the validity of the significance tests (Johnston, 1972, pp. 408–420, but especially p. 418).

In large samples the statistical significance of structural coefficients is not always of consequence (e.g., Duncan and Featherman, 1973, or Hauser, 1973). In such cases relatively inconsequential structural coefficients may be statistically significant by virtue of the number of degrees of freedom. Unless theoretical arguments override, such coefficients could be deleted and either the R^2s recalculated or an overall test of fit of the simpler causal system to the observed data made (see Chapter 4 for a discussion of χ^2 tests of fit). If the simplified causal system does not appreciably decrease R^2 or significantly alter the fit to observed data overall, then parsimony dictates deletion despite statistical significance.

Overall tests of fit of the causal system to the observed data can be undertaken when at least one of the structural equations is overidentified. Fink (Chapter 4) discusses such procedures for nonrecursive systems and so they will not be repeated here. Note however that the procedures discussed by Fink involve estimating coefficients in structural equations *all at once* (a full information method) rather than one equation at a time (a limited information method). Such techniques can be less desirable under certain conditions as was discussed in footnote 3.

Finally, the magnitude of covariation among the disturbance variables can be used as an indicator of the susceptibility of the posed model to threats due to spuriousness. In the communication literature Salteil and Woelfel (1975) have used this information as a basis for respecifying the structure of the initial model. In essence, the size of the correlation among two disturbance variables, say ζ_1 and ζ_2, raises suspicion concerning the causal linkages specified between their endogenous variables η_1 and η_2. If the most direct causal linkage between η_1 and η_2 is deleted from the system and the coefficients reestimated, then, if the correlations among residuals drop significantly, there is some basis for concluding that the dropped causal linkage should not have been specified in the first place. Salteil and Woelfel reduce the complexity of their model by just such an inspection–deletion–reestimation procedure. It should be noted, however, that because such a procedure is post hoc, it should be applied hesitatingly and, more importantly, demands a retesting of the modified causal system on a new data set. Of course, if deletion of one or more causal linkages between the culprit endogenous variables does not succeed in dropping the absolute magnitude of the correlation among the pertinent residuals, then the researcher is faced with an environment of disturbances that are not independent, and future work with the causal system must be expanded to include these significant spurious causal agents.

IV. ESTIMATION IN SIMPLE CAUSAL MODELS WITH TIME-SERIES DATA

A. Introduction

The estimation procedures discussed until this point have presumed that the sample data were cross sectional only. What if the data were obtained across adjacent time periods rather than over adjacent cross sections of a population? Would such data place demands upon estimation and hypothesis-testing procedures different from those discussed earlier? In general the answer is yes.

There are two significant reasons to be concerned with time-series data. First, cross-sectional models permit estimation only under the condition that the system has equilibrated or stopped changing; otherwise, estimates of variances and covariances will differ immediately after measurement has occurred. Unless there exists some clear indication that the process under study either has equilibrated or is changing very slowly, dynamic modeling is required.

Second, time-series data are required whenever one poses a substantive question involving change. Such questions have always been deeply embedded in the theoretical concerns of communication researchers: how does group structure change over the group's history (Bales, 1950; Ellis & Fisher, 1975); how do attitudes change in response to a stream of external messages (Hovland, Janis, and Kelly, 1953); how does overt message intimacy, message intensity, or speech and silence durations change as the other's overt message characteristics change (Jourard, 1971; Cozby, 1973; Natale, 1975; Feldstein & Welkowitz, 1978)? The answer to such questions of a process nature (Brooks & Scheidel, 1968; Berlo, 1960; Smith, 1972) that does not pervert the process into a static pseudo-process by means of careful but ecologically invalid experimental designs requires time-series data.

B. Varieties of Time-Series plus Cross-Sectional Data

Certain distinctions will help locate the discussion of the next several pages in the general problem of analyzing time-series data. First, our concern is with multiple variable rather than single variable systems; that is, structural equation systems remain the focus in this section as they were in the section on cross-sectional data. Box and Jenkins (1976) and Glass, Willson, and Gottman (1975) offer extensive treatment of model building with univariate time series.

Second, the structural equations discussed in this section are limited to the recursive variety; nonrecursive systems are not considered. As Hibbs (1974, p. 304) notes, "Simultaneous equation formulations . . . present additional complications . . . [which] in any case have yet to be resolved completely." Attempts to develop useful estimation procedures for causal systems with loops and with lagged endogenous variables (therefore, time-series data) have been made by Amemiya (1966), Fair (1970), and Sargan (1961). Rather than focus on a general N-equation time dependent causal system with one-directional influence, we shall consider with no loss in generality the simplest, a two-equation system:

$$\eta_1(t) = \beta_{12}\eta_2(t - 1) + \gamma_{11}\eta_1(t - 1) + \zeta_1(t) \tag{27}$$

$$\eta_2(t) = \beta_{21}\eta_1(t - 1) + \gamma_{22}\eta_2(t - 1) + \zeta_2(t) \tag{28}$$

This system consists of two variables η_1 and η_2 which are predicted by their own values in the prior time period and the value of the other variable in the prior period. Thus, each equation consists of an endogenous variable, a lagged endogenous variable, and an exogenous variable. The structural simplicity of the above system should not mislead the reader. The problems and procedures in estimating the βs and γs for Eqs. (27) and (28) can be generalized to any causal system with one-directional causal influence and lagged endogenous variables as predictors regardless of the number of exogenous predictors or the size of the time lag.

Third, we will assume that the data available to estimate the βs and γs in Eqs. (27) and (28) consists of both time-series (TS) and cross-sectional (CS) observations. In addition, we shall consider only the case in which the TS data is sufficient to carry out individual analyses for each cross section which might be pooled later if appropriate. Recent articles by Hannan and Young (1977) and Simonton (1977) explore the case in which there are few TS points and many CS observations. These cases are statistically simpler than the one discussed here.

The discussion proceeds as follows: (1) the analysis of a system like Eqs. (27) and (28) for each CS is presented, (2) suggestions for pooling across CS are offered, and (3) an example of mutual influence in speech latency in dyadic conversations is presented.

C. Autocorrelated Disturbances and Lagged Endogenous Variables

Let us suppose that Eqs. (27) and (28) were to be estimated using standard MR techniques one equation at a time. Focusing on Eq. (27) without any loss of generality the MR would be carried out on

$$\eta_1(t) = \beta_{12}\eta_2(t - 1) + \gamma_{11}\eta_1(t - 1) + \zeta_1(t) \tag{29}$$

where for the first cross section

$$\eta_1'(t) = (\eta_{12}(t_2), \ldots, \eta_{12}(t_T))$$
$$\eta_2'(t - 1) = (\eta_{21}(t_1), \ldots, \eta_{21}(t_{T-1})) \tag{30}$$
$$\zeta_1'(t) = (\zeta_{11}(t_2), \ldots, \zeta_{11}(t_T))$$

where the prime indicates transposition. In other words a regression analysis would be run on a string (column) of data which are the time-series observations. The observations over time are treated much as if they were other cross sections.

To carry out separate MR analysis on the two-equation system, (27) and (28), requires (1) that each equation meet the assumptions of a standard multiple regression and (2) that the equations are not simultaneous (that is, the disturbance variables must be uncorrelated). The pertinent assumptions (for time-series data) are:

(1)   The disturbance variables must be uncorrelated over time.
(2)   The predictor variables should be nonstochastic [that is, they should be fixed (Kmenta, 1971, pp. 297 ff.)].
(3)   The predictor variables in each equation must be independent of the disturbance variable in that equation.

What are the chances that a model like Eqs. (27) and (28) meet these three assumptions? The first assumption is not likely to be met since its violation represents the commonly occurring situation in which some relatively stable (in time) variable is spuriously affecting both η_1 at time $t - 1$ and at time t (similarly for η_2). Since this is a likely and empirically frequent occurrence, the researcher can expect data gathered across time to exhibit (usually positive) autocorrelation.

Even if assumption (1) were to hold, assumption (2) cannot be true since both Eqs. (27) and (28) have as predictors lagged endogenous variables which are stochastic variables. The consequence of having stochastic predictors usually is a violation of assumption (3) (Wannacott & Wannacott, 1970, pp. 150–152). If predictor and disturbance variables within an equation are correlated, then the usual OLS (i.e., MR) procedures yield estimates of the βs and γs which are consistent (i.e., unbiased in large samples) but not efficient (i.e., have unknown variance properties in both small and large samples). Thus, the three assumptions do not seem to be able to be met individually for the case of Eqs. (27) and (28).

Unfortunately, the estimation problems are even more serious when all three assumptions simultaneously fail to be met. Whenever the structural equation to be estimated contains a lagged endogenous variable [and, hence, assumption (2) is violated] *and* the disturbance variables are correlated [assumption (1) is violated], then two serious results obtain for the model of Eqs. (27) and (28): (1) the disturbances will necessarily be correlated across the equations so that they will not be separable and (2) the predictor and disturbance variables within each equation will be neither independent nor contemporaneously uncorrelated (Kmenta, 1971, p. 302) so that MR estimates will not even be consistent (rather, they will be biased even in large samples; see Hibbs, 1974, pp. 291–292).

Before considering alternative procedures to MR for estimating the βs and γs of Eqs. (27) and (28) under different violations of assumptions, a question

TABLE II

Effects of Violation of Assumptions on Parameter Estimates when Multiple Regression Is Applied to Eqs. (27) and (28)

Assumptions		Properties of estimates				Consequences
		Small sample		Large sample		
Lagged variable	Auto-correlation	Unbiased	Efficient	Consistent	Asymptotic efficiency	
No	No	Yes	Yes	Yes	Yes	Use MR; usual desirable properties hold.
No	Yes	Yes	No	Yes	No	*Tends* to inflate individual significance tests and r^2; depends upon degree and type of autocorrelation process.
Yes	No	No	No	Yes	Yes	Use MR; large sample preferred since small sample properties unclear.
Yes	Yes	No	No	No	No	When autocorrelation is positive, impact of lagged endogenous is exaggerated and that of exogenous depressed.

of pragmatics must be raised. Just how serious are the violations of the assumptions when MR is (inappropriately) used as an estimation technique? Table II summarizes these effects as reported by Hibbs (1974), Hannan and Young (1977), and Kmenta (1971). It is clear that the most serious obstacles to useful MR estimation are posed by the presence of autocorrelation in the disturbance variables especially when that autocorrelation is coupled with lagged endogenous variables. In the latter case, the estimates of the parameter values cannot be trusted even in large samples.

In the following pages, alternative estimation procedures are considered for the two problem cases: Case I, autocorrelation but no lagged variables and Case II, autocorrelation and lagged variables. Unfortunately, there is one additional complication. In both Case I and Case II, the alternative procedures will depend upon knowing the form of the relationship among the disturbance variables which produces the autocorrelation. When this form is known due to a priori theory or research, then the alternative estimation procedures will reduce to simple MR analyses on transformed data. For the sake of easy reference, let us refer to these as Cases IA and IIA. When the form of the disturbance is *not* known, then estimation must be preceded by an analysis of the time dependencies in the residuals; call these Cases IB and IIB.

D. Alternative Estimation Procedures with Autocorrelated Disturbances

1. CASE IA: AUTOCORRELATED DISTURBANCES (FORM KNOWN) WITHOUT LAGGED VARIABLES

In the event that the lagged variables are absent form Eqs. (27) and (28), $\gamma_{11} = \gamma_{22} = 0$ and the system to be estimated is

$$\eta_1(t) = \beta_{12}\eta_2(t - 1) + \zeta_1(t) \tag{31}$$

$$\eta_2(t) = \beta_{21}\eta_1(t - 1) + \zeta_2(t) \tag{32}$$

with each of the disturbance variables autocorrelated across time in some known fashion. Three classes of autocorrelation processes are treated in the statistical literature (Glass *et al.*, 1975; Box & Jenkins, 1976): autoregressive processes, moving average processes, and mixed autoregressive–moving average processes.

The basic form of a first-order (or lag-1 time unit) autoregressive process is

$$\zeta_1(t) = \phi_1\zeta_1(t - 1) + \nu_1(t) \tag{33}$$

where $\nu_1(t)$ is an error term uncorrelated with $\zeta_1(t - 1)$ and with prior values of ν_1. The autoregressive process implies that the correlations among errors decrease as the lag time between errors to be correlated increases since it is assumed that $-1 < \phi_1 < 1$. A second-order autoregressive process would be described by

$$\zeta_1(t) = \phi_{11}\zeta_1(t - 1) + \phi_{12}\zeta_1(t - 2) + \nu_1(t) \tag{34}$$

The error at t clearly depends not only on the value of the prior disturbance but also that at two periods prior. The correlations between errors at different size lags will also decrease as the lag size increases (because of the constraints on ϕ_{11} and ϕ_{12}) but the decrease will be less rapid than the first-order process when ϕ_{11} and ϕ_{12} are the same sign. While the autoregressive process can be obviously generalized to third and higher orders, most researchers in time series note that a second-order process is usually sufficient to describe the behavior of most autoregressive disturbance processes (Hibbs, 1974; Wheelwright & Makridakis, 1975).

Moving average processes ascribe the subsequent values of the disturbances $\zeta_1(t)$ to weighted sums of the prior nonautocorrelated random shocks $\nu_1(t - 1)$. The order of the moving average is determined by the number of prior values which determine the value of the disturbance at time t. A first-order moving average process is described by

$$\zeta_1(t) = \omega_1 \nu_1(t - 1) + \nu_1(t)$$

and a second-order process by

$$\zeta_1(t) = \omega_{11} \nu_1(t - 1) + \omega_{12} \nu_1(t - 2) + \nu_1(t)$$

As Hibbs (1974, pp. 272–277) nicely shows the autocorrelation for a first-order moving average process is zero for all lags greater than 1, for a second-order process is zero for all lags greater than 2, and so forth. Once again this process can be generalized to higher orders but is usually unnecessary.

An autoregressive moving average process is simply the superposition of the previous two processes at some order for the autoregressive process and at some (perhaps different) order for the moving average process. For our purposes, this complexity is unnecessary as long as we are aware that such additions are possible, should the data require it (Glass, et al., 1975, pp. 97–101).

To estimate the parameters in Eqs. (31) and (32), let us assume that the disturbance autocorrelations are known to be generated by the commonly observed first-order autoregressive process

$$\zeta_1(t) = \phi_1 \zeta_1(t - 1) + \nu_1(t) \tag{35}$$

$$\zeta_2(t) = \phi_2 \zeta_2(t - 1) + \nu_2(t) \tag{36}$$

The goal is to use our a priori knowledge about the form of the disturbances to improve the quality of the estimates of β_{12} and β_{21} beyond those provided by MR. In particular the MR estimates are not efficient.

Asymptotically efficient estimates of β_{12} and β_{21} in the face of first-order autoregressive disturbances can be obtained by carrying out a generalized least squares (GLS) analysis of Eqs. (31) and (32) separately. Equations (31) and (32) can be treated separately because in the absence of lagged endogenous variables the correlation between ζ_1 and ζ_2 due to the lag structure is zero even with autocorrelated disturbances (Kmenta, 1971, p. 587). As is well known in the econometric literature, GLS yields consistent and asymptotically efficient estimates of the structural parameters (in this case β_{12} and β_{21}) when consistent estimates of certain confounding parameters (in this case ϕ_1 and ϕ_2) can be obtained. What is not so obvious in reading discussions about GLS is that GLS is nothing more than MR after the data have been appropriately transformed.

Since Eqs. (31) and (32) are separable, let our discussion focus on Eq. (31) only with similar remarks for Eq. (32) following by analogy. The procedure is as follows: Estimate β_{12} in Eq. (31) by using ordinary multiple regression yielding β_{12} and, more importantly, a consistent estimate of $\zeta_1(tj)$ for each observation-time unit tj. Call these estimates $\hat{\zeta}_1(tj)$. Now regressing these estimated residuals according to

$$\hat{\zeta}_1(tj) = \phi_1 \hat{\zeta}_1(tj - 1) + \nu_1(tj)$$

across all tj observations will yield a consistent estimate of ϕ_1, $\hat{\phi}_1$.

With this estimate in hand, the raw data can be transformed and GLS accomplished by a third set of regressions. The transformations for the raw data are (Hibbs, 1974, p. 269):[12]

$$\eta_1^*(tj) = \eta_1(tj) - \hat{\phi}_1 \eta_1(tj - 1), \qquad j = 2, \ldots, T \tag{37}$$

$$\eta_2^*(t_1) = \left[1 - \left(\hat{\phi}_1\right)^2\right]^{1/2} \eta_2(t_1) \tag{38}$$

$$\eta_2^*(tj) = \eta_2(tj) - \hat{\phi}_1 \eta_2(tj - 1), \qquad j = 2, \ldots, T - 1 \tag{39}$$

This transformation in essence removes from each current value of the variable that which is due to the prior value of the same variable. Now that this purification has taken place a third regression is run on the transformed variables according to

$$\eta_1^*(t) = \beta_{12} \eta_2^*(t - 1) + \zeta_1^*(t) \tag{39a}$$

which will yield estimates of β_{12} (and β_{21} when carried out there) which are consistent and asymptotically efficient. Thus the usual significance tests on β_{12} and R^2 are now less troubling than in the straight MR case of Eq. (31) without purification.[13]

The purification of the statistical testing procedure is bought at some cost. The researcher must run three different regressions rather than one and must

---

[12]If the disturbance process is not first-order autoregressive, then the general procedure outlined in the text still holds. However, for higher-order autoregressive or moving average processes the estimation is somewhat messier but is masterable. The transformations of the raw data would be analogous to this first-order autoregressive case but, again, messier (see Hibbs, 1974, pp. 269–278, 282, note 30 for a more complete discussion).

[13]Based upon Monte Carlo studies by Rao and Griliches (1969), Hibbs (1974, p. 283, note 31) suggests that GLS should be undertaken when $|\phi_1| > 0.3$ but not otherwise, regardless of the significance of the Durbin–Watson Statistic obtained in the regression of Eq. (31).

transform the original data before the final regression. However, each of these tasks can be accomplished within the standard MR software as long as the program has options to carry over the residuals and has reasonably flexible transformation options on the input data. The return will be estimates of β which are less likely to be inflated.

2. CASE IB: AUTOCORRELATED DISTURBANCES (FORM UNKNOWN) WITHOUT LAGGED VARIABLES

This case is identical to the previous one [that is Eqs. (31) and (32)] except that there is *no* presumption that the form of the process generating the disturbances is known *a priori*. Thus, the primary task is to determine the form of the disturbance process and then to proceed as in Case IA.

To determine the form of the disturbance process, we follow the guidelines discussed by Box and Jenkins (1976) for modeling a time series. First, however estimates of the $\zeta_1(t)$ and $\zeta_2(t)$ must be obtained by regressing $\eta_1(t)$ on $\eta_2(t-1)$ to obtain estimates of the residuals, $\zeta_1(t)$, and regressing $\eta_2(t)$ on $\eta_1(t-1)$ to obtain estimates of the residuals $\zeta_2(t)$. This yields two separate time series for each of the disturbances and the methods of Box and Jenkins can be applied to each of the residual series separately.

In order to use Box and Jenkins techniques, we need the autocorrelations (AC) and partial autocorrelations (PAC) between pairs of residual estimates for different time lags. That is we need the lag -1 correlation $\rho_{\zeta_1}(1)$ which is the correlation between $\hat{\zeta}_1(t)$ and $\hat{\zeta}_1(t-1)$, the lag-2 correlation $\rho_{\zeta_1}(2)$ which is the correlation between $\hat{\zeta}_1(t)$ and $\hat{\zeta}_1(t-2)$, etc. We also need the lag-1 PAC controlling for the other time units; that is, $\rho_{\zeta_1.23\ldots T}(1)$, $\rho_{\zeta_1.132\ldots T}(2)$, $\rho_{\zeta_1.124\ldots T}(3)$, etc. These ACs and PACs can be obtained directly from the usual printout of the regression of $\hat{\zeta}_1(t-1)$, $\hat{\zeta}_1(t-2)$, $\hat{\zeta}_1(t-3)$, etc., onto $\hat{\zeta}_1(t)$ to the highest order PAC desired. The highest order is usually determined by T, the number of observations. Both Hibbs and Box and Jenkins suggest that the order generated should be no greater than $T/4$ or $T/5$. But since we expect the autoregressive, moving average, or mixed disturbance process to be no greater than order 2, ACs and PACs of order 4–6 probably will suffice to get some idea of the nature of the disturbance process. Let us arbitrarily choose the maximum order to be 5 which presumes 20–25 time-series observations. If the estimated residuals are arrayed as

$$
\begin{bmatrix} \hat{\zeta}_1(6) \\ \vdots \\ \hat{\zeta}_1(k) \\ \vdots \\ \hat{\zeta}_1(T) \end{bmatrix}
=
\begin{bmatrix} \hat{\zeta}_1(5) & \hat{\zeta}_1(4) & \hat{\zeta}_1(3) & \hat{\zeta}_1(2) & \hat{\zeta}_1(1) \\ \vdots & & & & \vdots \\ \hat{\zeta}_1(k-1) & & \cdots & & \hat{\zeta}_1(k-5) \\ \vdots & & & & \vdots \\ \hat{\zeta}_1(T-1) & & \cdots & & \hat{\zeta}_1(T-5) \end{bmatrix}
\begin{bmatrix} \alpha_1 \\ \alpha_2 \\ \alpha_3 \\ \alpha_4 \\ \alpha_5 \end{bmatrix}
\tag{40}
$$

$+$ error terms

and run through a standard MR program, then (1) the routinely produced correlation matrix will contain the elements corresponding to $\rho_{\zeta_1}(1)$, $\rho_{\zeta_1}(2)$, $\rho_{\zeta_1}(3)$, $\rho_{\zeta_1}(4)$, and $\rho_{\zeta_1}(5)$, and (2) the regression coefficients α_1, α_2, α_3, α_4, α_5 will routinely be printed along with the associated PAC coefficient $\rho_{\zeta_1.2345}(1)$, $\rho_{\zeta_1.1345}(2)$, $\rho_{\zeta_1.1245}(3)$, $\rho_{\zeta_1.1235}(4)$, $\rho_{\zeta_1.1234}(5)$. A similar procedure for ζ_2 yields the necessary information for modeling the other residual series.

Determining the form of the disturbance process is a matter of inspecting the ACs and PACs relevant to certain criteria. These criteria, described by Glass *et al.* (1975, p. 98), Hibbs (1974, p. 281), and Davis and Lee (Chapter 14, this volume), are based on the fact that (1) a purely autoregressive process of order p exhibits ACs which decrease in absolute value slowly as the time lag increases and (2) the PACs of an autoregressive-only process of order p cut off after lag p. On the other hand, (3) a purely moving average process of order q has ACs which cut off after lag q and (4) has PACs which decrease in absolute value slowly as the time lag increases. Finally, (5) a mixed disturbance process of order p in autoregression and order q in moving average exhibits ACs and PACs which both decrease slowly in absolute value as the time lag increases. Thus, one should obtain a rough estimate of the type of disturbance process by using the criteria just given and inspecting the plot of the ACs and PACs as a function of time lag. For example, if the graphical display for our example were as in Fig. 6, then we would conclude that the disturbance process is an autoregressive process of order 1 described theoretically by $\zeta_1(t) = \phi_1 \zeta_1(t - 1) + \nu_1(t)$.

Mere inspection of the graphical display of the ACs and PACs may not be sufficient for some applications; statistical tests of significance may be desirable or necessary. Such tests are generally available for autoregressive but not for moving average processes (Glass *et al.*, 1975, pp. 98–99; Hibbs, 1974, pp. 280–281). For autoregressive processes Bartlett (1946) has shown that the variance of $\hat{\rho}$ of order τ is approximately $(1/T)(1 + 2(\hat{\rho}^2(1) + \hat{\rho}^2(2) + \cdots + \hat{\rho}^2(\tau - 1)) = \hat{\sigma}_{\hat{\rho}(\tau)}$ so that the ratio of $\hat{\rho}(\tau)$ to $[\hat{\sigma}_{\hat{\rho}(\tau)}]^{1/2}$ tests the significance of $\hat{\rho}(\tau)$ by comparison (in the conventional way) to the unit normal curve. An estimate of the variance of the PAC was established by Quenouille (1949) as $1/T$ so that the ratio of any order PAC to $1/T^{1/2}$ tests the significance of that PAC also by comparison to the unit normal curve. While these tests are only approximate, they can sometimes serve as more precise guides than eyeballing the AC and PAC curves as a function of lag time.

Once the form of the disturbance process is established, then Case IB degenerates into Case IA and the procedures of Case IA should be followed. Obviously, Case IB requires a considerable increase in data manipulation over Case IA but the additional effort is aimed at buying information about the form of the disturbances which were either already known in Case IA or were (appropriately or inappropriately) presumed.

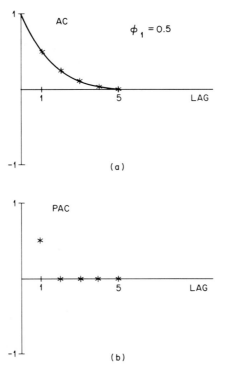

FIG. 6. (a) Autocorrelations and (b) partial autocorrelations for a first-order autoregressive process.

3. CASE IIA: AUTOCORRELATED DISTURBANCES (FORM KNOWN) WITH LAGGED ENDOGENOUS VARIABLES

As Table II suggests, estimation of the structural coefficients in Eqs. (27) and (28) by means of MR when there is autocorrelation does not even yield estimates of βs and γs which are consistent. That is, even in large samples the magnitudes both of the structural coefficients and their standard errors are untrustworthy. There are two reasons for this: The predictors in Eqs. (27) and (28) are correlated with the residuals and the equations are simultaneous (necessarily correlated across disturbances).

Case IIA assumes that the effects of the lagged endogenous variables are nonzero and that the form of the disturbances is known. For the sake of simplicity and because they are most common, let us assume that both disturbances are generated by a first-order autoregressive process as described by Eqs. (35) and (36).

By analogy to Case IA it would be desirable to obtain consistent estimates of $\zeta_1(tj)$ and $\zeta_2(tj)$ for each tj and then regress these estimates according to Eqs. (35) and (36). This would yield the necessary estimates of ϕ_1 and ϕ_2 so that the procedures of Case IA could be followed. The problem is how to obtain consistent estimates of $\zeta_1(tj)$ and $\zeta_2(tj)$.

An interesting variant of the instrumental variables techniques will yield consistent estimates as follows. First, consider the logic of the following trick. By Eqs. (27) and (35)

$$\eta_1(t) = \beta_{12}\eta_2(t-1) + \gamma_{11}\eta_1(t-1) + \zeta_1(t)$$
$$= \beta_{12}\eta_2(t-1) + \gamma_{11}\eta_1(t-1) + \phi_1\zeta_1(t-1) + \nu_1(t) \qquad (41)$$

But

$$\zeta_1(t-1) = \eta_1(t-1) - \beta_{12}\eta_2(t-2) - \gamma_{11}\eta_1(t-2)$$

so that substituting this expression into Eq. (41) yields

$$\eta_1(t) = \beta_{12}\eta_2(t-1) - (\gamma_{11} + \phi_1)\eta_1(t-1)$$
$$- \beta_{12}\phi_1\eta_2(t-2) - \gamma_{11}\phi_1\eta_1(t-2) + \nu_1(t) \qquad (42)$$

The same procedure would yield a similar equation for $\eta_2(t)$. Equation (42) has a desirable form since the disturbance term $\nu_1(t)$ is independent of all of the predictors in Eq. (42) and is assumed not to be autocorrelated. Hence, Eq. (42) and the analogous equations for $\eta_2(t)$ could be separately estimated by standard MR procedures to yield consistent estimates of the structural coefficients.

Let us next consider the procedures implied by the preceding approach:

(1) Regress $\eta_1(t)$ on $\eta_1(t-1)$, $\eta_2(t-1)$, $\eta_1(t-2)$, and $\eta_2(t-2)$ according to

$$\eta_1(t) = \alpha_1\eta_1(t-1) + \alpha_2\eta_2(t-1) + \alpha_3\eta_1(t-2) + \alpha_4\eta_2(t-2) + \nu_1(t)$$

(2) The desired structural coefficients are found by

$$\hat{\beta}_{12} = \hat{\alpha}_2, \qquad \hat{\phi}_1 = \hat{\alpha}_4/(-\hat{\alpha}_2), \qquad \hat{\gamma}_{11} = \hat{\alpha}_1 + (\hat{\alpha}_4/\hat{\alpha}_2)$$

(3) If $\hat{\phi}_1$ is not too large (say, less than .3 in absolute value), it is probably not unwise to go back to the original regression Eq. (27) for estimates of the standard errors.

(4) If $\hat{\phi}_1$ is hefty, then, since $\hat{\phi}_1$ is consistent, it can be used in a GLS analysis by transforming the data according to Eqs. (37)–(39) as in Case IA. According to Hibbs (1974, p. 296) this second pass should improve the precision of the estimates of βs and γs and because of the desirable properties of GLS estimates give standard errors which are asymptotically efficient.

Case IIA is not unlike the previous cases in that variations of standard MR techniques can yield estimates of the structural coefficients which are consistent and asymptotically efficient. The trick described in Eqs. (41) and (42) makes Case IIA estimable by removing from each equation the effects of the assumed first-order autoregression in the errors. Unfortunately, such a trick is not possible in Case IIB since knowledge of the form of the autocorrelation process is not available.

4. Case IIB: Autocorrelated Disturbances (Form Unknown) with Lagged Endogenous Variables

Quite frankly, the statistical literature offers no unequivocal solution to the full problem of Case IIB. As both Hannan and Young (1977) and Hibbs (1974, p. 298, note 57) note, the best that the researcher can hope for in Case IIB is consistent estimates of the structural coefficients. No known statistical procedure will yield estimates which are asymptotically efficient. Hence, confidence in significance tests must be limited.

Through the time of Hibbs's useful review, little small sample Monte Carlo evidence was available to evaluate alternative estimators for the equation system of Case IIB [that is, Eqs. (27) and (28) with disturbances assumed correlated in some unknown way]. Recently, Hannan and Young (1977) reported the results of a Monte Carlo study pertinent to Case IIB. They conclude that of the six estimation procedures studied, a synthetic technique called instrumental variables–modified generalized least squares (IV–MGLS hereafter) outperformed other consistent and inconsistent estimation techniques in small samples and under a variety of conditions on the magnitude of autocorrelation and cross-equation correlation. Based upon these results, we will consider only the IV–MGLS estimation technique as discussed by Hibbs.[14]

Despite its formidable name, IV–MGLS is actually nothing more than the sequential application of estimation procedures already encountered in this paper. Let us outline the procedure stepwise and then comment on it (see Hibbs, 1974, pp. 297–298):

(1) The coefficients to be estimated are β_{12}, β_{21}, γ_{11}, γ_{22} from Eqs. (27) and (28), their variances, significance, and R^2 under the assumption that disturbances are autocorrelated. Focus on Eq. (27) for simplicity of exposition.

(2) Regress the lagged endogenous variable $\eta_1(t)$ on whatever good instrumental variables are available using the criteria discussed earlier; $\eta_2(t-1)$ may be a good candidate although $\eta_2(t-2)$ may be required. This yields $\hat{\eta}_1(t)$.

(3) Use $\hat{\eta}_1(t)$ in place of $\eta_1(t)$ in the original regression so that $\eta_1(t+1)$ is regressed on $\hat{\eta}_1(t)$ and $\eta_2(t)$ yielding the second-stage estimates $\hat{\beta}_{12}$ and $\hat{\gamma}_{11}$. These two regressions complete the two-stage instrumental variables portion of the estimation.

---

[14]The IV-MGLS procedure discussed by Hannan and Young (1977) is considerably *less* general than that discussed by Hibbs. In particular, Hannan and Young presume that the disturbance process among the errors is such that "disturbances for the same unit are correlated at the same magnitude no matter how distant they are in time" [p. 61]. This type of process seems too specialized to warrant general adoption. Modeling the disturbance process as Hibbs advocates seem wiser in the exploratory stages of time series investigations. Kmenta (1971, p. 508–517) presents an overview of standard assumptions in pooling time series and cross sectional data including that advocated by Hannan and Young.

(4)   Use $\hat{\beta}_{12}$ and $\hat{\gamma}_{11}$ with the original raw data to generate consistent estimates of the disturbances $\hat{\zeta}_1(tj)$ for lag tj.

(5)   The disturbances $\hat{\zeta}_1(tj)$ can now be used exactly as they were used in Case IB to (a) determine the form of the disturbance process using the standard time-series correlogram techniques; (b) transform the data as required by the form of the disturbance process; and (c) regress the transformed endogenous on the transformed endogenous and exogenous variables to yield MGLS estimates of the βs and the γs.

While this procedure requires a good deal of data manipulation and remanipulation, no step requires the use of software different from that of MR. Thus, the researcher with facility in MR software can, with some perserverance successfully use that facility to manage statistically more intractable problems. The usual t values, R^2s, Fs, etc., printed by an MR package would after step (5c) be IV–MGLS estimates and, hence, should be interpreted with some caution even in large samples. However, without other guidance the IV–MGLS significance tests are probably better than nothing. Overall the increased costs in data handling buy estimates of the structural coefficients which are otherwise hopelessly intertwined with the disturbances of both equations.

E. The Pooling of Cross Sections

The previous four cases carried out estimation on a dyad-by-dyad basis. In communication research it is more frequently the case that multiple cross sections are available and the researcher concerned with a parsimonious description valid over cross sections. This is the question of pooling cross sections. How the pooling occurs depends upon three factors: (1) the number of cross sections, (2) the assumptions one is willing to make about autoregression, and (3) the similarity of disturbance processes across cross sections.

The question of pooling cross sections only concerns similarities and differences in the process generating correlation among errors. Each CS is assumed to follow the same structural equation system [Eqs. (27) and (28)]. If not, the CS units must be separated into groups with members of each group having the same structural equation. Assuming that each CS obeys the same structural equation, then pooling turns on the differences among error processes.

If the number of cross sections is small, then it is feasible to carry out individual time-series analyses on each cross section (the number of time-series points permitting). Making no further assumptions about the disturbance processes, the CS and TS data would be pooled in a vector of observations *after* the raw data had been transformed to remove the effects of autoregression. That is, pooling would take place on the η^* or transformed data.

If the number of cross sections is so large as to make it unfeasible to carry out a time-series analysis for each CS, then some other strategies are available. The simplest strategy is to presume that all CS have the same error-generating process (say first-order autoregressive) and have approximately the same autocorrelation coefficient; that is, $\phi_{11} = \phi_{12} = \cdots = \phi_{1k}$ where ϕ_{1j} is the first-order autocorrelation for the jth CS. In this case, the raw CS and TS data are pooled at the outset and Cases I and II proceed using the average of the ϕ_{1j} values across CS for transforming the data (Kmenta, 1971, p. 512). The only other reasonable strategy is to sample the CS and carry out case-by-case analyses on the subsample, hoping that the subsample will show that each CS has approximately the same disturbance process. If so, then the entire sample would be transformed according to the observed disturbance process in the subsample.

F. A Case Study: Switching Pause Matching in Two-Person Conversations

Since Chapple's (1942) early work on the patterns of activity matching in two-person conversations, researchers have been attracted to the observation that individuals often become more similar across several discussions in their average durations of certain overt communication behaviors such as vocalization length, pause length, and switching pause length. It is possible that this "tracking and adjustment" process may be a deeply ingrained psychological process which makes itself felt in many other overt communication behaviors as Webb's explanations imply (Webb, 1972).

Most researchers (Feldstein & Welkowitz, 1978) believe that if there is a systematic matching process between the overt communication behaviors, then that process is not only subtle but also takes place only over lengthy periods of association. For example, Natale (1975) has observed that in initial encounters matching in various indices of talk and silence does not occur. The conventional wisdom is that matching is a long term process; there is, in short, no moment-to-moment matching. On my own view, I fail to see how matching over long periods could take place without some matching, albeit subtle, in the moment-to-moment tracking presumed to co-occur with floor switching. Also, methodologies employed to uncover the matching process have not in general been time-series methods but rather have been typically ANOVA techniques. Such techniques usually beg the moment-to-moment question in favor of matching across grosser time units. The search for moment-to-moment matching requires not only time-series data but the methodologies appropriate to those data.

The data to be reported here are a reanalysis of some data reported sketchily by Cappella (1976).[15] In particular, we will consider whether matching of switching pause durations (lag time between switch of speaker and listener roles) occurs systematically over a single 20-minute conversation. The

---

[15]The data to be presented in these sections are actual data but represent a carefully selected set of 3 experiments out of 12 run. The complete set will be reported in a subsequent paper. The reader is cautioned not to make generalizations from these 3 experiments (i.e., dyadic conversations).

question then is whether person A's switching pauses are becoming more similar to those of B and vice versa over the conversation. Such observations have been made for interviewee's adjusting to interviewers (Matarazzo, 1965) and have been made across several informal social conversations between the same persons (Jaffe & Feldstein, 1970). Is the same true when the time units shrink from conversations to individual turns?

The process of matching between persons 1 and 2 can be described mathematically by Eqs. (27) and (28). The lagged endogenous variables are retained because, as Jaffe and Feldstein (1970) have noted and as we have replicated (Cappella, 1976), there is a strong consistency in individual probabilities of responses over time both within and across conversations. Such a consistency must be retained in the matching process since otherwise each person's behavior would be continually changing in response to the random fluctuations in the other's behavior. Such a process is neither observed empirically nor suggested by common sense experience. Thus, γ_{11} and γ_{22} should both be nonzero and should be positive in sign. Similarly β_{12} and β_{21} should be nonzero and if the matching process is convergent (as it should be if it is truly matching) then either β_{12}, β_{21}, or both should be positive. If both were zero, there would be no matching in the dyad; if both were negative, then each person would be "moving away" from the other; if one were negative, then one person would be moving away while the other was not adapting or was in fact matching.

What about the disturbance process? Here there seem to be two options, both of which will be discussed. First, there exists some evidence that the talk–silence process is first order rather than higher order (Jaffe & Feldstein 1970; Hayes, Meltzer, and Wolfe, 1970) so that whatever the form of the disturbance process it would at most be first order. The *form* of the disturbance is more likely to be akin to an autoregressive disturbance than to a moving average process since whatever disturbances intervene are likely to be slowly forgotten thus paralleling the exponentially decreasing curves of most short term memory studies (Kintsch, 1977). Thus, the first assumption to be made is that the disturbance process is first-order autoregressive. Second, despite the preceding arguments, it may be wise to assume nothing about the *form* of the disturbance process, only that there exists such a disturbance process. This will be the second assumption.

1. CASE IIA: SWITCHING PAUSE MATCHING WITH FIRST-ORDER AUTOREGRESSION

If we assume that the disturbance process is a first-order autoregressive one, then the data fall under Case IIA. In order to show some of the problems in analyzing and interpreting results we shall consider first the results for each cross section (i.e., dyad) and then for the cross section plus time-series pooled data.

a. Individual Analysis The trick which Case IIA employs makes possible the separate analysis of each person in each of the three experiments. Thus, the regression

$$SP_A(t) = \alpha_1 SP_A(t - 1) + \alpha_2 SP_B(t - 1)$$
$$+ \alpha_3 SP_A(t - 2) + \alpha_4 SP_B(t - 1) + \zeta_A(t) \tag{43}$$

(where SP_A = As switching pause duration) was run for each of the persons (A and B) in each of the three experiments. The regression coefficients, their associated probabilities of significance, and the autoregression parameter ($\phi = \hat{\alpha}_4/(-\hat{\alpha}_2)$) are presented in Table III. There are several obsservations to be made concerning these data: (1) The effects of B's duration of switching pause is either positively related or unrelated to that of A; (2) the effects of A's length of switching pause is either positively related or unrelated to A's subsequent switching pause; (3) the lag-2 effects are essentially unrelated to A's duration of switching pauses; and (4) the estimates of first order autocorrelation, ϕ, are very unstable from case to case.

The instability in ϕ is somewhat more perplexing at first. ϕ ranges from -2.22 to $+.508$. The problem with interpreting this coefficient arises from the fact that it is a ratio of two other estimates each with its own confidence interval. Since $\hat{\alpha}_4$, the numerator for ϕ, has such a wide confidence region (in four of six cases the standard error of estimate is considerably larger than the estimate of $\hat{\alpha}_4$ itself), it is difficult to treat ϕ with much degree of trust. Since the estimates of $\hat{\gamma}_{11}$ and $\hat{\gamma}_{22}$ which are the lag-1 effects for Case IIA are given by $\hat{\alpha}_1 - \hat{\phi}_1$, then these estimates are also highly unstable with wide confidence regions and, hence, cannot be trusted. As these data show, one of the unresolved difficulties with the techniques of Case IIA is what to do with estimates of ϕ (and hence the estimates of α) when the coefficients which constitute ϕ, $\hat{\alpha}_2$ and $\hat{\alpha}_4$, are not statistically stable. My own biases would be to trust ϕ only when both $\hat{\alpha}_2$ and $\hat{\alpha}_4$ are significant or when $\hat{\alpha}_2$, the denominator, is statistically significant and $\hat{\alpha}_4$, the numerator, is not significantly different from zero. In the latter case ϕ would be presumed to be near zero. These two cases should be the most common empirical situations which the researcher faces. If $\hat{\alpha}_4$ were significant and $\hat{\alpha}_2$ not, then the data may be exhibiting second-order characteristics which require reformulation of the model. In the case where neither $\hat{\alpha}_2$ nor $\hat{\alpha}_4$ is significant at some preassigned level, it is not clear what importance should be attributed to ϕ at all. But a nonsignificant $\hat{\alpha}_2$ suggests that the original model requires reformulation since the key independent variable has failed to achieve significance.

Given the above interpretive guidelines three of six ϕ values in Table III are probably in the vicinity of zero ($-.500$, $-.115$, $-.237$, and possibly .474) while the other three are indeterminate given the nonsignificant $\hat{\alpha}_2$s (.508, -2.22, and probably .474). In order to take advantage of clear trends in the individual analyses and to test for the presence of individual, partner, or dyad differences in these data the individual cross sections were pooled with the time-series data.

The generally positive relationship between B's effect on A suggests that at the individual dyad there is some kind of matching process taking place in the

TABLE III

CASE IIA RESULTS: INDIVIDUAL EFFECTS ON THE OTHER'S DURATION
OF SWITCHING PAUSE

Experiment 3 ($T = 107$; $N = 1$)

	Person 1		Person 2	
	Coeff. (Std. err.)	Prob.[a] (d.f. = 102)	Coeff. (Std. err.)	Prob. (d.f. = 102)
α_1 (A's lag-1 effect on A)	.210 (.101)	.040	− .090 (.098)	.360
α_2 (B's lag-1 effect on A)	− .061 (.137)	.655	.162 (.071)	.025
α_3 (A's lag-2 effect on A)	.015 (.103)	.881	− .014 (.098)	.882
α_4 (B's lag-2 effect on A)	.031 (.141)	.824	.081 (.073)	.270
$\phi (= \hat{\alpha}_4 / - \hat{\alpha}_2)$ 1st order correlation	.508		− .500	

Experiment 7 ($T = 140$; $N = 1$)

	Person 1		Person 2	
	Coeff. (Std. err.)	Prob. (d.f. = 135)	Coeff. (Std. err.)	Prob. (d.f. = 135)
α_1 (A's lag-1 effect on A)	.281 (.087)	.001	− .028 (.086)	.742
α_2 (B's lag-1 effect on A)	.148 (.079)	.062	.137 (+.093)	.140
α_3 (A's lag-2 effect on A)	− .034 (.085)	.688	.143 (.086)	.096
α_4 (B's lag-2 effect on A)	.017 (.080)	.825	− .065 (.093)	.482
$\phi (= \hat{\alpha}_4 / - \hat{\alpha}_2)$ 1st order correlation	− .115		.474	

[a] Probability of significance of the individual coefficient by the t ratio.

TABLE III (continued)

	Experiment 12 ($T = 124$; $N = 1$)			
	Person 1		Person 2	
	Coeff. (Std. err.)	Prob. (d.f. = 119)	Coeff. (std. err.)	Prob. (d.f. = 119)
α_1 (As lag-1 effect on A)	.095 (.091)	.299	.046 (.091)	.611
α_2 (Bs lag-1 effect on A)	.131 (.066)	.048	.105 (.126)	.404
α_3 (As lag-2 effect on A)	−.049 (.093)	.599	.104 (.093)	.264
α_4 (Bs lag-2 effect on A)	.031 (.066)	.633	.233 (.128)	.069
$\phi (= \hat{\alpha}_4/-\hat{\alpha}_2)$ 1st order correlation	−.237		−2.22	

length of switching pause exhibited even over single conversations as short as 20 minutes. The generally positive relationship between A's lag-1 switching pause and A's subsequent switching pause suggests that the change in switching pause is accounted for partially by the other's influence and partially by the baseline which is A's own prior activity. These results are in basic agreement with those reported elsewhere in the literature on matching (cited earlier) but support the existence of matching in short run moment-to-moment cases.

b. Cross-Sectional and Time-Series Pooled Data   In the model of Eqs. (27) and (28) the equations are perfectly symmetrical. As soon as the equations are made separable (as by the trick of Case IIA) and one pools the cross sections together, then the two-equation system can be treated as a single equation of the form

$$SP_A(t) = \alpha_1 SP_A(t-1) + \alpha_2 SP_B(t-1)$$
$$+ \alpha_3 SP_A(t-2) + \alpha_4 SP_B(t-2) + \zeta_A(t) \qquad (44)$$

with six cross sections and a total of 740 observations. The trick of removing the correlation between equations makes possible a single data string 740 observations long with no autocorrelation among the observations (one hopes). The single equation model asks the question, Is there matching in switching pause duration across individual conversations as a group?

Rather than run the regression of Eq. (44) initially, a model which includes the aforementioned four independent variables along with a series of dummy variables was run using a hierarchial procedure with groups of variables being entered in a prespecified order. The groups and their order of entry were: (1) the four switching pause variables in Eq. (44), (2) two dummy variables representing the three dyads or experiments, (3) four interactions, the products of the dyad dummies with $SP_A(t - 1)$ and $SP_B(t - 1)$, (4) three-person dummies to distinguish the four participants, and (5) three-partner dummies to distinguish the four partners. This procedure permitted a test of differences in regression coefficients between dyads, differences due to the dyad, the person, and the person's partner. Since none of these 12 predictors was significant at $\alpha = .05$ they will not be presented.

The absence of these differences suggests that no dyad showed a matching process any different from the baseline dyad. The absence of individual difference and dyad differences suggests that the mean response in switching pause duration was not different between any person or any dyad and the baseline person or dyad, respectively. Partners did not affect mean duration of switching pause for the speaker as compared to the baseline partner.

The positive results for the matching process for the pooled cross sections are presented in Table IV.

Besides the results for the Case IIB regression, regression coefficients for a simple multiple regression are also presented. Most striking is the similarity of the coefficients of the two analyses. That is, the effect of B's length of switching pause on A and A's lagged effect on self is almost identical in the two cases. The reason for this is obvious when one looks more carefully at ϕ. The numerator of ϕ, $\hat{\alpha}_4$, is not significantly different from zero while the denominator, $\hat{\alpha}_2$, is. Thus, $\hat{\phi}$ is probably not to be interpreted as significantly

TABLE IV

CASE IIA: CROSS-SECTIONAL PLUS TIME-SERIES REGRESSIONS FOR EXPERIMENTS

Case IIA regressions ($NT = 740$)		Ordinary regressions ($NT = 740$)	
Coeff. std. error	Prob. df = 733	Coeff. std. error	Prob. df = 737
α_1 .097 (.037)	.009	α_1 .112 (.037)	.002
α_2 .110 (.037)	.003	α_2 .121 (.037)	.001
α_3 .059 (.037)	.111		
α_4 .020 (.037)	.584		
ϕ	$-$ .182		
Overall $F(4,735) = 6.91$, $p < .0000$, $R = .19$		Overall $F(2,737) = 11.87$, $p < .0000$, $R = .18$	

different from zero. Even being liberal, $\hat{\phi}$ is probably a small enough autocorrelation to ignore.

If ϕ is zero or at least negligible, then the trick of Case IIA is unnecessary and $\hat{\alpha}_1 = \hat{\gamma}_{11}$ and $\hat{\alpha}_2 = \hat{\beta}_{12}$ directly. The lag-2 independent variables in Eq. (44) are unnecessary and Case IIA reduces to a case of simple multiple regression with no autocorrelation in the errors. Furthermore, the typical next step in Case IIA, refining the coefficients by undertaking a transformation of the data (i.e., generalized least squares), is unnecessary.

Table IV also bears out the substantive hypothesis of a matching process in switching pause duration with A's subsequent pause lengths dependent on B's prior pauses and A's own prior pauses. As the R value reported in Table IV shows, the matching process is very weak, explaining less than 4% of the variance. On the other hand, the reader must keep in mind that this is a very subtle process occurring over a brief duration (20 minutes) with no attempt to manipulate its occurrence. Other studies which have reported much stronger matching effects (Feldstein & Welkowitz, 1978; Jaffe & Feldstein, 1970; Chapple, 1942) have used either matching over several separate meetings (e.g., eight one-half hour sessions in the Jaffe & Feldstein data), matching of average durations of switching pauses across persons, or both. The data reported here exhibit matching between pairs of persons during a brief discussion and on a moment-by-moment basis.

2. CASE IIB: SWITCHING PAUSE MATCHING WITH CORRELATED ERRORS

In Case IIA one assumes that the pattern of relationship among errors is first-order autoregressive and, while there may be good reason to make such an assumption, it could be invalid. Case IIB does not make such a presumption but only assumes that some relationship exists among the disturbances. Case IIB involves a five-step data manipulation procedure: (1) instrumental variables to generate a predicted value for the lagged independent variable, (2) regression to obtain consistent estimates of γ and β and, hence, the error terms, (3) modeling the error terms to determine the form of the disturbance, (4) transforming the original data to remove dependencies in the dependent and independent variables according to the results of step (3), and (5) regressing the transformed data according to the original model to obtain sharper estimates of the β and γ terms.

Steps (3)–(5) are important not because of the estimates of the βs and γs provided but rather because the estimates of the standard errors, the error variance, and R^2 output from the regressions of step (2) are not even asymptotically efficient rendering significance tests problematic. However, steps (1) and (2) are not mere preliminaries to the important steps (3)–(5) since they do provide consistent estimates of the desired parameters. So if the researcher wished to get a "ball park" estimate of β and γ without the complex data manipulations of steps (3)–(5), then steps (1) and (2) alone can provide such estimates but not (in general) trustworthy tests of hypotheses.

Just such a procedure was undertaken with the data from experiments 3, 7, and 12. The results are presented in Table V. Two instrumental variables were tried: B's switching pause duration lagged one time unit and the same variable lagged two time units. Since the regression effects of both on A's switching pause were very similar, the lag-1 instrument was used since it showed a higher correlation with the dependent variable. Using $SP_B(t - 1)$ as the instrument, predicted values for $SP_A(t)$, $S\hat{P}_A(t)$, were generated, punched onto cards, and used as the independent variables along with $SP_B(t)$, the original data, to generate estimates of β and γ. The results from the stage 2 regressions show that both β and γ have the same qualitative effects as in Case IIA. In the present case we would conclude that the speakers and their partners exhibited matching in switching pause duration and showed a susceptibility to influence from their own prior switching pauses. Of course, the standard errors and R^2 values would not generally be trusted in Case IIB but the similarity among the standard errors for β and R^2 values in Case IIA, Case IIB, and the simple regressions (Table IV) suggests that the low correlation among errors is a correct interpretation of the behavior of this process. The larger point estimate of γ in Case IIB compared to Case IIA and the ordinary regressions is somewhat disturbing but might be explained as follows: if there is a *negative* autocorrelation between the error at time 1 and that at time 2 as the estimate of ϕ in Table IV suggests, then the actual estimate of the effect of A on A's subsequent pausing should be *larger* than the estimate provided by Case IIA and the ordinary regressions. Since the procedures of Case IIB are presumably taking such effects into account, a negative autocorrelation between adjacent errors should deflate the estimate of γ as provided by ordinary regression. In fact, in Case IIA if ϕ were to be treated as significantly different from zero, then the estimate of γ would be

TABLE V

CASE IIB: CROSS-SECTIONAL PLUS TIME-SERIES REGRESSIONS FOR EXPERIMENTS 3, 7, AND 12.

Results for instrumental variables	Results for stage 2 instrumental variables
Using $SP_B(t - 1)$ as an instrument:	
$\quad SP_A(t) = \alpha SP_B(t - 1) + \zeta(t)$	$SP_A(t + 1) = \beta SP_B(t) + \gamma S\hat{P}_A(t) + \zeta(t + 1)$
$\quad\quad \hat{\alpha} = .137$	$\hat{\gamma} = .875, \quad p = .001$
$\quad\quad (.037)$	$\quad (.268)$
	$\hat{\beta} = .123, \quad p = .001$
	$\quad (.037)$
$F(1,738) = 14.4, \quad p = .0002$	$F(2,731) = 12.56, \quad p < .0000$
	$R^2 = .033$
Using $SP_B(t - 2)$ as an instrument:	
$\quad SP_A(t) = \alpha SP_B(t - 2) + \zeta(t)$	
$\quad\quad \hat{\alpha} = .063$	
$\quad\quad (.037)$	
$F(1,738) = 2.97, \quad p = .08$	

$.097 - (-.181) = .278$ for a stronger self-effect than we concluded was warranted by the data.

The only resolution of the discrepancy in γ estimates between Case IIA and IIB is to continue the steps of Case IIB through (3) to (5) to ascertain whether there exists an overall negative autocorrelation between adjacent errors or a negligible one.[16]

More firm conclusions about the coefficient measuring the matching process, that is, β, can be offered. Across all three procedures, ordinary regression, Case IIA, and Case IIB, the influence of partners on speakers' duration of switching pause remained positive and of almost identical magnitude. This similarity across estimation procedures bodes well for the robustness of the small effect which is represented by β. Until clear guidelines about the types of autocorrelation processes common to substantive problems in communication research arise from extensive experience with live data (as they have in economics), researchers would be wise to employ alternative estimation procedures to maximize confidence in the interpretation of results.

V. CONCLUSION

What must the researcher know to analyze and to estimate a system of causal relationships? Those of us who are researchers and theorists first and statisticians last need to know what we *must* know, not what we should know, to correctly handle newly developing data sets. First, this essay has treated a special case of causal systems, one in which each variable is indicated by one and only one observable indicator. Multiple indicators are discussed by Fink (Chapter 4). Second, two broad classes of causal systems are distinguished here and must be treated separately by the analyst: those at rest or equilibrium, static ones, and those which are moving and changing, dynamic ones.

Within the class of static causal systems, the researcher adept at multiple regression procedures should be able to handle estimation in any causal system equation by equation with only a few tricks added to the statistical repertoire. First, the researcher must be aware of the effects on the typical estimation which a priori assumptions about disturbances will have. Second, the researcher must be aware of the effects on the possibility of estimation which the measurement or nonmeasurement of exogenous variables will have. Third, the identification status of an equation determines the possibility of estimation and the type of estimation required. Identification status is a new concept to most researchers trained in single MR and ANOVA but it is a very general concept across statistical procedures whose study will be rewarded outside the domain of causal systems. Researchers are advised to acquire familiarity with this concept. Fourth, despite their fancy names and

---

[16]Subsequent detailed analyses of residuals confirms the absence of autocorrelation.

their number, estimation in static causal systems can for most researchers in most applications be reduced to MR (i.e., OLS) or MR twice (i.e., 2SLS).

While the complexities of structural equation modeling procedures seem to have delighted the early translators of these methods from econometrics to the other social and behavioral sciences, it is only their reduction to the most important distinctions which will lead to widespread use by substantively motivated researchers. Such use will produce the data which will be the criterion of vindication or repudiation of this statistical alchemy.

For the class of dynamic causal systems, the review presented here is less comprehensive than is ideal. The situations discussed and the example presented of cross-sectional plus time-series data were biased toward the case of a few cross sections and lengthy time series. Obviously, there are other possibilities which are as common, if not more common, than large T, small N data sets. For the case of large T, small N time series emphasis was placed on the manipulation of data within the standard multiple regression routines. Obviously, time-series data require a considerable amount of manipulation. The researcher trained in MR and with access to software permitting carryover of residuals and of regression coefficients and with flexible data transformation procedures can produce sophisticated and useful results.

In general, the researcher wishing or needing to conduct large T data analyses in the causal domain (as opposed to univariate time series) must first and foremost become familiar with the description, effects, detection, and removal of autocorrelation in the disturbance variables. The effects of auto-correlated disturbances on point estimation and hypothesis testing under various conditions are summarized in Table II. The detection and description of autocorrelation processes depends on the pattern of autocorrelation and partial autocorrelation of *consistent* estimates of the disturbance variable at various time lags. The first stage of any causal time-series analysis revolves around this detection and description process. Either the form of the autocorrelation is presumed to be of a particular type or some consistent estimation technique must be used to obtain trustworthy estimates of the residuals which can then be subject to correlogram inspection. The final stage of a causal time series involves using the knowledge presumed or gained about the autocorrelation in the disturbances to transform the original data to a purified form in which autocorrelation is absent from the errors. This step usually involves some sort of differencing techniques. Overall, the researcher can accomplish these techniques with a flexible MR computer routine. The greatest barrier to the adoption of such procedures (beside the requirement for lengthy time series which is often prohibitive) is a reoriented thought process. The researcher must come to see time-series data as inextricably intertwined with their errors and to visualize the autocorrelation detection and removal steps as a kind of systematic unraveling process. Once the data are unraveled then, from the point of view of hypothesis testing and estimation, they can be treated no differently than one would treat a set of cross-sectional observations.

References

Ayres, F. *Matrices*. New York: Schaum's Outline Series, McGraw-Hill, 1962.

Amemiya, T. Specification analysis in the estimation of parameters of a simultaneous equation with autoregressive residuals. *Econometrica*, 1966, **34**, 283–306.

Bales, R. F. *Interaction process analysis: A Method for the study of small groups*. Reading, Massachusetts: Addison-Wesley, 1950.

Bartlett, M. S. On the theoretical specification of sampling properties of autocorrelated time series. *Journal of Royal Statistical Society*, Ser. *B*, 1946, 8.

Berlo, D. *The process of communication*. New York: Holt, 1960.

Blalock, H. M. *Causal inferences in non-experimental research*. New York: Norton, 1964.

Blalock, H. M. *Theory construction: From verbal to mathematical theories*. Englewood Cliffs, New Jersey: Prentice-Hall, 1969.

Blalock, H. M. (Ed.). Causal inferences, closed populations, and measures of association. *Causal inferences in the social sciences*. San Francisco, California: Jossey-Bass, 1971.

Blalock, H. M. *Social statistics*. (2nd ed.) New York: McGraw-Hill, 1972.

Bohrnstedt, B. W., and Carter, T. M. Robustness in regression analysis. In H. L. Costner (Ed.), *Sociological methodology* 1971. San Francisco, California: Jossey-Bass, 1971.

Boudon, R. In A. B. Blalock & H. M. Blalock (Eds.), *Methodology in social research*. New York: McGraw-Hill, 1968.

Box, G. E. P., and Jenkins, G. M. *Time series analysis*. (2nd ed.) San Francisco, California: Holden Day, 1976.

Brooks, R. D., and Scheidel, T. M. Speech as process: A case study. *Speech Monographs*, 1968, **35**, 1–7.

Cappella, J. N. An introduction to the literature of causal modeling. *Human Communication Research*, 1975, **1**, 362–377.

Cappella, J. N. Modeling interpersonal communication systems as a pair of machines coupled through feedback. In G. R. Miller (Ed.), *Explorations in interpersonal communication*. Beverly Hills, California: Sage Publ., 1976.

Cappella, J. N. *The concept of cause in structural equation modeling*. Unpublished manuscript, Department of Communication Arts, Univ. of Wisconsin, Madison, Wisconsin, 1978.

Chapple, E. D. The measurement of interpersonal behavior. *Transactions of the New York Academy of Science*, 1942, **4**, 222–233.

Christ, C. *Econometric models and methods*. New York: Wiley, 1966.

Costner, H. L. Theory, deduction, and rules of correspondence. *American Journal of Sociology*, 1969, **75**, 245–263.

Cozby, P. C. Self disclosure: A literature review. *Psychological Bulletin*, 1973, **79**, 73–91.

Davis, D. K., and Lee, J. W. Time series analysis models for communication research. In P. R. Monge and J. N. Cappella (Eds.), *Multivariate techniques in communication research*. New York: Academic Press, 1980.

Draper, N. R., and Smith, H. *Applied regression analysis*. New York: Wiley, 1966.

Duncan, O. D. Path analysis: Sociological examples. In H. M. Blalock (Ed.), *Causal models in the social sciences*. San Francisco, California: Jossey-Bass, 1971.

Duncan, O. D. *Introduction to structural equation models*. New York: Academic Press, 1975.

Duncan, O. D., and Featherman, D. L. Psychological and cultural factors in the process of occupational achievement. In A. S. Goldberger and O. D. Duncan (Eds.), *Structural equation models in the social sciences*. New York: Seminar Press, 1973.

Ellis, D. G., and Fisher, B. A. Phases of conflict in small group development: A markov analysis. *Human Communication Research*, 1975, **1**, 195–210.

Fair, R. C. The estimation of simultaneous equation models with lagged endogenous variables and first order serially correlated errors. *Econometrica*, 1970, **38**, 507–515.

Feldstein, S., and Welkowitz, J. A chronography of conversation: In defense of an objective approach. In A. W. Siegman and S. Feldstein (Eds.), *Nonverbal behavior and communication*. Hillsdale, New Jersey: Lawrence Erlbaum, 1978.

Fink, E. L. Structural equation modeling: Unobserved variables. In P. R. Monge and J. N. Cappella (Eds.), *Multivariate techniques in communication research*. New York: Academic Press, 1980.

Fisher, F. M. The choice of instrumental variables in the estimation of economy-wide econometric models. In H. M. Blalock (Ed.), *Causal Models in the social sciences*. San Francisco, California: Jossey-Bass, 1971.

Glass, G. V., Willson, V. L., and Gottman, J. M. *Design and analysis of time series experiments*. Boulder, Colorado: Colorado Associated Univ. Press, 1975.

Goldberger, A. A. *Econometric theory*. New York: Wiley, 1964.

Goldberger, A. S. On Boudon's method of linear, causal analysis. *American Sociological Review*, 1970, **35**, 97–101.

Goldberger, A. S., and Duncan, O. D. *Structural equation models in the social sciences*. New York: Seminar Press, 1973.

Hannan, M. T., and Young, A. A. Estimation in panel models: Results on pooling cross-sections and time-series. In D. R. Heise (Ed.), *Sociological methodology 1977*. San-Francisco, California: Jossey-Bass, 1977.

Hargens, L. L. A note on standardized coefficients as structural parameters. *Sociological Methods and Research*, 1976, **5**, 247–255.

Harris, R. J. The uncertain connection between verbal theories and research hypotheses in sociology. *Journal of Experimental Social Psychology*, 1976, **12**, 210–219.

Hauser, R. M. Disaggregating a social-psychological model of educational attainment. In A. S. Goldberger and O. D. Duncan (Eds.), *Structural equation models in the social sciences*. New York: Seminar Press, 1973.

Hayes, D., Meltzer, L., and Wolf, G. Substantive conclusions are dependent upon techniques of measurement. *Behavioral Science*, 1970, **15**, 265–269.

Hays, W. *Statistics for psychologists*. New York: Holt, 1963.

Heise, D. R. Problems in path analysis and causal inference. In E. F. Borgatta and G. W. Bohrnstedt (Eds.), *Sociological methodology 1969*. San Francisco, California: Jossey-Bass, 1968.

Heise, D. R. *Causal analysis*. New York: Wiley, 1975.

Heise, D. R. Group dynamics and attitude-behavior relations. *Sociological Methods and Research*, 1977, **5**, 259–288.

Hibbs, D. A. Problems of statistical estimation and causal inference in time-series regression models. In H. L. Costner (Ed.), *Sociological methodology 1973–74*. San Francisco, California: Jossey-Bass, 1974.

Hotchkiss, L. A technique for comparing path models between subgroups. *Sociological methods and research*, 1976, **5**, 53–76.

Hout, M. A cautionary note on the use of two-stage least squares. *Sociological Methodology and Research*, 1977, **5**, 335–345.

Hovland, C. I., Janis, I. L., and Kelley, H. H. *Communication and persuasion*. New Haven, Connecticut: Yale University Press, 1953.

Huber, K. C. An overview of five widely distributed statistical packages. In P. R. Monge and J. N. Cappella (Eds.), *Multivariate analysis in communication research*. New York: Academic Press, 1980.

Jaffe, J., and Feldstein, S. *Rhythms of dialogue*. New York: Academic Press, 1970.

Johnston, J. *Econometric methods* (2nd ed.). New York: McGraw-Hill, 1972.

Joreskog, K. G. A general method for the analysis of covariance structures. *Biometrika*, 1970, **74**, 213–218.

Joreskog, K. G. A general method for estimating a linear structural equation system. In A. S. Goldberger and O. D. Duncan (Eds.), *Structural equation models in the social sciences*. New York: Seminar Press, 1973.

Jourard, S. *Self disclosure*. New York: Wiley, 1971.

Kerlinger, F. N., and Pedhazur, E. J. *Multiple regression in the behavioral sciences*. New York: Holt, 1973.

Kintsch, W. *Memory and cognition.* (2nd ed.) New York: Wiley 1977.

Kmenta, J. *Elements of econometrics.* New York: Macmillan, 1971.

Land, K. C. Principles of path analysis. In E. F. Borgatta (Ed.), *Sociological methodology 1969.* San Francisco, California: Jossey-Bass, 1968.

Land, K. C. Identification, parameter estimation, and hypothesis testing in recursive sociological models. In A. S. Goldberger and O. D. Duncan (Eds.), *Structural equation models in the social sciences.* New York: Seminar Press, 1973.

Matarazzo, J. D. The interview. In B. B. Wolman (Ed.), *Handbook of Clinical Psychology.* New York: McGraw-Hill, 1965.

McClelland, P. D. *Causal explanation and model building in history, economics, and the new economic history.* Ithaca, New York: Cornell Univ. Press, 1975.

Monge, P. R. *Causal antecedants of structure in large-scale communication networks.* Unpublished paper, Department of Speech-Communication, San Jose State Univ., 1975.

Monge, P. R. Multivariate multiple regression in communication research. In P. R. Monge and J. N. Cappella (Eds.), *Multivariate techniques in communication research.* New York: Academic Press, 1980.

Namboodiri, N. K., Carter, L. F., and Blalock, H. M. *Applied multivariate analysis and experimental designs.* New York: McGraw-Hill, 1975.

Natale, M. Convergence of mean vocal intensity in dyadic communication as a function of social desirability. *Journal of Personality and Social Psychology*, 1975, **32**, 790–804.

Nie, H. H., Hull, C. H., Jenkins, J. G., Steinbrenner, K., and Bent, D. H. *SPSS: Statistical package for the social sciences.* New York: McGraw-Hill, 1975.

Quenouille, M. H. Approximate tests of correlation in time series. *Journal of the Royal Statistical Society, Series B*, 1949, **11**.

Rao, P., and Griliches, F. Small sample properties of several two-stage regression methods in the context of autocorrelated errors. *Journal of the American Statistical Society*, 1969, **64**.

Sargan, T. D. The maximum likelihood estimation of economic relationships with autoregressive residuals. *Econometrica*, 1961, **29**.

Salteil, J., and Woelfel, J. Inertia in cognitive processes: The role of accumulated information in attitude change. *Human Communication Research*, 1975, **1**, 333–344.

Simon, H. A. *Models of man.* New York: Wiley, 1957.

Simon, H. A. *The sciences of the artificial.* Cambridge, Massachusetts: MIT Press, 1969.

Simon, H. A. Spurious correlation: a causal interpretation. In H. M. Blalock (Ed.), *Causal models in the social sciences.* Chicago, Illinois: Aldine-Atherton, 1971.

Simonton, D. K. Cross-sectional time-series experiments: Some suggested statistical analyses. *Psychological Bulletin*, 1977, **84**, 489–502.

Smith, D. H. Communication research and the idea of process. *Speech Monographs*, 1972, **39**, 174–182.

Wannocott, R. J., and Wannocott, T. H. *Econometrics.* New York: Wiley, 1970.

Watzlawick, P., Beavin, J., and Jackson, D. *The pragmatics of human communication.* New York: Norton, 1967.

Webb, J. T. Interview synchrony: An investigation of two speech rate measures. In A. W. Siegman and B. Pope (Eds.), *Studies in dyadic communication.* Oxford: Pergamon, 1972.

Werts, C. E., Joreskog, K. G., and Linn, R. L. Identification and estimation in path analysis with unmeasured variables. *American Journal of Sociology*, 1973, **78**, 1469–1484.

Wheelwright, S. C., and Makridakis, S. *Forecasting models for management.* New York: Wiley, 1970.

Wright, S. The method of path coefficients. *Annals of Mathematical Statistics*, 1934, **5**, 161–215.

Wright, S. Path coefficients and path regressions: Alternative or complementary concepts? In H. M. Blalock (Ed.), *Causal models in the social sciences.* Chicago, Illinois: Aldine-Atherton, 1971.

Zetterberg, H. *On theory and verification is sociology.* (3rd ed.) New York: Bedminster Press, 1965.

Chapter 4

UNOBSERVED VARIABLES WITHIN STRUCTURAL EQUATION MODELS

EDWARD L. FINK

Department of Communication
Michigan State University
East Lansing, Michigan

I. OVERVIEW

In this chapter, the role of unobserved variables within structural equation models will be examined. The discussion will be presented in four sections. First, structural equation models and unobserved variables will be defined and related to more traditional approaches such as factor analysis and multiple regression. Next, the steps necessary to create a linear structural equation model will be reviewed, including the role of theory, statistical assumptions, the identification problem, and procedures for estimating and evaluating a model. Third, applications will be provided from within the

MULTIVARIATE TECHNIQUES
IN HUMAN COMMUNICATION RESEARCH

context of communication as a social science, and a complete example will be presented. The final section will consider problems and extensions of this approach.

II. PRELIMINARIES

A. Linear Structural Equation Models

A linear structural equation model is a set of one or more linear equations which are presumed to relate values of variables in some population. The relation between any given predicted variable and its predictors in an equation is presumed to be *structural*, which is considered either a causal or an identity relation. In a structural relation, the variability of each predicted variable is assumed to be "completely explained" by its predictors. By a "causal" relation we will mean that the predictor of a variable is theoretically necessary within the model (cf. Heise, 1975, pp. 3–33, and Cappella, Chapter 3, this volume). By "identity relation" we mean a relation in which a predicted variable is defined as a specific linear combination of its predictors without error (see Kmenta, 1971, pp. 580–581). In distinction to these two kinds of structural relations, we have what, for contrast, may be called "merely correlational" relations. Note that the distinction between "structural" and "merely correlational" is a function of the level of analysis posited within a model, as well as an indicator of the extent to which an empirical theorist is willing to make explicit that which verbal theory often leaves vague or ambiguous.

The notion of "complete explanation," which seems at first a relatively demanding restriction, is actually handled very simply: provide in each causal (nonidentity) structural equation one additional term that represents "that which the empirical variables leave unexplained." One such term added to an equation will then permit such an equation within the domain of a linear structural equation model.

The linear structural equation model represents three separate statements. First, it explicitly is a *mathematical structure*, with general mathematical or logical properties. Like any other such system of equations, we can, in the abstract, consider conditions of its solvability. For example, without any knowledge as to the content (empirical referent) of the variables, we know that the two-equation system,

$$a = 2b - 7$$
$$a = 8b - 37 \qquad (1)$$

has the unique solution $b = 5$, $a = 3$. Either equation in isolation would not have yielded this unique solution. We will return to consider aspects of this particular issue later in the section on identification. The point here is that the mathematical structure of a model may be studied without reference to empirical content.

Second, a linear structural equation model is a statement about an empirical domain, the world "out there." There are two linkages to the empirical domain that are significant. First, objects need to be defined and assigned a quantity (value) for each attribute (variable) required for a given theory. This is *measurement*, which consists of (1) a set of rules for the definition of objects and the assignment of numbers to each object being considered (the theory of measurement), and (2) the actual assignment of the numbers as values of variables (the process of measurement) (cf. Meyer, 1975, p. 3; Torgerson, 1958, pp. 9–40). The second linkage to the empirical domain is that the relation of the abstract variables of the mathematical model is considered *isomorphic to the empirical relations* of these variables. To state

$$\eta = 2\xi - 7 \qquad (2)$$

within a structural model is to say that a change in ξ "brings about" a change in η, and that, under appropriate conditions, such as the existence of system equilibrium, the relation of η and ξ will be as prescribed in Eq. (2).[1]

The third statement implicit within a structural equation model is that the model represents (or is evaluated as if it represents) an *invariant structure*. That is, we consider that the function that describes the change that ξ brings about in η in Eq. (2) may be replicated over observers and over time. Several meanings of invariant are possible; most restrictively, a structure is invariant only if each population coefficient of the structure is in fact constant over time. In sample terms, this suggests testing a model with different cross-sectional or time-series samples to see if, in fact, the resulting estimated coefficients differ significantly. This statement of invariance, however, suffers from incompleteness; first, a theory being modeled generally will contain boundary conditions, initial conditions, or other special conditions that need to be explicated in order to create a true test of invariance. For example, Boyle's law, relating the temperature, pressure, and volume of a gas, assumes weak interactions among gas molecules; when this is untrue, the law does not hold. Yet, rather than say the law is false, we say it is true under specified conditions. [For other examples of special conditions, see Cunningham (1963) and Petrovskii (1969, pp. 330ff.).] The implications and difficulties of the idea of invariance are discussed by Duncan (1975, pp. 151–159; see also Cortes, Przeworski, & Sprague, 1974). To achieve model invariance with cross-sectional data,[2] equilibrium values of the process under examination would be

---

[1]For a discussion of the equilibrium assumptions implicit in modeling, see Heise (1975, pp. 226ff), Miller (1971), Nurmi (1974, pp. 172ff), Strotz and Wold (1960), and Turner and Stevens (1959). While Miller (1971) indicates that our *estimation* techniques do not require an equilibrium assumption, the next issue to be discussed addresses the necessity of an equilibrium assumption for appropriate model interpretation and evaluation.

[2]In cross-sectional data, the objects or units of analysis have no significant order among themselves apart from that provided by the variables included in the model. This is contrasted here with time-series data (or more generally, series data), in which we generally have one object at many ordered points (e.g., time points). In these terms, a panel study consists of two cross sections on the same objects, one cross section being "shifted" in time from the other. We will consider panel data cross sectional.

necessary; for invariance with time-series data, stationarity or invertibility (see Hibbs, 1974) are necessary conditions. One further thought: As social scientists, we often assume that the level of invariance achieved in the "hard," "real," or "physical" sciences (each adjective conveys the distinction very poorly) is quite good. And yet, we find the following: "There has not been a single date in the history of the law of gravitation when a modern significance test would not have rejected all laws and left us with no law (Jeffreys, 1948, as quoted in Nelder, 1968, p. 314)." Invariance is invented more than discovered, and the tools of the theorist need to allow for this invention.

Now some key terms will be defined before examining the utility of this approach.

A linear structural equation model consists of one or more *structural equations*, which express theoretical relations between variables; the theory contained may be measurement theory, substantive theory, or both. The variable to be predicted in a given structural equation is a *dependent variable*; a predictor variable in a given equation with a priori substantive theoretical meaning is an *independent variable*; and a predictor variable without a priori substantive theoretical meaning which is added for purpose of "complete explanation" is an *error*.[3] Unobserved substantive variables may appear in a model as independent or dependent variables, while an error variable is always an unobserved independent variable.[4] A substantive variable is unobserved if we consider that it has one or more indicators that may have some variability unsystematically or nonlinearly associated with a relevant theoretical construct, while the unobserved variable itself is assumed to be perfectly linearly associated with that same construct. In this sense, true score variables, factors, and latent variables from classical test theory (psychometrics) are examples of nonerror (substantive) unobserved variables (see Lord & Novick, 1968). These unobserved variables are considered not to have any errors of measurement which contaminate the observed scores or indicators from which they are analytically created.

A substantive unobserved variable is *exogenous*[5] to a model if it never occurs as a dependent variable in any structural equation of the model; it is an effect of unspecified causes. A substantive unobserved variable which appears one or more times as a dependent variable is defined to be *endogenous* to the model. Indicators of exogenous substantive unobserved variables

---

[3]Errors are also referred to as "disturbances," "residuals," or (for uncorrelated over time errors), "white noise," sometimes with the term "random" or "stochastic" as a modifier. Some different kinds of error will be distinguished later. We are not distinguishing sample from population errors at this point.

[4]This classification of variables conforms to Griliches (1974, pp. 976–977), but, as he indicates, is not without criticism.

[5]What we are calling exogenous, econometricians would call "predetermined," which they divide into "exogenous" and "lagged endogenous." These latter distinctions are more convenient for discussing time-series models (see Kmenta, 1971, p. 532). Exogenous substantive unobserved variables can also be defined by their independence with regard to all errors in the model.

are defined as exogenous, and indicators of endogenous substantive unobserved variables are defined as endogenous. For convenience, indicators will
be treated as being exclusively exogenous or endogenous.

B. Utility of the Approach

In the brief preceding section, we have provided a framework to consider
structural models and unobserved variables within them. This approach has
several desirable features for estimating and evaluating theoretical relationships. First, when more than one structural equation is considered, this
approach promotes (but does *not require*) use of full information methods of
system estimation, as employed in three-stage least squares and full information maximum likelihood techniques. This means that all variable relations
may be collectively incorporated in estimation, and, in addition, may be
simultaneously subjected to potential test. For example, suppose we have the
following hypothetical cross-sectional model[6]:

$$\eta_1 = \gamma_{11}\xi_1 - \beta_{12}\eta_2 + \zeta_1$$
$$\eta_2 = \gamma_{22}\xi_2 - \beta_{21}\eta_1 + \zeta_2 \tag{3}$$

We may diagram this as shown in Fig. 1. In this model, ξ_1 and ξ_2 represent
exogenous substantive unobserved variables, η_1 and η_2 represent endogenous
substantive unobserved variables, and ζ_1 and ζ_2 represent errors included to
yield complete explanation of η_1 and η_2, respectively.[7] The arrow represents a
causal impact, and double-headed curved arrows represent possible correlations (or covariances) between variables which are not to be statistically
explained in causal terms within the model. (Assumptions incorporated in
model construction will be discussed later.) If one were to use simple
regression (i.e., ordinary least squares[8]) to estimate the model coefficients
$(\gamma_{11}, \gamma_{22}, -\beta_{12}, -\beta_{21}, \sigma_{12}, \sigma_{\zeta_1}^2, \sigma_{\zeta_2}^2, \sigma_{\xi_1}^2, \sigma_{\xi_2}^2, \sigma_{\zeta_1\zeta_2})$, the obtained estimates

---

[6]The approach to notation and estimation taken here is from the work of Karl Jöreskog and
his associates (see, e.g., Jöreskog, 1970, 1973, 1974; Werts, Jöreskog, and Linn, 1973; Werts,
Linn, and Jöreskog, 1971; Werts, Rock, Linn, and Jöreskog, 1976). Unless otherwise stated, all
models discussed will be cross sectional and all variables will be mean corrected (i.e., have mean
of zero).

[7]In structural equation models, the "impact" of a variable is the product of its coefficient (its
"transmission") and its variance. In the case of an error variable, we can determine its "impact,"
but cannot allocate this "impact" to the separate factors of coefficient and variance (i.e., these
parameters are underidentified). Hence, we may either arbitrarily set the coefficient equal to one
and "solve" for the variance of the error term, or arbitrarily set the variance equal to one, and
"solve" for the coefficient. In the examples that follow, we assume that the coefficient associated
with any error term is (implicitly) equal to one. Hence, no algebraic symbol for the coefficient of
an error term will be provided.

[8]Ordinary least squares in the single equation case will provide coefficient estimates identical
to those obtained by maximum likelihood; these estimates will also be best (minimum variance)
linear unbiased estimates.

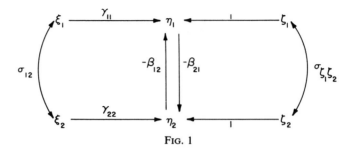

$$\text{Fig. 1}$$

would be biased[9] due to the possibly nonzero covariances between η_1 and ζ_2, and between η_2 and ζ_1. These nonzero covariances come about from two sources: the casual impact of η_1 and η_2 on each other, and the possible covariance of ζ_1 and ζ_2. A single-equation technique of estimation such as two-stage least squares will yield estimates of the coefficients which will in general be consistent[10] but not asymptotically efficient.[11] By creating a linear causal model the investigator is making all the interrelationships among theoretical variables explicit, and this mode of presenting a system of interrelations suggests system estimation techniques. Asymptotically efficient techniques do exist, and are increasingly available. Use of these techniques (when their assumptions are plausible) is the first potential benefit of the approach presented here.

A second benefit of the structural model approach using unobserved variables is that we may analytically decompose our causal model into three interdependent subsystems while estimating the coefficients of these subsystems simultaneously. The first subsystem is the theoretical subsystem. In general, verbal theories relate variables without explicitly considering problems of measurement. The unfortunate distinction between theory and method in social science often results in measurement being relegated to the "methodologist" rather that the "theorist." The unobserved variable approach allows us to consider the theoretical causes and effects of interest to be true (reliable) variables, and the relations between these unobserved variables will be estimated as the "fundamental parameters of the mechanism that generated the data" (Goldberger, 1973, p. 3; see also Isaac, 1970).

The two remaining subsystems are the measurement submodel relating the exogenous variables (unobserved and observed), and the measurement submodel relating the endogenous variables (unobserved and observed). In most

---

[9]"$\hat{\theta}$ is an unbiased estimator of θ if $E(\hat{\theta}) = \theta$" (Kmenta, 1971, p. 157). E represents the expected value operator or the mathematical expectation.

[10]"$\hat{\theta}$ is a consistent estimator of θ if plim $\hat{\theta} = \theta$" (Kmenta, 1971, p. 165). Here "plim" represents the probability limit. This may be interpreted as meaning that the bias $[E(\hat{\theta}) - \theta]$ and variance of a consistent estimator approach zero as the sample size approaches infinity.

[11]An estimator is asymptotically efficient if it is a consistent estimator with an asymptotic distribution with finite mean and variance and with the smallest asymptotic variance of all consistent estimators (see Kmenta, 1971, pp. 164–167). Use of cross-equation covariances to improve efficiency of estimation is discussed by Griliches (1974, pp. 978ff).

research, the statistical relation between a theoretical variable (here represented by the unobserved variable) and its one or more indicators is likely to
be arbitrary and hence statistically inefficient. We may consider several cases
for this point. In a single-equation model, our coefficient of causal impact will
be the usual regression coefficient, and it will be biased if there is measurement error in the predictor variables (Blalock, 1972, p. 414; Bohrnstedt &
Carter, 1971, p. 133; Isaac, 1970). If we treat predictor variables as if they are
true (reliable) variables, estimates of theoretical coefficients will be in error
even with an infinite size sample. In multiequation systems, measurement
errors result in biased estimates of more complex form (Bohrnstedt & Carter,
1971, p. 139). Again, treating fallible measures as theoretical variables is
misleading, and we rarely know the extent to which results are biased.

Several procedures to combine indicators to create somewhat more reliable
composites are often employed, typically involving a linear composite of the
original indicators. Examples include simple addition of indicators and
factor-analyzing and factor-weighting indicators; either procedure may be
performed on standardized (mean of zero, standard deviation of one) or
unstandardized indicators. Any simple addition implicitly weights each variable as a function of its covariance (unstandardized case) or correlation
(standardized case) structure with the other indicators included as elements of
the composite. Each of these procedures treats a measurement submodel
independently of the theoretical submodel, and thus fails to include the
complete pattern of theoretical relations in the creation of an unobserved
variable. For example, let us examine the factor model shown in Fig. 2. The
corresponding equations are

$$y_1 = \lambda_{y_1}\eta + \varepsilon_1$$

$$y_2 = \lambda_{y_2}\eta + \varepsilon_2$$

$$y_3 = \lambda_{y_3}\eta + \varepsilon_3 \tag{4}$$

(This assumes a linear model; cf. Hunter & Cohen, 1974.) The ys represent
indicators of an underlying variable η, which is unobserved. The εs represent
errors of measurement, and ζ represents the disturbance component of η.
Under the assumption that $\text{Cov}(\zeta, y_i) = \text{Cov}(\zeta, \varepsilon_i) = \text{Cov}(\varepsilon_i, \varepsilon_j) = \text{Cov}(\eta, \varepsilon_i)$
$= 0$ for all $i, j, i \neq j$, and that the variance of η equals one, we may create the

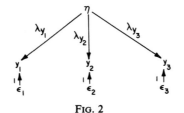

FIG. 2

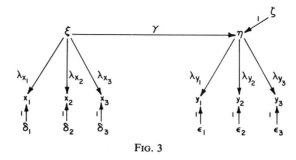

FIG. 3

following estimates of the λs:

$$\lambda_{y_1} = \left[\left[\mathrm{Cov}(y_1, y_2) \cdot \mathrm{Cov}(y_1, y_3) \right] / \mathrm{Cov}(y_2, y_3) \right]^{1/2}$$

$$\lambda_{y_2} = \left[\left[\mathrm{Cov}(y_1, y_2) \cdot \mathrm{Cov}(y_2, y_3) \right] / \mathrm{Cov}(y_1, y_3) \right]^{1/2}$$

$$\lambda_{y_3} = \left[\left[\mathrm{Cov}(y_1, y_3) \cdot \mathrm{Cov}(y_2, y_3) \right] / \mathrm{Cov}(y_1, y_2) \right]^{1/2} \tag{5}$$

[See Duncan (1972) for the derivation; "Cov" represents covariance.]

However, if our model had η as an effect of another theoretical variable, ξ, a complete model might look like that shown in Fig. 3. This full model incorporates the following additional equations:

$$x_1 = \lambda_{x_1}\xi + \delta_1$$

$$x_2 = \lambda_{x2}\xi + \delta_2$$

$$x_3 = \lambda_{x3}\xi + \delta_3$$

$$\eta = \gamma\xi + \zeta \tag{6}$$

The first three of these equations comprise the exogenous measurement submodel. The fourth equation is our understanding of the theoretical (causal) relationship between the substantive unobserved variables ξ and η, and the unobserved "error in equation" (the variable that completes the prediction of η), ζ. The additional information regarding the covariance structure of the observed variables is useful to obtain maximally efficient estimates in this situation; for example, the population model requires that the covariance between x_1 and y_1 be the product of λ_{x_1}, γ, and λ_{y_1}. Estimating a measurement model in isolation of a theoretical model amounts to excluding information that in general would result in more efficient estimation (cf. Blalock, 1969a; Costner, 1969; Hauser & Goldberger, 1971; Jöreskog & Goldberger, 1975; Siegel & Hodge, 1968).

It should be noted that the two desirable features of structural equation models dealt with up to this point both concern using assumptions or information about errors to create more efficient model estimation. The first feature entailed using information concerning "errors in equations," represented here by ζs. Use of this error information is most associated with the work of econometricians in the study of linear regression. The second error, "error in variables" (measurement error), represented by δs and εs, is most associated with the work of psychometricians in the study of factor analysis.

A third advantage of the linear structural model approach is that maximum likelihood estimation algorithms are readily available to create estimates of model coefficients and have additional features for model testing.[12] Maximum likelihood estimates of population parameters are values of the population parameters that are most likely to have generated the observed sample data given specific distributional assumptions. In the univariate case, if we wish to estimate a parameter θ with sample data $x_1, \ldots, x_n$, and we let $L(x_1, \ldots, x_n|\theta)$ represent the likelihood of this particular sample result given θ, the principle of maximum likelihood, if accepted, requires that we choose as our estimate of θ that value making $L(x_1, \ldots, x_n|\theta)$ take on its largest value.[13] In order to utilize this procedure, distributional assumptions are required so that the likelihood function can be specified. Following this specification, a likelihood equation is generated for each parameter to be estimated, which consists of the derivative (or partial derivative) of the logarithm of the likelihood function with respect to the parameter set equal to zero to find an extremum.[14]

If we assume that our observed endogenous variables are multinormal or that the observed variables are jointly normal,[15] we can generate maximum likelihood estimates appropriately relating the substantive unobserved variables to each other and relating the observed variables to the relevant unobserved variables in the measurement submodels. Under general conditions, maximum likelihood estimates are consistent and asymptotically efficient, and standard errors based on large sample (asymptotic) variances are obtainable. This means that each estimated coefficient can be statistically tested and evaluated.

In addition, tests of the overidentifying restrictions (see Section III.C) of a complete structural equation model with unobserved variables may be made. A statistic distributed approximately χ^2 in large samples may be computed to test various null hypotheses. A general null hypothesis is that the specified restrictions of the model are correct, contrasted with the alternative hypothesis that the population covariance matrix is any positive definite matrix. In addition to this general test, a test may be made comparing the specified

---

[12]Generalized least squares procedures are also possible (see Jöreskog, 1974, pp. 3–4). However, they are not as readily available, nor are their estimation and hypothesis testing features as fully developed.

[13]This definition is adapted from Hays (1963, p. 213). See also Hanushek and Jackson (1977, pp. 344–348), Kmenta (1971, pp. 174–182), and Meyer (1975, pp. 311–330).

[14]The logarithm is used because it converts a multiplicative function into an additive function, which is generally more mathematically tractable.

[15]This assumption may be met by having fixed values for the substantive unobserved exogenous variables and normally distributed error terms (equation errors and measurement errors) (see Hanushek and Jackson, 1977, p. 312n; cf. Jöreskog and Goldberger, 1975, p. 633).

model with a specific alternative; in this case, the χ^2-test of the difference between the models is the difference between the χ^2 of the two models evaluated separately by the general test. See Jöreskog (1974, p. 4) for caveats concerning these procedures (see also Costner & Schoenberg, 1973; for tests of related interest, see Schoenberg, 1972; Specht & Warren, 1975).

The approach presented here, due to developments by Jöreskog and his associates and using maximum likelihood estimation, provides a great deal of flexibility. For example, except for computer program limitations, coefficients may be constrained to particular values or constrained to be equal to other coefficients in the model. This means that estimates from previous studies can be incorporated in a new model. In addition, constraints conformable with theory may be imposed to help achieve model identification (see Section III.C). It should be noted that we always implicitly constrain a covariance or other coefficient to be zero when we assume an association or effect is absent. Coefficients not constrained to a specified value or to a specified equality are defined as free parameters which are to be estimated.

In summary, the structural equation model with unobserved variables has the following advantages when its assumptions are plausible:

(1)   specification of theoretical and measurement relations simultaneously, together with statistical assumptions, which allows

(2)   consistent and efficient estimation of a total model, which allows

(3)   use of statistical inference for global tests (of overidentifying restrictions) on complete models, as well as the usual tests on single coefficients, which results in

(4)   parsimonious estimation and evaluation of complex theoretical systems.

III. MODEL FORMULATION, ESTIMATION, AND EVALUATION

A. Relating Theory and Model

The creator of a structural model of the kind discussed here is often in the uneviable position of being identified as a methodologist, a peculiar appellation which suggests anti-theoretical or nontheoretical interests. The approach taken here is that scientific theory of a rather powerful form has been expressed using the tools of mathematics, and that the job of theory construction, as Blalock (1969b) indicated in his book on the topic, is to move "from verbal to mathematical formulations." For the kinds of formulations herein proposed, it is probably most appropriate to start by considering processes of change and accounting for that change through linear equations.[16] If it is

---

[16]For a discussion of the concept of process, see Arundale (1971). The discussion that follows considers causal rather than identity relations of a structural equation model, since identity relations are not estimated.

proposed that the process of change is linear (e.g., by linear differential or difference equations), then the corresponding structural equation model will also be linear (see, e.g., Coleman, 1968, p. 435ff.). This is not meant to suggest that only the linear form is appropriate for the study of change, but rather that our initial formulations often begin this way. Furthermore, "linear in equation" models are not necessarily "linear in variables"; as examples, the following are all linear equations:

$$\eta = \gamma_1\xi + \gamma_2\xi^2 + \zeta, \qquad \eta = \gamma \log \xi + \zeta,$$

$$\eta = \gamma\xi_1\xi_2 + \zeta, \qquad \eta = \gamma|\xi_1 - \xi_2| + \zeta \qquad (7)$$

In each case, we may create a "new" variable which, after replacement, will result in an equation that appears linear. For example, letting $\xi' = \xi^2$, the first equation becomes

$$\eta = \gamma_1\xi + \gamma_2\xi' + \zeta \qquad (8)$$

This may also be done in the other equations. In addition, some nonlinear equations may be treated by appropriately transforming variables to create a linear form (see, e.g., Kmenta, 1971, pp. 451–472).

The second suggestion for formulating a model is to consider boundary conditions, initial conditions, and/or other special conditions and to use variables of sufficient abstraction so that invariant outcomes are at least plausible a priori. It seems to this author that variables like "years of schooling" are involved in relations that are so spatio-temporally specific that it is hard to imagine conditions under which these variables could yield invariant relations. Such models, in the absence of abstraction, are ultimately of historical (idiographic) rather than theoretical (nomothetic) character.

The notion of process requires restricting endogenous variables to state variables at the core of the process, and restricting exogenous variables to prior state variables or to variables that are believed to markedly shift the equilibrium values of the system being modeled. When conceived of in this way, our equation system has a certain sense of closure. A variable is often considered solely because another investigator found it to be interesting, or found its coefficient statistically significant in a given equation; it should not be assumed automatically that such variables enter into invariant relations. Further, since people, including theorists, can make a plausible argument[17] for almost any variable "making a difference," a model may quickly become complex and relatively meaningless. The scientific ideal of parsimony should always make us suspicious of unwieldy models not having achieved a sufficient level of abstraction.

Endogenous variables in a structural model are best conceived of as continuous variables[18]; if measured by bounded scales (such as probabilities),

---

[17]See Duncan (1975, p. 89) on the consequences of adding variables arbitrarily.

[18]Note that a discontinuous process or discrete structure may be discovered by means of relatively continuous variables, so this does not exclude finding that a variable (as opposed to its measurement theory) is discrete "in nature" (cf. Kac, 1969, p. 699nl).

they will often require mathematical transformation if they are to meet the statistical assumptions required to estimate and test a structural equation model. Exogenous variables may be conceived of as continuous or discrete, depending on the kind of explanation they are expected to provide in the model.

In the model formulation, the substantive unobserved exogenous variables should not be perfectly linearly associated with each other (i.e., perfectly multicollinear). The theoretical analog of this statistical constraint is that our exogenous factors should be analytically independent. Often in social science we find this a difficult constraint because key variables are highly interrelated in the population. For example, the educational and occupational attainments of heads of households in models of status attainment have been found to be moderately linearly related (Blau & Duncan, 1967, p. 169). Given this finding, the investigator should question whether the exogenous factors are in fact conceived of as analytically independent. One thought experiment that may be conducted is to try to imagine a situation in which one can experimentally manipulate each exogenous factor without changing the values of the other exogenous factors. Variables that are "manipulatable" in this sense are likely to be more fruitful for causal modeling, because they are more likely to be relatively empirically independent of other exogenous factors (and hence be nonmulticollinear) and because they are more attractive to social policy analysis. (In addition, it is the suspicion of this author that analytically independent variables are likely to be more theoretically fruitful in the long run.)

Theories are often constructed by use of "naive analogy" with other systems, by finding principles of system conservation or equilibrium (Cunningham, 1963) or finding principles of optimization or adaptation (cf. Simon, 1957, p. 165). These techniques leave open the content of the theory, and here advice is difficult. The preceding guidelines, while being quite general, suggest the kinds of relations that are best considered within a structural model. The approach taken here is that while theoretical concerns should not be sacrificed or distorted by method, methods do "exert pressure for new foci of theoretical interest" and research does exert "pressure for clear concepts" (Merton, 1948). While material on theory construction is often helpful (see McDermott, 1975, for a bibliography on the topic), we have not yet routinized the development of theoretical insight. However, it is important that the theorist understand what methods of analysis imply for theory construction, so that methodological tools may be used effectively and intelligently.

B. Model Notation and Assumptions

The most general notation for structural modeling comes from Jöreskog's work (e.g., 1973) and will be adopted here. Let $\boldsymbol{\eta}' = (\eta_1, \ldots, \eta_m)$ represent the set of substantive unobserved endogenous variables, $\boldsymbol{\xi}' = (\xi_1, \ldots, \xi_n)$

represent the set of substantive unobserved exogenous variables, and $\zeta' = (\zeta_1, \ldots, \zeta_m)$ represent the (unobserved) errors of prediction. Then

$$\underset{(m \times m)}{\mathbf{B}} \underset{(m \times 1)}{\boldsymbol{\eta}} = \underset{(m \times n)}{\boldsymbol{\Gamma}} \underset{(n \times 1)}{\boldsymbol{\xi}} + \underset{(m \times 1)}{\boldsymbol{\zeta}} \tag{9}$$

represents the theoretical relations of the model (see Chapter 3 for the development and explication of this matrix equation). Let $\mathbf{y}' = (y_1, \ldots, y_p)$ and $\mathbf{x}' = (x_1, \ldots, x_q)$ represent the observed endogenous and exogenous variables, respectively, and $\boldsymbol{\varepsilon}' = (\varepsilon_1, \ldots, \varepsilon_p)$ and $\boldsymbol{\delta}' = (\delta_1, \ldots, \delta_q)$ represent errors of measurement in $\mathbf{y}$ and $\mathbf{x}$, respectively. It will also be assumed that ζ is uncorrelated with ξ, that $\mathbf{B}$ is nonsingular, and the errors of measurement (ε, δ) are uncorrelated with η and ξ, and that ε and δ are uncorrelated (Jöreskog, 1973, p. 86). The two matrix equations

$$\underset{(p \times 1)}{\mathbf{y}} = \underset{(p \times m)}{\boldsymbol{\Lambda}_y} \underset{(m \times 1)}{\boldsymbol{\eta}} + \underset{(p \times 1)}{\boldsymbol{\varepsilon}}, \qquad \underset{(q \times 1)}{\mathbf{x}} = \underset{(q \times n)}{\boldsymbol{\Lambda}_x} \underset{(n \times 1)}{\boldsymbol{\xi}} + \underset{(q \times 1)}{\boldsymbol{\delta}} \tag{10}$$

represent the measurement submodels of the endogenous and exogenous variables. Let $\boldsymbol{\Phi}$ and $\boldsymbol{\Psi}$ be the covariance matrices of ξ and ζ respectively, and $\boldsymbol{\theta}_\varepsilon$ and $\boldsymbol{\theta}_\delta$ the covariance matrices of ε and δ, respectively. The covariance matrix of $(\mathbf{y}', \mathbf{x}')$ imposed by the model is

$$\underset{([p+q] \times [p+q])}{\boldsymbol{\Sigma}} = \begin{bmatrix} \boldsymbol{\Lambda}_y(\mathbf{B}^{-1}\boldsymbol{\Gamma}\boldsymbol{\Phi}\boldsymbol{\Gamma}'\mathbf{B}'^{-1}) + \mathbf{B}^{-1}\boldsymbol{\Psi}\mathbf{B}'^{-1})\boldsymbol{\Lambda}'_y + \boldsymbol{\theta}_\varepsilon & \boldsymbol{\Lambda}_y\mathbf{B}^{-1}\boldsymbol{\Gamma}\boldsymbol{\Phi}\boldsymbol{\Lambda}'_x \\ \boldsymbol{\Lambda}_x\boldsymbol{\Phi}\boldsymbol{\Gamma}'\mathbf{B}'^{-1}\boldsymbol{\Lambda}'_y & \boldsymbol{\Lambda}_x\boldsymbol{\Phi}\boldsymbol{\Lambda}'_x + \boldsymbol{\theta}_\delta \end{bmatrix} \tag{11}$$

Let $\mathbf{S}$ equal the sample estimate of the population covariance matrix. Assuming either than $\mathbf{x}$ is fixed and $\mathbf{y}$ multinormal, or that $\mathbf{x}$ and $\mathbf{y}$ are jointly multinormal, allows use of maximum likelihood procedures; the log-likelihood function, omitting constants, is

$$F = \log|\boldsymbol{\Sigma}| + \mathrm{Tr}(\mathbf{S}\boldsymbol{\Sigma}^{-1}) \tag{12}$$

which is to be minimized with respect to the parameters to be estimated. This procedure requires that $\boldsymbol{\Sigma}$ be nonsingular. In large samples we may test the overidentifiying restrictions of the model by a χ^2 statistic [a function of the minimized value of F in Eq. (12)]. For this general null hypothesis (that the restrictions are correct), contrasted with the alternative hypothesis that $\boldsymbol{\Sigma}$ is any positive definite matrix, the number of degrees of freedom of the test is equal to the number of variances and nonredundant covariances in $\boldsymbol{\Sigma}$ minus the number of independent parameters estimated under the model (r):

$$df = \frac{1}{2}(p + q)(p + q + 1) - r \tag{13}$$

An additional assumption is that units are cross-sectionally independent, which usually implies simple random sampling has been employed.

The preceding assumptions allow estimation and inference if the structural model to be estimated is identified. We have mentioned "identification" and "overidentifying restrictions" many times; we now turn our attention to identification.

C. Model Identification

A structural equation model is an explicit statement of causal relations. When making inferences by the experimental method, we attempt to randomize or control those factors that may make a difference, so that the effects of the factors of interest, our manipulated variables, can be evaluated. The population assumption that the ξs and ζs are independent is the statistical analog to randomization and is necessary if we are to be able to estimate effects within the model. However, we must be sure that the theoretical assumptions and constraints we have placed on the model are sufficient so that infinite sets of coefficients do not exist which will equally satisfy the mathematical requirements of the model. For example, the first equation in Eq. (1),

$$a = 2b - 7 \tag{14}$$

represents the infinite set of (a, b) values that geometrically define a particular line. Adding one linearly independent equation to Eq. (14) will result in a unique solution for (a, b). With population data we assume that all theoretical constraints in the model can be met exactly if we correctly solve for model parameters.

In model estimation with sample data (in which we assume the possibility of sampling error), we impose statistical criteria to choose among competing estimates. We will wish to choose that set of estimates which is at least statistically consistent and also which has relatively small variance (either in the small sample or asymptotic sense). In the general structural equation model that has been considered, we constrain or treat as free parameters each element in $\mathbf{B}$, $\mathbf{\Gamma}$, and $\mathbf{\Psi}$ (matrices of the theoretical submodel), in $\mathbf{\Lambda}_x$, $\mathbf{\Lambda}_y$, $\mathbf{\Theta}_\varepsilon$, and $\mathbf{\Theta}_\delta$ (matrices of the measurement submodels), and in $\mathbf{\Phi}$ (which is relevant to all submodels); $\mathbf{\Sigma}$ is a function of all these structural specifications, as indicated by Eq. (11). Several structures may generate the same $\mathbf{\Sigma}$; these are defined to be *equivalent* (Jöreskog, 1973, p. 87). Parameters having the same value in all equivalent structures are *identified*; if all model parameters are identified, the model is identified (Jöreskog, 1973, p. 87; see also Wiley, 1973).

Identification may be considered logically and empirically. A minimal logical requirement for a model to be identified is that the number of distinct model parameters to be estimated must be equal to or less than the number of nonredundant variances and covariances observed in our data. A stronger logical requirement, which is difficult to examine in complex models, is that each individual parameter to be estimated may be demonstrated to be an algebraic function of the observed variances and covariances in our data.

Finally, even if this strong logical requirement can be met, we may have data incapable of providing a finite set of defined estimates for the coefficients of the model. This is the *empirical* requirement of identification. In what follows, all three requirements will be considered, but we will always examine the minimal logical requirement for every model we present. This is a necessary, but not sufficient, condition for model identification.

A general model combines theoretical and measurement submodels, and identification of these submodels has been examined in the literature; the econometric literature has considered identification in regression to estimate the theoretical submodel (e.g., Kmenta, 1971, pp. 539–550; Hanushek & Jackson, 1977, pp. 254–264), and the psychometric literature on factor analysis has considered identification of the measurement submodels [as indeterminacy of factor structures; see, e.g., the discussions by Hanushek and Jackson (1977, pp. 304–308) and by Jöreskog (1974, pp. 23–24)]. If the theoretical and measurement submodels considered separately are identified (given our assumptions concerning independence of errors), the model will be identified, but the model may be identified in the absence of this condition (cf. Wiley, 1973, p. 81).

The minimal logical requirement for identification considers the degrees of freedom for the general χ^2-test previously discussed. The number of degrees of freedom relates how much (apparent) information one expects to retrieve from the model, compared to how much information is apparently put into it. Let us consider some examples. In the following Examples 1–3, consider the substantive unobserved variables as being identically equal to omitted observed variables.

Example 1 $\mathrm{Cov}(\zeta_1, \zeta_2) = 0$ by assumption (Fig. 4). Our *information input* = 3 (nonredundant elements of **S**). The *information outflow* (parameters to be estimated) = 4 (2 in **B**, 2 in **Ψ**). This model is *underidentified* (input minus outflow = -1).

Example 2 $\mathrm{Cov}(\xi, \zeta) = 0$ by required assumption (Fig. 5). *Information input* = 3 (nonredundant elements of **S**). *Information outflow* = 3 (1 each in **Γ**, **Φ**, and **Ψ**). The model appears *exactly identified* ("just identified"); input minus outflow = 0, i.e., this model has 0 degrees of freedom.

Example 3 $\mathrm{Cov}(\zeta_1, \zeta_2) = 0$ by assumption (Fig. 6). [This implies $\mathrm{Cov}(\eta_1, \zeta_2) = 0$.] *Information input* = 6 (nonredundant elements of **S**). *Information outflow* = 5 (1 in **Φ**, 1 in **Γ**, 1 in **B**, and 2 in **Ψ**). This model appears

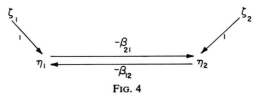

FIG. 4

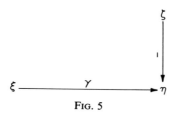

FIG. 5

overidentified; input minus outflow = 1; i.e., this model has 1 degree of freedom. With sample data we could estimate $-\beta_{21}$ in two ways (one "extra" estimate) if $\text{Cov}(\xi, \eta_1) \neq 0$:

$$-\hat{\beta}_{21} = \text{Cov}(\xi, \eta_2)/\text{Cov}(\xi, \eta_1), \qquad -\hat{\beta}_{21} = \text{Cov}(\eta_1, \eta_2)/\text{Var}(\eta_1) \qquad (15)$$

In general, these estimates are not expected to be equal when we use sample data. The second estimate of $-\beta_{21}$ may be efficiently obtained from ordinary least squares regression of η_2 on η_1.

In Examples 4–6, assume $\text{Var}(\eta) = 1$[19], and $\text{Cov}(\eta, \varepsilon_i) = \text{Cov}(\varepsilon_i, \varepsilon_j) = \text{Cov}(\varepsilon_i, \zeta) = 0, i \neq j$.[20]

Example 4 (Fig. 7). *Information input* = 3 (nonredundant elements of **S**). *Information outflow* = 4 (2 in Λ_y, 2 in Θ_ε). This model is underidentified.

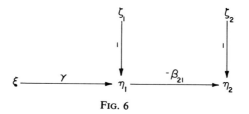

FIG. 6

[19]For purposes of identification, it is necessary to specify a metric for each ξ and η; this may be done by normalizing its variance (e.g., by setting it equal to 1), or by constraining one of its associated λs. [In addition, the diagonal entries of **B** are set equal to 1 (see Wiley, 1973, pp. 78–79).] As an example, the three indicator model expressed by Eq. (4) results in the nonlinear equations

$$\text{Cov}(y_1, y_2) = \lambda_{y_1}\lambda_{y_2} \text{Var}(\eta),$$
$$\text{Cov}(y_1, y_3) = \lambda_{y_1}\lambda_{y_3} \text{Var}(\eta),$$
$$\text{Cov}(y_2, y_3) = \lambda_{y_2}\lambda_{y_3} \text{Var}(\eta)$$

Establishing a value for either one λ or $\text{Var}(\eta)$ results in this model being identified if no covariances are zero.

[20]Note that η is endogenous even though it is predicted only by ζ. Equivalent models may be specified with ξs, xs, and δs.

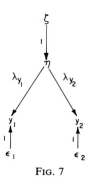

FIG. 7

Input minus outflow $= -1$. Certain additional constraints (e.g., assuming $\lambda_{y_1} = \lambda_{y_2}$) will identify this model.

Example 5   Consider as Example 5 the three indicator model represented in Fig. 2. *Information input* $= 6$ (nonredundant elements of $\mathbf{S}$). *Information outflow* $= 6$ (3 in Λ_y, 3 in Θ_ε). If the covariances in Eq. (5) are not zero, the model is exactly identified [for solution, see Eq. (5)]. Input minus outflow $= 0$, i.e., 0 degrees of freedom.

Example 6   (Fig. 8). *Information input* $= 10$ (nonredundant elements of $\mathbf{S}$). *Information outflow* $= 8$ (4 in Λ_y, 4 in Θ_ε). This model appears *overidentified*. Input minus outflow $= 2$. Notice that we can estimate each λ three ways (2 "extra" estimates) *if* none of the denominators equal zero; for example,

$$\hat{\lambda}_{y_1} = \left[\left[\operatorname{Cov}(y_1, y_2) \cdot \operatorname{Cov}(y_1, y_3)\right]/\operatorname{Cov}(y_2, y_3)\right]^{1/2}$$

$$\hat{\hat{\lambda}}_{y_1} = \left[\left[\operatorname{Cov}(y_1, y_2) \cdot \operatorname{Cov}(y_1, y_4)\right]/\operatorname{Cov}(y_2, y_4)\right]^{1/2}$$

$$\hat{\hat{\hat{\lambda}}}_{y_1} = \left[\left[\operatorname{Cov}(y_1, y_3) \cdot \operatorname{Cov}(y_1, y_4)\right]/\operatorname{Cov}(y_3, y_4)\right]^{1/2} \tag{16}$$

The first three models were "econometric"; the last three "psychometric." A full model, as in Fig. 3, would be evaluated as follows:

Example 7   Assume errors of measurement uncorrelated with ξ and η, and with each other, and ζ uncorrelated with ξ. Further, $\lambda_{x_1} = \lambda_{y_1} = 1$ by

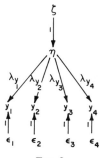

FIG. 8

constraint (see footnote 19). *Information input* = 21 (nonredundant elements of **S**). *Information outflow* = 13 (2 in Λ_y, 2 in Λ_x, 3 in Θ_δ, 3 in Θ_ε, and 1 each in Γ, Ψ, and Φ). This model appears *overidentified*. Input minus outflow = 8.

The computation of the degrees of freedom of the model to evaluate the level of identification (or the number of overidentifying restrictions) must be done with caution. In a given model, some parameters may be underidentified and some may be overidentified. A necessary condition for a model to be identified is that the degrees of freedom (input minus outflow) as specified in Eq. (13) must be nonnegative, but this is not a sufficient condition, since it does not tell us if the constraints that are imposed are "strategic," in that they result in all parameters being at least exactly identified. Further, a nonnegative number of degrees of freedom is still only a logical condition and says nothing about the numerical value of the entries in matrix **S** (which may, for example, reflect multicollinearity). In Examples 3, 5, and 6, the level of "empirical" (as opposed to "logical") identification explicitly depended on various covariances not being equal to zero. In the general structural equation model, if **B** is in fact singular, the model cannot be estimated. It should be realized that for an underidentified parameter, an infinite set of consistent estimates can be obtained regardless of sample size; in the exactly identified case, the model may be estimated but is not subject to a χ^2-test; in the overidentified case, the model may be estimated *and* its overidentifying restrictions may be tested.[21] The more parameters we require to be estimated from a given covariance matrix, the "less identified" the model becomes. Duncan's moral is pertinent here: "Underidentification, not 'causal inference,' is achieved by 'letting the data decide which way the causal arrow runs.' The data cannot decide this matter, except in the context of a very strong theory ... " (Duncan, 1975, p. 87). Note that a model may be estimated in which certain coefficients are of low magnitude; for all practical purposes, large standard errors for the resulting coefficients can suggest that the model is "empirically underidentified" (for a related discussion, see Land & Felson, 1978).

IV. BASIC APPLICATIONS AND AN EXAMPLE

A. Some Basic Applications

In this section some models broadly applicable to cross-sectional (including panel) data will be presented. These models are quite flexible and can be readily adopted by investigators for somewhat different data structures.

Costner (1971) and Alwin and Tessler (1974), among others, have considered using structural equation models to evaluate experimental data. Consider

---

[21]A model may be overidentified and yet multiple, though finite, sets of estimates may be obtainable even with population data. Typically, one chooses one of the sets of estimates in this situation. See Fink and Mabee (1978).

the model shown in Fig. 9. *Information input* = 15 (nonredundant elements of **S**). *Information outflow* (to be estimated) = 12 (1 each in **B**, **Γ**, **Φ**; 2 in Λ_y, 4 in **Θ**$_\varepsilon$, and 3 in **Ψ**). This model provides a structure for an experiment in which the "true" variable implicated by a single experimental manipulation is linearly related to the experimental outcomes. This model can be expanded easily to represent multifactor experiments. In addition, curvilinear and interaction effects may be included by means of appropriate coding (see, e.g., Cohen & Cohen, 1975; Kerlinger & Pedhazur, 1973). ξ represents the experimental manipulation and is identically equal to an observed variable whose values are the numerical labels that the experimenter uses to specify the experimental condition of each unit of the study. The observed variables y_1 and y_2 represent manipulation checks, which are variables that are assumed directly responsive to the "true" manipulation that each unit receives (η_1). The observed variables y_3 and y_4 represent indicators of the effect of the experiment. For example, ξ could represent the manipulation of anxiety in the Schachter (1959, p. 20ff.) study, η_1 could represent the true levels of anxiety experienced by the subjects, and η_2 could represent affiliative tendency. The ys are indicators of their respective ηs. If this model were estimated and seemed plausible, we would have confidence that the effects hypothesized are channeled through the appropriate causal paths. If this model failed, exploratory analyses could be performed to see if the theoretical coefficient of interest ($-\beta_{21}$) is able to be evaluated even though the full model is flawed (e.g., by demand characteristics). Note that various nontheoretically appropriate models can be established in which, e.g., Cov(ξ, y_3) would differ significantly from zero and yet which would not necessitate $-\beta_{21}$ being significantly different from zero. The model as specified is apparently over-identified, and thus seems testable.

Many studies have been concerned with the effects of measurement error in panel analysis, or in "separating reliability and stability in test–retest correlation" [Heise (1969); an elaborate presentation of these issues is given

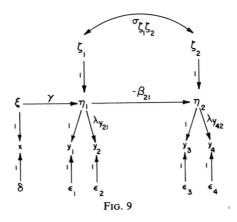

FIG. 9

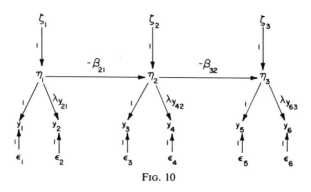

FIG. 10

by Wheaton, Muthén, Alwin, & Summers (1977)]. To deal with these issues, the model shown in Fig. 10 is proposed. *Information input* = 21 (nonredundant elements of **S**). *Information outflow* = 14 (2 in **B**, 3 in **Ψ**, 3 in Λ_y, 6 in Θ_ε).

The model represents two congeneric measures ("y even" and "y odd") taken at three points in time; each pair of measures is associated with a given η. This model poses a stringent test, in that the ζs are constrained to be uncorrelated. In fact, serial correlation among all errors is assumed absent.

As an example of this model, suppose the ηs represent (unobserved) communication skill, the odd-numbered ys representing skill evaluated by judges observing subjects, and the even-numbered ys representing subjects' skill at evaluating the communications of others. We can use this model to examine the stability of the underlying "true" skill. Time enters into this model implicitly; the same model estimated with greatly different time intervals may actually be modeling different systems. Consider how the model would be interpreted if the time interval were a few seconds as compared to a few years (cf. Heise, 1975, pp. 206–207). Of course, a time interval appropriate to the process being modeled must be selected (cf. Arundale, 1971).

An interesting modification of the above model is that shown in Fig. 11. *Information input* = 21 (nonredundant elements of **S**). *Information outflow* = 20 (2 in **B**, 5 in **Ψ**, 7 in Λ_y, 6 in Θ_ε).

In this version, we consider the possibility of a factor that is associated with odd-numbered ys and a different factor that is associated with the even-numbered ys. These new factors may be conceived of as representing the particular *method* of evaluating communicator skill, or the particular *trait* which is independent of the general communicator skill variable. This way of formulating the model is in recognition of the recent work using structural equation models to examine the "multitrait–multimethod matrix" (see, e.g., Alwin, 1974). As presented, the model is apparently overidentified.

In many situations we may have a model appearing somewhat similar to the one in Fig. 11. For example, suppose that in an experiment judgements by four observers are used to provide indicators of both the exogenous and

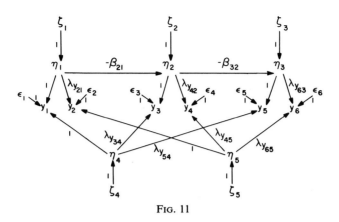

FIG. 11

endogenous substantive unobserved variables. This would result in the experimental model (as in Fig. 9) being modified to incorporate observer factors, and, with assumptions concerning the covariances among the ζs, the model can usually be identified. A similar idea is found in Werts, Jöreskog, and Linn (1976).

The three models diagrammed in Figs. 9–11 suggest ways in which theoretical questions may be associated with the analytical technique of utilizing unobserved variables within linear structural equation models. In the next section an example of "nonrecursivity," or mutual simultaneous causation, will be presented.

B. A Nonrecursive Example

Let us define a model in which **B** can be constructed to be triangular (i.e., by appropriately subscripting the ηs) as a *recursive model* (cf. Kmenta, 1971, p. 538; Strotz & Wold, 1960). If **B** cannot be constructed to be triangular, the model will be defined as *nonrecursive*. If **B** cannot be triangular, this means that there is direct or indirect causal *feedback* among (between) the ηs. In the following example, the model is nonrecursive since each of the two ηs is viewed as a cause of the other η. Nonrecursive models reflect, in particular, limiting forms (over time) of causal relations in recursive models under equilibrium (Strotz & Wold, 1960). An example of a nonrecursive model is found in Eq. (3).

In the present example, data from an experiment concerning the relation of humor and embarrassment (Fink & Walker, 1977) are reanalyzed to examine the interdependence of embarrassment and laughter. In the original study, 60 male subjects engaged in embarrassing interactions with female interviewers by telephone, and their interactions were coded for laughter and embarrassment (among other variables) by trained judges listening on extension telephones. Relative status of the subject as compared to the interviewer (three levels), and the anticipation of future interaction with the interviewer (two levels) were experimentally manipulated; the number of others present with the subject during the course of the telephone interview was provided by the subjects and serves as a control variable. Laughter and embarrassment were measured by magnitude estimation techniques on theoretically continuous scales with nonnegative values.

In the model, we define ξ_1 and ξ_2 to be identically equal to status equality (x_1) and number of others (x_2), respectively. Laughter (η_1) and embarrassment (η_2) are each indicated by two observed (coded) variables. The table of relevant data (Table I), the diagram of the model (Fig. 12), the equations for the creation of the matrices of the model, and the parameter estimates (Table II) for the model follow. Higher values of x_1 indicate more inequality.

TABLE I

DESCRIPTIVE STATISTICS AND INTERCORRELATIONS AMONG OBSERVED VARIABLES[a]

		Mean	(S.D.)	y_1	y_2	y_3	y_4	x_1	x_2
y_1	Laughter 1	12.88	(9.63)	1.					
y_2	Laughter 2	12.82	(9.05)	.99	1.				
y_3	Embarrassment 1	13.17	(2.75)	.00	− .05	1.			
y_4	Embarrassment 2	13.72	(2.58)	− .02	− .07	.85	1.		
x_1	Status equality	2.00	(1.43)	− .23	− .24	.11	.02	1.	
x_2	Number of others	1.22	(1.52)	.18	.22	− .29	− .32	− .23	1

[a]$N = 60$ for each variable except x_2, for which $N = 59$. Variables marked "1" were coded by Observer 1, and those marked "2" by Observer 2.

TABLE II

ESTIMATES OF PARAMETERS FOR NONRECURSIVE MODEL RELATING LAUGHTER AND EMBARRASSMENT[a, b]

$$\mathbf{B} = \begin{bmatrix} 1.000 & -1.166 \\ .079 & 1.000 \end{bmatrix} \qquad \mathbf{B^*} = \begin{bmatrix} 1.000 & -.285 \\ .323 & 1.000 \end{bmatrix}$$

$$\mathbf{\Gamma} = \begin{bmatrix} -1.251 & 1.671 \\ -.201 & -.425 \end{bmatrix} \qquad \mathbf{\Gamma^*} = \begin{bmatrix} -.187 & .267 \\ -.123 & -.277 \end{bmatrix}$$

$$\mathbf{\Psi} = \begin{bmatrix} 90.000 & \text{(Symmetric)} \\ .598 & 5.311 \end{bmatrix} \qquad \mathbf{\Psi^*} = \begin{bmatrix} .994 & \text{(Symmetric)} \\ .027 & .981 \end{bmatrix}$$

$$\mathbf{\Lambda}_y = \begin{bmatrix} 1.000 & .000 \\ .951 & .000 \\ .000 & 1.000 \\ .000 & 1.110 \end{bmatrix} \qquad \mathbf{\Lambda}_y^* = \begin{bmatrix} 9.516 & .000 \\ 9.052 & .000 \\ .000 & 2.327 \\ .000 & 2.538 \end{bmatrix}$$

$$\mathbf{\Theta}_\varepsilon = \begin{bmatrix} 2.155 & 0 & 0 & 0 \\ 0 & .000 & 0 & 0 \\ 0 & 0 & 2.146 & 0 \\ 0 & 0 & 0 & .008 \end{bmatrix} = \mathbf{\Theta}_\varepsilon^*$$

[a]$\chi^2 = 12.2653$; df $= 3$; $p < .05$.
[b]Starred matrices are parameter estimates created by standardizing the ξs and ηs so that they have unit variance. Estimates of $\mathbf{\Phi}$ matrix not reported here; see footnote 22.

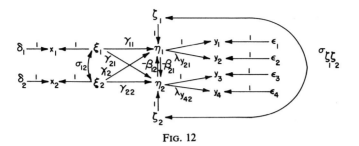

FIG. 12

Theoretical submodel   (The spacing of the equations below should assist the reader in creating the matrices.)

$$\eta_1 = \qquad\qquad -\beta_{12}\eta_2 + \gamma_{11}\xi_1 + \gamma_{12}\xi_2 + \zeta_1$$

$$\eta_2 = -\beta_{21}\eta_1 \qquad\qquad + \gamma_{21}\xi_1 + \gamma_{22}\xi_2 + \zeta_2$$

$$\begin{bmatrix} 1 & \beta_{12} \\ \beta_{21} & 1 \end{bmatrix}\begin{bmatrix} \eta_1 \\ \eta_2 \end{bmatrix} = \begin{bmatrix} \gamma_{11} & \gamma_{12} \\ \gamma_{21} & \gamma_{22} \end{bmatrix}\begin{bmatrix} \xi_1 \\ \xi_2 \end{bmatrix} + \begin{bmatrix} \zeta_1 \\ \zeta_2 \end{bmatrix}$$

$$\mathbf{B}\boldsymbol{\eta} = \boldsymbol{\Gamma}\boldsymbol{\xi} + \boldsymbol{\zeta}$$

Measurement submodel (exogenous)

$$x_1 = 1\xi_1 \qquad + \delta_1$$

$$x_2 = \qquad 1\xi_2 + \delta_2$$

$$\begin{bmatrix} x_1 \\ x_2 \end{bmatrix} = \begin{bmatrix} 1 & 0 \\ 0 & 1 \end{bmatrix}\begin{bmatrix} \xi_1 \\ \xi_2 \end{bmatrix} + \begin{bmatrix} \delta_1 \\ \delta_2 \end{bmatrix}$$

$$\mathbf{x} = \boldsymbol{\Lambda}_x\boldsymbol{\xi} + \boldsymbol{\delta}$$

(Note that $\boldsymbol{\Theta}_\delta$ will be a 2×2 null matrix since we assume no error in our "measures" of x_1 and x_2. Hence, $\boldsymbol{\Theta}_\delta$ will not be estimated).

Measurement model (endogenous)

$$y_1 = 1\eta_1 \qquad\qquad + \varepsilon_1$$

$$y_2 = \lambda_{y_{21}}\eta_1 \qquad\qquad + \varepsilon_2$$

$$y_3 = \qquad\qquad 1\eta_2 + \varepsilon_3$$

$$y_4 = \qquad\qquad \lambda_{y_{42}}\eta_2 + \varepsilon_4$$

$$\begin{bmatrix} y_1 \\ y_2 \\ y_3 \\ y_4 \end{bmatrix} = \begin{bmatrix} 1 & 0 \\ \lambda_{y_{21}} & 0 \\ 0 & 1 \\ 0 & \lambda_{y_{42}} \end{bmatrix}\begin{bmatrix} \eta_1 \\ \eta_2 \end{bmatrix} + \begin{bmatrix} \varepsilon_1 \\ \varepsilon_2 \\ \varepsilon_3 \\ \varepsilon_4 \end{bmatrix}$$

$$\mathbf{y} = \boldsymbol{\Lambda}_y\boldsymbol{\eta} + \boldsymbol{\varepsilon}$$

Level of apparent identification: Information input = 20. Information outflow = 17($\mathbf{B}$, 2; $\mathbf{\Gamma}$, 4; $\mathbf{\Psi}$, 3; $\mathbf{\Lambda}_y$, 2; $\mathbf{\Theta}_\varepsilon$, 4; $\mathbf{\Phi}$, 2).[22]

Substantively, the interesting part of the model (if correctly structured) is the finding that laughter reduces embarrassment while embarrassment increases laughter; however, the confidence in the model is not great, as the χ^2-test results in the rejection of the null hypothesis that the overidentifying restrictions imposed on the data are correct. The χ^2-test is a large sample test, and a sample of 60 is small, so that we cannot consider the test definitive. One finding supportive of the model is that the correlation of ζ_1 with ζ_2 is about zero (.03). This suggests that no significant variables independent of ξ_1 and ξ_2 causing both laughter and embarrassment have been omitted. However, the proportion of variance explained in both laughter and embarrassment in this model is extremely low.

If multiple indicators of the substantive unobserved endogenous variables had not been employed, the model would have been underidentified; only by changing the structure would it have been possible to estimate the nonrecursivity between laughter and embarrassment. Duncan (1969) discusses this case in more detail. Note that the measurement submodels and theoretical submodel are identified, estimated, and tested together; the model forms a single logical structure.

V. ISSUES IN MODEL CONSTRUCTION

In this section, we will briefly discuss general questions that arise in model construction.

A. Robustness

Robustness refers to the ability of a statistical procedure to provide accurate decisions even when one or more of its assumptions are violated. In linear structural equation models with unobserved variables, a typical assumption that might be suspect is that of multinormality, and the implicit corollary of continuous, unbounded scales at least for the observed endogenous variables. For example, in a study using the analytic procedures we have discussed (Wiley, Schmidt, & Bramble, 1973), concern was expressed for the limited continuity of subtest scores, so some subtests were combined so that the multivariate normality assumption would be more plausible. The assumption of multivariate normality is relevant to two points: first, the maximum likelihood technique requires a distributional assumption for estimation;

---

[22]Note that the elements of $\mathbf{\Phi}$ will contain the variance of x_1, x_2, and their covariance. Since $x_1(\equiv \xi_1)$ is an experimentally manipulated variable, its variance is fixed, not estimated, and therefore $\mathbf{\Phi}$ has two elements to be estimated, rather than three. For this reason, $\mathbf{S}$ has 20 rather than 21 nonredundant elements.

second, the assumption enters into the χ^2-test for goodness of fit. Transformations to eliminate heteroscedasticity are often effective in creating normality in data (Smith, 1976), and may be applied here. In addition, alternative models for categorical data exist (e.g., Goodman, 1972) so that the investigator is not limited to the procedures we have discussed. The full implications of violations of these assumptions are not clear, but creating relatively continuous endogenous variables should be quite seriously considered prior to data collection if the technique outlined in this chapter is going to be employed for analysis.[23]

A second issue concerns the confidence one places in a structural equation model when the structure one has posited is theoretically questionable. We indicated that the estimation method employed "full information"; if the information is erroneous, errors of estimation should contaminate all coefficients (and they clearly contaminate the test of the overidentifying restrictions of the model as a whole). Strong theory allows powerful inference, and there is no substitute for theory. Many models are so poorly thought out in terms of canons of theory construction that they should be rejected before the data have been collected! Omitting key variables, including irrelevant variables, and using the wrong functional form of relationship are all errors of specification, and a model is worth very little if serious errors of specification are made.

B. Scaling and Validity of Measurement

One controversy that has received much consideration in the social sciences is the use of standardized (mean 0, standard deviation of 1) observed variables in model construction. If standardized variables are used, the correlation matrix **R** rather than the covariance matrix **S** is used as the data to be analyzed. By analyzing **R** the investigator is making irrelevant the units of the scales (metric) on which the original data were collected, and creates a situation in which all variables have equal variance. As Heise (1975, pp. 126–127) indicates, and as Schoenberg (1972) demonstrates, loss of the variances in the data by standardization results in an inability to compare data from samples drawn from populations that differ with respect to variances. Standardizing data is typically resorted to when the particular scales used are viewed as arbitrary and irrelevant; rather than obscuring meaningful results by standardizing, we suggest creating scales that are meaningful. [For statistical issues in standardizing, see Bielby and Kluegel (1977, p. 300n) and Harris (1975, pp. 174–175); for somewhat different view, see Hargens (1976).]

A second, related issue of measurement in structural equation models concerns how one selects the multiple indicators for an unobserved variable. Clearly, an observed variable must have as one of its components the "true"

---

[23]For assessing multivariate normality, see Andrews *et al.* (1973).

variable which it indicates in the model. However, the structural model approach cannot perform magic. Any construct without coherently related indicators should strike the social scientist as problematic. The issue really concerns measurement by fiat versus fundamental measurement (Torgerson, 1958, pp. 21–25). A strong proposal is that each indicator of the same unobserved variable be required to reflect theoretically equivalent operations (or operations that may be transformed to equivalence), and that these operations consist of fundamental or derived measurements. In that case, the label we attach to an unobserved variable would not be problematic (cf. Land, 1970). We cannot attempt to create or test social science theory always utilizing ad hoc or arbitrary indicators, and expect social science to match the development of the physical sciences, in which the concerns for precision and dimensional analysis of measures have gone hand in hand with theoretical progress.

C. Alternative Modes of Model Evaluation

The traditional evaluative tools which are assumed to be familiar to the reader consist of significance tests for correlations, for individual coefficients, and for covariances between errors (mentioned in Section IV.B), and the χ^2-test of goodness of fit for an overidentified model. Each provides evidence which is limited by the assumptions and constraints it was necessary to impose when constructing the model. In addition, we may examine the entries of the residual matrix (Σ minus S) to see where the model is performing poorly; this last procedure must be done carefully, for it is easy to use the information in Σ minus S to reconstruct a model which is incorrectly specified but which seems to fit; without new data, any statistical "test" will not be maintaining an appropriate α level (see Costner & Schoenberg, 1973; Bielby & Kluegel, 1977). Furthermore, other things being equal, more parsimonious (overidentified) models will do a poorer job when the residual matrix Σ minus S is considered. Either adding paths (coefficients to be estimated) to lessen entries in the Σ minus S residual matrix or removing paths because of statistical nonsignificance has its pitfalls.

Analysis of errors for their size, homoscedasticity, mutual independence, and independence with included variables is a fruitful way to evaluate some assumptions of a model. In this way, violations of normality, linearity, and other specification errors can be examined; see Rao and Miller (1971, pp. 112–126) for a discussion of the regression case, and Burt (1973) for a discussion in the context of path analysis. Monge (Chapter 2) discusses some of these techniques.

Two other techniques may be used to evaluate a model, especially if we have time-series data. Computer simulation may be used to look at the predictive capability of a model. Several measures have been developed to evaluate model performance by simulation; see, e.g., Pindyck and Rubinfeld (1976). A second evaluative tool is to use the structural coefficients of our theoretical submodel (elements of **B** and Γ) to create a differential or difference equation model (see Blalock, 1969b; Coleman, 1968; Doreian & Hummon, 1977), and assess this model qualitatively for its stability. An unstable solution may call into question the validity of some models when theory or other empirical evidence suggests a stable outcome. This makes the structural equation model problematic.

A final issue concerns the too literal adherence to the statistical tests one may perform, using this technique or any other. One should not ignore one's ordinary critical capabilities in evaluating a model. While "seat of the pants" techniques are always suspect as biased, it should be realized that the trained investigator is invaluable to the evaluation of a model; the investigator is the person who looks at the results and judges that the data have been mispunched or miscoded, or that a type II error may have been committed. The proposed χ^2-test is best used cautiously (Jöreskog, 1974, p. 4); research on the statistical power of this test should be done so that this, too, may be taken into account when evaluating a model. Nevertheless, statistical techniques should be the servants, not the masters, in the theory building process; given the large number of ways a model may be evaluated, judgment rather than reflex is what is required.

D. Data Over Time and Theory Building

In all of the examples that have been presented, cross-sectional data have been used. With time-series data, and with some panel data, it is possible to estimate models that can be related to differential or difference equation models. These latter models are often the form in which scientific laws are constructed or discovered. Even simple causal structures may be concealed in the absence of overtime data (Carlsson, 1972). In addition, invariance of structural coefficients cannot be expected in over time data if different time intervals are used by different investigators (Coleman, 1968); however, differential equation model coefficients will be invariant regardless of the time interval chosen, if the model is correct and well estimated.

An additional criticism of cross-sectional structural models may be made on philosphical grounds, challenging the use of the term "causal" applied to relations obtained from data that are gathered at one point in time (cf. Nurmi, 1974). With cross-sectional data, we must assume that all our units are equilibrated, and we must interpret the coefficients of causal impact with this in mind (see footnote 1); the plausibility of this assumption may be questioned. Criticisms of the use of cross-sectional data for causal modeling have some validity, and data gathered at many time points should probably be considered a requirement for the more rigorous testing of most theories in the social sciences. The linear structural equation model technique with or without unobserved variables is not necessarily tied to cross-sectional data; it may be used to handle some time-series data structures. Models of differential equations (as opposed to structural equations) may be what theory building ultimately requires, but we nevertheless need the statistical tools to efficiently and consistently estimate structural models that have prediction and measurement error, so that consistent estimates for the mathematical models can be created.

VI. RETROSPECT

An attempt has been made to discuss key issues in a relatively new technique in the social sciences: structural equation models with unobserved variables. This technique is a synthesis of regression and factor-analytic models. We have indicated the utility and assumptions of the approach, given some applications and one example in detail, and discussed theory building with this technique. It is hoped that the reader realizes that while there may be no royal road to social science theory, some paths may be more attractive than others; under some conditions, this approach may be one such path.

ACKNOWLEDGMENTS

The author wishes to thank Timothy Mabee, James J. Noell, Katrina Simmons, Carol Stein, and Joseph Woelfel for discussion concerning ideas presented herein. Unfortunately, errors remaining are those of the author.

References

Alwin, D. F. Approaches to the interpretation of relationships in the multitrait-multimethod matrix. In H. L. Costner (Ed.), *Sociological methodology 1973–1974*. San Francisco, California: Jossey-Bass, 1974. Pp.79–105.

Alwin, D. F., and Tessler, R. C. Causal models, unobserved variables, and experimental data. *American Journal of Sociology*, 1974, **80**, 58–86.

Andrews, D. F., Gnanadesikan, R., and Warner, J. L. Methods for assessing multivariate normality. In P. R. Krishnaian (Ed.), *Multivariate analysis*, Vol. 3. New York: Academic Press, 1973. Pp. 95–116.

Arundale, R. B. The concept of process in human communication research (Doctoral dissertation, Michigan State University, 1971). *Dissertation Abstracts International*, 1971, **32**, 1816B. (University Microfilms No. 21–23,157.)

Bielby, W. T., and Kluegel, J. R. Statistical inference and statistical power in applications of the general linear model. In D. R. Heise (Ed.), *Sociological methodology 1977*. San Francisco, California: Jossey-Bass, 1977. Pp. 283–312.

Blalock, H. M., Jr. Multiple indicators and the causal approach to measurement error. *American Journal of Sociology*, 1969, **75**, 264–272. (a)

Blalock, H. M., Jr. *Theory construction*. Englewood Cliffs, New Jersey: Prentice-Hall, 1969. (b)

Blalock, H. M., Jr. *Social statistics* (2nd ed.). New York: McGraw-Hill, 1972.

Blau, P. M., and Duncan, O. D. *The American occupational structure*. New York: Wiley, 1967.

Bohrnstedt, G. W., and Carter, T. M. Robustness in regression analysis. In H. L. Costner (Ed.), *Sociological methodology 1971*. San Francisco, California: Jossey-Bass, 1971. Pp. 118–146.

Burt, R. S. *The theory construction potential of path analysis: An interdisciplinary perspective.* Albany, New York: State University of New York at Albany International Center for Social Research, 1973.

Carlsson, G. Lagged structures and cross-sectional methods. *Acta Sociologica*, 1972, **15**, 323–341.

Cohen, J., and Cohen, P. *Applied multiple regression/correlation analysis for the behavioral sciences.* Hillsdale, New Jersey: Lawrence Erlbaum Associates, 1975.

Coleman, J. S. The mathematical study of change. In H. M. Blalock, Jr. and A. B. Blalock (Eds.), *Methodology in social research.* New York: McGraw-Hill, 1968. Pp. 428–478.

Cortes, F., Przeworski, A., and Sprague, J. *Systems analysis for social scientists.* New York: Wiley, 1974.

Costner, H. L. Theory, deduction, and rules of correspondence. *American Journal of Sociology*, 1969, **75**, 245–263.

Costner, H. L. Utilizing causal models to discover flaws in experiments. *Sociometry*, 1971, **34**, 398–410.

Costner, H. L., and Schoenberg, R. Diagnosing indicator ills in multiple indicator models. In A. S. Goldberger and O. D. Duncan (Eds.), *Structural equation models in the social sciences.* New York: Seminar Press, 1973. Pp. 167–199.

Cunningham, W. J. The concept of stability. *American Scientist*, 1963, **51**, 425–436.

Doreian, P., and Hummon, N. P. Estimates for differential equation models of social phenomena. In D. R. Heise (Ed.), *Sociological methodology 1977.* San Francisco, California: Jossey-Bass, 1977. Pp. 180–208.

Duncan, O. D. Some linear models for two-wave, two-variable panel analysis. *Psychological Bulletin*, 1969, **72**, 177–182.

Duncan, O. D. Unmeasured variables in linear models for panel analysis. In H. L. Costner (Ed.), *Sociological methodology 1972.* San Francisco, California: Jossey-Bass, 1972. Pp. 36–82.

Duncan, O. D. *Introduction to structural equation models.* New York: Academic Press, 1975.

Fink, E. L., and Mabee, T. I. Linear equations and nonlinear estimation: A lesson from a nonrecursive example. *Sociological Methods and Research*, 1978, **7**, 107–120.

Fink, E. L., and Walker, B. A. Humorous responses to embarrassment. *Psychological Reports*, 1977, **40**, 475–485.

Goldberger, A. S. Structural equation models: An overview. In A. S. Goldberger and O. D. Duncan (Eds.), *Structural equation models in the social sciences.* New York: Seminar Press, 1973. Pp. 1–18.

Goodman, L. A. A modified multiple regression approach to the analysis of dichotomous variables. *American Sociological Review*, 1972, **37**, 28–46.

Griliches, Z. Errors in variables and other unobservables. *Econometrica*, 1974, **42**, 971–998.

Hanushek, E. A., and Jackson, J. E. *Statistical methods for social scientists.* New York: Academic Press, 1977.

Hargens, L. L. A note on standardized coefficients as structural parameters. *Sociological Methods and Research*, 1976, **5**, 247–255.

Harris, R. J. *A primer of multivariate statistics.* New York: Academic Press, 1975.

Hauser, R. M., and Goldberger, A. S. The treatment of unobservable variables in path analysis. In H. L. Costner (Ed.), *Sociological methodology 1971.* San Francisco, California: Jossey-Bass, 1971. Pp. 81–117.

Hays, W. L. *Statistics for psychologists.* New York: Holt, 1963.

Heise, D. R. Separating reliability and stability in test-retest correlation. *American Sociological Review*, 1969, **34**, 93–101.

Heise, D. R. *Causal analysis.* New York: Wiley, 1975.

Hibbs, D. A., Jr. Problems of statistical estimation and causal inference in time-series regression models. In H. L. Costner (Ed.), *Sociological methodology 1973–1974.* San Francisco, California: Jossey-Bass, 1974. Pp. 252–308.

Hunter, J. E., and Cohen, S. H. Correcting for unreliability in nonlinear models of attitude change. *Psychometrika*, 1974, **39**, 445–468.

Isaac, P. D. Linear regression, structural relations, and measurement error. *Psychological Bulletin*, 1970, **74**, 213–218.

Jöreskog, K. G. A general method for the analysis of covariance structures. *Biometrika*, 1970, **74**, 239–251.

Jöreskog, K. G. A general method for estimating a linear structural equation system. In A. S. Goldberger and O. D. Duncan (Eds.), *Structural equation models in the social sciences*. New York: Seminar Press, 1973. Pp. 85–112.

Jöreskog, K. G. Analyzing psychological data by structural analysis of covariance matrices. In D. H. Krantz, R. C. Atkinson, R. D. Luce, and P. Suppes (Eds.), *Contemporary developments in mathematical psychology*, Vol. 2. San Francisco, California: Freeman, 1974. Pp. 1–56.

Jöreskog, K. G., and Goldberger, A. S. Estimation of a model with multiple indicators and multiple causes of a single latent variable. *Journal of the American Statistical Association*, 1975, **70**, 631–639.

Kac, M. Some mathematical models in science. *Science*, 1969, **166**, 695–699.

Kerlinger, F. N., and Pedhazur, E. J. *Multiple regression in behavioral research*. New York: Holt, 1973.

Kmenta, J. *Elements of econometrics*. New York: Macmillan, 1971.

Land, K. C. On the estimation of path coefficients for unmeasured variables from correlations among observed variables. *Social Forces*, 1970, **48**, 506–511.

Land, K. C., and Felson, M. Sensitivity analysis of arbitrarily identified simultaneous-equation models. *Sociological Methods and Research*, 1978, **6**, 283–307.

Lord, F. M., and Novick, M. R. *Statistical theories of mental test scores.* Reading, Massachusetts: Addison-Wesley, 1968.

McDermott, V. The literature on classical theory construction. *Human Communication Research*, 1975, **2**, 83–103.

Merton, R. K. The bearing of empirical research upon the development of social theory. *American Sociological Review*, 1948, **13**, 505–515.

Meyer, S. L. *Data analysis for scientists and engineers*. New York: Wiley, 1975.

Miller, A. D. Logic of causal analysis: From experimental to nonexperimental designs. In H. M. Blalock, Jr. (Ed.), *Causal models in the social sciences*. Chicago, Illinois: Aldine-Atherton, 1971. Pp. 273–294.

Nelder, J. A. Regression, model-building, and invariance. *Journal of the Royal Statistical Society*, Series A, 1968, **131**, 303–315.

Nurmi, H. Social causality and empirical data reduction techniques. *Quality and Quantity*, 1974, **8**, 159–180.

Petrovskii, I. G. Ordinary differential equations. In A. D. Aleksandrov, A. N. Kolmogorov, and M. A. Lavrent'ev (Eds.), *Mathematics: Its content, methods, and meaning*, Vol. 1 (S. H. Gould and T. Bartha, translators). Cambridge, Massachusetts: MIT Press, 1969. Pp. 311–356.

Pindyck, R. S., and Rubinfeld, D. L. *Econometric models and economic forecasts*. New York: McGraw-Hill, 1976.

Rao, P., and Miller, R. L. *Applied econometrics*. Belmont, California: Wadsworth, 1971.

Schachter, S. *The psychology of affiliation.* Stanford, California: Stanford Univ. Press, 1959.

Schoenberg, R. Strategies for meaningful comparison. In H. L. Costner (Ed.), *Sociological methodology 1972*. San Francisco, California: Jossey-Bass, 1972. Pp. 1–35.

Siegel, P. M., and Hodge, R. W. A causal approach to the study of measurement error. In H. M. Blalock, Jr. and A. B. Blalock (Eds.), *Methodology in social research*. New York: McGraw-Hill, 1968. Pp. 28–59.

Simon, H. A. *Models of man.* New York: Wiley, 1957.

Smith, J. E. K. Data transformations in analysis of variance. *Journal of Verbal Learning and Verbal Behavior*, 1976, **15**, 339–346.

Specht, D. A., and Warren, R. D. Comparing causal models. In D. R. Heise (Ed.), *Sociological methodology 1976*. San Francisco, California: Jossey-Bass, 1975. Pp. 46–82.

Strotz, R. H., and Wold, H. O. A. Recursive vs. nonrecursive systems: An attempt at synthesis. *Econometrica*, 1960, **28**, 417–427.

Torgerson, W. S. *Theory and methods of scaling*. New York: Wiley, 1958.

Turner, M. E., and Stevens, C. D. The regression analysis of causal paths. *Biometrics*, 1959, **15**, 236–258.

Werts, C. E., Jöreskog, K. G., and Linn, R. L. Identification and estimation in path analysis with unmeasured variables. *American Journal of Sociology*, 1973, **78**, 1469–1484.

Werts, C. E. Jöreskog, K. G., and Linn, R. L. Analyzing ratings with correlated intrajudge measurement errors. *Educational and Psychological Measurement*, 1976, **36**, 319–328.

Werts, C. E., Linn, R. L., and Jöreskog, K. G. Estimating the parameters of path models involving unmeasured variables. In H. M. Blalock, Jr. (Ed.), *Causal models in the social sciences*. Chicago, Illionois: Aldine-Atherton, 1971. Pp. 400–409.

Werts, C. E., Rock, D. A., Linn, R. L., and Jöreskog, K. G. Comparison of correlations, variances, covariances, and regression weights with or without measurement error. *Psychological Bulletin*, 1976, **83**, 1007–1013.

Wheaton, B., Muthén, B., Alwin, D. F., and Summers, G. F. Assessing reliability and stability in panel models. In D. F. Heise (Ed.), *Sociological methodology 1977*. San Francisco, California: Jossey-Bass, 1977. Pp. 84–136.

Wiley, D. E. The identification problem for structural equation models with unmeasured variables. In A. S. Goldberger and O. D. Duncan (Eds.), *Structural equation models in the social sciences*. New York: Seminar Press, 1973. Pp. 69–83.

Wiley, D. E., Schmidt, W. H., and Bramble, W. J. Studies of a class of covariance structure models. *Journal of the American Statistical Association*, 1973, **68**, 317–323.

Chapter 5

MULTIVARIATE ANALYSIS OF VARIANCE: TECHNIQUES, MODELS, AND APPLICATIONS IN COMMUNICATION RESEARCH

ARTHUR P. BOCHNER
Department of Speech
Temple University
Philadelphia, Pennsylvania

MARY ANNE FITZPATRICK
Department of Communication Arts
University of Wisconsin
Madison, Wisconsin

I. INTRODUCTION

Multivariate analysis of variance (MANOVA) is a set of data analytic procedures used to assess research models which map linear relationships between independent variables with fixed values and completely determined outcomes on a set of multiple response variables. Most social scientists have learned univariate analysis of variance in the context of classical experimental design. However, it is now widely recognized that the differences between analysis of variance and multiple linear regression are minor when research is conceptualized in the terms of a general linear model. Indeed, the same analysis of variance results can be produced by using the more versatile and general methods of linear multiple regression (Bottenberg & Ward, 1960; Bradley, 1968; Cohen, 1968; Cohen & Cohen, 1975; Overall & Klett, 1972; Woodward & Overall, 1975).

In this chapter, multivariate analysis of variance will be explained in the language of the general multivariate linear model and examined, in part, as a general case of multiple linear regression. This chapter is basically written from the classical point of view in which an analysis of *all* linear combinations of the individual responses is taken as obviously a good thing. From time to time, however, we shall point to a different approach that is discussed more fully in Chapter 16, Section XX. The presentation is addressed to the practicing researcher who is familiar with univariate analysis of variance and multiple regression approaches to it (Cohen, 1968; Cohen & Cohen, 1975) and also has a fairly complete grasp of elementary matrix algebra.

We view MANOVA as a six step data-analytic strategy designed to answer five specific questions: (1) What are we testing? (2) How should we test it? (3) Are the results significant? (4) How significant? (5) What do the results mean? Thus, MANOVA will not be described as an isolated statistical technique but rather as a design and analysis process for testing and developing models. As we conceptualize them, MANOVA procedures involve (1) stipulating a model to be tested; (2) choosing a method to evaluate the model; (3) testing the significance of model parameters; (4) producing the best model to explain the data; (5) obtaining best estimates for the significant terms in the model; and (6) interpreting the results.

II. MODELS

In a multivariate experiment with k independent variables and p response variables, MANOVA offers a test for the existence of at least one linear combination—one discriminant function—of the p responses which will reject the null hypothesis of no differences for each of the k effects tested. The significance procedure enables the investigator to select the most prominent such discriminant function. If global significance is identified, other multivariate tests may be used to help explain the variation in the original p variates in terms of more synthetic variates, further linear combinations— further discriminant functions—that account for a substantial share of the variation in the original set of variates.

Significance testing is, however, only a part of the total data analysis process. We view data analysis as essentially a problem of model fitting. Underlying the design and analysis of most behavioral research is a conceptual or mathematical model that attempts to explain the response(s) of human subjects in terms of specified parameters of interest (independent and/or concomitant variables). In the theory- or hypothesis-generating stage of research, the model is a verbal or symbolic one which stipulates expected relations between independent and dependent variables. In the analysis stage, after quantified responses for the classification conditions have been obtained, the model is an algebraic equation which assumes that a term on one side of the equation can be represented—explained and/or predicted—by a term or set of terms on the other side of the equation. From the model point of view, data analysis involves estimating the numerical values (coefficients) for the various terms of the model, i.e., fitting the model to the data. Data analysis may also involve the comparison of several alternative models for the same data, when the objective is to determine which model explains the data most satisfactorily.

A. Univariate Models

Consider, for example, three commonly applied univariate (ANOVA) models:

$$y_{ij} = \mu + \varepsilon_{ij} \tag{1}$$

$$y_{ij} = \mu + \alpha_j + \varepsilon_{ij} \tag{2}$$

$$y_i = \alpha + \beta_1 x_{i1} + \varepsilon_i \tag{3}$$

These three equations depict three different linear models for explaining a single quantified response. Models (1) and (2) are *experimental design models* for univariate research. The term y_{ij} signifies the single quantified response for subject i in group j. Subject i may have been randomly assigned to group j, as is true in most research classified as experimental; or he may have been identified as a member of group j by the researcher on the basis of his score(s) on a test used for classification purposes, e.g., personality, aptitude, a communication apprehension measure, I.Q., or membership in a particular intact group (all Americans, all males, etc.).

The symbol μ represents a fixed parameter or population constant, usually interpreted as the general or overall mean of the j groups prior to experimental treatment. Actually, the value of μ is typically estimated by calculating the mean of all observations, $\sum y_{ij}/n$, in the entire experiment *after* exposure to the experimental treatments.

The term ε_{ij} represents the error associated with the measurement of subject i in group j; it is conventionally assumed that this error is random and normally distributed for each j group, having a mean value of zero and common variance. Errors for each of the i subjects in the j groups are conventionally assumed to be independent. ε_{ij} is estimated as the deviation of subject i in treatment j from the j treatment group mean.

The only difference between model (1) and model (2) is the single term α_j, which stands for the effect of the jth experimental treatment. The simplest experiment, a case in which a single independent variable is manipulated in two ways to determine its effect on one dependent variable, is essentially a test of model (2) against model (1). If there are significant differences between the means of the two groups, model (2) fits the data more satisfactorily than model (1); if there are no differences model (1) is the more satisfactory of the two.

Consider the following example: An investigator is interested in studying the effect of physical attractiveness on impression formation. Subjects are randomly assigned to three experimental conditions. In treatment group one, α_1, subjects are shown pictures of extremely attractive individuals (as previously determined by ratings of expert judges) and asked to rate each picture on a seven-interval warm/cold scale. In treatment group two, α_2, subjects are shown pictures of moderately attractive individuals and asked to rate each picture on the seven-interval warm/cold scale. In treatment group three, α_3, the same procedure is followed for a series of extremely unattractive individuals. The mean score for each subject's group of ratings is tabulated; then, the treatment means for each of the three groups is calculated. An analysis-of-variance F-test is used to determine whether the three treatment effects are equal. In most statistics texts, this is referred to as the test of the null hypothesis of equality of group means, $H_0 : (\mu_1 = \mu_2 = \mu_3)$, where $\mu_1 = \mu + \alpha_1$, $\mu_2 = \mu + \alpha_2$, and $\mu_3 = \mu + \alpha_3$. If the F-test does not exceed the critical value, e.g., $p < .05$ or $p < .01$, then the investigator concludes that there are no "significant" differences among the treatment means. Thus, $\alpha_j = 0$ and model (1) provides the best fit. If there is a significant difference among the means, then $\alpha_j \neq 0$ and model (2) is fitted. Should model (2) be chosen, the investigator would proceed to estimate the difference among the three attractiveness treatment groups and to interpret the warm/cold scores in terms of the fixed treatment conditions.

Model (3) is a simple regression model with one predictor variable, x_1, and one criterion variable, y_i. The symbol β signifies a weight or *partial regression coefficient* used to optimize the prediction of y. The constant term α is used to equalize the two sides of the equation by exploiting the differences in scaling among x and y variables; ε_i is the error term. When there is only a single predictor (x variable), the model is referred to as a *simple regression model*; when there is more than one predictor, it is a *multiple regression model*.

Most classification or experimental research in the social and behavioral sciences is designed to test analysis-of-variance models incorporating two or more independent variables. There are two models which are frequently employed: the *main class* or *main effects* model and the *full class* model. The main class model is represented by

$$y_{ijk} = \mu + \alpha_j + \beta_k + \varepsilon_{ijk} \qquad (4)$$

which assumes the additivity of two main effects, an A classification variable (α) and a B classification variable (β). The *full class* model is given by

$$y_{ijk} = \mu + \alpha_j + \beta_k + (\alpha\beta)_{jk} + \varepsilon_{ijk} \qquad (5)$$

which includes an interaction or nonadditive term $(\alpha\beta)_{jk}$ reflecting the extent to which the main effects are not equally effective (additive) across all levels of the other factor(s), i.e., the A classifications across the B treatments and/or the B treatments across the A subclasses.

Similarly, most prediction studies incorporate multiple predictors. For example, the algebraic multiple-regression model for a study in which three measured predictors, I.Q., undergraduate grade point average, and interview rating scores, are used to predict success in graduate school would be

$$y_i = \alpha + \beta_1 x_{i1} + \beta_2 x_{i2} + \beta_3 x_{i3} + \varepsilon_i \qquad (6)$$

the symbols being identical to those of model (3) but expanded to include the additional predictor variables.

When students are first introduced to analysis-of-variance models such as Eqs. (2), (4), and (5) and regression models such as Eqs. (3) and (6), they are often left with the impression that analysis of variance and multiple regression are very different techniques applicable to very different types of research problems. Analysis of variance is typically conceptualized as a method of analyzing group differences when the data are experimental. The independent variables are categorical; subjects either belong to a given treatment group or they do not. Analysis of variance is used to reveal whether or not there are statistically significant differences among the group means. Regression models, on the other hand, are sometimes thought to be applicable only to prediction studies in which independent variables are measured rather than categorically assigned and usually are measured on interval scales. Criterion scores predicted by the computed partial regression coefficients are compared statistically with the observed scores to determine whether a significant portion of the variance in the criterion is attributable to the predictors, or to state it another way, whether any or all of the regression coefficients are nonzero.

The distinctions between analysis of variance and multiple regression are more apparent than real and more a matter of convenience than of necessity. Most problems suitable for analysis of variance can be handled by multiple regression methods with approximately equivalent results, although the reverse is not always true. Underlying both cases is a more inclusive general linear model (Finn, 1974, p. 5):

$$y_i = \sum_j a_j x_{ji} + \varepsilon_i \qquad (7)$$

In the most common analysis of variance case, the x_j are categorical; observations are assigned a 1 if members and a 0 if nonmembers of a given j

group. In the most common regression case, the x_j are scores on measured variables. The a_j are the coefficients which are multiplied by the x_j to produce the closest approximation possible for the y_i. The difference between the predicted scores (approximations) and the actual scores are the ε_i, the errors. When the independent variables are fixed parameters, the results will be the same no matter what type of analysis is applied to the data. When the regression model is used, the α_j and β_k parameters of Eq. (4), for example, are the partial (multiple) regression coefficients. The parameter values for these terms may be calculated by dummy coding the effects in a manner summarized later in this article (also see Cohen & Cohen, 1975; Overall & Klett, 1972; Woodward & Overall, 1975).

Researchers sometimes assume erroneously that analysis-of-variance models permit inferences about causal relationships between independent and dependent variables, but regression models do not. The inferences to be drawn from analysis-of-variance tests, however, rest solely on the manner in which those data were gathered. These tests are just as valid when group membership is based on nonrandom assignment of cases as when membership is determined randomly, though their meaning is different. If data are gathered from randomly assigned subjects (or other experimental units) then causal inferences are legitimate no matter whether these data are categorical or measured or whether they are analyzed by ANOVA or regression techniques. Random assignment is the only recognized condition which justifies the interpretation of significant differences as causal (Tukey, 1978).

B. The MANOVA Model

Models (2)–(6) are univariate models. These models depict cases in which each subject provides only one response, y_i. Each effect parameter, regression coefficient, or covariate (for example, pretest scores) in the model is evaluated in terms of its impact on only one response. Since each subject provides only the one score ($p = 1$), the $N \times p$ matrix of scores for all subjects sampled is a column vector of length N.

Practically all analysis-of-variance models, whether univariate or multivariate, can be represented in matrix terms as

$$\mathbf{Y} = \mathbf{XB} + \mathbf{E} \qquad (8)$$

In Eq. (8), $\mathbf{Y}$ is the $N \times p$ matrix of subject responses. The rows of this matrix are the N research subjects; the columns are the p responses. $\mathbf{Y}$ is a column vector in the univariate case, because there is only one p variate, i.e., one response for each subject. In the multivariate case, the $\mathbf{Y}$ matrix contains as many columns as there are responses.

On the right-hand side of Eq. (8), $\mathbf{X}$ is the $N \times k$ analysis-of-variance model matrix. This matrix contains a row for each of the n subjects and a column for each of the k parameters in the model. The k parameters typically include an estimate for the grand mean, μ, and effects terms, α, β, etc. In analysis-of-variance cases, the effects are independent variables with categorical values. These values are represented in the model matrix by means of a dummy code. Each of the N observations is assigned a 1 if it is a subclass member of that parameter, or a 0 if it is not. Hence, the model matrix is a matrix of 0's and 1's, designating whether a given observation contains a given parameter or not. A 1 signifies that the unit (subject) is a member of that class (parameter); a 0 signifies nonmembership. For example, the model matrix for a *main effects*, 2×2 factorial design (no interaction parameter) representing

$$Y_{ijk} = \mu + \alpha_j + \beta_k + \varepsilon_{ijk} \qquad (9)$$

would be diagrammed[1] in the following manner:

$$\mathbf{X} = \begin{bmatrix} 1 & 1 & 0 & 1 & 0 \\ 1 & 1 & 0 & 0 & 1 \\ 1 & 0 & 1 & 1 & 0 \\ 1 & 0 & 1 & 0 & 1 \end{bmatrix}$$
$$\mu \quad \alpha_1 \quad \alpha_2 \quad \beta_1 \quad \beta_2$$

Each of the N observations for this experimental design would be coded in a manner identical to one of the rows in this matrix. Therefore, each of these rows actually refers to a subclass in the experimental design.

The matrix $\mathbf{B}$ in Eq. (8) is the $k \times p$ matrix of fixed parameters. The k parameters (effects) are estimated from the sample data and tested for significance to determine whether any or all of them differ significantly from zero. The matrix of fixed parameters contains one row for each of the k treatments and one column for each of the p responses. In the univariate case $\mathbf{B}$ is a $k \times 1$ column vector, whereas in the multivariate case, there are as many columns as there are response variables. Thus, one can see that embedded within any multivariate analysis of variance, there are p univariate analyses (see e.g., Woodward & Overall, 1975).[2] Moreover, the sum of squares

---

[1]We have chosen arbitrarily to use the main class model for our example. The full class model would, of course, be represented in a similar fashion. For the 2×2 full class case, four columns would be added to the model matrix in order for the interaction parameters, the $(\alpha\beta)_{jk}$, to be estimated and tested for significance. The four additional columns would represent sequentially the following parameters: $(\alpha\beta)_{11}$, $(\alpha\beta)_{12}$, $(\alpha\beta)_{21}$, and $(\alpha\beta)_{22}$.

[2]Since there are p univariate analyses implanted within any multivariate analysis of variance, one might naturally ask, why not do them? What is to be gained by doing MANOVA? Actually there are three choices available to any investigator whose data consist of multiple responses. The first option is to conduct the p univariate analyses. This analytic strategy is generally discouraged because the dependent variables are likely to be correlated, making the separate F-tests nonindependent. Moreover, if one computes only the p univariate tests, then no information is provided about the exact probability that at least one of the p tests will exceed some critical decision level. For these reasons, advocates of multivariate models indubitably reject the unprotected univariate strategy: "Whenever variables consist of multiple measures of the same construct, a multivariate

and cross products can also be used, almost as easily, to provide a similar univariate analysis for any linear combination of the elementary responses. Thus, if q such linear combinations are chosen, we have the option of considering $p + q$ univariate analyses, one for each elementary response and one for each selected linear combination of responses.

In Eq. (8), E is the $N \times p$ matrix of errors. This matrix is frequently referred to as the *residual matrix*, since it reflects the extent to which the estimates of Y based on the products of XB are in error, i.e., do not fit $(E = Y - XB)$, where Y is the matrix of predicted scores and XB is the matrix of observed scores. It is assumed that the errors for any pair of subjects are independent; conversely, errors for each of the N subject's p measures will be correlated. The distributional assumptions for the E matrix have been outlined in detail by Finn (1974, pp. 211–214).

The major computational objective of ANOVA/MANOVA is to produce an estimate of B ($\hat{B}$) which will minimize the sum of squared residuals in the sample data. These are referred to as the *least squares estimates* of effects. In other words, least squares principles are used to determine a $\hat{B}$ which makes the deviations of observed scores from predicted scores as small as possible.

III. CONSTRUCTING MANOVA MODELS

How are multivariate models actually tested through analysis of variance? As indicated earlier, the central question is, Does the hypothesized model fit the data? To answer this question, we must first obtain estimates for each term in the model, and then test the estimates for "significance" to determine how well they "explain" the observed data. It is usually assumed that a given

---

test statistic is appropriate for deciding whether or not the hypothesis is supported. Univariate F ratios for a single effect are *not* independent and will tend to compound sampling and decision errors" [Finn, 1974, p. 309].

A second alternative is to use MANOVA. This strategy has the advantage of producing an F-test for between-group differences which is comprehensive of the p univariate analyses, thus protecting the investigator against excessive decision errors. MANOVA also provides a set of coefficients which represents statistically the optimal linear combination of response variates for discriminating between the groups (the primary discriminant function). Some writers have argued that optimal linear combinations are misleading or of little interest (Finney, 1956), but this position has been challenged by numerous social and educational researchers who believe that such information can broaden a researcher's understanding of what variables to examine under what conditions and with what subjects (Cramer and Bock, 1966; Harris, 1975; Pruzek, 1971).

A third alternative is to construct a few simple composites (linear combinations of the univariate responses), q in number, to go with the p univariate responses, and to test all $p + q$ in a univariate fashion, adjusting decision rates to $5\%/(p + q)$ or $1\%/(p + q)$. Tukey (1978) has outlined some tentative rules and an algorithm for selecting composites appropriately. The approach advocated by Tukey appears to overcome some of the criticisms engendered by the p univariate strategy just mentioned, but it is too early to tell how this method will stack up against alternatives in producing usable and interpretable results. As Tukey himself acknowledges: "It will take time to learn how it works and how to tune it to work better" [p. 489].

parameter explains the data well if it accounts for a significant portion of the variation in **Y**.

In practice, there are actually two questions to be asked about each parameter in the model: (1) Is the effect greater than chance, i.e., statistically significant? (2) If so, how important is it, i.e., what is the magnitude or size of the effect?[3] The classically conventional statistical procedure is to compute a significance test—usually a univariate or multivariate F— for each effect in the model, adjusting the test for all other effects in the hypothesized model. Parameters (effects) in the original model that do not exceed the critical level, e.g., $p < .05$, are then removed from the model and new estimates, referred to as "best estimates," for the nonzero terms are computed for the reduced model (Finn, 1975, p. 206). The "new" estimates may then be used to evaluate the magnitude of the effects.

There are actually three steps involved in the testing and revising of models by means of multivariate analysis of variance. First, estimates are obtained for each parameter in the full model. This is referred to as the *estimation* stage. Second, the initial estimates are tested for significance. This is the *significance testing stage*. Third, null parameters are dropped from the model and new estimates are obtained for the nonzero parameters, so that an appropriate interpretation of their magnitude and importance can be made. This is the *reestimation stage*. (The researcher should keep in mind that dropping terms from the model to be fit often changes the meaning of the remaining terms.)

The process of testing and estimating effects would be straightforward were it not for one serious problem. The model matrix, **X**, in Eq. (8) which is used to estimate analysis-of-variance parameters will frequently contain linearly dependent columns, i.e., some of the columns are expressed as linear combinations of others. To use the language of linear algebra, **X** in Eq. (8) is a matrix of *deficient rank*.

Consider, for example, a model matrix, **X**, for estimating the parameters of Eq. (9) ($Y_{ijk} = \mu + \alpha_j + \beta_k + \varepsilon_{ijk}$):

$$\mathbf{X} = \begin{bmatrix} 1 & 1 & 0 & 0 & 0 \\ 1 & 0 & 1 & 0 & 0 \\ 1 & 0 & 0 & 1 & 0 \\ 1 & 0 & 0 & 0 & 1 \end{bmatrix}$$

$$\mu \quad \alpha_1 \quad \alpha_2 \quad \beta_1 \quad \beta_2$$

As is usually the case, matrix **X** contains more columns than rows. Moreover, some of the columns are expressed as linear combinations of others. For example, column 1 is equal to the sum of columns 2, 3, 4, and 5. When at least one vector (column) can be expressed as a linear combination of other

---

[3]Large sample sizes can, of course, produce significant parameters ($p < .05$ or $p < .01$) that account for a very small proportion of the variance and are therefore of little substantive *importance*.

vectors in the set (for example, $1 = 2 + 3 + 4 + 5$), then the vectors are said to be *linearly dependent*. Analysis of variance models are normally models of deficient rank (more columns than rows) with linearly dependent columns. Understanding the consequences of producing a model matrix of deficient rank is vital, for when the model matrix is of deficient rank it is not possible to obtain unique estimates for all of the parameters in the model. In the present example, we want to estimate five parameters (the five columns), but we have only four *degrees of freedom* (the rank of the matrix is four) to work with. The model is of deficient rank. Thus, we cannot estimate all of the parameters. The number of parameters which can be estimated is restricted to the number of subclasses in the research design which in the present case is four.

Deficient rank seems to pose a serious dilemma for the testing of analysis-of-variance models. We ordinarily want to test the significance of each term in the model, but we cannot because not all of the effects can be estimated without bias. And without unbiased estimates, we cannot conduct meaningful significance tests.

Fortunately, there is a practical solution to this problem. Few researchers are actually interested in estimating and testing the parameter values of every subclass in the experimental design. Instead, most research focuses attention on a subset of critical comparisons among or between subclass means. Since science is grounded in the notion of comparison and contrast, *it is the linear combinations among subclasses, not the subclasses themselves, that are of most scientific concern*. Hence, one viable solution to the problem of deficient rank is to construct new parameters for the model, a procedure referred to as *reparameterization* (Finn, 1975). The *reparameterized model* contains only linear combinations of the parameters that can be estimated without bias. Thus, the researcher can overcome the problems of deficient rank by choosing the linear combinations of effects that most directly reflect the scientific issues to which the research is addressed.

Finn (1974) has shown that reparameterization involves converting the general model (8), $\mathbf{Y} = \mathbf{XB} + \mathbf{E}$, into

$$\mathbf{Y} = \mathbf{K(LB)} + \mathbf{E} \tag{10}$$

$\mathbf{L}$ is defined as an $e \times k$ matrix, with $e \leq j$, the number of subclasses (treatment groups) in the experimental design or the total degrees of freedom among means. We can estimate without bias as many parameter values as there are degrees of freedom for significance testing. Instead of estimating all of the original k parameters, only the e parameters (which are linear combinations of the k parameters), equal to the rank of the model for significance testing, are estimated. Thus, contrasts among parameters are substituted for the original model parameters. The rows of $\mathbf{L}$ are linear combinations of the rows of $\mathbf{X}$ in Eq. (8), i.e., the original parameters. $\mathbf{K}$ provides the new model matrix necessary for estimating the terms in the reparameterized model. It is a matrix of full rank, containing as many parameters as there are subclasses in the experimental design.

IV. SELECTING CONTRASTS

The most general application of MANOVA consists of cases in which not all of the parameters are estimable. To cope with this situation, the investigator reconstructs the original model, substituting linear combinations of the effects of primary interest (which are each uniquely estimable) for the original parameters. Any linear combination of the original parameters (of a given kind) whose coefficients sum to zero is referred to as a contrast. That is, contrasts are the linear combinations which are substituted for the original parameters (Bock & Haggard, 1968).

The decision one makes about what linear combinations to estimate is crucial, for it is the contrasts that are estimated and tested for significance, not the original parameters themselves. There are only two restrictions placed on the construction of a contrast matrix. The number to be estimated cannot exceed the degrees of freedom in the model, and the coefficients for each estimate must sum to zero. The researcher has the option of testing for significance either the single contrasts individually or all the contrasts of a given sort (described in the following) collectively. Unless a corresponding reduction is made in α, the critical p value, the significance testing of single contrasts individually can lead to unrecognized increases in the overall error rate.

Finn (1974) has described four types of contrasts frequently employed by behavioral scientists to compare sets of means in experimental designs. These are *deviation contrasts*, in which each of the $k - 1$ parameters, k_j, is compared with k, the general mean of all k_j; *simple contrasts*, in which each of the $k - 1$ parameters is compared to a control or comparison group; *Helmert contrasts*, in which each $k - 1$ group effect is contrasted with the mean of succeeding group effects, in a stepwise order; and *orthogonal polynomial contrasts*, in which group means are examined to determine whether a polynomial function underlies their relationship to the independent variable.

Suppose, for example, that an investigator were interested in estimating the optimal amount of fear arousal to use in a persuasive message about the dangers of cigarette smoking. The investigator designs an experiment in which four randomly assigned groups of subjects are exposed to a persuasive message about cigarette smoking. Each group of subjects hears a slightly different message. Group 1, the control group, listens to a standard message without any fear arousing stimuli. Group 2 receives a similar message with a low fear appeal. Group 3 gets a message with a moderate fear appeal. And Group 4 hears a message, similar to the others, but with a strong fear appeal. The investigator collects post-test scores on a multidimensional measure of attitudes toward cigarette smoking from the subjects in all four groups (all of the subjects are heavy cigarette smokers who have smoked for at least 10 years).

The investigator now has several options available for comparing the four groups. For example, he may want to determine whether any of the three arousal conditions (Groups 2–4) was more effective than the average effectiveness of all the messages combined. This test could be accomplished by utilizing *deviation* contrasts. The general mean for all of the N subjects, k, would be contrasted against the mean of Group 2 (low fear arousal), Group 3 (moderate fear arousal), and Group 4 (strong fear arousal), as follows:

Deviation contrasts[a]
k − Group 2 (low fear arousal)
k − Group 3 (moderate fear arousal)
k − Group 4 (strong fear arousal)

[a]k = the general mean for all subjects tested.

A second option available to the investigator would be to employ *simple* contrasts in order to determine whether each (or any) of the fear arousal conditions provided a significant gain in effectiveness over the control group (Group 1). The means for each of the three arousal conditions would be contrasted against the mean for the control group in the following manner:

Simple contrasts
No fear arousal − low fear arousal
No fear arousal − moderate fear arousal
No fear arousal − strong fear arousal

A third option would be to compare each effect with the average of those which precede it. This approach would provide a test of the hypothesis that linear increases of fear appeal progressively enhance the persuasiveness of the message. Contrasts of this sort are referred to as Helmert contrasts. For our example, these would be described as follows:

Helmert contrasts	
No fear arousal −	low fear arousal
Average of no fear arousal and low fear arousal −	moderate fear arousal
Average of no fear arousal, low fear arousal, and moderate fear arousal −	strong fear arousal

Although a thorough treatment of how to construct and interpret contrast matrices would be desirable, we have only enough space to stress two important points about the choice of contrasts. First, contrasts must be chosen on the basis of the research design and hypotheses. Since the contrasts must be chosen in advance of the data analysis, careful thought must be given to the available options. For many research problems, either simple or deviation contrasts will be appropriate. When there is a clear theoretical ordering to the treatment groups, such as in repeated measures designs or longitudinal research, Helmert or polynomial contrasts may be more beneficial. Second, the choice of contrasts determines what is to be tested by the significance tests. The number and nature of the contrasts affects the calculation of the estimates; different contrasts produce different estimates, and the deletion or addition of contrasts changes the remaining estimates. A more advanced and detailed consideration of contrasts may be found in the text by Finn (1974) and the articles by Bock & Haggard (1968) and Pruzek (1971).

V. MANOVA TEST CRITERIA

As a statistical technique, analysis of variance is generally understood as a method for dividing the variation observed in a single dependent variable into different parts, each part being identified as a *source of variance*. The magnitude of variation due to each source is tested to determine whether it accounts for more variation than expected under the null hypothesis. Variance is defined as the square of the standard deviation of a variable X. Analysis of variance partitions variance by dividing the sum of squares, $\Sigma(x - \bar{x})^2$, into additive parts. Once separated from the other parts, each source of variance can be tested for its unique contribution to criterion variance.

The most popular means of testing the significance of independent sources of variance is the univariate F-test. Originally developed by R. A. Fisher for the analysis of experiments in the field of agriculture, the F-test is most commonly applied to test the null hypothesis of equal group means against the most general alternative, inequality of group means. The F-test reveals only an overall relationship among the treatment means with respect to the dependent variable. The means are either equal or unequal; no other inferences are appropriate.

Multivariate analysis of variance extends the concept of dividing up variance for a single dependent variable to that of partitioning variance for a group of dependent variables. For every step in statistically dividing up the variance for a univariate analysis of variance, there is a corresponding step in MANOVA. MANOVA begins with a matrix product of a score vector and its transpose. The score vectors are used to compute sums of squares and cross-products matrices for each source of variance—total, main effects, interactions, and within cells—involved in the testing of a given model.

The computational steps involved in dividing up the sources of variance for MANOVA are cumbersome and difficult to explain to students lacking substantial mathematical preparation. Since our objective in this chapter is to stress the logic and pragmatic principles of MANOVA in order to facilitate greater understanding of its uses, we will not pursue an explanation or description of these calculations any further. Readers interested in a more formal presentation of the computational algorithms associated with MANOVA may consult any of an increasing number of multivariate analysis texts for this information (see, e.g., Bock, 1975; Cooley & Lohnes, 1971; Finn, 1974; Morrison, 1967; Overall & Klett, 1972; Tatsuoka, 1971, Timm, 1975). With the widespread availability of high speed electronic computers and canned computer programs, it is unlikely that many of us will ever be called on to actually calculate these matrices by hand. Moreover, a firm grasp of how to interpret tests of multivariate hypotheses is far more crucial to the practically minded researcher struggling to understand perplexing data than is the capacity to actually compute these statistics. We believe it is possible to be a user without being a doer. (Being a doer without being a user would be worst of all.)

In the experimental sense of contrasting group differences, analysis of variance involves a test for the effect of k treatments. The means of a number of different treatments are tested for departure from the null hypothesis of no differences. When the data include only one score from each subject, the difference among means can vary in only one dimension. Then the means for different conditions can be plotted on a single line, since any inequality among the means must be restricted to one dimension—the single line.

Such simplicity is not possible when the data reflect multiple responses for each subject. In the special case of MANOVA, the null hypothesis is that no differences exist among treatment mean *vectors*, each vector containing the p means for one of the treatment groups. If the null hypothesis cannot be accepted, then the treatment mean vectors are considered unequal, but this inequality need not be confined to one dimension except when $k = 2$. The multivariate measurement space involves s dimensions, s being equal to the lesser of p (the number of response variables) and degrees of freedom for the hypothesis $(k - 1)$. Thus, in a three-degrees-of-freedom test for a main effect involving four treatment groups and four response variates, there would be three orthogonal dimensions in the measurement space; i.e., three independent dimensions. Differences among the population means may occur in any or all of these dimensions.

We have raised the issue of dimensionality because each of the MANOVA test statistics assess group differences by applying different criteria to the multivariate measurement space (see, e.g., Olson, 1976, p. 580). Unlike univariate analysis of variance, which provides an invariant F-test for differences among group means, different MANOVA test statistics may produce conflicting results about statistical significance when applied to the same data.

The four MANOVA test criteria most commonly used for significance testing are (1) Roy's largest root, R (Roy, 1953); (2) Hotelling's trace, T (Hotelling, 1951); (3) Wilks' likelihood ratio, W (Wilks, 1932); and (4) Pillai–Bartlett's trace, V (Bartlett, 1939; Pillai, 1955). All of these tests operate under the same set of assumptions as univariate F-tests, translated to the multivariate case: the additive linear model with independently sampled errors from a multivariate normal population with a common covariance matrix. Each of these tests assesses the s dimensions in the multivariate measurement space, but each conceptualizes the s dimensions in a slightly different manner.

The four criteria test different functions of the *eigenvalues*, the values of the characteristic roots associated with the sum of squares and cross-products matrices being tested. Roy's largest root defines a single eigenvalue reflecting maximum between-group variability relative to within-group variability. Hotelling's trace sums the roots; Wilks' likelihood ratio multiplies the roots, placing a restriction on the boundaries of their values; and Pillai–Bartlett also places a restriction on the range of eigenvalues, but sums rather than multiplies them.

Given these differences among the test criteria, a choice of a test statistic for a particular study can be a complicated and important matter. Olson, on the basis of a thorough consideration of each test's power and robustness, recommends Pillai–Bartlett over the others (Olson, 1976). Among the four criteria studied, Pillai–Bartlett withstood moderate departures from normality and homogeneity of variance the best, without sacrificing the power to detect differences (Olson, 1976). According to Olson, when large samples are utilized, V, W, and T are approximately equal in power. R should be avoided whenever possible: " . . . the largest root R is apt to be both wasteful of information and susceptible to substantial distortion due to a single deviant eigenvalue" [Olson, 1976, p. 583].

VI. NONORTHOGONAL ANALYSIS OF VARIANCE

In this section, we address the problem of selecting a data analysis strategy appropriate for testing specific research hypotheses by means of analysis of variance. When there are an equal number of observations in each of the treatment subclasses of the research design, the analysis-of-variance results will be identical no matter which of the least squares regression methods to be described is chosen. Designs in which there are equal numbers of subjects in each treatment are called balanced or orthogonal designs. These designs are referred to as orthogonal because the correlation among the estimates of the classification parameters—main effects and interactions—would be exactly zero if within-cell variances were in fact equal. Thus, the test of each parameter is unaffected by the tests of the other parameters in the model except when they share the same error term. Conversely, research designs which permit unequal or disproportionate numbers of observations in the treatment subclasses are called *unbalanced* or *nonorthogonal designs* because tests of the parameters are not independent of one another. The consequence of unequal frequencies is nonzero correlation among the estimates of the classification parameters, even when within-cell variances are equal. Unlike orthogonal cases, nonorthogonal research designs provide a special problem for the data analyst.

For many years, the conventional wisdom on analysis of variance was to insist upon balanced designs. As Bock (1975) has advised, "If possible, equal numbers of units should be assigned to each treatment," [Chapter 5, p. 6]. And, Timm (1975), viewing the problem from a statistical vantage point, concurs: "Due to the complexities in analyzing nonorthogonal designs generally, the best solution to the problem is not to have unequal N_{ij}'s . . . " [p. 526]. On the other hand, it is sometimes impossible or undesirable to strictly control the number of observations in each treatment group. Many research problems simply do not permit random assignment of subjects to classes, and randomization itself cannot guarantee an equal number of observations in each cell of the research design. Even when randomization is possible, there are many occasions when it is more realistic to assume that frequencies among classification groups will be unbalanced.[4]

Many researchers have handled the problems imposed by nonorthogonality by randomly eliminating cases in certain treatment groups until all the cell frequencies are equal, thereby transforming a nonorthogonal design into an orthogonal one. However, certain least squares procedures (Method 1, which follows) will provide exactly the same analysis-of-variance results for nonorthogonal data that would be produced *for the same problem* if the data were orthogonal (see, e.g., Overall, Spiegal, & Cohen, 1975; Woodward & Overall, 1975, p. 31). More importantly, the artificially balanced design produced by eliminating cases, randomly or otherwise, will generally have lower power to detect statistical differences than the identical nonorthogonal analysis of variance with greater total N. Clearly, there is little to recommend the

---

[4]In any of these cases, it is very important for the researcher to understand, *before data analysis begins*, exactly what, if anything, has been assigned at random. If subjects come in bundles, and only bundles are assigned at random (for example, intact classrooms assigned at random, but as a whole, to experimental conditions), then conventional statistical analyses, e.g., analysis of variance, should stop at the bundle level, at least so far as significance is concerned, for variability appearing *within* bundles will be biased downward in comparison with a proper error term.

practice of artificially balancing designs. Instead, researchers need to recognize that several different methods are available for analyzing nonorthogonal data, each method being appropriate only for certain research problems.

Least squares regression methods provide the most general and flexible approach for handling analysis of variance problems. Under certain conditions (to be described), general least squares methods will produce results identical to those derived from the classical computations for conventional experimental design models. Least squares methods have the additional capacity to test hypotheses that are ordinarily untestable by conventional analysis of variance (for example, Method 3 below). However, the flexibility of general least squares methods places a heavier burden on the data analyst. There are now several different types of analysis to choose from, and each type of analysis may produce different results. The researcher must, therefore, know in advance exactly what hypotheses are to be tested.

The first step in applying general least squares methods to the analysis of classification data is to construct a design matrix. Overall and Klett have developed a useful set of procedures, termed *effects coding*, for constructing the design matrix (Overall & Klett, 1972). A dummy variate, 1, 0, -1, code is used to identify each subject's treatment classifications and interactions. A 1 signifies that the subject is a member of that treatment or interaction class; a 0 means he is not a member, and a -1 code means he is a member of the class left out of the design matrix. The -1 code must be used because of the normal restriction that only $a - 1$ and $b - 1$ degrees of freedom are available for estimating main effects, A and B, etc. An extended example of effects coding for a factorial design problem is given by Overall and Klett (1972, pp. 444–447; for a more detailed treatment of dummy and effect coding see Cohen & Cohen, 1975, pp. 173–176, 188–195, and Kerlinger & Pedhazur, 1973, pp. 116–153).

Once the design matrix has been constructed, the data are ready to be analyzed by the appropriate least squares method. When the design is completely balanced, each method described below will produce exactly the same results. But when the design is nonorthogonal, correlation among the classification variables will be introduced and, consequently, different methods of analysis will produce different results. In the next section, we consider three general methods for analyzing nonorthogonal data from factorial studies.

A. Method 1

Method 1 is referred to as the *general linear model* or *regression* method. A conventional multiple regression solution is provided for all of the effects in the model simultaneously, each effect being adjusted for *all* other effects in the model. This method is sometimes called the full linear-model analysis, because main effects and interactions are treated equally, each effect being adjusted for all of the others. For example, in an $A \times B$ factorial arrangement, the A effect is estimated by adjusting for the B and AB interaction; the B effect is estimated by adjusting for the A and AB interaction; and the AB interaction is estimated by adjusting for the A and B main effects. Although Method 1 is commonly associated with a regression rather than a classical experimental design approach, Overall, Spiegal, and Cohen (1975) have demonstrated that for nonorthogonal cases Method 1 constitutes the closest analog to conventional analysis-of-variance for balanced factorial designs. *Only Method 1 provides a fully simultaneous analysis of both main effects and interactions.* Woodward and Overall (1975) have developed a computer program to accomplish Method 1 analyses for multivariate problems, i.e., when multiple response variates are utilized.

B. Method 2

Method 2 is referred to as the *classical experimental design* approach. This method provides a test for the additive "main class" model, with interaction effects tested only for the purpose of protecting against violations of the additivity assumption. Each main effect is estimated by adjusting for all other main effects, but interactions are disregarded. Interactions, on the other hand, are tested by adjusting for *all* other terms in the model, main effects and interactions. In the case of an $A \times B$ factorial design, the estimate of A is adjusted only for B, and the estimate of B is adjusted only for A; however, the test for AB interaction is adjusted for *both* A and B. In more complicated designs, the rules are similar but have to be more detailed. Methods 1 and 2 produce exactly the same estimates for interactions, but the manner in which main effects are estimated is clearly different for the two methods. It is important to understand that Method 2 tests main class hypotheses that are considerably different from the fully simultaneous tests provided by Method 1. The SPSS multiple-classification analysis program contains a default option which causes the program to execute a Method 2 analysis for univariate problems. A computer program reported in Overall and Klett (1972) may be used to produce a Method 2 multivariate analysis in a single run through the computer. Finn's multivariance program (Finn, 1974) may also be used to accomplish a Method 2 MANOVA, but it is somewhat more complicated to use and is more appropriate for Method 3 problems.

C. Method 3

Method 3 is referred to as a *hierarchical* method. Hypotheses are tested in sequence. The first hypothesis is tested as if it stood alone, all other effects being ignored. Then, the second hypothesis is tested, adjusting only for the effect which preceded it. Tests of successive main effects and interactions are carried out by adjusting each effect for all other effects which precede it in the testing order. The model specified by the investigator determines the order in which effects are tested. The notion of order is central to the analysis strategy of Method 3, since each effect is adjusted *only* for the effects which precede it. For example, in an $A \times B$ factorial design in which an investigator specifies an A, B, AB ordering of effects, the A effect would be estimated first, ignoring B and AB; B would be estimated next, adjusting for A but ignoring AB; AB would be estimated last, adjusting for both A and B. Like other stepwise statistical procedures, Method 3 provides a test for the idiosyncratic significance of each effect, above and beyond the ones which are tested before it. Finn's MULTIVARIANCE favors a Method 3 approach, but permits tinkering with the order of effects, i.e., reordering the parameters. When the researcher decides in advance to apply Method 3 to several different orders, with significance demanded in every order, Method 3 becomes the most rigorous approach to significance testing, since effects ordered last will be significant only if they *add* something substantial to the explanation of criterion variation. Significance in each order can be appropriately required as a criterion for determining nonzero parameters. However, the converse of this rule should not be used to delete terms from the model, since significance in any order is likely to be quite adequate evidence for retention.

D. Choosing a Method

The essential differences among the three types of nonorthogonal analysis of variance are shown in Table I. Knowing which method to choose for a particular case is indeed a knotty problem. Although statisticians have frequently debated the matter, the debates have been restricted largely to the issue of similarity between orthogonal and nonorthogonal solutions for experimental cases (see e.g., Appelbaum & Cramer, 1974; Gocka, 1973; O'Brien, 1976; Overall *et al.*, 1975; Rawlings, 1972). And even for this limiting case no consensus has been achieved. Hence, the general advice, "choose the method most desirable for your problem," may not be very helpful. Yet, a choice must be made, and the importance of the choice must not be underestimated, since interpretation depends largely on the method employed.

TABLE I

EFFECTS ADJUSTED FOR IN THE APPLICATION OF THREE METHODS OF NONORTHOGONAL ANOV IN THE $A \times B$ FACTORIAL CASE

Effects assessed	Method 1 Regression	Method 2 Classical	Method 3 Hierarchical
A main effect	B, AB	B	None
B main effect	A, AB	A	A
AB interaction	A, B	A, B	A, B

On partly empirical, but largely logical, grounds we offer the following advice. First, when the data have been generated through an experimental strategy that could conceivably have produced a balanced distribution of cases among the treatment subclasses *and* there is no priority given to any one or set of effects over others, use Method 1. Overall and his colleagues (1975) have shown that only Method 1 yields parameter estimates that are equivalent in the nonorthogonal case to conventional ANOVA solutions for balanced factorial designs. If any of the interactions are significant, suitable caution should be exercised in the interpretation of main effects.

Second, though many statisticians tend to favor the clarity and elegance provided by Method 2, there is, in our opinion, little empirical or logical justification for the wide application of this method in the realm of social and behavioral research. We can think of very few research situations in which it is appropriate to assume on an a priori basis that no true interactions exist. Social phenomena are almost always influenced by interactions among two or more independent variables. Indeed, one of the most important clashes in the history of social psychology has been prompted by the recognition, among many of the leading American social psychologists, that main effects have not proven to be constant across social contexts—an insight that has led to a crisis of confidence in both the prevailing research methods and the knowledge existent in the field (see, e.g., Cronbach, 1975; Gergen, 1973, 1976). Given the prevailing evidence in support of pervasive interaction effects, we can see little reason to recommend Method 2.

Third, Method 3 is appropriate whenever a researcher can assign a theoretical or pragmatic priority to effects. Hypotheses tested under this type of analysis are not ordinarily equivalent to those tested by conventional analysis of variance for orthogonal designs with the same independent variables and should not usually be interpreted as if they were. If a theory stipulates a temporal, progressive (developmental), or hierarchical ordering to the effects, Method 3 may constitute the best way to test the theory. In established research domains, investigators may be interested in improving the capacity to predict outcomes; thus the critical variables hypothesized to enhance prediction would be tested last, to determine whether they add something unique to criterion prediction over and above the established predictors. One advantage to a Method 3 analysis is that it reduces the possibility that theoretically less important effects will cancel out the more important ones, since the effects are assigned importance, i.e., ordered by priority, before testing begins (Overall & Klett, 1972). There is nothing inherently wrong with utilizing a Method 3 approach to test the significance of parameters in several different orderings provided that the risk of compounding statistical error rates beyond the nominal level is taken into account, e.g., as one alternative to this problem, by adjusting the experimentwise type 1 error rate to incorporate different α levels for each test of significance within each different ordering of the parameters. If Method 3 analyses of different orders lead to more than trivially different results (recall that we consider the difference between $p < 4\%$ and $p < 6\%$ to be trivial), then the only appropriate conclusion is that the data *alone* do not provide an adequate basis for deciding whether a certain part, or all, of the effect should be attributed to one independent variable rather than another. In the presence of such results, the investigator is obligated to identify the difficulty of interpreting such results before allowing any theoretical predispositions he may hold to dictate the importance of one independent variable over any other(s).

E. A Data Analytic Example

In this section, we present a hypothetical example designed to highlight some of the major characteristics of nonorthogonal MANOVA. The data for this problem were originally presented by Woodward and Overall (1975, p. 27) to illustrate the application of multiple regression methods to MANOVA problems. We have taken the liberty to relabel Woodward and Overall's independent and response variables to conform to our own interest in marital communication research.

The simulated research problem involved the study of two types of marital couples, *conflict avoiders and conflict engagers*, in two types of simulated conflict situations. The two types of couples were randomly assigned to the two different experimental situations. In the first condition, couples were asked to act out a disagreement involving a difference of opinion about what television program to watch on a Monday evening at 9:00 P.M.—Monday Night Football or an educational special on sex role socialization of young children. This condition was referred to as the *low relational threat treatment*. In the other experimental condition, couples were asked to role play a more emotional conflict episode in which the male, who has been growing increasingly detached from his wife, is confronted by his spouse, who desperately yearns for his affection. This situation was labeled the *high relational threat treatment*.

The videotaped interactions for each of the couples in each of the experimental treatments were observed by trained raters who made interval-scaled judgments about the degree of cognitive/rational, rejection, and emotional communication involved in each one minute segment for each couple. These three scales constituted the dependent variables for this study.

Table II shows a factorial display of the observed cell means and n per cell for each of the three dependent variables in each of the four subclasses. The crucial hypothesis of the research was whether the type of couple would explain variation in the multivariate vector of communication responses—cognitive, rejection, emotional—above and beyond what could be explained by the type of conflict episode—high or low threat. A nonorthogonal design of this type does not permit the unbiased testing of both main effects simultaneously, because the sums of squares obtained for the two independent variables are not independent.

TABLE II

FACTORIAL DESIGN DISPLAY FOR EXAMPLE PROBLEM

Type of couple	Communication measures	Type of conflict episode		High threat –low threat
		High threat	Low threat	
Avoiders	Cog. style	20.12	21.52	1.40
	Rejection	22.40	21.89	– .51
	Emotional	28.46	27.44	– 1.02
		$n = 16$	$n = 10$	
Engagers	Cog. style	17.61	19.46	1.85
	Rejection	23.07	21.26	– 1.81
	Emotional	29.80	28.31	– 1.49
		$n = 7$	$n = 11$	
Avoiders– A–E engagers	Cog. style	2.51	2.06	
	Rejection	– .67	.65	
	Emotional	– 1.34	– .87	

A Method 3 stepwise nonorthogonal solution was applied to the data, the main effect for marital type being entered *after* the main effect for conflict episode. Simple one-degree-of-freedom tests, c-contrasts, were planned for each of the estimable effects. One contrast was stipulated for each estimable term in the model. Not all of the between-group degrees of freedom can be utilized, since one contrast must be reserved for the "general mean" term, in order for the estimated linear parametric functions to produce least squares estimates for each treatment group in the design (Bock & Haggard, 1968, p. 115). The contrasts stipulated for the present analysis were (1) general mean; (2) high threat–low threat; (3) avoiders–engagers; and (4) threat-by-avoiders interaction (one degree of freedom only). These contrasts were necessary for the significance testing of the full model. However, it may be desirable to drop some parameters that do not produce significant differences from the model after significance testing in order to produce "better" estimates of the cell means for the reduced model, provided that the consequent change in meaning of the fitted parameters is carefully considered at the end. Most problems run in conjunction with this algorithm ordinarily require two passes through the computer, one for parameter estimation and significance testing, the other for reestimation of the nonzero parameters.

For the sample problem, effects were tested in the order stipulated by the contrast vectors: (1) general mean; (2) threat, eliminating general mean; (3) marital type, eliminating general mean and threat; (4) threat × marital type, eliminating threat, marital type, and general mean.

Of course, there are many occasions when there simply is no theoretical or logical basis for ordering effects in the model. When more than one main effect is of interest, contrasts must be reordered so that tests which are not confounded by the other parameters may be calculated (Finn, 1974, p. 326). For example, we may want to estimate and test for significance the threat treatment after concluding that the marital type effect is nonzero. To do so, we must reorder the contrast vectors, placing the threat parameter *after* the test for marital type. By reordering the contrasts in this manner, we should produce a test of the threat condition, eliminating the significant marital type parameter. Unless the analysis is carried out for two different orderings of the main effects, we cannot determine the "unbiased" effect of each (Finn, 1974, p. 326). When nonorthogonal designs are employed, one must give careful consideration to the initial ordering of effects, as well as to the total number of effects to be tested. The more often effects are reordered for significance testing, the more likely it is that type 1 error rates will be excessively inflated beyond their nominal values for some of the tests, when significance in any *one* order at the nominal level is used as the standard of judgment. If one wishes to test the parameters in several orders, it is probably best to require significance at the nominal level in each order tried or to divide the nominal level by the number of orders tested and establish that figure as the standard of judgment, significance in any one order at that level being considered sufficient.

Table III shows the multivariate-analysis-of-variance summary table for the original ordering of effects. The significance tests are interpreted in the reverse order of computation, i.e., the last test is interpreted first and so on. Interpretation of the parameters continues until a significant F value (or latent root value) is encountered. Once a significant F is found, testing usually stops, since further tests would be difficult to interpret in the presence of significant parameters of a more complex nature, e.g., main effects in the presence of interactions. This procedure is governed by the logic of Method 3 analysis. One may, as previously noted, reorder the parameters, eliminating

TABLE III

MULTIVARIATE ANALYSIS OF VARIANCE SUMMARY TABLE FOR EXAMPLE PROBLEM

Source	df	Latent roots, λ	Test, F	p
Constant	1	—	—	—
Episodes, eliminating constant	1	1.60	20.38	.0001
Marital type, eliminating constant and episodes	1	3.93	49.75	.0001
Episodes × marital type, eliminating constant, episodes, and marital type	1	.27	3.40	.03
Within (residual)	40	—	—	—

those of a higher order found to be significant, in order to obtain "valid" tests of lower order effects (see Finn, 1974, pp. 324–326, for further elaboration of this point).

The inspection of the results begins with the test for an episodes × marital type interaction. Finding this term significant (Table III), we would stop testing and attempt to interpret the interaction. Significant interactions do not invalidate main effects, but they do complicate interpretations (see, e.g., Scheffé, 1959, p. 110).

For the sake of example, let us assume that the interaction term was not significant. We could, of course, argue that the results justify proceeding to the tests for main effects because of the marginal magnitude of the interaction effect ($p < .03$). Compared to the multivariate F for the main effects, the value of the interaction parameter is not very large.

The results reported in Table III show a sizable effect for the "unbiased" test of marital type. If we were committed to a Method 3 analysis, we would probably stop here and interpret the differences among the marital type groups.

Assume for the sake of example that we are also interested in obtaining an unbiased test of the episodes effect. Table IV shows the results of the multivariate analysis of variance when the episode parameter is reordered *behind* the marital type parameter. We can see from these analyses that the correct—that is unbiased—tests for the two main effects produce highly significant results and that the unbiased tests are substantially different from the biased ones.

Just how strong are these effects? Assuming a nonsignificant interaction parameter, one convenient way to assess the magnitude of the main effects is to reestimate the contrasts, using only the nonzero main effects parameters (and thus somewhat redefining them). The null interaction parameter is omitted from the model and new estimates are computed for the remaining terms in the model.

TABLE IV

MULTIVARIATE ANALYSIS OF VARIANCE FOR REORDERING OF MAIN EFFECTS

Source	df	Latent roots, λ	Test, F	p
Constant	1	—	—	—
Marital type, eliminating constant	1	2.96	37.49	.0001
Episodes, eliminating constant and marital type	1	2.58	32.64	.0001
Within (residual)	40	—	—	—

TABLE V

LEAST SQUARES ESTIMATES OF EFFECTS AND STANDARD ERRORS FOR ESTIMATES OF
SUBGROUP MEAN VECTORS

Contrast	Dependent variable		
	Cognitive style	Rejection	Emotional
High threat–low threat	− 1.58 (.25)	1.05 (.24)	1.21 (.35)
Avoiders–engagers	2.28 (.25)	− .01 (.24)	− 1.09 (.35)

Table V shows the least squares estimates and standard errors of these estimates (in parentheses) for the contrasts of interest. From these results, we can see that relative to their standard errors the largest differences are between high and low threat episodes for cognitive acts (-1.58) and between avoiders and engagers (2.28), also for cognitive acts. Apparently low threat episodes produce more cognitive acts, especially for conflict avoiders who are more predisposed toward cognitive than emotional interaction. There is also a sizeable difference between high and low threat episodes for rejecting acts (1.05). As we might expect, assuming the absence of a nonzero interaction, the higher the threat, the greater the potential for rejecting messages. (Recall that the data being interpreted are synthetic, not real.) In the next section, we consider other procedures for interpreting between-group hypotheses for MANOVA problems.

VII. INTERPRETING SIGNIFICANT DIFFERENCES

One advantage of MANOVA is its capacity to examine simultaneously the influence of one or more independent variables on a *set* of response variables. When the mutivariate test criterion exceeds the critical value of alpha, the researcher can conclude that a nonchance relationship exists between the independent and response variables and that there exists at least one linear combination of responses which significantly discriminates among the k treatments. But researchers are seldom interested only in making global statements of this sort. Most research calls for a much richer and more detailed analysis than that provided by an overall MANOVA test for the equality of mean vectors. Of primary concern are such questions as (1) What dimensions underlie the overall relationship between the independent and response variables? (2) Which linear combinations of response variables account for maximal separation of the treatment groups? (3) Can any of these response variables be eliminated from future work with these treatment groups? (4) How important is each variable or set of variables for each of the treatment groups, e.g., how much variance is accounted for by each of the elementary responses and/or q linear combinations? We usually want to know the nature and quantity of the relationships among groups and responses and the part each group and/or variable plays in these relationships.

To probe these questions, researchers may choose from a variety of available techniques, each of which is helpful for interpreting a particular type of between-group hypothesis. In this section, we describe the application of some of the statistical techniques which may be employed to help interpret differences among groups.

A. Univariate F-Tests

Embedded within each multivariate analysis of variance are p univariate analyses of variance or, if q linear combinations of responses have been chosen, $p + q$ univariate analyses of variance, one for each elementary response and one for each chosen linear combination. The values of these univariate F-tests may be used to reveal the direction and magnitude of each category's influence on each dependent variable (Finn, 1974, pp. 320–321; Wilkinson, 1975). Although these univariate F-tests do seem to provide a certain ease of interpretation, they also tend to reduce a complex multivariate problem to a series of simpler univariate ones. By examining dependent variables as if they were uncorrelated, i.e., without adjusting statistical decision rates, the researcher tacitly assumes that the univariate F value for each variable is unrelated to the F values of the others. (For an alternative interpretation and solution to this problem see Chapter 16, Section xx.) When there are more than two or three variates, this strategy is likely to compound decision errors and lead to conclusions which will not be replicated.

A researcher interested in assessing the importance of each dependent variable without assigning an order of priority to these variables can protect against inflated error rates by setting a critical level of $5\%/p$ for each univariate F-test. For example, with 5 dependent variables the critical level for each test would be set at .01 ($5\%/5$); with 10 response measures, alpha would be .002 ($5\%/10$ for each test). In this manner, one can retain the simplicity of a univariate analysis without excessively compounding error rates. And if it is desired to include q linear combinations of the responses, as well as the p elementary responses, it is only necessary to divide by $p + q$ instead of by p.

B. Step-down F Analysis

In step-down F analysis, the researcher begins by stipulating an a priori ordering of the dependent variables. The contribution of each dependent variable is then tested for contribution to between-group differences, by eliminating variates which precede it in the established order. Thus, the order in which the variates are tested makes a difference, both in the outcome and interpretation of results. One would not choose to do step-down analysis unless the response variates could be logically ordered, e.g., by complexity (simple to complex) or by time (first to last).

By computing step-down F values, the researcher can detect whether most of the between-group variation is concentrated in the earlier simple measures, or whether more complex measures are needed to explain the differences among groups. Although each dependent variable is interpreted separately, step-down analysis is clearly a multivariate technique, since the F values are calculated by taking into account the correlations among several or all of them, after the first. Finn (1974, pp. 322–323) and Stevens (1972, pp. 503–506) have described the computation and interpretation of step-down F(s) in detail. One important suggestion, offered by Stevens (1972, p. 505), is that researchers should report the amount of variance in each of the dependent variables accounted for by the classification variable. For the step-down procedure, this statistic is a variant of the univariate measure of association, η^2 $[\eta_i^2 = \mathrm{df_b}F_i/(\mathrm{df_b}F_i + \mathrm{df_w})]$, where $\mathrm{df_b}$ stands for degrees of freedom between groups and $\mathrm{df_w}$ stands for degrees of freedom within groups. This statistic should always be included in the summary of results.

C. Discriminant Analysis

Discriminant analysis is a mathematical maximization procedure which defines the major differences among the classification variables as orthogonal dimensions that do the best job of separating the groups. In discriminant analysis, differences among the classes are characterized as weighted linear combinations of the entire set of dependent variables that have the mathematical property of maximally dividing the groups (see Chapter 6). Each discriminant function identified is uncorrelated with the other discriminant functions (in the particular set of data at hand). The number of discriminant functions is defined as the lesser of $k - 1$, one less than the number of groups, or p, the number of dependent variables. For example, with five groups and six dependent variables, four discriminant functions could be identified. The first function would be the single weighted composite of dependent variables that provides maximal variation between groups relative to variation within groups. Successive discriminant functions also provide maximum separation between groups relative to within groups and all correlations among the functions are exactly zero (see Overall & Klett, 1972).

Interpreting a discriminant analysis is no simple matter. Of primary importance are the standardized coefficients or weights assigned to each variate on each discriminant function. To interpret these weights, the researcher must examine both the sign and the magnitude of the weight. Variables with the same algebraic sign may perhaps be interpreted as defining a cluster for a given discriminant. The sign merely indicates which variables go together on the discriminant of interest. The magnitude of the standardized coefficients must also be taken into account. There are no exact guidelines about how large a coefficient should be to warrant serious interpretive consideration. It is safe to assume, however, that the absolute magnitude of a coefficient reveals something of the importance of that variate for separating the groups *on that discriminant*.

An alternative way to interpret the discriminant function coefficient is through the use of the canonical structure matrix (Porebski, 1966). This matrix reveals the correlation of each dependent variable with the discriminant being considered. The variables with the highest correlations are the most responsible for the between-group differences.

As another interpretive aid, we have found it useful in our own research to compute and graph each group's centroid (weighted mean) on each significant discriminant function. Others have suggested graphing the variable–discriminant function correlations (Andrews, 1972; Mulaik, 1972; Stevens, 1972; Van der Geer, 1971). Such pictorial representations often illuminate the meaning of the functions for the groups involved in the research.

Difficulties do arise when the discriminant function strategy is adopted, primarily because the coefficients must be interpreted with the same caution necessary for regression coefficients. A number of chapters in this volume discuss the difficulties that are encountered when interpreting regression coefficients (see, e.g., chapters 2–4 and 6).

D. Simultaneous Confidence Tests

The simultaneous interval method may be used to determine and test confidence regions for point estimates. Like its analog in univariate analysis, the Scheffé procedure, this test applies a constant alpha probability level to all linear contrasts of the treatment groups. Since the probability level is invariant for all comparisons, the test lacks power (Hummel & Sligo, 1971; Wilkinson, 1975). Examples of this procedure may be found in the unpublished work of Di Salvo (1970) and Bochner (1971). Confidence regions that some authorities consider much more likely to be useful can be based upon the parallel univariate analyses at $5\%/p$ or $5\%/(p + q)$ already hinted at, particularly if studentized-range procedures are used in place of F-tests in each of the p or $p + q$ univariate analyses.

VIII. SUMMARY AND CONCLUSIONS

We have touched upon a number of important issues associated with the application of MANOVA to communication research. By encompassing all the data in one analysis, multivariate analysis of variance may (but will not always) provide a clear and organized account of a very complex piece of research. Rather than computing significance levels for each response variable separately, MANOVA produces one probability statement for the entire set of dependent variables. The researcher is thereby protected from being misled by partial results. MANOVA is not, however, the only acceptable way to handle conventional research problems when the data involve multiple responses. Some scholars are convinced that adjusting univariate decision rates to $5\%/p$ or $5\%/(p + q)$ offers adequate protection as well.

We conclude our presentation by underscoring the following points:

(1) MANOVA is just as appropriate for the analysis of nonexperimental data as it is for the analysis of experimental data. Social scientists are turning away from the traditional preoccupation with fixed-condition experiments. One consequence of this trend is a more active consideration of nonexperimental conditions under which one can make strong and legitimate generalizations about causal connections between independent variables and responses. Strict lines are sometimes drawn between analysis of variance and regression as research models. Under the general linear model, however, these divisions are seen as arbitrary and largely unnecessary. For example, Model 1 analysis of variance is merely a special case of general linear regression analysis.

(2) The widespread availability of computer programs for multivariate analysis now makes it possible to study a large number of variables without giving much prior thought to the selection of independent and dependent variables. But, as any experienced multivariate data analyst will tell you, "garbage in; garbage out!" Multivariate research can neither be planned nor interpreted without using your head. The more complex the research and analysis, the more important it is to have some advance notion about what one wants most to find out and what one expects to happen. There is no substitute for a carefully conceived hypothesis or a compelling theory. Unless the dependent variables form some conceptually meaningful set, any analysis of multivariate data will more likely confuse than inform the researcher about the meaning of data.

(3) MANOVA is best thought of as a means of testing formal models. The interpretation of results should therefore emphasize the extent to which data fit or do not fit the hypothesized model. Models should be taken for what they are—tools to assist data exploration—and nothing more. Researchers should guard against the ever present danger of hypostatizing their models and thereby impoverishing opportunities for insight and understanding.

(4) MANOVA proceeds in three distinct stages: estimation, significance testing, and reestimation. Preoccupation with significance testing should not be permitted to persist. Estimation should be given more attention than it has received in the past from communication researchers. As a standard practice, we believe researchers should compute and report estimates of variance components and, whenever possible, raw-score regression coefficients.

(5) MANOVA procedures provide an excellent opportunity to isolate the optimal linear combinations of elementary responses of most importance in a given domain of research, i.e., those that carry the most assignable variance.

Through discriminant analysis and related procedures, thoughtful researchers can determine which variables offer the greatest potential payoffs for future research with particular traits, constructs, and concepts. This aspect of MANOVA needs to be exploited. In short, MANOVA should lead to a better understanding of what responses ought to be studied and in what contexts to study them.

(6) There is no longer any need to insist upon perfectly balanced research designs. In particular, researchers need to become better acquainted with general least squares approaches to nonorthogonal analysis of variance. Different methods of analysis are appropriate for different problems. Interpretation of results must take into account the specific method used to partition the variance.

(7) As with other methods of multivariate analysis, MANOVA requires a willingness to pursue relentlessly the meaning of one's data. As Cronbach (1975) said, "There are more things in heaven and earth than are dreamt in our hypotheses, and our observations should be open to them." We must not stop looking at our data merely because our hypothesis has been rejected or accepted. Rather, we should continually be searching for clues reflecting unexpected, serendipitous, or unusual relationships among the variables. Multivariate data are too rich to be discarded without maximum effort at exposition and extrapolation. Surely, our capacity to develop explanatory concepts will be enlarged as our vision of how to analyze and interpret multivariate data is expanded.

ACKNOWLEDGMENTS

The authors wish to thank Peter Monge, Joseph Capella, Jack Hunter, and Jane Edwards for their comments on earlier versions of this manuscript. We are especially grateful for the careful and constructive criticism provided by John Tukey of Princeton University.

References

Andrews, D. F. Plots of high dimensional data. *Biometrika*, 1972, **28**, 125–136.

Appelbaum, M. I., and Cramer, E. M. Some problems in the nonorthogonal analysis of variance. *Psychological Bulletin*, 1974, **81**, 335–347.

Bartlett, M. S. A note on tests of significance in multivariate analysis. *Proceedings of the Cambridge Philosophical Society*, 1939, **35**, 180–185.

Bochner, A. P. *A multivariate investigation of machiavellianism and task structure in four-man groups*. Unpublished Ph.D. dissertation, Bowling Green State Univ., 1971.

Bock, R. D. *Multivariate behavioral methods in behavioral research*. New York: McGraw-Hill, 1975.

Bock, R. D., and Haggard, E. A. The use of multivariate analysis of variance in behavioral research. In D. K. Whitla (Ed.), *Handbook of measurement and assessment in behavioral sciences*. Reading, Massachusetts: Addison-Wesley, 1968. Pp. 100–112.

Bottenberg, R., and Ward, J. H. *Applied multiple linear regression analysis*. Department of Commerce, Office of Technical Services, 1960.

Bradley, H. E. Multiple classification analysis for arbitrary experimental design. *Technometrics*, 1968, **10**, 13–28.

Cohen, J. Multiple regression as a general data-analytic system. *Psychological Bulletin*, 1968, **70**, 426–443.

Cohen, J., and Cohen, P. *Applied multiple regression/correlation analysis for the behavioral sciences*. Hillsdale, New Jersey: Lawrence Erlbaum Associates, 1975.

Cooley, W. W., and Lohnes, P. R. *Multivariate data analysis*. New York: Wiley, 1971.

Cramer, E. M., and Bock, R. D. Multivariate analysis. *Review of Educational Research*, 1966, **36**, 604–617.

Cronbach, L. J. Beyond the two disciplines of scientific psychology. *American Psychologist*, 1975, **30**, 116–127.

Di Salvo, V. S. *A multivariate analysis of variance investigation of the effects of information processing ability, amount of task relevant information, and group climate on group behavior*. Unpublished Ph.D. dissertation, Bowling Green State Univ., 1970.

Finn, J. D. *A general model for multivariate analysis*. New York: Holt, 1974.

Finney, D. J. Multivariate analysis of agricultural experiments. *Biometrics*, 1956, **12**, 67–71.

Fitzpatrick, M. A. *A typological examination of communication in enduring relationships*. Unpublished Ph.D. dissertation, Temple Univ., 1976.

Gergen, K. J. Social psychology as history. *Journal of Personality and Social Psychology*, 1973, **26**, 309–320.

Gergen, K. J. Social psychology, science, and history. *Personality and Social Psychology Bulletin*, 1976, **2**, 373–383.

Gocka, E. F. Regression analysis of proportional cell data. *Psychological Bulletin*, 1973, **80**, 28–30.

Harris, R. J. *A primer of multivariate statistics*. New York: Academic Press, 1975.

Hummel, T. J., and Sligo, J. R. Empirical comparison of univariate and multivariate analysis of variance procedures. *Psychological Bulletin*, 1971, **76**, 49–57.

Hotelling, H. A. A generalized T test and measure of multivariate dispersion. In J. Neyman (Ed.), *Proceedings of the Second Berkeley Symposium on Mathematical Statistics and Probability*. Berkeley, California: Univ. of California Press, 1951, Pp. 23–41.

Kerlinger, F. N., and Pedhazur, E. J. *Multiple regression in behavioral research*. New York: Holt, 1973.

Morrison, D. F. *Multivariate statistical methods*. San Francisco, California: McGraw-Hill, 1967.

Mulaik, S. A. *The foundations of factor analysis*. New York: McGraw-Hill, 1972.

O'Brien, R. J. Comment on some problems in the nonorthogonal analysis of variance. *Psychological Bulletin*, 1976, **83**, 72–74.

Olson, C. L. On choosing a test statistic in multivariate analysis of variance. *Psychological Bulletin*, 1976, **83**, 579–586.

Overall, J. E., and Klett, C. J. *Applied multivariate analysis*. New York: McGraw-Hill, 1972.

Overall, J. E., Spiegal, D. K., and Cohen, J. Equivalence of orthogonal and nonorthogonal analysis of variance. *Psychological Bulletin*, 1975, **82**, 182–186.

Pillai, K. C. Some new test criteria in multivariate analysis. *Annals of Mathematical Statistics*, 1955, **26**, 117–121.

Porebski, O. R. Discriminatory and canonical analysis of technical college data. *The British Journal of Mathematical and Statistical Psychology*, 1966, **19**, 215–236.

Pruzek, R. M. Methods and problems in the analysis of multivariate data. *Review of Educational Research*, 1971, **41**, 163–190.

Rawlings, R. R., Jr. Note on nonorthogonal analysis of variance. *Psychological Bulletin*, 1972, **77**, 373–374.

Roy, S. N. On a heuristic method of test construction and its use in multivariate analysis. *Annals of Mathematical Statistics*, 1953, **24**, 220–238.

Scheffé, H. *The analysis of variance*. New York: Wiley, 1959.

Stevens, J. P. Four methods of analyzing between variation for the K-group MANOVA problem. *Multivariate Behavioral Research*, 1972, **7**, 499–522.

Stevens, J. P. Step-down analysis and simultaneous confidence intervals in MANOVA. *Multivariate Behavioral Research*, 1973, **8**, 391–402.

Tatsuoka, M. M. *Multivariate analysis: Techniques for educational and psychological research*. New York: Wiley, 1971.

Timm, N. H. *Multivariate analysis: With applications in education and psychology*. Monterey, California: Brooks/Cole, 1975.

Tukey, J. Personal correspondance. 1978.

Van de Geer, J. P. *Introduction to multivariate analysis for the social sciences*. San Francisco, California: Freeman, 1971.

Wilkinson, L. Response variable hypotheses in the multivariate analysis of variance. *Psychological Bulletin*, 1975, **82**, 408–412.

Wilks, S. S. Certain generalizations in the analysis of variance. *Biometrika*, 1932, **24**, 471–494.

Woodward, J. A., and Overall, J. E. Multivariate analysis of variance by multiple regression methods. *Psychological Bulletin*, 1975, **82**, 21–32.

Chapter 6

DISCRIMINANT ANALYSIS IN COMMUNICATION RESEARCH

MARGARET L. MCLAUGHLIN

Division of Speech Communication
Texas Tech University
Lubbock, Texas

I. OVERVIEW OF DISCRIMINANT ANALYSIS

Discriminant analysis is a multivariate statistical technique of broad utility which may be employed in those many instances in which the investigator has obtained scores on a battery of variables for two or more groups. Discriminant analysis is frequently employed in the social sciences for hypothesis testing alone: it provides for a multivariate-analysis-of-variance (MANOVA) test of the hypothesis that the vectors of means for K groups on a battery of p variates are significantly different. While the "overall" significance tests in

MULTIVARIATE TECHNIQUES
IN HUMAN COMMUNICATION RESEARCH

discriminant analysis and one-way MANOVA are identical in the case of three or more groups, the investigator using discriminant analysis for hypothesis testing may be seeking to discover if the mean vectors for the K groups differ significantly in *more than one way*. What we are looking for in discriminant analysis is a set *or sets* of weights which have the property that when they are applied to the raw scores on the p variables, and the scores on the weighted variables are then summed to make a new *composite variable*, Y, the K group means on that composite variate will be maximally different (although not necessarily *significantly* different). These sets of weights are known as *discriminant functions*. The number of such discriminant functions will always be equal to the number of groups minus one or the number of variables, whichever is the smaller. Scores produced by the application of the first discriminant function to the p variables will be uncorrelated with scores produced by the similar application of successive functions. The MANOVA routines found in the more popular statistical packages for the computer do not ordinarily provide separate significance tests for among-group differences associated with each of the successive discriminant functions. If the investigator believes that there may be several mutually exclusive dimensions, or subsets of the independent variables, along which the K groups differ, then discriminant analysis would be the technique of choice. This is especially the case when the number of groups is large (> 3).

A further aspect of discriminant analysis which is attractive to many investigators is that the discriminant function coefficients (the elements of the weighting vector) serve, when standardized, as a basis for comparing the variates in terms of their relative ability to distinguish the K groups. These coefficients are interpreted in much the same way as factor loadings in factor analysis or standardized weights in multiple regression.

Discriminant analysis is frequently employed in taxonomic research. In such studies the investigator may have a variety of aims, including the evaluation of a new taxonomic instrument and the subsequent assignment of a number of unclassified "cases" (e.g., fossils) to one of K groups on the basis of this same instrument. The investigator might obtain at least a partial evaluation of the new taxonomic measure by determining, using discriminant analysis as a hypothesis testing technique, whether or not groups of *previously classified* cases differ significantly on one or more linear combinations of the new items. The investigator might then wish to use the validated taxonomic measure to group unclassified cases. This is ordinarily a rather simple matter of assigning a new case to that group whose mean score on the composite variate(s) Y is closest to its own.

The investigator who is interested in using discriminant analysis will soon discover that the widely used statistical packages such as SPSS (Nie, Hull, Jenkins, Steinbrenner, & Bent, 1975) and BMD (Dixon, 1975) are set up for execution of the hypothesis testing and classification aspects of discriminant analysis in the same computer run. (See Chapter 17 for a discussion of the various statistical packages.) This is a fortunate state of affairs, for it reflects what ought to be going on in the laboratory. For example, suppose that a researcher has a battery of language variables, such as number of self-references or number of body-part references in one-hundred word language samples, which purportedly could serve as an instrument for the diagnosis of adolescent schizophrenia. If there were no significant differences on the instrument between normal adolescents and previously diagnosed schizoids, then its potential for use in classifying as-yet undiagnosed individuals would probably by quite low. The hypothesis testing aspect of discriminant analysis is often a necessary prelude to the use of discriminant scores in classification.

Discriminant analysis has a very broad range of applications: the following are only a few.

(1) Discriminant analysis may be used to test the MANOVA hypothesis that K groups differ significantly on p variates, especially, in the case where $K \geqslant 3$, that there are two or more orthogonal linear composites of the p variables along which significant differences occur. For example, a researcher arranges to observe subjects engaging in a 10-minute interaction with (a) a stranger of the opposite sex (b) a stranger of the same sex: subjects have been instructed prior to the interaction to learn as much as possible about each other. Questions occurring during the interaction are coded into 10 content categories by frequency. The researcher hypothesizes that the three dyad types (F/F, M/M, F/M) will differ significantly *along two dimensions*, the first characterized primarily by the use of questions with *social–emotional* content (for example, family and friendship), the second characterized primarily by variables reflecting *instrumental* content (e.g., work or study).

(2) Discriminant analysis may be used for *post hoc* comparisons in MANOVA. For example, in a factorial MANOVA for which the row effect has been found significant, discriminant analysis may be used to determine how the treatment levels are related to the dependent measures, just as in the application previously described. If significant column or interaction effects are found, they may be studied similarly (Tatsuoka, 1971).

(3) Discriminant analysis may be used to evaluate diagnostic instruments. For example, a new diagnostic for which significant differences have been found between *sedative abusers* and *narcotic abusers* may be said to be cross-validated if the instrument is successful in classifying persons who have already been assigned on the basis of another, established measure.

(4) Discriminant analysis may be used for assigning individuals to groups (e.g., types of therapy, courses of study, medication levels). It is presupposed that (a) individuals of the type being assessed (cancer victim/noncancer victim, for instance) do tend to differ significantly on the variables from which the discriminant function was formed and (b) that the diagnostic has been cross-validated.

II. FUNDAMENTALS OF DISCRIMINANT ANALYSIS

A. Underlying Assumptions of Discriminant Analysis

The assumptions underlying discriminant analysis are described briefly. The consequences of a violation of one or more of these assumptions will be dealt with in Section III.A.

(1) *Multivariate normality.* It is assumed that the p independent variables have a multivariate normal distribution in each of the populations from which the K groups are sampled.

(2) *Homogeneity of the population dispersions.* It is assumed that the population variance–covariance matrices $\Sigma_1, \Sigma_2, \ldots, \Sigma_k$ are equal: consequently one may speak of a common covariance matrix Σ.

(3) *Mutual exclusivity and exhaustiveness of K groups.* In general, it is assumed that the dependent variable, group membership, is categorical and not susceptible of continuous measurement (Eisenbeis and Avery, 1972).

If the linear discriminant function is used in classification, it will prove to be the optimal assignment rule (Lachenbruch, 1975) if the population means and covariances are known. Classification will generally be suboptimal when estimates of the population parameters must be made from sample values.

B. Extraction of Discriminant Functions

We shall begin by stating the *discriminant problem* for a simple two-group case. Let use assume that we have drawn a sample from each of two bivariate normal populations (say, *monolinguals* and *bilinguals*) with, respectively, sample sizes N_1 and N_2. The population covariance matrices are known to be equal. We have measures on two variables, X_1 and X_2, for each of the $N_1 + N_2$ subjects. One way to put the discriminant problem, in this case, is as follows: What linear combination of the two variables X_1 and X_2 will result in (univariate) score distributions, for the two groups, with minimal overlap? In other words, how can we weight the subjects' score vectors such that the resulting composite scores for monolinguals are as different as possible from those of bilinguals?

Let us approach the problem from a slightly different angle. Consider the schematic representation (Fig. 1) of the "data swarms" for the two samples just described. The points M_1 and M_2 are the respective *centroids* for the two samples. Now consider the unclassified case"?," with a score vector [35, 15]. This case seems to be more similar to the "average" bilingual subject with respect to variable X_1; however, the case more closely resembles the typical monolingual with respect to variable 2. Assignment of the case to a group will obviously have to be a function of an overall resemblance to some particular *combination* of X_1 and X_2 (Tatsuoka, 1970).

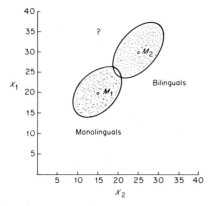

FIG. 1. Schematic representation of two bivariate normal distributions:

$$M_1 = [20, 15], \quad M_2 = [30, 25], \quad ? = [35, 15].$$

It should be clear that the ease of classifying such a new case is related to the amount of *overlap* between the pair of distributions: when the two distributions are widely separated, the probability of an incorrect assignment ordinarily will not be very great (Van de Geer, 1971). Separation is not just a function of the distance between the two group centroids, it is also determined by the variability of the scores *within* each of the groups. Ideally, we would want the separation of the group means to be as large as possible relative to the within-group dispersions (Van de Geer, 1971). Put another way, we want to maximize the ratio of the between-group variance to the variance within groups. This maximization is accomplished by projecting the points from our two distributions onto some new vector $Y = v_1 X_1 + v_2 X_2$ along which the group distributions are as distinct as possible. The discriminant problem, simply stated, is to find such a vector (Van de Geer, 1971).

The discriminant problem was formulated by Fisher (1936), who developed the discriminant function as a linear combination of p variates $Y = \mathbf{X}'\mathbf{V} = v_1 X_1 + v_2 X_2 + \cdots + v_p X_p$, where the vs are coefficients to be applied to raw scores on the p variables. The vs are chosen to maximize the between variation in our new composite variable, Y, relative to the within variation. These vs are the *direction cosines* for the vector Y (Van de Geer, 1971).

For K groups, the ratio of between to within-group sums of squares in Y can be written as a function of the vector of weights $\mathbf{v}$:

$$\frac{\text{sum of squares between in } Y}{\text{sum of squares within in } Y} = \frac{\mathbf{v}'\mathbf{B}\mathbf{v}}{\mathbf{v}'\mathbf{W}\mathbf{v}} = \lambda$$

where $\mathbf{B}$ is the between-groups sums of squares and cross-products matrix and $\mathbf{W}$ is the pooled within-groups SSCP matrix (Tatsuoka, 1971). The ratio thus derived, λ, is known as the *discriminant criterion*.

The equation to be solved for the set of weights $\mathbf{v}$ which maximizes λ is, after reduction (Tatsuoka, 1970),

$$(\mathbf{B} - \lambda\mathbf{W})\mathbf{v} = 0$$

The reader may have realized by now that finding the discriminant function(s), the set(s) of weights applied to raw scores to maximize group separation, is analogous to finding a factor in principal components analysis: mathematically, it amounts to discovering the patterns of linear dependence in a set of variables from the eigenvalues and associated eigenvectors of a matrix whose entries reflect the comparative degrees of association among the variables.

A variety of algorithms may be found for solving the discriminant problem. Tatsuoka (1970, 1971), rewriting $(\mathbf{B} - \lambda\mathbf{W})\mathbf{v} = 0$ as $(\mathbf{W}^{-1}\mathbf{B} - \lambda\mathbf{I})\mathbf{v} = 0$, presents a method for extracting the nonzero latent roots of $\mathbf{W}^{-1}\mathbf{B}$ (solving $|\mathbf{W}^{-1}\mathbf{B} - \lambda\mathbf{I}| = 0$). In the event that $\mathbf{W}$ turns out to be singular (has a zero determinant), the eigenvalues are extracted from the equation $|\mathbf{B} - \lambda\mathbf{W}| = 0$ (Tatsuoka, 1970). Alternative algorithms are given by Overall and Klett (1972), Eisenbeis and Avery (1972), and Tatsuoka (1971).[1]

Whatever the algorithm employed, it would appear to be the current vogue to compute discriminant functions in conjunction with a stepwise method of variable selection. We shall consider the appropriateness of this procedure, in the context of statistical inference, at a later point. Let us assume for the moment that we are using the algorithm by which we extract the latent roots and vectors of $\mathbf{W}^{-1}\mathbf{B}$. In very general terms, we say that at any given "step," the discriminant function will be obtained from a product matrix $\mathbf{W}^{-1}\mathbf{B}$ whose entries represent only those q variates out of p which contribute significantly to discrimination among the K groups.

C. Significance Testing in Discriminant Analysis

For K groups, a chi-square test of the equality of the group centroids is performed on the statistic *Wilks' lambda* (Bartlett, 1934). Lambda is the

---

[1]Overall and Klett (1972) propose extracting the latent roots and vectors of the matrix $\mathbf{V}^{-1}\mathbf{B}\mathbf{V}'^{-1}$, where $\mathbf{B}$ is the between-groups SSCP matrix, and $\mathbf{V}^{-1}$ is the lower triangular matrix which results from computing the triangular square-root inverse of $\mathbf{W}$, the within-groups SSCP matrix. The resulting eigenvectors are premultiplied by $\mathbf{V}'^{-1}$ to obtain the weighting coefficients. Eisenbeis and Avery present as an alternative solving of the determinantal equation $|\mathbf{W} - \mathbf{\Psi T}| = 0$, where $\mathbf{T}$ is the "total" SSCP matrix $(\mathbf{B} + \mathbf{W})$ and the tth root Ψ_t is equal to $1 \; (1 + \lambda_r + 1 - t)$ where $t = 1, \ldots, r$ (Eisenbeis & Avery, 1972).

An alternative suggested by Tatsuoka (1971) is the canonical correlation approach. In this method $K - 1$ dummy group membership variables are coded as criterion variables. The matrix $\mathbf{S}_{pp}^{-1}\mathbf{S}_{pc}\mathbf{S}_{cc}^{-1}\mathbf{S}_{cp}$ is formed, where $\mathbf{S}_{pp}$ is the SSCP matrix of the p predictor variates, $\mathbf{S}_{pc}$ is the SP matrix between predictors and criterion variables (dummy group membership variates), $\mathbf{S}_{cp}$ is the transpose of $\mathbf{S}_{pc}$, and $\mathbf{S}_{cc}$ is the SS vector of the criterion variables. The elements of the eigenvector which corresponds to the square root of μ_1^2, the largest root of $\mathbf{S}_{pp}^{-1}\mathbf{S}_{pc}\mathbf{S}_{cc}^{-1}\mathbf{S}_{cp}$, are the weights which maximize the correlation between the set of p variates and the group membership variables: they are roughly equivalent to the elements of the eigenvectors associated with the largest root of $\mathbf{W}^{-1}\mathbf{B}$ (Tatsuoka, 1971).

ratio of the determinant of $\mathbf{W}$, the pooled within-groups SSCP matrix, to the determinant of $\mathbf{T}$, the total SSCP matrix: $\Lambda = |\mathbf{W}|/|\mathbf{T}|$. Lambda varies between zero and unity, where zero indicates that none of the variation in the discriminant space is within groups. Lambda subtracted from unity is equal to the canonical R^2 (Fisher, 1940) where R^2 represents the proportion of variance in the discriminant space attributable to between-group differences.

The reader will recall that the number of discriminant functions, or sets of weighting coefficients, is equal to p or $K - 1$, whichever is smaller. Each of the linear combinations $Y = v_1 X_1 + v_2 X_2 + \cdots + v_p X_p$ can be tested separately for significance. In the K-group case where $K \geqslant 3$, a significant "overall" value of lambda implies that *at least* the first linear combination of the variates is significant (Tatsuoka, 1970). This first test indexes the *conjoint* effect of all of the functions. Successive tests may be performed for each of the discriminant functions extracted to determine if they are significant in producing group separation when the effect of the previously extracted, consequently more "important" function(s), has been removed. Procedures for these successive tests are given in Tatsuoka (1970, 1971): they are routinely performed for the SPSS user. When $K = 2$, the significance level associated with Wilks' lambda is the significance level associated with the single discriminant function.

A second statistic which is important in discriminant analysis is Mahalanobis' δ^2. δ^2 is a measure of the distance between two populations, and is given by $(\mu_1 - \mu_2)'\Sigma^{-1}(\mu_1 - \mu_2)$. To put it another way, δ^2 is an index of the distance between the means of two populations expressed in standard score units. Recall that we transform a raw score to a standard score by subtracting from the particular X_i the mean of X and then dividing through by σ_x: $Z_{x_i} = (X_i - \bar{X})/\sigma_x$. We may consider $(\mu_1 - \mu_2)'(\mu_1 - \mu_2)$ as a squared analog to the expression $(X_i - \bar{X})$, and Σ^{-1} as a squared multivariate analog of σ_x: in matrix algebra, "division" by Σ is accomplished by multiplication by Σ^{-1}. We may also consider $(\mu_1 - \mu_2)'(\mu_1 - \mu_2)$ and Σ^{-1} as analogs, respectively, to between and within variance estimates. The reader will recall that in Section II.B the discriminant problem was described as the maximization of between-group differences relative to the dispersion within groups: it is to this ratio that δ^2 is proportional.

δ^2 may be used to test the hypothesis that the centroids for some pair of the K groups differ significantly. The test used by SPSS and BMD is

$$ F = \left[(N - K - p + 1)N_i N_j / p(N_i + N_j) \right] \delta_{ij}^2 / (N - K) $$

with p and $N - K - p + 1$ degrees of freedom, where N equals $N_1 + N_2 + \cdots + N_k$, and N_i, N_j are the sample sizes for groups i and j. In practice, sample values of $\bar{\mathbf{X}}_k$ and $\mathbf{S}^{-1}$ are substituted for the corresponding population parameters. When the population parameters are unknown, the Mahalanobis squared distance, symbolized by D^2, is given by $(\bar{\mathbf{X}}_1 - \bar{\mathbf{X}}_2)'\mathbf{S}^{-1}(\bar{\mathbf{X}}_1 - \bar{\mathbf{X}}_2)$.

A complete account of the interrelationships among the multivariate statistics employed in testing the significance of discriminant functions may be found in Porebski (1966).

D. Interpretation of Findings

The user of one of the packaged statistical programs may find a bewildering array of "functions" on the printout. SPSS, for example, prints out a "classification function," an "unstandardized discriminant function," and a "standardized discriminant function." BMD outputs a "classification function," and a matrix called "coefficients for canonical variables." What do these terms mean?

a. Classification function (SPSS, BMD)   For each of the K groups there will be a vector of variable weights $\hat{\mathbf{B}}_i$ and a constant $\hat{\alpha}_i$. They will appear in matrix form. The classification function is used to assign individuals to groups. Consider the score vector of subject s. S's classification score for group 1 is obtained by (1) summing the products of S's raw scores on the p variables and the p corresponding weights $\hat{b}_1$ and (2) adding the constant $\hat{\alpha}_1$. A score is computed similarly for groups $2 - K$. Subject S should be assigned to that group for which $[(\Sigma_{i=1}^{p} \hat{b}_i X_i) + \alpha_i]$ is largest. The values of the $\hat{b}_i$ are obtained by inverting the pooled within-groups covariance matrix and post-multiplying it by the vector group means. The α_i values are given by $-\frac{1}{2}\bar{\mathbf{X}}_i'\mathbf{\Sigma}^{-1}\bar{\mathbf{X}}_i$.

b. Unstandardized discriminant function (SPSS)   This is a $(p \times (K - 1))$ matrix giving the coefficients v_i of the normalized eigenvectors of $\mathbf{B}^{-1}\mathbf{W}$, plus a constant for each of the K groups. To obtain the *discriminant scores* for an individual, the products of the raw scores and the unstandardized coefficients v_i are summed and added to the constant term, which is analogous to an intercept in linear regression. The score will be in standard form. Each individual will have as many discriminant scores as there are discriminant-functions: they may be interpreted as coordinates of S's location in discriminant space. The matrix which is used to calculate the discriminant scores in BMD is labeled *coefficients for canonical variables*. In the case where $K = 2$, the coefficients for the "second canonical variable" should be ignored, owing to an associated eigenvalue of zero.

c. Standardized discriminant function (SPSS)   This is a $(p \times (K - 1))$ matrix of discriminant coefficients v_i^* which are obtained by premultiplying the (unstandardized) v_i by the square root of the corresponding diagonal element w_{ii} of the matrix $\mathbf{W}$ (Tatsuoka, 1971). The absolute magnitude of the v_i^* give us an idea of the relative importance of each of the variables to group separation.

E. Linear and Quadratic Classification

1. LINEAR CLASSIFICATION

The basic task of a classification scheme is to answer the following question: Given that subject i has a set of scores $X_{1i}, X_{2i}, \ldots, X_{pi}$ on a battery of p variates, from which of K populations is [the subject] likely to have been sampled? [Tatsuoka, 1975, p. 261]. When we speak of likelihood in the technical sense we refer to *probability density*. If we construct two density functions $f_1(\mathbf{X})$ and $f_2(\mathbf{X})$, for the populations Π_1 and Π_2, the height of the curve $f_k(\mathbf{X})$ represents, for any given score combination $\mathbf{X}$, the probability density at such a point (Tatsuoka, 1975).

The very simplest kind of classification rule, for the two-group case, calls for assigning an observation to Π_1 if

$$f_1(\mathbf{X})/f_2(\mathbf{X}) \geqslant P_1/P_2$$

where P_1 is the prior probability that a case would actually arise from Π_1 (Eisenbeis & Avery, 1972) and P_2 is the prior probability that a case would actually arise from Π_2. (The problem of estimating prior probabilities is addressed in Section IV.B) If the prior probabilities are *equal*, then the ratio on the right-hand side will be equal to unity, and consequently for any instance in which $f_1(\mathbf{X}) \geqslant f_2(\mathbf{X})$ the case will be assigned to Π_1.

As it happens, the ln of the ratio $f_1(\mathbf{X})/f_2(\mathbf{X})$ reduces to $-\frac{1}{2}[\hat{X}_1^2 - \hat{X}_2^2]$, where $\hat{X}_1^2$, for Π_1, equals $(\mathbf{X} - \boldsymbol{\mu}_1)'\boldsymbol{\Sigma}^{-1}(\mathbf{X} - \boldsymbol{\mu}_1)$, and $\hat{X}_2^2$ for Π_2 is equal to $(\mathbf{X} - \boldsymbol{\mu}_2)'\boldsymbol{\Sigma}^{-1}(\mathbf{X} - \boldsymbol{\mu}_2)$ (Eisenbeis & Avery, 1972; Tatsuoka, 1975). These two expressions reflect the squared Mahalanobis' distances of the score vector $\mathbf{X}$ from the respective centroids $\boldsymbol{\mu}_k$ of the two populations Π_1 and Π_2. The reader will notice further that the univariate analog of $(\mathbf{X} - \boldsymbol{\mu}_k)'\boldsymbol{\Sigma}^{-1}(\mathbf{X} - \boldsymbol{\mu}_k)$ is $(X - \mu)^2/\sigma^2$, a squared normal deviate. A standardized deviate squared is a chi-square with one degree of freedom (Tatsuoka, 1975). When a case is assigned to that population Π_i for which $f_i(\mathbf{X}) \geqslant f_j(\mathbf{X})$ (assuming equal prior probabilities), then it is assigned to membership in that population for which the case's score vector $\mathbf{X}$ deviates the least from the population mean. To put it another way, an observation is assigned to the population for which the squared Mahalanobis' distance from $\mathbf{X}$ to the population centroid is smallest.

The available computer packages usually assign cases to groups on the basis of *posterior probabilities*. A case is assigned to that population for which its posterior probability of membership is greatest, following Bayes (Lachenbruch, 1975):

$$P_0(\Pi_i|\mathbf{X}) = \frac{P_i f_i(\mathbf{X})}{P_i f_i(\mathbf{X}) + P_2 f_2(\mathbf{X}) + \cdots + P_k f_k(\mathbf{X})}$$

where $P_0(\Pi_i|\mathbf{X})$ is the posterior probability that the score vector $\mathbf{X}$ is a member of Π_i, and P_i is the prior probability of belonging to Π_i.

The posterior probabilities printed out by SPSS and SAS are given by

$$P_0(\Pi_i|\mathbf{X}) = \frac{P_i \exp\left[-0.5\hat{X}_i^2\right]}{P_1 \exp\left[-0.5\hat{X}_1^2\right] + P_2 \exp\left[-0.5\hat{X}_2^2\right] + \cdots + P_k \exp\left[-0.5\hat{X}_k^2\right]}$$

where, using sample values of $\overline{\mathbf{X}}_k$ and $\mathbf{S}_w^{-1}$ (the inverted within-groups covariance matrix) to estimate the parameters $\boldsymbol{\mu}_k$ and $\boldsymbol{\Sigma}^{-1}$, $\hat{X}_k^2(\mathbf{X}) = (\mathbf{X} - \overline{\mathbf{X}}_k)'\mathbf{S}_w^{-1}(\mathbf{X} - \overline{\mathbf{X}}_k)$. Here $\mathbf{X}$ is the p-variable score vector for subject i, and $\overline{\mathbf{X}}_k$ is the centroid or vector of sample means on the p variables for group K.

We may be able to simplify classification considerably by substituting the subject's discriminant score vector $\mathbf{Y}$ for the score vector $\mathbf{X}$, and the Kth group centroid $\overline{\mathbf{Y}}_k$ on the discriminant function(s) for the group centroid $\overline{\mathbf{X}}_k$. Then $\hat{X}_k^2 = (\mathbf{Y} - \overline{\mathbf{Y}}_k)'\mathbf{S}_w^{-1}(\mathbf{Y} - \overline{\mathbf{Y}}_k)$. If we use the discriminant scores corresponding to all $K - 1$ of the discriminant functions, the posterior probabilities will be the same as if the p-variate score vector $\mathbf{X}$ had been used, provided that the group covariance matrices are equal. Investigators frequently employ discriminant scores based on the significant discriminant functions only.

The posterior probabilities may be modified by including in the preceding equation terms reflecting the *costs of misclassifying* an observation for each of the populations under study. (For an account of practical problems in estimating misclassification costs, the reader is referred to Section IV.B.) These terms c_k, where $\Sigma c_1 + c_2 + \cdots + c_k = 1$, act as a correction factor on the $\hat{X}^2$ estimates (Overall and Klett, 1972). Taking both prior probabilities and misclassification costs into account, the posterior probability $P_0(\Pi_i|\mathbf{X})$ becomes

$$\frac{c_i P_i \exp\left[-0.5\hat{X}_i^2\right]}{c_1 P_1 \exp\left[-0.5\hat{X}_1^2\right] + c_2 P_2 \exp\left[-0.5\hat{X}_2^2\right] + \cdots + c_k P_k \exp\left[-0.5\hat{X}_k^2\right]}$$

Misclassification costs are difficult to establish with any degree of precision. There are currently no options in SPSS, BMD, or SAS for including such estimates in the computation of the posterior probabilities.

2. QUADRATIC CLASSIFICATION

It is generally advisable that a test for homogeneity of the K group covariance matrices be performed prior to using the minimum $\hat{X}^2$ classification rules just given. If the group covariance matrices are unequal, estimates of the posterior probabilities computed from $\hat{X}^2$ values in which the population covariance matrix $\boldsymbol{\Sigma}$ is estimated by $\mathbf{S}_w$ (the pooled covariance matrix) will be less than optimal.

The investigator may test the null hypothesis $\boldsymbol{\Sigma}_1 = \boldsymbol{\Sigma}_2 = \boldsymbol{\Sigma}_k$ by means of Box's "M" test (Box, 1949). This test is available in both SPSS and SAS: in the latter, an option is available such that if H_0 is rejected at $p < .10$, *quadratic* classification will be employed. In quadratic classification, the $\hat{X}_k^2$

estimates for the deviation of $\mathbf{X}$ (the subject's score vector) from the group centroids $\overline{\mathbf{X}}_k$ are based on the *separate* covariance matrices for each of the K groups. Thus $\hat{X}_k^2 = (\mathbf{X} - \overline{\mathbf{X}}_k)'\mathbf{S}_k^{-1}(\mathbf{X} - \overline{\mathbf{X}}_k)$ where $\mathbf{S}_k$ is the within-groups covariance matrix for group K, which is used in place of the pooled covariance matrix $\mathbf{S}_w$ as an estimate of $\boldsymbol{\Sigma}$.

III. ISSUES AND OPTIONS IN DISCRIMINANT ANALYSIS

A. Failure to Meet Assumptions

One of the assumptions underlying discriminant analysis is that the p independent variables have a *multivariate normal distribution*. A common violation of this assumption occurs when the variables are categorical (coded 0 or 1) and follow a multinomial distribution. Typically, categorical independent variables are employed in discriminant analysis when presence/absence measurement (Lachenbruch, 1975; Sokol and Sneath, 1963) has been made (for example, presence or absence of wings) or when the data is demographic in nature (sex, political affiliation, and so forth). Gilbert (1968) compared the performance of the linear classification rule (actually, the variety in which a case is assigned to Π_i on the basis of the classification function described in Section II.D) to other classification rules including a multinomial model, in assigning cases on the basis of a set of "qualitative" variables. She found that linear classification was only slightly less efficient than the other procedures in terms of the probabilities of misclassfication. Similar results for categorical variables have been reported by Moore (1973).

However, the outlook for using linear classification on nonnormal variables with distributions other than the multionomial is somewhat less bright. Lachenbruch, Sneeringer, and Revo (1973) tried out the effectiveness of the linear rules on three continuous but nonnormal sets of variables for which the original multivariate normal set X_p underwent, respectively, log, logit, and $\sinh^{-1}$ transformations. The performance of the linear rules was found to be quite poor in classifying cases on the basis of the transformed variables.

An alternative to discriminant analysis for distributions with unknown parameters is *nearest-neighbor* analysis (Fix & Hodges, 1951; Cover & Hart, 1967), which is available in SAS. The program allows for the inclusion of prior probability estimates.

A second assumption of discriminant analysis which is frequently violated is *equality of the group covariance matrices*. As the reader will recall, the Box test of the null hypothesis $\boldsymbol{\Sigma}_1 = \boldsymbol{\Sigma}_2 = \boldsymbol{\Sigma}_k$ is a must if discriminant analysis is to be used to classify cases; further, quadratic classification rules are in order if H_0 is rejected. As far as the hypothesis $\boldsymbol{\mu}_1 = \boldsymbol{\mu}_2 = \boldsymbol{\mu}_k$ is concerned, nonhomogeneity of the covariance matrices tends to bias the test in favor of the null hypothesis (Holloway & Dunn, 1967).

Gilbert (1969) has studied the effect of unequal variance–covariance matrices on the efficiency of the linear classification procedures, as compared to the quadratic, for the case where Σ_i is a multiple d of Σ_j. In her sampling study Gilbert systematically varied d, T^2 (a relative of Mahalanobis' D^2, the distance between populations), the prior probabilities, and the number of independent variables. Gilbert found that the linear rule worked best when the prior probabilities were quite unequal ($\Pi_1 = .8333$) and T^2 was large. The reduction in the probability of misclassification obtained from the use of the quadratic form was greatest when the prior probabilities were equal, T^2 was small, and the number of variables was large. Lest the reader assume that quadratic classification is always called for when the covariance matrices are unequal, it should be noted that Marks and Dunn (1974) found fairly poor performance by the quadratic procedures when the sample sizes were small.

As a footnote to the importance of the covariance estimates in classification, the reader is urged to examine the interesting article by Bartlett and Please (1963) on discrimination in the case where there are *zero* mean differences between populations, yet unequal covariance matrices.

A third assumption which underlies discriminant analysis is that the populations from which the K groups are sampled are *discrete* and that they exhaust the criterion of interest. In other words, it is inappropriate, when classification is the desired outcome of a discriminant analysis, to take a continuous variable, for example, apprehensiveness, split the sample at the median, and pronounce the two halves Π_1 ("high apprehensives") and Π_2 ("low apprehensives"). Alternatively, such groupings as "top 10%" and "bottom 10%" do not make two populations, nor do they exhaust the criterion.

A considerable amount of research has been carried out on the effects of an initial misclassification of cases. Lachenbruch (1966) employed a procedure in which he first established, on the basis of two populations with correctly assigned members, the true probability of misclassification under the linear rule. He then grouped randomly drawn cases from Π_2 with the first population, Π_1, and recalculated the probabilities of misclassification. He found that for large samples there was little increase in misclassification probability as a function of this misclassification of the initial samples. The asymptotic results for discriminant analysis given initial random misclassification were developed by McLachlan (1972). His results were generally in agreement with those of Lachenbruch. However, in a more recent study, Lachenbruch (1974) found that for *nonrandom* initial misclassification—when an observation is misclassified because (1) it is close to the mean of the wrong population or (2) it is an unlikely member of the correct population, as well as being close to the mean of the wrong one—the results were quite different. The true probabilities of misclassification are not worsened as a result of initial nonrandom misclassification: when the effects of "outliers" are removed, the general result is a better separation of the two populations. But the *apparent error rate*, which is obtained by reclassifying cases by the function computed from same cases, is grossly inflated on the optimistic side.

The median split strategy is quite likely to lead to initial misclassification of cases close to the sample mean if the criterion variable to be split is distributed normally. Consequently we should expect the "percent of correct classification" (the apparent error rate) which turns up on the printout in SPSS and BMD to be quite inflated when the "populations" resulted from a median split on a continuous criterion variable.

Tests of the hypothesis that a score vector **X** did not arise from *either* of two populations may be found in Rao (1965), for the case where population parameters are known, and in McDonald, Lowe, Smidt, and Meister (1976), for populations for which the parameters are estimated from sample values and the samples are small.

Occasionally an investigator will needlessly partition a continuous variable in order to "meet" the demands of the discriminant model. A pertinent example of such a misuse of discriminant analysis is the 1975 study, by Rosenfeld and Plax, of personality determinants of leadership. The avowed purpose of the study was to determine which subscales of a number of personality measures (California Psychological Inventory, Edwards Personal Preference Schedule, Tennessee Self-Concept Scale, among others) could be isolated as correlates of, respectively, autocratic and democratic leadership styles. The criterion variable, leadership style, was measured by the Sargent and Miller Leadership Questionnaire. However, rather than let the criterion vary continuoulsy, the investigators employed a median split to assign subjects to criterion groups. Such a procedure not only represents a loss of information but also introduces unnecessary error into the measurement of the criterion. A multiple regression analysis would have been more appropriate.

B. Missing Values

Occasionally the investigator will run up against the problem of *missing values*: the score vector for one or more of the cases will be incomplete. There are several alternatives available for dealing with missing values. One is simply to omit the entire case from the computations. This is the standard procedure in BMD, SAS, and SPSS, although the latter has an option by which the user may elect that all cases, regardless of missing values, be included in the computations: apparently the variable means are substituted for the missing elements(s).

Jackson (1968) has argued that omission of cases with missing values may produce a biased result: estimates of population parameters may be poor even when there are only a few, randomly distributed missing values. Furthermore, it may well be that one or two items are systematically ignored by some homogeneous subset of respondants. For example, certain kinds of subjects may be more prone than others to refuse to characterize themselves with respect to age, race, sex, marital status, or income. To eliminate such cases on the basis of missing values on a few variates may result in a considerable misestimate of population characteristics with respect to other variables.

Jackson studied the missing values problem by comparing (1) a discriminant analysis where a systematically deleted set of values was replaced by the variable means to (2) a discriminant analysis where these "missing values" were estimated by an elaborate iterative regression method (Federspiel, Monroe, & Greenberg, 1959) to (3) a discriminant analysis of the cases with deleted values replaced. She found that estimation of missing values by the variable means was not appreciably inferior to the iterative method when the criterion was the percentage of cases misclassified. The former method has the added advantages of being simple and economical.

C. Sample Size

The question of *sample size* in discriminant analysis has not received a great deal of attention from researchers. Many investigators have relied on the old rule of thumb that estimates of population parameters are unreliable unless there are at least 10–20 cases for each independent variable in the analysis. Lachenbruch (1968) conducted research to determine the necessary sample sizes to obtain error rates within a specified closeness to the optimum error rates. The needed sample sizes were found to vary considerably with the number of variables and the size of the squared distance between populations. The reader is urged to consult Lachenbruch's table for specific problems. In general, however, it was shown that the greater the group separation δ (the Mahalanobis' distance with parameters known), the smaller the necessary sample size; and the greater the number of variables, the greater the necessary sample size. To be within .01 of the optimum error rate, one ought to have about ten times as many observations as variables when the groups are very distinct ($\delta = 3$), and about twenty times as many observations as variables when the separation of groups is not very great ($\delta = 1$) (Lachenbruch, 1975).[2]

D. Number of Independent Variables

In some studies the investigator may be faced with a trade-off between inclusiveness and discriminatory efficiency. As a general rule, increasing the *number of independent variables* decreases the accuracy of classification. Van Ness and Simpson (1976) report a simulation study designed to determine the increase in Mahalanobis' distance necessary to offset increasing the number of variables in the score vector, for two linear, one quadratic, and two nonparametric algorithms. For instance, with a linear algorithm (unknown covariances), when the number of variates p was equal to 10, a classification

---

[2]Increasing the sample size will cause the *apparent* error rate to increase.

accuracy rate of .75 was obtained with a Mahalanobis δ of only 1.8, while with p equal to 20, an accuracy rate of .75 was not achieved until δ was equal to 2.4. For a quadratic discriminant analysis, the classification accuracy rate for $p = 2$ was $\approx .74$ at $\delta = 1.4$, while for $p = 5$, an accuracy rate as high as .74 required an increase in the Mahalanobis' distance from 1.4 to 1.8. The reader is urged to consult the Van Ness and Simpson tables for specific problems.

E. Stepwise Methods

The reader who first becomes familiar with discriminant analysis through the manual accompanying one of the popular statistical packages may well assume that a *stepwise* discriminant analysis is the preferred approach to hypothesis testing. Lachin and Schachter (1974) have shown, however, that highly significant between-group differences will frequently be found when a stepwise discriminant analysis is employed, even though there may be no real differences between the groups on the full set of p independent variables. The authors point out that in the reduced-model overall F-test, that is, in the test of the hypothesis that the K groups differ significantly on a linear combination of some *subset q* of the p variables, a new *random variate*, the number of variables selected, is added for which the test statistic does not account. We know that when p is large, we are likely to get some spuriously "significant" differences. Some of the spuriously discriminating variables will undoubtedly be entered into the discriminator set during the stepping procedure. Lachin and Schachter recommend that the full p-variate discriminant analysis be used for testing $\mu_1 = \mu_2 = \mu_k$: it is their claim that the stepwise Fs are "worthless." Lachenbruch (1975) suggests that variables be entered only until the overall alpha level reaches .05: he contends further that usually no more than three to five variables can "safely" be selected before noise factors enter in.

The stepwise procedure, however, appears to have much to recommend it to the investigator who wishes to select some subset of the full p-variable set to use in classification. Weiner and Dunn (1966) studied the results of classification based on discriminant analysis, using discriminant functions formed from subsets of varying sizes selected from an original set of 25 variates. There were four variable subsets of size 10, four of size five, and four of size two. Each of these variable subsets of a given size was formed according to one of four selection schemes: (1) those 10 (or 5, or 2) variables were included with the largest Student t between the sample means; (2) those 10 (or 5, or 2) variables were included that had the largest standardized discriminant coefficients; (3) those 10 (or 5, or 2) variables were included which were the first to be entered in a stepwise regression program which at each step reduces the residual sum of squares as much as possible; (4) those 10 (or 5, or 2) variables were included which were the first selected at random. For each classification run, equal prior probabilities and misclassification costs were assumed. An analysis of the proportion of misclassifications attributable to each of the four selection methods indicated that the stepwise selection procedure was considerably better than the other methods for the 10-variable sets, and roughly comparable to the Student t for smaller sets. The procedure of selecting those variates with the largest standardized discriminant coefficients was generally associated with larger proportions of misclassification (Weiner and Dunn, 1966).

There are a number of different stepwise selection methods available. The SPSS user may choose from among methods in which variables are entered or removed so as to (1) minimize Wilks' lambda (WILKS); (2) maximize D^2 between the least distinct groups (MAHAL); (3) minimize the residual sum of squares, summed over pairwise comparisons (MINRESID); (4) maximize the smallest F between pairs of groups (MAXMINF); (5) maximize the increase in Rao's V (RAO) (Klecka, 1975).

Experience tends to indicate that the different methods produce similar, and often identical, results, particularly when $K = 2$. This is not surprising considering that Wilks' lambda, which is minimized in method WILKS, is equal to $(1 - R^2)$, which is minimized pairwise in method MINRESID. Further, the pairwise F ratio which is maximized in MAXMINF is based on D^2, which is maximized in MAHAL. It seems reasonable to opt for the method in which the overall Wilks' lambda is minimized when there are more than two groups; the pairwise procedures for maximizing D^2 and/or F may not be fully effective if there are several groups, yet only a few "steps," as may be the case if there are only a few "good" variables. The MAHAL option in which D^2 is maximized would be a good choice in the case of two groups. See Cochran (1964) for an account of the effect of intercorrelations among the independent variables on variable selection with D^2.

McLachlan (1976) has proposed a method of variable selection in which the selection criterion is based on the increase in the conditional risk (probability of misclassification) associated with the deletion of a variable. McCabe (1975) has developed a FORTRAN program which computes statistics, including Wilks' lambda, for all $2^p - 1$ possible subsets of p variables. Using this method the investigator could find the "best" two-variable subset, the best five-variable subset, and so forth. [Finn (1974) and others have argued, however, that the test statistics associated with such procedures are invalid.] McKay (1976) has recently developed a procedure to find all possible subsets of variates which are not significantly less effective discriminators than the full p-variable set, in which the true significance levels and Type I family error rate can be determined.

IV. PRACTICAL PROBLEMS IN CLASSIFICATION

A. Test Space versus Reduced Space

One of the issues that arises in discriminant analysis is whether to classify in the *test space* or in the *discriminant space*. The reader will recall that ordinarily a score vector $\mathbf{X}_i$ is assigned to that group K for which $(\mathbf{X} - \overline{\mathbf{X}}_k)'\mathbf{S}^{-1}(\mathbf{X} - \overline{\mathbf{X}}_k)$ is the least. The researcher may wish to classify cases on the basis of the original $(p \times 1)$ score vectors and the group centroids on the p variables: this is known as the test space method (Lohnes, 1961). Alternatively, the vector of discriminant scores $\mathbf{Y}_i$ and the centroid $\overline{\mathbf{Y}}_k$ may be substituted for, respectively, $\mathbf{X}_i$ and $\overline{\mathbf{X}}_k$: this is known as the discriminant space method. When the population covariance matrices are equal, the results of classification will be the same for either method (Lohnes, 1961; Tatsuoka, 1971). When this condition does not hold, the classification results of the two methods will be similar, as a rule, but not identical. Huberty and Blommers (1974) found that the error rate was lower for the discriminant space method than for the test space method when the proportion of misclassification was determined in a cross-validation setting, where the error rate was computed for a hold-out sample rather than the "calibration" sample from whose score vectors the discriminant function was developed.

Tatsuoka (1971) argues that classification ought to be based on discriminant scores computed from the *significant discriminant functions only*. He makes the point that in using only the significant functions, the risk of dependence on spurious differences which may have arisen as a result of sampling error is reduced. If on the other hand the significant discriminant functions account for no more than, say, 60–75% of the variation in the discriminant space, the investigator may be losing considerable information by eliminating nonsignificant discriminants prior to classification.

B. Estimation of Prior Probabilities and Misclassification Costs

Arriving at appropriate estimates of *prior probabilities* and *misclassification costs* are two of the most difficult tasks in discriminant analysis. If the criterion variable on which the K groups were originally classified were, for example, sex, race, or marital status, and if the sample were truly representative, then the researcher should have little trouble establishing the prior probabilities. However, it is more likely that not very much will be known about the distribution of the criterion variable in the population. In this case, sample sizes may be used to estimate the prior probabilities so long as the samples are selected not from two separate populations but from one single population (Lachenbruch, 1975). A brief but provocative examination of the estimation of prior probabilities is given in Tatsuoka (1971).

Misclassification costs will rarely be figured with any accuracy: consequently caution is urged in departing from the assumption of equal misclassification costs in computing the posterior probabilities. Suppose, just for the moment, that a medical researcher were interested in developing a means of determining which persons having suffered dog bite should undergo a series of preventative injections against rabies. Since rabies is usually quite fatal, it is obviously the more costly error to classify an individual into Π_1 ("no shots") when in fact the individual should have been assigned to Π_2 ("shots").

On the other hand, those persons wrongly assigned to Π_2 will undergo a notably unpleasant series of injections which they could safely have foregone. An additional factor which undoubtedly would have to be considered would be the risk of legal liability attendant upon the misclassification of an individual into Π_1. On the other hand, there is a small proportion of the population which has a natural immunity against rabies: this should somewhat reduce the risk of assignment to Π_1. Were extreme caution to prevail, at some point the respective misclassification costs might become so disparate (say, $C_1 = .01$, $C_2 = .99$) that their influence on the assignment rule would wipe out the effects of the variables making up the discriminant. The complexity of the factors which the researcher must juggle would seem to preclude any generally acceptable cost estimates.

The study that follows typifies the current usage of discriminant analysis in diagnostic evaluation. Although the study was generally quite well designed, errors in the assumptions made by the researchers about prior probabilities and misclassification costs cast considerable doubt upon their claims.

Weiner and Weiner (1974) used stepwise discriminant analysis to determine whether or not the clinical observation of toy play behavior was of any diagnostic utility in distinguishing between normal and retarded children. Such an unobstrusive measure, one which would eliminate the need for subject–diagnostician interaction, appeared to the investigators to be particularly desirable.

Twenty institutionalized retardates (3- and 6-year-olds) and 40 normal children (again, 3- and 6-year-olds) were videotaped during play with such toys as blocks, jump ropes, and dolls. Raters viewing the tapes recorded at 20-second intervals the presence or absence of ten play behaviors, such as pushing and pulling, throwing, pounding, oral contact, and separation of parts. For each S the dependent measures were the number of times the presence of activity was observed in each of the ten toy play categories.

Three stepwise discriminant analyses were conducted: between 6-year-old retardates and 6-year-old normals; between 6-year-old retardates and 3-year-old normals; between 3-year-old normals and 6-year-old normals. Significant differences were obtained for all three of the comparisons.

Weiner and Weiner claimed to find that toy play observation was fairly effective in differentiating normals and retardates of the same chronological age: the proportion of correct classification, *based on the researchers' assumption of equal prior probabilities and equal costs of misclassification*, was 85%.

It is not possible to have a great deal of confidence in the results of the Weiner and Weiner study. In the first place, the researchers have confused prior probabilities with sample sizes. The a priori probabilities refer to the likelihood of an observation's actually belonging to each of the populations under study (Eisenbeis & Avery, 1972). It should be obvious that it is *not* equally probable, in the larger society, for a child to be retarded or normal. The most common estimate of the proportion of mentally retarded in the population is about 3% (Schreiber, 1970), although the figure will vary as a function of the age and socioeconomic level of the target population. Weiner and Weiner however, used a sample of *institutionalized* retardates. The incidence of institutionalized mentally retarded in the United States has been estimated at about .63 per thousand (Penrose, 1949). Although this figure was compiled many years ago, it is still regarded as an upper bound. [The incidence of grave mental retardation has declined in recent years as a result of improved standards in health services and nutrition (Akesson, 1975).] The prior probabilities should have been adjusted to reflect more closely the incidence of grave retardation.

Whether or not the costs of misclassification are equal would depend to a great degree upon the extent to which the diagnostic results would be regarded as final. If a trainable, mildly retarded child were classified as normal by the "appropriate" authorities, it is not unlikely, assuming no follow-up testing, that the child would be denied access to immediately needed services such as special education and medical treatment and might eventually be denied income maintenance of the type provided by O.A.S.D.I., for a "normal" child is not apt to be reclassified as a retarded adult. It is much more probable that there will be follow-up tests for the normal child misclassified as a retardate, since mental retardation is a symptom of a great many conditions, environmental, psychological, and neurological. At any rate, the changes of unwarranted institutionalization ought to be slim, especially considering that only about 4% of the retarded are institutionalized (Schreiber, 1970). It would appear, then, that if the diagnostic is to be used as a preliminary screening device, the costs of misclassification will probably be considerably more profound for the retardate than for the normal.

C. Determining Error Rates

Another practical problem encountered by the researcher is the estimation of classification errors (Lachenbruch and Mickey, 1968). The *optimum error rate*, assuming that the common population covariance matrix Σ is known, is given by $\Phi(-\frac{1}{2}\delta)$, where Φ is the cumulative normal distribution function and $\delta^2 = (\mu_2 - \mu_1)'\Sigma^{-1}(\mu_2 - \mu_1)$ (Lachenbruch, 1967). The sample-based error rate, with Σ assumed known, given for Π_1, is

$$\Phi\left(\left[(\overline{X}_2 - \overline{X}_1)'\Sigma^{-1}\{\mu_1 - \tfrac{1}{2}(\overline{X}_1 + \overline{X}_2)\}\right] \Big/ \left[\{(\overline{X}_2 - \overline{X}_1)'\Sigma^{-1}(\overline{X}_2 - \overline{X}_1)\}^{1/2}\right]\right)$$

(Moran, 1975). This is referred to as the *actual error rate*, which means the probability that a new case actually belonging to Π_1 will be misclassified. The *estimated error rate*, given by $1 - \Phi(D/2)$, where $D^2 = (\overline{X}_2 - \overline{X}_1)'S^{-1}(\overline{X}_2 - \overline{X}_1)$, is a biased estimate of the actual error rate based on the sample means and the pooled within-group covariance matrix (Lachenbruch, 1975; Moran, 1975).

Suppose that we had obtained discriminant scores for samples from two populations, Π_1 and Π_2, as shown in Fig. 2. Suppose that the Mahalanobis D^2 between the two samples were 4.50. What is the *estimated error rate* for Π_1; that is, what is the probability of misclassifying an observation arising from Π_1 into Π_2? It should be clear from Fig. 2 that such errors of classification will occur when individuals from Π_1 obtain Y scores greater than C, where C is equal to precisely one-half the Mahalanobis distance D between $\bar{Y}_1$ and $\bar{Y}_2$ (Overall and Klett, 1972). In other words, the probability of misclassification will be equal to the size of the shaded area under $f_1(Y)$. We determine the size of this area by looking up the ordinate at C in the normal table (Lachenbruch, 1975). Since C is equal to $D/2$, we need only find the area under the normal curve above a Z score of $D/2$ or 1.06: that proportionate area is equal to .1446. The proportionate error rate for Π_2 is given by the size of the striped area under $f_2(Y)$: it is also equal to .1446. Lachenbruch cautions that the estimated error rate may be of little use for small samples or nonnormal data (Lachenbruch, 1975). DiPillo (1976) has introduced a modification of the estimated error rate in which the ridge technique is used to offset the biasing effect of small sample sizes. Moran (1975) has developed exact expressions for the expected values of the actual error rate and the estimated error rate.

As a rule, the researcher will not know the population parameters: consequently the optimal error rate and the actual error rate will not be susceptible to computation. If the sample sizes are small, or if the data are "not quite normal," or if there are more than two groups, the estimated error rate will be less than useful. Three alternatives remain, however: (1) the *apparent error rate*; (2) the *"jackknife" error rate*; (3) the *"hold-out" error rate*. The apparent error rate is the proportion of cases in the original sample (that is, the same sample used to develop the assignment rule) which are misclassified by that rule. This type of error rate estimation is routinely performed in SPSS, BMD, and SAS. The apparent error rate has a pronounced optimistic bias, which decreases as the sample sizes become large. The "jackknife" error rate is the proportion of misclassification associated with a classification rule formed $(N_1 + N_2 + \cdots + N_k)$ times, with a different observation held out each time (Lachenbruch, 1967). This method of error estimation, which is available in

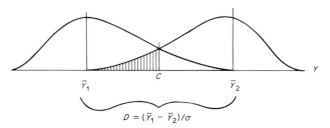

$$D = (\bar{Y}_1 - \bar{Y}_2)/\sigma$$

FIG. 2. Misallocation regions for two populations.

BMD, is rated by Lachenbruch and Mickey (1968) as the runner-up to the estimated error rate. The third method of error estimation, which is rejected by Lachenbruch on the practical grounds of cost, is based on the hold-out sample. In this method, a portion of the sample is withheld for cross-validation of the performance of the assignment rule. Cost notwithstanding, the hold-out method gives a much better approximation to the actual error rate than does the apparent error rate to its parametric counterpart. The hold-out method is easily implemented by the use of the SAS discriminant analysis program.

V. RESEARCH EXAMPLE

Edwards' (1973) theory of the early environmental antecedents of interpersonal styles led him to the development of the situational preference inventory, an instrument which may be used to characterize individuals as to their preferred or *primary* mode of social interaction. The situational preference inventory (SPI) classifies persons into one of three categories of social adaptation style. The *analytic* style, characterized by intellectualism, independence, and a tendency to psychological/sociological interpretation of the behavior of self and others, has been found to be associated with a permissive early environment in which minimal demands for conformity are made, and aggression is tolerated. For individuals preferring the *cooperational* and *instrumental* styles, parental approval was much more contingent upon "acceptable" behavior. The cooperational style, characterized by altruism and self-sacrifice, tends to develop in an environment in which the main task of the child is to win the love and approval, through ingratiation and self-denial, of the parent of the opposite sex. The instrumental style, characterized by a reliance upon authority and custom to structure interaction, appears to be the product of an early environment in which the demands are many, punishment is swift and sure, and parental approval is purchased by obedience (Edwards, 1973).

Suppose that a researcher has been able to classify a sample of 15 persons[3] as primarily analytic, cooperational, or instrumental in interpersonal style. Suppose further that the researcher had obtained scores, for the same individuals, on the following variables: (1) Factor 1 ("approach avoidance") of the unwillingness-to-communicate scale (Burgoon, 1976); (2) Factor 2 ("reward") of the unwillingness-to-communicate scale; (3) the total score on the predispositions toward verbal behavior scale (Mortenson, Arnston, & Lustig, 1977); (4) the total score on the Wheeless self-disclosure scale (Wheeless, 1976). The

---

[3]The data presented in this miniature example are a subset of a much larger data set: ordinarily the researcher would attempt to obtain a minimum of 80 subjects for a three-group problem in which the probable extent of group separation was not known in advance.

TABLE I

COMMUNICATION TRAITS OF ANALYTICS, COOPERATIONALS, AND INSTRUMENTALS;
MEANS AND STANDARD DEVIATIONS, ORIGINAL SAMPLE

Communication traits	Analytics, $N = 5$		Cooperationals, $N = 5$		Instrumentals $N = 5$	
	$\bar{X}$	σ	$\bar{X}$	σ	$\bar{X}$	σ
Willingness-to-communicate (approach/avoid)	50.40	3.51	45.00	7.71	41.00	4.44
Willingness-to-communicate (reward)	55.20	7.26	63.60	2.19	58.80	8.79
Predisposition towards verbal behavior	104.20	10.69	94.60	8.82	86.60	9.56
Self-disclosure	137.40	16.52	128.00	19.86	111.20	22.75

means and standard deviations for analytics, cooperationals, and instrumentals on these four variables are given in Table I. The researcher had hypothesized that instrumental subjects would have the lowest scores on this combination of variates; that is, that instrumentals actively avoid opportunities to communicate, find communication unrewarding, are nontalkative, and are reluctant to disclose. Analytics were predicted to have just the opposite profile on the combination of variables. Further, the researcher believes that this variable combination, or some subset thereof, would provide a good index of the individual's situational preference. How can discriminant analysis be used to test these speculations?

In the *inferential* phase of the discriminant analysis we test not one but two and possibly more null hypotheses. The first of these, H_1, is a test of the equality of the variance–covariance matrices for the analytics (Group 1), cooperationals (Group 2), and instrumentals (Group 3): H_1: $\Sigma_1 = \Sigma_2 = \Sigma_3$. We perform this test for two reasons. The first is to determine whether or not the data meet the assumption of homoscedasticity. This is not to say that if H_1 is rejected, the analysis must be abandoned. It would imply, however, that power of the test for the equality of the group centroids might be low. Additionally, the decision rule employed during the classification phase of discriminant analysis probably should be quadratic if H_1 is rejected.

Applying the Box test for homogeneity of variance to the sample data, we find that the covariance matrices for the three groups are indeed significantly different ($X^2 = 34.4359$, df $= 20$, $p < .0233$). Thus H_1 is rejected, implying that should all four of these variates be retained for classification, the assignment rule will have to be based on the group covariance matrices, rather than the pooled covariance matrix $\mathbf{S}_k$.

We proceed next to our test of the hypothesis that the centroids on the four variables are equal for analytics, cooperationals, and instrumentals: $H_2 = \mu_1$

$= \mu_2 = \mu_3$. Actually, for the present example, two such tests are needed. The reader will recall that ordinarily $K - 1$ discriminants are extracted from the matrix $\mathbf{W}^{-1}\mathbf{B}$. In the case of three groups, there may be two discriminants which produce among-group separation such that H_2 can be rejected. First the conjoint effect of both discriminant functions is tested. Should this test yield a X^2 which is significant at the specified confidence level, then (1) H_2 is false, and (2) at least the first discriminant function is significant. We may then proceed to determine if the second function is significant after the effects of the first have been removed.

With each of the eigenvalues λ_r of $\mathbf{W}^{-1}\mathbf{B}$ there is associated an independent chi square, V, which equals (Tatsuoka, 1970)

$$2.3026\left[N - 1 - \tfrac{1}{2}(P + K)\right] \log(1 + \lambda_r)$$

The conjoint effect of all the discriminant functions is determined by a chi-square test, with $P(k - 1)$ degrees of freedom, of the *sum* of the Vs associated with each eigenvalue. We may then determine if the linear combination of variates associated with the second function is significant by removing from the "sum" the V term corresponding to the largest eigenvalue (Tatsuoka, 1970).

To test the null hypothesis, a *direct* or nonstepwise discriminant analysis is performed on the sample data using SPSS. [The same analysis may be carried out using BMDs stepwise program P7M by setting the F-to-enter and F-to-remove parameters equal to zero, provided that all of the variables pass the tolerance test (Lachin and Schachter, 1974).]

The discriminant functions, standardized and unstandardized, and their respective eigenvalues are given in Table II. The first (unstandardized) discriminant function is the normalized eigenvector corresponding to the

TABLE II

STANDARDIZED AND UNSTANDARDIZED DISCRIMINANT FUNCTIONS, COMMUNICATION TRAITS OF ANALYTICS, COOPERATIONALS, AND INSTRUMENTALS[a]

Communication trait	Standardized functions		Unstandardized functions	
	Function 1	Function 2	Function 1	Function 2
Willingness-to-communicate (approach–avoidance)	− .5100	− .3091	− .0793	− .0480
Willingness-to-communicate (reward)	.3462	− .5924	.0484	− .0828
Predispositions toward verbal behavior	− .3245	.3505	− .0278	.0300
Self-disclosure	− .4182	− .4328	− .0194	− .0201
Constant			5.8230	6.7556

[a]Eigenvalues: $\lambda_1 = 2.9349$; $\lambda_2 = .3459$. Relative percentages: $\lambda_1 = 89.46$ $\lambda_2 = 10.54$.

TABLE III

SUMMARY STATISTICS, DISCRIMINANT FUNCTIONS:COMMUNICATION TRAITS OF ANALYTICS, COOPERATIONALS, AND INSTRUMENTALS

Discriminant function	Canonical R	Wilks' lambda prior to removal of function	X^2	df	P
1	.864	.1888	17.503	8	.025
2	.507	.7430	3.119	3	.374

largest root of $\mathbf{W}^{-1}\mathbf{B}$; the corresponding standardized function is obtained by multiplying each unstandardized coefficient V_i by $(w_{ii})^{1/2}$.

Table III presents the summary statistics associated with the two discriminant functions, including the X^2 significance test of the associated Wilks lambdas. For the conjoint effect of the two discriminants, Wilks' lambda = .1888 ($X^2 = 17.503$, df $= 8, p < .025$), meaning that only about 19% of the variation in the discriminant space remains unaccounted for by among-group differences.

The null hypothesis may thus be rejected: the conjoint effects of the $K - 1$ functions, and the independent effect of the first function both produce significant differences among analytics, cooperational, and instrumentals. However, removal of the variation accounted for by the first function increases Wilks' lambda to .7430, a value for which the associated chi-square is not statistically significant ($p < .374$). Table IV presents the matrix of F ratios for the pairwise (group-to-group) contrasts. These are the Fs associated with the Mahalanabis D^2 between groups. The analytic–instrumental differences are significant at $p < .05$, while the analytic–cooperational differences just miss significance at $p < .075$.

TABLE IV

F MATRIX, GROUP-TO-GROUP CONTRASTS: CONJOINT EFFECTS OF TWO DISCRIMINANT FUNCTIONS

	Analytics	Cooperationals	Instrumentals
Analytics			
Cooperationals	3.3304		
Instrumentals	6.3743[a]	1.3681	

[a] $p < .05$, df $= 4, 9$.

TABLE V

GROUP CENTROIDS IN THE DISCRIMINANT SPACE

	Function 1	Function 2
Analytics	-1.0616	.1313
Cooperationals	.2222	$-.4043$
Instrumentals	.8394	.2730

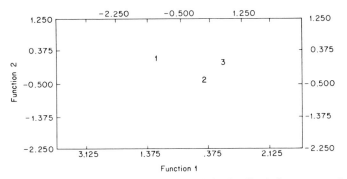

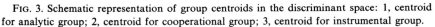

FIG. 3. Schematic representation of group centroids in the discriminant space: 1, centroid for analytic group; 2, centroid for cooperational group; 3, centroid for instrumental group.

Table V gives the coordinates of the three groups in the discriminant space (see also Fig. 3). Function 1 serves primarily to contrast the analytic and instrumental groups. Looking back to Table II, we find that an individual with a high score on Function 1 would avoid communication, avoid self-disclosure, and would not be inclined to talkativeness but might find communication rewarding. The primary effect of Function 2 is to separate cooperationals from instrumentals. An individual with a high score on Function 2 would be characterized primarily by a feeling that communication was unrewarding—that friends and family were not always honest and that one's opinions were of not much consequence (Burgoon, 1976). Although the X^2 associated with this second function is not statistically significant, in light of the earlier finding that the power of the test of H_2 might be low, it is quite probable that with a larger sample size the function would have been significant. Consequently, it is worth interpreting.

In the *classification* phase of our study, our first step ordinarily would be to determine the prior probabilities and misclassification costs. Although there is a disproportionately small number of instrumentals in the larger sample from which these subsamples were selected, for the present purpose of illustration we will assume that the prior probabilities are .33 for each group. The same simplifying assumption of equality will be made for the misclassification costs.

Since it has already been established that the centroids for the three groups are significantly different, it would now be appropriate to use a stepwise procedure to select the best of the discriminating variables. The Wilks' lambda selection criterion would probably be the best choice, since the objective is to find some subset of the four original variables which will maximize *overall* separation among the three groups.

The results of the stepwise analysis are given in Tables VI and VII. As it happens, the combination of just two of the variables, unwillingness-to-communicate, Factor 2, and predispositions toward verbal behavior, are sufficient to reduce Wilks' lambda to .3294. The group centroids in the

TABLE VI

STANDARDIZED AND UNSTANDARDIZED DISCRIMINANT FUNCTION COEFFICIENTS,
STEPWISE PROCEDURE: COMMUNICATION TRAITS OF ANALYTICS,
COOPERATIONALS, AND INSTRUMENTALS[a]

Communication traits	Standardized functions		Unstandardized functions	
	Function 1	Function 2	Function 1	Function 2
Willingness-to-communicate (reward)	− .5492	.7404	− .0768	.1035
Predispositions toward verbal behavior	.7248	.4811	.0621	.0412
		Constants	− 1.3592	− 10.0458

[a]Eigenvalues: $\lambda_1 = 1.6345$; $\lambda_2 = .1519$. Relative percentage: $\lambda_1 = 91.5$; $\lambda_2 = 8.5$.

reduced space are: Group 1, $\overline{Y}_1 = .8698$, $\overline{Y}_2 = 1.0406$; Group 2, $\overline{Y}_1 = -.3709$, $\overline{Y}_2 = .4335$; Group 3, $\overline{Y}_1 = -.4989$, $\overline{Y}_2 = -.3929$. Again the effect of Function 1 is to separate analytics and instrumentals, while the effect of Function 2 is to contrast cooperationals and instrumentals. A high score on Function 1 corresponds to a high predisposition toward verbal behavior and a low evaluation of the reward aspect of communication—the typical analytic pattern. A high scorer on Function 2 is typically a cooperational with a mild predisposition toward verbal behavior and a very high evaluation of communication as rewarding. The two-variable function yields some improvement over the four-variable functions in pairwise group separation: analytics and cooperationals are significantly different ($F = 6.3305$, df $= 2,11, p < .05$) as are analytics and instrumentals ($F = 7.5225$, df $= 2, 11, p < .01$), although cooperationals and instrumentals do not differ significantly ($F = .8924$, df $= 2, 11, p > .05$).

Our next step is to evaluate the effectiveness of these two independent variables as predictors of situational preferences. A Box test on the two-variable covariance matrices showed that they were significantly different ($X^2 = 11.2454$, df $= 6, p < .081$). We will thus perform a quadratic classification in the test space (the most conservative procedure) using the SAS

TABLE VII

SUMMARY STATISTICS, DISCRIMINANT FUNCTIONS OBTAINED FROM STEPWISE
PROCEDURE: COMMUNICATION TRAITS OF ANALYTICS, COOPERATIONALS,
AND INSTRUMENTALS

Discriminant function	Canonical R	Wilks' lambda prior to removal of function	X^2	df	p
1	.788	.3794	12.772	4	.012
2	.363	.8681	1.627	1	.202

TABLE VIII

RESULTS OF CLASSIFICATION FOR TWO-VARIABLE
QUADRATIC ASSIGNMENT RULE: APPARENT ERROR RATE
AND HOLD-OUT ERROR RATE[a]

From group	Classified into group		
	1	2	3
1	(100%)	(0%)	(%)
	33%	33%	33%
2	(0%)	(100%)	(0%)
	0%	100%	0%
3	(0%)	(60%)	(40%)
	50%	0%	50%

[a](X%) is apparent error rate; **X%** is hold-out error rate.

discriminant analysis program. The goal of the analysis is to obtain both the apparent error rate (the proportion of cases in the original sample which are misclassified by the minimum X^2 rule) and the "hold-out" error rate (the proportion of cases in a hold-out sample which are misclassified by the same rule).

The results of the classification based upon the quadratic assignment rule are given in Table VIII. The apparent error rate is 80%. Errors in reclassifying the original subjects occur only for instrumentals, three of whom are mistakenly classified as cooperationals. The holdout error rate is a less impressive .67. While all of the holdout cooperationals are correctly assigned, two-thirds of the analytics and one-half of the instrumentals are misassigned. This latter error rate would probably be considerably better had the original sample been a good bit larger: apparently the cooperationals in both samples are very similar, but this is not the case for the analytics and instrumentals.

We may conclude, then, that there is a subset of the original variables which will predict situational preferences, but with a only moderate degree of accuracy.

VI. FUTURE TRENDS IN DISCRIMINANT ANALYSIS

The next decade should usher in a much more widespread application of such developments as *logistic discrimination* (Efron, 1975) and *time-series discrimination* (Azen & Afifi, 1972; Shumway & Unger, 1974). While logistic discrimination has been shown to have a lesser asymptotic efficiency than normal discrimination, it is, in theory, more robust (Efron, 1975). In the logistic model, the probability that a case belongs to Π_1 given a score vector **X** is equal to $\exp(\alpha_0 + \beta'\mathbf{X})/[1 + \exp(\alpha_0 + \beta'\mathbf{X})]$, and the probability of Π_2

given X is $1/[1 + \exp(\alpha_0 + \beta'X)]$, where α_0 is given by

$$\ln(P_1/P_2) - \tfrac{1}{2}\left(\mu_1'\Sigma^{-1}\mu_1 - \mu_2'\Sigma^{-1}\mu_2\right)$$

and β' is given by $(\mu_1 - \mu_2)\Sigma^{-1}$(Efron, 1975).

Shumway and Unger (1974) have considered the problem of assigning a $(T \times 1)$ normal stationary time series X to one of two discrete categories: their example of such a problem is the allocation of events to one or the other of the categories "explosion" and "earthquake" on the basis of seismic records. The methods they have developed are spectral approximations to linear discriminant analysis which maximize either detection probabilities or information rates. Methods for the discriminant analysis of time dependent data which will have more appeal to the mathematically unsophisticated researcher have been developed by Azen and Afifi (1972). Suppose that observations are made at successive times t ($t = 0, 1, 2, \ldots, n, N$) on i cases arising from two populations Π_1 and Π_2. These observations may be t discriminant scores Y_i, obtained by computing the discriminant function for separating Π_1 from Π_2 at each of the points in time. Final classification is made on the basis of a discriminant function in which the variables are, respectively, the slope and intercept of the regression of Y on time (t): $Y = \alpha + \beta t$. These slopes and intercepts are calculated differently according to which of two models the researcher assumes. Under Model I it is assumed that the mean of Π_k is a linear function of time, while under Model II it is assumed that the mean for each case is a unique linear function of time.

For an account of other recent developments in discriminant analysis, such as *constrained discrimination* and *sequential discrimination*, the reader is referred to Lachenbruch (1975).

References

Akesson, H. O. The concept and prevalence of mental defect. In J. M. Berg, H. Lang-Brown, D. A. A. Primrose, and B. W. Richards (Eds.), *Proceedings of the the Third Congress of the International Association for the Scientific Study of Mental Deficiency*, Vol. 2. Warsaw: Polish Medical Publ., 1975.

Azen, S. P., and Afifi, A. A. Two models for assessing prognosis on the basis of successive observations. *Mathematical Biosciences*, 1972, **14**, 169–176.

Barr, A. J., Goodnight, J. H., Sall, J. P., and Helwig, J. T. *A user's guide to SAS*. Raleigh, North Carolina: Sparks Press, 1976.

Barlett, M. S. The vector representation of a sample. *Proceedings of the Cambridge Philosophical Society*, 1934, **30**, 327–340.

Barlett, M. S., and Please, N. W. Discrimination in the case of zero mean differences. *Biometrika*, 1963, **50**, 17–21.

Box, G. E. P. A general distribution theory for a class of likelihood criteria. *Biometrika*, 1949, **36**, 317–346.

Burgoon, J. K. The unwillingness-to-communicate scale: development and validation. *Communication Monographs*, 1976, **43**, 60–69.

Cochran, W. G. On the performance of the linear discrimination functions, *Technometrics*, 1964, **6**, 179–190.

Cover, T. M. and Hart, P. E. Nearest neighbor pattern classification. *IEEE Transactions on Information Theory*, 1967, **IT-13**, No. 1, 21–27.

DiPillo, P. J. The application of bias to discriminant analysis. *Communications in Statistics*, 1976, **A5**, 843–854.

Dixon, W. J. (Ed.). *Biomedical computer programs*. Los Angeles, California: Univ. of California Press, 1975.

Edwards, C. N. Interactive styles and social adaptation. *Genetic Psychology Monographs*, 1973, **87**, 123–174.

Efron, B. The efficiency of logistic regression compared to normal discriminant analysis. *Journal of the American Statistical Association*, 1975, **70**, 892–898.

Eisenbeis, R. A., and Avery, R. B. *Discriminant analysis and classification procedures: theory and applications*. Toronto: Heath, 1972.

Federspiel, C. F., Monroe, R. J. and Greenberg, B. G. *An investigation of some multiple regression methods for incomplete samples*. Univ. of North Carolina, Institute of Statistics, Mimeo Series, No. 236, August, 1959.

Finn, J. D. *A general model for multivariate analysis*. New York: Holt, 1974.

Fisher, R. A. The use of multiple measures in taxonomic problems. *Annals of Eugenics*, 1936, **7**, 179–188.

Fisher, R. A. The precision of discriminant functions. *Annals of Eugenics*, 1940, **10**, 422–429.

Fix, E. and Hodges, J. L., Jr. *Discriminatory analysis: non-parametric discrimination: Consistency properties*. Report No. 4, Project No. 21-49-004, School of Aviation Medicine, Randolph Air Force Base, Texas, 1959.

Gilbert, E. S. On discrimination using qualitative variables. *Journal of the American Statistical Association*, 1968, **63**, 1399–1412.

Gilbert, E. S. The effect of unequal variance-covariance matrices on Fisher's linear discriminant function. *Biometrics*, 1969, **25**, 505–515.

Holloway, L. N., and Dunn, O. J. The robustness of Hotelling's T^2. *Journal of the American Statistical Association*. 1967, **62**.

Huberty, C. J., and Blommers, P. J. An empirical comparison of the accuracy of selected multivariate classification rules. *Multivariate Behavioral Research*, 1974, **9**, 61–84.

Jackson, E. C. Missing values in linear multiple discriminant analysis. *Biometrics*, 1968, **24**, 835–843.

Klecka, W. R. Discriminant analysis. in N. H. Nie, C. H. Hull, J. G. Jenkins, K. Steinbrenner, and D. H. Bent (Eds.), *SPSS: Statistical package for the social sciences*. (2nd ed.) New York: McGraw-Hill, 1975. pp. 434–467.

Lachenbruch, P. A. Discriminant analysis when the initial samples are misclassified. *Technometrics*, 1966, **8**, 657–662.

Lachenbruch, P. A. An almost unbiased method of obtaining confidence intervals for the probability of misclassification in discriminant analysis. *Biometrics*, 1967, **23**, 639–645.

Lachenbruch, P. A. On expected probabilities of misclassification in discriminant analysis, necessary sample size, and a relation with the multiple correlation coefficient. *Biometrics*, 1968, **24**, 823–833.

Lachenbruch, P. A. Discriminant analysis when the initial samples are misclassified II: non-random misclassification models. *Technometrics*, 1974, **16**, 419–424.

Lachenbruch, P. A. *Discriminant analysis*. New York: Hafner Press, 1975.

Lachenbruch, P. A. and Mickey, M. R. Estimation of error rates in discriminant analysis. *Technometrics*, 1968, **10**, 1–111.

Lachenbruch, P. A., Sneeringer, C., and Revo, L. T. Robustness of the linear and quadratic discriminant function to certain types of non-normality. *Communications in Statistics*, 1973, **1**, 39–56.

Lachin, J. M., and Schachter, J. On stepwise discriminant analyses applied to physiologic data. *Psychophysiology*, 1974, **11**, 703–709.

Lohnes, P. R. Test space and discriminant space classification models and related significance tests. *Educational and Psychological Measurement*, 1961, **21**, 559–574.

Marks, S. and Dunn, O. J. Discriminant functions when covariance matrices are unequal. *Journal of the American Statistical Association*, 1974, **69**, 555–559.

McCabe, G. P., Jr. Computations for variable selection in discriminant analysis. *Technometrics*, 1975, **17**, 103–109.

McDonald, L. L., Lowe, V. W., Smidt, R. K., and Meister, K. A. A preliminary test for discriminant analysis based on small samples. *Biometrics*, 1976, **32**, 417–422.

McKay, R. J. Simultaneous procedures in discriminant analysis involving two groups. *Technometrics*, 1976, **18**, 47–53.

McLachlan, G. J. Asymptotic results for discriminant analysis when the initial samples are misclassified. *Technometics*, 1972, **14**, 415–422.

Mclachlan, G. J. A criterion for selecting variables for the linear discriminant function. *Biometrics*, 1976, **32**, 529–534.

Moore, D. H., II. Evaluation of five discrimination procedures for binary variables. *Journal of the American Statistical Association*, 1973, **68**, 399–404.

Moran, M. A. On the expectation of errors of allocation associated with a linear discriminant function. *Biometrika*, 1975, **62**, 141–148.

Mortenson, C. D., Arnston, P. H., and Lustig, M. The measurement of verbal predispositions: scale development and application. *Human Communication Research*, 1977, **3**, 146–158.

Nie, N. H., Hull, C. H., Jenkins, J. G., Steinbrenner, K., and Bent, D. H. (Eds.), *SPSS: statistical package for the social sciences.* (2nd ed.) New York: McGraw-Hill, 1975.

Overall, J. E., and Klett, C. J. *Applied multivariate analysis.* New York: McGraw-Hill, 1972.

Penrose, L. S. *The biology of mental defect.* London: Sidgwick & Jackson, 1949.

Porebski, O. R. On the interrelated nature of the multivariate statistics used in discriminatory analysis. *The British Journal of Mathematical and Statistical Psychology*, 1966, **19**, 197–214.

Rao, C. R. *Linear statistical inference and its applications.* New York: Wiley, 1965.

Rosenfeld, L. B., and Plax, T. G. Personality determinants of autocratic and democratic leadership. *Speech Monographs*, 1975, **42**, 203–208.

Schreiber, M. (Ed.) *Social work and mental retardation.* New York: John Day Company, 1970.

Shumway, R. H., and Unger, A. N. Linear discriminant functions for stationary time series. *Journal of the American Statistical Association*, 1974, **69**, 948–955.

Sokal, R., and Sneath, P. *Principles of numerical taxonomy.* San Francisco, California: Freeman, 1963.

Tatsuoka, M. M. *Discriminant analysis: the study of group differences.* Selected Topics in Advanced Statistics, an Elementary Approach, No. 6. Champaign: Institute for Personality and Ability Testing, 1970.

Tatsuoka, M. M. *Multivariate analysis: Techniques for educational and psychological research.* New York: Wiley, 1971.

Tatsuoka, M. M. Classification Procedures. In D. J. Amick and H. J. Walberg (Eds.), *Introductory multivariate analysis for educational, psychological, and social research.* Berkeley, California: McCutchen Publ., 1975. Pp. 257–284.

Van de Geer, J. P. *Introduction to multivariate analysis for the social sciences.* San Francisco, California: Freeman, 1971.

Van Ness, J. W., and Simpson, C. On the effects of dimension in discriminant analysis. *Technometrics*, 1976, **18**, 175–187.

Weiner, E. A., and Weiner, B. J. Differentiation of retarded and normal children through toy-play analysis. *Multivariate Behavioral Research*, 1974, **9**, 245–252.

Weiner, J. M., and Dunn, O. J. Elimination of variates in linear discrimination problems. *Biometrics*, 1966, **22**, 268–275.

Wheeless, L. R. Self-disclosure and interpersonal solidarity: measurement, validation, and relationships. *Human Communication Research*, 1976, **3**, 47–61.

Chapter 7

CANONICAL CORRELATION

RAYMOND K. TUCKER
School of Speech Communication
Bowling Green State University
Bowling Green, Ohio

LAWRENCE J. CHASE
Communication Studies Department
California State University
Sacramento, California

I. INTRODUCTION

Fewer test statistics have enjoyed greater popularity than has the Pearson product-moment coefficient of correlation. The reasons are clear: correlation is a measurement of the relationship existing between two variables. And the

MULTIVARIATE TECHNIQUES
IN HUMAN COMMUNICATION RESEARCH

existence of a significant relationship is of great scientific interest in virtually every research domain. In fact, nearly every major statistical model employed by the behavioral scientist has as its primary goal the assessment of relationships. Recently, however, interest in studying the degree to which a single pair of variables are related has declined. Several factors have contributed to this decline.

The major factor is the frustration that accompanies working with only a single pair of variables. Even if a correlation coefficient is impressively high, the researcher is left with the empty feeling of not knowing whether the variables per se represent scientifically meaningful constructs or whether they contribute only a small amount of variance to a larger construct. Since most of the important constructs in the behavioral sciences are thought to consist of clusters of variables it is reasonably safe to conclude that any two variables are likely to represent only a portion of a construct. Working with variables rather than constructs has the effect of muddying the theoretical waters and of producing research results that are misleading and unreplicable.

A second factor contributing to the decline of interest in binary correlation is that the interpretation of large numbers of bivariate correlations is simply too difficult a task.

Finally, there is the issue of time and resources. The executing of many bivariate correlational studies over a long period is uneconomical. A single multivariate study is by far the better research buy.

Because of these and other limitations associated with simple correlation, interest has shifted to multivariate research models which do not constrain the researcher to the study of only two variables at a time. Canonical correlation ($\mathbf{R}c$) is representative of this class of models. The logic of the model and the mathematics associated with the computational algorithm were detailed by Hotelling (1935, 1936). Canonical correlation has been available since 1935. Few behavioral scientists have employed the model, however, because of the high level of mathematical abstraction associated with the algorithm. Additionally, the computation of a canonical correlation is an arduous task that is best accomplished by computer. And until computers came into widespread use few researchers could afford the enormous investment in time.

$\mathbf{R}c$ may be employed to study the relationships between any two sets of linearly related variables. The only restriction is that there be a minimum of two variables in each set. With one variable in one set and two or more in a second, a multiple regression obtains. Single variables in each set, of course, resolve to a problem of simple correlation.

Essentials of the Model: An Overview

A canonical correlational analysis begins with the computation of four intercorrelation submatrices representing within- and between-set correlations. Assume that Set 1 has five variables and Set 2 three variables. The resulting supermatrix is depicted as follows:

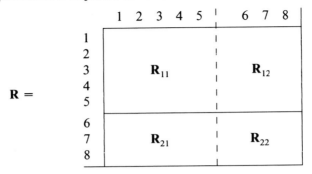

where $\mathbf{R}_{11}$ represents the intercorrelations of Set 1 variables, $\mathbf{R}_{12}$ represents the correlation of Set 1 with Set 2 variables, $\mathbf{R}_{21}$ represents the transpose of the $\mathbf{R}_{12}$ submatrix, $\mathbf{R}_{22}$ represents the intercorrelations of the Set 2 variables. Next the basic canonical relationship (BCR) matrix is formed. This involves multiplications of the submatrices:

$$\left[\mathbf{R}_{22}^{-1} \quad \mathbf{R}_{21} \quad \mathbf{R}_{11}^{-1} \quad \mathbf{R}_{12} \right]$$

The solution of an $\mathbf{R}c$ problem involves the extracting of two sets of *weights* simultaneously, one for each variable set. These weights, similar to the beta weights of multiple regression, are applied to each subject's original data scores to form linear composites called *canonical variates*. The canonical correlation coefficient is the Pearson product-moment correlation between pairs of canonical variates for each root.

A second set of weights may be extracted to account for residual variance. Root 2 weights can be expected to differ from those extracted from the first root. Additional sets of weights are obtained until 100% of the variance has been extracted. The number of sets of weights that can be extracted is equal to the number of variables in the smaller set. Hence, the number of roots is likewise equal to the number of variables in the smaller set. An $\mathbf{R}c$ analysis, then, extracts unique sets of weights for each root. In our example, weights for a maximum of three roots can be extracted since the smaller set contains three variables.

The $\mathbf{R}c$ algorithm operates so as to produce pairs of canonical variates for each root that are maximally correlated. Variates formed from successive roots are orthogonal to (uncorrelated with) all previous variates.

Roots are tested for statistical significance using Bartlett's (1941) χ^2 test. The null hypothesis is that the canonical correlation coefficient is equal to zero.

The extracting of weight sets for each root is referred to in the mathematical literature as an eigenstructure problem. From the BCR matrix, roots and eigenvectors are extracted. The eigenvectors, usually normalized, are the canonical weights.

A fundamental problem in canonical correlation is how the canonical variates are to be interpreted. As in factor analysis interest centers on the nature of each dimension. Historically, researchers examined the size and configuration of the weights in each set. Variates were labeled by noting the variables associated with the highest weights. Many researchers continue to rely on the weights to interpret canonical variates. For reasons to be explained later, however, we advocate interpreting canonical variates by examining the canonical component *loadings*. Loadings represent the correlations of the original data variables with the derived canonical variates.

The determination of sets of canonical variates has been the classic motivation for conducting an **R**c analysis. A confusion that continues in the literature, however, is exactly what the correlation of the pairs of canonical variates means. The **R**c coefficient is a direct measure of the correlation of the variates. **R**c^2 (the root) indicates the amount of variance shared by the *variates*. It is not a measure of the variance shared by the two *sets* of variables. To assess the degree to which the sets overlap, an index of redundancy is utilized. It assesses the amount of variance in the Set 1 variables predictable from a knowledge of the Set 2 variables, and vice versa. The index we suggest for this purpose is the one developed by Stewart and Love (1968).

II. HYPOTHETICAL RESEARCH EXAMPLE

Behavioral researchers have expressed frequent concern over the experimental artifact problem. In any research involving human subjects the possibility exists that the data is resulting from sources other than the investigator's experimental manipulations, or from a combination of artifact and manipulation. Among other undesirable effects, this can produce theoretical confusion as studies fail to replicate. In this hypothetical research example we focus on five potential sources of artifact. These constitute the Set 1 variables:

(1)   *S*'s evaluation of the physical environment (the room) in which the study is conducted.

(2)   *S*'s attitude toward forced (nonvoluntary) participation in the study.

(3)   *S*'s reported degree of evaluation apprehension as a result of participating in the study.

(4)   *S*'s assumed knowledge of the purpose of the study.

(5)   *S*'s rating of the attractiveness of the experimenter (the research assistant who administered the study).

The Set 2 variables:

(6)   *S*'s attitude toward the concept *capital punishment*.

(7)   *S*'s rating of the attractiveness of the communicator.

(8) S's rating of the communicator's attitude.
(9) S's rating of the communicator's public speaking ability.
(10) S's evaluation of the persuasive message.

Ss are randomly assigned to one of six experimental groups. An identical tape-recorded pro-capital punishment message is presented to each group. The experimental variations are (1) the experimental assistant and (2) the physical environment, i.e., the room in which the experiment is conducted. It is hypothesized that at least one significant relationship exists between the two sets of variables. Specifically, it is hypothesized that subjects who react positively to the room,

exhibit a positive attitude toward being a nonvolunteer subject,
report little evaluation apprehension,
feel they understand the purpose of the study, and
rate the experimenter positively on the attractiveness variable,

will exhibit positive attitudes toward the concept *capital punishment*,
rate the communicator higher on attractiveness, attitude, and public speaking ability, and will rate the persuasive message more positively.

The results are presented in Table I.

Turning to Root 1, we note that the χ^2 test indicates significance at $p < .0001$. The $\mathbf{R}c$ coefficient is high, .91. The root, $\mathbf{R}c^2, = .83$. These indicators suggest that the canonical variates are indeed highly correlated. Hence interpretation of the first root is in order.

Next, attention is directed to the vector of canonical component loadings for both sets. In a manner analogous to factor analysis the loadings define the nature of the canonical variates. Since the vector of variables for both sets is uniformly high, interpretation is facilitated.

Not surprising, the Set 1 vector seems to be defining an experimental artifact variate; the Set 2 vector a generalized attitude toward the experiment. Specifically, subjects who rate the room positively, report a positive attitude toward the participation requirement, express little evaluation apprehension (note the negative sign), feel they understand the purpose of the experiment, and rate the experimenter high on attractiveness—tend also to rate the concept *capital punishment* higher, rate the experimenter higher on attractiveness, attitude, and public speaking ability, and evaluate the persuasive message higher—thus lending support to the hypothesis.

Canonical variates, as noted earlier, are linear combinations of the original data variables. The $\mathbf{R}c$ coefficient represents the correlation of the variates for each root. Individual pairs of variates are formed by multiplying original data variables by the vector of weights for each root–set combination. Assume S_1 scored 7, 6, 1, 5, and 4 on the Set 1 variables, and 6, 5, 5, 6, 7, on the Set 2 variables. The canonical variate pair for that subject is computed by multiplying each score by the corresponding weight and summing:

TABLE I

CANONICAL STRUCTURE HYPOTHETICAL RESEARCH EXAMPLE

	Root 1 Loading	Root 1 (Weight)	Root 2 Loading	Root 2 (Weight)	Root 3 Loading	Root 3 (Weight)	Root 4 Loading	Root 4 (Weight)	Root 5 Loading	Root 5 (Weight)
Set 1 Variables										
1. Evaluation of physical environment	.92	(.28)	−.38	(−1.85)	.09	(.24)	.05	(.21)	.00	(.15)
2. Attitude toward forced participation	.92	(.15)	.18	(.77)	.03	(1.12)	.14	(1.30)	.31	(1.87)
3. Evaluation apprehension	−.92	(.15)	.12	(.23)	.07	(.62)	.36	(2.11)	.08	(.44)
4. Knowledge of purpose of study	.93	(.16)	.11	(.27)	.33	(2.77)	.00	(.33)	.08	(.47)
5. Attractiveness of the experimenter	.96	(.32)	.14	(1.07)	.07	(.80)	.06	(.90)	.22	(1.89)
Redundancy:	.72		.00		.00		.00		.00	
Set 2 Variables										
6. Attitude toward concept *capital punishment*	.97	(.58)	.18	(1.13)	.00	(.30)	.16	(1.05)	.10	(.75)
7. Communicator's attractiveness	.73	(.01)	.22	(.53)	.43	(.88)	.20	(.04)	.44	(1.14)
8. Communicator's attitude	.87	(.15)	.02	(.36)	.00	(.68)	.50	(1.72)	.01	(.56)
9. Communicator's public speaking ability	.88	(.08)	−.35	(1.14)	.30	(1.53)	.09	(.12)	.08	(1.00)
10. Evaluation of the persuasive message	.90	(.25)	−.33	(.87)	.13	(1.23)	.01	(.38)	.24	(1.40)
Redundancy:	.63		.00		.00		.00		.00	
	Rc = .91		Rc = .37		Rc = .17		Rc = .12		Rc = .01	
	Rc^2 = .83		Rc^2 = .14		Rc^2 = .03		Rc^2 = .01		Rc^2 = .00	

Total redundancy: Set 1 given Set 2 = .72; Set 2 given Set 1 = .63.

Tests of significance:

Root 1, χ^2 = 342.9644 with df = 25, $p < .0001$
Root 2, χ^2 = 132.5421 with df = 16, $p < .0085$
Root 3, χ^2 = 117.7148 with df = 19, $p < .5632$
Root 4, χ^2 = 112.3401 with df = 14, $p < .6735$
Root 5, χ^2 = 111.0230 with df = 11, $p < .8796$

For Set 1:

$$(7 \times .28) + (6 \times .15) + (1 \times .15) + (5 \times .16) + (4 \times .32)$$
$$= 1.96 + .90 + .15 + .80 + 1.28$$
$$= 5.09 = S_1$$

canonical variate, Set 1

For Set 2:

$$(6 \times .58) + (5 \times .01) + (5 \times .15) + (6 \times .08) + (7 \times .25)$$
$$= 3.48 + .05 + .75 + .48 + 1.75$$
$$= 6.51 \ S_1$$

canonical variate, Set 2.

Turning to the redundancy analysis we find that the total set overlap is restricted to the first root. The redundancy for Set 1, given a knowledge of Set 2, is .72. Moving from the opposite direction, the redundancy of Set 2, given a knowledge of Set 1, is .63. Note that the index differs depending upon direction, i.e., which set is computed given knowledge of the second set. A classic error in many $\mathbf{R}c$ analyses is to treat the canonical correlation coefficient as a measure of set overlap. The $\mathbf{R}c$ coefficient is a measure of the correlation between pairs of canonical variates for a given root. The index of redundancy is a measure of the degree of variable set overlap. It may also be viewed as the proportion of variance in Set 1 predictable from Set 2, and vice versa.

In summary, the Root 1 canonical variates are highly correlated. In addition, the two variable sets exhibit considerable redundancy.

The picture for Root 2 is strikingly different from that of the first root. First, the loadings are substantially lower as is the $\mathbf{R}c$ coefficient of .37. This is typical of successive roots in $\mathbf{R}c$ analyses since they contain residual variance, i.e., variance not associated with earlier roots. The $\mathbf{R}c$ is above the rule of thumb figure of .30; and the χ^2 test indicates significance at the $p < .0085$ level. These indicators suggest that this root also may contain scientifically meaningful information.

Set 1 is dominated by the first variable, evaluation of the physical environment, which is negatively loaded. Since the other variables are much lower than $-.38$ (in an absolute sense) attention may be limited to the first variable only. Set 2 is dominated by Variables 9, 10, and 7, in that order. The dimension suggests (note the negative signs) that subjects who report displeasure with the room in which the experiment was held have a moderate tendency to rate the communicator attractive but, on the other hand, to rate his public speaking ability lower. In addition, there is some tendency to devalue the persuasive message.

If interest lies solely in the relationships of the canonical variates, then the second root would seem to provide additional information of interest. The variates, uncorrelated with the first root variates, share 14% common variance as indicated by the size of the root. This, of course, represents only a small amount of shared variance. So conclusions regarding the relationship should be guarded despite the significant χ^2.

Should the researcher be interested in the degree to which the two sets span the same measurement space (redundancy), the analysis would terminate with Root 1. The redundancy index for Root 2 indicates that the two sets contain zero overlapping information, regardless of direction. This result illustrates vividly the differences that can obtain between the correlation of the canonical variates, on the one hand, and the amount of redundancy information contained in the variable sets on the other.

Summarizing Root 2, the **R**c coefficient indicates that the canonical variates are significantly correlated. The redundancy analysis, however, reveals zero set overlap.

Roots 3, 4, and 5 can be essentially ignored for several reasons. First, none is significant by χ^2 test. Second, the **R**c coefficients are less than the suggested .30 lower limit. Finally, the sets contain zero redundant information.

Before we leave this hypothetical research example we wish to stress the fact that other statistical models would normally be applied to the data base in addition to **R**c. A multiple discriminant analysis, for example, would reveal those variables maximally differentiating the six experimental groups.

III. RESEARCH DESIGNS UTILIZING THE **R**c MODEL

Whether a given statistical model should be employed in a research design should be decided by its appropriateness to the research goal. In the multivariate case, the researcher has a virtual arsenal of models from which to choose. Hence it is well to spend some time reflecting upon what might constitute an optimum choice. The general conditions under which **R**c might be an appropriate choice are those in which the goal is an assessment of the relationship between two sets of linearly related variables. The basic question the researcher must answer is this: What is the logical, theoretical basis for pitting the Set 1 variables against the Set 2 variables? This implies that the research project has evolved from a relevant theoretical base, that the literature has been assessed, and that the research problems will be best answered by studying the relationship of these specific sets of variables rather than two other sets. Each variable entering into the analysis, then, is selected for its theoretical relevance and meaningfulness.

The research designs discussed below represent a few of the ways in which the **R**c model can be used to answer research questions. The best way to view the prototypical studies is heuristically. That is, each design should be viewed in the light of additional research uses it might suggest. In the final analysis, the **R**c model can be used in any research provided it is appropriate and that it provides unambiguous answers to the research questions.

A. Naturally or Experimentally Paired Subjects

Research on paired subjects includes investigations involving, for example, husbands and wives, two children in the same family, or engaged couples. Wolff (1976) utilized the design in a study of self-disclosure between husbands and wives. The measuring instrument was Jourard's (1971) 21-item self-disclosure questionnaire. The Set 1 and 2 variables were identical. Wolff was interested in determining the degree of similarity of self-disclosure patterns within the marital dyads. Expressed somewhat differently, the research goal was to discover the extent to which the couples spanned the same measurement space on the Jourard test.

Naturally paired subject research is appropriate in any dyadic situation. The word "natural" is perhaps something of a misnomer inasmuch as truly naturally formed dyads are probably rare. The term is used only to differentiate it from similar research in which the subjects are paired by the investigator for the purposes of the research. Example: a professor and a student.

B. Test Relationships

The relationship existing between different types of tests has been studied extensively by researchers utilizing $\mathbf{R}c$. Most have been conducted by counseling psychologists. Typical of the research in this area is a study by Stewart (1971). This investigator pitted eight subscales from the Interest Assessment Scales against seven subscales comprising the Omnibus Personality Inventory. The motivation for the study was the existence of a trend, documented by Stewart, toward the drawing of inferences about personality attributes based on patterns of scores from interest inventories. The study was designed to examine the extent to which a strong relationship did in fact exist between the two tests.

Persuasion researchers might use $\mathbf{R}c$ in this instance to assess the degree of relationship existing between, for example, Likert-type attitude scales versus semantic differential scales. Research of this kind has been carried out by such researchers as Osgood, Suci, and Tannenbaum (1957); but they did not utilize the $\mathbf{R}c$ model. Subjects would be given both tests with Likert scales constituting the Set 1 variables, and semantic differential scales the Set 2 variables. Under conditions of a substantial canonical correlation, a decision might be made to utilize only one of the tests in subsequent research.

C. Academic Practice

Researchers can investigate the relationship of class characteristics to student evaluations of professors utilizing $\mathbf{R}c$. In this case Set 1 variables might consist of class size, grade point average, time/day of class meetings, whether the course is elective or required, etc. Set 2 variables might include ratings of the professor on such items as general teaching ability, homework, sense of humor, interest in students—to mention a few.

Personality or attitudinal characteristics may also figure into research on course evaluations. An investigator may wish, for example, to determine how alienation and anomie scores are related to course evaluations. Results could, for example, suggest that the more alienated students tend to be, the more negative are their evaluations of instructors.

D. Experimental Artifact Research

For several years behavioral scientists have expressed concern over the potential confounding effect experimenters can have on the outcome of experiments. Much of the more important research in this area has been summarized by Rosenthal and Rosnow (1969). The phenomenon has been studied from numerous angles; but well-conceived multivariate studies are clearly lacking. Tucker and Chase (1976) detailed a paradigm designed to investigate the problem in the persuasion domain. These authors suggested that measurements be taken on evaluation of the communicator and attitude toward the topic of the communication (Set 1 variables), evaluation of the experimenter, attitude toward serving as a nonvolunteer subject, and reported evaluation apprehension generated by participating in the experiment (Set 2 variables). A significant relationship between the two sets of variables might provide the basis for inferences such as more attractive experimenters are associated with higher scores on attitude tests. Findings of this nature, if consistently demonstrated, could have marked effects on the design of per-suasion–attitude change studies.

E. Mass Communication and Marketing

Rc research has been carried out most extensively by two groups of researchers: counseling psychologists and marketing researchers. Investiga-tors in this latter group tend to look upon Rc as a "natural" model because of their strong interest in relating personality characteristics to consumer brand and product preferences. In fact, a relatively new research domain called psychographics has as its principal goal the study of just such kinds of relationships. Sparks and Tucker (1971) utilized Rc to study the structural relationships existing between product use variables (Set 1) and personality traits (Set 2). Such information can be of value to the mass media, e.g., television networks, in terms of determining the optimum time to run product commercials.

F. Test Construction

A problem sometimes facing communication researchers utilizing pre-test–posttest designs is that of obtaining equivalent forms of the measuring instrument. Twenty scale items can be administered to a sample. Then the items can be divided into two equal sets of ten corresponding, say, to a pretest and a posttest. The structure resulting from the $\mathbf{R}c$ analysis would indicate that canonical variate associated with the first set (pretest) that is maximally related to the canonical variate of the second set (posttest).

G. Message Construction

As an aid in determining how elements, e.g., "pieces" of evidence, are related to a set of attitude subtests a researcher may choose to employ $\mathbf{R}c$. Such research could lead to the development of theories related to argumentation, persuasion, and public debate. A simple design in this area might begin with the construction of a five-minute persuasive communication containing five one-minute pieces of evidence: e.g., testimony, statistical data, real example, hypothetical example, and analogy. Each of these items (Set 1) could be rated as to persuasiveness or convincingness. Set 2 variables might consist of a series of five subtests of attitude toward the position advocated by the communicator. The $\mathbf{R}c$ analysis could provide indications as to which of the evidence pieces relates most positively to high scores on the attitude subtests.

IV. RESEARCH EXAMPLES

A. The Construction of Equivalent Forms of an Attitude Test

Over a period of years the senior author has developed sets of unidimensional attitude scales. For one 12-item set, designed to measure attitude toward the concept *annual medical checkups*, it was desired to obtain two equivalent forms for use in a univariate pretest–posttest persuasion experiment.

The $\mathbf{R}c$ analysis involved the pitting of the first six variables against the second six. Concern was with the obtaining of sets of weights to be applied to subjects' scores such that the resultant test items, when summed to composite scores, would be maximally correlated. The weight structure for the first root is presented in Table II. The $\mathbf{R}c$ coefficient, .88, the corresponding root, .77, and the test of significance, $p < .0001$—these provided compelling evidence that the canonical variates were highly correlated. The second root was not statistically significant; in addition the $\mathbf{R}c$ coefficient was less than .30. Hence attention was confined to Root 1.

Since factor analyses identified each of the 12 variables as determining a general evaluative factor, the labeling of the variates corresponding to the two sets was considered unnecessary.

The pattern of weights presents an interesting illustration of how different multivariate models operating on the same data base, can produce divergent results. Factor analyses of the data typically produced uniformly high correlations of each variable with a first general factor. Factor analysis, of course,

TABLE II

CANONICAL WEIGHTS FOR ROOT 1 EQUIVALENT FORMS STUDY

Set 1		Set 2	
Variable	Weights	Variable	Weights
1. Good–bad	.80	7. Valuable–worthless	.77
2. Right–wrong	.35	8. Wise–foolish	.66
3. Useful–useless	.40	9. Just–unjust	.09
4. Intelligent–stupid	.61	10. Approve–disapprove	.22
5. Nice–awful	.15	11. Honest–dishonest	.21
6. Fair–unfair	.29	12. Responsible–irresponsible	.51

$\mathbf{R}c = .88$, $\mathbf{R}c^2 = .77$, $\chi^2 = 342.9644$ with   df $= 25$, $p < .0001$

analyzes within-set variance. Canonical correlation analyzes between-set variance and weights the variables in such a way as to maximize the correlation of the variates.

Examination of the weights indicates that the variables in both sets contributed unequally to the construction of the canonical variates. For Set 1 most heavily weighted are Variables 1 and 4, at .80 and .61, respectively. The remaining variables are weighted considerably less than either of these. The Set 2 variables exhibit even greater variation. Variable 7 clearly dominates, followed closely by Variables 8 and 12. The weight for Variable 9 indicates that its contribution to the construction of the canonical variate is negligible compared to most of the other variables in the set.

In terms of the research goal the $\mathbf{R}c$ analysis was quite satisfactory. Since the variates were found to correlate highly there is justification for using the weights to construct equivalent forms of the tests for use in later experimentation.

B. Hinman and Tucker's Study of Student Evaluations of Communication Instructors

Hinman and Tucker (1978) completed an $\mathbf{R}c$ analysis, $N = 2479$, of student responses to 20 selected items related to the evaluation of communication instructors at a midwestern state university. Six variables comprised Set 1:

(1) Status of the student: freshman to senior (positive = senior).
(2) Student's cumulative grade point average (negative = high average).
(3) Final grade expected (negative = high grade).
(4) Evaluation of instructor's fairness (negative = fair).
(5) Evaluation of instructor's academic standards (negative = high).
(6) Amount of effort put into the course (negative = very much).

Fourteen variables (7)–(20) were assigned to Set 2:

(7)   Organization of course material.
(8)   Preparation for class.
(9)   Enthusiasm and interest in course.
(10) Assignments, e.g., clear to vague.
(11) Concept selection, e.g., selects important ideas.
(12) Encouragement of class discussions, questions.
(13) Poise and self-confidence.
(14) Examinations, e.g., thought-provoking questions.
(15) Mastery of subject.
(16) Ability to maintain student interest.
(17) Tolerance, e.g., encourages differences of opinion.
(18) Sense of humor.
(19) Instructor–student relationship.
(20) Overall teaching skill.

Set 2 variables were scored 1–6 with 1 indicating the highest score on the item, 6 the lowest. This explains the numerous negative loadings, especially in Root 1.

The authors designed the study in order to determine if variables that are, strictly speaking, unrelated to actual classroom teaching behavior do in fact influence instructor evaluations. The analysis is displayed in Table III.

The first two roots were statistically and practically significant. The R_c coefficient of .20 for Root 3, while significant, accounted for only 4% shared variance. It was dropped from further consideration.

1. THE FIRST ROOT

The Set 1 vector is dominated by Variables 5 and 4, in that order—and, to a lesser extent, by Variable 6. The authors chose to label the variate "professional integrity." The Set 2 vector defines a generalized instructor evaluation variate. Though Variables 7, 8, 16, and 20 dominate, virtually all of the variables, with the exception of Variable 14, are heavily loaded.

Interpretation of the dimension is evident. Students who rate an instructor's academic standards high, perceive him/her to be fair, and who put greater effort into the course—these students tend to rate that instructor higher on all 14 teaching-related variables.

2. THE SECOND ROOT

Root 2 accounted for only 13% shared variance. However, the size of the sample suggests that the relationship of the variates should be evaluated. Set 1 Variables 4 and 5 are again dominant with Variables 3 and 6 also making strong contributions. The main difference between the roots seems to be the elevation of Variable 3, expected grade, from $-.24$ in Root 1 to $-.40$. The

TABLE III

CANONICAL STRUCTURE INSTRUCTIONAL EVALUATION STUDY

Set		Variable	Root 1[a, c] Loadings	(Weights)	Root 2[b, c] Loadings	(Weights)
1	1.	Student status: freshman to senior	− .11	(−.0897)	− .04	(−.0777)
	2.	Cumulative grade point average	− .03	(.0573)	.12	(.2091)
	3.	Expected grade	− .24	(−.0048)	− .40	(−.3148)
	4.	Fairness of instructor	− .78	(−.5875)	− .57	(−.7171)
	5.	Instructor's academic standards	− .81	(−.5704)	.50	(.6362)
	6.	Student effort	− .43	(−.1512)	.40	(.2779)
2	7.	Course organization	− .81	(−.1766)	.07	(−.0596)
	8.	Class preparation	− .80	(−.2050)	.22	(.2947)
	9.	Enthusiasm—interest	− .77	(−.1181)	.10	(.2094)
	10.	Assignments	− .60	(−.0123)	− .31	(−.4482)
	11.	Concept selection	− .77	(−.1152)	− .00	(−.0674)
	12.	Encourages discussion	− .63	(−.0123)	.07	(.2008)
	13.	Poise—self-confidence	− .62	(−.0678)	.18	(.1961)
	14.	Examinations	− .41	(−.0814)	− .25	(−.2039)
	15.	Subject mastery	− .71	(−.1271)	.30	(.4269)
	16.	Ability to maintain interest	− .83	(−.1800)	.06	(.1468)
	17.	Tolerance	− .57	(−.0881)	− .39	(−.2716)
	18.	Sense of humor	− .65	(−.0409)	− .20	(−.1214)
	19.	Instructor–student relationship	− .66	(−.1260)	− .55	(−.7099)
	20.	Overall teaching skill	− .80	(−.0218)	.04	(.1102)

[a]Root 1: $Rc = .67$, $Rc^2 = .45$, $\chi^2 = 2049.3928$, df $= 84, p < .0001$. Redundancy: Set 1 given Set 2 $= 11\%$, Set 2 given Set 1 $= 22\%$.
[b]Root 2: $Rc = .36$, $Rc^2 = .13$, $\chi^2 = 533.1296$, df $= 65, p < .0001$. Redundancy: Set 1 given Set 2 $= 2\%$, Set 2 given Set 1 $= 1\%$.
[c]Total redundancy: Roots 1 and 2: Set 1 given Set 2 $= 13\%$, Set 2 given Set 1 $= 23\%$.

most powerful variables associated with the Set 2 variates are 19, 17, 10, and 15, in that order.

The Set 1 variate is not easily labeled. How is a student parsimoniously described who tends to expect a high grade, who puts only average (or less) effort into the course, who perceives the instructor to be fair, but who also rates that instructor low on academic standards? After considerable unproductive discussion the authors concluded that an "average student syndrome" seemed as reasonable a label as any. Interpreting the loadings in Set 2 likewise presents something of a challenge. But since the heaviest loadings are associated with Variables 19 and 17 it would seem justifiable to label that variate—tentatively at any rate—a kind of "human relations" variate. The loadings suggest, then, that students who rate the instructor fair, but low on academic standards, who expect a high grade, and who put minimal effort into the course tend to rate him/her high on instructor—student relationships, tolerance, clarity of assignments, and knowledge of subject matter.

Does the second root make substantive sense? Or is it more representative of a statistical artifact? The questions cannot be answered with any degree of certainty. To be sure, the root was not nearly as interpretable as was Root 1. Therefore the researcher could conceivably restrict the analysis to the first root. Before making this decision, however, it would be well to consult with experts in the discipline directly related to the study, in this case educational research or educational psychology. Configurations of variables that seem unintelligible to the unsophisticated can sometimes be interpreted by those with advanced training in the specialized area.

3. HIGH LOADINGS—LOW LOADINGS

The process of interpreting canonical variates typically involves focusing on the loadings with the highest absolute value. But what can be said of the most heavily loaded variable in a set? Answer: It is the variable that most highly predicts the variate in the opposite set. In Root 1, for instance, student ratings of the instructor's academic standards (Variable 5) is the best single predictor of the generalized course evaluation variate associated with Set 2. Likewise, the instructor's ability to maintain class interest (Variable 16) is the best single predictor of the "professional integrity" variate of Set 1.

Finally, how are low loadings, including those that approach zero, to be interpreted? Simply put, they are unrelated to the variate in the opposite set. Looking again at Root 1, the loading of $-.03$ for Variable 2 indicates that grade point average is entirely unrelated to the overall evaluation of the instructor, a finding likely to be of considerable importance to educational theorists.

4. REDUNDANCY ANALYSIS

The analysis to this point has focused on the nature and strength of relationships existing between the pairs of canonical variates. The final step in the analysis was computation of the redundancy index for the first two roots.

Virtually all of the redundancy was associated with the first root as evidenced by the figures in Table III. Set 2, given Set 1, contained 22% predictable information; and Set 1, given Set 2, contained 11%. The redundancy figure for the second root once again dramatizes the potential differences that can result between canonical variate relationships and variable set relationships. While the variates were significantly related the set redundancy approached zero. Combining roots, the redundancy figures increased to 13% and 23% for Sets 1 and 2, respectively.

V. THEORETICAL AND PRACTICAL PROBLEMS

Although the literature relating to $\mathbf{R}c$ is far from extensive and comparatively few researchers have employed the model, a number of issues have arisen regarding its use and its limitations. Some of the criticisms are the result of a misunderstanding concerning what $\mathbf{R}c$ is capable of accomplishing. But others are reasonable and must be taken seriously. $\mathbf{R}c$, in brief, has its limitations. It is still in an evolutionary stage. The next few years should see many of the uncertainties surrounding its use disappear. In addition, research in progress points to an enlargement of the capabilities of the model. Canonical correlations with more than two sets, which is not readily available today, is likely to become routine in the future. In addition, a variety of rotations of the canonical vectors is likely to become common practice.

A. Psychometric Adequacy

Questions as to the overall soundness of the $\mathbf{R}c$ model have arisen over the years. A frequently expressed reservation lies in the area of the interpretability of canonical structures. Critics point out that $\mathbf{R}c$ analyses are difficult to relate to substantive areas, that the statistical entities that result often bear little relation to the real world. The basic criticism is, Do the structures make theoretical, or substantive sense, or do they represent statistical artifacts?

The answer is that the relationship structures resulting from an $\mathbf{R}c$ analysis may or may not make substantive sense. And this is true of any multivariate statistical model. Factor analysts, for instance, have often noted that a given factor may be uninterpretable. The more general issue is how statistical structures of any kind should be assessed.

First, it seems clear enough to seasoned multivariate researchers that far too much emphasis is placed on the results of a statistical analysis. Researchers often seem overly concerned with computer printouts: loadings, coefficients, correlations. The better course is not to place total reliance on statistical results per se. The safer, more productive course, is to assess the statistical output as it relates to the substantive area under consideration. This implies that the researcher treat the findings as a set of indications which, when studied in the context of current knowledge in the area under investigation, can contribute to the theoretical development of that area. The $\mathbf{R}c$ model is psychometrically sound. But it cannot perform miracles on the data base. It is maximally powerful when its results are studied within the context of existing theory.

B. Canonical Weights—Canonical Loadings

In the hypothetical research example a distinction was made between canonical weights and canonical component loadings in terms of the functions they serve. To review briefly, weights are used to construct canonical variates. Loadings represent correlations of original data variables with canonical variates.

For years researchers have used the weights to interpret the nature of canonical variates. However, in 1964 Merideth (1964) published an article critical of this practice. His recommendation was that rather than focus on the weights the researcher would be better advised to place the interpretation on the loadings. The logic underlying the choice of loadings over the weights is intimately connected with the issue of the stability of those weights, or the problem of "bouncing betas." In brief, statistical models involving the extraction of beta weights, such as multiple regression and canonical correlation, produce weights that are characterized by instability. The weights tend to shrink across samples. The reasons are many; but essentially a substantial error factor is likely to be responsible. When samples are small and are neither well defined, homogeneous, nor random, large quantities of sample-specific covariation can result. In addition, the problem can be aggravated by less than optimum conditions surrounding the execution of the study.

In order to gain insight into the relative stability of weights versus loadings, Thorndike and Weiss (1973) executed a comprehensive cross-validation study. They found the loadings to hold up more firmly under cross-validation than the weights.

A critical aspect of the problem is rarely discussed. Which of two possible interpretations does the researcher wish to focus upon? A direct analogy to factor analysis is helpful at this point.

It is a matter of empirical fact that the loadings in a factor structure matrix —the correlations of variables with factors—may differ from the matrix of factor score coefficients in the case of, for example, the regression estimates model. Now typically it is the factor structure matrix that is interpreted. But the factor score coefficients are the weights used in the construction of factor scores. Canonical component loadings are analogous to factor structure coefficients; weights to factor score coefficients. So if the construction of the canonical variates is of concern, then attention should be directed to the contributions of the weights. They constitute an operational definition of the canonical variates. If research interest lies in assessing the correlations of the canonical variates with the original data variables, then, as is standard practice in the interpretation of factor analytic structures, attention should focus on the loadings. It seems clear to the present authors that interpreting the loadings is appropriate for the bulk of communication research. Indeed it is our opinion that researchers who choose to interpret the weights should present a logical basis for doing so.

C. Variables and Samples

Rc seeks to maximize the relationships of variables. It works most effectively when there is an adequate number of variables to interrelate. Hence researchers are encouraged to input as many well chosen, theoretically relevant variables as is considered necessary to the attainment of the research goal. There are both practical and computer limits, however. Hence the number of variables and their characteristics should be given careful consideration.

Theoretical relevance should be the primary criterion for variable inclusion. This normally results from the researcher's investigation into the theoretical and research literature. It is a time-consuming process that few researchers relish. But unless a thorough search is made, the investigator runs the risk of omitting a substantively important variable. Since the canonical model maximizes variate correlations, each potential variable should be studied for its possible relationship to the other variables both within its own set and between the second set. The process constitutes what is called an *a priori* analysis. In such an analysis variables are included only when it seems plausible that they will contribute to the definition of the variate in a theoretically meaningful way.

Common sense suggests that if only a few variables, i.e., four or five, are of interest, then studying the ordinary correlations existing among them may be all that is necessary. An Rc analysis would hardly be justified. When the number climbs to say eight or more then it becomes more difficult to assess the thrust of the variable relationships. At this point, an Rc analysis might be very fruitful indeed. The issue is twofold: First, some theorists posit a well-defined relationship between the number of dependent variables and necessary sample size. Weiss (1972), for instance, suggests a minimum of twenty subjects per measured variable. Weiss is virtually the only scholar who offers a recommendation as to what constitutes an adequate sample for a canonical analysis. We offer this advice: Small samples should be avoided. We define a sample as small if it consists of fewer than 100 subjects. Second, while hard evidence is not available to us at this time, our experience suggests that a minimum of 200 subjects is needed for a scientifically useful Rc analysis. In studies involving over 12 variables the sample size should be increased accordingly. As with any study in the human communication domain the researcher is seeking well-defined, stable data indicators. The enemy is always the error component; and large samples are needed to combat the influence of this error on the data.

One issue remains to be discussed concerning the number of variables to be included in an Rc analysis: that of the effects of including very large numbers of variables, e.g., 100 or more. It is known in the language of information theory as a signal-to-noise problem. The difficulty, briefly stated, is that large numbers of variables can submerge fine distinctions and permit only gross, strong, relationships to emerge. Further, the uncritical inclusion of numerous variables into an Rc analysis will inevitably lead to interpretation problems. We cannot advocate strongly enough the need for restraint. In brief, "shotgun empiricism" rarely solves important research problems.

D. Method Specific Results

Behavioral scientists tend to become wedded to specific research models. There are those whose answer to every research problem is to apply factor analysis, path analysis, or canonical correlation. Two problems are associated with this kind of behavior.

The first is that the researcher may be inclined to try to fit the research problem to the model. This is permissible as long as the research goals can in fact be best answered by utilizing that particular statistical model. Sometimes it cannot, at least without some bending. The better course is to find the statistical model that best fits the research goals.

There is a second reason for avoiding an overdedication to one research model. Its essence is contained in the word *heteromethod*. It suggests that multiple types of analyses are more likely to produce results that stand up under replication. The consistent use of a single method can introduce ambiguity inasmuch as there is no way of assessing the extent to which the obtained results are at least partially due to the specific method of analysis. The results, in other words, can be method specific. Human communication researchers are often faced with problems involving several independent and dependent variables. And certainly nobody would be so naive as to suggest that there is only one correct method of attacking these problems. In this perspective it seems entirely reasonable that the same body of research data might be analyzed using several of the research procedures discussed in this volume.

E. Cross-Validation and Replication

That canonical structures may be highly unstable from sample to sample was suggested earlier. We have addressed the issue of "bouncing betas"; and we have noted that canonical weights can exhibit considerable instability. Concern over this fact has led researchers to call for cross-validation procedures as a routine part of any canonical analysis. To review, the issue is this: Sample-specific covariation, error, chance—these may be capitalized upon in such analyses as canonical correlation. Under these conditions inferences concerning the population parameters, based on the sample, can be misleading. Future researchers may be unable to replicate the structures—neither the weights nor the loadings. To reduce the possibility of this occurring, we suggest a cross-validation be executed:

(1) The sample must be of sufficient size to permit dividing it into two subsamples, a main sample and a hold-out sample.
(2) Execute the $\mathbf{R}c$ analysis.
(3) Apply the weights obtained in the main sample to the hold-out group.

To the extent the canonical variates formed in this manner lead to $\mathbf{R}c$ coefficients similar to those of the first subsample—to that extent can the researcher be reasonably assured that the obtained structures are relatively stable.

Replication is a second method for assessing the reliability of $\mathbf{R}c$ structures. Replication involves repeating the study on a comparable sample. If the original structures emerge from the replication then confidence that they may in fact be good representations of the population structures is increased. Replication is the ultimate criterion of science. Regardless of sample size or the brilliance of the design and execution, the ultimate question is, Are the results replicable?

While replication is advocated by many, it is accomplished by few. The history of the behavioral sciences, including human communication research, is one of a failure to replicate. This condition has caused critics of behavioral science to question the value of conducting such research. Unfortunately some replication research is so sloppily carried out that it contains the seeds of its own failure. Because replication is so crucial to the development of theory, the researcher should exercise care in executing such studies. Before replications involving strategic variations are carried out we advocate the executing of "exact" replications.

Executing an exact replication employing the canonical correlation model would demand that the researcher adhere to the following criteria:

(1)   that the sample be of sufficient size and have demographic character-istics similar to those found on Ss in the study being replicated;

(2)   that the dependent variables be identical;

(3)   that the methods of administering the study be as nearly identical to the original as possible.

Studies unable to meet these minimal criteria cannot qualify as exact replica-tions and should not be reported as such.

VI. SUMMARY AND RECOMMENDATIONS

(1)   Canonical correlation is a multivariate procedure for maximizing the correlation between linear combinations of two sets of variables. These composite, weighted linear combinations are known as canonical variates.

(2)   The weights used to determine canonical variates are extracted from a basic canonical relationship matrix. For each root, a vector of weights is extracted—one for Set 1 and one for Set 2. These weights, sometimes referred to as beta weights because of their similarity to the partial regression weights of regression analysis, are the eigenvectors that have been extracted from the BCR matrix. Hence, canonical correlation—like factor analysis and discrimi-nant analysis—is essentially an eigenstructure problem.

(3)   A root represents the amount of variance extracted. It is also a direct indicator of the amount of variance shared by the pairs of canonical variates.

There are as many roots as there are variables in the smaller set. Each root explains variance not associated with the preceding root. The canonical variates for the second root are maximally correlated and are orthogonal (uncorrelated) to the first root. The same condition holds true for all successive roots.

(4) Roots are tested for significance via Bartlett's (1941) χ^2 test. Statistically significant roots may or may not be practically significant. The size of the $\mathbf{R}c$ coefficient should also be considered. Coefficients of less than .30 are considered trivial.

(5) Canonical component loadings represent correlations between canonical variates and original data variables. They are analogous to the structure loadings of a factor analysis. Whether the weights or the loadings should be used for interpretation purposes has been a source of controversy. In general, if interest lies in interpreting the nature of the constructed canonical variates, then the weights should be relied upon. If, however, the relationship of the canonical variates to the original data variables is the goal (as is customary in factor analysis) then the loadings should be interpreted. In the general case we advocate interpreting the loadings.

(6) A given $\mathbf{R}c$ root structure may not necessarily make theoretical sense. If the first root cannot be meaningfully interpreted in terms of existing theory, then that root may be abandoned in favor of interpreting the second or third root. It is assumed that these latter roots are both practically and statistically significant. In general the results of an $\mathbf{R}c$ analysis should be considered suggestive of a potential structure existing in the population. Statistical models produce statistical structures. Substantive interpretations must be made by the researcher.

(7) The relationship between the two *sets* of variables can be assessed via redundancy analysis. This index provides an indicator of shared variance, predictability, or the amount of overlap existing between the two variable *sets*. It is referred to as a redundancy index because it provides a measure of the amount of overlap (redundant information) in one set, given that information is available concerning a second set, and vice versa. The index is asymmetric. That is, it assesses redundancy for Set 1 given a knowledge of Set 2; and for Set 2 given a knowledge of Set 1.

(8) $\mathbf{R}c$ analyses must be based on large samples. Consider a ratio of 20 subjects per dependent variable the lower limit. Results obtained on small samples may contain large quantities of error or sample-specific covariation, with the consequence that the obtained structures cannot be replicated.

(9) Theoretically relevant and interesting variables should be included in an $\mathbf{R}c$ analysis. Inputting massive numbers of variables, however, may lead to important distinctions becoming literally buried. An a priori analysis should be conducted. Each variable should be evaluated in terms of its potential substantive relationship both to the variables within its own set and to the variables in the second set. This will provide a theoretical benchmark to aid interpretation of the structures.

(10) **R**c may be used in conjunction with other statistical models. The utilization of more than one method of analysis increases the probability that the results are not method specific.

VII. TECHNICAL SUPPLEMENT: THE REDUNDANCY ALGORITHM

Computation of the redundancy index (Stewart and Love, 1968) is provided by Dr. Roger Wimmer of the University of Georgia. A detailed description of the study is not necessary to the explanation of the procedure. The study examined the relationship between mass media variables and voter practices in the 1972 campaign. Interested readers are invited to examine the complete work, Wimmer's doctoral dissertation, Bowling Green State University, 1976.

SET 1 VARIABLES = POLITICAL INTEREST
SET 2 VARIABLES = MEDIA USED FOR POLITICAL INFORMATION

Set	Root 1[a]		Root 2[b]		Root 3[c]		Root 4[d]	
	Loadings	(Weights)	Loadings	(Weights)	Loadings	(Weights)	Loadings	(Weights)
Set 1								
1. Always Vote	.4700	(.2359)	.7713	(.8744)	.2707	(.3285)	.2639	(−.3182)
2. Attention	.7875	(.6131)	−.0650	(−.1667)	−.3138	(−.5036)	.3405	(.4575)
3. Party Worker	.3798	(.0217)	−.5253	(−.1583)	.3561	(.0603)	−.6089	(−.8723)
4. Organization	.2835	(.1451)	−.2926	(−.1137)	.8431	(.8734)	.3315	(.6539)
5. Money	.6978	(.4944)	−.1201	(−.0726)	.1184	(−.0405)	−.1323	(−.0928)
Set 2								
6. Newspaper	.9184	(.6425)	.3050	(1.1632)	.0696	(.2057)	.2421	(.1689)
7. Radio	.4708	(.0234)	−.4302	(−.4341)	.7024	(1.0751)	.3161	(.1488)
8. Magazines	.8302	(.4602)	−.3812	(−.5780)	−.1181	(−.2349)	−.3892	(−.9502)
9. Television	.6357	(.0265)	.3943	(−.6041)	−.2577	(−.7866)	.6115	(.8867)

[a]Root 1, $\mathbf{R}c$ = .4309, $\mathbf{R}c^2$ = .1857, χ^2 = 722.0415, df = 20, $p < .0001$.
[b]Root 2, $\mathbf{R}c$ = .1355, $\mathbf{R}c^2$ = .0184, χ^2 = 86.6083, df = 12, $p < .0001$.
[c]Root 3, $\mathbf{R}c$ = .0777, $\mathbf{R}c^2$ = .0060, χ^2 = 29.2699, df = 6, $p < .0001$.
[d]Root 4, $\mathbf{R}c$ = .0583, $\mathbf{R}c^2$ = .0034, χ^2 = 10.5499, df = 2, $p < .0052$.

Since redundancy is a nonsymmetric index, computation is done for either Set 1 given Set 2, or Set 2 given Set 1. In this example, the computation for Set 1 given Set 2 is provided.

Step 1 The first value to be obtained is the sum of squares for each canonical loading ($\mathbf{R}c_i$). Square each loading in each root and sum ... $\Sigma(\mathbf{R}c_i)^2$. For Root 1:

$$(.4700)^2 + (.7875)^2 + (.3798)^2 + (.2835)^2 + (.6978)^2 = 1.5526$$

Step 2 Divide 1.5526 by the number of variables (M) in the set. This equals the variance extracted for that root.

$$\text{VE} = \Sigma(\mathbf{R}c_i)^2/M = 1.5526/5 = .3105.$$

Step 3 Multiply VE by $\mathbf{R}c^2$ for Root 1 (.1857) to obtain the redundancy ($\overline{\mathbf{R}}$) for Root 1:

$$\overline{\mathbf{R}} = \text{VE} \times \mathbf{R}c^2 \quad \text{or} \quad \overline{\mathbf{R}} = .3105 \times .1857 = .0577 \quad \text{(for Root 1 of Set 1)}$$

Step 4 The same procedure is followed for the remaining roots. For Root 2:

$$(.7713)^2 + (-.0650)^2 \cdots + (-.1201)^2 = .9776.$$

$$\text{VE} = .9776/5 = .1955, \quad \overline{\mathbf{R}} = .1955 \times .0184 = .0036$$

For Root 3:

$$(.2707)^2 + (-.3138)^2 + \cdots + (.1184)^2 = 1.0235$$

$$\text{VE} = 1.0235/5 = .2047, \quad \overline{\mathbf{R}} = .2047 \times .0060 = .0012$$

For Root 4:

$$(.2639)^2 + (.3405)^2 + \cdots + (-.1323)^2 = .6835$$

$$\text{VE} = .6835/5 = .1367, \quad \overline{\mathbf{R}} = .1367 \times .0034 = .0004$$

Step 5 Total VE for Set 1 equals sum of the VEs for each root in the set:

$$.3105 + .1955 + .2047 + .1367 = 84.74\%$$

THE COMPLETE REDUNDANCY TABLE

COMPONENTS OF REDUNDANCY FOR CANONICAL CORRELATION: POLITICAL INTEREST VERSUS MEDIA USED FOR POLITICAL INFORMATION

Set	Root	$\mathbf{R}c$	$\mathbf{R}c^2$	VE	$\overline{\mathbf{R}}$
1[a]	1	.4309	.1857	.3105	.0577
	2	.1355	.0184	.1955	.0036
	3	.0777	.0060	.2047	.0012
	4	.0583	.0034	.1367	.0004
2[b]	1	.4309	.1857	.5396	.1002
	2	.1355	.0184	.1447	.0027
	3	.0777	.0060	.1446	.0009
	4	.0583	.0034	.1710	.0005

[a]Total variance extracted from Set 1 = 84.74%; $\overline{\mathbf{R}}$, total redundancy for Set 1, given Set 2 = 6.29%.

[b]Total variance extracted from Set 2 = 1.00; $\overline{\mathbf{R}}$, total redundancy for Set 2, given Set 1 = 10.43%.

Step 6   Total $\overline{\mathbf{R}}$ for Set 1 equals the sum of the $\mathbf{R}$s for each root:

$$.0577 + .0036 + .0012 + .0004 = 6.29\%$$

Notes: (1) To compute $\overline{\mathbf{R}}$ for Set 2, the same procedure is followed. (2) The sum of VE for smaller set is always $= 1.00$. (3) Interpretation of individual $\overline{\mathbf{R}}$ is generally in order when equal to or greater than 5%. (4) There are no significance tests for $\overline{\mathbf{R}}$. It is used only as a summary index.

References

Bartlett, M. S. The statistical significance of canonical correlations. *Biometrika, 1941,* **32**, 29–38.

Hinman, D., and Tucker, R.K. *A canonical analysis of student evaluations of communication instructors.* Unpublished manuscript, Bowling Green State Univ., 1978.

Hotelling, H. The most predictable criterion. *Journal of Educational Psychology*, 1935, **26**, 139–142.

Hotelling, H. Relations between two sets of variates. *Biometrika*, 1936, **28**, 321–377.

Jourard, S. M. *Self-disclosure.* New York: Wiley (Interscience), 1971.

Merideth, W. Canonical correlations with fallible data. *Psychometrika*, 1964, **29**, 55–65.

Osgood, C., Suci, G., and Tannenbaum, P., *The measurement of meaning.* Urbana, Illinois: Univ. of Illinois Press, 1957.

Rosenthal, R., and Rosnow, R. L. (Eds.), *Artifact in behavioral research.* New York: Academic Press, 1969.

Sparks, D. L., and Tucker, W. T. A multivariate analysis of personality and product use. *Journal of Marketing Research*, 1971, **8**, 67–70.

Stewart, L. H. Relationships between interests and personality scores of occupation-oriented students. *Journal of Counseling Psychology*, 1971, **18**, 31–38.

Stewart, D. K., and Love, W. A. A general canonical correlation index. *Psychological Bulletin*, 1968, **70**, 160–163.

Thorndike, R. M., and Weiss, D. J. A study of the stability of canonical correlations and canonical components. *Educational and Psychological Measurement*, 1973, **33**, 123–134.

Tucker, R. K., and Chase, L. J. Canonical correlation in human communication research. *Human Communication Research*, 1976, **3**, 86–96.

Weiss, D. J. Canonical correlation analysis in counseling psychology. *Journal of Psychology*, 1972, **19**, 241–252.

Wimmer, Roger D. *A multivariate analysis of the use and effects of the mass media in the 1968 presidential election.* Unpublished doctoral dissertation, Bowling Green State Univ., 1976.

Wolff, L. O. *Self-disclosure in the marital dyad.* Unpublished doctoral dissertation, Bowling Green State Univ., 1976.

Chapter 8

FACTOR ANALYSIS

JOHN E. HUNTER

Department of Psychology
Michigan State University
East Lansing, Michigan

I. INTRODUCTION

There have been three main approaches to factor analysis: trait theory, dust bowl empiricism, and cluster analysis. Trait theory was developed by men such as Spearman (1904, 1927), Thurstone (1935, 1947), and Cattell (1946, 1965). For trait theory, the basic question to be answered by a factor analysis is, What are the fundamental traits which underlie a given set of observed variables? They are also identified by their use of "communalities" in their factor analyses.

Dust bowl empiricism was a reaction against trait theory that stemmed both from the general Zeitgeist of behaviorism in psychology and from a tendency to want to keep factor analysis linked to purely mathematical

MULTIVARIATE TECHNIQUES
IN HUMAN COMMUNICATION RESEARCH

computations rather than content oriented models. Strong supporters of this school include Thompson (1951), the younger Kaiser (1963), and Peter Schoenemann (personal communication). The identifying characteristic of dust bowl empiricists is their belief that the business of factor analysis is the prediction of one set of numbers from another set of numbers. There are two varieties among this group. One group sees factor analysis as a procedure for replacing a large and unwieldy set of observed variables by a smaller set of summary variables which preserve most of the information in the larger set. The other group sees factor analysis as a procedure for generating a small table of numbers which represents the main properties of the much larger correlation matrix between the observed variables. These groups are distinguished from one another in that the first group does factor analysis "with ones in the diagonal" while the other group uses "communalities." Since the second group is solely concerned with factor analysis as a mathematical procedure, they will be ignored here (though they do normally espouse techniques which are the same as the other dust bowl empiricists except for the use of communalities).

The cluster analysts are a growing group of heretics within the body of psychometricians, but are an immense group within the body of people doing empirical work in psychology. Some of the better known cluster analysts are Holzinger (1944), Tryon (1959), and Bailey (Tryon & Bailey, 1970). The basic idea in cluster analysis is that data come in two levels: (1) a microscopic level (usually called "items") of highly error laden measurements, and (2) a macroscopic level of combined or summarized measurements (usually called "scales" or "tests" or "indexes") which are closer to the desired perfect measurement of some theoretically given variable (usually called a "true score" or "construct"). In a cluster analysis the set of observed variables is partitioned into groups or clusters of variables in such a way that those variables in a given cluster are thought to be measures of the same underlying construct. This clustering of the data either fits the observed correlations or else the cluster analysis model must be rejected for that partition. In most data sets it is possible to fit a cluster analysis to the data by modifying the clusters, i.e., dropping variables which do not fit the cluster into which they have been put or adding variables which were inadvertently put in some other cluster. If a cluster analysis is done "with ones in the diagonal," then the corresponding factors are ordinary scales, i.e., the sum of the items which made up the cluster. If the cluster analysis is done with "communalities," then the resulting factors are the hypothetical perfectly measured constructs which underlie each cluster.

This chapter is intended to be an exposition of these three approaches to factor analysis, not an evaluation of them. However, since my own beliefs will be visible between the lines, let me state my own position. As an undergraduate I read Cattell and Thurstone and I was excited by trait theory. As a graduate student I became disenchanted with trait theory and became a dust bowl empiricist. As a professor I have worked through actual empirical studies in which we have tried to find out something about people from analyses of survey data of the sort normally analyzed by factor analysis. After the first such serious project, I became convinced that the questions asked by traditional factor analysis—be it trait theoretic, or dust bowl—are simply irrelevant to real research. In particular, I became convinced that there can be no more useless final form of data display than a set of factor loadings. I have found cluster analysis to be a meaningful approach in those 95% of the studies where there was no need for a nonlinear model such as itemetrics or Guttman scaling.

A number of excellent textbooks have now been written for factor analysis, including those by Harman (1967) and Mulaik (1972), but especially the one by Gorsuch (1974).

II. THE DUST BOWL EMPIRICISTS

Consider factor analysis as it is viewed by the "dust bowl empiricists." Their contention is that whatever else a factor might be, it must be an observable variable. They argue that it must be possible to compute a person's score on each factor, i.e., a factor must be an exact function of the original variables. For example, if there are 150 original variables, $X_1, X_2, \ldots, X_{150}$, then a linear factor would take the form

$$F = b_1 X_1 + b_2 X_2 = \cdots + b_{150} X_{150} \tag{1}$$

where b_1 are weighting coefficients.

What is the purpose of a factor analysis to a dust bowl empiricist? He sees factor analysis as a method of data reduction; his main objective is to replace the original 150 variables by a small set of "summary variables," say $F_1, F_2, \ldots, F_{16}$. The question for such an analysis is, How much of the variance in the full set of original variables is accounted for by the smaller set of factors? This question generates an "ideal" solution in the sense that the ideal factors are those which account for the maximum possible variance. When Hotelling (1933) solved this problem, he called these factors the "principal components."

The phrase "the amount of variance accounted for by the factors $F_1, F_2, \ldots, F_k$" is *defined* to mean the squared multiple correlation, R^2, of the given variable onto the factors $F_1, F_2, \ldots, F_k$. Thus for each observed variable X_i, the amount of variance accounted for by the factors $F_1, F_2, \ldots, F_k$ is defined to be

$$R^2_{X_i \cdot F_1, F_2, \ldots, F_k} \tag{2}$$

The total variance in the set of observed variables accounted for by the K

factors would thus be

$$\sum_{i=1}^{150} R^2_{X_i \cdot F_1, F_2, \ldots, F_k} \tag{3}$$

The principal components can then be defined successively by

(1)   The first principal component is that linear combination of the observed variables which has the largest possible sum of squared correlations with the observed variables.

(2)   The second principal component is that linear combination of the observed variables which is uncorrelated with the first principal component which increases the squared multiple correlations for the two factors by maximal amount.

(3)   The third principal component is defined to be that linear combination of the original variables which is uncorrelated with the first two principal components and which increases the squared multiple correlations for the three factors by a maximal amount.

(4)   And so on . . . . The kth principal component is that linear combination of the original variables which is uncorrelated with the first $k - 1$ principal components and which adds the maximum amount possible to the sum of squared multiple correlations of the original variables onto the k principal components.

Table I presents a hypothetical correlation matrix and the principal components of that correlation matrix. Table Ia presents the correlations. Variables 1–4 can be thought of as four items from a text labeled "fear of public speaking"; they are highly but not perfectly correlated. Variables 5–8 can be thought of as four items from a test labeled "fear of inadequacy" which has been given to undergraduate students in secondary education; they too are highly but not perfectly correlated. The correlations between items from the two different sets are large because a fear of public speaking will lead to worries as to future inadequacy in teaching (since secondary teaching relies heavily on lecturing), however, they are not nearly so large as the correlations between items in the same set.

Table Ib presents the correlations between the eight original variables and the eight principal components which can be constructed from them. The number of principal components is equal to the number of variables, because none of the variables can be perfectly predicted from the others, as is true of nearly all data sets. However, the basis of the theory of principal components is that not all of the factors will be kept, i.e., only the first several are to be used as summary variables for the whole set. How many should be kept? There is no arbitrary answer to this question; the investigator must make up his mind how much of the variance he wishes to account for. The amount of variance accounted for by each successive principal component is smaller than the one before (or at least no larger), and hence the first several factors should account for far more of the variance in the data than the later factors.

TABLE I

THE INTERCORRELATIONS AND PRINCIPAL COMPONENTS FOR A HYPOTHETICAL SET OF EIGHT VARIABLES

(a) The correlations

	X_1	X_2	X_3	X_4	X_5	X_6	X_7	X_8
X_1	1.00	.64	.64	.64	.32	.32	.32	.32
X_2	.64	1.00	.64	.64	.32	.32	.32	.32
X_3	.64	.64	1.00	.64	.32	.32	.32	.32
X_4	.64	.64	.64	1.00	.32	.32	.32	.32
X_5	.32	.32	.32	.32	1.00	.64	.64	.64
X_6	.32	.32	.32	.32	.64	1.00	.64	.64
X_7	.32	.32	.32	.32	.64	.64	1.00	.64
X_8	.32	.32	.32	.32	.64	.64	.64	1.00

(b) The principal components factor loadings for the correlation matrix in (a) (decimals omitted)

	F_1	F_2	F_3	F_4	F_5	F_6	F_7	F_8
X_1	72	45	52	0	0	0	0	0
X_2	72	45	-17	0	49	0	0	0
X_3	72	45	-17	0	-24	0	42	0
X_4	72	45	-17	0	-24	0	-42	0
X_5	72	-45	0	52	0	0	0	0
X_6	72	-45	0	-17	0	49	0	0
X_7	72	-45	0	-17	0	-24	0	42
X_8	72	-45	0	-17	0	-24	0	-42

The first principal component accounts for 52% of the variance in the entire set of eight original variables in Table Ia. The second accounts for 20%, and the remaining six principal components account for 4.5% of the variance each. Thus a typical investigator might keep only the first two factors and thus account for 72% of the variance.

For the dust bowl advocates, the meaning or nature of the principal components is an unimportant consideration, names such as Factor 1, Factor 2, ... are fine. However, most users of factor analysis are unhappy with this approach and proceed to an interpretation anyway. Table Ia shows that the principal components in this hypothetical example are substantively rather strange. The first component correlates with all the variables equally and might be interpreted as "generalized fear," but the second component correlates positively with fear of public speaking items and negatively with fear of inadequacy items. What might that factor be? Unfortunately, there is no simple answer to the interpretation of principal components. The cluster analyst, however, can answer this question: The second principal component is the difference score for the cluster score of the first four items minus the cluster score for the last four items.

Because of the peculiar properties of the principal components, most factor analysts have rejected the use of principal components as a final solution to the problem. Instead they turn to a set of factors which is mathematically equivalent to the principal components, but which has more interpretable factors: these are called the "rotated" factors. The most widely used method of "rotating" the principal components to an alternative set of factors is Kaiser's (1958) VARIMAX procedure. The next most widely known method is the QUARTIMAX procedure from which Kaiser derived his method, which was independently discovered by Carrol (1953), Saunders (1953), and Neuhaus and Wrigley (1954). Technically, the shift from the principal components to a mathematically equivalent set of factors is called an "orthonormal transformation."

The definition of VARIMAX factors depends on the number of summary variables to be saved. If two summary variables are to be saved, then two principal components are rotated; if three variables are to be saved, then three principal components are rotated and so on. This fact is brought out in Table II which shows four sets of VARIMAX factors: those produced by rotating three components, four components, and finally eight components. The VARIMAX factors produced by rotating five, six, or seven principal components were deleted in consideration of space.

Another point is made in considering the different sets of factors in Table II; the meaningfulness of the VARIMAX factors depends on the number of factors rotated. If just two components are rotated, then the structure of the VARIMAX factors clearly shows the basic cleavage in the data. The first factor correlates .83 with each of the fear of public speaking items and .19 with each of the fear of inadequacy items, while the second factor correlates .83 with the adequacy items and .19 with the public speaking items. However, if three principal components are rotated, then a strange factor emerges which loads highly only on item 1. If four components are rotated, then strange factors emerge which have high loadings only on item 1 or only on item 5, respectively. This pattern reaches its ultimate if all eight principal components are rotated; each of the eight VARIMAX factors has a high

TABLE II

Two, Three, Four, and Eight VARIMAX Factors for the Principal Components in Table Ib (Decimals Omitted)

Two VARIMAX factors		Three VARIMAX factors			Four VARIMAX factors				Eight VARIMAX factors							
83	19	57	18	80	57	17	80	8	87	27	27	27	10	10	10	10
83	19	84	18	16	84	18	16	8	27	87	27	27	10	10	10	10
83	19	84	18	16	84	18	16	8	27	27	87	27	10	10	10	10
83	19	84	18	16	84	18	16	8	27	27	27	87	10	10	10	10
19	83	18	83	8	17	57	8	80	10	10	10	10	87	27	27	27
19	83	18	83	8	18	84	8	16	10	10	10	10	27	87	27	27
19	83	18	83	8	18	84	8	16	10	10	10	10	27	27	87	27
19	83	18	83	8	18	84	8	16	10	10	10	10	27	27	27	87

loading on only one variable. The technical explanation for this phenomenon lies deep in matrix algebra and appears to have no useful substantive interpretation. However, the trait theorists and the cluster analysts *do* have an explanation; they argue that these strange factors are an artifact of failing to distinguish between common and unique variance (trait theorists) or between true scores and error of measurement (cluster analysts). According to their models, no more than two factors should ever be considered for this data.

However, even if only two principal components are rotated, there is still an interpretational problem with the resulting VARIMAX factors. By definition, VARIMAX factors are uncorrelated. Thus, to assert that the first factor is "fear of public speaking" and the second factor is "fear of inadequacy" is to assert that these variables are uncorrelated. Yet, there is a correlation of .32 between any item representing fear of public speaking and any item representing fear of inadequacy. Most dust bowl empiricists interpret these facts to mean that naming factors is unwise and that factors are better left uninterpreted.

Some empiricists have tried to get around the problem of judging solutions for meaningfulness (which they regard as basically unscientific) by inventing a rule for determining the number of factors on a numerical basis. A number of such rules have been offered, the most famous of which is "Kaiser's rule" which is, Stop factoring when the eigenvalues go below one in value. The problem is that every such rule has been shown to be based on reasoning that ultimately proves to be in whole or in part false. For example, the error in Kaiser's derivation was found by Levine and Hunter (1971).

There is a fly in the ointment of the summary variable approach which has received little attention. The set of observed variables is "replaced" by the principal components only in the sense of analysis. The principal components are actually calculated from the observed variables. Thus principal components do *not* generate a reduced number of variables in the sense of reducing the number of measurements required in future research on the same factors. A technique similar in spirit to principal components has been developed by Hunter (1972) to which a best subset of the observed variables is used as the set of factors to summarize the data. Hunter calls his method "maximal decomposition." However, he warns that this technique is not suited to data at the level of "items," i.e., unsummarized very poor measurements, but is designed for studies using scales or other "molar" measurements with relatively little error of measurement.

SOP: The Standard Operating Procedure for the Interpretation of Factors

Once a person has gotten a factor analysis back from the computer center, his first question is usually, What are those factors? At this point many dust bowl empiricists will squirm in their chair and try to make an argument that factor interpretation is a risky and hence inherently unscientific business. So the investigator goes off and asks somebody else what he would do. The procedure that we shall outline is the *Scuttlebutt* method, and as we shall see later, it has severe drawbacks. But if you want to know what is done in most of the studies in the current literature, here it is.

The first step is to select a magic number to represent a "high" loading. The classic number is .30, though the reasons for this are lost in history. A number of people have switched over to using the standard .05 significance level. This level would be $1.96/N - 1$, where N is the number of observations on which the correlation was calculated, for a factor analysis done with ones in the diagonal (and larger to an unknown extent in a factor analysis done with communalities). Some people look at their output before deciding what a "high" loading is in their study. In any case, once a magic number has been chosen, then a "salient list" is drawn up for each factor; that is, all the variables with a high loading on that factor are listed (remember that $r = -.60$ is just as much "high" as is $r = +.60$.) On the basis of that list, a hypothesis as to the nature of the factor is made. Usually that hypothesis takes the form of a name for the factor.

What are the crucial errors made in applying this method of salient lists? Remember that just because the computer does not print the correlations between the factors, that does not mean the correlations between factors do not exist. The correlation between any two principal components, for example, is 0. So if you find that you want to name one factor "friendliness" and another factor "gregariousness," just remember that those factors are not correlated!!!

III. TRAIT THEORY: SURFACE TRAITS AND SOURCE TRAITS

When we look at people or ask them questions or consider particular behaviors, we are observing their "surface traits." The correlations between surface traits are often all so low they suggest that there is no structure to personality, that behaviors are mostly independent, etc. But this is not true. The problem is that there are so many ways of accomplishing the same purpose in external behavior that any given behavior will have a large random component that is composed of (1) randomness in the subject's response itself, (2) trivial situational determinants, (3) trivial semantic misinterpretations, etc.

Underlying the infinity of surface traits that represent the vagaries of momentary behavior, we presume that there exists a more stable motivational structure which represent s the person's basic purposes and desires in life. The variables which describe that structure are the "source traits" which are the heart of all personality theories. The fundamental simplicities which those theories have attempted to capture are shown mathematically by the fact that the number of source traits is not only finite, but very small.

If there are an infinite number of surface traits, but only a finite number of source traits, then how do we find the source traits? First, we must gather data on a large and representative sample of surface traits. The term "representative" implies that the selection of surface traits must be broad enough to involve *all* the source traits, and must not be so concentrated on a few aspects of personality that some source traits are related to only one or two surface traits.

Let $X_1, X_2, \ldots, X_{150}$ be set of surface traits. Let $F_1, F_2, \ldots, F_{16}$ be the fundamental source traits. Then for each surface trait there is a multiple regression equation for that surface trait in relation to the source traits; i.e., we can write

$$X_1 = a_{i1}F_1 + a_{i2}F_2 + \cdots + a_{i16}F_{16} + e_i \tag{4}$$

where e_i is the error in predicting the surface trait X_i from the source traits $F_1, F_2, \ldots, F_{16}$ and the a_{ij} are the regression weights. Thus, by definition we have

$$r_{e_i F_1} = r_{e_i F_2} = \cdots = r_{e_i F_{16}} = 0 \tag{5}$$

Since the surface traits are trivial except insofar as they relate to the source traits, they carry no mathematical information about each other that is not also given in the source traits, i.e., the errors $e_1, e_2, \ldots, e_{150}$ in predicting each surface trait from the source traits $F_1, F_2, \ldots, F_{16}$ are essentially garbage and in particular the errors $e_1, e_2, \ldots, e_{150}$ are uncorrelated with each other, i.e.,

$$r_{e_i e_j} = 0 \quad \text{if} \quad i \neq j \tag{6}$$

Trait theorists are split on one important point: Are the underlying source traits correlated or uncorrelated? We shall first consider the problems in finding uncorrelated or "orthogonal" source traits or factors. We shall later return to this question and comment on finding correlated traits by "rotating" principal axis factors. Cluster analysis can be regarded as a more radical method of finding correlated source traits. But for the moment we shall assume that the underlying source traits are independent of one another, i.e.,

$$r_{F_i F_j} = 0 \quad \text{if} \quad i \neq j \tag{7}$$

How would a set of uncorrelated factors be related to the original data? The answer is this: The underlying factors account for all the correlations that exist between the observed variables (to within sampling error). Thus, if the basic statistical facts about the factors are known, then from those facts we should be able to "predict" all the correlations between the observed variables. What are the basic facts? For *uncorrelated factors*, the regression weights in the model

$$X_i = a_{i1}F_1 + \cdots + a_{i16}F_{16} + e_i \tag{8}$$

are in fact simply the correlations between factors and variables, i.e.,

$$a_{ij} = r_{X_i F_j} \tag{9}$$

The matrix of factor variable correlations is called the *factor structure matrix* and is designated $\mathbf{A}$, and we shall find a formula that yields the correlations between the original variables from the factor loadings in the matrix $\mathbf{A}$. What is the relationship between the observed matrix, $\mathbf{R}$, and the unknown matrix, $\mathbf{A}$? The fact is that all the observed correlations must be accounted for by the entries of $\mathbf{A}$, and the equation which does it is this: If the factors are *uncorrelated*, then

$$r_{ij} = \sum_{k=1}^{16} a_{ik} a_{jk} \qquad \text{if} \quad i \neq j \tag{10}$$

For those who know matrix algebra, this formula says that if $i \neq j$, then r_{ij} is the dot product of the ith and jth rows of the factor structure matrix. What if $i = j$? If $i = j$, then $r_{ij} = r_{ii} = 1$ whereas the dot product for the diagonal is

$$\sum_k a_{ik} a_{jk} = \sum_k a_{ik}^2 < 1 \tag{11}$$

That is, the dot product formula *does not work for the diagonal entries* of the observed correlation matrix, only for the off-diagonal entries.

The formula generates a number for the case $i = j$. Let us give that number a name: let us call it the "communality" of the variable X_i and let us denote the communality by h_i^2. That is, we define the communality h_i^2 by the formula

$$h_i^2 = \sum_{k=1}^{16} a_{ik} a_{jk} = \sum_{k=1}^{16} a_{ik}^2 \qquad \text{for} \quad j = i \tag{12}$$

The communality of X_i is not an observed value; the communality is not known until we have solved for the matrix $\mathbf{A}$. But what would it be if it were known? If the factors are *uncorrelated*, then the communality of variable X_i is the sum of squared correlations between X_i and the factors $F_1, F_2, \ldots, F_{16}$, which is, in fact, the squared multiple correlation of X_i as a function of $F_1, F_2, \ldots, F_{16}$; i.e.,

$$h_i^2 = R_{X_i}^2 \cdot F_1 F_2 \cdots F_{16} \tag{13}$$

The communality of X_i is the proportion of variance in X_i that is accounted for by the common factors.

The importance of communalities is that all the early methods of solving the previous equations for the factor structure $\mathbf{A}$ had to assume that the communalities were known. That is, the early factor analysts were all caught in the following bind: to calculate the communalities, you must know the factor structure $\mathbf{A}$; but to calculate the factor structure, you must know the communalities. The many methods for getting out of that bind are known collectively as "the problem of estimating the communalities." Any book on factor analysis will have at *least* one full chapter devoted to estimating the communalities. Some of the more well-known methods are the method of tetrad differences (Spearman, 1904), the largest correlation, Guttman's (1956) squared multiple correlations or SMCs, the iterative method (Thurstone, 1931), maximum likelihood factor analysis (Lawley, 1940), canonical factor analysis (Rao, 1955), alpha factor analysis (Kaiser & Caffrey, 1965), minres factor analysis (Harmen, 1967), etc. Note that most of the fancy "methods of factor analysis" are really fancy methods of estimating communalities.

What's the best method? That is a big debate. For the population correlation matrices or huge samples (say $N > 300$), the Guttman SMCs are a good but expensive estimate. For normal samples ($100 < N < 300$) or for small samples ($N < 100$), the Guttman SMCs are *terrible* (and just as expensive); like any multiple correlations they are very sensitive to small sample problems of capitalizing on chance. In fact, for most small sample problems (say 70 variables, 88 subjects), the typical value for a Guttman SMC is inflated by sampling error to .98. That is, for sample data, the use of Guttman SMCs may in fact be the inadvertent use of *unities* in the diagonal.

Once the communalities have been estimated, then we replace the diagonal entries of the correlation matrix (i.e., the unities) by the corresponding communalities. This new matrix with communalities down the diagonal is called the "reduced correlation matrix" and is denoted $\tilde{\mathbf{R}}$. For the *reduced* correlation matrix the dot product formula should hold for all entries, i.e., placing communalities in the diagonal makes the formula work for the diagonal as well as the off-diagonal entries.

In matrix algebra, our formula for "reproducing" the correlations from the factor loading can be written in a very simple way:

$$\tilde{\mathbf{R}} = \mathbf{A}\mathbf{A}^1 \qquad (14)$$

i.e., the reduced correlation matrix is the product of $\mathbf{A}$ and its transpose $\mathbf{A}^1$. Thus the problem of finding the unknown factors becomes the algebraic problem of "factoring" the reduced correlation matrix into two terms, $\mathbf{A}$ and $\mathbf{A}^1$. How is this "factoring" done? You simply apply to the reduced correlation matrix the methods already developed for factoring the correlation matrix itself, i.e., cluster analysis, principle components, square root analysis, maximal decomposition, etc. In terms of numerical frequency, the most common method is that of principal components. However, when applied to a matrix with communalities, the method of principal components is called "principle axis factor analysis" and produces "principal axis factors."

The central problem in calculating the factor structure matrix $\mathbf{A}$ can be described as "when do you stop factoring?" Basically, the question here is one of sampling error. If our assumption $\tilde{\mathbf{R}} = \mathbf{A}\mathbf{A}^1$ is true and we have perfect communality estimates, then any method of factoring will produce a clear cut answer: It will generate exactly 16 factors and at that point the correlation matrix will be reproduced perfectly. But for sample data its a different story. The fit of the model to the observed correlation matrix can *never* be perfect since sampling error cannot be eliminated. A number of statistical rules have been proposed, but nobody with any experience believes in them: none of them "work" in practice. So it is a matter of judgment, and that means it is basically up to the person doing the study to assess which solution fits his purposes.

Once a given number of principal axis factors has been obtained, then the focus of attention shifts to alternate solutions, i.e., to "rotating" the principal axis factors. The theory of rotation is exactly the same for the present case of factors from a matrix with communalities as it was for factors from a matrix with unities in the diagonal. To replace the uncorrelated factors is to "perform an orthogonal rotation." To replace the uncorrelated principal axis factors by a mathematically equivalent set of *correlated* factors is to "perform an oblique rotation." At least 90% of all current factor analyses finish with one orthogonal rotation procedure: VARIMAX. Most of its competitors are much more expensive and yield only negligible differences.

The preceding two paragraphs give the impression that you should first determine the number of factors and then rotate. Indeed, most theoretical papers are written this way. But practice is very different. In practice, any worthwhile computer program will print the rotation of every set of principal axis factors up to some point, i.e., the rotation of the first two, the rotation of the first three, etc. The practical factor analyst then scans through these to pick out the "best" number of factors. What most people report of this scanning is that up to some point, the factors appear to be substantively "blurred," i.e., the variables which load on the same factor do not appear consistent with any hypothesis. The problem is that you are considering too few factors. If there are not as many factors as there are content domains, then some factors must have loadings from variables from more than one content area. In particular, it is common for an early principal component to be defined in terms of two or more correlated content domains while later components correspond to the differences between these domains. This fact is true for both large and small data sets.

On the other hand, the behavior of VARIMAX (or principal components for that matter) as the number of factors becomes larger depends on sample size. For large samples, once a certain number of factors is passed, the VARIMAX factors tend not to change; the new factor is added without altering those which went before. Usually this new factor looks like garbage to the substantive eye and is therefore rejected as sampling error.

For small samples, the end process is very different. No matter how far you go the VARIMAX factors keep changing. But the change is from something meaningful to something strange, i.e., from gold to garbage. At this point it is time to quit and go back. You have now reached the point where the sampling error is as large or larger than the real residuals representing small factors. That is, for small data sets you are usually forced to quit earlier than would be true if the sample were larger.

A. Correlated Factors and "Oblique" Rotation

In the consideration of the VARIMAX factors generated in Table II, it was noted that even though factors might be associated with different content domains, there are contradictions in tying uncorrelated factors to those contents. That is, the correlations between individual variables representing those domains suggest that the corresponding domain traits should also be correlated. Therefore, most trait theorists have insisted that orthogonal rotations cannot yield the real source traits. If you do an oblique rotation, then there are several important technical questions that should concern you. First, if the factors are correlated, then the regression weights in

$$X_i = a_{i1}F_1 + \cdots + a_{i16}F_{16} + e_i \tag{15}$$

are *not* the same as the correlations between variables and factors, i.e.,

$$a_{ik} \neq r_{X_iF_k} \tag{16}$$

Instead, the matrix of regression weights $\mathbf{A}$ is called the "factor pattern matrix" and the matrix of variable-factor correlations is called the "factor structure matrix." If we denote the factor structure matrix by $\mathbf{R}_{XF}$, then $r_{X_iF_j} = \sum_{k=1}^{16} a_{ik}c_{kj}$ where c_{kj} is the correlation between F_j and F_k, which in matrix rotation is

$$\mathbf{R}_{XF} = \mathbf{A}\Phi \tag{17}$$

where $\mathbf{A}$ is the factor pattern matrix and Φ is the matrix of correlations between factors.

Second, if the factors are correlated, then the dot product formula for reproducing the correlations between the observed variables is no longer correct. Instead we have

$$r_{ij} = \sum_{k=1}^{16} \sum_{m=1}^{16} a_{ik}c_{km}a_{mj} \tag{18}$$

where $c_{km} = r_{F_kF_m}$, which is the correlation between the kth and mth factors. In matrix notation this is

$$\tilde{\mathbf{R}} = \mathbf{A}\Phi\mathbf{A}^1 \tag{19}$$

Not that this means that our earlier formula for the communality is also wrong for correlated factors.

Third, there are serious computational problems with existing oblique rotation schemes. Each person who has introduced a new scheme (say

OBLIMAX, EQUAMAX, PROMAX, etc.) has successfully shown that previous schemes do not work very well. So do not expect any miracles from oblique rotation at this point in history.

Fourth and sadly, there is the problem of computer programs. Oblique rotation programs are notorious for having unsuspected "bugs." So if your results look fishy, maybe you have caught a bug. And even if the program works right, there is the question of what is printed. Under the guise of "factor loading," some programs print the factor pattern, some print the factor structure, and some print an irrelevant matrix called the "reference vector structure." These will all be very different matrices, and woe unto the scientist who looks at one while thinking it is the other. Moreover, the situation is not getting better, it is getting worse. People in the field are currently printing new and more bizarre versions of the reference vector structure and calling it a "pattern."

Once the factor pattern or structure matrix is found, then only one question remains: What are the factors that have been found? The classic answer to this question has already been discussed under the rubric SOP, and need not be repeated here.

B. An Example

Table III contains the principal axis factor analysis of the correlation matrix in Table Ia with communalities in the diagonal (all communalities in this pure error-free example being .64 by any criterion). The critical feature of Table III is the number of factors: just two. Thus, as claimed by the classical trait theory, any matrix of variables from the same general domain will ultimately prove to have a small number of common factors.

TABLE III

THE FACTOR ANALYSIS OF THE CORRELATION MATRIX IN TABLE I WITH
COMMUNALITIES IN THE DIAGONAL

(a) The principal axis factors of Table I with communalities			(b) The VARIMAX factors of Table 1 with communalities		
	F_1	F_2		F_1	F_2
X_1	.70	.40	X_1	.78	.22
X_2	.70	.40	X_2	.78	.22
X_3	.70	.40	X_3	.78	.22
X_4	.70	.40	X_4	.78	.22
X_5	.70	− .40	X_5	.22	.78
X_6	.70	− .40	X_6	.22	.78
X_7	.70	− .40	X_7	.22	.78
X_8	.70	− .40	X_8	.22	.78

Table IIIb contains the VARIMAX rotation of the principal axis factors shown in Table IIIa. The notable feature of this table is that the VARIMAX factors show the symmetry of the two clusters in a more straightforward way than do the principal axis factors.

IV. CLUSTER ANALYSIS

A. Background Remarks

A cluster analysis begins with a partitioning of the variables into groups or clusters. For example, in Table, I, variables X_1 to X_4 might be measures of anxiety while variables X_5 to X_8 might be measures of depression. Once such a set of clusters has been given, two things are possible. First, *regardless of whether or not it is meaningful*, we can always define a set of factors by summing (or averaging) the variables in each cluster. In general, we will refer to such factors as the observed cluster sums. Such a variable might also be called a "scale" or "test" or "index." On the other hand, we would not normally form such sums unless we thought that they would, in fact, be meaningful. What constitutes a "meaningful" sum? There are a number of possible answers. We shall consider one such answer: The variables constitute alternate measures of the same underlying variable.

Suppose that the variables in some given cluster are, in fact, equivalent measures of some one underlying variable. Then that cluster of variables is related in a specific way to a large set of *un*measured variables: the variables present are a sample of all variables which would also be equivalent measures of the same underlying variable as those in the cluster. Tryon (1959) called such a set of variables a "domain" (though most other writers have used the term domain more generally then that). That is, if a cluster of variables are all equivalent to one another, then they are equivalent to some *particular* underlying variable. Let us call that variable the cluster true score. Then what we have said is that if a cluster of variables is equivalent to one another, then they define a domain of variables which are all equivalent to one another because they all are versions of the same underlying variable, the cluster true score. If the cluster of variables are equivalent to one another, then the observed cluster sum can be regarded as an estimate of the cluster true score in the usual sense of that term in classical reliability theory.

There are two ways to think of cluster analysis: as a mathematical model of the structure of a set of variables or as a computational procedure. As a computational procedure, "cluster analysis" is the same as "oblique multiple groups factor analysis" in which the factors are defined to be the sum or "centroid" of the variables in the designated group of variables. However, this definition has a different meaning depending on whether communalities are placed in the diagonal or whether the diagonal of the correlation matrix is left as unities. If ones are left in the diagonal, then the oblique multiple groups procedure produces the factor loadings for the set of cluster sums or indexes of the designated groups of variables. If communalities are placed in the diagonal of the correlation matrix, then the numbers produced by the oblique multiple groups procedure may or may not be factor loadings. If the variables in a given cluster satisfy the assumptions of the cluster analysis model, then the entries for the corresponding factor are estimates of the factor loading for the hypothetical construct which underlies the variables in that cluster. However, if the variables in a given group do not satisfy the assumptions of the cluster analysis model, then the "loadings" for that factor are garbage and have no statistical meaning.

That is, cluster analysis is really a form of multivariate reliability theory in which each group of variables is considered to be a fallible measure of the same trait. If cluster analysis is done with ones in the diagonal, then each factor is related to the variables in its group as a test score is related to its items. If a cluster analysis is done with communalities in the diagonal, then each factor is related to the variables in its group as the true score is related to the items. Within cluster analysis, a factor analysis with communalities is related to the same factor analysis without communalities in the same way that correlations corrected for attenuation are related to the uncorrected correlations.

Cluster analysis goes beyond the oblique multiple groups computational procedure in two ways: (a) It specifies a particular model which then yields an interpretation of the numbers calculated and (b) it provides specific tests which the data must meet before the model is viewed as valid. That is, cluster analysis specifies the conditions which must be met before the oblique multiple groups procedure is meaningful.

Table IV shows the oblique multiple groups factors of the correlation matrix in Table I calculated with and without communalities. It is especially important at this time to note that the factors produced by a cluster analysis are correlated. For the cluster analysis with ones in the diagonal, the factors correlate .43. For the cluster analysis with communalities, the correlation is still higher, .50. This reflects the fact that the effect of communalities is to cause the correlation between the factors to be corrected for attenuation. That is, if the reliability of each cluster sum in Table IVa were calculated using Cronbach's (1951) coefficient alpha, then those reliabilities would each be found to be

$$r_{FF} = 4(.64)/\left[3(.64) + 1\right] = .88 \tag{20}$$

If a correlation of .43 is corrected for attenuation assuming each variable has a reliability of .83, then the correlation corrected for attenuation is precisely the correlation found for the cluster analysis with communalities, $r_{F_1F_2} = .50$.

There are two ways in which the cluster analysis model might fail to fit the data. First, one or more of the clusters might consist of variables which are not, in fact, alternate measures of the same underlying trait. Second, the relations among the alternate measures might not be linear. In particular, many domains of achievement testing (math, for example) have found that items are not related to the underlying trait by straight lines, but by ogival curves. In such cases, the appropriate mathematical model for the data is not factor analysis, but "probit analysis" or "logit analysis," both of which are special cases of "itemetrics" (Lord & Novick, 1968; Urrv. 1974). Hunter

TABLE IV

THE CLUSTER ANALYSIS OF THE CORRELATION MATRIX IN TABLE I.

(a) The cluster analysis with ones in the diagonal

	X_1	X_2	X_3	X_4	X_5	X_6	X_7	X_8	F_1	F_2
X_1	1.00	.64	.64	.64	.32	.32	.32	.32	.91	.35
X_2	.64	1.00	.64	.64	.32	.32	.32	.32	.91	.35
X_3	.64	.64	1.00	.64	.32	.32	.32	.32	.91	.35
X_4	.64	.64	.64	1.00	.32	.32	.32	.32	.91	.35
X_5	.32	.32	.32	.32	1.00	.64	.64	.64	.35	.91
X_6	.32	.32	.32	.32	.64	1.00	.64	.64	.35	.91
X_7	.32	.32	.32	.32	.64	.64	1.00	.64	.35	.91
X_8	.32	.32	.32	.32	.64	.64	.64	1.00	.35	.91
F_1	.91	.91	.91	.91	.35	.35	.35	.35	1.00	.43
F_2	.35	.35	.35	.35	.91	.91	.91	.91	.43	1.00

(b) The cluster analysis with communalities in the diagonal

	X_1	X_2	X_3	X_4	X_5	X_6	X_7	X_8	F_1	F_2
X_1	.64	.64	.64	.64	.32	.32	.32	.32	.80	.40
X_2	.64	.64	.64	.64	.32	.32	.32	.32	.80	.40
X_3	.64	.64	.64	.64	.32	.32	.32	.32	.80	.40
X_4	.64	.64	.64	.64	.32	.32	.32	.32	.80	.40
X_5	.32	.32	.32	.32	.64	.64	.64	.64	.40	.80
X_6	.32	.32	.32	.32	.64	.64	.64	.64	.40	.80
X_7	.32	.32	.32	.32	.64	.64	.64	.64	.40	.80
X_8	.32	.32	.32	.32	.64	.64	.64	.64	.40	.80
F_1	.80	.80	.80	.80	.40	.40	.40	.40	1.00	.50
F_2	.40	.40	.40	.40	.80	.80	.80	.80	.50	1.00

(1975) has written a simple introduction to this material in the context of mathematically determining racial bias in a set of test items.

B. Testing a Cluster for Unidimensionality

A perfect cluster is a set of variables which all measure exactly the same underlying trait. In that sense, each cluster represents but one dimension in the data. Thus, a perfect cluster is said to be unidimensional. There are three tests for the unidimensionality of a cluster: (1) homogeneity of content, (2) internal consistency, and (3) parallelism.

1. HOMOGENEITY OF CONTENT

The most important property of a cluster is a substantive, rather than a statistical one: Do the variables in a cluster all measure the same thing from a substantive point of view? To say "yes" to this question is to claim to have a theory of the content of the variables under consideration. For example, consider the items: (1) I like to bet on football. (2) I avoid football "pools." These items are logically equivalent in their content although the second must be reverse scored to match the first. However, if you believe that some people are "acquiescent" in their response to items, then you would predict that those persons would say "yes" to both items despite the reversed content. If such a theory were true, then the two items would *not* be homogeneous in content.

There are two reasons why homogeneity of content is the most important property of a cluster. First, there is the interpretation of the factors in the cluster analysis. The meaning of the cluster sum or cluster true score is clear to exactly the same extent as the content of the cluster is homogeneous in content (and vice versa!) Second, assessing the relation between the results of one study and the results of another (i.e., is a result replicated or is it not?) can only be carried out to the extent that the correspondence between variables can be assessed. Comparison of variables in different studies is entirely a matter of homogeneity of content in the variables.

2. INTERNAL CONSISTENCY

If the variables in a cluster are all measures of the same underlying trait, and if the relations between the variables are linear, then the correlations among those variables must satisfy a condition first stated by Spearman (1904) which is not called "unit rank." (If proper communalities are placed in the diagonal of the correlation matrix for the variables in the cluster, then that matrix has rank one in the sense of matrix algebra.) In other words, the correlations of the variables in a given cluster should form a Spearman matrix.

Strictly speaking, this means that the correlations should satisfy a certain product rule. Let the correlations of the variables in the cluster be denoted r_{ij}. Then the Spearman condition is that there exist a set of numbers g_i such that the correlation between two variables X_i and X_j, i.e., r_{ij}, must be the product of the numbers g_i and g_j. That is, the Spearman condition is that we can find numbers g_i such that for each off-diagonal correlation

$$r_{ij} = g_i g_j \tag{21}$$

If the Spearman condition is satisfied, then the set of numbers g_i have a straightforward interpretation,

$$g_i = r_{X_i F} \tag{22}$$

where F is the cluster true score. That is, g_i is the factor loading for X_i where the cluster analysis is done with communalities in the diagonal. The product rule is then one of the conventional theorems of reliability theory:

$$r_{X_i X_j} = r_{X_i F} r_{X_j F} \tag{23}$$

The communality for the variable X_i then takes on a special meaning as well:

$$h_i^2 = g_i^2 = r_{X_i F}^2 \tag{24}$$

That is, in a Spearman matrix, the *communality* of a variable is the same as its *reliability*. (However do not confuse the reliability of a given variable with the reliability of the cluster sum obtained through cluster analysis with ones in the diagonally. The reliability of the cluster sum is given by coefficient alpha.)

In practice, the test for a rank one correlation matrix is simpler than Spearman's test. If all the variables have about the same quality in measuring the underlying trait, i.e., if each variable in the cluster has about the same amount of error, then the correlations among the variables in that cluster will be "flat," i.e.,

$$r_{X_i X_j} = r_{XX} \tag{25}$$

where the single number r_{XX} is the correlation between any two of the variables in that cluster. For example, in Table I, any two variables in the cluster X_1 to X_4 have the same correlation $r_{XX} = .64$. Of course, in a real sample correlation matrix, the correlations will never all be exactly equal, but only equal to within sampling error. A statistical test for this is given in Hunter (1977).

If a cluster fails the Spearman test, then it will usually fail that test in a straightforward way: the variables in the cluster will form subclusters which are not perfectly correlated with each other. For example, suppose that the investigator had believed that all the variables in Table I were alternate measures of "emotional instability." Then he would have found that the variables form two subclusters, the anxiety subcluster X_1 to X_4 and the depression subcluster X_5 to X_8, where the correlations between variables not in the same subcluster (always .32 in Table Ia) are less than the correlations between variables in the same subcluster (always .64 in Table Ia).

If the cluster analysis has been done with communalities, then there is another test for internal consistency which is not derived from Spearman's unit rank criterion, but which follows from the rest of his theory: A cluster should correlate more highly with its own cluster true score than with any other cluster true score. This test is completely useless if the cluster analysis was done with ones in the diagonal because the "part whole correlations" are "spuriously" high in this case (see Hunter, 1977).

3. PARALLELISM

If two variables are measures of the same thing, then not only should they correlate with each other, but they should correlate in a similar manner with other things. In particular, if two variables are both measures of the same thing, and they both have equal quality as measures of that trait, then they should have exactly the same correlation with any other variable whatsoever. That is, if X_1 and X_2 are both measures of the same trait F, and if $r_{X_1 F} = r_{X_2 F}$, then for any variable Y we should have

$$r_{X_1 Y} = r_{X_2 Y} \tag{26}$$

Thus, if the correlation matrix for a given cluster is flat (to within sampling error), then for any other variable in the study the variables X_i in the cluster should satisfy the rule

$$r_{X_1 Y} = r_{X_2 Y} = r_{X_3 Y} = \cdots \tag{27}$$

to within sampling error. There is a statistical test for this in Hunter (1977).

Where do we look to assess a cluster for parallelism? The best place to look is at the bottom of the cluster analysis at the correlations between variables (as column headers) and factors (as row headers). For example, the item–cluster correlations for the second cluster in Table IVb are

	X_5	X_6	X_7	X_8	
F_1	.4	.4	.4	.4	(28)
F_2	.8	.8	.8	.8	

The correlations with F_2 are the correlations between the items of the second cluster and the second cluster true score (i.e., the "part–whole" correlation for the second cluster) itself, and therefore irrelevant. However, the correlations with F_1 are very much relevant and we see that in this perfect example those correlations are all exactly equal, i.e., to .4.

If the variables in the cluster are not all equal in quality, then the situation is somewhat more complicated. But basically the story is this: If one of the variables has poorer quality than the others, then its correlations with all other variables will be somewhat lower than the corresponding correlations for the better measures. Greater detail can be found in Hunter (1977).

In the literature on factor analysis and reliability theory, there has been long and considerable discussion of internal consistency. Yet the important formulas in either field are the formulas for correction for attenuation, and those formulas depend on parallelism which is rarely mentioned as such. Furthermore, it has been my experience that parallelism is a far better method for discovering bad items than is the test for internal consistency. In particular, the test for parallelism will detect those items which are masquerading as "weak" items in a cluster to which they do not belong.

V. THE MYSTERY OF TRAIT THEORY

To the dust bowl empiricist who uses ones in the diagonal of his correlation matrix, there is no mystery as to the nature of his factors. Each factor is just a linear function of the observed variables which is intended to act as a summary variable. This becomes even more prosaic in cluster analysis with ones in the diagonal: each factor is just the average score on the variables which make up the corresponding cluster. Cluster analysis with communalities is only a shade less plain: each factor is what the observed variable would have been had the observed variable been measured perfectly.

But in trait theory with its source traits and surface traits, with its communalities and unique factors, the factors seem to be on a different conceptual level from the observed variables. In a word, the factors in trait theory are "mysteries" whose nature must be discovered by some leap of intuition as to the fundamental nature of the mind. The purpose of this section is strip the mystery from the factors in trait theory and reveal their prosaic nature for all to see.

Consider the equation of the first variable in our 16-factor world:

$$X_1 = a_{11}F_1 + a_{12}F_2 + \cdots + a_{1,\,16}F_{16} + e_1 \tag{29}$$

What is the nature of the "unique factor" e_1? The unique factor e_1 is not correlated with any other variable in the study, not with any of the common factors nor with any other unique factor. Furthermore, the unique factor is not correlated with any other variable in the general domain which the observed variables sample. If it were, then it would mean that the nature of the common factors in the study depends on the particular variables chosen, and this would be regarded as a serious design error by a trait theorist. Thus, we come to the bottom line: The unique factor e_1 is correlated with nothing in the world that is of any interest to anyone. But, this means that the "unique factor" of trait theoretic factor analysis is exactly the "error" of classical reliability theory!! What then is the true score?

Let T_1 be the true score for X_1. Then by definition

$$T_1 = X_1 - e_1 = a_{11}F_1 + \cdots + a_{1,\,16}F_{16} \tag{30}$$

That is, there is *no* error in the equation linking the true score T_1 to the factors $F_1, F_2, \ldots, F_{16}$. The true scores for the observed variables are to the trait theory factors as the observed scores are to the dust bowl summary variables in a factor analysis without communalities. But, this suggests that the factors obtained using communalities are nothing more than summary variables for the observed variable true scores, i.e., perfectly measured summary variables. And indeed, this is precisely the case. The perfect linear equations linking the true scores to the common factors can always be solved to yield the factors in terms of the true scores. Thus, for every factor F_k, there is a set of weights $b_{k1}, b_{k2}, \ldots, b_{kn}$ such that

$$F_k = b_{k1}T_1 + b_{k2}T_2 + \cdots + b_{kn}T_n \tag{31}$$

In particular the principal axis factors of the observed variables are just the principal components of the true scores.

A. Factor Analysis with Communalities

When the correlation matrix in Table I was factor analyzed with communalities, there were no longer eight principal axis factors, but only two. This implies that there is so much redundancy in this matrix that we can account for all eight variables in terms of two factors. Where is this redundancy?

Consider the cluster analysis on this same data. We had perfect fit to the cluster model. Thus, we know that the first four variables are all measures of the same underlying variable and we know that the last four variables are all measures of the same underlying variables. That is, from the cluster analysis we know that

$$T_1 = T_2 = T_3 = T_4 = F_1, \qquad T_5 = T_6 = T_7 = T_8 = F_2$$

So there is no mystery to the redundancy: the first four true scores are the same and the last four true scores are the same.

What then is the relation of the principal axis factors to the cluster true scores? Let the principal axis factors be denoted PA_1 and PA_2. Then in *raw* score form,

$$PA_1 = F_1 + F_2 = T_1 + T_5, \qquad PA_2 = F_1 - F_2 = T_1 - T_5$$

To obtain the principal axis factors in standard score form, PA_1 must be divided by the square root of the variance form, PA_1 must be divided by the square root of the variance of $F_1 + F_2$ or $2 + 2(.5) = 3$ and PA_2 must be divided by the standard deviation of the difference or the square root of $2 - 2(.5) = 1$.

What about the VARIMAX factors? The VARIMAX factors are linear functions of the principal axis factors and hence, must be linear functions of the cluster true scores. Let the VARIMAX factors be denoted by V_1 and V_2. Then in raw score form

$$V_1 = F_1 - .27F_2 = T_1 - .27T_5, \qquad V_2 = F_2 - .27F_1 = T_5 - .27T_1$$

There has been a great deal written about the "advantages" of uncorrelated predictors, is there not a price paid for using orthogonal factors? Consider the present example. If F_1 is anxiety and F_2 is depression, then what is the substantive meaning of the VARIMAX factors

$$V_1 = \text{anxiety} - .27 \text{ depression}, \qquad V_2 = \text{depression} - .27 \text{ anxiety}$$

There are those who would argue that the VARIMAX factors like the principal axis factors are "artifactually" orthogonalized versions of the basic cluster true scores. Furthermore, it should be noted that the basic facts for a correlation matrix with three or more clusters becomes even worse: the amounts subtracted from the basic cluster true scores to produce orthogonality depend not only on the correlations between clusters, but on the number of variables in each cluster as well.

B. Hidden Assumptions in Principal Components

The basic premise in the use of ones in the diagonal is the assumption that in that fashion you side step all the messy questions of reliability or true scores or unique factors or etc. But is this really true? Consider the following fact: No one ever recommends keeping *all* of the principal components (or their VARIMAX equivalents). Rather, the idea is that only a "few" of the principal components will be considered while the rest are dropped. But, once some of the principal components are to be dropped, then there has been an implicit decision as to what information in the correlation matrix is of interest and what information is trivial. That, in turn, raises this question: Is the eigenvalue a measure of the *importance* of a given principal component?

Consider an example. Suppose that because of the easy availability of measures such as high school and college grade point average, we put together a variable set in which there are eight measures of intelligence, two measures of anxiety, and 140 other variables. The principal component that sums the intelligence measures will have an eigenvalue about four times as large as that for the principal component that sums the anxiety measures. Can we then conclude that intelligence is four times as important as anxiety? Certainly not, the ratio of eight measures to two measures was determined by expedience. The importance of a principal component is a function of its substantive composition, not its eigenvalue.

To summarize the argument to this point: The usual practice is to use only the first few of the principal components as summary measures and to drop the rest. This implies that the importance of the principal components with small eigenvalues is less than the importance of those with large eigenvalues and this is nonsense. Is there then any substance to the widespread practice of ignoring the smaller principal components? Certainly this practice cannot be justified in all data sets, but in those where the cluster analysis model holds, there is foundation for such assumptions.

Let us consider the substantive nature of the principal components in the example of Table I. Let us denote the principal components by $PC_1, PC_2, \ldots, PC_8$. Then in raw score form

$$PC_1 = X_1 + X_2 + X_3 + X_4 + X_5 + X_6 + X_7 + X_8$$
$$PC_2 = X_1 + X_2 + X_3 + X_4 - X_5 - X_6 - X_7 - X_8$$
$$PC_3 = X_1 + X_2 - X_3 - X_4,$$
$$PC_4 = X_5 + X_6 - X_7 - X_8$$
$$PC_5 = X_1 - X_2,$$
$$PC_6 = X_3 - X_4,$$
$$PC_7 = X_5 - X_6,$$
$$PC_8 = X_7 - X_8$$

What do these variables become if we make the cluster analytic assumptions which we know to fit Table I? According to the cluster analytic model,

$$X_i = F_1 + e_i \quad \text{for} \quad i = 1, \ldots, 4,$$
$$X_i = F_2 + e_i \quad \text{for} \quad i = 5, \ldots, 8$$

where F_1 is the cluster true score for the first cluster and F_2 is the cluster true score for the second cluster. If we denote the two cluster sums by C_1 and C_2, then we have

$$C_1 = X_1 + X_2 + X_3 + X_4, \qquad C_2 = X_5 + X_6 + X_7 + X_8$$

From which we obtain the formulas for the principal components:

$$PC_1 = C_1 + C_2,$$
$$PC_2 = C_1 - C_2$$
$$PC_3 = e_1 + e_2 - e_3 - e_4,$$
$$PC_4 = e_5 + e_6 - e_7 - e_8$$
$$PC_5 = e_1 - e_2,$$
$$PC_6 = e_3 - e_4,$$
$$PC_7 = e_5 - e_6,$$
$$PC_8 = e_7 - e_8$$

In these formulas we see a striking split between the first two principal components and the remaining six. The first two principal components are given in terms of the cluster sums while the remaining six components are each defined solely in terms of the error variables e_1 to e_8. Thus, the cluster analytic model *dictates* that the last six principal components be dropped. On the other hand, the cluster analytic model also reveals that the principal components are an artifactual and usually meaningless transformation of the cluster sums C_1 and C_2. Furthermore, this is just as true of the VARIMAX factors V_1 and V_2 which have the substantive composition

$$V_1 = C_1 - .27C_2, \qquad V_2 = C_2 - .27C_1$$

That is, the VARIMAX components are also an artifactual orthogonalization of the cluster sums.

This situation becomes fundamentally more complicated in data sets with three or more clusters, and especially difficult in data sets in which the basic clusters have greatly different numbers of variables. Under such conditions, the eigenvalue for an error component may be larger than the eigenvalue representing a small cluster or a cluster which is highly correlated with other clusters. That is, for data sets in which there are three or more clusters (i.e., the *usual* data set), the principal components may not be substantively ordered if listed by the size of their eigenvalues.

C. Sampling Error in Factor Analysis and Cluster Analysis

Contrary to popular belief, the effect of sampling error in factor analysis is very different from its impact in multiple regression. In multiple regression, the beta weights are typically more different from one another than are the zero order correlations, because the influence of other variables are being partialed out. The usual effect of sampling error is to exaggerate the difference between beta weights for variables that are alternate measures of the same thing while randomly effecting the beta weights for variables measuring different underlying traits. Thus, the smaller the sample, the greater the likelihood of obtaining different beta weights for variables which have the same meaning.

But in factor analysis, differences in correlation are not exaggerated, but blurred. That is, factor analytic formulas *average* correlations and hence produce patterns of loadings which show *less* variation over the variables in a cluster than do the zero order correlations themselves. In fact, if the clusters are properly given, then factor analysis actually yields better and better estimates of the factor loadings as the number of variables is increased!

However, there is a string attached to the preceding argument: the clusters must be properly known. But, if the determination of the clusters is on purely statistical grounds, then the clusters are determined from the data set and hence may not be correctly given by error-laden small sample data. For example, suppose a small four-item cluster is embedded in 144 other variables. Then, if we put those variables first in the matrix, then the factor loadings with and without sampling error for a sample of size 50 might look like

Population: .50 .50 .50 .50 .0   .0   .0   .0   . . .

Sample: .78 .36 .22 .34 .14 $-.28$ $-.28$ .28   . . .

If the cluster were known before hand, the random error poses little problem here, since the average loading for cluster members is clearly differentiated from the average loading of nonmembers. But, if the cluster composition is not known, then there is a severe problem: there are 144 chances for sampling error to produce garbage loadings that are bigger than the loadings for the cluster members. The results of this garbage is that people using factor analysis interpret fewer factors on a smaller sample than they would on a larger sample. Hence, they give a cruder picture of the correlation matrix for a smaller sample than they would for a larger sample.

If the cluster analysis model fits the population correlation matrix, then cluster analysis will always give better estimates of population parameters than will principal components and rotation (i.e., the oblique multiple groups loadings will be more accurate than any possible oblique rotation of the principal components). The reason for this is that principal components allow the defining coefficients of the factor to wobble from sample to sample depending on the wobble in the correlations, while the cluster analysis holds the defining weights of each factor rigidly at 0 and 1. In a cluster analysis, the nature of errors is different: a variable might be falsely included in a cluster or a variable might be falsely left out of a cluster.

Cluster analysis improves on factor analysis in three ways: (1) the requirement of content homogeneity, (2) the use of a "residual cluster," are (3) parallelism criterion. Consider the problem of placing a variable into a cluster to which it does not belong. Such a variable would have to satisfy three criteria: First, in order that the cluster in which it is placed meet the criterion of internal consistency, the invalid item would have to correlate highly with the corresponding cluster true score. However, this is a single-correlation criterion and may happen with fairly high probability, particularly if the item would correctly fall in a cluster which is highly correlated with the one in which it has been misplaced. Second, the item would have to be parallel to all the other items in that cluster. That is, the invalid item would have to have several correlations fall in the same region as the correlations for the valid items. This is a several-correlation criterion and is much less likely to occur by chance. For example, if an item had to have correlations that were plus plus plus by chance, then only one in eight items would qualify even though the probability of meeting any one criterion was .5. Thus, parallelism has proved to be an excellent screening device for chance item membership. Third, if the item is to remain in a cluster in which it has been placed, then it must not lead to a cluster which is inhomogeneous in content. That is, the false item must exactly match the content of the other items in the cluster. But, if the investigator sets a high criterion for homogeneity of content (and I cannot recommend this too strongly), then this would be virtually impossible. Note that a careful content requirement is independent of sample size and should be just as effective with $N = 50$ as with $N = 500$. Finally, every good cluster analysis is run with a "residual cluster." This residual cluster acts as a carrier for items which do not belong to clusters in which they were initially placed. Eventually one of three things happens to these items: (1) They are placed in the correct cluster (unlikely if not done initially), (2) they are placed with other items from the residual cluster to form a cluster that was initially missed, or (3) they are dropped from the study. What sorts of items are ultimately dropped? These are items which do not correlate with anything else in the matrix (which may be good items that need replication in order to provide good measurement on a dimension not adequately tapped in the study); items which statistically belong in some cluster that they do not fit in content; and items which belong to some cluster in content, but which do not meet the statistical criteria. The last two item types are especially important since they represent a large portion of the error term in cluster analysis. Items which fit statistically, but not in content are items which would be incorrectly placed into clusters by blind statistical techniques and, in my experience over perhaps 30 studies, would not cross-validate. Thus, these items represent errors that factor analysis would make which are avoided in cluster analysis. Items which fit content, but not the statistical criteria are of two types: (a) They are excellent candidates for sampling error in a cluster analysis, i.e., the nonfit of their statistics may well be sampling error, and (b) they represent cases where there is a subtle content factor which the investigator does not recognize (in which case the item definitely belongs in the residual set). Of these two types, only type (a) represents an error for cluster analysis. How serious is this error? From a substantive point of view, placing an item in the residual set can never be a serious error in determining the quality of the items that are left, since they must stand alone anyway. That is, the identification of the true score is just as clear without the additional item and it is still possible in future work to replace that item by another suitable measure. Thus, the only price incurred by falsely placing an item in the residual set is that the reliability of the index that would be formed for that cluster would be lower for having fewer items, and that is not a substantive error. Finally, the residual set prevents an error which is fundamental to principal components: it allows an item to be eliminated from the study if it does not fit the general pattern of the content of that study. This is especially important in terms of items which statistically (or even in content) cross over two clusters. Isolated items of this type end up in the residual set of a cluster analysis and hence do not mess up the definitional process as applied to the clusters in question. That is, in cluster analysis it is not true that every item must be forced in somewhere, whereas in principal components this is required by definition. In particular, an item which is falsely left out of one cluster will not be placed in another, but will be placed in the residual set on the basis of content.

D. Cluster Correlations

One last note on cluster analysis. After the final alteration of the original clustering and after the residual set has been dropped and after the cluster analytic model has been shown to fit the remaining data, then there is one last set of numbers to be dealt with: the correlations among the cluster true scores. But this is not a defect of cluster analysis, for it represents the essence of a multivariate study for those who are substantively oriented. From a substantive point of view, the cluster or factor analysis is really just a preparatory step to looking at the correlations among the molar measures which have been created from the original variables. Indeed, many people who would enter into a cluster analysis are hoping that it will just be a pro forma step showing that their established measuring devices work as they think they do. Their sole interest is in the cluster correlations.

What do you do with the cluster correlations? How about second order factors or maximal decomposition (Hunter, 1972) or path analysis? Any post factor analytic examination of the data is bound to add immeasurably to the information gained from the study.

VI. SUMMARY

Three general approaches to factor analysis have been presented here: the dust bowl empiricist approach which defines factors as linear combinations of the observed variables, the trait theory approach which defines factors as linear combinations of observed variable true scores, and cluster analysis which requires that the variables split into clusters each of which is a set of indicators for one underlying trait (in which the factors obtained using communalities are derived by correcting the factors obtained with ones in the diagonal for error of measurement). If the cluster analysis model fits the data, then cluster analysis is a superior technique in terms of both conceptual usage and in terms of statistical estimation. The other models are potentially more general than cluster analysis, but this generality has rarely been the point of an empirical study. Rather, the theoretical interpretability of a factor analysis has been assessed in terms of "simple structure," which is a criterion for factor loadings that is mathematically equivalent to the cluster analysis model assumptions. Moreover in actual usage, factors are interpreted in terms of their "salient lists," i.e., each factor is interpreted as a generalization of the variables which correlated highly with it. That is, in actual usage, people treat factor analysis as if it were cluster analysis. Thus, cluster analysis fits normal interpretation patterns which are actually inconsistent with the mathematical properties of orthogonal factors.

But the most telling difference between cluster analysis and classic forms of factor analysis lies in the *further* analysis of the data. After factors are obtained, a factor analysis is terminated. But after clusters have been formed, a cluster analyst turns to the analysis of the correlations between the clusters. And it is these correlations which are actually the target of most multivariate research. It is the correlations between traits that reveal the causal processes which are the dominant interest in most fields of science.

In short, the main difference between cluster analysis and other forms of factor analysis is that cluster analysis distinguishes between the *measurement* model which assesses the extent to which various variables are indicators of certain traits and the *causal* model which seeks to explain why the various traits are correlated as they are. It should be noted in passing that this difference also extends to some of the less well-known forms of classic factor analysis such as confirmatory factor analysis and LISREL as developed by Joreskog (1970).

References

Carrol, J. D. An analytical solution for approximating simple structure in factor analysis. *Psychometrika*, 1953, **18**, 23–28.
Cattell, R. B. *The description and measurement of personality*. New York: World Book, 1946.
Cattell, R. B. *The scientific analysis of personality*, London: Penguin Books, 1965.
Cronbach, L. J. Coefficient alpha and the internal structure of tests. *Psychometrika*, 1951, **16**, 297–334.
Ferguson, G. A. The concept of parsimony in factor analysis. *Psychometrika*, 1954, **19**, 281–290.
Gorsuch, R. L. *Factor analysis*, Philadelphia, Pennsylvania: Saunders, 1974.
Guttman, L. "Best possible" systematic estimates of communalities, *Psychometrika*, 1956, **21**, 273–285.
Harman, H. H. *Modern factor analysis*, Chicago, Illinois: Univ. of Chicago Press, 1967.
Holzinger, K. J. Factoring test scores and implications for the method of averages. *Psychometrika*, 1944, **9**, 155–167.

Hotelling, H. Analysis of a complex of statistical variables into principal components. *Journal of Educational Psychology*, 1933, **24**, 417–421, 498–520.

Hunter, J. E. Maximal decomposition: an alternative to factor analysis. *Multivariate Behavioral Research*, 1972, **1**, 243–268.

Hunter, J. E. *A critical analysis of the use of item means and item-test correlations to determine the presence or absence of content bias in achievement tests.* Paper presented at the National Institute of Education conference on test bias, Annapolis, Maryland; December, 1975. To be published in a book of proceedings of that conference.

Hunter, J. E. *Psychological measurement: Reliability, cluster analysis, construct validity, and the multitrait multimethod analysis.* Unpublished manuscript, Department of Psychology, Michigan State Univ., 1977.

Jöreskog, K. G. A general approach to confirmatory factor analysis. *Psychometrika*, 1969, **34**, 182–202.

Jöreskog, K. G. A general method for the analysis of covariance structures. *Biometrika*, 1970, **57**, 239–251.

Kaiser, H. F. The varimax criterion for analytic rotation in factor analysis. *Psychometrika*, 1958, **23**, 187–200.

Kaiser, H. F. Image analysis. In Chester W. Harris (Ed.), *Problems in measuring change.* Madison, Wisconsin: Univ. of Wisconsin Press, 1963.

Kaiser, H. F, and Caffrey, J. Alpha factor analysis. *Psychometrika*, 1965, **30**, 1–14.

Lawley, D. N. The estimation of factor loadings by the method of maximum liklihood. *Proceedings of the Royal Society of Edinburg*, 1940, **60**, 64–82.

Levine, R., and Hunter, J. E. Statistical and psychometric inference in principal components analysis. *Multivariate Behavioral Research*, 1971, **6**, 105–116.

Lord, F. M., and Novick, M. R. *Statistical theories of mental test scores.* Reading, Massachusetts: Addison-Wesley, 1968.

Mulaik, S. A. *The foundations of factor analysis*, New York: McGraw-Hill, 1972.

Neuhaus, J. O., and Wrigley, C. The quartimax method: An analytical approach to orthogonal simple structure. *British Journal of Statistical Psychology*, 1954, **7**, 81–91.

Rao, C. R. Estimation and tests of significance in factor analysis. *Psychometrika*, 1955, **20**, 93–111.

Saunders, D. R. *An analytic method for rotation to orthogonal simple structure.* Research Bulletin 53-10, Princeton, New Jersey: Educational Testing Service, 1953.

Spearman, C. General intelligence, objectively determined and measured. *American Journal of Psychology*, 1904, **15**, 201–293.

Thomson, G. H. *The factorial analysis of human ability.* Boston, Massachusetts: Houghton Mifflin, 1951.

Thurstone, L. L. Multiple factor analysis. *Psychological Review*, 1931, **38**, 406–427.

Thurstone, L. L. *The vectors of the mind.* Chicago, Illinois: Univ. of Chicago Press, 1935.

Thurstone, L. L. *Multiple factor analysis.* Chicago, Illinois: Univ. of Chicago Press, 1947.

Tryon, R. C. Domain sampling formulation of cluster and factor analysis. *Psychometrika*, 1959, **24**, 113–135.

Tryon, R. C., and Bailey, D. E. *Cluster analysis.* New York: McGraw-Hill, 1970.

Urry, V. W. Approximations of item parameters of mental test models and their uses. *Educational and Psychological Measurement*, 1974, **34**, 253–269.

Chapter 9

CLUSTERING

KLAUS KRIPPENDORFF

The Annenberg School of Communications
University of Pennsylvania
Philadelphia, Pennsylvania

I. CLUSTERING

Clustering seeks to group or to lump together objects or variables that share some observed qualities or, alternatively, to partition or to divide a set of objects or variables into mutually exclusive classes whose boundaries reflect differences in the observed qualities of their members. Clustering thus extracts typologies from data which in turn represent a reduction of data complexity and may lead to conceptual simplifications.

MULTIVARIATE TECHNIQUES
IN HUMAN COMMUNICATION RESEARCH

Clustering should not be confused either with the analysis of the groupings made by subjects or with the assignment of objects to the categories in which they belong.

Clusters emerge from the interaction between the characteristics that are manifest in multivariate data and the assumptions that are built into the procedure. The recognition of these assumptions pertains to problems of validity, to which much of the paper and its conclusion are devoted.

Clustering originated in anthropology (Driver and Kroeber, 1932) and in psychology (Zubin, 1938; Tryon, 1939) in response to the need for empirically based typologies of cultures and of individuals. Computational problems hindered the initial development of these ideas. But by the early 1960s clustering techniques emerged in a variety of other disciplines, including biology (Sokal and Sneath, 1963). Applications are now so numerous that references to them would fill a book (see Sneath and Sokal, 1973). Problems to which clustering has found answers range from counting dust particles and bacteria, to land allocation in urban planning and political campaigning. Clustering has proven useful especially in psychology, anthropology, sociology, political science, economics, management, geography, and literature— virtually the whole spectrum of the behavioral and social sciences (Bailey, 1975) in which data do not exhibit the determinism of the natural sciences and theories are based on types, categories, and differentiations that knowingly omit some of the less significant variations in the observed phenomena.

In communication research, clustering provides a valuable tool for identifying cliques from sociometric or communication network type data, for example, or for detecting "invisible colleges" as manifest through citations of literature in scientific publications. Clustering is also used for grouping concepts that appear highly associated in given messages into stereotypes, for developing emic as opposed to etic type categories for content analysis from receiver responses, or for detecting redundant questionnaire items that may be explained by a common underlying variable. Clustering may also be used to simplify the representation of complex communication systems and thus provides the pretext for other forms of analysis including modeling.

As clustering has been applied to more and more diverse subject areas, clustering procedures have, themselves, grown in variety. I will not attempt to present a survey of either. Rather, based on the belief that all clustering techniques follow a few basic principles, with ample room open for further applications and developments of details, I shall discuss some of the options an analyst faces when deciding among existing clustering procedures or when assembling one for his special purpose, and I shall discuss some of the implications such choices have regarding computational efforts, validity and interpretability of results. This chapter provides in a sense a collection of *tools for evaluating what exists* and for *constructing anew what is needed* when multivariate data are to be analyzed by what has become known as clustering.

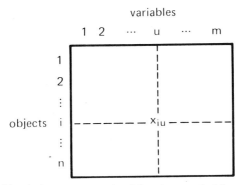

Fig. 1. An $n \times m$ matrix of data in canonical form.

II. CANONICAL FORM OF DATA

Figure 1 depicts the canonical form of data for clustering. It is an $n \times m$ matrix X with entries x_{iu} denoting measures of some sort. The common interpretation of this matrix is that each of n objects is described in terms of m values, each pertaining to a different variable. The rows of this matrix are m-tuples or vectors with m components. The variables may have different metrics, nominal, ordinal, interval, and ratio metric, and may have any number of degrees of freedom. This includes binary variables as a special case.

It is basic to clustering that a matrix X whose variables have the *same metric throughout* can be interpreted in two ways, as objects $\times$ variables and as a variables $\times$ objects, for it is then possible to cluster objects in terms of variables, variables in terms of objects, and indeed both in terms of each other. For example, the matrix in Table I can be depicted either as in Fig. 2 or as in Fig. 3. Figure 2 depicts distances between objects as would be required when objects are clustered in terms of the values on their descriptive variables. In Fig. 3 distances between variables are depicted in an object space with variables X and Y shown to be in close proximity.

TABLE I

DATA MATRIX WITH RATIO METRIC ENTRIES

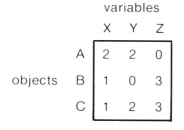

	X	Y	Z
A	2	2	0
B	1	0	3
C	1	2	3

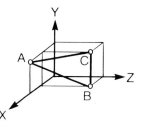

FIG. 2. Distances between objects in a space of variables.

An important distinction is whether data are "complete." If some of the entries x_{iu} are not known or are unavailable for analysis, data are incomplete and require that special assumptions be adopted to compensate for the missing entries. This chapter considers complete data only.

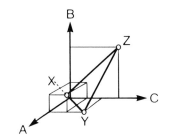

FIG. 3. Distances between variables in a space of objects.

III. RELEVANCE OF DATA

It is important that the variables that are chosen as descriptive of the objects in a sample be relevant to the attempted clustering. Individuals can be categorized in terms of their income, occupation, and social status, in terms of psychopathologies, in terms of physical conditions, their weight, height, strength, in terms of their life styles, etc. The choice among descriptive variables depends on the purpose of the clusters that are expected to emerge. While sampling theory provides statistical criteria for choosing among the *objects* of a population, criteria are less clear for choosing among the potentially infinite universe of possible *variables*.

Generally, variables that either vary randomly or remain constant in the data may be ignored in cluster analysis as they provide little help in differentiating among objects. Also redundant variables (different measures of the same underlying dimension) should be avoided for they only increase computational efforts. The identification of constant, random, and redundant variables can be accomplished by a variety of analytical techniques. For example, factor analysis has been used to identify orthogonal variables. These could be said to be least redundant.

Except for the removal of constant, random, and redundant variables, the researcher requires a theory or at least good intuition to decide on the relevance of the remaining variables to a given problem. For example, a researcher wishing to cluster psychotherapeutic patients for the purpose of standardizing clinical treatments should derive his variables from existing theories about such treatments. Similarly, a researcher attempting to develop typologies for social organization of industrial enterprises must be careful to include all of the variables that sensible writers have associated with industrial organizations. In using theoretical writings to identify relevant variables, however, the researcher may encounter three basic difficulties. First, different theories may be concerned with different levels of aggregation, for example, alienation, an individual's state, versus vertical organization, a characteristic of formal structure in which individuals take part. Second, theoretical concepts may be abstract and multidimensional. Authoritarianism, for example, may not be measurable by a single variable. Finally, variables may not have the same weight. For example, "education" has more influence than "sex" on the formation of social groups focusing on academic topics, but the reverse is true for humor, social stereotypes, and economic expectations.

In summary, the researcher should choose variables which are on the same level of abstraction, equal in weight, and logically independent of each other. But most of all such variables should feed into a theory or conceptual system that renders the description of the objects of analysis meaningful specimens for clustering.

Though a lack of relevance may greatly complicate the interpretation of clustering results, this is a problem that is extraneous to the process of clustering and can therefore be mentioned only in passing. Section X will examine a second source of difficulties of interpretation. The following Sections IV and V are concerned with properties and forms of data.

IV. ORDINALITY OF DATA

Like all other multivariate techniques, clustering methods are used in identifying certain patterns within available data and differ mainly in the way they define, recognize, and represent such patterns.

When clustering is defined as "a technique for grouping objects that are in close *proximity* to each other," one has a biordinal (of the order two) conception of the pattern in mind that clusters are to represent. Biordinal techniques either accept or immediately convert data into distances, differences, similarities, disagreements, correlations, etc. Distances, etc., are quantitative expressions for relations between *two* objects or between *two* variables. They have exactly *two* arguments and belong to the class of *binary* relations. Biordinal clustering procedures yield clusters whose members stand to each other in a certain *pairwise* relationship, proximity being one example.

TABLE II

DATA MATRIX WITH BINARY ENTRIES

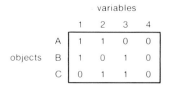

There exist more complex relations, however, that cannot be decomposed without loss into a set of binary relations. This is easily demonstrated and provides the ground for the distinction between *biordinal* and *multiordinal* clustering techniques.

Suppose one is given a 3 by 4 matrix X as in Table II with binary attributes, 0 or 1, in all cells.

The distances or associations between the pairs of objects in Table II will have to be defined on three two-dimensional contingency matrices depicted as Table III. The uniform distribution of probabilities in these matrices indicates that the pairwise co-occurrence of attributes may be due entirely to chance. A biordinal clustering technique would therefore find no justification for merging objects into clusters. However, when objects are examined in triples rather than in pairs, one finds a strong tertiary relation present. This becomes obvious when the data in Table II are represented three-dimensionally as in Table IV.

An example of a relation between three objects that is fully explainable in terms of any two of its three component binary relations is given as Table V. Here, biordinal clustering would be perfectly justifiable for there is nothing unique about the combination of the three objects that could not be expressed in binary terms.

TABLE III

CONTINGENCY MATRICES CONTAINING NO ASSOCIATION IN PAIRS

	B 0	B 1		C 0	C 1		C 0	C 1
A 0	.25	.25	A 0	.25	.25	B 0	.25	.25
A 1	.25	.25	A 1	.25	.25	B 1	.25	.25

TABLE IV

CONTINGENCY MATRIX CONTAINING A TERTIARY ASSOCIATION

TABLE V

CONTINGENCY MATRICES CONTAINING PAIR ASSOCIATIONS ONLY

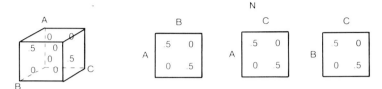

The point of this demonstration is that relations of lower ordinality do not imply anything about the presence or absence of relations of higher ordinality. Biordinal clustering techniques are therefore powerless in the presence of multiordinal relations. And when biordinal techniques are employed nevertheless, it is implicitly assumed that objects are linearly related as in Table V.

Moreover, while data in canonical form are fully capable of exhibiting multiordinality, when such data are transformed into distances, similarities, etc., higher-order relations among objects are irretrievably lost [for more details and a calculus for higher-order relations in data see Krippendorff (1976, 1980)].

The significance of higher-order relations in reality and inherent in multivariate data cannot be underestimated. It is well known, for example, that the behavior of a social group cannot be inferred from the knowledge of the pairwise interactions between its members. There often are great qualitative differences between two-person interaction and three-person interaction, coalition formation being just one example requiring three or more parties. Even in chemistry, most man-made substances emerge when a certain number and quantity of elementary substances meet under suitable conditions, for example, in the presence of a catalyst. What does emerge cannot be predicted from known effects that any pair of elementary substances may have on each other. Or, if the components of electronic equipment have more than one input and/or more than one output, their behavior can no longer be described by a two-valued function. The switching network is then more complex precisely because the whole is different from the sum of the input–output relations of its parts. The difference between a whole and its parts is variously called organization, synergy, interaction effects, or a Gestalt, and points directly to the difference between binary and higher-order relations. Unfortunately not all multivariate techniques are capable of exploring the multiordinal character of the data to which they are applied.

The choice between biordinal and multiordinal clustering techniques should be made dependent on the nature of the data. Whenever objects form natural clusters on the basis of wholistic qualities similar to those just mentioned, multiordinal techniques are called for. If the choice of a biordinal technique is dictated by their availability, the researcher should at least be aware of or measure in quantitative terms what his clusters will omit.

V. DERIVED FORM OF DATA: DISTANCES

Biordinal clustering usually starts with data in the form of a square matrix D whose entries d_{ij} measure some distance, difference, or dissimilarity either (and generally) between all pairs of objects or (provided they possess the same metric) between all pairs of variables. See Fig. 4.

Distances between the same objects must be zero. Otherwise, distances must be positive and symmetrical:

$$d_{ii} = 0, \qquad d_{ij} \geqslant d_{ii}, \qquad d_{ij} = d_{ji}$$

In order to possess at least interval metric properties within many-dimensional space, distances must also satisfy the triangle inequality:

$$d_{ik} \leqslant d_{ij} + d_{jk}$$

and in some cases the ultrametric inequality (Jardine and Sibson, 1971; Johnson, 1967):

$$d_{ik} \leqslant \max(d_{ij}, d_{jk})$$

Data may also be represented through measures of similarity, agreement, resemblance, or correlation, s_{ij}. Similarities and distances are inversely related with the least similar objects giving rise to large distances and small distances reflecting strong resemblances. Similarity measures may be converted into distance measures, for example by

$$d_{ij} = s_{ii} - s_{\min} - s_{ij}$$

$$d_{ij} = (s_{ii} - s_{\min} - s_{ij})^{1/2}$$

$$d_{ij} = (s_{ii} - s_{ij})/(s_{ii} - s_{\min})$$

$$d_{ij} = \left[(s_{ii} - s_{\min})(s_{ii} - s_{ij})\right]^{1/2}$$

objects

	1	2	$\cdots$	j	$\cdots$	n
1	d_{11}	d_{12}	$\cdots$	d_{1j}	$\cdots$	d_{1n}
i	d_{i1}	d_{i2}	$\cdots$	d_{ij}	$\cdots$	d_{in}
$\vdots$	$\vdots$	$\vdots$		$\vdots$		$\vdots$
$\vdots$	$\vdots$	$\vdots$		$\vdots$		$\vdots$
n	d_{n1}	d_{n2}	$\cdots$	d_{nj}	$\cdots$	d_{nn}

FIG. 4. A n^2 matrix of distances.

The latter is my generalization of Gower's (1966) transformation, developed to convert similarity measures that range between 0 and +1. A useful conversion for correlation coefficients has been suggested by Tukey (1977):

$$d_{ij} = 1 - r_{ij}^2$$

It expresses the degree to which two objects are linearly related (positive *or* negative) and takes its maximum value when the objects are statistically independent. This serves as an example that distances and similarities can have many different interpretations which need to be understood before a clustering is attempted. Motivations for these conversion formulas cannot be given here.

I shall now give several distance and similarity measures and show how some of the more familiar measures can be regarded as special cases. For this purpose I shall first define four kinds of differences, one for each metric, then present methods of standardizing such differences across different metrics, and finally present a few key distance and similarity measures.

Difference notions depend on the metric of the variables involved. This may be seen in the comparison between nominal and interval data. Nominal data are characterized by qualitative distinctions without any implied order. Thus a nominal value matches with another or it does not and all mismatching pairs differ to the same degree. Interval data, on the other hand, recognize an ordering of values that allows additions and subtractions. Differences then become a function of their algebraic difference and may be large or small. These intuitive notions can be given rigorous forms: For *nominal* scales the difference between two values x_{iu} and x_{ju} of the uth variable is

$$\Delta_{ij,\,u} = \begin{cases} 0 & \text{iff} \quad x_{iu} = x_{ju}, \\ 1 & \text{iff} \quad x_{iu} \neq x_{ju} \end{cases}$$

For *ordinal* variables in which merely the rank orders count, such a difference is a function of the number of ranks above and below the two values to be compared. With

$$x_{iu}^* = 1 + \frac{1}{n}\left[\sum_{x_{ku} > x_{iu}} n_{x_{ku}} - \sum_{x_{ku} < x_{iu}} n_{x_{ku}} \right]$$

and x_{ju}^* defined analogously, the difference in ordinal scales becomes

$$\Delta_{ij,\,u} = \left| x_{iu}^* - x_{ju}^* \right|$$

For variables with *interval* metric the difference is as just discussed:

$$\Delta_{ij,\,u} = \left| x_{iu} - x_{ju} \right|$$

and for variables with *ratio* metric, the difference may be expressed by

$$\Delta_{ij,\,u} = \left| x_{iu} - x_{ju} \right| / \left| x_{iu} \right| + \left| x_{ju} \right|$$

If both x_{iu} and x_{ju} are positive, as should be expected in ratio-level measurements, then the ratio difference is a modification of Lance and Williams'

(1967) Canberrametric. All of these differences are taken from Krippendorff (1973), where also the motivations for their form may be found.

The most obvious way of aggregating differences across variables into a measure of *distance* is by summing some power r of it:

$$d_{ij} = \left[\sum_{u=1}^{m} (\Delta_{ij,\,u})^r \right]^{1/r}$$

When $r = 1$, differences $\Delta_{ij,\,u}$ are assigned equal weights and are merely summed. When variables are moreover dichotomous, d_{ij} becomes the Hamming distance (Hamming, 1950). For $r = 2$, d_{ij} corresponds to the familiar Euclidean distance in multidimensional space which has been used since Heinecke (1898). The distance is common in research on the semantic differential (Osgood, Suci, and Tannenbaum, 1957) and has been discussed in the cluster analysis literature by Sokal and Sneath (1963), Gower and Ross (1969), and many others. Generally an increase in the exponent r increases the impact of larger differences over smaller ones and thereby affects the nature of the clusters formed.

The Euclidean distance is appropriate when all variables possess the same metric but not when the metric of the variables differs. Variables then will have to be standardized. There seem to be three *methods of standardizing distances* across different metrics.

The *first* is a *reduction* of the power of the metric of all variables *to the least powerful metric* among the variables. The possible metrics may be listed in order of increasing power: nominal, ordinal, interval, ratio. Thus if there are ratio scales (e.g., numerical age, income in dollars) and ordinal scales (e.g., variables containing such values as "most conservative," "somewhat conservative," "neutral"), the values of all variables would then have to be regarded merely by their rank within the set of all values. Similarly, when binary attributes occur, all variables would then have to be dichotomized (e.g., above or below a certain age, income, liberal versus conservative).

A *second* method is to transform all values x_{iu} so that their *range* falls within the interval 0 and 1 (Sokal and Sneath, 1963; Gower, 1971). The transformed value may be expressed as

$$x'_{iu} = \frac{x_{iu} - \min_u(x_{ku})}{\max_u(x_{ku}) - \min_u(x_{ku})}, \qquad k = 1, \ldots, n$$

where $\min_u(x_{ku})$ and $\max_u(x_{ku})$, $k = 1, \ldots, n$, represent the smallest and largest values in u, respectively. This method, however, is inapplicable to nominal metric variables, and if applied to ordinal data, it would assume interval characteristics that are not there.

A *third* method, and one that I prefer, is to standardize the *variance* in each variable before summing. For this purpose one computes a variable-specific weight:

$$w_{u(r)} = \left[\sum_{i=1}^{n} \sum_{j=1}^{n} (\Delta_{ij,\,u})^r \right]^{-1}$$

so that

$$\hat{\sigma}_u^r = \sum_{i=1}^{n} \sum_{j=1}^{n} w_{u(r)}(\Delta_{ij,\,u})^r = 1$$

for each variable. The weighted distance then follows the form proposed by Bock (1974):

$$d_{ij} = \left[\sum_{u=1}^{m} w_{u(r)}(\Delta_{ij,\,u})^r \right]^{1/r}$$

Evidently, when $r = 2$ and all $w_{u(2)} = 1$, the distance becomes again the Euclidean distance.

Another generalization of the Euclidean distance has been proposed by Mahalanobis (1936). For $n > m$, let the $m \times m$ covariance matrix Σ have entries:

$$\sigma_{uv} = \frac{1}{n} \sum_{i=1}^{n} (x_{iu} - \bar{x}_{.u})(x_{iv} - \bar{x}_{.v})$$

where $\bar{x}_{.u}$ and $\bar{x}_{.v}$ are the means in variable u and v, respectively. Let the inverse of this matrix Σ^{-1} have entries σ^{uv}, then the Mahalanobis distance is defined by

$$d_{ij} = \left(\sum_{u=1}^{m} \sum_{v=1}^{m} \sigma^{uv} \Delta_{ij,\,u} \Delta_{ij,\,v} \right)^{1/2}$$

It is noticeable that the Mahalanobis distance depends on all n objects simultaneously with its range in fact a function of n:

$$0 \leqslant d_{ij} \leqslant (2n)^{1/2} \qquad \text{and} \qquad \sum_{i=1}^{n} \sum_{j=1}^{n} d_{ij}^2 = 2mn^2$$

The Mahalanobis distance also eliminates the effects of possible correlations among pairs of variables on the distance between two objects. And it is relatively independent of the ranges in each variable. The Mahalanobis distance is not applicable across different metrics, but this drawback might be corrected by standardizing the variance in each variable according to the third method just discussed. Accordingly, the corrected covariance matrix Σ^* has then entries

$$\sigma_{uv}^* = w_{u(1)} w_{v(1)} \sigma_{uv}$$

and the corrected distance becomes

$$d_{ij} = \left(\sum_{u=1}^{m} \sum_{v=1}^{m} \sigma^{*uv} w_{u(1)} w_{v(1)} \Delta_{ij,\,u} \Delta_{ij,\,v} \right)^{1/2}$$

A most common similarity measure is the product–moment correlation coefficient r_{ij} which is defined by

$$r_{ij} = \frac{\sum_u x_{iu} x_{ju} - \bar{x}_{i.}\bar{x}_{j.}}{\left(\sum_u x_{iu}^2 - \bar{x}_{i.}^2\right)\left(\sum_u x_{ju}^2 - \bar{x}_{j.}^2\right)}$$

where $\bar{x}_{i.}$ and $\bar{x}_{j.}$ are the mean values for objects i and j, respectively. This reliance on mean values presupposes that all variables possess interval or ratio metrics.

While the correlation coefficient can easily be converted into a distance measure by one of the conversion formulas, its interpretation as a similarity measure is not too clear. $r_{ij} = 0$ denotes statistical independence, and $|r_{ij}| = 1$ denotes that variables are linearly dependent. Nonlinear relationships and relations of higher ordinality reduce the value of $|r_{ij}|$, however. The difference between positive and negative values of r_{ij} adds another difficulty to the interpretation of the coefficient as a similarity measure. For example, it is not too obvious whether two objects between which a strong negative linear relation exists should thereby be regarded as similar or different.

Opinions on the use of correlation coefficients for clustering vary considerably in the literature. (For additional arguments see Section X.)

In an approach to multiordinal clustering of nominal data, Krippendorff (1969, 1974) used information theoretical measures to asses the loss of structure in many-dimensional spaces caused by the grouping of the objects' qualitative descriptions. The notion of structure here considered may be paraphrased by "interdependent differentiation," "trans-information," "multiple-order interaction," or "relational entropy" and might be said to be the opposite of redundancy and randomness. The loss in the amount of structure due to the elimination of qualitative distinctions in one or more variables can be expressed by several distances between two objects. I shall define only one here. Let $n_{\langle i \rangle}$ be the number of objects with the description $\langle x_{i1}, \ldots, x_{iu}, \ldots, x_{im} \rangle$, $n_{x_{.u}}$ be the number of objects described in terms of x in the uth variable, and $n_{x_{iu}}$ be the number of objects that share the value x in the uth variable with the object i. The total amount of structure within the m-dimensional space—that is, the total amount of relatedness manifest in the m-valued distribution of objects—is

$$T = \sum_i \frac{n_{\langle i \rangle}}{n} \log_2 \frac{n_{\langle i \rangle}}{n} - \sum_{u=1}^{m} \sum_x \frac{n_{x_{.u}}}{n} \log_2 \frac{n_{x_{.u}}}{n}$$

And the distance between two objects i and j becomes the loss in structure when all hyperplanes within which i and j are located are to be merged.

To express this, the two m-tuples $\langle x_{i1}, \ldots, x_{iu}, \ldots, x_{im} \rangle$ and $\langle x_{j1}, \ldots, x_{ju}, \ldots, x_{jm} \rangle$ are considered to be composed of two parts i_C and $k_{\bar{C}}$ and j_C and $k_{\bar{C}}$, respectively, where C is a set of variables within which $\langle i \rangle$ and $\langle j \rangle$ differ. With a loss function defined by

$$\text{Loss}(a, b) = \begin{cases} 0 & \text{iff} \quad a = b \text{ or } n_a = 0 \text{ or } n_b = 0, \\ (n_a + n_b) \log_2(n_a + n_b) - n_a \log_2 n_a - n_b \log_2 n_b & \\ & \text{otherwise} \end{cases}$$

the loss in structure, expressed as a distance, becomes

$$d_{ij} = T(\text{before}) - T(\text{after merging } i \text{ and } j)$$

$$= \frac{1}{n} \left[\sum_C \sum_{k_{\bar{C}}} \text{Loss}(\langle i_C k_{\bar{C}} \rangle, \langle j_C k_{\bar{C}} \rangle) - \sum_{u=1}^{m} \text{Loss}(x_{iu}, x_{ju}) \right]$$

This distance is small when objects are redundant, i.e., have many values in common, and values with respect to which the objects differ carry little information. The distance is large when the descriptions of objects represent significant differentiations within the m-dimensional space. Like the Mahalanobis distance, the preceding takes all objects into consideration that share some values with either of the two objects being compared. But, unlike the Mahalanobis distance, it takes account of the multiordinal nature of the distribution of objects and does not assume any ordering of values.

For binary attributes, 0 or 1, in all variables several simple distances have been used. To simplify the notation, let me represent the matching and mismatching of attributes associated with objects i and j in terms of a 2 by 2 contingency table:

		j		
		1	0	
i	1	a	b	e_i
	0	c	d	$1 - e_i$
		e_j	$1 - e_j$	1

$$a = \frac{1}{m} \sum_{u=1}^{m} x_{iu} x_{ju}, \quad e_i = \frac{1}{m} \sum_{u=1}^{m} x_{iu}$$

where a is the proportion of matching ones between i and j, b is the proportion of mismatches with is zeros co-occurring with js ones, etc. (the distance d_{ij} is not to be confused with the proportion d). In these terms, the Euclidean distance becomes

$$d_{ij} = (b + c)^{1/2}$$

and two simple matching coefficients used by Zubin (1938) and Jaccard (cited in Sokal & Sneath, 1963), respectively, are

$$d_{ij} = b + c \qquad \text{and} \qquad d_{ij} = a + b + c$$

Yule's association coefficient

$$s_{ij} = (ad - bc)/(ad + bc).$$

has also been used as a similarity measure (Sokal & Sneath, 1963).

Space does not permit a review and discussion of the many distance and similarity measures which are possible and have actually been applied in clustering. The user of any clustering technique that starts from distance or similarity data must ascertain though that these measures possess the metric properties that the clustering technique requires and that the assumptions implied by the choice of a particular distance measure conform to what the clusters are expected to represent. Specifically, multiordinal relations are not manifest in distance or similarity data. Multiordinal clustering techniques require continuous interaction with data in their canonical form because they are capable of retaining such relations.

VI. GOALS AND COMPUTATIONAL EFFORTS

A major problem of all multivariate techniques is the amount of computation required to produce results. Since the number of cells in a many-dimensional space grows exponentially with the number of dimensions, such numbers often approach limits of computability before data can be considered rich enough to contain interesting information. Virtually all multivariate analysis algorithms rely on computational shortcuts to reduce this effort and thereby impose assumptions on the way data are processed. Cluster analysis is no exception and the user should know what is involved.

While all clustering procedures yield groupings of objects or variables according to some criterion, the specific task may be one of the following:

(a) selecting that subset of a set of objects which contains a designated object in relation to which criteria for inclusion into the subset, class, type, or cluster are defined.

(b) selecting that partition of a set of objects into a specified number of exhaustive and mutually exclusive subsets, classes, types or clusters, the parts of the partition, of which each is in a specifiable sense optimal under the numerical restriction.

(c) selecting that partition of a set of objects into any number of exhaustive and mutually exclusive subsets which satisfies a specified criteria of optimality.

(d) selecting that binary decision tree which contains only partitions satisfying (b) including the partition satisfying (c).

Table VI shows how the number of alternatives among which decisions need to be computed grows with the number of objects to be clustered. With only $n = 10$ objects, task (a) presents 512 alternatives, which is a manageable and unproblematic number. But task (c) requires the evaluation of 116 thousand partitions, a number that approaches practical limits of computation, while task (d) with its 2.6 billion decision trees already exceeds computational limits. The lesson to be drawn from any extension of numbers n of this table into the domain of theoretical significance is that practical clustering procedures cannot compute alternatives *simultaneously* but must proceed *iteratively*, in irreversible steps. It is in the *form* of iteration that *hierarchical clustering schemes* emerge.

Two iterative clustering procedures can be distinguished: The successive *partitioning* of a set of objects into more and smaller subsets (classes or clusters) and the successive *merging* of objects into fewer and larger subsets (classes or clusters). Sneath and Sokal (1973) call the former technique *divisive* and the latter *agglomerative*. With a vertical bar separating the parts of a partition among four objects, a, b, c, and d, these two options are depicted in Fig. 5 as a path through a partition lattice from top to bottom or from bottom to top, respectively.

While either option results in the choice of one out of $n!(n-1)!2^{n-1}$ binary decision trees, their computational efforts are rather different as the following table of the number of alternatives may show:

	1st step	2nd step	$\cdots$
Successive partitioning:	$2^{n-1}-1$	between $2^{(\frac{1}{2}n-1)}-1$ and $2^{n-2}-1$	$\cdots$
Successive merging:	$\dfrac{n(n-1)}{2}$	$\dfrac{(n-1)(n-2)}{2}$	$\cdots$

Numerically, when $n = 100$, the first step of successive partitioning poses about 10^{30} alternative partitions to chose from, a practical impossibility, whereas successive merging calls for the evaluation of only 4950. While successive partitioning cuts these numbers down rather quickly, the first step is evidently prohibitive.

Finally, computation is affected by two further distinctions. The first was suggested by Lance and Williams (1967). They define a *combinatorial strategy* as one in which the original input matrix (of distances or of data in canonical form) is successively transformed, becomes smaller and simpler, and thereby reduces the computational effort by each step. In contrast, in a *noncombinatorial* strategy all computations are based on the original input which must therefore be maintained throughout. Obviously, combinatorial strategies are more efficient. Furthermore, I should like to distinguish between two combinatorial strategies: *distance-recursive* strategies in which each distance matrix is derived from its preceding distance matrix, and *data-recursive* strategies in

TABLE VI

COMPUTATIONAL EFFORTS OF FOUR DIFFERENT CLUSTERING TASKS

	$n:$ 1	2	3	4	5	6	7	8	9	10
(a) Number of subsets of which g is a member, 2^{n-1}	1	2	4	8	16	32	64	128	256	512
(b) Number of partitions into k parts, $\sum_{j=0}^{k-1}(-1)^j\dfrac{(k-j)^n}{j!\,(k-j)!}$										
$k = 1$	1	1	1	1	1	1	1	1	1	1
2		1	3	7	15	31	63	127	255	511
3			1	6	25	90	301	966	3,025	9,330
4				1	10	65	350	1,701	7,770	34,105
5					1	15	140	1,050	6,951	42,525
6						1	21	266	2,646	22,827
7							1	28	462	5,880
8								1	36	750
9									1	45
10										1
(c) Total number of partitions, $\sum_{k=1}^{n}\sum_{j=0}^{k-1}(-1)^j\dfrac{(k-j)^n}{j!\,(k-j)!}$	1	2	5	15	52	203	877	4,140	21,147	115,975
(d) Number of binary decision trees, $\dfrac{n!\,(n-1)!}{2^{n-1}}$	0	1	3	18	180	2,700	56,700	1,587,600	57,153,600	2,571,912,000

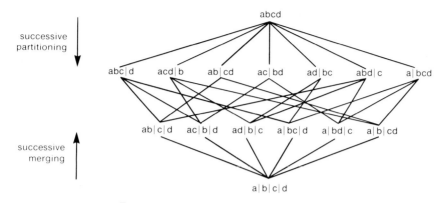

FIG. 5. Partition lattice involving four objects.

which it is the canonical representation of data which is successively modified. The latter is exemplified in Table VII. Distance recursive strategies are at least m times (m = the number of variables) as efficient as data recursive methods.

Of course, computational advantages must be weighted against the amount of information that combinatorial strategies lose. Computational shortcuts can not bypass questions of validity.

VII. PRESENTATION OF RESULTS

The conceptualization of multivariate data is difficult. We are just not accustomed to seeing point distributions in four-or-more-dimensional spatial representations and it is this fact that often serves as a motivation for applying multivariate statistical analyses. All multivariate techniques transform such data. Even though analytical results may appear simple, it is often difficult to relate the transforms of these data to the original observations. This section does not deal with questions of meaningfulness and of the adequacy of the transformations for producing a result. It is rather concerned with several ways the results of a clustering process might be visualized leaving the conceptualization of the process for Section IX.

A. Dendrograms

The most important form of representing clustering results is the dendrogram (see Fig. 6) which is a tree-like structure whose branches terminate at the objects being clustered. The lengths of its branches indicate differences in homogeneity, or heterogeneity within clusters being merged or partitioned. Dendrograms are nothing but a more sophisticated form of listing objects by their membership in clusters: Each horizontal cut through a dendrogram

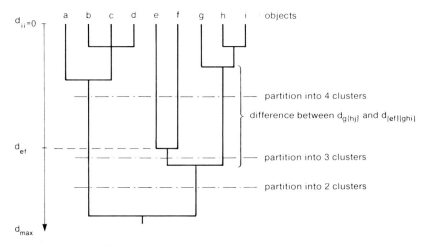

FIG. 6. Dendrogram representation of clustering.

indicates one of several partitions of the set of objects, the height between this cut and the original (unclustered) objects indicates the level of homogeneity or heterogeneity lost in the partition.

Dendrograms are particularly suited to represent a large number of objects and the whole history of a clustering process whether it proceeds by successive merging or partitioning. Relatively long stems between branching points indicate to the researcher where relatively large jumps in heterogeneity occur and might suggest cutoff points at which partitions might be meaningful.

Figure 7 represents a small section of a dendrogram obtained by clustering 299 sales appeals in television commercials (Dziurzinski, 1978) by the strong association method (see Section IX).

Johnson (1967) used a modified dendrogram which is particularly suited for computer printouts (Fig. 16).

B. Spatial Representations for Biordinal Clustering

By far the most appealing form of representation depicts the proximities among objects in some space and indicates clusters by drawing their boundaries. Since proximities are an essential ingredient of Gestalt perception, groupings are much easier to visualize when similarities, correlation, and the like are expressed as distances. Figures 8 and 9 exemplify such a representation in one and in two dimensions.

When three dimensions are involved, the representation is somewhat more cumbersome although still possible. Spatial representations in four or more dimensions become virtually unreadable however. Since many multivariate data consist of objects that are characterized by many more than three variables, the use of spatial representations of clustering results is extremely limited. But since two- or three-dimensional representations are so common,

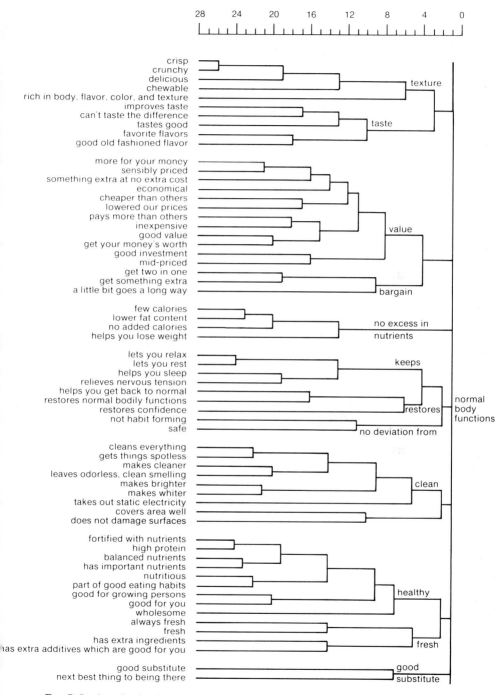

FIG. 7. Section of a dendrogram for television advertising appeals (after Dziurzynski, 1978).

FIG. 8. One-dimensional spatial representation of clusters.

researchers have either ignored the many-dimensional character of the distances between objects and approximated them by distances in two- or three-dimensional representations or else have employed dimension reducing techniques, such as factor analysis, that yield visually representable distributions of objects in a space with orthogonal dimensions. Since the size of the resulting clusters and distances between them are then distorted in the visual representation, numerical values for these may have to be added to indicate their true quantitative relationship. These are omitted in Fig. 10, which is the visualization of a taxonomy of the Enterobacteri aceae (Lysenko & Sneath, 1959).

It should be reemphasized that spatial representations with their emphasis on proximity carry strong biordinal biases. Higher-order relations among three or more objects have no obvious spatial form.

C. Reordered Distance Matrices

Several authors, among them Sneath and Sokal (1973), suggest that the results of distance recursive merging be represented by reordering the entries of the initial distance matrix D^0 so that the proximity of rows (and columns) reflect the rank ordering of distances between objects. However, when the initial distances are rearranged not by their rank but by the hierarchical ordering that any iterative clustering process imposes, one obtains a reordered distance matrix, such as in Fig. 11, in which entries are "blocked" into sections representing distances within and between clusters, respectively. The

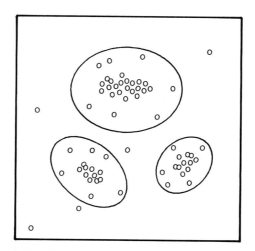

FIG. 9. Two-dimensional spatial representation of clusters.

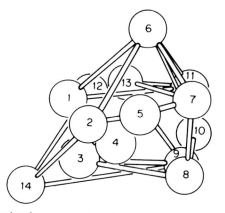

FIG. 10. Three-dimensional representation of many-dimensional clusters (Sneath & Sokal, 1963, with permission of W. H. Freeman and Company).

reordering of distance matrices does not reveal, however, the motivation for multiordinal clusters. It is instructive primarily when clustering proceeds from distances and is biordinal.

D. Prototypes and Centroids

It is often desirable to identify an object, real or hypothetical, that is most representative of a cluster. Such an object is called the prototypical object or centroid, respectively. *Centroids* locate a given cluster, in multivariate space. In monothetic clustering schemes, the centroid is that m-tuple of values that

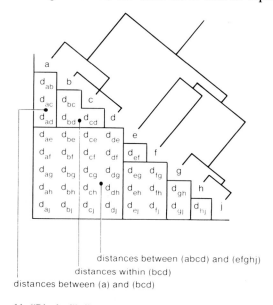

FIG. 11. "Blocked" distance matrix and associated dendrogram.

all objects in a cluster share. Since the objects in clusters emerging from polythetic techniques (see Section VIII) need not have any value in common, the centroid may then be quite abstract and is often unidentifiable in terms of data in canonical form. In either case, there may not exist a real object in the sample that coincides with the hypothetical centroid of a cluster. The object closest to the centroid of a cluster may then be chosen as the *prototype* of the cluster.

In single linkage clustering methods (see Section VIII) and those that employ measures of differences *between* rather than *within* clusters, centroids have no clear theoretical justification because clusters have this chain-like appearance and heterogeneities are not accounted for by these methods. The computation of centroids and the identification of prototypes is thereby not excluded however.

When data are in canonical form and biordinal clustering proceeds from distances, the centroid of the cluster G becomes the m-tuple

$$\langle \bar{x}_{G1}, \ldots, \bar{x}_{Gu}, \ldots, \bar{x}_{Gm} \rangle$$

where $\bar{x}_{Gu}$ is the arithmetic mean of values of the uth variable over objects in cluster G when that variable has interval metric, the median when that variable has ordinal metric, and the mode when that variable is unordered.

Otherwise, the researcher tends to be restricted to identify the prototype of a cluster by

$$\min_{g \in G}(d_{gG}) \leftrightarrow g \text{ is the prototypical object of } G$$

in which d_{gG} stands for the heterogeneity measure chosen. In diametric clustering

$$d_{gG} = \max_{j \in G}(d_{gj})$$

whereby the prototype g is the one closest to the center of the circle circumscribing the objects in G. In variance-type clustering,

$$d_{gG} = \left(\frac{1}{n_G - 1} \sum_{j \in G} d_{gj}^r \right)^{1/r}$$

and when $r = 1$, the prototype occupies a position close to the mean of the cluster. Large values for r make that position more responsive to the skewness of the distribution of objects within a cluster.

In multivariate classification the prototype of a cluster is defined as that object which, when removed from the cluster, causes the least amount of structure loss within the cluster. With $n_{\bar{g}u} = n_{Gu} - n_{gu}$ and $n_{\langle \bar{g}_c k_{\bar{c}} \rangle} = n_{\langle G_c k_{\bar{c}} \rangle} - n_{\langle g_c k_{\bar{c}} \rangle}$ for simplicity of notation,

$$d_{gG} = \frac{1}{n} \left[\sum_C \sum_{k_{\bar{c}}} \text{Loss}(\langle \bar{g}_c k_{\bar{c}} \rangle, \langle g_c k_{\bar{c}} \rangle) - \sum_{u=1}^{m} \text{Loss}(\bar{g}u, gu) \right]$$

If the proportion $n_{\langle g_c k_{\bar{c}}\rangle}/n_{\langle G_c k_{\bar{c}}\rangle}$ = constant for all objects that share some values with g, then $d_{gG} = 0$ and g is both prototype and centroid of the cluster G.

Two drawbacks of representing clusters by prototypes are that there may exist objects that are actually more representative (closer to the centroid) of a cluster than those occurring in the sample and that there may exist many different objects for which d_{gG} is equal and minimum. The first problem is one of sampling and the second, one of measurement.

E. Other Multivariate Techniques

Insofar as it provides a single partition of canonically represented objects, clustering adds to the m descriptive values each object's membership in some cluster. Such an indication of membership can be regarded as the $(m + 1)$st descriptive variable and thus expands the initial $n \times m$ matrix of data in canonical form to an $n \times (m + 1)$ matrix. This expanded matrix may be subjected to a variety of other multivariate techniques, for example, multiple discriminant techniques yielding explanations of the clusters in terms of the features that discriminate.

The results of clustering can be subjected to factor analysis to obtain a more efficient system of coordinates for representing these clusters (see Chapter 8). The results of different clustering techniques can be compared by cross-tabulations, etc. In fact, there is no limit to the use of other analytical techniques for describing and exploring the nature of the clusters that have been obtained as well as in preparing the data for subsequent clustering.

VIII. PROPERTIES OF EMERGING CLUSTERS

The aggregate or shared properties of objects within a cluster, the boundaries around clusters, the relations between clusters, the tree-like dendrograms describing either the history of merging objects into classes or the history of partitioning sets of objects into subsets are all expected to be based on given data. Once the criteria for iterative merging or partitioning are set, the clusters that do emerge develop certain properties that should not be an artifact of the procedure. Decision criteria for clustering must therefore be based on measures that characterize *sets of objects*. This section presents several measures on clusters of two or more objects and in terms of three dimensions of classification:

Difference measures versus heterogeneity measures

Single linkage measures versus multiple linkage measures

Polythetic measures versus monothetic measures

The distinction between biordinal and multiordinal clustering is also reflected in these measures and the formal conditions imposed on such measures depend to a large part on the computational approach taken, i.e., whether the procedure is distance recursive or data recursive and whether clusters are formed by partitioning (divisive) or by merging (agglomerative). Naturally the number of combinatorially possible clustering criteria exceeds those actually realized, and of those available only a few can be discussed here.

The differentiation between *difference* measures and *heterogeneity* measures is conceptually simple but the implications are far from obvious. Applied to clusters (classes of objects), difference measures quantitatively assess differences *between two* different clusters whereas heterogeneity measures assess differences *within one* cluster. Both are divergent generalizations of the distance between two objects. When a third object is added to a cluster of two, a difference measure assesses the difference between the third object and either one or both of the two objects already merged while a heterogeneity measure assesses some difference among all three objects regardless of how they were brought together and thereby assigns equal weight to each object involved.

Notationally, d_{EF} will be used to denote the *heterogeneity* of the union of two sets of objects, whereas $d_{E|F}$ will be used to denote the *difference* between the two sets. The distance d_{ij} between two objects i and j then is the special and overlapping case at which $E = \{i\}$ and $F = \{j\}$.

In these terms, and without reference to details, several formal requirements on the use of these measures as decision criteria for clustering can be stated. For *distance recursive* procedures, both heterogeneity and difference measures must satisfy analogous conditions:

$$d_{EE} \geqslant 0$$

$$d_{EF} \geqslant d_{EE}, \qquad\qquad d_{E|F} \geqslant 0 \qquad\qquad \text{Positive}$$

$$d_{EF} = d_{FE}, \qquad\qquad d_{E|F} = d_{F|E} \qquad\qquad \text{Symmetrical}$$

$$d_{EF} \leqslant d_{EG} + d_{GF}, \qquad d_{E|F} \leqslant d_{E|G} + d_{G|F} \qquad \text{Triangle inequality}$$

to which the following may have to be added:

$$d_{EF} \leqslant \max(d_{EG}, d_{GF}), \qquad d_{E|F} \leqslant \max(d_{E|G}, d_{G|F}) \qquad \text{Ultrametric inequality}$$

These conditions correspond to those for distances between two objects except that the heterogeneity within a cluster, d_{EE}, may exceed zero and the difference between a cluster and itself, $d_{E|E}$, is meaningless by definition.

For *data recursive* procedures these formal requirements may be relaxed to the following two conditions:

(1) Decision criteria must not decrease with each upward move in the partition lattice (merging) and must not increase with each downward move in the partition lattice (partitioning). For any three clusters E, F, and G, at

any stage in the clustering process,

$$\max(d_{GG}) \leqslant \min(d_{EF})$$

For difference measures this does not apply generally. However, if one interprets $d_{G|G}$ as that distance which served as criterion to merge two clusters into G, then, while some differences within G may exceed $d_{E|F}$, at least under a successive merging strategy,

$$\max(d_{G|G}) \leqslant \min(d_{E|F})$$

This condition favors heterogeneity measures because whenever G is the union of E and F, $d_{GG} = d_{EF}$. For difference measures the condition must be rephrased to read: The largest of the differences that lead to the formation of a cluster must not exceed the smallest difference between any pair of clusters *at that stage at which that cluster was formed.*

(2) Ideally, decision criteria should also be independent of the order of cluster formation:

$$d_{\{ijk\}\{ijk\}} = d_{\{i\}\{jk\}} = d_{\{ij\}\{k\}} = d_{\{ik\}\{j\}}$$

This is again satisfied by heterogeneity measures but not by difference measures. Some of the implications of this failure will become apparent in the following.

The second dimension of classification refers to whether clusters are characterized by a *single representative linkage* between two objects or whether the measure aggregates *multiple linkages into a single index.* I shall exemplify the two dimensions by several individual and polythetic measures for biordinal clusters.

	Difference	Heterogeneity
Single linkage:	Connectedness	Diameter
Multiple linkage:	Average linkage	Variance

Clusters that are characterized by the *connectedness* of their members (Johnson, 1967; single linkage clustering according to Sokal & Sneath, 1963) stem from the simplest form of clustering with difference measures: Clusters are formed by merging objects in the increasing order of their distances, i.e., by merging those clusters that contain at least one object each, which is least distant *across* cluster boundaries. Thus, the two clusters E and F, if they are to be merged to form the cluster G, satisfy the criterion:

$$\min_{E,F}(d_{E|F}) = \min_{E,F}\left(\min_{i\in E, j\in F}(d_{ij})\right)$$

The difference $d_{E|F}$ in this criterion is crucially dependent on the history of the formation of the cluster. It is the distance between two objects within G that at the point of the last addition to the cluster was the smallest distance between objects of all different clusters formed prior to G. Within a cluster it is then possible to find distances between members that are larger or smaller than the distance on account of which the cluster was formed.

While leading to an extremely simple form of computation (in fact it can be done manually by inspection of the distance matrix D without any arithmetical computation), the weakness of this criterion lies in its tendency to form long chains that often bridge otherwise perfectly meaningful clusters. Some of the peculiar clusters that this criterion will produce are illustrated in the spatial representation of Fig. 12. The use of difference measures generally and in conjunction with single linkage conceptions of those measures in particular allows clusters to "grow out of control."

Clusters may be characterized by the largest distance between their members, called their *diameter*. The technique minimizing the diameter of a cluster is variably called the complete linkage method (Sokal & Sneath, 1963), compact clustering (Lorr, cited in Cureton, Cureton, & Durell, 1970), or the diameter method (Johnson, 1967) and controls for what single-linkage clustering omits, namely, that extreme differences within a cluster stay within bounds. The largest distance within a cluster G, the diameter, is

$$d_{GG} = \max_{i,j \in G} (d_{ij})$$

The diameter of a cluster is a heterogeneity measure but it takes only one distance as representative of the cluster as a whole. In the formation of clusters that minimize this measure, a successive merging procedure will join at each step those two clusters whose most distant objects have the smallest distance across all pairs of clusters. Thus, by analogy to MacNaughton-Smith (1965) and Johnson (1967), if E and F are merged to form a new cluster G,

$$d_{GG} = \min_{E,F} (d_{EF}) = \min_{E,F} \left(\max_{i \in E, j \in F} (d_{ij}) \right)$$

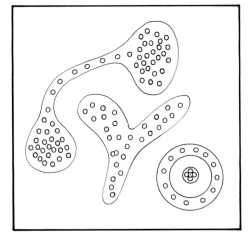

FIG. 12. Clusters for single-linkage method.

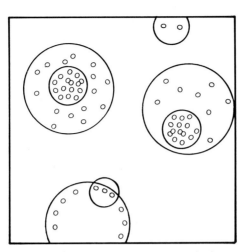

FIG. 13. Clusters for diametric method.

Compared with the connectedness criterion, the diameter criterion yields relatively compact clusters. But such clusters have several peculiar properties. First, there is the tendency of clusters to become circular and equal in diameter. Second, the number of objects within a cluster, the density of its population, has no bearing on the way clusters are formed. Third, and a corollary of the second, a center need not exist for such clusters. Figure 13 illustrates some of the typical clusters diametric clustering will yield. These clusters are shown at two stages of formation.

Average linkage clustering (Sokal & Sneath, 1963) extends the notion of connectedness to an aggregate measure of all distances between two clusters. So Bock (1974) defines the average distance between two clusters by

$$d_{E|F} = \frac{1}{n_E n_F} \sum_{i \in E} \sum_{j \in F} d_{ij}$$

The criterion to merge E and F into G, generalized to any power, then is

$$\min_{E,F}(d_{E|F}) = \min_{E,F} \left(\frac{1}{n_E n_F} \sum_{i \in E} \sum_{j \in F} d_{ij}^r \right)^{1/r}$$

Another average linkage criterion is Pearson's (1926) coefficient of racial likeness:

$$\min_{E,F}(d_{E|F}) = \min_{E,F} \left[\frac{1}{m} \sum_{u=1}^{m} \frac{(\bar{x}_{Eu} - \bar{x}_{Fu})^2}{(\sigma_{Eu}/n_E) + (\sigma_{Fu}/n_F)} \right]^{1/2}$$

in which $\bar{x}_{Eu}$ is the arithmetic mean of values in E of variable u, and σ_{Eu} is the variance within E regarding the uth variable. The coefficient has been used by Rao (1948, 1952), Sokal and Sneath (1963), and several others. The coefficient makes the difference between two clusters a function of the variance within both and is thus not a "pure" average linkage measure but belongs to the same family.

Both difference measures work against the chainlike appearance of clusters typical of the connectedness criterion but do not eliminate it completely. Their clusters are less compact than those using corresponding heterogeneity measures. Difference measures simply do not optimize homogeneity within a cluster. Once two clusters are merged, the distances that contributed to that decision are no longer referred to in subsequent clustering steps.

Clusters with minimum *variance* between their objects are achieved by taking all distances within a prospective cluster into account. Accordingly, a multiple linkage measure of heterogeneity *within* a cluster G is

$$d_{GG} = \left(\frac{1}{n_G(n_G - 1)} \sum_{i,j \in G} d_{ij}^r \right)^{1/r}$$

and to minimize this heterogeneity, clusters E and F are merged into G when

$$d_{GG} = \min_{E,F}(d_{EF}) = \min_{E,F} \left(\frac{1}{(n_E + n_F)(n_E + n_F - 1)} \sum_{i,j \in E,F} d_{ij}^r \right)^{1/r}$$

When the exponent $r = 1$, d_{GG} is the mean distance within the objects of a cluster and its use as a decision criterion assures that this mean distance is kept at a minimum. When $r = 2$, d_{GG} is the standard deviation within a cluster. And, since the variance is the square of the standard deviation, clustering with $r = 2$ also might be said to minimize the variance within clusters. Sokal and Sneath (1963) termed the latter index, the taxionomic distance.

Variance-type heterogeneity measures compensate for a large distance within a cluster by several smaller distances within that cluster. Clusters with equal heterogeneity in this variance sense may thus be different in diameter. However, as r increases in value, larger distances are weighted increasingly heavily on the measure so that r in fact controls the conservatism of the clustering procedure. The higher the exponent r the more compact the clusters that emerge. Some typical clusters that variance methods will identify are depicted in Fig. 14.

The relationship between variance-type difference and heterogeneity measures is easily illustrated by the following equality in which $r = 1$ for both the average linkage between clusters and the mean distance within the union of two clusters:

$$(n_E + n_F)(n_E + n_F - 1)d_{EF} = n_E(n_E - 1)d_{EE} + n_E n_F d_{E|F} + n_F(n_F - 1)d_{FF}$$

This equality reveals the difference measure $d_{E|F}$ to be *only one part* of the heterogeneity measure d_{EF}. If used as a clustering criterion, $d_{E|F}$ ignores the heterogeneities d_{EE} and d_{FF} of the clusters being merged and thus minimizes some property other than a characteristic of all the objects in the merging cluster. This accounts for what was suggested earlier, that difference measures

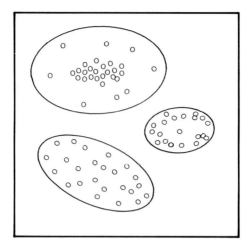

FIG. 14. Clusters for variance method.

tend to let clusters "grow out of control" and are for this reason inferior to measures of heterogeneity.

Clusters may also be *polythetic* or *monothetic* (Sokal & Sneath, 1963). In a monothetic cluster *all members share* some properties. Objects are admitted to a cluster because a large number of their characteristics match. In a poly-thetic cluster, members need not hold any value in common. They need only be similar in some respect and this similarity may be expressed by a high correlation, by a larger proximity between values, or by the sharing of values between pairs rather than among all members of a cluster. Distance recursive techniques yield polythetic clusters only and all clustering criteria discussed so far are also polythetic in result.

An example of a monothetic clustering technique is Krippendorff's (1975) strong associative clustering of binary attribute data. Key to the technique is the successive enumeration of the attributes that are shared among all members of a cluster. Since this number cannot be obtained from agreements between pairs, the enumeration must be data recursive. And seeking to correct observed agreement on attributes by what is due to chance, one of the more convincing coefficients turns out to be a generalization of Benini's (1901) measure of association. With a_G as the proportion of attributes shared among objects in G and e_i as the proportion of attributes associated with the object i of G, the coefficient, converted into a heterogenity measure by $d_{ij} = 1 - s_{ij}$ and stated as a decision criterion for merging E and F into G, is

$$d_{GG} = \frac{\min_{i \in G}(e_i) - a_G}{\min_{i \in G}(e_i) - \prod_{i \in G} e_i} = \min_{E,F}(d_{EF}) = \min_{E,F}\left(\frac{\min_{i \in E,F}(e_i) - a_{EF}}{\min_{i \in E,F}(e_i) - \prod_{i \in E,F} e_i}\right)$$

It is the proportion of the observed disagreement on attributes shared within G to the disagreement of chance matching.

A graphical representation of typical clusters resulting from this monothetic, heterogeneity measure is difficult precisely because multiordinal
clusters defy spatial representations. Further elaboration of the measure and
an example are found in Section IX. This heterogeneity measure exemplifies a
measure that does not satisfy the triangle inequality and would thus not lend
itself to distance recursive clustering.

An example of a polythetic multiordinal and variance-type technique is
multivariate classification. It is a method by which clusters are formed neither
by grouping objects in terms of their variables nor by grouping variables in
terms of their objects (all of which might produce one univariate classification
or clustering scheme) but by clustering variables in terms of each other,
interactionally so to speak, using the distribution of objects in multivariate
space as a reference for the interaction. Krippendorff (1969, 1974) developed
the technique from information theory. The simplest decision criterion is
given in the section on distances. And the recursive form of the heterogeneity
measure is presented in Section IX where details are elaborated. This measure
assesses the amount of multivariate structure lost within the m-dimensional
space when some of the terms within variables are no longer differentiated. It
can be interpreted as expressing the amount of multivariate information that
can no longer be transmitted due to the formation of clusters in each
dimension or as the amount of relational entropy lost within a cross-classification of m separate clustering schemes, one for each variable. What this
clustering technique achieves is a more efficient representation of the objects
involved, one that reduces the m-dimensional space in volume without much
loss in the essential relationship (see Figs. 20 and 21 for examples). Since the
complexity of the resulting cluster again defies a simple graphical representation, Fig. 15 offers a two-dimensional diagram of the nature of the clusters
that the technique might identify.

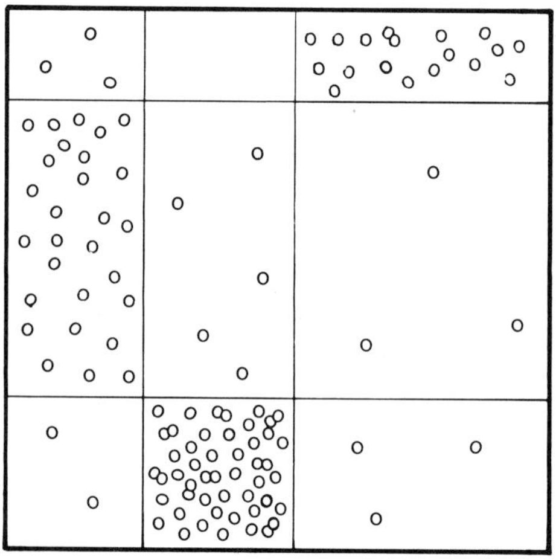

FIG. 15. Clusters for multivariate classification method.

In conclusion, it is evident that the choice of clustering criteria is the most important determinant of the kind of clusters that do emerge and the kind of properties these clusters are thereby able to represent. The classification of these properties merely serves to clarify principal differences between clustering criteria and the emerging properties of clusters. Examples are more numerous for difference than for heterogeneity measures, for single than for multiple linkage procedures, for polythetic than for monothetic clusters. The reliance of biordinal rather than multiordinal conceptions of properties is striking, and the fact that I did not exemplify the results of partitioning approaches to clustering is indicative of suspicious white spaces on the map of all combinatorially possible clustering techniques.

IX. CLUSTERING ALGORITHMS

An algorithm is a stepwise procedure that is completely specified (leaves no alternative undecidable) and transforms some input into some output. Clustering algorithms accept data as input either in their canonical form of a data matrix X or in their derived form of a distance matrix D. The output of a clustering algorithm either identifies a cluster containing a given object, produces some partition, i.e., a set of clusters, satisfying some criterion of optimality, or it gives a decision tree that contains partitions all of which satisfy some criterion of optimality.

Because of the insurmountable efforts required to compute clusters, partitions, and decision trees simultaneously, demonstrated previously, algorithms must be defined recursively. A recursive algorithm is one that is applied to some initial set of data, yielding an output to which it is applied again and again until some terminating criterion is met. Recursive clustering algorithms work themselves stepwise either down a partition lattice (through successive partitioning) or up the partition lattice (through successive merging). After the first step, a recursive algorithm avoids references to the initial data and transforms only its transforms.

This section presents four different algorithms for clustering objects or variables. The algorithms are chosen for their distinctive features: successive partitioning versus successive merging, biordinal clustering versus multiordinal clustering, data recursive versus distance recursive, monothetic versus polythetic, etc. The algorithms presented here do not exhaust all alternatives however. A researcher has many more options than are given here.

A. The Johnson Algorithm

The first example of a clustering algorithm is taken from Johnson (1967), who formalizes the two single-linkage clustering techniques previously discussed. Since both are distance-recursive merging techniques and proceed identically except for their clustering criteria, I shall describe only one here, the algorithm for diametric clustering. The Johnson algorithm is extremely simple, speedy in execution, and therefore inexpensive to use, which might explain its widespread application.

Given: The $n \times n$ matrix of distances $(d_{ij}^s) = D^s$ at the initial $s = 0$.

Step 1 Search for the smallest distance, $\min_{E \neq F}(d_{EF}^s)$ in the $(n - s) \times (n - s)$ matrix D^s.

Step 2 Print or store on a history record: $s + 1$, E, F for which d_{EF}^s is minimum and merge all pairs of objects in E and F into G.

Step 3 Compute a new $(n - s - 1) \times (n - s - 1)$ matrix of distances in D^{s+1} from D^s by replacing all entries with references to E and F by

$$d_{GI}^{s+1} = \max(d_{EI}^s, d_{IF}^s) \qquad \text{for all } I \neq E, F \text{ in } D^s$$

Step 4 Set $s \leftarrow s + 1$, return the new D^s to Step 1 unless either the smallest distance d_{EF}^{s-1}, now d_{GG}^s, exceeds a specified limit, the number of remaining clusters $n - s$ falls below a specified number, or any other terminating criterion is satisfied.

Step 5 Print results and terminate.

For an illustrative example, Johnson uses data obtained from a psycho-acoustic study of 16 principle consonants which are listed here across Fig. 16. The numbers down the left-hand side are similarity values that were obtained in the study and are here associated with each merging as indicated. Apparently the resulting clusters correspond to the distinctive features presumed by Miller and Nicely (1955) who provided these data. At the level of five clusters the 16 phonemes divide into a hierarchy, as depicted in Fig. 17.

	p	t	k	f	θ	s	ʃ	b	d	g	v	ð	z	ʒ	m	n
—	·	·	·	·	·	·	·	·	·	·	·	·	·	·	·	·
2.635	·	·	·	·	·	·	·	·	XXX	·	·	·	·	·	·	·
2.234	XXX	·	·	·	·	·	·	·	XXX	·	·	·	·	·	·	·
2.230	XXX	·	·	·	XXX	·	·	·	XXX	·	·	·	·	·	·	·
2.123	XXX	·	·	·	XXX	·	·	·	XXX	·	·	XXX	·	·	·	·
1.855	XXXXX	·	·	XXX	·	·	·	XXX	·	·	XXX	·	·	·
1.683	XXXXX	·	XXXXX	·	·	XXX	·	·	XXX	·	·	·
1.604	XXXXX	·	XXXXX	·	·	XXX	·	·	XXX	XXX
1.525	XXXXX	·	XXXXX	·	·	XXX	·	XXXXX	XXX
1.186	XXXXX	·	XXXXX	·	XXX	XXXXXXX	XXX
1.119	XXXXX	·	XXXXX	XXXXX	XXXXXXX	XXX
0.939	XXXXX	XXXXXXX	XXXXX	XXXXXXX	XXX
0.422	XXXXXXXXXXXXX	XXXXX	XXXXXXX	XXX
0.302	XXXXXXXXXXXXX	XXXXXXXXXXXXX	XXX
0.019	XXXXXXXXXXXXX	XXXXXXXXXXXXXXXX
0.000	XXXXXXXXXXXXXXXXXXXXXXXXXXXXXXXX

FIG. 16. Computer printable dendrogram for phoneme clusters (Johnson, 1967).

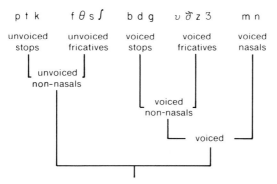

FIG. 17. Typology for phonemes derived from clustering (Johnson, 1967).

B. The CONCOR Algorithm

The second example of a clustering algorithm is taken from Breiger, Boorman, and Arabie (1975). It is the only effective partitioning algorithm I know that is applicable to a wide variety of data. CONCOR is the acronym of "convergent correlation" which designates the iterative application of correlations to yield stable indications of dependencies which are in turn used to partition a set of objects or variables into two parts. The use of correlations identifies the method as a biordinal partition technique.

Given: The $n \times m$ matrix $(x_{iu}) = X$ with interval metric in each variable u.

Step 1 Compute the $n_G \times n_G$ matrix of product-moment correlations $_t(r_{ij}^s)_G = {}_tR_G^s$ for the initial $s = 0$ and $r = 0$ where the initial set G is the set of all $n_G = n$ objects.

Step 2 Compute the $n_G \times n_G$ matrix of product-moment correlations $_{t+1}(r_{ij}^s)_G = {}_{t+1}R_G^s$ from all pairs i and j in $_tR_G^s$ and iterate this step to create from $_0R_G^0 = {}_0R_G^s$, $_1R_G^s$, $_2R_G^s$, $_3R_G^s$, ... until all entries r_{ij}^s of $_wR_G^s$ approximate within a specified limit the value $+1$ or -1.

Step 3 Permute $_wR_G^s$ into the bipartite form:

	E	F
E	$+1$	-1
F	-1	$+1$

Step 4 Print or store on a history record: $s + 1$, the partition of G into E and F, and decompose the original correlation matrix $_0R_G^0$ into and store separately the two submatrices, the $n_E \times n_E$ matrix $_0R_E^0$ and the $n_F \times n_F$ matrix $_0R_F^0$.

Step 5   Set $s \leftarrow s + 1$, search for the largest remaining matrix $_0R_I^0$, and return that matrix as $_0R_G^s$ to Step 2 unless either s exceeds a specified limit or the number n_G of the largest cluster falls below a specified number.

Step 6   Print results and terminate.

The authors developed this algorithm for clustering a variety of sociometric data and profiles of either objects or variables between which correlations can be computed. This requires that all variables possess interval metric. There is no reason, however, to restrict the use of this algorithm to canonical forms of data and to variables with interval metrics. Since the principal feature of the algorithm is that correlations are computed iteratively, any matrix of distances or similarities with appropriate interval metric properties could be entered at Step 1 in place of $_0R_G^0$.

The authors have applied this algorithm to many sets of data and report that with $n = 70$ and the cutoff point for $r_{ij} = .999$, no more than 11 iterations are needed to approximate stability conditions. This keeps the required computational effort within practical limits. Apparently, while there are a few theoretical examples of a knife-edge character in which the iteration of correlations does not converge to the bipartite form, actual data that would lead to indecisions of this sort have not been encountered.

The interpretation of the CONCOR clusters is difficult however. As the authors recognize, the procedure does not use measures of homogeneity or heterogeneity as decision criteria, and while it is easy to understand when correlations are positive within clusters and negative across, such an understanding is indeed difficult when one is concerned with correlations of correlations of correlations ... that might be 11 times removed from the data. Nevertheless Breiger, Boorman, and Arabie have compared CONCOR results with a variety of results obtained from other clustering techniques and found them convincing. Its clusters seem to be very similar to those obtained by clustering techniques based on a connectedness criterion.

C. The Strong Association Algorithm

In the next example I shall attempt to illustrate how a very simple multiordinal clustering procedure works and also how the required decision criteria may be formulated recursively to keep computational efforts small. It will be recalled that the computational effort of multiordinal clustering is generally magnified by the fact that such techniques require constant interaction between the procedure and data in their canonical form. Since clustering, to be practical, must proceed recursively, measures that keep account of the increasing heterogeneity in the emerging clusters should be defined recursively as well, else the procedure would have to return to the original data at each step and thereby annul the computational advantage of recursion.

The algorithm for strong association of 2^m data (Krippendorff, 1975) was developed in this way. It is applicable to binary attribute data where the attributes to be shared within clusters are assigned the value $x_{iu} = 1$ and the absence of this attribute the value $x_{iu} = 0$. In terms of the 2×2 contingency matrix defined in Section V, Krippendorff's generalization of Benini's association coefficient, which is converted here to a suitable heterogeneity measure by $d_{ij} = 1 - s_{ij}$. is

$$d_{EF} = \frac{\min_{i \in E, F}(e_i) - a_{EF}}{\min_{i \in E, F}(e_i) - \prod_{i \in E, F} e_i}$$

where, in terms of the canonical form of data, $e_i = m^{-1}\sum_{u=1}^{m} x_{iu}$ is the proportion of attributes present in object i, $a_{EF} = m^{-1}\sum_{u=1}^{m}\prod_{i \in E, F} x_{iu}$ is the proportion of attributes shared within E and F, $\min_{i \in E, F}(e_i)$ is the largest possible proportion of attributes that could be shared within E and F, and $\prod_{i \in E, F} e_i$ is the expected proportion of attributes that would be shared if their co-occurrence were due to chance.

It turns out, all these components of the measure can be defined in terms of one matrix and two quantities for each cluster at the initial $s = 0$ and at any $s + 1$ from s. At $s = 0$ and from the initial $n \times m$ matrix X^0 with entries x_{iu}, the maximum proportion of attributes in cluster $\{i\}$, containing just one member, is

$$\mu^0_{\{i\}} = \frac{1}{m} \sum_{u=1}^{m} x_{iu} = e_i$$

and so is the initial probability of attributes in that one-object cluster:

$$\rho^0_{\{i\}} = \frac{1}{m} \sum_{u=1}^{m} x_{iu} = e_i$$

At each prospective merger of two clusters E and F into G, these quantities change as follows:

$$\mu^{s+1}_G = \min(\mu^s_E, \mu^s_F), \qquad \rho^{s+1}_G = \rho^s_E \rho^s_F$$

And the $(n - s) \times m$ matrix X^s becomes the $(n - s - 1) \times m$ matrix X^{s+1} by

$$x^{s+1}_{Gu} = x^s_{Eu} x^s_{Fu}$$

So that the measure of heterogeneity for merging E and F into G becomes a function of values solely available at the preceding iteration:

$$d^{s+1}_{GG} = d^s_{EF} = \frac{\min(\mu^s_E, \mu^s_F) - m^{-1}\sum_{u=1}^{m} x^s_{Eu} x^s_{Fu}}{\min(\mu^s_E, \mu^s_F) - \rho^s_E \rho^s_F}$$

This recursive formulation provides the key to the following surprisingly efficient algorithm:

Given: The $n \times m$ matrix $(x^s_{iu}) = X^s$ at $s = 0$ with the presence of an attribute denoted by $x_{iu} = 1$ and its absence by $x_{iu} = 0$.

Step 1   For $i = 1, 2, \ldots, n$ set $\mu_{\{i\}}^s = \rho_{\{i\}}^s = m^{-1}\sum_{u=1}^{m} x_{iu}$.

Step 2   Compute the $(n - s) \times (n - s)$ distance matrix $(d_{EF}^s) = D^s$ from the $(n - s) \times m$ matrix X^s by

$$d_{EF}^s = \frac{\min(\mu_E^s, \mu_F^s) - m^{-1}\prod_{u=1}^{m} x_{Eu}^s x_{Fu}^s}{\min(\mu_E^s, \mu_F^s) - \rho_E^s \rho_F^s}$$

Step 3   Search for $\min(d_{EF}^s)$ in D^s and for this smallest distance, print or store on a history record: $s + 1$, $\min(d_{EF}^s)$, E, F, the newly assigned label G, and D^s if required.

Step 4   Compute those recursive accounts that are affected by the merger of E and F into G:

$$\mu_G^{s+1} = \min(\mu_E^s, \mu_F^s), \quad \rho_G^{s+1} = \rho_E^s \rho_F^s, \quad x_{G_u}^{s+1} = x_{Eu}^s x_{Fu}^s, \quad s \leftarrow s + 1$$

Step 5   Return the reduced $(n - s) \times m$ matrix X^s to Step 2 unless either $\max(d_{GG}^s)$ exceeds a specified value or any other terminating criterion is satisfied.

Step 6   Print result and terminate.

The example given in Table VII starts with an initial data matrix X^0 describing 10 objects in terms of 16 variables. When the distribution of attributes are examined in this matrix, one may discover that the attributes of object j are fully contained in the attributes of the ith object, yielding, as it should, a distance of $d_{ij}^0 = 0$. Since monothetic clusters are represented by the attributes its objects share, the cluster $\{i, j\}$ then takes on the attributes i and j have in common, here those of j, which may be seen in the subsequent transform of the data matrix. Also objects e and f show the strongest possible association which $d_{ef}^0 = 0$ indicates. At the third iteration it is the objects g and h that are found least different. In terms of the 2×2 contingency table, the distance would be computed as follows:

$$
\begin{array}{ccccc}
 & & \multicolumn{2}{c}{g} & \\
 & & 0 & 1 & \\
\hline
 & 0 & \frac{6}{16} & \frac{2}{16} & \\
h & & & & \\
 & 1 & \frac{1}{16} & \frac{7}{16} & \frac{8}{16} \\
\hline
 & & & \frac{9}{16} & 1 \\
\end{array}
$$

$$d_{gh} = \frac{\min\left(\frac{8}{16}, \frac{9}{16}\right) - \frac{7}{16}}{\min\left(\frac{8}{16}, \frac{9}{16}\right) - \frac{8}{16}\frac{9}{16}} = .29$$

d_{gh} of D^3 then appears in D^4s diagonal as associated with the cluster $\{g, h\}$. So the process continues as indicated in Fig. 18.

TABLE VII

HISTORY OF TRANSFORMS OF DATA IN CANONICAL FORM, EXAMPLE

	X^s	D^s											
a	0 1 1 1 0 1 1 1 0 1 1 1 1 0 1 0	.00											
b	1 0 1 1 1 1 0 1 0 1 1 0 1 0 0 1	.96	.00										
c	1 0 1 1 0 1 1 1 1 1 0 0 1 1 0 1	1.16	.64	.00							$s = 1$		
d	0 0 1 0 1 1 1 1 0 1 1 0 0 1 1 0	.71	.89	1.07	.00								
e	0 0 1 1 1 1 1 1 1 1 1 0 0 1 1 0	.83	.96	.87	**.00**	.00							
f	0 1 1 0 0 1 1 0 0 1 1 1 0 0 1 1	.36	1.19	1.42	.76	1.07	.00						
g	1 1 0 0 1 1 1 0 0 0 1 1 0 0 0 1	1.20	1.00	1.60	1.14	1.60	.57	.00					
h	1 1 0 0 1 0 1 0 0 0 1 1 1 1 0 1	1.42	1.19	1.42	1.27	1.78	1.02	.29	.00				
i	0 1 0 1 1 1 1 0 1 0 0 1 0 1 1 1	1.28	1.60	1.28	1.19	.96	.89	.67	.89	.00			
j	0 1 0 1 1 0 1 0 0 0 0 1 0 1 1 0	.91	1.91	1.83	.98	.91	.98	.86	.65	**.00**	.00		
a	0 1 1 1 0 1 1 1 0 1 1 1 1 0 1 0	.00											
b	1 0 1 1 1 1 0 1 0 1 1 0 1 0 0 1	.96	.00										
c	1 0 1 1 0 1 1 1 1 1 0 0 1 1 0 1	1.16	1.00	.00							$s = 3$		
de	0 0 1 0 1 1 1 1 0 1 1 0 0 1 1 0	.42	.68	.63	.00								
f	0 1 1 0 0 1 1 0 0 1 1 1 0 0 1 1	.36	1.19	1.42	.54	.00							
g	1 1 0 0 1 1 1 0 0 0 1 1 0 0 0 1	1.20	1.00	1.60	.82	.57	.00						
h	1 1 0 0 1 0 1 0 0 0 1 1 1 1 0 1	1.42	1.19	1.42	.91	1.02	**.29**	.00					
ij	0 1 0 1 1 0 1 0 0 0 0 1 0 1 1 0	.50	1.17	1.00	.56	.66	.62	.44	.00				
a	0 1 1 1 0 1 1 1 0 1 1 1 1 0 1 0	.00											
b	1 0 1 1 1 1 0 1 0 1 1 0 1 0 0 1	.96	.00										
c	1 0 1 1 0 1 1 1 1 1 0 0 1 1 0 1	1.16	.64	.00							$s = 4$		
de	0 0 1 0 1 1 1 1 0 1 1 0 0 1 1 0	.42	.68	.63	.00								
f	0 1 1 0 0 1 1 0 0 1 1 1 0 0 1 1	**.36**	1.19	1.42	.54	.00							
gh	1 1 0 0 1 0 1 0 0 0 1 1 0 0 0 1	.82	.77	1.02	.80	.55	.29						
ij	0 1 0 1 1 0 1 0 0 0 0 1 0 1 1 0	.50	1.17	1.00	.56	.66	.52	.00					
af	0 1 1 0 0 1 1 0 0 1 1 1 0 0 1 0	.36											
b	1 0 1 1 1 1 0 1 0 1 1 0 1 0 0 1	.97	.00										
c	1 0 1 1 0 1 1 1 1 1 0 0 1 1 0 1	1.05	.64	.00							$s = 5$		
de	0 0 1 0 1 1 1 1 0 1 1 0 0 1 1 0	**.45**	.68	.63	.00								
gh	1 1 0 0 1 0 1 0 0 0 1 1 0 0 0 1	.64	.77	1.02	.80	.29							
ij	0 1 0 1 1 0 1 0 0 0 0 1 0 1 1 0	.56	1.17	1.00	.56	.52	.00						
adef	0 0 1 0 0 1 1 0 0 1 1 0 0 0 1 0	.45											
b	1 0 1 1 1 1 0 1 0 1 1 0 1 0 0 1	.67	.00										
c	1 0 1 1 0 1 1 1 1 1 0 0 1 1 0 1	.68	.64	.00							$s = 6$		
gh	1 1 0 0 1 0 1 0 0 0 1 1 0 0 0 1	.92	.77	1.02	.29								
ij	0 1 0 1 1 0 1 0 0 0 0 1 0 1 1 0	.79	1.17	1.00	**.52**	.00							
adef	0 0 1 0 0 1 1 0 0 1 1 0 0 0 1 0	.45											
b	1 0 1 1 1 1 0 1 0 1 1 0 1 0 0 1	.67	.00										
c	1 0 1 1 0 1 1 1 1 1 0 0 1 1 0 1	.68	**.64**	.00							$s = 7$		
ghij	0 1 0 0 1 0 1 0 0 0 0 1 0 0 0 0	.88	.96	.98	.52								
adef	0 0 1 0 0 1 1 0 0 1 1 0 0 0 1 0	.45											
bc	1 0 1 1 0 1 0 1 0 1 0 0 1 0 0 1	**.75**	.64										
ghij	0 1 0 0 1 0 1 0 0 0 0 1 0 0 0 0	.88	1.08	.52							$s = 8$		
abcdef	0 0 1 0 0 1 0 0 0 1 0 0 0 0 0 0	.75											
ghij	0 1 0 0 1 0 1 0 0 0 0 1 0 0 0 0	**1.01**	.52								$s = 9$		

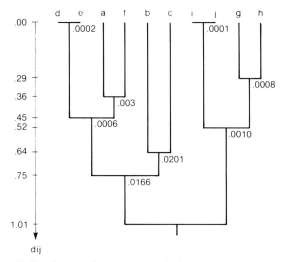

Fig. 18. Dendrogram for strong association clustering, an example.

The researcher now has to decide which partition is the most meaningful one, that is, at what level clusters are most convincingly interpretable. This is in part an intuitive decision but it can be strengthened by statistical considerations. In this example the null hypothesis (that the sharing of attributes within clusters is due to chance) can be rejected on significance levels indicated in the dendrogram at each point of merger. One can see that the significance level drops sharply after the sixth step and one might on these grounds be led to accept the partition of the ten objects into four clusters as optimal. However, the attributes then still overlap. A perfect differentiation between clusters is achieved only before the last step, at a point at which the two remaining clusters share no attributes anymore, with 7 out of the 16 variables providing the basis of the differentiation. All others dropped out.

D. The Multivariate Classification Algorithm

This example presents a clustering technique that does not cluster objects for their own sake, but rather uses them as a vehicle for simplifying their multivariate description. The description of these objects is a qualitative one; i.e., variables have the nominal metric throughout. Given a many-dimensional distribution of objects, the task of the clustering procedure is to reduce the representational space of this distribution not in dimensionality but in size without or with only a small amount of losses in structure within this space. Clusters then emerge not in one variable (e.g., the set of objects) and in terms of all other variables, rather, clusters emerge in all variables simultaneously, each in terms of all others. What is thereby taken account of is that the clustering within one variable may interact with the clustering in another variable and that higher-order dependencies within data are allowed to enter such interactions. The most distinctive feature of this algorithm is that it optimizes the representation of multiordinal relations in data by the simultaneous clustering of values within many variables.

I am presenting here a version of the algorithm that is a considerable simplification of the one initially published (Krippendorff, 1974) and although multivariate classification provides several choices of heterogeneity measures, only the information theoretical measure of the amount of loss in structure will be used in the example. Since the procedure is a multiordinal one, and hence proceeds data recursively, the recursive formulation of loss functions is a key factor to the algorithm's practicality.

The algorithm yields several (as many as there are variables) hierarchical clustering schemes for the qualities in terms of which objects are described.

Given: The $n \times m$ matrix $(x_{iu}) = X$, all variables with nominal metric (unordered values).

Step 1 Reduce the $n \times m$ matrix X to an $(n - s) \times m$ matrix X^s containing $n - s$ unique objects i to each of which is assigned the frequency $n_{(i)}$. Compute frequencies $n_{x._u} = \sum_{i=1}^{n-s} n_{x_{iu}}$ for each value x occurring in variable u. (From here on X^s serves as a matrix of indices only.) Set $d^s_{\{i\}\{i\}} = 0$ for all $i = 1, 2, \ldots, n - s$.

Step 2 With the function

$$\text{Loss}(a, b) = \begin{cases} 0 & \text{iff} \quad a = b \text{ or } n_a = 0 \text{ or } n_b = 0, \\ (n_a + n_b) \log_2(n_a + n_b) - n_a \log_2 n_a - n_b \log_2 n_b \\ \text{otherwise} \end{cases}$$

with $n_{x_{Eu}}$ denoting the frequency of the value x_{Eu} within variable u in terms of which objects in cluster E are characterized, and with the m-valued description of each object divided into two parts, E_C and $K_{\bar{C}}$, so that $n_{\langle E_C K_{\bar{C}} \rangle}$ denotes the number of objects that share values x_{ic} within the set C of variables with objects in E but differ with respect to the remaining variables $\bar{C}$, now then compute the new $(n - s) \times (n - s)$ distance matrix D^s, replacing missing distances only, by

$$d^s_{EF} = d^s_{EE} + d^s_{FF} + d^s_{E|F}$$

where

$$d^s_{E|F} = \frac{1}{m} \left[\sum_C \sum_{K_{\bar{C}}} \text{Loss}(\langle E_C K_{\bar{C}} \rangle, \langle F_C K_{\bar{C}} \rangle) - \sum_m^{u=1} \text{Loss}(x_{Eu}, x_{Fu}) \right]$$

and where the sum over C refers to all subsets of variables in C whose values differ between E and F.

Step 3 Search for $\min_{E, F}(d^s_{EF})$ in D^s and print or store on a history record $s + 1$, D^s if desired, $\min_{E, F}(d^s_{EF})$, and for this minimum: E, F, the newly assigned label G, and for all values $x_{Eu} \neq x_{Fu}$: $x_{Eu}, x_{Fu}, x_{Gu}, u$.

298 KLAUS KRIPPENDORFF

Step 4   Merge E and F into G by modifying for all $x_{Eu} \neq x_{Fu}$ and u:

$$n_{x_{Gu}} = n_{x_{Eu}} + n_{x_{Fu}} \qquad n_{x_{Eu}} = n_{x_{Fu}} = 0$$

for all clusters whose objects share some value x with values in $K_{\bar{C}}$ of E and F:

$$n_{\langle G_C K_{\bar{C}} \rangle} = n_{\langle E_C K_{\bar{C}} \rangle} + n_{\langle F_C K_{\bar{C}} \rangle}, \qquad n_{\langle E_C K_{\bar{C}} \rangle} = n_{\langle F_C K_{\bar{C}} \rangle} = 0$$

and

$$d_{GG} = d_{EF}, \qquad d_{EI} = d_{IF} = 0 \qquad \text{for all} \quad I \neq E, F$$

recompute s so that the number of unique objects or clusters is $n - s$.

Step 5   Return altered accounts to Step 2 unless either $\max(d_{GG})$ exceeds a specified limit, the number of clusters $n - s$ falls below a specified number, or any other terminating criterion is satisfied.

Step 6   Print results and terminate.

Note that d_{EF} measures the amount of structure lost by merging E and F. Within the three dimensions u, v, and w, if $x_{Eu} = x_{Fu}$ are the values E and F share, the distance between E and F expresses the difference it would make to the total amount of structure in the data when (with K denoting clusters other than E or F) all triples $\langle x_{Ku}, x_{Kv}, x_{Ew} \rangle$ and $\langle x_{Ku}, x_{Kv}, x_{Fw} \rangle$, $\langle x_{Ku}, x_{Ev}, x_{Kw} \rangle$ and $\langle x_{Ku}, x_{Fv}, x_{Kw} \rangle$, and $\langle x_{Ku}, x_{Ev}, x_{Ew} \rangle$ and $\langle x_{Ku}, x_{Fv}, x_{Fw} \rangle$ would no longer be differentiated. The sum over C then assures that all clusters are merged whose objects share some value with E or F in v, in w, and in both vw. What d_{EF} assesses is the effect of collapsing not only the point E and F but also all planes on which these points are located (see Fig. 19).

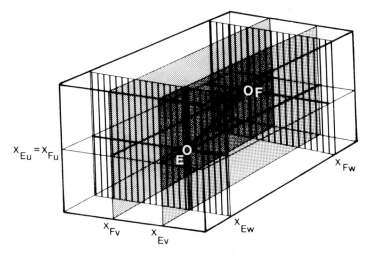

FIG. 19. A multivariate clustering step in three-dimensional space.

The implementation of the previously published version of the multivariate classification algorithm used an extremely wasteful form of storage (objects occupied cells in an m-dimensional array) and more complicated accounting devices that made the procedure reach computational limits before practical results could be obtained. The preceding algorithm is currently under investigation.

What multivariate classification accomplishes might best be illustrated graphically in Fig. 20. Suppose a three-valued characterization of a sample of objects finds all objects distributed as in the left space. There is a lot of redundancy in the values used for describing these objects and there is also some structure manifest in the distribution. Multivariate classification would now attempt to eliminate this redundancy by grouping variables in such a way that the remaining space contains as much of the initial structure as possible. In the illustration on the right of the original distribution no structure is lost. The algorithm boiled the initial representation down to its essentials.

In another, somewhat more artificial example, consider the schematic figure of a man as in Fig. 21. The clustering of values in the horizontal dimension first eliminates the duplication of columns, here due to symmetry, and yields the figure to the right of the original, showing no loss. The clustering of values in vertical dimension eliminates all duplication of rows and yields the figure below the original, showing no loss either. Clustering in both dimensions yields the resultant figure below and right of the original, also showing no loss in structure. (At this point it might be said that the example is misleading insofar as the algorithm does not recognize proximities between rows and columns which are important in Gestalt perception.) The original figure can be reconstructed from the figure below and right of the original by inverse application of the hierarchical clustering that emerged in each variable.

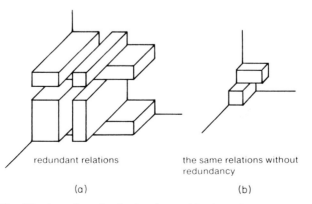

redundant relations   the same relations without
                               redundancy

(a)   (b)

FIG. 20. Simplification of a distribution by multivariate classification. (a) Redundant relations; (b) the same relations without redundancy (Krippendorff, 1974).

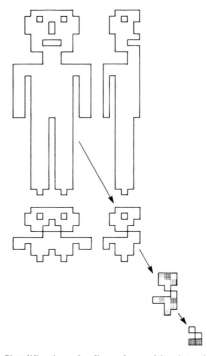

FIG. 21. Simplification of a figure by multivariate classification.

Further simplification of the figure results in losses which are indicated here by shading. When such losses occur they cannot necessarily be evaluated from either dimension in isolation. Losses in structure are losses in interaction effects and thus require that losses be inspected simultaneously for all variables involved. Continuing the classification one might reach the figure in the extreme lower right corner. The two final steps would wipe out the structure in this simple figure. Where to stop the clustering is a question of applying suitable termination criteria on the process.

It should be mentioned that a variety of clustering algorithms appear in Hartigan (1975) whose work was published after this was substantially completed.

X. VALIDATION AND VINDICATION

Clustering procedures compute clusters, often regardless of how strong the patterns permeate the data these clusters aim to represent. In any distribution of objects in space, even in an entirely random one, some objects are bound to be closer to each other or more similar than are others. Even when neighboring objects are approximately equidistant, the slightest inequality can provide the kick that starts a clustering sequence rolling. Testing for the statistical significance of the clusters that do emerge in the process therefore is an important safeguard against attempts to interpret the results of a clustering process when an underlying pattern is spurious or does not exist in fact. The minimum requirement is to test one of two null hypotheses: that the co-occurring qualities shared within a cluster are due to chance or that the objects of different clusters are drawn from the same population.

But evidence for the statistical significance of clusters should be seen only as a prerequisite for entering into validity considerations. Only when null hypotheses can be rejected with confidence might one find empirically meaningful interpretations of clustering results. When clustering turns out to be due to chance or an artifact of the procedure, their potential validity may be soundly questioned.

Although I am quite aware of existing typologies for kinds of validation, let me focus here on only two types that Feigl (1952) termed validation and vindication. In the context of this application, *validation* is a mode of justification according to which the results of a particular analytical procedure are justified by showing the structure of that procedure to be derivable from general principles or theories that are accepted quite independently of the procedure to be validated, while *vindication* is a mode of justification that renders a particular analytical procedure acceptable on the grounds that its results lead to accurate predictions (to a degree better than chance) regardless of the details of the procedure. The rules of deduction and induction are essential to validation while the relation between means and particular ends provide the basis for vindication. In focusing on these two kinds of justification, I take for granted that the procedure is reliable, that successive clustering is order invariant, that distances and homogeneity measures satisfy required conditions, etc., all of which can be justified on logical grounds. I also take for granted that data are relevant in the sense considered earlier, for it is inconceivable that valid clusters can be obtained from irrelevant data.

Two not necessarily separate questions pertain to the *validation* of clustering procedures. First, exactly what features of objects are characterized when data enter the procedure in their derived form as distance or similarity measures, and are these features and the omission of others justifiable on theoretical or on empirical grounds? And second, exactly what does a clustering procedure optimize; which clustering criteria does it employ; and how do the measures that characterize the emerging clusters relate to a theory about how objects become associated, group themselves, or are clustered in reality?

Regarding the first question, it should be noted that there are great differences between how product-moment correlations, Euclidean distances, or information losses conceptualize and quantitatively assess dissimilarities between objects. For example, the product-moment correlation assesses the degree to which two objects are linearly related. A positive r_{ij} indicates that the values of two objects increase in the same direction, while a negative r_{ij}

indicates such an increase to be in the opposite direction. But $r_{ij} = +1$ does not imply $i = j$. The underlying concept of resemblance is a very peculiar one, and the researcher who wishes to cluster on the basis of a correlation matrix must establish that available knowledge about the nature of the objects would indeed lead to this conception. Product-moment correlations assume that objects i and j are related by $a_j x_{ju} + b_j = a_i x_{iu} + b_i$ for all variables u and that similarity is independent of the constants a and b. Obviously this does not conform to intuition, which suggests that two objects are maximally similar only when $i = j$, that is, $x_{ju} = x_{iu}$ for all of the u. Pearson's intraclass correlation coefficient satisfies this condition, the product-moment coefficient does not.

An examination of whether the formal properties of the underlying distance or similarity measures are defensible ought to be made before any clustering for a particular purpose is undertaken. Failure to provide such validating evidence makes it otherwise difficult to interpret findings in the light of a given theory.

One common way of bypassing the validation of distances is to input data in the form of subjective difference or similarity ratings obtained from a sample of subjects. If the researcher is indeed interested in clustering subjective difference or similarity judgments, two problems tend to arise: One is the variance that such judgments invariably entail and the other is that such judgments ought to satisfy the formal conditions of a distance.

Answers to the second question pertaining to the validation of clustering criteria pose even greater problems. To decide on the acceptability of a clustering criterion, the researcher must first decide on the properties his clusters are to represent. Given such a designation of purpose the researcher must then examine the principles underlying the formation of the groupings in reality that a clustering attempts to approximate or predict. In order to complete the validation, the researcher must finally demonstrate consistency between the decision criteria, difference or heterogeneity measures employed in the clustering procedure on the one side and knowledge about the natural processes on the other. This knowledge may take the form of an established theory, of hard empirical evidence, or in its weakest form, of grounded intuition. Wherever such knowledge comes from, validation may rely on it.

For example, if the resulting clusters are expected to predict how individuals form cliques or other social forms of organization, then knowledge about the way such social groupings emerge is indispensable in the validation of a procedure. The knowledge that cliques and social groups possess synergetic-organizational-Gestalt qualities and that their formation cannot be predicted from information on the interaction within pairs of individuals would render biordinal techniques invalid from the start (unless the effect were insignificantly small). To be valid, a multiordinal technique would then have to replicate the social process involved.

Another crucial option is whether clusters are formed on the basis of differences between clusters or heterogeneities within. The chainlike clusters resulting from the connectedness method have already been contrasted with the compactness of the diameter method. The knowledge that all similarities or distances within a cluster will determine its boundaries with other clusters lends validity to a minimum heterogeneity criterion. In contrast, the knowledge that significant similarities and distances follow a hierarchical pattern, representing differences between clusters while neglecting those within, would lend validity to a minimum difference criterion. A hypothetical example of a situation in which a difference measure might be superior to a heterogeneity measure would be a certain form of communication within a social organization in which communication occurs primarily *on the same level* of the organizational hierarchy and *between minimally different* parts of the organization and is secondary or absent *across different levels* of such a hierarchy and *within* these parts. Such an implicit hierarchical conception of difference would be inappropriate when an organization is formed on the basis that members share certain properties, that communication within is larger or more important than communication across the parts of an organization, etc.

It is often more difficult to apply available evidence about natural groupings on a given clustering technique than to formalize such evidence into a computable clustering criterion. The development of the strong association technique by Krippendorff (1975) is a case in point. It started with a problem in content analysis where the development of emic or indigenous as opposed to etic or imposed categories is a common problem. The task was to develop a reliable coding instrument for advertising appeals in categories that are close to those used by television viewers. For this purpose Dziurzynski (1978) asked subjects to group about 300 appeals culled from commercials into categories that seemed most meaningful to them. In observing the subject's justifications one often finds some like this: "If i and j are together, then k must be in the same category, but if h and i are in the same category then k cannot join them." Those are typical *multiordinal* arguments. The task was to form clusters among aspects based on *agreements* among subjects regarding the grouping. The formalization of the notion of agreement, which ought to be maximum when groups are either identical or when one is included in the other, leads to an association coefficient which has been discussed in the preceding. The correspondence was taken as validating evidence.

To summarize, validation asks whether the way information is processed within a clustering procedure is consistent with the way such information would be processed in the real world, while vindication asks the a posteriori question of whether the results of a clustering procedure correspond with independently obtained evidence about clusters.

The most obvious form of *vindication* is to establish correspondence between the results of a clustering procedure and the results obtained by other methods (including by independent observation). Since clusters obtained by other methods must always be available for such comparisons, vindication primarily yields information about the efficiency or simplicity and only secondarily about the adequacy of the underlying structure.

So, when developing the partitioning algorithm CONCOR and probably because correlations of correlations of . . . is a concept that is far removed from penetrations by intuition, Breiger *et al.* (1975) compared their results with those obtained by a variety of other clustering techniques. The finding that CONCOR results approximate those obtained by the connectedness method makes the procedure vindicatively acceptable but only to the extent the results of this connectedness method are already known to be valid in a particular application.

In another example of vindication, we asked subjects to group sets of words according to perceived semantic similarities. Since the multivariate classification algorithm was developed by formalizing certain theories of contextual meanings, if the theories and their algorithmic implementation are correct, then computational results and subjective clusters are expected to be in high agreement. In this case we were fortunate to be able to vary certain computational parameters and found, to our surprise, that the weakest clustering criterion resulted in the best fits. This may serve as a warning against the assumption that the validity of clustering procedures increases with their complexity.

In vindication experiments, the variability of a clustering technique is a deceptive virtue, however, for it is always possible to find a computational approximation to an independently obtained set of clusters. This possibility is exemplified in work done by Lance and Williams (1967) who showed with Fig. 22 how changes in value of one variable of their clustering criterion causes extremely different dendrograms to emerge from the same data. The danger is that once one considers oneself free to play with the clustering criteria, one can "prove" anything, and since the computation then merely supports what is already known, the proof given is "empty."

Vindication allows all conceivable clustering options to be tested against empirical evidence, but its aim is to find that option which produces *consistently* high agreements within the empirical domain chosen. A single "convincing match" means very little. Carefully used, vindication provides a method for generalizing or for confining the success of a particular clustering procedure.

The researcher who does not have independently obtained clusters at his disposal might be led to believe that the computational results "make sense" or are "acceptable on intuitive grounds." But a better way of rendering such results plausible is to get into the very procedure that produced them and to show that the procedure is, at least ideally, a homomorphic representation of the processes known to explain the phenomena under consideration. All users of clustering techniques should be expected to make at least some effort at validation when publishing their results.[1]

---

[1]Referring to the comments on this section by Tukey (see Chapter 16, Section B), I disagree that validation is impossible or dangerous but I am perfectly happy with his words: "All users of clustering techniques should be expected to make at least some effort (a) to explain why they

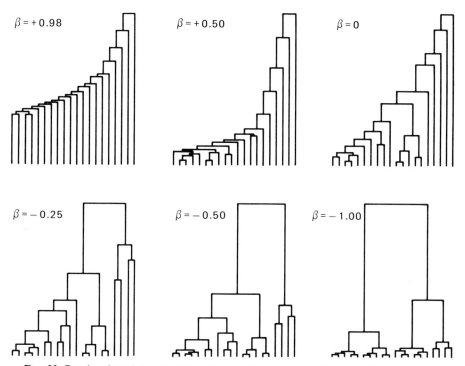

FIG. 22. Results of applying six different clustering criteria on the same objects (Lance & Williams, 1967, with permission of British Computer Society).

XI. SUMMARY—CONCLUSION

This chapter explores clustering as a multivariate technique in communication research and does so with several kinds of users in mind.

There is, first, the researcher who wants to make use of data stemming from clustering, either for a secondary analysis by different techniques, for supporting practical decisions, or simply, to understand published findings. If he seeks a level of understanding beyond the Presentation of Results he will want to acquaint himself with Validation and Vindication, needs to be able to

---

chose the methods used and (b) to make as clear as is reasonable the tentative character of clustering results in general and the degree to which this applies to those they describe."

This section is merely intended to put into focus the fundamental relationship between the description of objects, the process of clustering and its results (all of which are very much guided by the researcher's choices), and the nature of the objects and the processes by which objects form groups, cliques, classes, lumps, associations, or Gestalts (which are not so much influenced by if not independent of the way they are analyzed). No multivariate technique can avoid some degree of artificiality and its results are, hence, always tentative to some extent. The task of validating an analytic technique is to justify and to explain the use of a procedure not in terms of aesthetics, convenience, or habit but in reference to knowledge about reality, however hypothetical this might be.

judge the Relevance and Ordinality of Data from which results are obtained and read particularly the section on Properties of Emerging Clusters, at least where it pertains to the clustering procedure actually used. He may then be able to judge whether given clustering results may be interpretable in view of his particular problem.

There is, second, the researcher who seeks to apply one of the available clustering procedures to his data, with the aim of data simplification, in search for a typology or to group or lump together phenomena that share certain characteristics. Such a user may need to know the form of data amenable to clustering: Canonical Form of Data and Derived Form of Data. He may want to become familiar with the Presentation of Results. And, after familiarizing himself with the basic ideas of Validation and Vindication, he may want to read all that needs to be known to understand what available clustering procedures do: Properties of Emerging Clusters, Ordinality of Data, Clustering Algorithms, etc. He may then be able to make intelligent choices among available procedures or find that the tasks he set for himself cannot be accomplished by Clustering.

There is, third, the researcher who wants to design his own special purpose clustering technique. Whether he is a computer programmer himself or delegates the writing of such a procedure to someone else, he ought to consider the warnings in Goals and Computational Efforts seriously before conceptualizing a Clustering Algorithm, taking most of the sections of this chapter and references to additional literature into account.

The chapter will be useful, fourth, to the computer programmer who will have to converse with empirically oriented social scientists when helping him either to implement, modify, or to develop anew suitable clustering procedures. Much too often have I found that differences in technical discourse prevent the full utilization of available analytical or intellectual resources. Computer programmers may be keenly aware of Goals and Computational Efforts and the nature of Clustering Algorithms but often lack understanding of the philosophical issues raised in Validation and Vindication and the special demands made by available social theory on the Properties of Emerging Clusters.

The chapter is on clustering. But several important issues point beyond this (here welcome) restriction, for example, the issue of validating the logic of an analytical procedure as opposed to merely vindicating its result or the issue of the ordinality in data and the ordinality a procedure can take. It is amazing that most current *multi*variate techniques are *bi*ordinal in structure and thus fail to deliver what their label seems to suggest. So far we have always thought in categories: variance analysis, multidimensional scaling, clustering, etc., each had its own purpose and assumptions. Ultimately these categorial distinctions need to be overcome by tying the processes they follow more directly to those of the empirical world. These issues are of concern, finally, to the methodologist and epistemologist of the social sciences.

References

Bailey, K. D. Cluster analysis. In D. R. Heise (Ed.), *Sociological Methodology 1975*. San Francisco, California: Jossey-Bass, 1975.

Benini, R. *Principii di demografia. No. 29.* Manuali Barbera de Scienze Guiviche Sociale e Politiche, Firenzi: Barbera, 1901.

Bock, H. H. *Automatische Klassifikation.* Gottingen: Vandenhoeck and Ruprecht, 1974.

Breiger, R. L., Boorman, S. A., and Arabie, P. An algorithm for clustering relational data with applications to social network analysis and comparison with multidimensional scaling. *Journal of Mathematical Psychology*, 1975, **12**, 328–383.

Cureton, H. R., Cureton, L. W., and Durell, R. C. A method of cluster analysis. *Multivariate Behavioral Research*, 1970, **5**, 101–106.

Driver, H. E., and Kroeber, A. L. Quantitative expression of cultural relationships. *University of California Publications in American Archeology and Ethnology*, 1932, **31**, 211–256.

Dziurzynski, P. S. *Development of a content analytic instrument for advertising appeals used in prime-time television commercials.* MA Thesis. Philadelphia: The Annenberg School of Communication, University of Pennsylvania, 1978.

Feigl, H. Validation and vindication: An analysis of the nature and limits of ethical arguments. In W. Sellars and J. Hospers (Eds.), *Readings in ethical theory*. New York: Appleton, 1952.

Gower, J. C. Some distance properties of latent root and vector methods used in multivariate analysis. *Biometrics*, 1966, **53**, 325–338.

Gower, J. C. A general coefficient of similarity and some of its properties. *Biometrics*, 1971, **27**, 857–872.

Gower, J. C., and Ross, G. J. S. Minimum spanning trees and single-linkage cluster analysis. *Applied Statistics*, 1969, **18**, 54–64.

Hamming, R. W. Error detecting and error correcting codes. *The Bell System Technical Journal*, 1950, **26**(2), 147–160.

Hartigan, J. A. *Clustering algorithms*, New York: Wiley, 1975.

Heinecke, F. Naturgeschichte des Herings. I. Die Lokalformen und die Wanderungen des Herings in den Europäischen Meeren. *Abhandlungen des Deutschen Seefischerei-Vereins*, 1898, **2**, i-cxxxvi, 1–223.

Jardine, N. and Sibson R. *Mathematical taxonomy*. New York: Wiley, 1971.

Johnson, S. C. Hierarchical clustering schemes. *Psychometrika*, 1967, **32**, 241–254.

King, B. Step-wise clustering procedures. *Journal of the American Statistical Association*, 1967, **62**, 86–101.

Krippendorff, K. *Computer programs for multivariate classification in content analysis, A proposal to the national science foundation*, Philadelphia, Pennsylvania: University of Pennsylvania, mimeo, 1969.

Krippendorff, K. *Reliability*. Philadelphia, Pennsylvania. Univ. of Pennsylvania, mimeo, 1973.

Krippendorff, K. An algorithm for simplifying the representation of complex systems. In J. Rose (Ed.), *Advances in cybernetics and systems*. New York: Gorden and Breach, 1974.

Krippendorff, K. *A method for strong associative clustering of 2^m data.* Philadelphia, Pennsylvania: University of Pennsylvania, mimeo, 1975.

Krippendorff, K. A spectral analysis of relations. Unpublished paper presented to the International Congress of Communication Sciences, Berlin, May 31, 1977. Philadelphia: The Annenberg School of Communications, University of Pennsylvania, mimeo, 1976.

Krippendorff, Klaus. *On the algorithm for identifying structures in multivariate data, including structures with loops.* Philadelphia: The Annenberg School of Communications, University of Pennsylvania, mimeo, 1980.

Lance, G. N., and Williams, W. T. A general theory of classificatory sorting strategies I. Hierarchical systems. *Computer Journal*, 1967, **9**, 373–380.

Lance, G. N., and Williams, W. T. A general theory of classificatory sorting strategies II. Clustering systems. *Computer Journal*, 1967, **10**, 271–277.

Lorr, M. A. A review and classification of typological procedures. Paper read at the meeting of the American Psychological Association, San Francisco, California, 1968.

Lysenko, O., and Sneath, P. H. A. The use of models in bacterial classification. *Journal of General Microbiology*, 1959, **20**, 284–290.

MacNaughton-Smith, P. Some statistical and other numerical techniques for classifying individuals. *Home Office Research Unit Report No. 6*, London: H. M. Stationary Office, 1965.

Mahalanobis, P. C. On the generalized distance in statistics. *Proceedings of the National Institute of Science India*, 1936, **2**, 49–55.

Miller, G. A., and Nicely, P. E. An analysis of perceptual confusion among some english consonants. *Journal of the Acoustical Society of America*, 1955, **27**, 338–352.

Osgood, C. E., Suci, J. C., and Tannenbaum, P. H. *The measurement of meaning*, Urbana, Illinois: Univ. of Illinois Press, 1957.

Pearson, K. On the coefficient of radical likeness. *Biometrica*, 1926, **18**, 105–117.

Rao, C. R. The utilization of multiple measurements in problems of biological classification. *Journal of the Royal Statistical Society*, 1948, **B10**, 159–193.

Rao, C. R. *Advanced statistical methods in biometric research*, New York: Wiley, 1952.

Sneath, P. H. A., and Sokal, R. R. *Numerical taxonomy*, San Francisco, California: Freeman, 1973.

Sokal, R. R., and Sneath, P. H. A. *Principles of numerical taxonomy*. San Francisco, California: Freeman, 1963.

Tryon, R. C. *Cluster analysis: Correlation profile and orthometric (factor) analysis for the isolation of unities in mind and personality*. Ann Arbor, Michigan: Edwards Brothers, 1939.

Tryon, R. C., and Bailey, D. E. *Clustering analysis*. New York: McGraw-Hill, 1970.

Tukey, J. W. Personal communication, 1977.

Zubin, J. A. A technique for measuring likemindedness. *Journal of Abnormal & Social Psychology*, 1938, **33**, 508–516.

Chapter 10

NONMETRIC MULTIDIMENSIONAL SCALING IN COMMUNICATION RESEARCH: SMALLEST SPACE ANALYSIS

ROBERT W. NORTON

Department of Communication
Purdue University
West Lafayette, Indiana

I. INTRODUCTION

Nonmetric multidimensional scaling maps a set of variables (objects, stimuli, people) into a set of points in a metric space such that variables that are similar by some empirical standard are close neighbors in the space, and variables that are dissimilar are distant neighbors from each other in the space.

Smallest analysis (SSA) (Guttman, 1968; Lingoes, 1973) is discussed here so that the reader will understand how the algorithm works. The logic of SSA readily transfers to similar nonmetric multidimensional algorithms such as Kruskal's (1964) M-D-SCAL and Young and Torgerson's TORSCA-9 (Torgerson, 1958; Young, 1968). In fact, Spence (1972) found only negligible

MULTIVARIATE TECHNIQUES
IN HUMAN COMMUNICATION RESEARCH

differences between these methods when he compared them through a Monte Carlo evaluation, based on 2160 scaling solutions. Though SSA is the focus of this discussion, it is believed that mastery of this technique eases the mastery of related nonmetric multidimensional methods.

In Section II, the SSA algorithm is explained and illustrated with a hypothetical example. In Section III, an actual communication study is reported using SSA. Clustering, dimensionality, and best predictors are discussed. Section IV discusses possible applications of nonmetric multidimensional scaling techniques in the study of attitude, group, and interpersonal behavior.

II. THE SMALLEST SPACE ANALYSIS ALGORITHM

Smallest Space Analysis is one of the newest multivariate methods in statistics. It is a nonmetric technique developed by Guttman (1968) and refined and computerized by Lingoes (1973). SSA can be used for an extraordinary variety of investigations requiring a rigorous multivariate analysis without the constraints of special assumptions.

Any matrix of relationships can be analyzed as long as the elements of the matrix function as similarities or dissimilarities. This includes Pearson's r, Spearman's rho, Goodman and Kruskal's gamma, Guttman's lambda, covariances, conditional probabilities, percentage differences, and post hoc mean differences.

Briefly, SSA is important to the communication researcher for these reasons.

(1) SSA is suitable for a fairly large number of variables. The technique can handle about 100 variables without getting too messy.

(2) The geometric output from SSA makes intuitive sense and thus can be quickly comprehended by the researcher and the audience.

(3) All the relationships in the distance matrix (usually, a correlation table) can be visually represented.

(4) It makes no special assumptions regarding the level of measurement. The following caveat is in order, however. *Although nonmetric multidimensional algorithms can use ordinal data, this is not to say that the researcher should prefer ordinal data. The researcher should use the best data that he or she is capable of gathering.*

(5) It makes no special assumptions regarding the linearity of data.

(6) It entails factor analytic solutions and provides solutions with the fewest number of dimensions.

(7) It provides a measure of "goodness of fit."

(8) It provides results which remain invariant under rotation.

(9) It eliminates decisions between orthogonal and oblique solutions.

(10) It identifies the amount of stress contributed by each variable in the solution.

(11)   It can be used for variables, situations, and people. For example, legislators could be plotted into a space based upon a distance matrix which is a function of voting records.

(12)   It keeps the researcher close to his data. The researcher must make decisions about variable clusters, interpretation of dimensions, and determination of organizing patterns.

(13)   It provides a molar solution which allows the researcher to simultaneously relate individual variables and clusters of variables.

With these advantages in mind, SSA will now be introduced by taking the reader through a step-by-step solution of a hypothetical example. The model is largely adopted from Lingoes and Roskam's (1973) explanation of multidimensional Euclidean methods. The mock example considers four subjects and four variables.

The basic approach of SSA is to assign ranks to a set of relationships (distances) among variables. *It is the ranks which are analyzed.* For this reason it is a nonmetric technique. At this point, the researcher should realize the essential difference between nonmetric and metric analyses. The researcher is committed to the importance of the order of the relationships. The magnitude of the relationships is ignored. For example, consider the correlations given in Table I. Because the ranks (lower triangular matrix) are the same, the SSA solution would be the same. Whether this matters depends upon the objectives of the researcher. It is the position of this chapter that the power of this technique is not diminished by focusing on ranks. The following steps show the process of the analysis.

(1)   Begin with a subject (s_k) by variable (x_i) matrix. In the example (see Table II), four subjects have raw scores across four variables. The raw scores could be from Likert scales, frequencies, absolute values, or any kind of distance relationships. This table is the raw score matrix.

(2)   Construct a table of relationships among the variables. In the example (see Table II), a table of correlation coefficients is used. Formally stated, $p =$ an r-element array of matrix of arbitrary indices of similarity (near) or dissimilarity (distant) between all pairs of n objects or variables having general p_{ij}, where $r = \frac{1}{2}n(n-1)$ and r pairs of subscripts are generated by taking for each subscript i a second subscript j such that $j = i + 1, i +$

TABLE I

Distance Matrices with Identical Nonmetric Structures[a]

	x_1	x_2	x_3		x_1	x_2	x_3
x_1:	—	.45	.98	x_1:	—	.02	.05
x_2:	2	—	.10	x_2:	2	—	.01
x_3:	1	3	—	x_3:	1	3	—

[a]The upper triangular matrix represents the correlations; the lower triangular matrix represents the rank order of the correlations.

TABLE II
SUBJECT BY VARIABLE MATRIX OF RAW SCORES

Subjects	Variables			
	x_1	x_2	x_3	x_4
s_1:	4	5	9	8
s_2:	2	4	8	7
s_3:	4	6	8	9
s_4:	5	5	10	10

$2, \ldots, n$ ($i = 1, 2, \ldots, n - 1$). Thus, the elements of an n-square matrix of relations of pairs of objects (where $p_{ij} = p_{ji}$) are symmetrically ordered in an array. Both the diagonal of the matrix and one-half of the off-diagonal elements are ignored. For example, Table III is the r-element array.

(3) Construct rank relationships based upon the r-element array. Assign the rank of 1 to the highest correlation, the rank of 2 to the second highest, and so on. This new array (see Table IV) is called Δ. Formally stated, let Δ be an $n \times n$ symmetric matrix of ranks, that is, $\Delta = r$-element array of real numbers with elements $\delta_{ij} = f(P_{ij})$ such that whenever $P_{ij} > P_{kl}$ (for similarity data), then either (a) $\delta_{ij} < \delta_{kl}$ (semistrong monotonicity when some p are tied and strong monotonicity when no p are tied) or (b) $\delta_{ij} \leqslant \delta_{kl}$ (weak monotonicity for no ties in P and semiweak monotonicity when ties exist in P) for all, i, j, k, and l, where $i \neq j$ and $k \neq l$; i.e., $\Delta \rightarrow P$ monotonically. These relationships would be reversed for dissimilarity data.

The Δ vector represents a monotonic transformation of the P vector having certain statistical properties in addition to the mathematical ones just defined.

TABLE III
P ARRAY OF R-ELEMENTS

	x_1	x_2	x_3	x_4
x_1:	—	P_{12}	P_{13}	P_{14}
x_2:	.65	—	P_{23}	P_{24}
x_3:	.76	.00	—	P_{34}
x_4:	.92	.63	.67	—

TABLE IV
Δ MATRIX: RANK RELATIONSHIPS OF P

	x_1	x_2	x_3	x_4
x_1:	—	δ_{12}	δ_{13}	δ_{14}
x_2:	4	—	δ_{23}	δ_{24}
x_3:	2	6	—	δ_{34}
x_4:	1	5	3	—

TABLE V

RECTANGULAR COORDINATES FOR FIG. 1

	Dimension I	Dimension II
x_1:	4.00	3.00
x_2:	8.00	3.00
x_3:	3.20	5.60
x_4	2.00	3.00

Its function is to weight the iterations for moving the configuration toward its goal and to form a basis for evaluating how well it is doing at any given iteration.

(4)   At this point, *arbitrarily* place the variable points in a space. Let X be an $n \times m$ matrix of rectangular coordinates (the arbitrary starting configuration), where n is the number of variables and m is the number of dimensions. X functions as the starting iteration designated as $X^{(0)}$ (see Table V graphed in Fig. 1). If the initial placement of the points is fairly close to relationships reflected in P, then fewer iterations are needed to reach a final solution.

(5)   Compute all possible distances, d_{ij}, between the points, using the Pythagorean theorem for right triangles. Formally stated, $D =$ an r-element vector of distances between the n points embedded in m-dimensional Euclidean space. These distances are calculated from X according to the standard distance formula

$$d_{ij} = \left[\sum_{a=1}^{m} (x_{ia} - x_{ja})^2 \right]^{1/2} \tag{1}$$

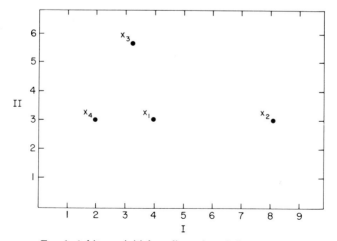

FIG. 1. Arbitrary, initial configuration of the variables.

For example, d_{23} is calculated as

$$d_{23} = \left[(8.00 - 3.20)^2 + (3.00 - 5.60)^2 \right]^{1/2} = 5.46$$

Given P, some initial configuration X, a fixed m, and the distances calculated from the d_{ij} formula, *the problem of nonmetric multidimensional scaling can be formulated in terms of the minimization of a function of two sets of unknowns, namely D and Δ.*

(6)   The problem is to get D as close as possible to Δ. Table VI reports the D matrix. Certain restrictions may be imposed on Δ vis-à-vis the D. One obvious solution to the problem is to use a normalized least squares function, which is called the "loss function." It is formally equivalent to Kruskal's (1964) stress. By definition, the loss function is

$$L = \left[\sum_{ij} (d_{ij} - \delta_{ij})^2 / \sum_{ij} d_{ij}^2 \right]^{1/2} = \Phi^{(0)} \tag{2}$$

The L for the example (see Table VII) would thus be calculated as $(2.83/101.34)^{1/2}$ or .17. So, the stress in the arbitrary, initial configuration using the Kruskal formula is .17. Conventionally, a solution with stress of .15 or greater is considered too high. In a "good" solution, L normally ranges from .00 to .15. The relatively high L for our example indicates that the initial configuration can be improved. Before showing how the configuration is adjusted, Guttman's (1968) algorithm will be presented.

Guttman's definition of fit and his loss function differ from Kruskal's L. He employs what are called "rank images" of the ds, denoted by d_{ij}^*. *The rank images are obtained by ranking the distances from low to high and placing them*

TABLE VI
D MATRIX OF DISTANCES IN FIG. 1

	x_1	x_2	x_3	x_4
x_1:	—	d_{12}	d_{13}	d_{14}
x_2:	4.00	—	d_{23}	d_{24}
x_3:	2.72	5.46	—	d_{34}
x_4:	2.00	6.00	2.86	—

TABLE VII
CALCULATIONS FOR *L*

	d_{ij}	δ_{ij}	d_{ij}^2	$(d_{ij} - \delta_{ij})$	$(d_{ij} - \delta_{ij})^2$
x_{12}:	4.00	4.00	16.00	.00	.00
x_{13}:	2.72	2.00	7.40	.72	.52
x_{14}:	2.00	1.00	4.00	1.00	1.00
x_{23}:	5.46	6.00	29.81	− .54	.29
x_{24}:	6.00	5.00	36.00	1.00	1.00
x_{34}:	2.86	3.00	8.18	− .14	.02

TABLE VIII

D^*MATRIX: RANK IMAGES OF D

	x_1	x_2	x_3	x_4
x_1:	—	d_{12}^*	d_{13}^*	d_{14}^*
x_2:	4.00	—	d_{23}^*	d_{24}^*
x_3:	2.72	6.00	—	d_{34}^*
x_4:	2.00	5.46	2.86	—

in the cells corresponding to the ranked cells of P. This new matrix is designated as D^*. For our example, it appears in Table VIII.

D^* has the following properties:

$$\sum_{ij} d_{ij}^* = \sum_{ij} d_{ij} \tag{3}$$

$$\sum_{ij} d_{ij}^{*2} = \sum_{ij} d_{ij}^2 \tag{4}$$

$$d_{ij}^* < d_{k1}^* \quad \text{if} \quad p_{ij} > p_{k1} \quad \text{(similarities)} \tag{5}$$

In addition, if there are no ties in P, D^* is said to meet the criterion of "semistrong monotonicity."

Both D^* and D are estimates of the unknown Δ and both use the information of P. Using these two variables, Guttman (1968) defined the following measure of raw fit:

$$\Phi^* = \sum_{ij} (d_{ij} - d_{ij}^*)^2 \tag{6}$$

Guttman defines Φ as follows:

$$\Phi = 1 - \left(\sum_{ij} d_{ij} d_{ij}^* \Big/ \sum_{ij} d_{ij}^2 \right) \tag{7}$$

From this, Guttman's loss function, K, a coefficient of alienation, may be computed as

$$K = \left[1 - (1 - \Phi)^2 \right]^{1/2} \tag{8}$$

The K for our example (see Table IX) is .08.

TABLE IX

CALCULATIONS FOR K

	d_{ij}	d_{ij}^*	$d_{ij} d_{ij}^*$	d_{ij}^2
x_{12}:	4.00	4.00	16.00	16.00
x_{13}:	2.72	2.72	7.40	7.40
x_{14}:	2.00	2.00	4.00	4.00
x_{23}:	5.46	6.00	32.76	29.81
x_{24}:	6.00	5.46	32.76	36.00
x_{34}:	2.86	2.86	8.18	8.18

(7)   Now the problem is to improve the fit of the arbitrary, initial configuration until Guttman's K or Kruskal's L is satisfactorily small. Guttman uses
the following iterative procedure:

$$x_{ia}^{(t+1)} = \frac{1}{n} \sum_j c_{ij}^{*(t)} x_{ja}^{(t)} \qquad (t = \text{iteration} = 0, \dots, \text{max}) \qquad (9)$$

to obtain a correction matrix which will improve the initial configuration.
Two formulas are needed to construct the correction matrix, C. For the
diagonal elements of C, the following formula is used:

$$\text{If} \quad i = j, \qquad \text{then} \quad c_{ij}^{*(t)} = 1 + \sum_k \frac{d_{ik}^*}{d_{ik}} \qquad (10)$$

For the off-diagonal elements of C, the following formula is used:

$$\text{If} \quad i \neq j, \qquad \text{then} \quad c_{ij}^{*(t)} = 1 - (d_{ij}^*/d_{ij}) \qquad (11)$$

Using both formulas in conjunction will provide the correction matrix.
   In our example, the diagonal of the matrix is determined by (10) where
$i = j$. For instance d_{44} is calculated this way:

$$d_{44} = 1 + \frac{2.00}{2.00} + \frac{5.46}{6.00} + \frac{2.86}{2.86} = 3.91$$

The off-diagonal cells are determined by (11) where $i \neq j$. Table X shows the
correction matrix, C.
   (8)   *A new set of rectangular coordinates can be generated by using the
correction matrix and the first set of coordinates, $X^{(0)}$.* For example, x_1 in
dimension I is calculated by multiplying the first column vector of matrix C
by the vector of dimension I (Table V):

$$x_{11}^{(1)} = \tfrac{1}{4}[(4.00)(4.00) + (0)(8.00) + (0)(3.20) + (0)(2.00)] = 4.00$$

In like manner, generate the remaining coordinates for $X^{(1)}$. Table XI shows
the new coordinates which will improve the initial configuration. With the
new coordinates, Kruskal's stress is reduced to .15. Guttman's coefficient of
alienation is reduced to .00. The iterative process is repeated as often as
needed until the fit is acceptable or until the rate of improvement is negligible. For a more detailed discussion of these steps, the reader is referred to
Lingoes and Roskam (1973).

TABLE X

CORRECTION MATRIX C

	x_1	x_2	x_3	x_4
x_1:	4.00	.00	.00	.00
x_2:	.00	4.01	− .10	.10
x_3:	.00	− .10	4.10	.00
x_4:	.00	.10	.00	3.91

TABLE XI

RECTANGULAR COORDINATES FOR IMPROVED SOLUTION

	Dimension I	Dimension II
x_1:	4.00	3.00
x_2:	7.99	2.94
x_3:	3.08	5.67
x_4:	2.16	3.01

This section has used a mock data set to provide a step-by-step explanation of smallest space analysis (SSA). These steps are all straightforward and do not require complicated procedures such as finding the inverse of a matrix. Even so, the results of SSA contain a wealth of information which can be deceptively simple to interpret or elegantly complex. The next section provides an example from a real data set focusing on a communication problem.

III. A COMMUNICATION STUDY USING SMALLEST SPACE ANALYSIS

Thanks to computer technology, multidimensional methods are often abused or misunderstood. Statistical results from packaged programs can be reported with a minimal understanding or appreciation. Factor analysis is probably one of the most frequently mistreated techniques; too often a bland and uninspiring presentation of factor loadings highlights and terminates a multivariate study.

Some multivariate methods, however, such as the nonmetric and metric scaling techniques, require greater involvement by the researcher in making decisions about the computer output and then "selling" the results to the public.

The identification or verification of organizing patterns (clusters, spatial manifolds, predictors) pressures the researcher to tie theory to observations. Furthermore, it structures expectations and generates nonobvious hypotheses. This kind of interaction is not mandated by techniques which do not capitalize on or emphasize ongoing decisions in multivariate analyses. Too often "packaged statistical programs" allow the researcher the convenience of multivariate consumption without the attendant understanding or appreciation of the power or limitations of the technique.

In this section, the results of a communication study are presented using SSA. The problem which focuses on communicator style was chosen because it shows SSA dealing with a large variable set and points to ways of clustering variables. Then, a simplified version of the same variable set is used to introduce the notion of spatial manifolds using SSA. Also, the simplified variable set is used to identify predictors in the SSA solution.

A. Communicator Style

Communicator style (Norton, 1978) deals with the way one communicates. The following mapping sentence expresses the design. The CSM (communicator style measure) has a four point scale ranging from "very strong agreement" with the statement to "very weak agreement" with the statement.

No independent variables and one dependent variable are embedded in the measure. Five items define each independent variable; six items define the dependent variable. In this example, 1086 subjects from introductory communication classes at the University of Michigan and Western Michigan University filled out the measure.

B. Clustering Variables

When a person first sees the graphical display of a SSA solution in which the researcher has drawn regions around variables, it often looks whimsical, reminding one of amoebae. *One of the critical problems with SSA* and similar techniques *is how to determine the regions in the solution.* In general, there are two strategies to do this: (1) identify dense clusters of points and (2) identify "strings" of points or points determining some kind of continuum. In the next section, ways to cluster variables will be discussed; in the section following, ways to identify continua will be discussed.

Clustering (in the sense of grouping or drawing a region around) variables is always a tricky problem involving subjective stipulation, but not capricious decisions. Simply stated, a cluster is an array of points geometrically represented in a space. The array is separable from other points for one of two reasons: (1) statistical association and/or (2) theoretical association. The cluster must yield a contiguous subspace; it must have a continuous boundary—of whatever shape required—which does not intersect a boundary of another cluster (Lingoes, 1977).

1. STATISTICAL ASSOCIATION

The author has found that McQuitty's (1957) elementary linkage technique is the single best interpretative tool to aid in identifying clusters. If the researcher is interested in grouping dense arrays of points, then the following statistical consideration should be a guide: *The average correlation within clusters/regions should be greater than the average correlation between clusters/regions.* If this is the case, then the researcher has a set of *disjointed* clusters. To the degree that the average correlation within cluster approaches in magnitude the average correlation between clusters, the researcher has a set of linked clusters. In the real world, the latter condition is most likely to be the case. But the statistical association should not be the researcher's only criterion to determine clusters; it should function in conjunction with the theoretical association.

2. THEORETICAL ASSOCIATION

In this example, the mapping sentence is used as a way to identify the expected clusters that interest the researcher a priori. The expectations are derived from synthesis and resynthesis of the literature, pilot studies, and discussions with colleagues doing similar work. So, in the CSM example, the expectation is that five items (see Table XII) for each subconstruct will form a cluster. That is, respective items for each subconstruct will fall into relatively the same part of the SSA solution; they will be relatively close neighbors of each other.

For example, in the CSM, the following five items—based on the operational definition of dominant style and the emergent definition of dominant style from the literature—make up the dominant subconstruct:

Item 5.   In most social situations I generally speak very frequently.

Item 7.   In most social situations I tend to come on strong.

Item 9.   I have a tendency to dominate informal conversations with other people.

Item 20.   I try to take charge of things when I am with people.

Item 44.   I am dominant in social situations.

If a contiguous boundary can be drawn around the five items, then they will be said to constitute a cluster which supports the initial expectation. The exact wording for each item and the a priori rationale for each subconstruct is discussed extensively elsewhere (Norton, 1978).

The results of a two-dimensional SSA solution of the 51 items is presented. Since it is impractical to report the original correlations and the derived coefficients, which include 1275 distances, the coordinates for the two-dimensional solution are reported in Table XIII. The coefficient of alienation with weak monotonicity is .25 which for the purposes of structural information in this example is not bad. Figure 2 shows the SSA solution. The three-dimensional solution, not reported here, has a better coefficient of alienation, but does not lead to different clusters.

TABLE XII

ITEMS POSITED FOR EACH SUBCONSTRUCT

Subconstruct	Item numbers	Subconstruct	Item numbers
Dominant	5, 7, 9, 20, 44	Open	1, 25, 26, 33, 38
Relaxed	4, 12, 16, 17, 36	Animated	6, 21, 24, 34, 42
Dramatic	22, 28, 30, 32, 39	Contentious	2, 10, 13, 37, 41
Attentive	15, 23, 27, 29, 45	Impression leaving	11, 14, 18, 31, 40
Communicator image	46, 47, 48, 49, 50, 51	Friendly	3, 8, 19, 35, 43

TABLE XIII

CoORDINATES FOR SSA SOLUTION[a]

Item	Dimensions I	Dimensions II	Item	Dimensions I	Dimensions II	Item	Dimensions I	Dimensions II
1	7	70	18	12	85	35	− 100	−42
2	− 65	56	19	49	− 23	36	46	44
3	48	− 100	20	− 6	60	37	− 24	50
4	89	86	21	− 13	− 8	38	65	−3
5	7	48	22	− 11	9	39	− 34	33
6	− 5	19	23	25	− 47	40	16	24
7	6	46	24	− 49	0	41	− 38	63
8	25	15	25	16	39	42	− 2	− 28
9	− 23	62	26	22	92	43	5	− 20
10	− 48	− 36	27	69	− 42	44	− 6	48
11	38	9	28	− 77	38	45	20	− 31
12	100	17	29	58	− 66	46	26	1
13	− 36	− 40	30	− 30	17	47	25	34
14	29	20	31	− 19	12	48	28	52
15	− 2	38	32	− 32	41	49	30	46
16	64	42	33	2	35	50	39	38
17	88	57	34	− 63	13	51	37	63

[a]These are *not* factor loadings. The scale − 100 to + 100 was used for convenience only.

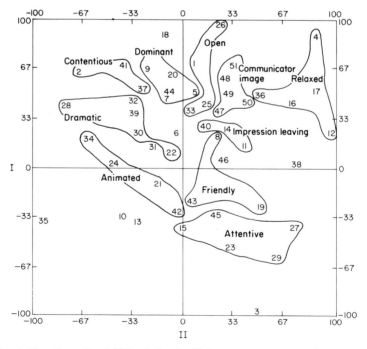

FIG. 2. Two-dimensional SSA solution for 51-item communicator style construct.

The subconstructs are well defined even in light of a large number of items. Four of the subconstructs, Relaxed, Attentive, Dominant, and Dramatic ended up with all original items located in approximately the same region, respectively. The dependent variable, Communicator Image, ended up with five out of six of the original items. Two of the subconstructs, Open and Animated, lost only one item. Even the three weakest subconstructs, Impression Leaving, Contentious, and Friendly, contained three of the original items, respectively.

Like factor analysis, where a given variable feasibly could load on more than one factor, some of the items could be cross-classified. For example, Item 31 ("the *way* I say something usually leaves an impression on people") is conceptually and stylistically related to Item 30 ("often I physically and vocally act out what I want to communicate"), and they are close neighbors to one another. Thus these items might legitimatly be cross-classified. Table XIV summarizes how the CSM clusters empirically survived in light of the initial, theoretical expectations.

An obvious advantage of SSA is that it helps to identify "bad" items for a subconstruct. For example, the Open subconstruct lost Item 38. It was a poorly worded and ambiguous item—"I would rather be open and honest with a person rather than closed and dishonest, *even if it is painful for that person.*" Similarly, Items 3 (Friendly), 35 (Friendly), and 18 (Impression Leaving) proved to be poor items.

Items 10 and 13 did not cluster with Contentious as expected. However, because they were close neighbors of one another and located in a different part of the space, it suggested that the CSM potentially had room for another subconstruct; it suggested that there was a "hole" in the structure of the communicator style construct. In subsequent revisions of the CSM, these items formed the basis for a new subconstruct—namely, a Precise style. So, here is an instance in which a nonobvious hypothesis emerged through SSA.

TABLE XIV

ITEMS FORMING CLUSTERS IN SSA SOLUTION

Subconstruct	Expected items defining cluster	Cross-classified close to cluster	Expected items missing cluster
Dominant	5, 7, 9, 20, 44		
Relaxed	4, 12, 16, 17, 36		
Dramatic	22, 28, 30, 32, 39	6, 31	
Attentive	15, 23, 27, 29, 45		
Communicator image	47, 48, 49, 50, 51		46
Open	1, 25, 26, 33		38
Animated	21, 24, 34, 42	6, 31	
Contentious	2, 37, 41		10, 13
Impression leaving	11, 14, 40	31, 6	18
Friendly	8, 19, 43		3, 35

Finally, Items 6 (Animated) and 31 (Impression Leaving) represent two instances in which cross-classification may be legitimate. Both items could signal a Dramatic style and simultaneously signal an Animated and Impression Leaving style.

The clusters in SSA provide additional information. SSA provides a direct indication of the cohesiveness of items within a cluster. If the array of points is dense, the cluster is highly cohesive. For example, the Dominant subconstruct is highly cohesive with a dense array of Items 9, 20, 44, 7, and 5. The Relaxed subconstruct is also cohesive with its array of items (4, 17, 16, 36, and 12), but not as dense as the Dominant cluster. The cohesiveness of the subconstructs should be of concern to the researcher. Ideally, if all the subconstructs were equally cohesive, it would be easier to compare the relative impact each independent variable has on a specified dependent variable. Of course, the "degree of cohesiveness" is subjectively stipulated.

Also, SSA provides a direct indication of the relationships of the clusters to each other. The point is illustrated by examining the location of various subconstructs. Attentive and Friendly are located in similar spaces. This was expected because the subconstructs conceptually overlap. Similarly, Dominant, Contentious, Dramatic, and Animated fall close to each other. Again, there is conceptual overlap for these style behaviors on at least one dimension. The dependent variable, Communicator Image (i.e., "I am a good communicator") is surrounded by the subconstructs Open, Impression Leaving, and Relaxed. These clusters should probably be best predictors of Communicator Image. This point will be examined further in subsequent sections.

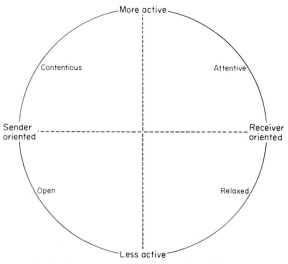

FIG. 3. Tentative model suggested by SSA solution.

Two observations emerge from the analysis of groups of clusters. First, there is an imbalance of highly visible style components such as Dominant, Impression Leaving, Dramatic, Contentious, and Animated. This imbalance should be corrected to enhance the development of the communicator style construct. Subconstructs related to Open, Attentive, Relaxed, and Friendly could strengthen the communicator style domain. Adding the "Precise style" as a subconstruct, for example, helps alleviate the imbalance.

Second, a tentative model is suggested by the SSA solution. Receiver-oriented behaviors such as Attentive are located in one part of the space. In the space opposite the Attentive subconstruct, sender-oriented behaviors are located such as Open. In like manner, less active style behaviors—that is, behaviors requiring less energy (Relaxed, for example)—are located in one part of the space; more active behaviors (Contentious) are located in the opposite space. So, the SSA solution suggests a tentative model (Fig. 3), which provides a guideline for improving the style domain and generates hypotheses about dimensionality that can be tested further.

C. Special Manifolds

In this section, the second strategy to deal with "strings" of points instead of dense arrays will be discussed. Both statistical and theoretical considerations shape the analysis in determining meaningful continua. In this example, the theoretical statements emerge post hoc in providing explanations for the continua. These explications, in turn, provide a priori expectations for the next round of data gathering.

For illustrative purposes, the items in each subconstruct are collapsed. For example, each item in the dominant subconstruct is standardized, summed, and averaged to obtain a total variable score for the cluster. Then this score is correlated with all other total scores of the respective clusters. The matrix in Table XV provided the initial input for the SSA solution.

Figure 4 shows the three-dimensional solution of the subconstructs. With semistrong monotonicity, the coefficient of alienation is .07. In general, any solution that has a coefficient of alienation of .15 or less is considered "good."

Spatial manifolds are aggregations of points satisfying given conditions. The types of manifolds range from very simple substructures such as a simplex to very complex substructures such as a radex, a multiplex, or a torex (Lingoes & Borg, 1977). Only the simplex will be discussed in this chapter.

A "simplex" is a set of variables through which a continuous line can be drawn so that the line does not bend back on itself. If all the variables within a set can be projected without any intransitivities onto such a line, then they determine a simplex.

Guttman (1965) recommends the following to discern a simplex pattern. Arrange the variables in the correlation table such that all the values in both

TABLE XV

CORRELATIONS AND DERIVED COEFFICIENTS AMONG COMMUNICATOR STYLE SUBCONSTRUCTS[a], [b]

Subconstructs		(1)	(2)	(3)	(4)	(5)	(6)	(7)	(8)	(9)	(10)
Dominant	(1)	—	60	102	107	88	142	178	76	156	72
Dramatic	(2)	.51	—	97	65	100	194	175	94	148	106
Contentious	(3)	.48	.41	—	143	102	193	187	166	190	140
Animated	(4)	.39	.54	.32	—	106	211	142	92	101	111
Impression leaving	(5)	.48	.45	.41	.42	—	129	99	106	101	58
Relaxed	(6)	.36	.26	.19	.22	.37	—	180	147	184	101
Attentive	(7)	.24	.31	.29	.37	.38	.28	—	160	59	124
Open	(8)	.48	.38	.32	.42	.40	.31	.33	—	118	61
Friendly	(9)	.35	.35	.25	.40	.39	.25	.50	.37	—	105
Communicator image	(10)	.59	.41	.36	.37	.54	.48	.38	.53	.42	—

[a]The lower triangular matrix represents the correlations; the upper triangular matrix represents the derived distances.

[b]Only the items which did not fall into the last column of Table XIV were standardized and averaged. In other words, "bad" items were excluded.

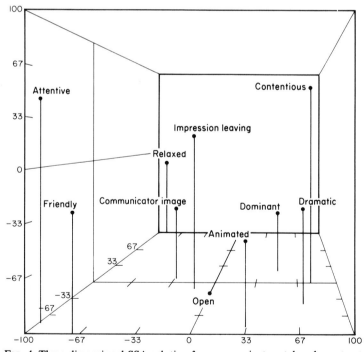

FIG. 4. Three-dimensional SSA solution for communicator style subconstructs.

TABLE XVI

SIMPLEXES IN THE VARIABLE SET

Simplex I	Simplex II	Simplex III
Relaxed	Attentive	Attentive
Communicator image	Friendly	Friendly
Dominant	Animated	Animated
Dramatic	Dramatic	Open
Animated	Dominant	Dominant

the rows and columns monotonially decrease away from the diagonal. If the same pattern occurs in the table of derived coefficients, then a simplex pattern is rigorously established.

In the simplified CSM data set, only three, five-variable simplexes out of 252 combinations are present. Table XVI reports them. Two kinds of simplexes are in the configuration.

Simplex I reflects a continuum anchored by communicative activity, dramatic and animated, which requires energy expenditure and allows tension release at one end and by communicative inactivity, relaxed, which conserves energy and reflects a state of already released tension.

Simplexes II and III reflect different continua. Nondirective communicative activity, attentive and friendly, anchor one end; directive communicative activity, dominant, anchor the other end.

Of course, it is too early to identify the exact nature of the continua at this point in the development of the communicator style construct. Nevertheless, this kind of analysis helps to generate ideas about the direction a comprehensive theory about communicator style might take. For this reason, SSA has powerful heuristic value.

D. Best Predictors

The most likely predictors of any variable in a SSA solution are the closest neighbors in the configuration. In the simplified data set, three subconstructs are relatively close to the dependent variable. Impression leaving is the closest variable in the three-dimensional solution with a derived coefficient of $d = 58$. The original coefficient, namely, the correlation between communicator image and impression leaving, is .54. Open is the second closest neighbor with $d = 61$ and the original distance of $r = .53$. Dominant is the third closest variable with $d = 72$; dominant is closest to communicator image in terms of the original distance, $r = .59$.

In short, the three best candidates for strong predictors of the dependent variable are impression leaving, open, and dominant. As it turns out, dominant and impression leaving are the best predictors in a least squares regression analysis (Norton, 1977).

E. Summary

The example showed how SSA could be used in clustering variables, analyzing spatial manifolds, and pinpointing best predictors. The clustering of the variables is closely connected to the correlation coefficients and is graphically shown in the SSA output. The SSA solution is a graphic analog of the original distances. Second, the search for underlying patterns within the configuration, in essence, is a search for the underpinnings of one's theory. In this case, simplexes were identified. In other SSA solutions, the theorist could search for patterns such as radexes, circumplexes, and cylindrexes (Levy & Guttman, 1975). Third, best predictors are suggested by the SSA solution simply as a function of being close neighbors in the configuration.

IV. OTHER SMALLEST SPACE ANALYSIS APPLICATIONS FOR THE COMMUNICATION RESEARCHER

The applications of nonmetric multivariate techniques range from mass media studies to interapersonal communication projects. This section points to applications in attitude change research, small group research, and interpersonal communication research. The examples which are alluded to are not meant to be comprehensive, only suggestive.

A. Attitude Change

There are many ways to use SSA and other nonmetric multivariate techniques in attitude change studies. McLaughlin's (1975) article on credibility judgments of well-known personalities is an excellent example of using these techniques.

The brief example presented here deals with perceived guilt relationships among the Watergate persona over two time periods. The analysis indicates that over time the image of relationships among the persona stabilized in such a way that Nixon graphically occupied the center of the SSA configuration, while the other aides were realigned. Figure 5—which incidently shows an alternative way to display SSA solutions—shows the analyses.

Two independent samples ($N_1 = 148$; $N_2 = 42$) were asked about their images relating to the guilt relationships among seven White House persona. The first sample was taken during the last week of the televised Wateragte hearings (second week in August); the second sample was taken during the second week of October. During the first time period, the hierarchy surrounding the President was being publicized. Nixon was still fending off charges of guilt and disassociating himself from the aides. During the second time period, Nixon had become a keystone figure and had become strongly associated with Haldeman in the public eye (Norton & Martin, 1974).

In sample 1, if a line is drawn through points 5 and 2, a continuum reflects the power positions of the people surrounding the President. Haldeman and

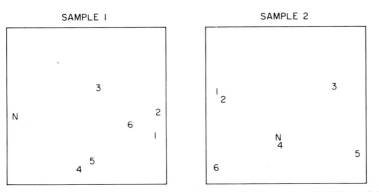

FIG. 5. SSA solutions of the Watergate persona in terms of guilt patterns (N, Nixon; 1, Dean; 2, Stans; 3, Mitchell; 4, Haldeman; 5, Ehrlichman; 6, McGruder).

Ehrlichman can be projected onto one end of the line; Stans can be projected onto the other end. Also, Nixon, if projected onto the line, falls into the correct power position.

The whole configuration shows Nixon disassociated from the others which coincides with the public image at the time. Two months later, however, Nixon was closely associated with Haldeman in terms of guilt perception. McGruder loses the early visibility which he had in the first sample and moves to a position of isolation, unassociated with anybody.

Clearly, nonmetric multivariate techniques provide useful tools for the person interested in attitude change research. In particular, they lend themselves to the following kinds of attitude research:

(1) *One shot study*: Nonmetric multivariate scaling techniques are useful for understanding variable sets in terms of clusters, spatial manifolds, and predictors for communication projects such as the first Ford–Carter debate, information diffusion about the shooting of George Wallace, and the alignment of abortion issues immediately after a Supreme Court decision.

(2) *Comparing configurations*: Configurations can be compared across samples, contexts, and time. For instance, SSA was used to demonstrate structural differences in attitudes toward cocaine users and nonusers (Norton, 1976). Also, SSA was used to compare configurations for two samples exposed to radically different newspaper stories about the Hearst kidnapping (Norton, 1974).

B. Group Communication

Nonmetric multidimensional scaling techniques not only help to examine group variables such as effectiveness, self-esteem, willingness to communicate, task accomplishment, and peer support but also allow a handy diagnosis of the group structure in which members are treated as variables. Laumann and Pappi's (1973) study of community elites is an outstanding example of such a treatment using SSA.

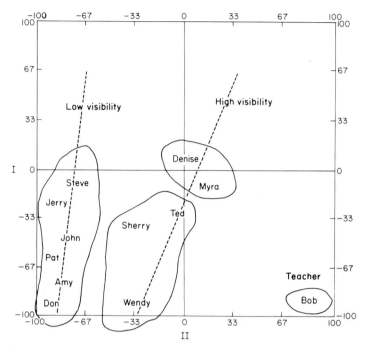

FIG. 6. SSA solution of attractiveness among class members and teacher.

The following example is but a modest indication of SSA being used to study coalitions. Twelve class members, including the teacher, participated in an attraction exercise. Each member of the class was given a white, blue, red, and yellow chip. They were asked to write down on a piece of paper the person they liked the best, the second best, the third best, and the fourth best. Then, they were instructed to give out the respective chips to the people listed. A triangular matrix was constructed by summing the rank values for each dyad. The matrix was used for the initial distance matrix for SSA. Figure 6 shows the solution.

The two-dimensional solution verified four, expected coalitions in the class (6, 7, 5, 11, 3, 12), (4, 1, 10), (9, 2), and (8). The coalitions remained stable over the semester. With one exception, the first coalition received the lowest grades. The third coalition (9, 2) received the highest grades.

A line drawn through points 10 and 9 defined the most visible members of the class and the most talkative ones. A line drawn through points 12 and 6 defined the low profile group and the least talkative ones. Within the visible group of people there was an interpretable continuum with the very vocal class members (9, 2) at one end and the moderately vocal class members (1, 4, 10) at the other end. The same relationship did not hold for the low profile group.

Several observations are in order. First, SSA can be used with an incomplete data set. Only the first four ranks provided the units of analysis in this example, but this was enough to construct a meaningful configuration.

Second, although the primary units of analysis concerned attractiveness, the coalitions and the continua suggested a potential explanation of the class structure which centered around "talkativeness." In short, the visible presentation of the configuration shaped expectations and explanations regarding why the structure formed the way it did.

C. Interpersonal Communication

Nonmetric multidimensional scaling techniques assist the researcher in generating theory. The communicator style construct exemplified this point. Also, these techniques aid in *confirming theory*. For example, Leary's (1957) frequently cited paridigm to diagnose personality through the use of an interpersonal checklist entailed a circular model defined by eight behaviors. Leary posited the model a priori. SSA could be used to *confirm the structure of the model*. If the interpersonal behaviors are in relation to each other as suggested, then analysis of empirical data should yield what Guttman (1965) calls a circumplex—a circular pattern in the configuration.

V. SUMMARY

Nonmetric multidimensional scaling attempts to place variables in the smallest possible space, the space with the lowest dimensionality, such that the distances between the variables in a coordinate space reflect the distances between the original coefficients. The strength of these techniques is not that it allows the researcher to discover new phenomena which cannot be discovered by other techniques. In principle, other techniques could lead the researcher to identical conclusions.

The strength of multidimensional scaling lies in the following reasons, which paraphrase Shepard's (1974) conclusions from his Presidential address at the annual meeting of the Psychometric Society:

(1) *These techniques provide a convenient, objective, and uniform way of representing the essential pattern underlying experimental results.* "Virtually the same, readily appreciated spatial picture may be obtainable despite the wide variations in nature or absolute numerical magnitudes of similarity data that arise from judgments, confusions, or reaction times."

(2) *These techniques probably provide a more statistically reliable set of relations in the nonmetric multidimensional solution than the set of relations in the original data.* Owing to the great reduction and hence averaging of data that the picture represents, the resultant configuration is likely to be more stable and replicable than the original coefficients.

(3)   *These techniques offer a quantitative method of psychologically calibrat-
ing or describing in a reduced, parametric way (that is, in a coordinate space) a
set of objects to be used in further experimental research or for the test of
theoreticl models.*

Finally, the position of this chapter is that the researcher does what is
necessary to understand the data set. Nonmetric multidimensional scaling
techniques are not touted as the ultimate in multivariate methods, but they
represent elegant and powerful tools which force the researcher to get
"intimately" involved with his data in terms of identifying clusters, spatial
manifolds, and predictors.

References

Elizur, D. *Adapting to innovation.* Jerusalem: Jerusalem Academic Press, 1970.

Gratch, M. *Twenty-five years of social research in Israel: A review of the work of the Israel
    Institute of Applied Social Research.* Jerusalem: Jerusalem Academic Press, 1973.

Guttman, L. A faceted definition of intelligence. *Studies in psychology, Scripta Hierosolymitana,*
    1965, **14**, 166–181.

Guttman, L. A general nonmetric technique for finding the smallest coordinate space for a
    configuration of points. *Psychometrika,* 1968, **33**, 369–506.

Kruskal, J. Multidimensional scaling by optimizing goodness of fit to a nonmetric hypothesis.
    Psychometrika, 1964, **29**, 1–27.

Laumann, E., and Pappi, F. New directions in the study of community elites. *American
    Sociological Review,* 1973, **38**, 212–230.

Leary, T. *Interpersonal diagnosis of personality: A functional theory and methodology for personality
    evaluation.* New York: Ronald Press, 1957.

Levy, S., and Guttman, L. *On the multivariate structure of wellbeing.* Jerusalem, Unpublished
    manuscript, 1975.

Lingoes, J. *The Guttman-Lingoes nonmetric program series.* Ann Arbor, Michigan: Mathesis
    Press, 1973.

Lingoes, J. (ed.) *Geometric representations of relational data.* Ann Arbor, Michigan, Mathesis
    Press, 1977.

Lingoes, J., and Borg, I. *Identifying spatial manifolds for interpretation.* Ann Arbor, Michigan,
    Unpublished manuscript, 1977.

Lingoes, J., and Roskam, E. A mathematical and empirical study of two multidimensional
    scaling algoritms. *Psychometric Monographs,* 1973, **38**, 93.

Lingoes, J., and Schoenemann, P. Alternative measures of fit for the Schoenemann-Carroll
    matrix fitting algorithm. *Psychometrika,* 1974, **39**, 423–427.

McLaughlin, M. Recovering the structure of credibility judgments: An alternative to factor
    analysis. *Speech Monographs,* 1975, **48**, 221–228.

McQuitty, L. Elementary linkage analysis for isolating orthogonal and oblique types and typal
    relevancies. *Educational and Psychological Measurement,* 1957, **17**, 207–229.

Norton, R. *Smallest space analysis for variable sets: Two methodological tools for attitude change
    research.* A paper presented at the meeting of the Speech Communication Association,
    Chicago, Illinois, December 1974.

Norton, R. *Best predictors concerning the legalization of cocaine.* A paper presented at the meeting
    of the International Communication Association, Portland, Oregon, April 1976.

Norton, R. Foundation of a communicator style construct. *Human Communication Research,*
    1978, **4**, 99–112.

Norton, R., and Martin, H. *A smallest space analysis of the Watergate persona.* A paper presented at the meeting of the Central States Speech Association, Milwaukee, Wisconsin, April 1974.

Shepard, R. Representation of structure in similarity data: Problems and prospects. *Psychometrika*, 1974, **39**, 373–421.

Spence, I. A Monte Carlo evaluation of three nonmetric multidimensional scaling algorithms. *Psychometrika*, 1972, **37**, 461–486.

Torgerson, W. *Theory and methods of scaling.* New York: Wiley, 1958.

Young, F. *A FORTRAN IV program for nonmetric multidimensional scaling*, Report No. 56. Chapel Hill, North Carolina: University of North Carolina, L. L. Thurstone Psychometric Laboratory, March 1968.

Young, F. Nonmetric multidimensional scaling: Recovery of metric information. *Psychometrika*, 1970, **35**, 455–473.

Chapter 11

MULTIDIMENSIONAL SCALING MODELS FOR COMMUNICATION RESEARCH

JOSEPH WOELFEL

East-West
Communication
Institute

and

Department of
Rhetoric and Communication
State University of New York at Albany
Albany, New York

JEFFREY E. DANES

Department of Business Administration
Virginia Polytechnic Institute and State University
Blacksburg, Virginia

I. INTRODUCTION

All measurement systems, whatever their type, share as a basic goal the determination of *difference* or separation among the elements measured. The crudest measurement systems are able to detect only the presence or absence of gross differences, while the most sensitive and precise measurement systems can reliably detect the smallest of differences and relate their magnitude to any other such difference as ratios. All measurement systems in practice lie along a continuum between these extreme points. These differences or separations among the elements scaled may be thought of as distances, and multidimensional scaling (MDS) capitalizes fully on the analogy to spatial distances implicit in the measurement model. MDS procedures construct a multidimensional space or map in which the objects scaled are arrayed such that the distances between any two objects in the map are functions of their measured distance from each other on the scaling instrument. To the extent that the measurement system used by the researcher yields outcomes toward the precise end of the measurement continuum, this spatial analogy becomes increasingly appropriate.

Although several variations of this analysis system exist (Carroll & Chang, 1970; Coombs, 1958; Harshman, 1972; Kruskal, 1964a, b; Lingoes, 1972; McGee, 1968; Pieszko, 1970; Shepard, 1962a, b; Torgerson, 1952, 1958; Tucker & Messick, 1963; Tucker, 1972), all share the central notion of a spatial coordinate system as a frame of reference within which symbols are arrayed and therefore "pictured." Insofar as they constitute projections of distances among points into a coordinate system, MDS procedures provide the closest analogy to mechanics in the social sciences.

The many variants of multidimensional scaling may be broadly classified as either "metric" or "nonmetric"; since Norton (in this volume) presents a chapter (Chapter 10) on one variant of nonmetric multidimensional scaling (smallest space analysis), no further elaborations will be made here.

II. METRIC MULTIDIMENSIONAL SCALING:
   THE CLASSICAL MODEL

The metric multidimensional scaling model was the first multidimensional scaling model developed and it is known as the "classical" approach. Following Young and Householder (1938) and Richardson (1938), among others, Torgerson (1952, 1958) is most well known for general improvements and dissemination of this approach. Unlike the nonmetric approach, the metric procedure begins with a precisely scaled $n \times n$ data matrix S (see Table I) and concludes with an identically precise multidimensional space. Any cell s_{ij} in this matrix represents the measured dissimilarity or difference between the ith and jth object or concept scaled. In a typical metric study as usually practiced in the communication field, two of the objects to be scaled are chosen as a "criterion pair" and the difference between them assigned a numerical value like 10 or 100. All other pairs are then compared as ratios to this criterion pair in a statement of the form: "If a and b are u units apart, how far apart are . . . and . . . ?" When there is more than one respondent, estimates of all samples responses are usually averaged within each cell s_{ij} across all sample members to yield the average dissimilarities matrix $\bar{s}$

(Gillham & Woelfel, 1977). The matrix of intercity distances in Table I is an ideal type of such a matrix.

Though its foundation can be traced back to the Greeks and beyond (Serota, 1974), the modern basis for metric multidimensional scaling was laid in 1938 when Young and Householder (1938) presented a technique for describing the location of points in a spatial configuration given only the separations (distances) among the points. Young and Householder (1938) converted the matrix of interpoint separations S into a matrix of scalar products B, whose elements b_{ij} are defined as

$$b_{ij} = \tfrac{1}{2}\left(s_{iP}^2 + s_{jP}^2 - s_{ij}^2\right) \tag{1}$$

where the point P is an arbitrary point in the space and is used as the origin of the space.[1] Although there is a unique B matrix for each point selected as the origin of the space, the separation relations among the points in the space remain invariant regardless of which point is selected as the origin.

Torgerson (1958) describes a procedure for locating the origin at the centroid of the space. The centroid is the exact center of the configuration of points, and Torgerson's procedure simply ensures that the resulting map or plot will be centered on the page. While functionally equivalent to the Young and Householder solution, Torgerson's procedure is more commonly used. Any element b^*_{ij} in Torgerson's (1958) "doubled centered" scalar products matrix is given by

$$b^*_{ij} = \tfrac{1}{2}\left(s_{ij}^2 - s_{.j}^2 - s_{i.}^2 + s_{..}^2\right) \tag{2}$$

where

$$s_{.j}^2 = \frac{1}{n}\sum_{i=1}^{n} s_{ij}^2, \qquad s_{i.}^2 = \frac{1}{n}\sum_{j=1}^{n} s_{ij}^2, \qquad s_{..}^2 = \frac{1}{n^2}\sum_{i=1}^{n}\sum_{j=1}^{n} s_{ij}^2.$$

That is, placing the origin of the space at the centroid (geometric center) of the space is accomplished by subtracting out the grand row and grand column means leaving only (in analysis of variance terms) the "interactions." Geometrically, any b^*_{ij} element represents

$$b^*_{ij} = \cos\theta_{ij}|R^i||R^j| \tag{3}$$

where $\cos\theta_{ij}$ is the cosine of the angle between the two vectors, $|R^i|$ the vector length of point i from the origin (centroid), and $|R^j|$ the vector length of point j from the origin (centroid).

Once the B^* scalar products matrix is obtained, establishing the coordinate system is fairly straight forward; it simply consists of a factorization of the B^* matrix. This factorization is identical to the factor analysis algorithm familiar to most communication researchers—the only difference is that the B^* matrix is input instead of the usual correlation matrix. It consists essentially

[1]The notation B, b and B^*, and b^* are taken from Torgerson (1958).

TABLE I

SEPARATIONS IN SPACE AMONG 16 SELECTED U.S. CITIES[A] ([A]1 UNIT = 1 KM)

City	(1)	(2)	(3)	(4)	(5)	(6)	(7)	(8)	(9)	(10)	(11)	(12)	(13)	(14)	(15)	(16)
(1) Atlanta	0															
(2) Boston	1508	0														
(3) Chicago	944	1369	0													
(4) Cleveland	891	886	496	0												
(5) Dallas	1160	2496	1292	1649	0											
(6) Denver	1950	2846	1480	1974	1067	0										
(7) Detroit	869	986	383	145	1607	1860	0									
(8) Los Angeles	2310	4177	2807	3297	2005	1337	3191	0								
(9) Miami	972	2019	1911	1749	1788	2777	1354	3764	0							
(10) New Orleans	682	2186	1340	1487	713	1741	1511	2692	1076	0						
(11) New York	1204	302	1147	652	2211	2624	1258	3944	1757	1884	0					
(12) PHoenix	2562	3701	2338	2814	1427	943	2719	574	3189	2117	3451	0				
(13) Pittsburgh	838	777	660	185	1721	2124	330	3437	1625	1478	510	2941	0			
(14) San Francisco	3442	4343	2990	3485	2386	1524	3364	558	4174	3099	4137	1051	3643	0		
(15) Seattle	3511	3979	2795	3260	2705	1643	3118	1543	4399	3381	3874	1792	3440	1091	0	
(16) Washington	874	632	961	492	1907	2404	637	3701	1485	1554	330	3191	309	3929	3849	0

of finding the eigenvectors of the B^* matrix. The output of this analysis will be a $k \times r$ matrix $R(\mu = 1, r; \alpha = 1, k)$ where each row $R^\mu_{(\alpha)}$ represents the projections of the αth concept or object (city, in the example of Table I) on a set of r orthogonal basis vectors e_μ. The fact that there is a single index (μ) shows it is a vector (no index would represent a scalar; two indices would represent a matrix, and so on). The (α) is placed within parentheses to show that it is not an index, but rather only a marker to describe which vector we are referring to. Furthermore, the index is superscripted to show that this vector refers to *observations* or *measured values*. (Superscripted quantities are called "contravariant"; subscripted quantities are called "covariant." R^μ, therefore, is a *contravariant vector*.)

Similarly, each of the e_μ represents a unit vector (the single index shows that it is a vector), and the fact that it is subscripted rather than superscripted indicates that each e_μ does not refer to observations of measured values but rather to an arbitrary reference vector onto which the measured or observed values ($R^\mu_{(\alpha)}$) are projected. Since it does not refer to measured values, it is a *covariant* vector and hence subscripted.

Each of these e_μ ($\mu = 1, r$) vectors represents a unit reference axis orthogonal to each other such reference axis, and thus the set of these basis vectors constitutes an ordinary r-dimensional Cartesian coordinate system. These vectors are usually called dimensions (sometimes factors or eigenvectors) and the fact that more than one such vector is usually needed to represent the configuration gives rise to the term "multidimensional scaling." In fact, it is always the case that $r \leqslant k - 1$, since any k points can always be represented on $k - 1$ orthogonal coordinates. Any three points, for example, can always be fit on a (two-dimensional) plane, but may in some cases be on a (one-dimensional) line. Factoring the centroid scalar products matrix (B^*) derived from the intercity distance matrix in Table I yields the results given in Table II and Fig. 1. Each column of Table II represents the projections of the cities on a reference vector e_μ; the first column, therefore, represents the projections of the cities on the first unit vector e_1, the second, their projections on e_2, and so on. The reader can easily verify that these columns are orthogonal by calculating the correlations among pairs of columns, all of which will be 0.0.

Each row of Table II represents the projection of one of the cities' position vector $R^\mu_{(\alpha)}$ on the e_μ basis vectors, thus the first row $R^\mu_{(1)}$ represents the projection of Atlanta's position vector on the space, so that $R^1_{(1)} = -808.7$ $R^2_{(1)} = 481.3$, etc. Moreover, since the transformation by which this solution is achieved is distance preserving, these numbers are to be understood in the original units of measure—in this case kilometers. Plots based on the first two dimensions (columns e_1 and e_2) of Table II are presented in Fig. 1. Actually, the figures in Table II have first been reflected (multiplied by -1) because the algorithm generated an inverted mirror-image of our conventional representation of the earth's surface—the algorithm, of course,

TABLE II

GALILEO COORDINATES OF 16 SELECTED CITIES IN A METRIC MULTIDIMENSIONAL SPACE NORMAL SOLUTION

	1	2	3	4	5	6	7	8
(1) Atlanta	−808.701	481.329	−26.846	−71.783	16.023	16.599	12.634	10.807
(2) Boston	−1677.183	−745.227	−184.542	85.696	−10.499	−27.056	−13.778	−8.615
(3) Chicago	−406.610	−363.631	110.592	−119.280	−.893	−7.731	−19.989	15.535
(4) Cleveland	−891.643	−403.765	54.297	−32.279	33.483	27.932	−8.801	−6.017
(5) Dallas	322.591	699.325	42.781	−152.488	−54.108	25.889	−16.486	−8.547
(6) Denver	1042.064	−82.214	156.341	−114.150	−11.267	−23.404	23.232	−7.455
(7) Detroit	−767.895	−473.812	73.193	−66.076	−13.045	4.508	1.460	−23.434
(8) Los Angeles	2268.293	367.182	18.883	128.831	86.748	−3.487	.092	−2.216
(9) Miami	−1326.834	1253.670	−256.774	102.060	−11.724	.826	5.017	−10.785
(10) New Orleans	−329.342	866.871	−51.591	−92.584	21.478	−16.044	−5.036	9.862
(11) New York	−1517.500	−480.943	−51.155	79.323	−22.697	9.141	5.351	23.699
(12) Phoenix	1733.251	541.157	52.360	−4.181	−17.993	−27.342	−6.725	5.051
(13) Pittsburgh	−1053.005	−319.613	21.158	−29.486	−5.232	3.694	28.170	2.261
(14) San Francisco	2529.978	−119.627	33.792	190.582	−54.348	25.969	.114	2.814
(15) Seattle	2240.414	−1172.344	−272.454	−88.105	.814	−.161	.044	.055
(16) Washington	−1357.579	−148.357	279.964	183.919	−8.741	−9.436	−5.304	−3.014

Eigenvalues (foots) of eigenvector matrix

	1	2	3	4	5	6	7	8
	3290982.656	6480979.446	310095.395	189689.444	22651.153	4969.506	2586.446	1974.062

Number of iterations to derive the root

	1	2	3	4	5	6	7	8
	4	4	24	4	44	7	9	13

Percentage of distance accounted for by individual vector

	1	2	3	4	5	6	7	8
	82.428	16.237	.777	.474	.057	.012	.006	.005

Cumulative percentages of real distance accounted for

	1	2	3	4	5	6	7	8
	82.428	98.665	99.441	99.915	99.972	99.984	99.991	99.996

Cumulative percentages of total (real and imaginary) distance accounted for

	1	2	3	4	5	6	7	8
	83.086	99.453	100.236	100.714	100.771	100.783	100.790	100.795

Trace 39598514.222
Number of dimensions in real space 9

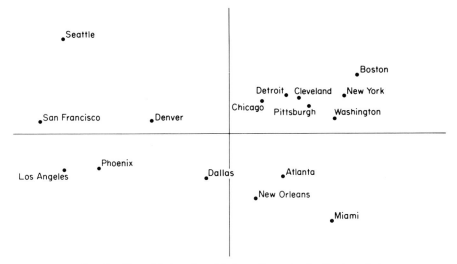

FIG. 1.   Plot of factors 1 and 2 from the unstandardized analysis.

cannot know which half of the world we like to consider the "top." Given this reflection, $R_{(1)}^1 = 808.7$ and $R_{(1)}^2 = -481.3$ tell us that Atlanta is 808.7 km east and 481.3 km south of the geographic center of these 16 cities.

It is worth noting also that two dimensions are enough to give a reasonably complete representation of these data. The third dimension (not plotted) represents the (minor) curvature of the earth; all the others represent rounding errors (the original data are not perfectly error-free). The determination of how many dimensions to retain is based solely on the relative sizes of the projections on the dimensions. When the projections are too small to be worth considering, or are within the precision of measure, they are ignored. As an aid in determining when they are "too small," we note that the squares of the projections on each factor sum to their corresponding eigenvalue, $\lambda_{(\mu)}$. (Note that μ is in parentheses, indicating that it is not an index; since $\lambda_{(\mu)}$ has no index it is a scalar.) That is,

$$\lambda_{(\mu)} = \sum_{\alpha=1}^{k} (R_{(\alpha)}^\mu)^2 \tag{4}$$

This value, $\lambda_{(\mu)}$, may be thought of in ANOVA terms as the amount of variance explained by the μth dimension. The total variance is called the trace (T) and is given by the sum of the eigenvalues, i.e., $T = \sum_{u=1}^{r} \lambda_{(\mu)}$. The proportion of variance explained by any single factor, therefore, is given by its eigenvalue divided by the trace, or

$$\%VAR = 100\lambda_{(\mu)}/T \tag{5}$$

Statistical tests for the significance of this ratio are not known in the MDS literature but the reader is referred to Barnett and Woelfel (1978) for a more thorough discussion of the question of dimensionality. These authors conclude that valuable information can be found in factors much smaller than typical practice usually retains, and they recommend retaining all or nearly all the dimensions, particularly when precise scaling procedures and large samples have been employed. (Most typical procedures now in use would ignore the small third dimension in this example and thus conclude that the world—or at least the United States—is flat.)

III. METRIC RATIOS, METRIC AXIOMS, AND "METRIC" SPACES

In the process of "measuring," the term metric usually refers to the initial *standard* for which other numerical values of separation are obtained by comparing these other magnitudes to the initial standard. As such, physical distances are *metric* ratios, proportions, or multiples of a consensually shared, prespecified distance: the meter. In the language of mathematics, however, the term "metric space" usually refers to a space which is isomorphic with certain prespecified axioms; for the metric Euclidean space, these axioms take the following form (cf. Blumenthal, 1961)

$$s_{ij} = 0 \quad \text{if and only if} \quad i = j \quad \text{(Positivity)}$$

$$s_{ij} = s_{ji} \qquad\qquad \text{(Symmetry)} \qquad (6)$$

$$s_{ij} + s_{jk} \geqslant s_{ik} \quad \text{for all} \quad i, j, \text{and } k \quad \text{(Triangle inequality)}$$

With the presence of positivity and symmetry, all that is needed to make the space "metric" is the requirement that any triangle formed by any three points be real; that is, that any side of a triangle not exceed the sum of the other two sides. These constraints are clearly met by the intercity distance of Table I. In communication research, however, the triangle inequality rule is usually violated by the original data set. Thus, when one is working with reliable metric ratios provided by human respondents, metric MDS frequently results in complex, non-Euclidean multidimensional spaces characterized by both real and imaginary eigenvectors in R.

The term "imaginary" has caused unfortunate misgivings among psychologists; some psychometricians have assumed that imaginary eigenvectors cannot be meaningful and, therefore, represent measurement error. Thus, if A is "close" to B, and B is "close" to C, the failure to find the logically expected "nearness" between A and C has usually been attributed to faulty data gathering procedures. Beginning with Shepard (1962a, b), Kruskal (1964 a, b), Guttman (1968), Lingoes (1972), and others have devised "nonmetric" procedures which eliminate triangle inequality violations by iteratively transforming data into a "metric space" of a prespecified number of dimensions.

Research by Danes and Woelfel (1975), Serota, Cody, Barnett, and Taylor (1975), and Woelfel (1977), among others, indicates, however, that respondents frequently and reliably report "inconsistent" separation judgments.

Collectively, these studies suggest that "inconsistent" separation judgments result from the differential interpretation of a given concept; that is, the meaning for a given symbol frequently varies with the context in which the symbol is presented. For example, "red" and "orange" may be conceived of as similar; "orange" and "tangerine" may be conceived of as similar; but "red" and "tangerine" may be viewed as very dissimilar. If such an example were quantified with metric ratio data, this would result in "inconsistent" separation and result in a complex multidimensional "metric" ratio space. In general, the spaces yielded by typical communication separation matrices are multidimensional and complex.

IV. STRUCTURE OF MULTIDIMENSIONAL SPACES: CLUSTERS AND ATTRIBUTES

Multidimensional scaling was conceived of primarily by psychologists to measure psychological structures, and early analyses usually were confined to efforts at identifying different characteristics that might be associated with different regions of the space. Five procedures for such analyses are most common. First is a simple "eyeball" approach, similar to the intuitive interpretation of factor analyses, where the investigators carefully scrutinize the plots of the configuration to determine obvious features. Very frequently the graphic simplicity of the multidimensional plot (e.g., Fig. 1) makes obvious facts concealed both by the separation matrix and other analytic procedures.

Second, many researchers frequently perform cluster analyses on either the separation matrix or the coordinate matrix R to identify meaningful clusters of elements. Those elements which cluster together are usually thought to possess some common characteristic(s). Interpretation of these analyses give precision to "eyeball" analyses, and the reader is referred to Chapter 9 for an explication of such procedures.

A third common analysis consists of attempts to locate linear arrays of "objects" which might express fundamental psychological attributes. If all the concepts in a space, for example, could be seen to lie on a line from "bad" to "good," a "good–bad" attribute might be inferred. Many early analysts, in fact, hoped or assumed that these attributes might correspond to eigenvectors or dimensions themselves, since they felt the basic attributes of experience would prove to be independent of each other, but few workers still hold to this view today (Rosenberg & Sedlak, 1972; Cody, Marlier, & Woelfel, 1976; Schmidt, 1972).

Very substantial evidence suggests rather that the orthogonal factors of the MDS space should be thought of only as a convenient reference frame (much like the numbered and lettered grids on street maps). Attribute lines may well take *any* orientation within this grid, and frequently the number of attributes found greatly exceed the number of eigenvectors.

This suggests a fourth common procedure for analysis of the structure of an MDS space. Locating such attribute vectors in the space can be accomplished very simply by capitalizing on the orthogonality constraints on the eigenvectors to yield the regression equation (see Gillham & Woelfel, 1977):

$$A = B_{(1)}R_{(1)}^{\mu} + B_{(2)}R_{(2)}^{\mu} + \cdots + B_{(r)}R_{(r)}^{\mu} \tag{7}$$

where A are the measured scores of the concepts scaled on any attribute scale, $B_{(i)}$ the standardized regression coefficients representing the cosines of the angles between the attribute vector A and the orthogonal $R_{(\alpha)}^{\mu}$ (due to the orthogonality constraint, the B_i are equal to the zero order correlations $r_{AR_{(\alpha)}^{\mu}}$), and $R_{(\alpha)}^{\mu}$ the eigenvectors (factors, axes, dimensions) of the solution. Even this procedure contains important flaws however. Among these are the assumptions implicit in (7) that each attribute or trait is equally salient or relevant for every element of the domain and that each trait is of infinite or at least indefinite length (Cody et al., 1976; Cody, 1976).

Fortunately, a fifth procedure which overcomes these and other problems requires simply that the words which describe traits (e.g., friendly, warm, sharp, unobtrusive, etc.) be included as concepts in the original separation judgments. Line segments between semantic "opposites" (e.g., good–bad) can be taken as finite attributes whose position and orientation vis-á-vis the other concepts in the domain are completely given by the scaling solution itself. Except for the difficulties due to respondent burden and other economic factors which occur when k (the number of concepts scaled) becomes large, this approach seems to be free of the problems inherent in the other methods. This procedure does not require that any empirical parameters be constrained in advance, but rather determines the number, length, and orientation of attributes by measurements.

V. THE COMPARISON OF MULTIDIMENSIONAL SPACES

As interesting and informative as these techniques are, by far the most interesting use of multidimensional scaling is for the comparisons of spaces across groups and across time, since these transformations provide the basis for projections of future events, causal analyses, and ultimately engineering applications.

Since the axes in a multidimensional space have an arbitrary orientation, some scheme of rotation and translation is necessary to "match" the spaces as closely as possible before such comparisons are undertaken. The transformation required is one which will minimize the discrepancy between spaces while leaving the measured distances within each space invariant. These transformations (frequently called "Procrustes" rotations to distinguish them from the analytic rotations—like "varimax" or quartimax"—common in factor analysis) are of great theoretical significance, since they establish a common frame of reference across respondents, observers, and time periods. Alternative choices of such transformations will result in different reference frames which will determine the form of regularities observed (Woelfel, 1977). In its most general form, this problem was solved independently by Cliff (1966) and Schonemann (1966). The general solution involves rotating a matrix of coordinates $R_{(\alpha)}^{\mu}$ at $t + 1$ about its center until the sum of the squared distances of each point in $R_{(\alpha)}^{\mu}$ at $t + 1$ from its counterpart in another space $R_{(\alpha)}^{\mu}$ at t is at a minimum. This transformation conserves position in that it minimizes total motion when t and $t + 1$ refer to times of measurement, or total difference if t and $t + 1$ refer to any arbitrary groups. Whenever two or more scaling solutions—or even factor analyses—are to be compared, Procrustes rotation is *required*; rotating all the spaces to a criterion like varimax or any other analytic solution will not minimize artifactual differences.

Under many circumstances it is desirable to weight these rotations. In an experiment, for example, in which some concepts are manipulated and others controlled, one would try to conserve the position of the unmanipulated concepts, but would expect the manipulated concepts to move freely. Under these conditions, the control concepts should be assigned unity weights and the manipulated concepts should be assigned zeros. Under more complicated conditions—such as those in which concepts were known to be measured with differential reliability—continuous variable weights may be assigned. The key function of these weights is to assign differential stability to the points across the rotations.

Coupled with the idea of rotation is the notion of translation. Translation means parallel displacement of the space, or relocation of the origin of the space. Translations represent changes in viewpoint in the space and are of great theoretical significance. It can easily be shown that distances within each data set remain invariant under both rotation and translation. Solutions to be weighted rotation problem, including translation to different origin, are presented in Woelfel *et al.*, (1979). While the Woelfel *et al.* solution is an iterative solution, it includes translation and is defined over complex coordinates as well as real. A direct, noniterative solution to the weighted Procrustes problem is presented by Lissitz, Schonemann, and Lingoes (1977), but the Lissitz solution does not include translation of origin and is defined only for real coordinates.

VI. COMPARISON OF SPACES: AN EQUALLY WEIGHTED LEAST SQUARES EXAMPLE

For the cross-sectional comparison of nine groups of subjects when comparing the identical concepts and using different criterion pairs (anchors) and different initial metrics (separations), Gordon (1976) used the rotation procedure given above with each concept given an equal weight.

The intent of Gordon's (1976) study was to evaluate whether the ratio judgements of separation scaling model (i.e., scales of the form: "if *a* and *b* are μ units apart, how far apart are *x* and *y*?; Danes and Woelfel, 1975) would yield equivalent solutions when subjects used different criterion pairs with different initial separation values. Four groups were given the larger criterion pair "children's comedy–crime drama" (CC) with an initial separation value of either 10, 25, 50, or 100 units; four groups were given the smaller criterion pair "family drama–medical drama" (FM) with an initial separation value of either 10, 25, 50, or 100 units. The ninth group who rated the identical concepts was instructed to " · · · keep a ten point scale in mind—

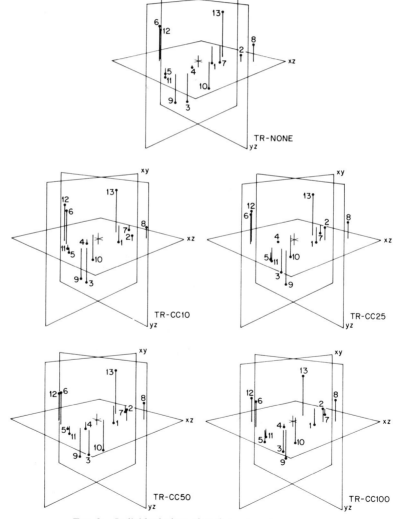

FIG. 2. Individual plots of each treatment.

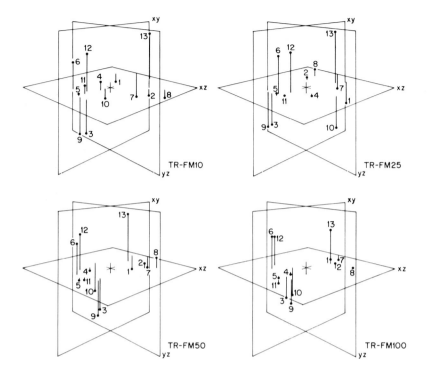

some concepts may be less than ten units apart and others may be more [p. 9]." Group sample size ranged from 92 to 112; a total of 863 subjects participated in their study. Each group rated the separations among the following 13 concepts:

1. Children's comedy
2. Adult situation comedy
3. Soap opera
4. Family drama
5. Medical drama
6. Crime drama
7. Fat Albert
8. All in the Family
9. General Hospital
10. The Waltons
11. Medical Center
12. The Streets of San Francisco
13. Me

On the basis of trace size, i.e., the total variance of each space, the nine matrices were rank ordered from the low 238.98 to high 45,100.99; the following order was obtained: CC10, None, FM10, CC25, FM25, FM50, CC100, and FM100. These results confirmed Gordon's (1976) expectations: (1) that the smaller the separation between the criterion pair, the larger the space (CC > FM), and (2) that the larger the numerical separation metric, the smaller the space. Leaving the "none" treatment out, multidimensional spaces were then computed and rotated to least squares congruence; the plot of these eight spaces appears in Fig. 2. The plot of the three principle planes appears in Fig. 3, the plot of the "none" and the CC10 group appears in Fig. 4.

Aside from the rotation illustration, the Gordon (1976) study illustrated two basic findings important for the ratio judgment of separation measurement procedure: (1) apparently subjects do perceive differential magnitudes of initial metric separations; that is, larger spaces were obtained when the criterion pair was smaller although the number assigned to that criterion pair remained the same; (2) although the spatial structure obtained from the "none" treatment was similar to the spatial stucture obtained from the CC10 treatment, the variance for the "none" group was almost three times as large as that obtained from the CC10 treatment group, a finding which indicates that the use of a criterion pair reduces the potential amount of "noise" in separation judgments as well as supplying a basic metric for the space.

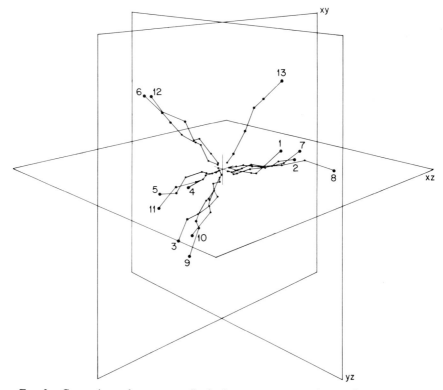

FIG. 3. Comparison of treatments. Beginning at concept number, each point represents the judgment of that concept using a different criterion pair. The order of treatments from outer to inner is: FM100, CC100, FM50, CC50, FM25, CC25, FM10, CC10 ("none" treatment not included, see Fig. 4).

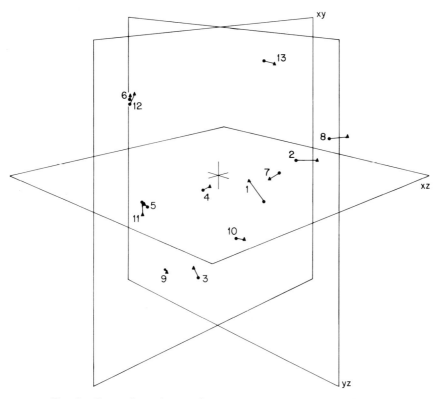

FIG. 4. Comparison of spaces for treatments "none" (▲) and CC10 (●).

VII. COMPARISON OF SPACES: AN UNEQUALLY WEIGHTED EXAMPLE

For the study 42 subjects estimated the separation among concepts using the same ratio judgments procedure used in the Gordon (1976) study; the concepts mapped were

1.	Sleeping	2.	Dreaming
3.	Daydreaming	4.	Intense concentration
5.	Marijuana high	6.	Good
7.	Depression	8.	Alcohol high
9.	Relaxation	10.	CTP
11.	Alpha wave mediation	12.	Transcendental meditation
13.	Reliable	14.	Message Source B
15.	Message Source A	16.	Me

Two days after the first (t_0) measurements were made, the subjects in this study received a letter from a well-known credible source (Source A), who advocated frequent daily practice of CTP, a deliberately undefined fictitious psychological activity—the "cortical thematic pause." After reading the letter from Source A, the subjects were then asked to estimate the concept relations again (t_1). Five days later a similar letter from a less credible source (Source B), who also advocated frequent CTP practice was delivered and the concepts scaled once again (t_2). Finally, a fourth (t_3) wave of data was collected two days later. It was expected that (1) two concepts CTP and Source A should converge after the reception of the first message, and that (2) the three concepts CTP, Source A, and Source B should converge after the reception of the second message. Those concepts not mentioned in either letter were expected to remain invariant.

Using separation matrices that consisted of averaged values for each measurement session, the second space was rotated to the first and in doing so, CTP and Source A were given weights of zero while the remaining concepts were assigned weights of unity. Further, the third space was rotated to the second and in doing so, CTP, Source A, and Source B were assigned weights of zero while the remaining concepts were again assigned unity values. Last, the fourth space was rotated in the same way to the third (see Fig. 5 and Table III). As Fig. 5 shows, at the t_2 measurement there is a triple convergence of Source A (15), the CTP (10), and the Me (16). At the t_3

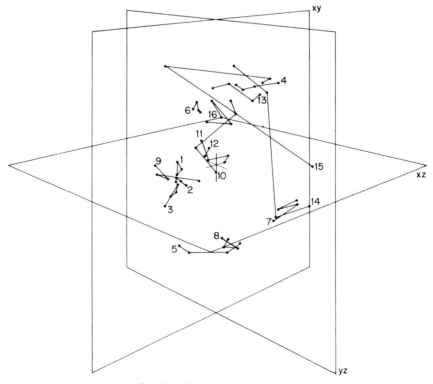

FIG. 5. Stable concepts rotation.

TABLE III

MEAN CHANGE SEPARATION VALUE (MOTION) AS A FUNCTION OF AN
UNEQUALLY WEIGHTED LEAST SQUARES CONCEPT–CONCEPT ROTATION

Concept	$t_0 - t_1$	$t_1 - t_2$	$t_2 - t_3$
(1) Sleeping	20.923	15.752	19.067
(2) Dreaming	14.539	18.902	19.285
(3) Daydreaming	22.033	12.331	17.785
(4) Intense concentration	20.110	17.462	14.972
(5) Marijuana high	21.858	24.396	16.136
(6) Good	30.317	23.736	13.200
(7) Depression	20.354	16.093	12.331
(8) Alcohol high	25.877	11.497	14.937
(9) Relaxation	31.861	16.341	26.256
(10) CTP	56.868[a]	67.708[a]	36.790[a]
(11) Alpha wave meditation	18.728	25.431	12.237
(12) Transcendental meditation	19.175	15.446	16.713
(13) Reliable	22.446	21.220	27.047
(14) Message Source B	27.933	71.548[a]	37.551[a]
(15) Message Source A	124.533[a]	74.952[a]	43.308[a]
(16) Me	24.766	25.259	23.889

[a] Denotes the concepts that were set to weights of zero; i.e., $m_i = 0$.

measure, there is a convergence of Source B (14), Source A (15), and the CTP (10), but a divergence (boomerang effect) of the Me (16). At time four, after no new manipulations, little interpretable motion is evident. (Table III reflects the magnitudes of these motions.) Note especially the small random motion (like Brownian motion) of the unmanipulated concepts. Although substantive interpretations of this experiment are beyond the scope of this chapter the main point is to show how the stable concepts rotation procedure can aid in the interpretation of multidimensional experiments.

VIII. MESSAGE DESIGN SYSTEMS

Among theoretical and applied communication specialists, it is commonly agreed that linking one's message topic with the appropriate message appeals increases the effectiveness of one's communications; but what are the "appropriate" message appeals? This section of this chapter presents a new analytic development for the design of optimum message strategies; that is, within a multidimensional analysis framework, the topic of discussion now turns to procedures designed specifically for the selection of the "best" message appeals for the design of *message content*.

Ego as a Concept

In the example given earlier, the concept "ego" (me, myself, my vote, my position, my purchase, my support, etc.) was mapped into the space as were the other concepts of concern. Within the multidimensional analysis frame-work, the concept "ego" and other such similar concepts appears to have special properties vis-à-vis behavior. In a political mass communication study, for example, Barnett, Serota, and Taylor (1975) have found the political candidate-ego separation to be inversely related to voting behavior; that is, that candidate which was nearest to "ego" received the largest share of the vote in a congressional election. Furthermore, earlier research by market researchers (e.g., Green & Carmone, 1972; Steffler, 1972) has found products nearest to the ego (e.g., my purchase or my choice) yield greater sales than those that are distant from the ego. Additionally, Jones and Young (1972) have found the separation between graduate students and graduate faculty to be predictive of communication frequency, as indicated by the formation of graduate committees.

A reanalysis of the data collected by Danes and Woelfel (1975) revealed a strong association between ego-concept separations and evaluation ($r = .93$) such that those concepts nearest to ego were rated the most favorable. However, Green, Maheshwari, and Rao (1969) did not find support for an ego-concept evaluation association. A casual reading of their work suggests that the lack of an association between preferences and the ego-concept separations may be due to the notion that many of the products scaled were out of economic reach; thus, although the subjects in their study preferred or liked certain products, they may have felt distant from them because they could not afford them. Nonetheless, there is ample empirical evidence indicat-ing that the ego-concept separation relationship is predictive of approach behavior; the message strategy discussed next capitalizes upon this relation-ship.

IX. THEORY

We begin by defining the vector space $R_{(\alpha)}^{\mu}$ where each of the contravariant vectors $R_{(\alpha)}^{\mu}$ represents the projections of the αth concept on a set of covariant (basis) unit vectors e_{μ}. In practice we expect the $R_{(\alpha)}^{\mu}$ to be the result of a multidimensional scaling analysis of a set of proximities data for k concepts where r is the number of dimensions retained. Therefore, we allow α to range over the number of concepts from 1 to k and μ over the number of dimensions from 1 to r.

We further designate the concept to be moved or manipulated (the "start" concept) as $R_{(s)}^{\mu}$ and the ideal point toward which it is to be moved as the "target" concept $R_{(t)}^{\mu}$. The object of the analysis thus becomes one of moving the start concept along the target vector $R_{(t)}^{\mu} - R_{(s)}^{\mu}$. For convenience, we first recenter the coordinate system with the start concept $R_{(s)}^{\mu}$ on the origin by the translation

$$R_{(\alpha)}^{\mu} = \bar{R}_{(\alpha)}^{\mu} - \bar{R}_{(s)} \tag{8}$$

where $R^\mu_{(\alpha)}$ is the position vector of the αth concept after recentering, $\bar{R}^\mu_{(\alpha)}$ the original position vector of the αth concept, $R^\mu_{(\alpha)}$ the original position vector of the concept to be manipulated (the "start" concept), $\alpha = 1, 2, \ldots, k$, and $\mu = 1, 2, \ldots, r$. Since $R_{(s)}$ (by definition the magnitude or length of $R^\mu_{(s)}$) now is zero, the target vector is given by $R^\mu_{(t)}$, which is represented in Fig. 6 as the "target vector."

While our understanding of the dynamics of such spaces is very rudimentary, the original procedure is motivated by a simple dynamic assumption: When two concepts in the space are associated (formally, when they are linked in an assertion of the form "x is y"), they converge relative to one another along the line segment connecting them. (This assumption is motivated solely by assuming each concept will move toward the other by the shortest path.) In Fig. 6, the sentence "the candidate is friendly" should therefore result in a motion of the candidate concept along the vector $R^\mu_{(p)}$ (predicted vector) in Fig. 6. As yet, insufficient data are available to warrant predictions of the magnitude of this motion, but its direction is clearly given from our starting assumption.

Based on this assumption, determination of a single optimal issue may be simply accomplished: First, the angle $\theta_{(p)(t)}$ between any predicted vector $R^\mu_{(p)}$ and the target vector $R^\mu_{(t)}$ can be conveniently calculated as

$$\theta_{(p)(t)} = \cos^{-1}\left[g_{\mu\nu} R^\mu_{(p)} R^\nu_{(t)} / R_{(p)} R_{(t)} \right] \tag{9}$$

where

$$R_{(p)} = |R^\mu_{(p)}| = \left[g_{\mu\nu} R^\mu_{(p)} R^\nu_{(p)} \right]^{1/2} \tag{10}$$

$$R_{(t)} = |R^\mu_{(t)}| = \left[g_{\mu\nu} R^\mu_{(t)} R^\nu_{(t)} \right]^{1/2} \tag{11}$$

and where the quantities $g_{\mu\nu}$ are given by the scalar products of the covariant basis vectors, i.e.,

$$g_{\mu\nu} = e^j_\mu e^j_\nu \tag{12}$$

The $g_{\mu\nu}$ can be shown to be a covariant tensor of the second rank which defines the metric properties of the space and is therefore referred to as the fundamental or metric tensor. If the covariant basis vectors e_μ are real and

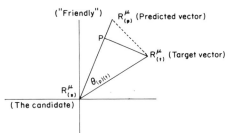

FIG. 6. Hypothetical representation of a multidimensional scaling space.

orthogonal, then the $g_{\mu\nu}$ take on the familiar form

$$g_{\mu\nu} = \delta_\nu^\mu = \begin{cases} 1 & \text{if } \mu = \nu, \\ 0 & \text{if } \mu \neq \nu \end{cases}$$

The numerator of the parenthetical expression in (9) is the tensor notation for the scalar product of $R_{(p)}^\mu$ and $R_{(t)}^\nu$; this alone may be seen as the product of the two vector lengths and the cosine of the angle between them. Dividing through by the vector lengths [given by (10) and (11)] leaves the cosine of the angle between them. That concept whose position vector forms the smallest angle with the target vector will represent the concept which lies most nearly in the *direction* of the "me" or ideal point. The amount of change advocated by this message strategy is given straightforwardly by the length of the predicted vector $R_{(p)}$, which is given by Eq. (10).

Although it is common practice for psychometricians to retain only real eigenvectors or dimensions, it is the prevailing practice of many communication researchers to perform metric analyses of ratio-scaled data averaged over very large samples, and most frequently all or nearly all eigenvectors are retained, including the imaginary eigenvectors (Woelfel, 1977). As we suggested earlier (Section II) these imaginary eigenvectors are the result of violations of the triangle inequalities usually found in empirical data sets. Since these violations occur reliably and frequently, communication researchers are usually unwilling to transform them away by nonmetric procedures, and must, therefore, make provision for them in analytic algorithms such as these.

Where the pth through rth roots are negative (corresponding to imaginary eigenvectors), the $g_{\mu\nu}$ are given by

$$g_{\mu\nu} = \begin{cases} 0 & \text{if } \mu \neq \nu, \\ 1 & \text{if } \mu = \nu < p, \\ -1 & \text{if } \mu = \nu \geqslant p \end{cases} \tag{13}$$

Given these considerations, and Eqs. (9)–(11), we can now solve any part of the triangle $R_{(s)}^\mu R_{(t)}^\mu R_{(p)}^\mu$ in Fig. 6. If the message equating the start concept $R_{(s)}^\mu$ with the concept $R_{(p)}^\mu$ were completely successful such that $R_{(s)}$ moved to $R_{(p)}$, then the distance between the start concept and target concept (after the message) would be given by the distance

$$S_{(pt)} = |R_{(p)}^\mu - R_{(t)}^\mu| \tag{14}$$

Such an outcome is very unlikely in most cases, since we could at best assume the point represented by $R_{(s)}^\mu$ would move only part of the distance toward $R_{(p)}^\mu$. The point P in Fig. 6 represents the orthogonal projection of $R_{(t)}^\mu$ on $R_{(p)}^\mu$ and gives the point of closest approach to $R_{(t)}^\mu$.

The length of this line segment is given by

$$|PR_{(t)}^\mu| = R_{(t)} \sin \theta_{(p)(t)} \tag{15}$$

where $\theta_{(pt)}$ is as given in (9). Similarly, the distance along $R_{(p)}^\mu$ that the start concept must travel to reach P is given by

$$PR^\mu_{(s)} = |PR^\mu_{(s)}| = |PR^\mu_{(t)}|/\tan \theta_{(pt)} \tag{16}$$

The percentage of change advocated that must be achieved for this message to have its maximum effect is given simply by

$$\Delta\% \max = 100|PR^\mu_{(s)}|/R_{(p)} \tag{17}$$

These calculations, along with an empirically measured estimate of the proportion of advocated change actually to be expected, provide ample data on the basis of which the optimal single issue may be chosen.

Multiconcept messages are very easily (and similarly) determined on the basis of an additional assumption: Messages average like vectors in the space. This is equivalent to the assumption that order effects (like primacy-recency) are negligible over the life of the message campaign. Based on this assumption, the position vectors or any two or more issues may simply be averaged to yield a resultant vector given (for two vectors) by

$$R^\mu_{(p)} = (R^\mu_{(\alpha)} + R^\mu_{(\beta)})/2 \tag{18}$$

This resultant vector is then taken as the predicted vector and the procedures just described are repeated.

Equation (18) can easily be generalized for n vector sums, although the number of such combinations of possible messages grows very rapidly as n becomes large.[2]

Evaluation of the degree of success of the message strategy is also simply a matter of determining the angles included between the predicted, target, and observed vectors over the time interval Δt. In practice, however, it is difficult to hold the origin of the space at $t + \Delta t$ precisely where it was at t, and so it is convenient to choose yet a different origin. In our work, we establish an origin at the centroid of the set of concepts not included or implicated in any message, and rotate the t and $t + \Delta t$ spaces to least squares best fit among only those unmanipulated concepts. This procedure may be seen as an effort to use the unmanipulated concepts to determine a stable frame of reference against which the relative motions of the manipulated concepts may be gauged. Time one variables transformed into these stable coordinates will be represented by barred tensors [e.g., $R^\mu_{(s)(t1)} = \bar{R}^\mu_{(s)}$] and time two variables will be represented by hats [e.g., $R^\mu_{(s)(t2)} = \hat{R}^\mu_{(s)}$] as shown in Fig. 7. (The reader should be careful to note that these bars do not mean "means," and the hats do not mean "predicted values" as is common in statistical usage.) Given these definitions we may define the predicted vector across the interval Δt as

$$R^\mu_{(p)} = \bar{R}^\mu_{(s)} - \bar{R}^\mu_{(p)} \tag{19}$$

The target vector across Δt is defined as

$$R^\mu_{(t)} = \bar{R}^\mu_{(t)} - \bar{R}^\mu_{(s)} \tag{20}$$

[2]In practice, the Galileo™ computer program with which we work computes all possible messages with up to four concepts to determine an "optimal message."

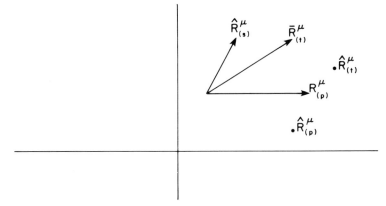

FIG. 7.   Multidimensional scaling space at t and $t + \Delta t$ represented on stable coordinates.

Similarly the observed motion vector is given by

$$R^{\mu}_{(0)} = \hat{R}^{\mu}_{(s)} - \bar{R}^{\mu}_{(s)} \tag{21}$$

Evaluation of the extent to which the start concept has moved as predicted is given simply by the angle between the predicted and observed vector, which is given by

$$\theta_{(p)(0)} = \cos^{-1}(g_{\mu\nu}R^{\mu}_{(p)}R^{\mu}_{(0)}/R_{(p)}R_{(0)}) \tag{22}$$

Also of interest is the extent to which the start concept has moved in the direction of the target, which is given by

$$\theta_{(t)(0)} = \cos^{-1}(g_{\mu\nu}R^{\mu}_{(t)}R^{\mu}_{(0)}/R_{(t)}R_{(0)}) \tag{23}$$

There are further considerations. While these equations are sufficient to indicate the basic structure of the procedures, many valuable modifications can be derived easily by the interested reader. One such example is the unweighted summation of vectors in multiconcept messages given by Eq. (18), which assumes each concept to be equally effective. This assumption may be relaxed by providing weights $\beta_{(\alpha)}$ such that (18) is replaced by

$$R_{(p)} = \sum_{\alpha} \beta_{(\alpha)}R^{\mu}_{(\alpha)} / \sum_{\alpha} \beta_{(\alpha)} \tag{24}$$

where $\beta_{(\alpha)}$ are estimated empirically by the regression equation

$$R^{\mu}_{(0)} = \sum_{\alpha} \beta_{(\alpha)}R^{\mu}_{(\alpha)} + e \tag{25}$$

where e is a least squares error term.

The equations presented here, it may be noted, are all difference equations, reflecting the "before–after" or "treatment–control" designs typical of current practice. Clearly the emphasis on process implicit in this paper suggests a much heavier emphasis on longitudinal designs. When such data sets become available, the transformation of these equations into differential form is straightforward, particularly when orthogonal MDS routines are chosen. Thus the infinitesimal displacement of the start vector $ds_{(s)}$ is given by

$$ds_{(s)} = \left[g_{\mu\nu} \, dR^{\mu}_{(s)} \, dR^{\mu}_{(s)} \right]^{1/2} \qquad (26)$$

where the $dR^{\mu}_{(s)}$ represent coordinate differentials. Similarly, the instantaneous velocity of the start vector at t is given by

$$v_t = ds_{(s)}/dt \qquad (27)$$

and the instantaneous acceleration of the start concept at t is

$$a_t = ds^2_{(s)}/dt^2 \qquad (28)$$

X. THREE-WAY MULTIDIMENSIONAL MODELS

The discussion thus far has focused on the $n \times n$ (where $n =$ the number of concepts) or two-way multidimensional model; now attention is given to the $n \times n \times d$ (where $d =$ the number of data sources) or three-way multidimensional model. This section considers multidimensional analyses which relate data sources, individuals, experimental treatments, groups, etc., to the universe of which they are a part.

These "three-way" models require special treatment because the relationship between the spaces of individuals and an aggregate space made from those of the individuals is not obvious. As Durkheim (1938) suggests:

> Currents of opinion, with an intensity varying according to the time and place, impel certain groups either to more marriages, for example, or to more suicides, or to a higher or lower birthrate, etc. · · · Since each of these figures contain all the individual cases indiscriminately, the individual circumstances which may have had a share in the production of the phenomenon are neutralized. · · · *The average, then, expresses a certain state of group mind* [italics added, p. 10].

Thus, if one is interested in the actions of this aggregate—i.e., who it will vote for, whether or not it will go to war, repress minorities, buy a product, etc., then analyses ought to be performed on an averaged separation matrix.

This aggregate, however, may have properties which are different from the properties (and attributes) of the individuals who comprise it, since, as Durkheim makes clear, aggregation tends to obscure individual or subcultural "points of view." Given two major "points of view" from, for example, racists and nonracists, aggregating the data obtained is likely to produce ambivalence—a viewpoint that is neither racist nor nonracist. From a change over time perspective, if the population or "culture" that the aggregate represents is initially homogeneous (i.e., characterized by a common point of view) and messages are introduced into that culture which polarize them into two groups, the averaged point of view obtained may misleadingly present to the researcher no discernible changes in that culture. The use of the average gives limited and sometimes misleading information regarding the conceptual changes occurring within a collection of individuals *as individuals*.

Individual Differences

One of the first individual difference MDS procedures was supplied by Tucker and Messick (1963), and their model is known as "points of view." In this method, a matrix of observations with rows representing pairwise separation judgments and columns representing individuals is orthogonally decomposed via the Eckart and Young (1963) procedure. The resulting factor space gives the number of "viewpoints" of those subcultures that are relatively homogeneous with respect to the separation judgments of the concepts scaled. A "viewpoint" is a factor (dimension) in the factor space of individuals, and a subculture consists of those individuals with high loadings on this factor.

Presenting a different point of view about "points of view," a number of three-way metric models have been created; the most widely used of these is Carroll and Chang's (1970) INDSCAL.

Carroll and Chang (1970) began the construction of their procedure by assuming that a set of r dimensions underlying the n stimuli are common to each data source, and while assuming commonality, they reasoned that some data sources would use some dimensions for distance judgments among stimuli, that others would not, and that some would differentially weight the dimensions of the common space. Diffferential weighting of a dimension, Carroll and Chang (1970) argued corresponds to the importance or salience of that dimension for a given data source.

The result of INDSCAL is two spaces: a common space and a subject space. The common space is quite similar to an aggregate space obtained by a two-way procedure (with the exception of possible nonorthogonal dimensions and the orientation of the dimensions). The subject space yields coordinate values for each data source which represents their weights on the dimensions of the common space. For each data source, the correlation between the reconstructed separation derived from the "private" space and the original separations is used as a goodness-of-fit measure. For the solution as a whole, the average of these correlations is used.

The INDSCAL solution, however, has some disadvantages. As is typical of psychometric practice, the centrality of the individual is paramount, and INDSCAL implies a set of different spaces, each one of which has an individual at the centroid from which originate a set of (generally oblique) attribute lines of varying length. Differential weighting of attributes is given by differential stretching and shrinking of these attribute lines. What INDSCAL cannot account for, however, are order inversions of concepts across data sources. Consider two hypothetical people who conceive of three concepts that are aligned differently on the *same* attribute. Person 1 conceives the separations shown in Fig. 8a, and person 2 conceives the separations shown in Fig. 8b. A metric analysis for person yields the unidimensional space shown in Fig. 8c, and a metric analysis for person 2 yields the unidimensional space shown in Fig. 8d. However, averaging the separations

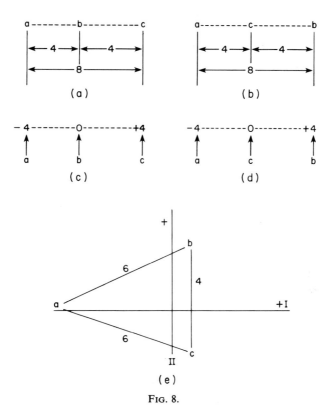

FIG. 8.

for these two individuals, and then analyzing the average $\bar{S}$ matrix does not yield a unidimensional space, as is illustrated in Fig. 8e.

Dimension I of the aggregate space does bear resemblance to the original attribute; however, an additional dimension emerges. In this space, note that no pattern of stretching or shrinking axes can account for this order inversion without the additional dimension. Why this is so can be shown by relaxing the requirement that each space be "subject centered" so that the different data sources may be free to locate at different points in the space as shown in Fig. 9.

Figure 9 shows two observers, x and y, situated among three stimuli, **A**, **B**, and **C**. From the viewpoint of x, these are arrayed along the continuum A_x in the order A, B, C. But to observer y, they appear to be arrayed along the A_y continuum in the order A, C, B. This can only be the case if A, B and C are *not* collinear in the joint space.

Marlier (1976) offers a solution to the "ordinal inversion" problem; the essence of Marlier's approach is the assumption that the aggregate space or cultural perception is "logically prior" to the individual viewpoint, and that individual perceptions (distortions) of the cultural "true" space are accounted

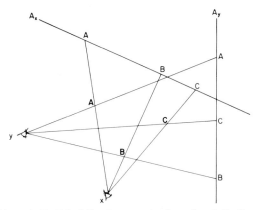

FIG. 9.   Three objects **A**, **B**, **C** (boldface) appear in the order A, B, C to the observer at x, but in the order A, C, B to the observer at y. For the observer at x, A, B, C represent the unidimensional continuum A_x; for the observer at y, A, C, B represent the unidimensional continuum A_y. The joint space, however, is two dimensional.

for by different locations of individuals in the space, much like the view of Tucker and Messick (1963). Given this assumption, Marlier's approach is simple: First, a set of individuals make separation judgments among the n concepts, one of which is "ego." Second all pairwise separation judgments among the $n - 1$ concepts exclusive of "ego" are averaged into an aggregate matrix $\overline{S}$, which is $(n - 1) \times (n - 1)$. Then m additional matrices $S_1, S_2, \ldots, S_m$ are constructed by augmenting $\overline{S}$ by adding the row and column of estimates of each individual's separation of each concept to him or herself. These m matrices are then orthogonally decomposed into multidimensional spaces and then rotated using the unequally weighted rotation procedure described earlier. Weights of zero (0) are assigned to the "egos" and weights of one (1) are assigned to the common, aggregate concepts. The result is one space which portrays the aggregate common concepts along with the individual "points of view"—points which represent the view of each data source (ego). The result is an analytic paradigm which produces an aggregate space in conjunction with potentially differing "points of view."

XI. APPLICATIONS

The MDS procedure may be applied in any situation where a set of objects may be described in terms of the dissimilarities among the members of the set. Any such set may be described by means of some kind of spatial representation, and the number of communication applications which fit this model is quite large. Whenever the reliability of the measures of dissimilarity is high (i.e., random error of measure is small), metric MDS is the appropriate procedure.

Nonmetric procedures may be called for when two conditions are fulfilled: (1) The data are relatively unreliable, i.e., the random component in the measurements is large, and (2) the configuration of the points is known a priori to be Euclidean, that is, the configuration of the domain meets the criteria of additivity, associativity, and triangle inequalities in Section III. This is so because all nonmetric procedures consider any failure of these axioms among the measured values (data) to be solely the result of error of measure, and iteratively and monotonically transform the measured values until they meet the metric axioms as closely as possible. (Differences in the actual monotonic transforming algorithm and differences in the operational definition of "as closely as possible" distinguish the various nonmetric procedures from each other.) If *either* of these conditions is not fulfilled, nonmetric procedures will *introduce* rather than remove error from the resulting configuration. On the other hand, while the metric procedure does not constrain the data to fit the metric axioms, they will yield a metric outcome if the (measured) data themselves fit those axioms. Put yet another way, nonmetric scaling places low confidence in the original measures and, therefore, *forces the solution* to fit the metric axioms; *metric* scaling places high confidence in the metric of the original measures and, therefore, *does not constrain the solution* to fit the metric axioms.

The metric MDS procedure is appropriately used, therefore, whenever the domain of inquiry can be expressed as a relatively reliable matrix of dissimilarities among a set of objects. There are several general classes of problems within the field of communication which meet this model quite well. The intercities distance matrix of Table I is an ideal type of a class of such data where the cities are examples of any node in general (in this case locations) and the distances are examples of some physical measure like distance. Network-type problems (see Farace and Mabee, Chapter 12 of this volume) are a special case of this type, particularly when interaction rates are measured in real (clock) time. Frequencies of interaction can often be measured with high reliability, and there is no reason currently in the literature why the spatial structure of communication networks should be expected to meet the metric axioms (i.e., to constitute a real Euclidean space).

Another generic type of communication domain for which metric MDS can be an effective tool is the domain of cognitive and cultural structures and processes. Cultural or cognitive domains have often been described as sets of objects (concepts, ideas, attributes, etc.) among which people discriminate. A cultural domain which has been investigated carefully in communication is the domain of voting, where the set of objects consists of issues within which are arrayed both candidates and voters (Serota *et al.*, 1977). Linguistics and language behavior constitutes another example in which the domain may be described as a set of symbols which differ in meaning among each other. Once again, estimates of the perceived differences among psychological or cultural objects can frequently be made with good precision, particularly in the case of cultural differences, which can be averaged over a large number of cases. And there is little theoretical basis for the assumption that the structure of cognitive or cultural elements should be Euclidean—in fact most current theory would probably oppose the rationality implicit in such a model.

Special cases of such cultural domains include markets and market segments, where products, services, candidates, etc., may be arrayed among attributes, issues, and other relevant cultural objects. Metric MDS has found important applications in both business and marketing.

Because of the availability of the rotation algorithm for least squares matching of spaces, metric MDS has found important comparative applications within all these domains. Quantitative measures of the similarity of multiple communication networks, for example, are straightforward, and comparisons of subcultures (e.g., male–female, black–white) or cultures are similarly made by means of the least squares rotation algorithm. Metric MDS has thus found important applications in cross-cultural communications.

Since the same procedures apply as well to multiple times of measure (as well as cross-group comparison) metric MDS has been used extensively for longitudinal or *kinematic* studies. Thus changes in communication networks, cultural beliefs, market opinions, and so on, have been extensively analyzed by metric MDS procedures. Whenever ongoing processes are interrupted or modified by some treatment (such as television viewing, or political debates, etc.), effects may be observed by means of metric MDS, and several such studies have been done (Stoyanoff; Barnett). Since processes are central to communication, the range of application is very wide.

When hypotheses about motion are added to process or kinematic MDS studies, *dynamic* models emerge, and such models have engineering applications in both prediction of future states or processes (like elections, cultural changes, changes in structure of communication networks) and active intervention in those processes. Thus the message generation model described in Section VIII has found useful application in marketing and political campaigning as well as in theoretical studies of the dynamics of cultural change (Cody, 1977) and attitude formation (Gillham & Woelfel, 1977).

ACKNOWLEDGMENTS

We are grateful for the assistance of Peter Monge, Joseph Cappella, John Tukey, John Hunter, Robert Norton, Edward L. Fink, James H. Watt, Bob Krajcik, and Ray Cirmo in the writing of this chapter, and to the Department of Communication at Michigan State University, the Department of Speech at the University of Connecticut, and the Communication Institute at the East-West Center, Honolulu, Hawaii, for assistance in the preparation of this manuscript. The authors are solely responsible for any errors.

References

Anderson, N., and Hovland, C. The representation of order effects in communication research. In C. Hovland (Ed.), *The order of Presentation in persuasion*. New Haven, Connecticut: Yale Univ. Press, 1957.

Anderson, N. Linear models for response measured on a continuous scale. *Journal of Mathematical Psychology*, 1964, 1, 121–142.

Anderson, N. H. Primacy effects in personality impression formation. *Journal of Personality and Social Psychology*, 1965, 2, 1–9.

Anderson, N. Information integration and attitude change. *Psychological Review*, 1971, **78**, 171–206.

Barnett, G., Serota, L., and Taylor, J. Campaign communication and attitude change: A multidimensional analysis. *Human Communication Research*, 1975, in press.

Barnett, G., and Woelfel, J. On the dimensionality of psychological processes, *Quality and Quantity*, 1978.

Blumenthal, N. *A modern view of geometry*. San Francisco, California: Freeman, 1961.

Carroll, J., and Chang, J. Analysis of individual differences in multidimensional scaling via and N-way generalization of Eckart-Young decomposition. *Psychometrika*, 1970.

Carroll, J., and Chang, J. *IDIOSCAL (individual differences in orientation scaling): A generalization of INDSCAL allowing indiosyncratic reference systems as well as an analytic approximation to INDSCAL*. Paper presented at the Annual Meeting of the Psychometric Society, Princeton, New Jersey, March 1972.

Carroll, J., and Wish, M. Multidimensional perceptual models and measurement methods. In E. C. Carterette and M. P. Friedman (Eds.), *Handbook of Perception*. Vol. 2. New York: Academic Press, 1974. Pp. 291–337. (a)

Carroll, J., and Wish, M. Models and methods for three-way multidimensional scaling. In D. H. Krantz *et al.* (Eds.), *Contemporary developments in mathematical psychology*. San Francisco, California: Freeman, 1974. Pp. 57–105. (b)

Cliff, N. Orthogonal rotation to congruence. *Psychometrika*, 1966, **31**, 33–42.

Cliff, N. The "idealized individual" interpretation of individual differences in multidimensional scaling. *Psychometrika*, 1968, **33**, 335–233.

Cody, M. *An application of the multiple attribute measurement model: Measurement and manipulation of source credibility*. Unpublished MA thesis, Michigan State Univ., East Lansing, Michigan, 1976.

Cody, M., Marlier, J., and Woelfel, J. *An application of the multiple attribute measurement model: Measurement and manipulation of source credibility*. Paper presented to the Annual Meeting of the Mathematical Psychology Convention, Lafayette, Indiana, 1976.

Cody, M., Marlier, J., and Woelfel, J. *An application of the multiple attribute measurement model: Measurement and manipulation of source credibility*. Paper presented to the Annual Meeting of the Mathematical Psychology Convention, Lafayette, Indiana, 1976.

Danes, J. *Message repetition and accumulated information: Meaningfulness as a measure of "inertial mass" for communication research*. Unpublished Manuscript, Department of Communication, Michigan State Univ. East Lansing, Michigan, 1975.

Danes, J., Hunter, J., and Woelfel, J. Belief change as a function of accumulated information. Submitted to *Human Communication Research*, 1976.

Danes, J., and Woelfel, J. *An alternative to the 'traditional' scaling paradigm in mass communication research: Multidimensional reduction of ratio judgments of separation. Paper presented to the International Communication Association Annual Meeting, Chicago, Illinois, April 1975.*

Day, G. Theories of attitude structure and change. In S. Ward and T. Robertson (Eds.), *Consumer behavior: Theoretical sources*: Englewood Cliffs, New Jersey: Prentice Hall, 1973.

Durkheim, E. *Rules of the sociological method*. Chicago, Illinois: Univ. of Chicago Press, 1938.

Eckart, C., and Young, G. The approximation of one matrix by another of lower rank. *Psychometrika*, 1963, 211–218.

Einstein, A. *Relativity*. Crown, New York, 1961.

Engle, J., and Light, M. The role of psychological commitment in consumer behavior: An evaluation of the role of cognitive dissonance. In F. Bass, C. King, and E. Pessemier (Eds.) *Applications of the sciences in marketing management*, New York: Wiley, 1968.

Fishbein, M., and Ajzen, I. *Beliefs, attitude, intention, and behavior*. Reading, Massachusetts: Addison-Wesley, 1975.

French, J. A formal theory of social power. *Psychological Review*, 1956, **63**, 181–194.

Fletcher, R., and Powell, M. A rapidly converging descent method for minimization. *Computer Journal*, 1963, **2**, 163–168.

Gillham, J., and Woelfel, J. *The Galileo system of measurement*. Human Communication Research, 1977.

Gordon, T. F. *Subject abilities to use metric MDS: Effects of varying the criterion pair*. Paper presented to the International Communication Association, Portland, Oregon, 1976.

Green, P., and Carmone, F. Marketing research application of nonmetric scaling methods. In K. Romney, R. Shepard, and S. Nerlove, *Multidimensional scaling*. Vol. 2, applications. New York: Seminar Press, 1972.

Green, P., Maheshwari, A., and Rao, V. Self concept and brand preferences: An empirical application of multidimensional scaling. *Journal of the Market Research Society*, 1969, **11**, 343–360.

Guttman, L. A general nonmetric technique for finding the smallest coordinate space for a configuration of points. *Psychometrika*, 1968, **33**, 469–506.

Harman, H. *Modern factor analysis*. Chicago, Illinois: Univ. of Chicago Press, 1967.

Harshman, R. *PARAFAC 2: Mathemaical and technical notes*. Univ. of California, Los Angeles, working papers in phonetics 22, March 1972.

Horan, C. Multidimensional scaling: Combining observations when individuals have different perceptual structures. *Psychometrika*, 1969, **34**, 139–165.

Hotelling, H. Analysis of a complex of statistical variables into principal components. *Journal of Educational Psychology*, 1933, **24**, 499–520.

Hunter, J., and Cohen, S. *Mathematical models of attitude change in the passive communication context*. Unpublished Book, Department of Psychology, Michigan State Univ. 1972.

Jones, L., and Young, F. Structure of a social environment: Longitudinal individual difference scaling for an intact group. *Journal of Personality and Social Psychology*, 1972, **24**, 108–121.

Klahr, D. A Monte Carlo investigation of the statistical significance of Kruskal's nonmetric scaling procedure. *Psychometrika*, 1969, **34**, 319–330.

Krippendorff, K. Values, modes, and domains of inquiry into communication. *Journal of Communication*, 1969, **19**, 105–133.

Kruskal, J. Multidimensional scaling by optimizing goodness of fit to a nonmetric hypothesis. *Psychometrika*, 1964, **29**, 1–27. (a)

Kruskal, J. Nonmetric multidimensional scaling: A numerical method. *Psychometrika*, 1964, **29**, 115–129. (b)

Kruskal, J. and Carroll, J. Geometric models and badness-of-fit functions. In P. R. Krishnaiah (Ed.), *Multivariate analysis II*. New York: Academic Press, 1969. Pp. 639–670.

Lingoes, J. A general survey of the Guttman-Lingoes nonmetric program series. In *Multidimensional scaling: Theory and applications in the behavioral sciences*, R. Shepard, A. Romney, and S. Nerlove (Eds.), Vol, I, Theory. New York: Seminar Press, 1972. Pp. 49–68.

Lissitz, R., Shonemann, P., and Lingoes, J. A solution to the weighted procrustes problem in which the transformation is in agreement with the loss function. *Psychometrika*, 1956, **21**, 1–17.

McGee, V. Multidimensional scaling of *N* sets of similarity measures: A nonmetric individual differences approach. *Multivariate Behavioral Research*, 1968, **3**, 233–248.

Pieszko, H. *Multidimensional scaling in Riemann space*. Unpublished doctoral dissertation, Department of Psychology, Univ. of Illinois at Urbana-Champaign, 1970.

Reeves, B. *A multidimensional analysis of children's perceptions of television characters.* Unpublished doctoral dissertation, Department of Communication, 1975.

Richardson, M. Multidimensional psychophysics. *Psychological Bulletin*, 1938, **35**, 659–660.

Rokeach, M. *Belief attitudes and values.* San Francisco, California: Jossey-Bass, 1958.

Rosenberg S., and Sedlak, A. Structural representations of perceived personality trait relationships. In A. K. Rumney, R. N. Shephard, and S. Nerlove (Eds.), *Multidimensional Scaling: Theory and Applications*, In the behavioral sciences, Vol. 2, Applications. New York: Seminar Press, 1972.

Saltiel, J., and Woelfel, J. Inertia in cognitive processes: The role of accumulated information in attitude change. *Human Communication Research*, 1975, **1**, 333–344.

Schmidt, C. Multidimensional scaling analysis of the printed media's explanation of the riots of the summer of 1967. *Journal of Personality and Social Psychology*, 1972, **24**, 59–67.

Schonemann, P., and Carroll, R. Fitting one matrix to another under choice of a central dilation and a rigid motion. *Psychometrika*, 1970, **35**, 245–255.

Scott, W. Attitude measurement. In G. Lindzey and E. Aronson (Eds.), *Handbook of social psychology*, Reading, Massachusetts: Addison-Wesley, 1968.

Serota, D. *Metric multidimensional scaling and communication: Theory and implementation.* Unpublished Master's Thesis, Michigan State Univ., 1974.

Serota, K., Cody, M., Barnett, G., and Taylor, J. Precise procedures for optimizing campaign communication. In R. Brent (Ed.), *Communication yearbook I*, Transaction Books, 1977. Pp. 475–494.

Shepard, R. Analysis of proximities: Multidimensional scaling with an unknown distance function. I. *Psychometrika*, 1962, **27**, 125–140. (a)

Shepard, R. Analysis of proximities: Multidimensional scaling with an unknown distance function. II. *Psychometrika*, 1962, **27**, 219–246. (b)

Shepard, R. Introduction to Volume I. In R. N. Shepard, A. K. Romney, and S. B. Nerlove (Eds.), *Multidimensional scaling: Theory and applications in the behavioral sciences*, Vol. I, Theory. New York: Seminar Press, 1972. Pp. 1–20.

Sherman, C. Nonmetric multidimensional scaling: A Monte Carlo study of the basic parameters. *Psychometrika*, 1972, **37**, 323–355.

Spence, I. A Monte Carlo evaluation of three nonmetric multidimensional scaling algorithms. *Psychometrika*, 1972, **37**, 461–486.

Stefflre, V. Some applications of multidimensional scaling to social science problems. In K. Romney, R. Shepard, and S. Nerlove (Eds.), *Multidimensional scaling*, Vol. 2, applications. New York: Seminar Press, 1972.

Torgerson, W. Multidimensional scaling: I. Theory and method. *Psychometrika*, 1952, **17**, 401–419.

Torgerson, W. *Theory and methods of scaling.* New York: Wiley, 1958.

Tucker, L. Relations between multidimensional scaling and three-mode factor analysis. *Psychometrika*, 1972, **37**, 3–27.

Tucker, L., and Messick, S. Individual difference model for multidimensional scaling. *Psychometrika*, 1963, **28**, 333–367.

Van Eeden, C. Maximum likelihood estimation of partially or completely ordered parameters. I. *Proceedings, Akademie van Wetenschappen, Series A*, 1957, **60**, 128–136. (a)

Van Eeden, C. Note on two methods for estimating ordered parameters of probability distrubutions. *Proceedings, Akademie van Wetenschappen, Series A*, 1957, **60**, 506–512. (b)

Whittaker, J. Resolution of the communication discrepancy issue in attitude change. In Carolyn W. Sherif and Muzafor Sherif (Eds.) *Attitude, ego-involvement, and change.* New York: Wiley, 1967, Pp. 159–177.

Wish, M. *An INDSCAL to studies analysis of the Miller-Nicely consonant confusion data.* Paper presented at the Annual Meeting of the Acoustical Society of American, Houstan, Texas, November 1970.

Wish, M., and Carroll, J. Applications of INDSCAL to studies of human perception and judgment. In E. C. Carterette and M. P. Friedman (Eds.), *Handbook of perception*, Vol. 2. New York: Academic Press, 1974. Pp. 449–491.

Woelfel, J. *Procedures for the precise measurement of cultural processes*. Unpublished manuscript, Department of Communication, Michigan State Univ., 1973.

Woelfel, J. *Metric measurements of cultural processes*. Paper presented to the Annual Meeting of the Speech Communication Association, Chicago, Illinois, 1974.

Woelfel, J. In D. P. Cushman (Ed.), *Foundations of cognitive theory*. 1977.

Woelfel, J., and Haller, A. Significant others, the self-reflexive act, and the attitude formation process. *American Sociological Review*, 1971, **36**, 74–87.

Woelfel, J., and Saltiel, J. *Cognitive processes as motions in a multidimensional space: A general linear model*. Unpublished manuscript, Department of Communication, Michigan State Univ., 1974.

Woelfel, J., Holmes, R., and Kincaid, D. L., *Orthogonal rotation to congruence for general riemann spaces*. Paper presented at 2nd Annual Workshop on Multidimensional Scaling, International Communication Association Annual Meeting, Chicago, Illinois, 1979.

Wold, H. Estimation of principle components and related models by interactive least squares. In P. R. Krishnaiah (Ed.), *Multivariate Analysis*. New York: Academic Press, 1966.

Young, F. Nonmetric multidimensional scaling: Recovery of metric information. *Psychometrika*, 1970, **35**, 445–473.

Young, G. and Householder, A. Discussion of a set of points in terms of their mutual distances. *Psychometrika*, 1938, **3**, 19–22.

Chapter 12

COMMUNICATION NETWORK ANALYSIS METHODS

RICHARD V. FARACE AND TIMOTHY MABEE*
Department of Communication
Michigan State University
East Lansing, Michigan

I. INTRODUCTION

The concept of a "communication network" has multiple origins in the broader literature on social networks. In sociometry, Moreno (1934) first interpreted patterns of social preferences between individuals as representing a network of human relations. Bavelas (1951) reported Leavitt's experiments in manipulating the communication channels of a small group. Bales (1950) measured the frequency of channel use in natural group interaction.

Some years later, Barnes (1972) described the conceptual and pragmatic importance of networks in anthropology, and Bott (1971) used anthropological methods to trace and compare the different interpersonal networks of

*Present Address: Office of Institutional Research, Michigan State University, East Lansing, Michigan

MULTIVARIATE TECHNIQUES
IN HUMAN COMMUNICATION RESEARCH

husbands and wives. Research in organizational communication has examined the relationship of communication network properties to such variables as morale and satisfaction (Shaw, 1964; Wigand, 1974a; Danowski & Farace, 1974).

The preceding examples show the generality of the concept of networks of social relations. Many of the techniques discussed in this chapter can be applied to a variety of social relations data; however, the examples and terminology used here will focus on communication relations.

Interest in the concept of networks of social relations, including networks of communication relations among people, implies a recognition of the complexity of social phenomena; a "network" is essentially a multivariate concept, requiring multivariate analytic techniques to reduce what are often large collections of data to a small number of network properties. Festinger, Schachter, and Back (1950) observe, "Without an adequate representational technique of handling such data the analysis of the exact patterns of interconnections among members of a group is virtually impossible unless the group is very small" [p. 132].

Monge and Day (1976) distinguish between two distinct kinds of multivariate approaches to complex data. The first approach uses *multivariate dependence models* of the data. A distinguishing feature of dependence models is the division of the variables into independent and dependent sets. The results are in the form of *predictions* of the dependent variable values, given the independent values. The second approach uses multivariate *inter*dependence models, or data reduction models. Here, no distinction is made among the variables; instead, the goal of the analysis is "to identify underlying simple structures which can parsimoniously represent the complexity in the data" [pp. 208–209]. The results usually consist of relatively few parameters which describe essential features of the data.

Krippendorff (1972) calls such an analytic device "explicit simplification procedures" and points out that these procedures are comparable to the processes of verbal–conceptual abstraction: Data of great complexity are reduced to a few simple concepts of practical utility.

Network analysis belongs in the second category of multivariate analysis. Its value lies in (1) its *replicability*, a property not shared by intuitive conceptual processes and (2) the *utility* of the resulting simplification in predicting other social phenomena. Thus, the value of network analysis in understanding complex social phenomena depends not only on the rigor of the analytic procedure, but also on the uses found for the simplified representation of social structure produced by the analysis.

A variety of analytic procedures which can be applied to network data are reviewed here and attempts are made to evaluate their usefulness for illustrating the complexity of human communication affairs. Special attention will be paid to the major network properties measured or implied by each procedure, because these properties must ultimately take their place in a theory of social structure if the network concept is to evolve as fruitfully as its intuitive appeal suggests it could.

II. BASIC CONCEPTS

Some general definitions will be helpful for comparing different multivariate analytic techniques that apply to networks. First, the entities composing the network will be called *nodes*. In many applications, the nodes of the network are people, but investigators have also studied the networks of relationships among groups (Danowski & Farace, 1974), organizations (Wigand, 1974b; Wigand & Larkin, 1975), among academic publications (Small, 1974a), and among generalized role categories (Burt & Lin, 1977). Many other interesting applications are conceivable.

The measured relationships between individual nodes will be called *links*. Links are usually specified between *pairs* of nodes. If the relationship represented by a link is bidirectional or symmetric (e.g., a correlation), there is one potential link for every pair of nodes in the network. If the relationship is *asymmetric*, like a sociometric choice, there are two potential links for every pair of nodes. Hence, if a network has N nodes, it has $N(N-1)/2$ symmetric pairwise links or $N(N-1)$ asymmetric links.

Links have been measured at each of Stevens' (1951) four levels of measurement: nominal (the relationship is present or absent), ordinal (rank of the frequency or importance of the relationship for the initiating or receiving node), interval, and ratio (strength or amount of the relationship). Occasionally, nonlinear measures are also used, such as correlations, which form polar scales.

The values of links may be measured directly or derived from other measurements. When the nodes are individuals, the most common direct measurement technique is to obtain reports from the individuals within the boundaries of the intended network. Bott (1971), for example, used face-to-face interviews with family members to gather information on their respondents' contacts with other persons. Jacobson and Seashore (1951) provided respondents with a list of potential network members and asked each person on the list to evaluate the frequency and importance of their contact with every other person. Conrath (1972) asked members of an organization to keep diaries of their communication contacts with other members. Unobtrusive measures (see, e.g., Martin & Ackoff, 1961) and mechanical means (Killworth & Bernard, 1976) have also been used to assess directly the links between network nodes.

Link measures derived from other data include correlations or other associational measures that are applied to cross-sectional data on the traits or activities of nodes. For example, Phillips and Conviser (1972) treated nodes (persons) as variables and assessed the strength of their relationships based on their co-participation in 14 social activities. Similarly, Griffith *et al.* (1974) measured the relationships between pairs of scientific publications as a function of the number of times each pair was cited together in another publication. Burt and Lin (1977) analyzed the content of newspaper articles for the co-occurrence of "actors," assigning each co-occurrence a weight based on the number of column inches devoted to the relationship, and adding the weighted co-occurrence to measure link strength.

It is often convenient and useful to distinguish several types of relationships between the nodes of a network. In Jacobson and Seashore's questionnaire, for instance, respondents separately reported their contacts on each of several topics, as well as specifying the medium of communication. Thus, each pair of nodes has not one but potentially several distinct types of links between it.

Networks analytic procedures which maintain distinctions between types of links are called *polythetic*, while those which use only a single type of link are called *monothetic* networks. Procedures which combine links of different types into one single type by simple or weighted averaging must be considered monothetic. No method of handling multiple types of links in a single analysis is now known to the authors; the development of a truly polythetic network procedure would be a major contribution to the methodology of network analysis.

A convenient way of arraying the pairwise links of a network is in the form of a square matrix, S, with each element s_{ij} corresponding to the link from the ith to the jth node. The values of the diagonal elements, s_{ii}, may be either 1, 0, or some other value, depending on the requirements of a particular analytic procedure. If the relationship represented by the links is symmetric, the resulting matrix is also symmetric. The matrix representation of links is attributed to Forsyth and Katz (1946). It is isomorphic with the graph representation used by Moreno. Table I and Fig. 1 show equivalent matrix and graphic representations of a network of three nodes using ratio-scaled asymmetric links.

TABLE I

HYPOTHETICAL LINK STRENGTH MATRIX

Respondent	Chosen nodes		
nodes	1	2	3
1	X	1	0
2	5^a	X	0
3	0	3	X

[a]Strength is the frequency of communication per week.

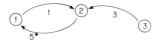

FIG. 1. Hypothetical sociogram corresponding to Table I. *Strength is the frequency of communications per week.

III. NETWORK PROPERTIES

The common goal of all network analytic procedures is to decipher the underlying structure implied by a particular link matrix. This general goal can be reached (or at least approached) by many different routes. Most procedures for network analysis are primarily directed towards decomposing the network into groupings or cliques of highly associated nodes.[1] In using these procedures, the investigator characterizes network structure by the number and size of cliques present and qualifies nodes in terms of their participation in cliques.

The criteria for detecting cliques are not well agreed upon and tend to vary considerably across procedures for network analysis. Most analytic methods, however, at least implicitly include some measure of the total amount of cohesion or structure in a subset of nodes as one criterion for the presence of a clique. When these measures are reported along with the clique membership results, the analysis becomes more useful, because it is possible not only to compare cliques within a network, and to compare entire networks quantitatively with regard to this fundamental property of amount of structure, but also to predict nonnetwork variables, such as homogeneity of beliefs and attitudes (e.g., Danowski & Farace, 1974) from measures of network structure. Various approaches to defining indices for the amount of network structure in terms of a link matrix are now discussed.

Regardless of whether a particular investigation or procedure emphasizes the detection of cliques or the quantification of structure, or employs a combination of these two methods for representing social structure, the properties revealed by network analysis procedures can be broken into three broad categories:

(1) properties of the *network as a whole*, including total amount of structure and various indications of the homogeneity of structure throughout the network. The latter property includes information about the number and size of detectable cliques, as well as the distribution of clique and node properties.

(2) properties of subnetworks such as *groups* or *cliques*, including the amount of structure binding the members of each clique, and the number of

---

[1]See Holland and Leinhardt (1975) and the discussion of Coleman's (1964) procedure that follows for exceptions.

members in each clique, and indicators of the relationship of each clique with other parts of the network.

(3) properties of the subnetworks associated with each individual *node*, including the role of the node in the network (e.g., whether or not the node is a clique member), and the amount of structure binding each node with others in the network.

Since clique detection methods are in general based upon some index of structure, we shall assume for the moment that cliques have been specified and proceed to review several alternative measures of their structure. This discussion applies equally well to the structure of the entire network but requires some modification when individual nodes are the focus.

A. Clique or Network Structure Measures

One of the most satisfactory indices of clique or network structure, from a statistical point of view, is Coleman's (1964) h_1 measure of "hierarchization" for an asymmetric binary link matrix. The observed distribution of links is compared with the distribution expected if the links were to occur randomly. Coleman suggests, however, that measures which take into account only the distribution of links will by definition not operationalize other important aspects of the network which "may be of most importance for theoretical concerns." He recommends, as an alternative, the "connectedness" of the network—the ratio of nonzero links to the total number of *possible* links—on the basis of work by Luce and Perry (1949).

This measure can then extend to indirect, multistep links: If a link matrix containing only ones and zeros is multiplied by itself, the result is a matrix containing the number of two-step paths from the ith node to the jth node, for all nodes. The ratio of the sum of these numbers to the number of possible two-step paths gives the two-step connectedness of the network. Coleman suggests continuing the multiplication operation until no new paths are added by the next multiplication. A summary measure of the connectedness density of a network therefore becomes the ratio of actually connected nodes to the total number of multistep connections possible.

When metric-level information is available in the link matrix, other measures of clique or network structure can be computed. A metric matrix is readily conceivable in spatial terms (Woelfel & Danes, 1977), suggesting *volume* as a measure of the structure in any subset of nodes. In a spatial representation, strong links are specified by *small* distances in the matrix, so volume is an inverse measure of structure.

Comparison across networks requires the use of a common or standardized unit of measurement for the links. Volume is not, however, a standardized measure of link connectedness. Volume depends not only on the unit used for measuring distances between nodes but also on the number of nodes. For comparisons across networks and groups of different size, a derivative measure, *density*, can be used. Density is defined as the number of nodes per unit volume. Further development of these concepts is needed to produce easily calculable indices that can be validated.

B. Measures of Node Properties

The simplest way of characterizing the network properties of individual nodes is to take the average number or strength of links to and from each node. These measures, like the hierarchization measure previously discussed, can be broadened to reflect other aspects of the subnetworks associated with each node. One alternative, which corresponds closely with the connectedness measure for cliques and networks, was proposed and implemented by Richards (1974c). Called "integrativeness," it measures the one-step connectedness density of those specific nodes that are directly linked with the starting node. The integrativeness of a node has a value of 0.0 when none of the nodes which are linked with the starting node are linked with each other and has a value of 1.0 when the nodes connected with the starting node are completely interlinked at the one-step level.

The metric equivalent of integrativeness is the density of nodes within a fixed radius of the target node.

The detection of cliques in a network makes it possible to characterize individual nodes in terms of their specific *roles* in the network. For most applications of network results, it is desirable to arrive at an unambiguous assignment of the clique membership role of each node, because the role of nodes then becomes a useful variable for analyses which relate network properties with other characteristics of the nodes (see, e.g., Wigand, 1974a). It also seems advisable to allow for nodes to be member of no clique, at least when it is possible for a node to have no links. Finally, special roles may be assigned to nodes which have many links to more than one clique, thus serving as *bridges* and *liaisons* between cliques (see Richards, 1974a; Farace, Monge, & Russell, 1977).

Finer investigation of the role of individual nodes within cliques has also been pursued. MacKenzie (1966) has argued for the importance of a measure of the centrality of individuals in a small group, defining this index in terms of the distribution of links with other individuals. A similar measure in spatially represented networks is the distance of each node from the center of the clique, defined as the vector addition of distances to all other nodes in the clique.

IV. CLIQUE DETECTION PROCEDURES

The general lack of agreement about the criteria for the detection of cliques in networks has a legitimate basis in the variety of existing conceptions and theoretic representations of social structure. Regrettably, the underlying assumptions are often left implicit and must be inferred from the measurement and data reduction operations performed. It is beyond the scope of this paper to provide the inferences and make the connections with communication theory, or with sociological and social psychological theory, of the major clique detection techniques. However, we shall focus, albeit briefly, on the measurement requirements and salient features of the operations performed in several currently used procedures. In various applications, different conceptions and criteria may be appropriate; for the purpose of this review, the important factors are (1) whether the criteria are well defined and (2) whether they appear to lead to interesting and potentially useful interpretations of cliques in terms of some research questions.

Major differences in clique criteria exist between the nominal procedures, which characterize the sociometric research tradition (for instance, a node usually may be a member of only one clique), and spatial procedures (where multiple clique membership may be allowed). Within these two broad categories of procedures, differences in the meaning of clique arise because of variations in detection and clustering methods, and because of different methods for measuring links. Because of the many ways in which procedures can vary, direct comparisons and judgments of relative merit are difficult, but contrasts will be drawn whenever they seem appropriate.

In addition to detecting cliques and providing measures of structural properties for the whole network, for cliques, and for individual nodes, a procedure for network analysis is particularly useful in a practical sense if it can accommodate data with many nodes and produce results at low cost. In describing specific procedures, we shall try to indicate typical network size limitations for available computer implementations. Processing costs vary widely with computer installations and, for some procedures, with network properties as well, so it is not feasible to give cost estimates.

A. Nominal Clique-Detection Procedures

The simplest link-strength matrix is a binary matrix, containing only a 1 or 0 in each cell to indicate the presence or absence of a relationship between the nodes. Initial work on discovering cliques of highly interconnected nodes in such data was reported by Luce and Perry (1949) and Luce (1950) and described and applied to social networks by Festinger et al. (1950). Luce and Perry (1949) provide the following definition of a clique: "A subset of the group forms a *clique* provided that it consists of three or more members each in a symmetric relation to each other member of the subset, and provided further that there can be found no element outside the subset that is in a symmetric relation to each of the elements of the subset" [p. 97]. Nodes may be members of more than one clique.

In Fig. 2, nodes 1–4 are clique members under the Luce and Perry definition, since each is connected to all other nodes in the clique by a symmetric link.

FIG. 2. Artificial symmetric network. Numbers in circles are nodes; lines indicate links between nodes.

Luce and Perry show that it is possible to determine which nodes are members of some clique as follows: (1) Make the link strength matrix symmetric by deleting unreciprocated links; (2) raise the symmetrized strength matrix to the third power (its cube); and (3) examine the main diagonal of the cubed matrix. Nodes corresponding to nonzero diagonal elements are members of cliques.

Table II shows the symmetric link matrix for the network in Fig. 2. The cube of the matrix is shown in Table III. Note in Table III that the only nonzero diagonal elements in Table III correspond to nodes 1–4, i.e., the "group" under the Luce and Perry definition.

However, Luce and Perry's procedure does *not* allow the investigator to determine precisely how many cliques there are, nor which nodes are members of which particular cliques. In simple cases, these goals can be accomplished by reviewing the symmetrized strength matrix for the specific patterns of symmetric relationships between nodes which are known to be members of cliques. A more serious difficulty with this approach (recognized by Luce and Perry) is that more complex or less complete structures cannot be considered cliques. For instance, sets of nodes which meet the criteria except for a few unreciprocated or missing links are excluded, by definition. Nodes 6–9 in Fig.

TABLE II
SYMMETRIC LINK MATRIX FOR ARTIFICIAL NETWORK[a]

	Node								
Node	1	2	3	4	5	6	7	8	9
1	—	1	1	1	0	0	0	0	0
2	1	—	1	1	0	0	0	0	0
3	1	1	—	1	1	0	0	0	0
4	1	1	1	—	0	0	0	0	0
5*	0	0	1	0	—	0	1	0	0
6	0	0	0	0	0	—	1	1	0
7	0	0	0	0	1	1	—	0	1
8	0	0	0	0	0	1	0	—	1
9	0	0	0	0	0	0	1	1	—

[a]This matrix corresponds exactly to the network diagram in Fig. 2. 1 indicates the presence of a link, 0 the absence of a link. The blocks indicate groupings of nodes (which may or may not be cliques, depending on the definition used). Node 5 links the two blocks.

TABLE III
CUBE OF LINK MATRIX FOR ARTIFICIAL NETWORK[a]

Node	Node								
	1	2	3	4	5	6	7	8	9
1	6	7	8	7	2	0	1	0	0
2	7	6	8	7	2	0	1	0	0
3	8	8	6	8	5	1	0	0	1
4	7	7	8	6	2	0	1	0	0
5	2	2	5	2	0	0	4	2	0
6	0	0	1	0	0	0	5	4	0
7	1	1	0	1	4	5	0	0	5
8	0	0	0	0	2	4	0	0	4
9	0	0	1	0	0	0	5	4	0

[a]Nodes 1–4 are nonzero on the diagonal, indicating clique membership; while nodes 5–9 are zero, indicating no clique membership.

2 and Table II have such a structure, since the addition of links between nodes 7 and 8 or between 6 and 9 would satisfy the connectedness criterion. For many purposes, it would be useful to be able to investigate the clique properties of looser groups than the one shown in Fig. 2.

Luce (1950) addresses this problem in a later paper. He bases a generalized definition of an *n-clique* on the concept of multistep connectedness discussed in the preceding section of this chapter. A set of three or more nodes is considered an *n*-clique if paths of *n* or fewer steps connect all members of the set. A matrix multiplication procedure is used to detect nodes which are members of *n*-cliques. It is easy to see by tracing the paths in Fig. 2 that nodes 6–9 do indeed satisfy the definition of a 2-clique, while node 5 joins the first four nodes under the new definition. The matrix multiplication method still does not identify the membership of each separate clique, however.

Harary and Ross (1957) address the problem of specific membership in *n*-cliques by showing that in networks with fewer than four cliques, at least one node in each clique must be a member of only that one clique. They give criteria for finding these "uncliqual" nodes and point out that all nodes connected with each node at *n* or fewer steps are members of a distinct clique. They are able to generalize their results by induction to networks having an indefinite number of cliques.

A different, but related, conception of connected cliques is proposed by Weiss and Jacobson (1955). Instead of weakening the complete, single-step connectedness criterion of Luce and Perry by formally allowing additional steps to complete the connections between clique members, they simply permit cliques to be *less* than fully connected. Their detection procedure consists of reordering the rows and columns of a symmetrized link matrix so that nodes who have contacts with each other are adjacent in the matrix. After "liaisons" are removed, the remaining nodes often fall into visibly separate, dense blocks, which they define as mutually exclusive cliques. They attempt to resolve less dense "gray" patterns by tentatively reclassifying key nodes as liaisons and reordering the nodes again, in an attempt to decompose the amorphous areas of the matrix into clearer, higher density aggregations. If the data in Table II were rearranged so that the nodes were placed in random order, this would indicate what a typical "starting" matrix would look like before the Jacobson and Seashore procedures were implemented. The resultant rearrangement should appear as shown in Table II.

In spite of the lack of specific, replicable criteria for both the reordering and the identification of cliques "by inspection" (both operations are carried out by hand), the Weiss and Jacobson method has interesting implications. It provides, for the first time, the possibility of assigning *roles* to the nodes, in terms of the clique structure of the network. Any node may be a member of one clique *or* may be an isolate, *or* may be a liaison by virtue of strong connections with more than one clique. Further, their procedures seem susceptible to rigorous formulation, though they themselves do not provide such a formulation. Richards' (1974b, 1975) NEGOPY program (see the last section of this chapter) uses and formalizes many of Weiss and Jacobson's ideas.

Other methods, some using criteria for clique detection which are unrelated to the connectedness criterion emphasized here, may also be used with binary network data. However, most of these methods also permit the use of metric (ordinal, interval, or ratio-scaled) data and hence will be dealt with in the next section. When binary data are used in such procedures, the data may be seen as possessing metric information with a very low power of resolution.

B. Metric and Ordinal Clique-Detection Procedures

The forerunner of the spatial procedures for clique detection is factor analysis. The link strength matrix for factor analysis of networks must be in the form of a correlation matrix. One possibility for the source of the matrix was mentioned in the section on link measurement: Correlations are calculated from cross-sectional co-occurrence data, using the nodes as variables and traits or activities as cases. Glanzer and Glaser (1959) describe a slightly different approach, involving the computation of correlations between the row vectors of an existing asymmetric link matrix. This approach is a special case of the one suggested first, with "chooses node *j*" as an activity.

Note that the analysis of correlation matrices derived in either way implies that the investigator is interested in a network based on *similarities* between the nodes with respect to traits, activities, or previously defined links, rather than the patterns of linkage among nodes. In the case of activities, an argument may be made for interpreting the correlations as indicators of an interdependence relationship, but the argument is rather weak for the activity of making a sociometric choice, which, after all, is stimulated by the investigator, rather than by the transmission of influence in the social setting of interest.

Yet another way to arrive at a suitable matrix for factor analysis and to avoid the similarity connotation in favor of a connectedness approach is to measure the links in such a way as to form a polar scale with values between minus one and one. If symmetric links are originally measured on a ratio scale, one transformation which might be used to achieve the desired polar scale is[2]

$$s'_{ij} = \begin{cases} \sqrt{s_{ij}/\max[S]}, & i \neq j, \\ 1, & i = j, \quad \text{a polar scale between 0 and 1.} \end{cases}$$

If the symmetric correlation or S' matrix is nonsingular, it can be orthogonally decomposed by factor analysis, i.e., transformed so that the input correlations are maintained (if principal components factor analysis is used), but the locations of the nodes are expressed in terms of an orthonormal basis (the N factors) rather than in terms of each other. Factors have been interpreted as cliques (see, e.g., Killworth and Bernard, 1973), but the problem of how many factors to use must be solved first, since there are as many factors as nodes in the decomposed matrix.

Factor loadings give the extent of involvement of each node with each factor; an arbitrary minimum value must be chosen (Killworth and Bernard use 0.6) or else every node will be a "member" of every factor. Even with a high cutoff, unique assignment of nodes to cliques is not guaranteed.

Oblique factor rotations allow the assessment of relationships between cliques in the same metric as the input matrix. The strength of an interclique relation is the cosine of the angle between the factors corresponding to each clique.

Standard factor analysis programs will handle up to about 100 nodes, with greater capacities available in some computer installations.

Factor analysis has been presented here primarily as an introduction to the concepts involved in multidimensional scaling (MDS). For metric MDS (MMDS), the links must be ratio scaled and (usually) symmetric. Since MMDS operates on a matrix of *distances* between nodes rather than link strengths, a transformation of the S matrix is necessary to prepare the data. The transformation may be of the form

$$d_{ij} = \begin{cases} 1/s_{ij}, & i \neq j \quad \text{and} \quad s_{ij} \neq 0, \\ 0, & i = j, \\ M, & s_{ij} = 0, \quad \text{and} \quad i \neq j \end{cases} \tag{1}$$

where M is a constant, $M > 1/s_{ij}$ for all i and j.

[2]This transformation is proposed as an example to clarify the relationship of factor analysis with other clique-detection methods which use a strength or distance matrix. See Lankford (1974) for several alternatives.

Using algorithms very similar to those of factor analysis, MMDS operates on the input distance matrix to place each node in a multidimensional space. The distance between every pair of nodes in the space is the same as the input distance. This sometimes results in a space with "imaginary" dimensions, or equivalently, the "warped" spaces of Riemann geometry and tensor calculus (see Woelfel and Danes Chapter 11 of this volume). There is nothing "wrong" with imaginary dimensions, except that many scaling methods discard them as irrelevant or uninterpretable, thus distorting the distances between some pairs of nodes in the space. Since imaginary dimensions are quite likely when MMDS is used with network data (depending somewhat on the value chosen for the constant, M), a scaling technique which retains the imaginary dimensions is recommended. One such technique is the Galileo program. Galileo will accept up to 45 nodes.

The interpretation, along with the disadvantages, of MMDS as a clique detection device is similar to that of factor analysis: Each of up to $N - 1$ dimensions may be a clique and each node may be associated with each clique. The problem of determining how many dimensions to retain remains. Barnett and Woelfel (1976) provide a number of solutions.

While MMDS in itself seems to have limited value as a clique-detection device, it appears to have useful application in the mapping of the "fine structure" within cliques discovered by other means and perhaps in describing the relationships between cliques. Further, it has the advantage of considerable methodological development in the area of graphically plotting changes in the distance matrix over time (see Woelfel and Danes Chapter 11 of this volume), a crucial and, until recently, neglected aspect of network analysis.

There exist a number of nonmetric or partially metric multidimensional scaling methods which can also be used for network analysis, with similar interpretations. Smallest space analysis (see Lingoes, 1972, and Norton, Chapter 10 of this volume), for instance, produces a spatial image of the network in which only the ranks of the input distances are respected. Kruskal, Young, and Seery (1975) provide an overview and some technical details of other ordinal methods, including MDSCAL and TORSCA. However, the utility of these methods for analyzing network data is not known, and some difficulty can be expected to arise from inconsistencies of link rankings given by different respondents.

Interpreting the dimensions of a space as cliques entails a considerable distortion of the usual sociometric meaning of a clique as a set of highly interconnected nodes. The nodes which lie on a line in space may still be very far apart (weakly linked). The distance matrix and its orthogonal decomposition contain far more than dimensional information; however, it might be useful to consider the spatial representation of a network as a detailed map with the nodes as scattered houses and the village boundaries not yet drawn in. By this analogy, the main task in identifying cliques becomes one of finding clusters (see Krippendorff, Chapter 9 of this volume) of closely spaced nodes in the spatial "map" of the network.

Among the best-known algorithms for finding clusters in multidimensional space are Ward's (1963) methods and two methods developed by Johnson (1967). All are agglomerative hierarchical methods: They add nodes to existing clusters in successive passes through the data, eventually producing a tree structure. Eventually all nodes end up in a single cluster; the problem is where to terminate the agglomerative procedure. See Anderberg (1973) for a discussion of several solutions for this difficulty. When a termination point is reached, the clusters are mutually exclusive, and some distant nodes may remain isolated.

Cluster analysis detects cliques which are highly structured in terms of the metric measures previously discussed in the section on network properties, since by definition clusters are relatively densely populated portions of the multidimensional space. All of the spatially derived properties of networks, cliques, and nodes are consistent with the structural implications of these methods. In addition, it seems possible and interesting in this context to investigate in some detail the relationships between cliques, perhaps in terms of closest, farthest, and average distances between members of different cliques.

In view of the apparent applicability of spatial clustering methods, it is surprising that they have been little used for the analysis of network data, although recent exceptions do exist. (See Breiger, Boorman, & Arabie, 1974, and the description of the SOCK program to follow.) Perhaps this is because the practical implementations of clustering methods are fairly new (Blashfield, 1976) and because much of their development and use has been in the fields of biology and cognitive psychology. A typical clustering program has a capacity of 100 modes, though Small (1974a) evidently has access to a program of much larger capacity.

C. Special Network Procedures

We turn now to a collection of procedures designed specifically for the analysis of sociometric and other linkage data. One such procedure is CONCOR, which Breiger et al. (1974) have compared extensively with some of the scaling and clustering procedures mentioned before.

CONCOR is essentially a metric hierarchical clustering algorithm. Unlike most general purpose clustering methods, which assemble nodes into larger and larger groups, CONCOR partitions the nodes into successively smaller groups. No specific criteria are given for stopping the partitioning.

An important step in the CONCOR procedure is the calculation of correlations between the rows (or columns) of the link strength matrix. This transforms the original linkage data into what Shepard, Rommey, and Nerlove (1972) call "profile" data. It produces clusters based on the similarity of nodes, rather than their linkage, as in the factor analysis of similar correlation matrices.

Though the authors tie this feature of their algorithm to the "block modeling" theory of sociometric data (Lorraine & White, 1971; see also White, Boorman, & Breiger, 1976), in the present context CONCOR would seem to be more applicable to (not necessarily square) matrices of trait or activity data such as that discussed by Phillips and Conviser (1972). CONCOR will accept unsquare matrices and should be very useful for discovering similarity clusters in such data. A recent analysis of the mathematical foundations of CONCOR shows that the program produces results which are formally similar to those of factor analysis (Schwartz, 1977).

CONCOR is solely a group-detection device and offers no measures of network properties, though if the results can be related to a metric space, the volume and distance measures associated with conventional cluster analysis could be used. This step seems doubtful, however, since the similarity measure used (correlation) is nonlinear. Two of the authors of the CONCOR description discuss structural measures in a separate context (Boorman & Arabie, 1972).

A particularly interesting feature of CONCOR is its ability to handle multiple kinds of association between the nodes, referred to previously as polythetic data. However, the three-dimensional polythetic data array is immediately collapsed by the program into an unsquare two-dimensional matrix, which appears from the authors' description to have the same effect as taking an unweighted sum or average of the different types of links, a feature which is available to any of the network procedures discussed, merely by preprocessing the data. Thus CONCOR is not truly polythetic in the sense of maintaining the distinction between types of links throughout the cluster-finding stage.

The node capacity of CONCOR is not known at present.

Killworth and Bernard's (1973) KBPAK is a collection of programs designed to process ordinal sociometric data of a particular type. [See Killworth & Bernard (1974a, b) for descriptions and evaluations of the data gathering method.] The essential feature of the data is that it is ranked within informants; i.e., each respondent ranks his/her frequency of contact with all other nodes; the node with the highest frequency receives the lowest rank, so the data matrix is more an ordinal distance matrix than a link strength matrix. After preprocessing to find the "minimum distance" between any pair of nodes, regardless of the number of steps involved (i.e., if two nodes who do not have much contact are each linked closely with a third node, the sum of the "short" links with the third node, plus a small penalty for the extra step, replaces the "long" link between the first two nodes), correlations are computed between the rows of the matrix, and the resulting correlation matrix is factor analyzed. Nodes having a loading of 0.6 or greater on any factor retained (how many are retained is not clear) are treated as a "tentative subgroup." Nodes with a loading factor of 0.3 or more on two or more factors are candidates for a special subgroup-linking "intermediary" role. Because correlations are computed, all results must be interpreted in terms of similarity rather than linkage.

Two methodological criticisms can be made of the KBPAK procedures. First, though the program description does not specify, it is assumed that the ordinary product-moment correlation is used. This may be unjustified in light of the ordinal scaling of the data; perhaps the Spearman rank-order correlation should be substituted. Second, it is difficult to understand the minimum-distance procedure, since factoring is based on the similarity of node preferences; the preprocessing distorts those preferences in an unknown fashion. Further, since the distances are ranked *within* respondents, there is no common metric for comparing them *across* nodes, as required by the minimum-distance procedure.

A major advantage of the KBPAK method, on the other hand, is its handling of some of the difficulties inherent in a factor analysis of networks. Ambiguity in assignment of nodes to cliques is greatly reduced, though not necessarily eliminated, by the high cutoff for factor loadings. More important is the creation of the special "intermediary" role, which allows for some consideration of the relations *between* cliques, even in the absence of a specific measure of the strength of those relations. Also interesting is the authors' insistence on the tentativeness of cliques and role assignments, and the importance of supplementary anthropological description of the network (Bernard & Killworth, 1973). This position may be compared with our own belief that network properties, if they are to be generally useful concepts, must be related to other theoretically important variables.

The KBPAK series will accept up to about 150 nodes, depending on the memory capacity of the computer used. It has been designed for easy portability between computing sites.

Alba and Gutman (1971) have written a package, called SOCK, for the analysis of binary sociometric data. Based on the concept of multistep paths (see the discussion of network structure properties, Section III), the program constructs one of several optional pairwise distance measures from either asymmetric or forced-symmetry data. The resulting distance matrix is then clustered by one of Johnson's (1967) hierarchical clustering methods, or mapped into a multidimensional space by a version of Kruskal's (1964) MDSCAL. Thus SOCK offers a combination of several of the spatial procedures previously discussed, together with linkage-derived preprocessing to achieve the necessary ratio scaled distances.

The key to understanding cliques produced by SOCK is the derivation of the distance measures. The first option for computing distances from the nominal linkage matrix is a weighted sum of the number of paths between two nodes, $d_{ij} = \sum_k a^{kP_k}$, where a is a constant chosen by the user (usually $0 < a \leqslant 1$), and P_k is the number of paths of length k between the nodes. Note that the average of this measure over all nodes would be a measure of total structure, which is closely related to Coleman's suggested network connectedness measure.

The second option is more complex and will only be described in general here. In this option, d_{ij} is made inversely proportional to the degree of overlap of two circles of radius k around nodes i and j, where k is again the number of steps in a path between the two nodes. Notice that when $k = 1$, the measure is a symmetric, inverted version of Richard's integrativeness measure.

Alba and Gutman do not mention any measures of network properties produced by their program, but several could easily be devised, based on information generated within the program. They give an example in which 1000 nodes are processed.

Richard's (1974a, b, c, 1975, 1976) NEGOPY program processes ratio scaled linkage measures in either asymmetric or forced-symmetry forms. The clique finding procedures consist of two stages. The initial detection stage is a unidimensional clustering procedure which is recognizably, if distantly, related to the matrix manipulation methods of Luce (1950). This stage has several user-adjustable parameters, which serve to emphasize its heuristic origins. Cliques tentatively identified by the first stage are then subjected to a series of formal criterion tests. The formal criteria are as follows:

(1) Each node must have at least p percent of its total link strength within the clique (p must be greater than 50% for unambiguous membership role assignment).

(2) The clique must be completely connected, using paths of length q or less.

(3) Removal of "critical" nodes or links must not cause the clique to become disconnected at the chosen path length.

In addition to detecting cliques, the NEGOPY program provides a number of network property measures, including the one-step connectedness density of cliques, and the integrativeness of individual nodes, previously discussed. Connectedness is not calculated for the network as a whole, perhaps because the large number of nodes the program is designed to handle might make such a calculation expensive. Node roles permitted include not only "clique member" and "isolate," but also "liaison" (nonmember node with strong ties to two or more cliques) and "bridge" (clique member with strong ties to another clique).

NEGOPY is designed to accommodate up to 4095 nodes. It is not portable, and is currently available at only a few Control Data Corporation (CDC) computer facilities.

V. CONTRASTS

The preceding section does not provide an exhaustive list of computerized techniques for network analysis. Rather, these methods were chosen for the

TABLE IV

NETWORK PROGRAM ASSUMPTIONS

Measurement assumption	Structure assumption	
	Similarity	Connectedness
Binary (nominal)	CONCOR	SOCK
Ordinal	KBPAK	
Interval or ratio		NEGOPY

availability of documentation and for their variety range of assumptions about social structure and data collection methods. They differ mainly in (1) the scaling of the link measures and (2) their use of a similarity versus a connectedness criterion for clique detection. These contrasts are shown in Table IV.

It should be pointed out that the clique membership findings of similarity-based procedures will often not differ from connectedness-based results that are limited to using two-step connections. This is because correlations or other similarity measures are usually based on the multiplication of some data matrix. For example, the matrix formulation for Pearson product-moment correlations is simply the expression (in terms of the standardized data matrix, X)

$$R = (1/n)X'X \qquad \text{(Van de Geer, 1971)}$$

and hence is proportional to the squared link matrix when the means and standard deviations of the rows are equal. The primary difference in connectedness procedures is that the original, one-step link matrix is always added to the squared link matrix before two-step cliques are sought. This follows from Luce's (1950) definition of an n-clique as a set of nodes which are completely connected at n *or fewer* steps.

Several studies have compared the results of various clique-detection procedures. As already mentioned, Breiger *et al.* (1974) have run the same sets of data on CONCOR and on a variety of scaling and clustering procedures. Likewise, Lankford (1974) has compared the results of several factor analytic and scaling procedures. Killworth and Bernard (1977) are conducting a "contest" to see which procedures produce the most consistent results when run using both error-free and error-filled data. No consistent set of guidelines has emerged from the comparisons performed up to now.

While such studies are valuable, the most useful contrasts among network analysis procedures should derive from the mathematical formulations of their operations. This paper has attempted to provide such contrasts whenever the mathematics were sufficiently well worked out.

Another useful approach to comparing network procedures, which should provide more general results than comparisons using a few sets of empirical data, are comparisons using a wide range of artificial sets of data. The artificial data can be configured to contain certain patterns of social interest. Edwards and Monge (1976) used this method for comparing network structure indices. Nosanchuk (1963) compared clique detection procedures by the same method. See also the comparison of clustering procedures by Blashfield described in the next section.

VI. PROBLEMS

The discussion so far has assumed that a social network is a thing unto itself, capable perhaps of being related to other social phenomena, but existing full grown and perceptible in the social milieu. This assumption simplifies the discussion of existing methods for network analysis, but it begs two questions. First, how do social networks arise, and second, how do they change in response to external stimuli?

The second question has a more straightforward answer in terms of the concepts developed here, so we shall consider it first. It is quite conceivable, though few examples will be found in the sociometric literature, to compare the properties of several networks defined by the same boundaries, but separated in time. For the summary measures defined on the entire network or on individual nodes, the statistical problem of how to assess the changes is straightforward, capable of solution by standard time-series regression methods (see, for introductory treatments, Nelson, 1973; Hibbs, 1974, 1977), or by repeated measures analysis of variance (Finn, 1969; Poor, 1973).

Of special interest would be attempts to predict changes in the network properties from external events, such as changing economic conditions or management styles. The amount of data required for such predictions would be quite large; at least 20 points in time are necessary for most time-series analyses. The limited budgets and short term nature of most social science research are major obstacles to obtaining such data, but it seems obvious that networks must be studied in this fashion if the network concept is to attain theoretical status commensurate with its intuitive appeal.

At the level of the clique, the problem of change over time is much more difficult to deal with. How does one compare one configuration of cliques with another? If the changes are small so that each clique at time 1 is readily identified with a similar clique at time 2, a variety of change measures are conceivable, including Cohen's (1960) kappa statistic for classification agreement. Monge (1971) reports one example of a study involving groups of fixed size whose emerging structure was examined at multiple time periods.

But suppose a clique decomposes over time into splinter groups? How, aside from observing that the decomposition has occurred, can the change be measured? Further, it is possible that no simple observation will fit the case—that the new configuration will bear no apparent relationship to the old. Roberts (1972) encountered such problems in examining the changing clique structure of a military organization over a period of two years.

Part of the answer to the difficulty of over time assessment may eventually come from methods described by Woelfel and Danes (Chapter 11 of this volume) for the comparison of multidimensional spaces over time. It is clear that most of the procedures for network analysis require much development in this regard, though it should be noted that Killworth and Bernard's KBPAK series of programs provides for the analysis of small changes in clique membership over a single time interval.

The question of how networks originate appears to be more of a conceptual question than an analytic problem at present. In collections of individuals, we may conceive that relatively stable network patterns arise as a consequence of a series of repeated communication events or social contacts. Some network investigations implicitly recognize this origin by asking respondents how frequently they talk to each other. A better example, though not a network study per se, is found in Katz and Lazarsfeld's (1955) investigation of interpersonal mediation of mass media influence. The investigators make a serious attempt to refer reported contacts to specific times and places so as to limit their influence to particular events. Their procedure is in itself a powerful check on the reliability of self-reported contacts and serves as well to clarify the validity issues in self-reported network data. But only very recently, in the area of small group research, is the possibility being investigated that the *sequence* of events may also be important in determining the social relationship between individuals.

A third issue that needs to be raised concerns the monolithic emphasis in network analysis on pairwise relationships. It should be clear that when social relationships are measured between two nodes at a time, an assumption is being made that when three people meet, the relationship between each of the three pairs is the same as when each pair meets separately. Such an assumption seems very difficult to justify (Krippendorff, 1976).

Fourth, it should be observed that most network analysis procedures assume perfect measurement: all nodes within the network boundary are assumed to have been measured, and each measurement is assumed to be unbiased and perfectly reliable. This assumption is untenable for most data sets. Since most of network analysis has no statistical basis,[3] the principal way of evaluating the effects of sampling and of random measurement error is by the Monte Carlo method, in which the results of many analyses with randomly disturbed data are compared to the "true" results. Some such work has been done on cluster algorithms by Blashfield (1976) which indicates that the effects of sampling, plus a random measurement error of up to 0.6 standard deviations, may be considerable. Johnson's two methods achieved median

[3]Two important exceptions have recently appeared. Granovetter (1976) shows how sample estimates of network connectedness can be made in very large networks, and Burt and Lin (1977) use multiple indicator models to assess link measurement validity and reliability.

coefficients of agreement in classifying nodes of .06 and .42, while Ward's minimum-variance methods achieved the highest agreement, a median of .77.

Research on the reliability and validity of the data used in communication network analysis is of major importance for the meaningful interpretation of the results of any investigation. As mentioned earlier in this chapter, the most typical source of data is respondent self-report of the amount (frequency and/or duration) or importance of communication contacts. Other means of data collection are diaries or "logs" of transactions, observations by trained coders, and the use of mechanical or electronic recording devices.

In the ideal, both the reliability and validity of a data collection procedure can be checked by comparing every data value with a known "true score." In practice, however, few investigators possess the information needed to obtain true scores. The best we can do is to compare the results obtained from independent procedures. Good agreement between the values produced by independent methods means we have succeeded in measuring *something* reliably. Krippendorff (1970) gives a generalized index of agreement.

If two very different procedures are used to measure the same conceptual variable, then agreement between the results of the two procedures provides a degree of confidence in the validity of the measurements. That is, the *something* we have measured appears to be what we intended to measure. Ultimately, however, the validity of the measurement remains a philosophical question which at best can be answered on utilitarian grounds after long experience with the procedure.

Several methodological issues are relevant in research on the reliability of communication network data; some examples follow. Each data collection technique is subject to measurement error of varying (and perhaps unknown) degrees. The time period over which techniques are compared must be appropriate to the techniques (for example, self-report will be subject to increasing error over time spans, while recording devices should be relatively insensitive to the time interval during which measurement takes place). The stimulus questions for which respondents provide data must be directly comparable. The measurement scales used for each technique should be as precise as the state of the art permits (and hopefully, interval or ratio rather than nominal or ordinal).

Preliminary work comparing data collection techniques has been recently reported by Killworth and Bernard (1976) and Bernard and Killworth (1977). In their first study, 21 deaf respondents who communicated via teletype were asked to rank the amount of communication each had with the others. At a later period in time, they maintained logs of their contacts over the teletype for three weeks. The investigators recognized that there might be true differences in the amount of communication at the time the ranking was done compared with the specific period used for the logs. The investigators found no relationship between the two sets of data. On the assumption that one of the two self-report measures (presumably the logging procedure) perfectly represented the respondent's behaviors, the investigators assert that respondents do not know their communication contacts with "any degree of accuracy" [p. 283]. This unequivocal conclusion does not appear warranted from the study, but the findings clearly suggest the importance of further research.

The later paper (Bernard and Killworth, 1977) is based on a study of 387 deaf respondents, 60 of whom were randomly selected and divided into two equal groups. The members of both groups indicated which of the 387 persons they communicated with. One group ranked and the other rated the amount of communication they had with their contacts for the *same* time period during which logs of teletype contacts were kept. The rankings and ratings each accounted for about 29% of the variance in the log data. These results were interpreted as further support for the conclusion that self-report data are an inadequate representation of communication contacts.

In this same paper, supplemental findings from other studies by the investigation are also given. Studies using direct observation in two office settings are compared with self-reported ranks of frequency of contacts. About 25% of the variance in observed frequency overlaps the self-reported frequency ranks. Another study, using mechanically recorded data from an amateur radio repeater station and self-report of amount of communication, covaries about 9%. The supplemental results are presented as further support for the inadequancy of self-report data.

These studies clearly identify the potential discrepancy between alternative data collection methods. It would be premature, however, to assume that the observational or mechanically recorded data are true scores, i.e., are error-free reflections of communication contacts. Observers made notations of contact at 15-minute or half-hour intervals; a great number of contacts could have taken place in the interim. The amateur radio operators could have bypassed the repeater station for their contacts; direct contacts among the respondents could account for the high error rate reported. The nature and types of errors in these "baseline" methods need further clarification.

It should also be noted that the self-report methods used by the investigators do not correspond to widely used methods for gathering communication network data, nor to the best available scaling practices. For example, ranking procedures require a respondent to make $n(n - 1)/2$ comparisons, where n is the number of contacts (if $n = 21$, 210 comparisons must be made). This is a difficult task, inherently prone to error, and quite likely to lead to low correlations with any criterion variable.

Similarly, the scales used for the accuracy investigations are quite limited and do not (apparently) provide a standard "yardstick" for respondents to use in assigning scale values. They may be overanchored and are bounded. Thus the scaling procedures used by Bernard and Killworth are not in accord with commonly accepted procedures such as those described in Torgerson

(1958). Improvements in scaling are warranted in further research on the relative merits of various data collection techniques.

We suggest that direct magnitude estimation techniques (Hamblin, 1974) be used to gather self-report data on amount of communication. Time in minutes would appear to be the most appropriate scale. Respondents should typically have a common reference for the standard unit, one minute. Therefore, no training in the scale would be needed.

Further study of procedures for acquiring data suitable for communication network analysis is clearly needed. The work of Bernard and Killworth provides an important contribution to the body of knowledge about the reliability of these procedures. Additional consideration should be given also to the validity question: for some research questions the respondents' *perceptions* of their communication contacts may be the true variable of interest, rather than their communication *behavior*.

Finally, there is the question of the validity of the current measures of network properties, that is, the mathematical formulas used to combine the links into summary statistics. Edwards and Monge (1977) note that past researchers have not systematically established the necessary monotonic relationship between each index and the structural attribute it is supposed to measure. The assumption is generally made that if an index reflects a desired property at its extreme values, it will also reflect it between those extremes. This assumption, however, implies that structure is a single attribute. In contrast, Edwards and Monge showed that *several* structural attributes may be manipulated largely independently of one another and that indices may reflect variations in several attributes at once. Thus it appears essential to select indices carefully, with an eye toward not only the structural attributes it is desired to measure, but also with a consideration for those which it is *not* desired to measure, so as to minimize the possibility that one's measurements of structure might be confounded by variations along unwanted structural attributes.

VII. CONCLUSIONS

This chapter has reviewed some of the fundamental bases for network analysis of social and/or communication relations and has provided a discussion of the important multivariate aspects of the technique. The emergence of working computerized algorithms makes it feasible for network research to become a component of, if not the focus of, communication studies in a variety of laboratory and field settings. In contrast to a decade ago, or perhaps just five years ago, the conceptual and operational tools available to researchers have increased dramatically. These developments would appear to forecast a steep growth curve in the amount of substantive knowledge to be accumulated about the emergence, stabilization, and dissolution of networks, and about the psychological, sociological, and other factors associated with these processes.

References

Alba, R. D., and Gutman, M. P. *SOCK—a sociometric analysis system*. Mimeograph, Univ. of Columbia and Univ. of Princeton, 1971.

Anderberg, M. R. *Cluster analysis for applications*. New York: Academic Press, 1973.

Bales, R. F. *Interaction process analysis: A method for the study of small groups*. Reading, Massachusetts: Addison-Wesley, 1950.

Barnes, J. Social networks. *Addison-Wesley Module* #26. 1972, pp. 1–29.

Bavelas, A. Communication patterns in task oriented groups. In D. Lerner and H. D. Lasswell (Eds.), *The policy sciences*. Stanford, California: Stanford Univ. Press, 1951.

Bernard, H. R., and Killworth, P. D. On the structure of an ocean-going research vessel and other important things. *Social Science Research*, 1973 **2**, 145–184.

Bernard, H. R., and Killworth, P. D. Informant accuracy in social network data II. *Human Communication Research*, 1977, **4**, 3–18.

Blashfield, R. K. Mixture model tests of cluster analysis: Accuracy of four agglomerative hierarchical methods. *Psychological Bulletin*, 1976, **83**, 377–388.

Boorman, S. A., and Arabie, P. Structural measures and the method of sorting. In R. N. Shepard, A. K. Romney, and S. B. Nerlove (Eds.), *Multidimensional Scaling*. New York: Seminar Press, 1972.

Bott, E. *Family and social networks* (2nd ed.). Glencoe, Illinois: The Free Press, 1971.

Breiger, R. L., Boorman, S. A., and Arabie, P. *An algorithm for blocking relational data, with applications to social network analysis and comparison with multi-multidimensional scaling*, Technical Report No. 244, Psychology and Education Series, Stanford, California: Stanford Univ., Institute for Mathematical Studies on the Social Sciences, 1974.

Burt, R., and Lin, N. Network time series from archival records. In D. Heise (Ed.), *Sociological Methodology* 1977. San Francisco, California: Jossey-Bass, 1977.

Cohen, J. A coefficient of agreement for nominal scales. *Educational and Psychological Measurement*, 1960, **20**, 37–46.

Coleman, J. S. *Introduction to mathematical sociology*. New York: Free Press, 1964.

Conrath, D. W. Communications environment and its relationship to organizational structure. *Management Science*, 1973, **20**, 586–603.

Danowski, J. A., and Farace, R. V. *Communication network integration and group uniformity in a complex organization*. A paper presented at the meeting of the International Communication Association, New Orleans, Louisiana, April 1974.

Edwards, J. A., and Monge, P. R. The validation of mathematical indices of communication structure. *Communication Yearbook I*, International Communication Association, 1977.

Farace, R. V., Monge, P. R., and Russell, H. *Communicating and organizing*. Reading, Massachusetts: Addison-Wesley, 1977.

Festinger, L., Schachter, S., and Back, K. *Social pressures in informal groups*. Stanford, California: Stanford Univ. Press, 1950.

Finn, J. D. Multivariate analysis of repeated measures data. *Multivariate Behavioral Research*, 1969, **4**, 391–413.

Forsyth, E., and Katz, L. A matrix approach to the analysis of sociometric data: A preliminary report. *Sociometry*, 1946, **9**, 229–235.

Glanzer, M., and Glaser, R. Techniques for the study of group structure and behavior: I. Analysis of structure. *Psychological Bulletin*, 1959, **5**, 317–332.

Granovetter, M. Network sampling: Some first steps. *American Journal of Sociology*, 1976, **81**, 1287–1303.

Griffith, B. C. *et al.* The structure of scientific literatures II: Toward a macro- and microstructure for science. *Science Studies*, 1974, **4**, 339–365.

Hamblin, R. L. Social attitudes: Magnitude measurement and theory. In H. M. Blalock, Jr. (Ed.), *Measurement in the Social Sciences*. Chicago, Illinois: Aldine, 1974.

Harary, F., and Ross, I. A procedure for clique detection using the group matrix. *Sociometry*, 1957, **20**, 205–215.

Hibbs, D. A. Problems of statistical estimation and causal inference in time-series regression models. In H. L. Costner (Ed.), *Sociological Methodology* 1973-74. San Francisco, California: Jossey-Bass, 1974.

Hibbs, D. A. On analyzing the effects of policy interventions: Box-Jenkins and Box-Tiao versus structural equation models. In D. Heise (Ed.), *Sociological Methodology* 1977. San Francisco, California: Jossey-Bass, 1977.

Holland, P., and Leinhardt, S. The statistical analysis of local structure in social networks. In D. Heise (Ed.), *Sociological Methodology* 1975. San Francisco, California: Jossey-Bass, 1975.

Jacobson, E., and Seashore, S. E. Communication practices in complex organizations. *Journal of Social Issues*, 1951, **7**, 28–40.

Johnson, S. C. Hierarchical clustering schemes. *Psychometrika*, 1967, **32**, 241–254.

Katz, E., and Lazarsfeld, P. F. *Personal influence*. New York: The Free Press, 1955.

Killworth, P. D., and Bernard, H. R. *The KBPAK—A collection of programs for the analysis of a social network*. Technical report no. BK-101-73. Arlington, West Virginia: Office of Naval Research, 1973.

Killworth, P. D., and Bernard, H. R. CATIJ: A new sociometric and its application to a prison living unit. *Human Organization*, 1974, **33**, 335–350. (a)

Killworth, P. D., and Bernard, H. R. *The CATIJ technique: Some descriptive tests of its adequacy*. A paper presented at the meeting of the American Sociological Association convention, Montreal, August 1974. (b)

Killworth, P. D., and Bernard, H. R. Informant accuracy in social network data. *Human Organization*, 1976, **35**, 269–286.

Killworth, P. D., and Bernard, H. R. Informant accuracy in social network data II. *Human Communication Research*, 1977, **4**(1), 3–18..

Krippendorff, K. Bivariate agreement coefficients for reliability of data. In E. F. Borgatta and G. W. Bohrnstedt (Eds.), *Sociological Methodology* 1970. San Francisco, California: Jossey-Bass, 1970. pp. 139–150.

Krippendorff, K. *An algorithm for simplifying the representation of complex systems*. A paper presented at the meeting of the International Congress of Cybernetics and Systems, Oxford, England, 1972.

Krippendorff, K. A spectral analysis of relations. Unpublished paper, Univ. of Pennsylvania, 1976.

Kruskal, J. B. Multidimensional scaling: A numerical method. *Psychometrika*, 1964, **29**, 115–129.

Kruskal, J. B., Young, F. W., and Seery, J. B. *How to use KYST, a very flexible program to do multidimensional scaling and unfolding*. Murray-Hill, New Jersey: Bell Laboratories, 1975.

Lankford, P. M. Comparative analysis of clique identification methods. *Sociometry*, 1974, **37**, 287–305.

Lingoes, J. C. A general survey of the Guttman-Lingoes non-metric program series. In R. N. Shepard, A. K. Romney, and S. B. Nerlove (Eds.), *Multidimensional Scaling*. New York: Seminar Press, 1972.

Lorraine, F., and White, H. C. Structural equivalence of individuals in social networks. *Journal of Mathematical Sociology*, 1971, **1**, 49–80.

Luce, D. Connectivity and generalized cliques in sociometric group structure. Psychometrika, 1950, **15**, 169–190.

Luce, D., and Perry, A. A method of matrix analysis of group structure. *Psychometrika*, 1949, **14**, 95–116.

MacKenzie, K. D. Structural centrality in communication networks. *Psychometrika*, 1966, **31**,

17–25.

Martin, M., and Ackoff, R. The dissemination and use of recorded scientific information, *Management Science*, 1961, **4**, 322–336.

Monge, P. R. *The evolution of communication structure.* Unpublished manuscript. Michigan State Univ., Department of Communication, 1971.

Monge, P. R., and Day, P. D. Multivariate analysis in communication research. *Human Communication Research*, 1976, **2**, 207–220.

Moreno, J. L. *Who shall survive? A new approach to the problem of human interrelations.* New York: Beacon, 1934.

Nelson, C. R. *Applied time series analysis for managerial forecasting.* San Francisco, California: Holden-Day, 1973.

Nosanchuk, T. A. A comparison of several sociometric partitioning techniques. *Sociometry*, 1963, **26**, 112–124.

Phillips, D. P., and Conviser, R. H. Measuring the structure and boundary properties of groups: Some uses of information theory. *Sociometry*, 1972, **35**, 235–254.

Poor, D. D. S. ANOVA for repeated measures: Two approaches. *Psychological Bulletin*, 1973, **80**, 204–209.

Richards, W. D. *Network analysis in large complex systems: Theoretical basis.* A paper presented at the meeting of the International Communication Association, New Orleans, April 1974 (a).

Richards, W. D. *Network analysis in large complex systems: Techniques and methods.* A paper presented at the meeting of the International Communication Association, New Orleans, April 1974. (b)

Richards, W. D. *Network analysis in large complex systems: Metrics.* A paper presented at the meeting of the International Communication Association, New Orleans, April 1974. (c)

Richards, W. D. *A manual for network analysis.* A report of the Institute for Communication Research, Stanford Univ., 1975.

Richards, W. D. *A coherent systems methodology for the analysis of human communication systems.* Technical Report #25. Stanford University Center for Interdisciplinary Research, March 1976.

Roberts, K. H. On looking at an elephant: An evaluation of cross-cultural research related to organizations. *Psychological Bulletin*, 1972, **74**, 327–350.

Schwartz, J. E. An examination of CONCOR and related methods for blocking sociometric data. In D. Heise (Ed.), *Sociological Methodology* 1977. San Francisco, California: Jossey-Bass, 1977.

Shaw, M. E. Communication networks. In L. Berkowitz (Ed.), *Advances in Experimental Social Psychology* (Vol. I). New York: Academic Press, 1964.

Shepard, R. N., Romney, A. K., and Nerlove, S. B. *Multidimensional Scaling.* New York: Seminar Press, 1972.

Small, H. G. *Mapping the speciality structure of the social sciences using the Social Science Citation Index.* Report to the National Science Foundation on Grant SOC73-09096, 1974. (a)

Small, H. G. Multiple citation patterns on scientific literature: The circle and hill models. *Information Storage and Retrieval*, 1974, **10**, 393–402. (b)

Stevens, S. S. Mathematics, measurement, and psychophysics. In S. S. Stevens (Ed.), *Handbook of Experimental Psychology.* New York: Wiley, 1951.

Torgerson, W. S. *Theory and Methods of Scaling.* New York: Wiley, 1958.

Van de Geer, J. P. *Introduction to multivariate analysis for the social sciences.* San Francisco, California: Freeman, 1971.

Ward, J. H. Hierarchical grouping to optimize an objective function. *Journal of the American Statistical Association*, 1963, **58**, 236–244.

Weiss, R., and Jacobson, E. A method for the analysis of the structure of complex organizations. *American Sociological Review*, 1955, **20**, 661–668.

White, H. C., Boorman, S. A., and Breiger, R. L. Social Structure from multiple Networks. I. Blockmodels of Roles and Positions. *American Journal of Sociology*, 1976, **81(4)**, 730–780.

Wigand, R. T. *Communication integration and satisfaction in a complex organization.* A paper presented at the meeting of the International Communication Association, New Orleans, Louisiana, April 1974. (a)

Wigand, R. T. *Interorganizational communication among complex organizations.* A paper presented at the meeting of the International Communication Association, New Orleans, Louisiana, April 1974. (b)

Wigand, R. T., and Larkin, T. J. *Interorganizational communication, information flow, and service delivery among social service organizations.* A paper presented at the International Communication Association, Chicago, Illinois, April 1975.

Woelfel, J., and Danes, J. E. New techniques for the multidimensional analysis of communication and conception (this volume)

Chapter 13

STOCHASTIC MODELING OF COMMUNICATION PROCESSES

DEAN HEWES

Department of Communication Arts
University of Wisconsin
Madison, Wisconsin

I. INTRODUCTION

The field of communication has always maintained a strong commitment to a process view of social interaction (Kibler & Barker, 1969), but only in recent years has the commitment come to fruition in positive research programs (Ellis & Fisher, 1975; Hawes & Foley, 1973; Hewes & Evans-Hewes, 1974). More and more researchers are recognizing the potential of various time-series techniques for the representation of communication process. For instance, researchers in attitude change (Anderson, 1954; Hewes & Evans-Hewes, 1974; Hewes, 1980; Hewes, Brazil, & Evans, 1977), group interaction (Ellis & Fisher, 1975; Hawes & Foley, 1973, 1976), leadership emergence (Binder, Wolin & Terebinsky, 1965) and nonverbal communication (Natale, 1976) have all found finite state stochastic models, a particular class of time-series models, to be highly useful investigative tools.

The purpose of this chapter is to introduce the conceptual framework and applications of finite state stochastic models to communication researchers.

In Section II a set of arguments is advanced to demonstrate the justifiability of discrete-state stochastic models as tools for communication research. The conceptual basis of stochastic models is outlined in Section III, which then focuses on typical classes of such models and their associated assumptions. In Section IV possible answers to the question Where do we go from here? are examined. Issues concerning conceptual and theoretical clarity and methodological sophistication are discussed.

A note of caution needs to be issued before proceeding. While I have attempted to be fair and accurate in presenting the case for stochastic modeling, this chapter is deliberately argumentative rather than descriptive. My purpose is to present the simpler forms of stochastic modeling in their best light (see Hewes, 1977 for a discussion of some of the more complex forms). Given recent criticisms of these forms of stochastic modeling in the communication literature (cf. Baird, 1977; Gouran, 1977; O'Keefe, 1977), a positive statement of the potential value of such models seems to be in order (see particularly Section II).

II. WHEN TO USE DISCRETE-STATE STOCHASTIC MODELS

The question posed by the section heading can be broken into two parts: (1) When are stochastic models useful? (2) When are discrete-state models useful? These two questions will be considered separately.

A. Stochastic Models

In order to determine the usefulness of stochastic models it is first necessary to define them. Anderson (1971, p. 164) suggests that stochastic models are "time series [models] in which the characteristic and useful properties appropriate to the time series are not the deterministic mean value functions but the probability structure itself." In other words, stochastic models are not primarily oriented toward predicting changes in the mean values of a process over time, but rather are best suited to predicting changes in probability distributions as a function of time.

In the deterministic (mean-value) framework, events, defined as dependent variables, are completely predictable *in principle* (cf. Box, 1966; Cattell, 1966; Hewes, 1975b). It is necessary only to locate all the antecedent conditions of the event to be predicted (Hempel & Oppenheim, 1948). For example, a researcher might wish to regress individuals' behavior (amount of contribution to a charity) on their attitude toward that act and the normative pressure to perform that act. The resulting regression equation, to the extent that it has a high variance accounted for, permits prediction of *individual* behavior. One merely needs to plug the target individual's particular scores on the independent variables into the regression equation in order to generate an expected value on the behavior. The ideal state of affairs in this sort of procedure is accounting for 100% of the variance in the dependent variable for the population, i.e., the goal is perfect prediction of individual events. Of course, this goal has not been attained.[1]

By contrast, stochastic models do not require the assumption that events are predictable in principle. Rather they assume that the probability distribution, or likelihoods, of events are predictable in principle. For example, a "fair" coin has two possible "events" which can result from flipping it; it can turn up heads or tails. No examination of antecedent conditions (for example, the number of heads that have resulted from previous flips) can tell us anything about the face that will appear on the next flip. However, the number of heads that will turn up over a large number of flips is entirely predictable. A *deterministic prediction of any particular event* in coin flipping is impossible, *but the likelihood that an event will occur* is entirely predictable. The stochastic description of this phenomenon is law-like; however, it achieves that status by focusing on distributional predictions rather than the prediction of events (Hempel, 1966).

One can legitimately argue that we, as a field, would lose something by trying to predict distributions rather than events. The reigning paradigm in the social sciences dictates that researchers seek deterministic, causal relationships among events (Seibold, 1977). By employing stochastic models, we would be abandoning the search for deterministic laws. This challenge is a serious one. Communication researchers should not blindly abandon a successful paradigm. Even temporary abandonment for specific purposes should be justified by the exigencies of the research question and the phenomena. Therefore, the *utility* of stochastic process models must be compared to their deterministic alternatives.

The justification for stochastic process models proceeds in three parts: first, I argue that the presumption of determinacy at the event level is not necessarily correct; second, I contend that no a priori case can be made for the general superiority of either deterministic or stochastic modeling; third, I suggest that specific applications strongly suggest the choice of stochastic, rather than deterministic, models. The point of these arguments is to overcome the presumption held by deterministic models in social science research. I do not contend that stochastic models are overall superior, but rather that they are *generally* a viable alternative to deterministic models and that they are *specifically* advantageous for certain kinds of theorizing.

1. THE ASSUMPTION OF EVENT-LEVEL DETERMINACY "AIN'T NECESSARILY SO"

Laplace (1796) argued vigorously that apparent randomness in the world was *solely* the result of our ignorance. While few scholars today would openly

[1]The point being made here is *not* that any particular methodology is inherently stochastic or deterministic. There are regression techniques which are stochastic by the definition offered here and there are versions of the models described in this paper which can be interpreted as being deterministic predictors of the dependent variable. If that variable is an *event*, the model is deterministic; if the dependent variable is a *probability*, the model is defined as stochastic.

defend such a position, covert faith in determinacy remains strong, as evidenced in discussions of the nature of error terms in mean-value models (e.g., Box, 1966; Christ, 1966). In fact, the pressure felt by stochastic modelers to justify their approach is symptomatic of the deterministic presumption (e.g., Coleman, 1964a, Chapter 1; Leik & Meeker, 1975, Chapter 11; Hewes, 1975b). However, gut level beliefs about determinacy do not necessarily make it so. The problem is that one cannot either prove or disprove the legitimacy of event-level determinacy. This fact has had such impact that researchers in many areas of physics have abandoned the search for determinacy altogether (cf. Bunge, 1973; Lenzen, 1938), rather than commit themselves to the more restrictive, deterministic position. The point is that we have no *objective* basis for conceiving of the world as deterministic. It could as easily "be" stochastic. If it could be, then it behooves us to try to conceive of it that way as well. Such conceptual flexibility is likely to be the key to progress in science.

2. The Generally Superior Utility of Deterministic Models Is Questionable

One rationale for employing deterministic models is that they generally have superior heuristic value. It is argued that a belief in determinism encourages researchers to dig deeper into causal processes so that they may reduce the error in their predictions. This argument is not definitive for four reasons. First, there is no reason why the search for undiscovered antecedent conditions requires a belief in determinacy (Rescher, 1970). Lack of fit between theoretical and observed probability distributions can and does encourage researchers to seek improvements in their stochastic models (cf. Diesing, 1971, Chapter 1). Second, errors of omission in stochastic models generally have known impact on the predictions of those models which serve as clues to the existence of the problem (e.g., Singer & Spilerman, 1974; Coleman, 1973) and inspire a search for undiscovered antecedent conditions. Third, the supposed heuristic value of deterministic models actually involves a commitment to inflexibility in research. Since we cannot know that the world is deterministic, we may encounter indeterminate relationships. If we are committed to deterministic explanation, this will result in a misplacement of energies in seeking antecedent conditions that may not exist (Hewes, 1980). By adoption a stochastic framework, we at least admit the possibility that laws may be observed which have linkages with associated probabilities of less than 1.00.[2] Fourth and finally, the breadth of actual applications of stochastic models is some indication of their utility (cf. Bailey, 1975; Bartholemew, 1967; Lee, Judge, & Zellner, 1970; Levine & Burke, 1972; Massy, Montgomery, & Morrison, 1970). No *unique* heuristic value has been demonstrated for the deterministic perspective. *Both* deterministic *and* stochastic models are useful tools for a wide variety of applications.

[2]This is not to say that in *some instances* predictions cannot be made deterministically. Stochastic relationships with probabilities of 1.00 are quite acceptable. The point is that not *all* relationships are deterministically predictable.

3. Specific Forms of Theorizing Suggest a Stochastic Framework

In particular, what I shall call *intra-individual theories of social action* would appear to be better rendered by stochastic models. Intra-individual theories of social action attempt to explain individual behavior in terms of mediating cognitive variables and/or internal predispositions. Most personality-based explanations of interaction (e.g., Gergen & Marlowe, 1970), a vast majority of theories of the message/attitude/behavior relationship (e.g., Cushman & McPhee, 1980), and individual-difference versions of rules theorizing (e.g. Mischel, 1964) are intra-individual theories of social action.

These theories share a common set of characteristics. First, they all represent the individual as responding to some force (normative or causal) which tends to produce regularity in that individual's social behavior. Second, the social situation in which the individual operates is viewed as being occupied by other individuals and environmental forces (a) which are not incorporated in the theory, (b) which are incorporated but which are not under the complete control of the individual, or (c) which are incorporated but which are not perfectly understood by the individual.[3] In short, intra-individual theories merely describe social action from the standpoint of individuals who are faced with a partially unpredictable social world not under their complete control.

If we accept this kind of theory as one important for communication, then the question remains, What should such a theory look like? A partial answer is that the theoretic linkages between internal variables (attitudes, beliefs, intentions, traits, etc.) and social actions must be stochastic for the following two reasons. If relevant external variables have been excluded [condition (a)], then logical or empirical determinism can hold only when the excluded variables remain constant across all tests of the theory, an assumption unlikely to be born out in fact (McClelland, 1975). The move to stochastic models is justified since the relationships between a *subset* of all relevant variables must be indeterminate even if relationships described by the *full* set are inherently determinate. Even with all variables included in the theory, if individuals lack perfect control of their environment and/or lack perfect understanding of it [conditions (b) and (c)], then any social action taken by the individual can be "blocked" by circumstances which individuals cannot control or anticipate (von Wright, 1971). Again a stochastic relationship between internal variables and social actions is justified.

Intra-individual theories are useful precisely because they explain individual human action from the standpoint of the individual. Accurate information, complete power, or both are not available to all individuals in all contexts; consequently such intra-individual theories of action *cannot* validly contain deterministic, causal linkages between internal variable and social behaviors. Stochastic representations more accurately describe the actual relationships between these variables while still permitting prediction, albeit

---

[3]Obviously conditions (b) and (c) could be included in the same theory.

at the level of distributions of events rather than at the single event level. Stochastic relationships would appear to be logically appropriate for the class of intra-individual theories at least.

B. Discrete-State Models

The previous discussion focused on the choice between stochastic and deterministic models for representing communication phenomena. In this section an argument is advanced to suggest the utility of discrete-state, as opposed to continuous, variables in model building. By "discrete-state models" I mean those models which are constructed using nominal or quasi-ordinal categorical variables rather that continuous (ordinal, interval, or ratio) variables.[4] The argument presented here, coupled with the conclusion from the previous discussion, is intended to supply a rationale for the use of discrete-state stochastic models in particular kinds of communication theories. This section of the overall rationale is divided into two parts. The first part concentrates on *pragmatic* justifications for representing events discretely. In the second part *in principle* arguments support the use of discrete models for specific classes of communication events.

1. DISCRETE-STATE MODELS HAVE PRAGMATIC ADVANTAGES OVER THEIR CONTINUOUS COUNTERPARTS FOR THE REPRESENTATION OF CERTAIN SOCIAL PHENOMENA

This point is documented by the problems associated with measurement of social science variables. Coleman (1964a) noted that measurement in the social sciences falls far short of the rigor achieved by more advanced sciences, being restricted to the nominal or ordinal levels at best. Why is this the case? Two answers suggest themselves. First, it may be that our measurement techniques are not advanced enough to produce the precision necessary to measure concepts at the interval or ratio levels.[5] Given the severe impediments to theory construction incurred by ordinal-level measurement (Wilson, 1971; Acock & Martin, 1974; Hewes, 1975b, 1976), discrete (nominal)

[4]As a point of clarification the distinction between "discrete" and "continuous" can be applied to two aspects of a stochastic model—time and states. Thus a continuous time model treats time as flowing without interruption and predictions can be made to any instant of this flow. Discrete time models reflect a view of time which moves by fits and starts; predictions can only be made to those instants which are measured; i.e., every other day, every five minutes, after every Presidential address, etc. Obviously there can be both discrete- and continuous-state models which reflect either discrete or continuous time. In other words, there are four possible kinds of models. For simplicity, this chapter will focus on discrete-state, discrete time models, although discrete-state, continuous time models will be mentioned.

[5]In 1978(a) I argued that there is sufficient reason to question the intervality of such common measures as the Thurstone scale, the semantic differential, and Likert-type scales. Even those attempts to introduce measurement techniques which claim to be ratio level can be said to have succeeded only by changing the nature of the phenomena that can be investigated.

measures may be the only viable option until our techniques of measurement improve.[6]

The second controversial interpretation of Coleman's claim is that some social phenomenon may only *exist* at lower levels of measurement; perhaps people do not cognitively represent certain kinds of information other than in a nominal or ordinal fashion. If this is the case, attempts to obtain higher-level measures are either doomed to failure or to sterile success. They would fail if individuals simply could not make interval or ratio judgments.[7] They would achieve a sterile success if individuals *could* make higher-level judgments when asked but *do not* under ordinary circumstances. Thus, measures obtained would be formally of the interval or ratio level but theoretically useless in trying to understand actual cognitive processes. Whatever is "really" the case, at this point in time there are pragmatic reasons for opting for discrete (nominal-level) models of communication phenomena. This is not to say that all theorists should or will do so, but merely that discrete models are a viable option that cannot be dismissed out of hand because they "only" employ nominal-level measurement.

2. DISCRETE-STATE MODELS ARE BETTER ABLE TO REPRESENT CERTAIN PHENOMENA THAN ARE THEIR CONTINUOUS COUNTERPARTS

For instance, some empirical evidence suggests that discrete-state processes better describe certain classes of phenomena. Greeno (1974) reports a number of studies which support a discrete picture of various types of learning (e.g., Bower, 1961; Greeno & Scandura, 1966). While many psychologists hold reservations to the claim that learning "is" a discrete process (e.g., Theios, 1972; Heine, 1970), the evidence generally suggest that discrete-state processes describe various types of learning as well as or better than their continuous counterparts.

This result is particularly important for two reasons. First, it suggests that nominal-level models of a significant phenomenon have proven highly successful. Second, the phenomenon (learning) itself undergirds a sufficiently large number of social science theories (cf. Shaw & Costanzo, 1970) that the utility of discrete models is potentially increased.[8] At the very least, learning theorists have provided us with some directions for devising ways in which to contrast continuous and discrete models of the same phenomenon.

[6]I am *not* arguing that ordinal measures are impossible. I am arguing that under present technology there are inherent problems with ordinal measures which inhibit theory construction to a greater degree than those possessed by "lower" level, nominal measures.

[7]In 1976 Gordon and DeLeo provided data which suggest that, in the case of Woelfel's system, this first possibility is unlikely.

[8]Great care must be exercised in stating this claim. For instance it must be recognized that highly controlled and contrived types of learning that take place in tests of mathematical learning theories are not always at the core of the metaphorical use of "learning" in many social science theories. Nevertheless, the discrete-state description of learning can and has been applied to higher-order phenomena, such as attitude change, with considerable success.

Stronger evidence for the special purpose use of discrete models comes from examination of the objects of study in social science. Very often these objects are best described in categorical terms. Consider the following example:

(a)   People are frequently conceived of as being categorized as discrete entities. Thus, some individuals are "leaders" and some are not; some are "bankers," or "rednecks" and some are not. To the extent that communication theories seek to capture the effect of differential roles on communication, the effect of communication on different roles, or the distinctive kinds of communication which identify differing roles, such theories must recognize the discrete nature of natural language descriptions of roles.

(b)   Many communicative acts and behaviors are also more realistically described as discrete phenomena. For instance, decisions can be described as dichotomous or polytomous variables over a wide range of instances—voting, buying or not buying a particular home, etc. This discrete representation of choice behavior has broad applicability for the study of the evolution of "common usages" in language (Lewis, 1969), analysis of social interaction (e.g. Bales, 1950; Fisher & Hawes, 1971), the investigation of rule-governed coordination (Cushman & Pearce, 1977), and the study of sequencing rules of behavior (e.g. Krivonos & Knapp, 1975, Hewes, 1978b). In short, for a large number of events of interest to the communication researcher, communication acts can be accurately regarded as discrete-state variables. Undoubtedly continuous representations can more accurately *describe* some events but, for a large class of phenomena, nominal level or partially ordered representations describe how we *communicate* about events.

The preceding discussion leads to the general conclusion that discrete models may be able to better represent certain phenomena than their continuous counterparts. I am asserting that no level of measurement is inherently "worse" than any other level simply because it has less powerful mathematical properties. The nature of the phenomena being measured and the pragmatic concerns of the researcher must also be taken into account. In the case of discrete-state models, nominal-level measurement would appear to be not only useful but positively justifiable for representing many communication phenomena.

C. Summary of the Rationale

In two previous sections I have tried to demonstrate the utility and theoretical justifiability of stochastic models and discrete-state models. Combined, these arguments suggest that the following kinds of communication theories would be realistically represented by discrete-state stochastic models: perceiver-based theories of social interaction; objective theories of social interaction based on nonomniscient observer data; theories of persuasion which have a discrete set of alternatives as an output; learning theoretic models of communication systems where uncertainty is considered to be an integral part of the process; theories of rule-governed behavior where the behaviors have ordinary language representations or are language acts themselves. Such models should be adopted not only because of pragmatic considerations but also because they realistically represent important classes of communication phenomena.

III. CONCEPTUAL BASES OF DISCRETE-STATE STOCHASTIC MODELS

In Section II, I presented an argument for the application of discrete-state stochastic models to some communication research. In this section I will address the more specific issues. The conceptual basis of discrete-state stochastic models will be elaborated, two different classes of such models introduced, the assumptions of those models discussed, procedures for testing those assumptions referenced, and theoretical implications drawn for communication.

A. Kinds of Regularity: The Starting Point for Stochastic Modeling

The ability to predict the probabilities of future events depends upon a systematic relationship between antecedent variables and subsequent probability distributions. For instance, if $p(t + j)$ is the probability that some event will occur at a point in time $t + j$ and $x_i(t + k)$s are i antecedent (causal, predictive, etc.) variables occurring at various points in time $t + k$, then we can describe regularities in $p(t + j)$ by the formula $p(t + j) = f(x_i(t + k))$ for some number of is and ks, $j \geqslant k$, $0 \leqslant i, j, k \leqslant \infty$ where i, j, and k are positive integers, and the f denotes some systematic relationship between the antecedent variables and the probability $p(t + j)$.

This kind of process can be described in a number of different ways depending on the nature of the xs, or antecedent variables. If the xs all refer to events of the same kind as the dependent variable, the system is called an *autoregressive sequence* or a *Markov process*. If the xs refer to both antecedent variables which define group membership (sex, SES, attitude similarity, etc.) and prior events similar to the dependent variable, the equation defines a *nonhomogeneous Markov process*. If the antecedent conditions are restricted to those similar to the dependent variable, the model is called a *homogeneous Markov process*. The simplest of these various models is *a first-order Markov chain* and is defined as $p(t + k) = f(x(t + k - 1))$. The probability of an event occurring during any time interval $t + k$ is a function of some event occurring during the immediately prior time interval, $t + k - 1$. The first-order Markov chain, because of its simplicity, serves as a particularly useful starting point in the application of discrete-state stochastic models in communication research.

To begin the analysis of Markov chains, let us choose the simplest "state space," or set of discrete categories, that is possible. A binary choice state space is obviously simplest and one which can be used to represent phenomena such as choosing to vote or not, continuing or terminating a relationship, etc. If we observe some dichotomous behavior over a large number of units of time, count the occurrences of each option and how often one option follows another, we could construct a description of how past occurrences of one option in the dichotomy are associated with the subsequent occurrence of the other option. Such data could be partially summarized by an index which indicates the rate of transition from one state to another over a given interval of time. For example, if two states in our state space are i and j then the rate of transition from i to j might be defined as:

$$q_{ij} = \frac{\text{number of events } i \text{ followed in the next time interval by event } j}{\text{number of events } i \text{ occurring across the entire time interval}}$$

Clearly, the magnitude of q_{ij} can be affected by the time interval employed. If the time interval is crucial, what time intervals should we choose? While the answer is not straightforward, there are at least two options. One option is to conceive of the time interval (Δt) as being extremely small; the other option is that Δt is measurably and meaningfully large. Let us consider both options.

1. CONTINUOUS TIME PROCESSES

If Δt is taken to be extremely small, then calculu serves as the deductive "language" for our theories of finite state stochastic processes. For instance, the relationship among transition probabilities can be expressed in the form of a differential equation:

$$dn_i = q_{ji} n_{j0} \, dt - q_{ij} n_{i0} \, dt \tag{1}$$

where dn_i is the change in the number of instances of event i over some time interval to be specified, n_{j0} is the instance of j during $t + 0$, n_{i0} is the number of instances of i during $t + 0$, q_{ji} are the probabilities of an event j being following by i and i being followed by j, respectively. Stated verbally, Eq. (1) can be characterized as follows: The change in the number of events $i(dn_i)$ is a function of the probability of an event i being followed by an event $i(q_{ji})$ during a specified period of time $)$ times the number of events j which exist for the process at its initiation (n_{j0}) *minus* the probability of an event i being followed by an event $j(q_{ij})$ during a specified unit of time (dt) times the number of events i which exist for the process at its initiation (n_{i0}). In other words, the increase or decrease in the number of some particular event is determined by how many you start with and the rate at which you add or subtract from that number.

In order to make predictions using Eq. (1), we need to divide through by dt:

$$dn_i / dt = q_{ji} n_{j0} - q_{ij} n_{i0} \tag{2}$$

If we solve Eq. (2) for dt, substitute $n - n_{i0}$ for n_{j0}, and then integrate dt over the interval $t + 0$ to $t + k$, and the left side of the equation over the interval n_{i0} to n_{ik} (see Coleman, 1964a, p. 131), we obtain the general equation for predicting n_{ik}:

$$n_{ik} = (n_{i0} + n_{j0})(q_{ji}/(q_{ji} + q_{ij}))$$
$$+ (n_{i0} - (n_{i0} + n_{j0})(q_{ji}/(q_{ji} + q_{ij})))e^{-k(q_{ji}+q_{ij})} \qquad (3)$$

Solutions such as Eq. (3) are indicative of the level of mathematics necessary to work with continuous time processes. Differential and integral calculus are unfamiliar to many social scientists so that deductions of the type just described cannot be made by many potential users of continuous time models. Fortunately Coleman (1964a), as well as Leik and Meeker (1975), has provided generalized solutions for many of the equations necessary for applying continuous time processes. Though the interested researcher might need to take these solutions on faith, application becomes possible.

A more serious problem arises because of the theoretical implications of continuous time assumption. The assumption underlying theories should not be dictated by an arbitrary choice of a logical calculus, at least as far as possible. The assumptions of the theory should come from our perceptions of the phenomenon being modeled. Therein lies the rub. While some discrete state processes clearly occur continuously, some clearly do not, and many fall in a gray area in between. For example, retention rates of information appear to decay continuously over time as do the effects of a persuasive message given no subsequent input (cf. McGuire, 1973). By way of contrast, the *input* of persuasive messages seems to occur at discrete and definable points in time, as do the performance of particular actions (voting, choosing to perform a cooperative behavior, etc.). In short, the continuous time assumption must not be made without first considering the nature of the phenomena being modeled.

2. Discrete Time Processes

Should the continuous time interpretation of Δt prove nonviable, an alternative is to assume that the time interval is measurably large. Markov models which make that assumption are called *discrete time Markov models*. Such models depend crucially on the size of the time interval chosen. This means that the time interval becomes a parameter of the model and, there-fore, of considerable theoretical interest. A properly specified theory of the phenomenon being modeled by a discrete time process *must* include a specified value for the time interval and a rationale for it.

There are a number of approaches for identifying the appropriate time interval, some empirical and some theoretical. Singer and Spilerman (1974) and Arundale (1976) have provided inductive procedures for identifying optimal values for the time interval. Typically these procedures presume the posited model is correct and work backward to locate the sampling interval which "best" fits a model of the type posited. Such procedures are ad hoc at best and should be avoided in favor of theoretical criteria for choosing the time interval when such criteria are available.

The nature of the time intervals can and should be drawn directly from the phenomena. For example, suppose we are modeling the process of attitude change in response to messages. It is entirely reasonable to consider the time intervals marking the occurrence of messages as discrete. Thus $t + 1$, $t + 2$, etc., do not represent "objective" time intervals measured continuously, but, rather, the occurrence of the first message $(t + 1)$, the second message $(t + 2)$, and so on. While the addition of a time interval parameter complicates the theory, it does produce a generally compensating benefit of simplifying the theory's deductive calculus, a point to be demonstrated in Section III.B.[9]

Once a choice between discrete and continuous time models has been made, it becomes necessary to determine the extent of the isomorphism between the stochastic model of the phenomenon and the phenomenon itself. The place to start in tests of fit is to determine how well the characteristic simplifying assumptions of the model are justified in actuality. For purposes of conceptual and mathematical simplicity, we will begin the search for assumptions by starting with those required by discrete time, discrete-state Markov chain. Once the assumptions required of this exceedingly simple model have been identified, we discuss their theoretical import, how to test for them, and how to rebuild the model if a particular assumption proves unjustified.

B. Testing and Modifying Fundamental Assumptions

A quick review of the discussion surrounding Eqs. (1)–(3) reveals that we have already made a number of implicit *assumptions* in the models presented so far. Consider the parameters q_{ji} and q_{ij} in Eqs. (1)–(3). In all instances these parameters were assumed to be constant over time. In fact, the general solution provided in Eq. (3) requires that both q_{ji} and q_{ij} remain unchanged as time proceeds. This assumption is often made in the case of discrete time Markov chain model as well. This time constancy assumption is called the *stationarity* assumption.

1. STATIONARITY

The reason for this assumption is straightforward. If predictability can be gained by positing some regular relationship between antecedent conditions and subsequent probabilities, then one way to assure predictability is to make that relationship constant over time. In the case of a discrete-state, discrete

---

[9]Throughout the remainder of this chapter I will take advantage of the mathematical simplicity of discrete time stochastic processes. My choice of presenting discrete time models is not to be taken as an endorsement of such models over other alternatives.

time Markov chain, the antecedent conditions are the previous states of the events. Since q_{ij} and q_{ji} define the nature of the relationship between prior states and the present state of events, these parameters must be assumed to be constant. An example may help to clarify this point.

Suppose that V_{t+k} is a vector of probabilities for two mutually exclusive and exhaustive events at $t + k$. If the two events are labeled i and j, $V_{t+k} = (p_i(t + k)p_j(t + k))$, where $p_j(t + k)$ is the probability that event j will occur during $t + k$. For instance, if probability of an intimate relationship between individuals having broken up (i) by $t + k$ is .35 and the probability of it stayed together (j) is .65, then $V_{t+k} = [.35 \ .65]$.

Let us introduce a further bit of notation labeled T, the *transition matrix*. T contains the elements q_{ii}, q_{ji}, and so on, in the following way:

$$T = \begin{bmatrix} q_{ii} & q_{ij} \\ q_{ji} & q_{jj} \end{bmatrix}$$

where q_{ii} in a discrete time system is the probability that event i will be followed immediately by another event i in the next time interval, q_{ij} is the probability that an event i will be followed immediately by an event j during the next time interval, etc. Further $q_{ii} + q_{ij} = q_{ji} + q_{jj} = 1.00$. In terms of our example, $q_{ii} = .75$ means that there is a 75% probability that, if a relationship was broken up during $t + k$, it will stay broken up at $t + k + 1$.

In these models one generally assumes that the probability vector at any time $t + k + 1$ is predictable by knowing that immediately prior value of V and the transition matrix.[10]

$$V_{t+k+1} = V_{t+k}T \tag{4}$$

If we can assume that T is a constant, that is, if we can assume that q_{ii}, q_{ij}, q_{ji}, and q_{jj} do not change with time, then the value of V for any time interval can be predicted using Eq. (4). Thus

$$V_{t+1} = V_{t+0}T \tag{5}$$

$$V_{t+2} = V_{t+1}T \tag{6}$$

$$V_{t+3} = V_{t+2}T \tag{7}$$

and so on, for any time interval.

Suppose that we substitute the right-hand side of Eq. (5) for V_{t+1} in Eq. (6) and then substitute the right-hand side of Eq. (6) for V_{t+2} in Eq. (7). This would yield

$$V_{t+3} = ((V_{t+0}T)T)T \quad \text{or} \quad V_{t+3} = V_{t+0}T^3$$

It turns out that for any value of $t + k$,

$$V_{t+k} = V_{t+0}T^k \tag{8}$$

[10]We will return to the basis of this "general assumption" shortly.

Equation (8) is a rather powerful generalization. Starting with any known probability vector V_{t+0} and a know transition matrix T, we can predict the probability vector for any time interval $t + k$ as long as T remains constant and two other assumptions are met. We will discuss these assumptions shortly.

To illustrate the power of Eq. (8), let us return to our example. If $V_{t+0} = [.35 \ .65]$ and

$$T = \begin{bmatrix} .75 & .25 \\ .60 & .40 \end{bmatrix}$$

then, for instance,

$$V_{t+2} = [.35 \ .65]\begin{bmatrix} .75 & .25 \\ .60 & .40 \end{bmatrix}^2, \quad V_{t+2} = [.35 \ .65]\begin{bmatrix} .5625 & .4375 \\ .4500 & .6500 \end{bmatrix}$$

$$V_{t+2} = [.4894 \ .5106] \tag{9}$$

Substantively Eq. (9) indicates that during $t + 2$ approximately 48.94% of the sampled population would have their relationship broken off given the initial probability vector values at $t + 0$, a constant transition matrix, and two other conditions to be specified. The expected cumulative percentages of broken relationships for any time interval could be estimated in the same fashion.

The assumption of stationarity is crucial to the predictive power of a whole class of stochastic models including Markov chains and various continuous-state models and autoregressive models (cf. Anderson, 1971; Box & Jenkins, 1970).[11] As a consequence, the assumption of stationarity must be empirically validated before other aspects of a Markov chain model are examined.

Anderson and Goodman (1957), as well as Kullback, Kupperman, and Ku (1962), provide a host of useful maximum likelihood tests for Markov chains, among them a test for stationarity. In order to test for stationarity one first pools the transition matrices for all available pairs of time periods (the transition matrices for $t + 0$ to $t + 1$ with $t + 1$ to $t + 2$ with $t + 2$ with $t + 3$, etc.). In practice this is accomplished by adding together the frequencies on which the transition matrices were based and computing a pooled transition matrix from the resulting pooled matrix of frequencies. Thus if $f_{ij}(1)$ equals the number of transitions between states i and j during $t + 0$ to $t + 1$ and $f_{ij}(2)$ equals the number of transitions between i and j during $t + 1$ to $t + 2$, then $f_{ij}(\cdot)$ equals the pooled transition frequency for $t + 0$ to $t + 2$. If $f_{ij}(\cdot)$ were divided by the total number of observations in state i across $t + 0$ to $t + 2$ ($f_{i.}(\cdot)$), the result will be $q_{ij}(\cdot)$ for the pooled transition matrix. This pooled transition matrix is then compared to each of the original transition matrices under the *null hypothesis* that any deviations are due to sampling

---

[11]While stationarity is crucial, it alone does not constitute a sufficient condition to ensure that $V_{t+0} = V_{t+0}T^k$. Two other assumptions, together with stationarity, become a sufficient set of conditions for this relationship to hold.

error alone. The *alternative* hypothesis is that some source of error, either systematic or random, greater than sampling error explains the deviations in fit between the pooled and individual transition matrices. Let us illustrate this with an example.

Hypothetical data presented in Tables I–III represent the results of a content analysis of dyadic interaction employing Rogers' relational coding scheme for dominance (cf. Rogers & Farace, 1975). Table I contains the occurrence of the three types of dominance statements at $t + 0$ cross-tabulated with the occurrence of the three types of dominance statements at $t + 1$.[12] Table II contains the same type of information for the time periods $t + 1$ and $t + 2$.

TABLE I

SEQUENTIAL STRUCTURE OF THE FREQUENCIES OF TYPES OF RELATIONAL REMARKS DURING THE TIME INTERVAL $T + 0$ TO $T + 1$

| Types of relational remarks at $T + 0$ | Types of relational remarks at $T + 1$ | | | |
	One-up	One-across	One-down	Row total
One-up	20	10	30	60
One-across	10	20	30	60
One-down	10	10	40	60
Column total	40	40	100	180

TABLE II

SEQUENTIAL STRUCTURE OF THE FREQUENCIES OF TYPES OF RELATIONAL REMARKS DURING THE TIME INTERVAL $T + 1$ TO $T + 2$

| Types of relational remarks at $T + 1$ | Types of relational remarks at $T + 2$ | | | |
	One-up	One-across	One-down	Row total
One-up	30	10	0	40
One-across	30	0	10	40
One-down	40	30	30	100
Column total	100	40	40	180

TABLE III

SEQUENTIAL STRUCTURE OF THE FREQUENCIES OF TYPES OF RELATIONAL REMARKS FOR THE POOLED TIME INTERVALS $T + 0$ TO $T + 1$ AND $T + 1$ TO $T + 2$

| Types of relational remarks | Types of relational remarks | | | |
	One-up	One-across	One-down	Row total
One-up	50	20	30	100
One-across	40	20	40	100
One-down	50	40	70	160
Column total	140	80	140	360

[12] To obtain this kind of data one might observe the interaction over some *interval* called $t + 0, t + 1$, etc. Clearly interactions do not occur *at* a particular point in time.

These two tables can be converted into three transition matrices which are used for testing the stationarity assumption; T_1, T_2, and $T_{(\cdot)}$ composed of elements $q_{ij}(1)$, $q_{ij}(2)$, and $q_{ij}(\cdot)$, respectively, where the $(\cdot)$ notation indicates parameters and matrices created by pooling the frequency data from Tables I and II. For example if the cell frequencies of the first table are divided through by their respective row totals

$$T_1 = \begin{bmatrix} .333 & .167 & .500 \\ .167 & .333 & .500 \\ .167 & .167 & .666 \end{bmatrix}, \qquad T_2 = \begin{bmatrix} .750 & .250 & .000 \\ .750 & .000 & .250 \\ .400 & .300 & .300 \end{bmatrix}$$

If we pool the two original tables we obtain Table III and we divide the cell frequencies through by the row totals, we obtain a pooled transition matrix, that is, a transition matrix pooled over both time intervals:

$$T_{(\cdot)} = \begin{bmatrix} .500 & .200 & .300 \\ .400 & .200 & .400 \\ .313 & .250 & .437 \end{bmatrix}$$

At this point all the information is available which we need to test whether the probabilities in T_1 and T_2 are stationary (constant) across times within the limits of sampling error. The statistical test has as its null hypothesis that the transition matrices are stationary $[q_{ij}(t+k) = q_{ij}(\cdot))$ for $1 \leqslant i, j \leqslant r$, and $1 \leqslant t \leqslant T]$ versus an alternative hypothesis that the transition matrices are not stationary $[q_{ij}(t + k) \neq q_{ij}(\cdot)]$. Rejection of the null hypothesis leads to a certain amount of ambiguity since the alternative hypothesis does not specify what, if any, relationship may exist between time and the changes in transition probabilities. For instance, in our example if we computed the fit for all 18 transition probabilities and summed those fits, we would have rejected the null hypothesis at a pre-set α of .001. The transition matrices T_1 and T_2 do not describe a stationary process. The process they *do* describe remains a mystery.

What does the result of this experiment imply conceptually? It simply means that some factor related to time or time itself must be incorporated in our explanation of the sequencing of statements of dominance. In particular, some explanation must be sought for the fact that one-up statements *are not* typically followed by one-up statements $[q_{11}(1) = .333]$ during the first two points in time (T_1) but *are* typically followed by one-up statements $[q_{11}(2) = .750]$ during the second and third points in time (T_2). Does the reason for the observed interaction involve the choice of a leader which was accomplished in $t + 1$ to $t + 2$? Did two dominant individuals revert to type after experiencing uncertainty in the initial interaction?

Clearly, a rejection of the null hypothesis of stationarity should inspire the search for more information about the phenomenon under investigation. This information could than be integrated with the transition matrix to form a more complete picture. For example, if the level of psychological uncertainty about the other person [$Un(t + 0)$] explains the predominance of one-down interacts [$q_{33}(1)$] in T_1, then the description of T_2 might be improved by theorizing that

$$q_{ij}(t + 0) = \beta_0 + \beta_1 q_{ij}(t - 1) + \beta_2 \, Un \, (t + 0) + E_{ij} \qquad (10)$$

The transition probability for any states i and j at some time t is dependent upon the transition probability between those same two states during the immediately prior transition period and the level of perceived uncertainty (Un) at time $t + 0$. The inclusion of the explanatory variable $Un(t + 0)$ permits exogenous information to influence the interaction patterns. Thus Eq. (10) could "explain" the failure to find over time regularity in dominance interaction patterns by adding more information concerning the context of that interaction. Hewes *et al.* (1977) have employed this approach with considerable success in modeling changes in behavior expectations in response to messages.

Equation (10) presents a number of methodological difficulties which can only be briefly mentioned here. For instance, the data set in Tables I and II does not allow for Eq. (10) to be tested. We have only one value each for $q_{ij}(t + 0)$, $q_{ij}(t - 1)$, and $Un(t + 0)$. We would need at least four transition matrices and three observations of levels of uncertainty to estimate all the unknowns in Eq. (10). Without this information we would have too few observations to estimate the parameters. Other problems manifest themselves as soon as we have enough observations to use Eq. (10) as a regression equation. There arise considerable difficulties in meeting the statistical assumption that the error terms of Eq. (10) are uncorrelated (Hibbs, 1974) and in obtaining efficient estimation of the parameters (cf. Lee *et al.* 1970; Madansky, 1959; Hewes, 1978c).

Perhaps more important than any of these difficulties, however, is the problem in bridging the theoretical gap between a rejection of the null hypothesis of stationarity and the specification of the form of that nonstationarity in a form such as Eq. (12). First of all, there is no guarantee that nonstationarity will be systematic; that is, there is no guarantee that the change in transition probabilities is *systematically* related to time or some time dependent variable. A rejection of the null hypothesis *only* means that, for the time intervals sampled, the transition probabilities were not constant over time. There is nothing to prevent them from varying randomly across time. Second, the specification of the relationship between the transition probabilities and some exogenous variables is not as straightforward as Eq. (10) implies. For instance, the dependent variable, $q_{ij}(t + 0)$, may be nonlinearly related to the independent variables. The specification of the type of nonstationarity, if it is systematic, represents a major theoretical and empirical undertaking in and of itself.

2. Order

In the previous discussion I observed that the assumption of stationarity is not the only assumption that needs to be made in the Markov chain model. Another necessary assumption, the *order* assumption, was explicitly introduced by requiring that the probability vector at any time $t + k + 1$ is predictable by knowing the immediately prior value of the probability vector at $t + k + 0$. It was this assumption that allowed us to assert Eq. (4),

$$V_{t+k+1} = V_{t+k}T$$

which was the starting point for the whole predictive process.

The order assumption can be formally stated as

$$q_{ij} = q_{klm \ldots ij} \tag{11}$$

where q_{ij} is the transition probability between state i and state j over the time interval $t + k$ to $t + k + 1$, and $q_{klm \ldots ij}$ is the same transition probability conditional on state occupancies prior to the occupancy of state i, i.e., prior to $t + k$. The preceding definition generally implies that in order to predict probabilities of state occupancy at $t + k + 1$ it is necessary only to have information *concerning the distribution* of state occupancy probabilities, i.e., the elements of V, at $t + k$. This is the sense in which the order assumption was employed in our previous discussion of the predictive power of the simple Markov chain [see Eqs. (4)–(8)].

Equation (11) actually describes only one kind of order assumption, a *first-order assumption*. This typical Markov chain assumption is so named because information from only *one* prior time period and the transition matrix are necessary in order to make predictions. One may have second-order Markov chains ($q_{kij} = q_{mp \ldots kij}$) or third-order Markov chains ($q_{klij} = q_{mp \ldots klij}$), etc. Even zero-order Markov chains are possible ($q_j = q_{klm \ldots ij}$), but these "Bernoulli series" models are generally of little interest to communication researchers except as benchmarks for more complex models or as models of processes at equilibrium.

If the wrong order is assumed for a process the predictions of equation would not hold. In order to test the order assumptions a variety of statistical tools are available (Kullback *et al.*, 1962; Chatfield, 1973); there are methods which test (1) whether the hypothesis is of the zeroth order versus the alternative hypothesis that the process is of the first or higher order, (2) whether the process is of the first order versus the alternative hypothesis that the process is of the second *or higher* order, and so on. A simple example might help both to clarify these order tests.

Suppose we are interested in whether or not "bids" to define a dyadic relationship are accepted or rejected (Folger & Puck, 1976). Since the power to accept or reject a bid suggests control in a relationship, developmental patterns in bid acceptance/rejection might be an *outcome* determined by antecedent variables such as tolerance for ambiguity, androgyny, or dogmatism of the participants. On the other hand, the trends in bid acceptance/rejection might be *precursors* of satisfaction with the relationship.

Whatever set of relationships are of interest, the simple Markov chain is a convenient place to begin analyzing these developmental trends. To demonstrate this point in the context of the order statistics already presented, consider the simplified hypothetical data set obtained from a large number of homogeneous dyads (dyads manifesting the same developmental patterns) (Table IV). The data in Table IV represent a hypothetical pattern of acceptance/rejection from the standpoint of *one* participant in the dyad. (Folger and Puck's "evasion" category has been excluded to simplify the example.)

The first null hypothesis posited is that these data describe a zero-order system. In order to test this hypothesis against its alternative, it is necessary to reduce the table to two transition matrices by collapsing across categories. Thus the transition matrix for $t + 0$ to $t + 1$ is given in Table V. The transition matrix for $t + 1$ to $t + 2$ appears in Table VI.[13]

In this example, the stochastic process described by these transition matrices significantly differs from a zero-order process ($p < .05$). That is, we

TABLE IV

FREQUENCIES OF BIDS ACCEPTED AND REJECTED DURING $T + 0$, $T + 1$ AND $T + 2$ REPRESENTED AS A SECOND-ORDER PROCESS

Bids accepted and rejected for $T + 0$ and $T + 1$	Bids accepted and rejected for $T + 1$ and $T + 2$				
	Accept ($T + 1$) and accept ($T + 2$)	Accept ($T + 1$) and reject ($T + 2$)	Reject ($T + 1$) and accept ($T + 2$)	Reject ($T + 1$) and reject ($T + 2$)	Row total
Accept ($T + 0$)/and accept ($T + 1$)	50	20	0	0	70
Accept ($T + 0$)/and reject ($T + 1$)	0	0	80	50	130
Reject ($T + 0$)/and accept ($T + 1$)	70	10	0	0	80
Reject ($T + 0$)/and reject ($T + 1$)	0	0	20	100	120
Column total	120	30	100	150	400

[13]The two transition matrices in Table V and VI are also nonstationary. One can construct a stationary first-order transition matrix that is better represented by a second-order process; therefore, there is no necessary link between higher-order processes and nonstationarity. One must remember, though, that if the process is of a higher order, then that *higher-order* transition matrix is what must be stationary.

reject the null hypothesis that this process is zero order in favor of the alternative hypothesis that it is of some higher order as yet unknown.

Here we encountered the problem of rejecting a *specific* null hypothesis in favor of the *unspecific* alternative hypothesis, that is, the null hypothesis that the process is of the first order versus the alternative hypothesis that the process is of the second or higher order. In this hypothetical example it turns out that the process is of the second order; therefore, we would have rejected the *null* hypothesis that the process was of the first order and, in a subsequent test, would have failed to reject the *null* hypothesis that the process is of the second order.

We are left with two problems to resolve: Once this series of tests is completed how do we *represent* and how do we *interpret* a second-order process? The first problem is rather easily resolved. The four-by-four raw-data matrix (Table IV) given at the beginning of this example can be converted into a second-order transition matrix by dividing all the cell entries through by their row sums. The second-order transition matrix for our hypothetical data thus becomes

$$T = \begin{bmatrix} .714 & .286 & .000 & .000 \\ .000 & .000 & .615 & .385 \\ .875 & .125 & .000 & .000 \\ .000 & .000 & .167 & .833 \end{bmatrix}$$

TABLE V

SEQUENTIAL STRUCTURE OF FREQUENCIES AND TRANSITION PROBABILITIES FOR RELATIONAL BIDS DURING THE TIME INTERVAL $T + 0$ TO $T + 1$

Bids at $T + 0$	Bids at $T + 1$[a]		Row total
	Accept	Reject	
Accept	50 + 20 = 70 (.35)	80 + 50 = 130 (.65)	200
Reject	70 + 10 = 80 (.40)	20 + 100 = 120 (.60)	200
Column Total	150	250	400

[a]Numbers in parentheses are transition probabilities.

TABLE VI

SEQUENTIAL STRUCTURE OF FREQUENCIES AND TRANSITION PROBABILITIES FOR RELATIONAL BIDS DURING THE TIME INTERVAL $T + 1$ TO $T + 2$

Bids at $T + 1$	Bids at $T + 2$[a]		Row total
	Accept	Reject	
Accept	50 + 70 = 120 (.80)	20 + 10 = 30 (.20)	150
Reject	80 + 20 = 100 (.40)	50 + 100 = 150 (.60)	250
	220	180	400

[a]Numbers in parentheses are transition probabilities.

It should be clear that the "states" in the second-order transition matrix, and consequently, in the probability vectors, are defined in terms of *two time-ordered* states from the first-order transition matrices, e.g., such second-order states as "accept at $t + k$ and reject at $t + k + 1$." [Miller (1952) has made available a more detailed account of the construction and application of second-order processes.]

As previously indicated, there is a second problem that confronts us once the order hypotheses have been tested; how do we interpret a second-order precess? The most frequently given answer is that we do not interpret second- or higher-order processes. A variety of methods are employed to avoid interpretation. For instance, Hawes and Foley (1976) used a power analysis of the statistical tests to justify treating a statistically identified second-order process as a first-order process. Cappella (1976) "eyeballed" his data to determine if it was other than a first-order, stationary process, though statistical tests would have undoubtedly revealed that the data was better represented by a higher-order process. Hayes, Melzer, and Wolf (1972) examined the mean proportion of uncertainty reduced by employing higher-order processes to demonstrate the lack of practical significance of increasing the order of the representational scheme.

The procedures employed by Cappella, Hawes, and Foley and Hayes *et al.* are justifiable and, in fact, highly advisable, since they are motivated by a desire for *mathematical simplicity*. Nonetheless, the practical value of mathematical simplicity can be overemphasized. The conventional wisdom in stochastic modeling implies that higher-order processes are too unwieldly to be of any practical use (Coleman, 1973). However, social interaction sequences might be more *accurately* explained by second-order processes.

> Given that interdependence is the crucial element from which a theory of organizations is built, *interacts* rather than acts are the crucial observables that must be specified. The unit of action by actor A evokes a specific response in actor B which is then responded to by actor A. This is the pattern designated a "double interact" by Barker and Wright (1955), and it is proposed by Hollander and Willis (1967) as the basic unit for describing interpersonal influence [Weick, 1969, p. 33]

Put another way, if the interact is the unit of analysis, then the double interact is the relationship to be analyzed. The double interact is simply a second-order transition probability in a matrix where *each state* indicates *who* performed a given communicative act at a given time period and *who* responded to it *how*.[14] Put another way, a second-order transition matrix of this type represents *who* said *what* to *whom* with *what effect* (Lasswell, 1948; see Hewes, 1977b, for a more detailed version of the argument).

[14] The probability of actor A's response at $t + k$ is contingent *both* on B's action at $t + k - 1$ *and* A's initial action at $t + k - 2$. In 1970 Lyman and Scott observed that much of the theorizing in social interaction is built on higher-order contingency models of human interaction.

Even when the double interact framework just described is not relevant to a particular problem, second- or higher-order processes may still be useful. For instance, in our acceptance/rejection transition matrix example, the process described was clearly of the second order. The second-order transition matrix reveals an interesting and potentially explainable pattern. If two bids in a row are either accepted or rejected the third bid will likely be treated in the same manner (processes 1 and 2); if the first bid is rejected and the second accepted, the third is likely to be accepted (process 3); if the first is accepted and the second is rejected, the third bid is likely to be accepted (process 4).

Process 1 is indicative of a relationship defining process where the initial bid turns out to be acceptable to both parties; the second and third bids confirm and reinforce the initially correct bid. Process 2 indicates a potentially irreconcilable disagreement over relational definitions while processes 3 and 4 indicate relationships fraught with initial uncertainty which is finally resolved. Thus, higher-order processes, such as the one stated previously, are often interpretable. While first-order processes may be more parsimonious, theoretical reasons for examining higher-order process should not be overlooked. Tests of the order assumption should be guided by an overall conceptual framework containing phenomenon-specific predictions and explanations for the outcome of the assumption testing.

3. HOMOGENEITY

The third fundamental assumption needed for Markov chain analysis is *homogeneity*. This assumption requires that the transition matrix T be representative of all individuals and/or subgroups in the sampled population.

Formally, the assumption requires that $T_a = T_b = \cdots = T_{(\cdot)}$ for all subgroups $(a, b,$ etc.) in the sampled population, where T_a and T_b are the transition matrices for subgroups a and b and $T_{(\cdot)}$ is the transition matrix for the whole population.

The reason for requiring homogeneity in Markov chain analysis is easily demonstrated. Suppose that T is created from a weighted average of the transition matrices in subgroups a and b; $T = xT_a + yT_b$, where x and y are weighting coefficients. In Markov chain analysis the transition matrix T is raised to powers for various computations such as predicting probability vectors [see Eq. (8)].

If T_a and T_b are both of the same order and have the same state space and described stationary processes, then each can be raised to the second power, for example, separately to make predictions to $t + 2$. If they are pooled together to recompose T, then

$$T^2 = xT_a^2 + yT_b^2 \tag{12}$$

According to the original pooling scheme, however, it was equally true that $T = xT_a + yT_b$, thus

$$T^2 = (xT_a + yT_b)^2$$

or

$$T^2 = xT_a^2 + xyT_bT_a + xyT_aT_b + Y^2T_b^2 \qquad (13)$$

It should be obvious that Eqs. (12) and (13) are not equivalent. The process described by a single transition matrix raised to a power is not necessarily the same as the process describing two separated subgroup transition matrices each raised to a power. In other words, *a single, pooled transition matrix is an inaccurate representation of processes in a heterogeneous population.*

If heterogeneity can invalidate a standard Markov representation, how do we detect violations of the homogeneity assumption? There are two ways to proceed: We can test for the effects of known or suspected sources of heterogeneity or we can perform a diagnostic test for unknown heterogeneity producing influences. The test for the effects of known or suspected sources of heterogeneity is very similar to the test employed earlier to detect non-stationarity (Anderson & Goodman, 1957; Kullback *et al.*, 1962). (In fact, nonstationarity is merely temporal heterogeneity.) The statistic tests the null hypothesis that the process is homogeneous against the alternative hypothesis that one or more of the subgroups possesses a transition matrix which differs systematically and substantially from the pooled, population transition matrix. Data gathered by Hewes and Evans-Hewes (1974) provide some insight into both the procedures and the interpretability of direct tests of homogeneity.

Hewes and Evans-Hewes were interested in examining the probability structure of attitude change in response to a message campaign. One issue which they examined was the possible influence of initial opinion and "sidedness" of the message on the transition probabilities of attitudes. Previous research suggested that the one-sided messages used in this study would produce different and more pronounced patterns of changes for those who were initially "for" the advocated policy option than for those initially "opposed" to it (for instance, Hovland, Lumsdaine, & Sheffield, 1949). Thus, Hewes and Evans-Hewes examined the transition matrices for those who were initially "for" and those who were initially "against" socialized medicine. Raw data pooled across four time periods from this experiment are presented in Tables VII and VIII.

These two transition matrices can be used to generate a third—a matrix created by presuming the process is homogeneous (with respect to initial opinion) and pooling the data from the other two raw data matrices. As before, the raw data matrices are converted into transition matrices by dividing each cell frequency through by the row total. The results of the operation on the three matrices are

$$T_f = \begin{bmatrix} .84 & .15 & .01 \\ .34 & .53 & .13 \\ .60 & .00 & .40 \end{bmatrix}, \quad T_a = \begin{bmatrix} .76 & .22 & .02 \\ .32 & .61 & .07 \\ .10 & .47 & .43 \end{bmatrix} \quad T_{(\cdot)} = \begin{bmatrix} .82 & .17 & .01 \\ .33 & .59 & .08 \\ .14 & .43 & .43 \end{bmatrix}$$

TABLE VII

SEQUENTIAL STRUCTURE OF FREQUENCIES OF ATTITUDE RESPONSES TO A QUESTION
CONCERNING SOCIALIZED MEDICINE FOR THOSE INITIALLY FAVORABLE[a]

Responses prior to messages	Responses subsequent to messages			
	For	Do not know	Against	Row total
For	146	26	1	173
Do not know	11	17	4	32
Against	3	0	2	5
Column total	160	43	7	210

[a]These data were taken from a study by Hewes and Evans-Hewes (1974) with the permission of the authors.

TABLE VIII

SEQUENTIAL STRUCTURE OF FREQUENCIES OF ATTITUDE RESPONSES TO A QUESTION
CONCERNING SOCIALIZED MEDICINE FOR THOSE INITIALLY OPPOSED[a]

Responses prior to messages	Responses subsequent to messages			
	For	Do not know	Against	Row total
For	51	15	1	67
Do not know	55	103	12	170
Against	5	24	22	51
Column total	111	142	35	288

[a]These data were taken from a study by Hewes and Evans-Hewes (1974) with the permission of the authors.

where T_f denotes the transition matrix for those initially for socialized medicine, T_a is the transition matrix for those against that issue, and $T_{(\cdot)}$ is the transition matrix created by pooling the frequency data from T_f and T_a under the assumption of homogeneity. The states of the matrices ("for," "do not know," and "against") are in the same configuration as in the raw data tables presented previously.

For these data the null hypothesis of homogeneity was rejected ($p < .01$) and, therefore, one anticipated source of heterogeneity identified. We now have evidence that the process of attitude change, in response to a one-sided message campaign, is heterogeneous with respect to initial opinion. If the other assumptions of the Markov chain were supported for the transition matrices *for each subgroup*, then we could predict the long term effects of this kind of campaign on both subgroups by working with the two transition matrices separately. Ultimately we should be able to determine how much attitude change was possible for either group and how many messages would be needed before the maximum practical effect could be realized.[15]

[15]Descriptive statistics which yield these two results are described in detail in a text by Derman, Gleser, and Olkin (1973, pp. 615–651).

Unfortunately, several issues remain unaddressed by the test of the data just reported. The fact that *one* source of heterogeneity has been located does not preclude others; the search for heterogeneity does not necessarily end with either the identification of the failure to identify a particular source. How do we locate other sources of heterogeneity? Further, if we cannot anticipate all possible sources of heterogeneity, how will that affect the predictive power of the model?

There are a number of moderately heartening answers to these two serious questions. To locate other sources of heterogeneity, we may proceed either by continued application of the described statistical test to other anticipated sources of heterogeneity or by means of a diagnostic test for unanticipated sources. Let us now consider the diagnostic approach. Coleman (1973) and Singer and Spilerman (1974) note that a characteristic indication of nonhomogeneity is a "deficient diagonal" in Markov chain predictions. This means that as a transition matrix is raised to powers greater than 1 (T^2, T^3, etc.), it tends to "overpredict" change. That is, the main diagonal in a transition matrix (running from the upper left corner to the lower right) raised to a power greater than 1 tends to have smaller probability values than those when the actual change over the observed time interval is examined. This diagnostic test can be applied to the Hewes/Evans-Hewes data as an illustration.

Suppose that we had not anticipated initial opinion as a source of nonhomogeneity. If we had anticipated some unknown source or sources of nonhomogeneity, then the diagnostic test would have proven useful. To execute this test we merely estimate the transition matrix for the whole sample, raise it to the second or a higher power depending on the available data, and compare those higher power transition matrices to actual observations. Observations of the higher power matrices are obtained by examining turnover tables for nonadjacent time periods. The actual values of T^2 could be obtained by looking at the turnover table for $t + 0$ to $t + 2$ or $t + 1$ to $t + 3$ while the actual values of T^3 could be obtained from turnover tables for $t + 0$ to $t + 3$ and $t + 1$ to $t + 4$.

Applied to the example this procedure yields the result:

$$T^2_{(\cdot)} = \begin{bmatrix} .69 & .26 & .05 \\ .41 & .52 & .07 \\ .12 & .44 & .44 \end{bmatrix}$$

whereas the expected value of T^2 under the assumption of homogeneity was

$$\hat{T}^2_{(\cdot)} = \begin{bmatrix} .73 & .24 & .03 \\ .50 & .36 & .14 \\ .33 & .45 & .22 \end{bmatrix}$$

$\hat{T}^2_{(\cdot)}$ was generated by raising the pooled transition matrix to the second power. $T^2_{(\cdot)}$ was obtained by examining the turnover table from $t + 0$ to $t + 2$. The effects of heterogeneity are apparent in the major diagonals of the two matrices. While the Markov chain tends to slightly underpredict values in the "for–for" transition (.73 versus .69), it vastly overpredicts change in the "do not know–do not know" transition (.36 versus .52) and again in the "against–against " transition (.22 versus .44). These results are characteristic of those produced by heterogeneity. The Markov predictions generally indicated greater tendencies to change than were observed. We have thus diagnosed the presence of heterogeneity.

Though this diagnostic test helps detect the presence of a violation of the homogeneity assumption, it is not without faults. There are several competing explanations for the deficient diagonal problem (cf. Coleman, 1973, Chapter 1; Hewes *et al.*, 1977). Even if these competing explanations can be ruled out, there still remains the problem of identifying the unknown sources of heterogeneity; this problem, however, need not be crippling. Being forced to look for other important variables is not necessarily bad. In fact, the "deficient diagonal" problem may be a positive benefit in that it focuses attention on missing sources of heterogeneity.

Before these sources are located, heterogeneity does not necessarily turn out to be a serious problem for prediction, though it does for explanation. Morrison, Massy, and Silverman (1971) have presented evidence that the effects of even moderately large heterogeneity on predictions are small. The Hewes/Evans-Hewes (1974) paper provided empirical support for that conclusion. Further, Singer and Spilerman (1974; Spilerman, 1972b) have developed a series of sophisticated models for incorporating heterogeneity from *unknown* sources into Markov models. If suspected sources of nonhomogeneity are identified, there are numerous techniques for incorporating them in Markov process models (cf. Hewes & Evans-Hewes, 1974; Ginsberg, 1972; Spilerman, 1972a). Thus heterogeneity, like the other violations of Markov chain assumptions, can yield theoretically meaningful insights and generate heuristically fruitful alternative models.

4. Miscellaneous

In previous sections we have examined the theoretical and statistical properties of Markov chain assumptions. We demonstrated that each of those three assumptions (stationarity, order, and homogeneity) was required for the predictive power of the Markov chain to be invoked. Communication researchers employing the Markov chain should test all these assumption before proceeding with the other analyses. Once these three assumptions have been examined there remain several fundamental properties of Markov chain models which should be considered. These are (a) the form of representation chosen for the state space and (b) "lumpability."

Consider one property of Markov chains most recently discussed by Conlisk (1976):

> One highly restrictive assumption, which is almost universal in Markov chain modeling, has received very little attention. This is the assumption that the transition probabilities governing an individual's moves across states do not

> depend on how other individuals in the population are distributed over other
> states. That is, one individual's behavior is independent of the behavior of other
> individuals. More simply, *social interaction among individuals is assumed away*.
> This is a remarkable assumption for a core model of social processes [p. 175,
> author's italics].

This assumption concerns the method by which transition probabilities are
estimated rather than the mathematical properties of the Markov chain itself;
nevertheless, it can pose serious problems for virtually every example of
Markov chain analysis cited in this chapter. For instance, much of the work
on chain models of small group interaction (Hawes & Foley, 1973; Ellis &
Fisher, 1975) can be questioned on the basis of this noninteractive assumption. The literature on small group interaction would hardly support the
assumption that social interaction does *not* have any influence on subsequent
behavior—the explicit assumption behind much of this research is precisely
the reverse (Fisher & Hawes, 1971; Weick, 1969, pp. 31–34). Further, the
attitude change research of Hewes and Evans-Hewes could well be under-
mined by a noninteractive assumption, especially in light of the potential
effects of social interaction on long term attitude change (e.g., Festinger,
1955).

Several avenues present themselves for resolving the problems precipitated
by the independent probabilities assumption. In attitude change research the
simplest solution is to ensure noninteraction of subjects by means of design,
instructions, and ex post facto manipulation checks. Hewes and Evans-Hewes
incorporated these approaches into their study. While such procedures do
limit generalizability to more naturalistic instances of overtime persuasion,
the problem of social interaction can be eliminated and its effects separated
from a direct one-step flow of persuasion processes.

This solution will not work for social interaction studies; however, for
studies of small group interaction, there are two other alternatives (which can
also be employed in attitude and behavior change studies). The first option is
to change the states employed in these studies. The traditional approach is to
restrict the states of the Markov chain to the categories in some coding
scheme. If, however, the states were redefined so that each state was described *both* in terms of a coding category *and* who enacted that coding
category, the problem would be resolved (e.g., Simon & Agazarian, 1967). As
Conlisk notes,

> It might be argued that a standard Markov chain can handle individual
> interaction if states are properly defined. Given K states for an individual and
> N individuals (or roles), there are K^N possible states for the population as a
> whole; and we might define a (K^N, K^N) transition matrix which takes the
> population from superstate to superstate as time passes. This idea does allow
> interaction since the transition probabilities could take account of all indi-
> vidual's behavior [p. 158].

Conlisk goes on to point out that this solution is intractable for large social
systems, but for small groups it may prove viable. The previous discussion of

double interact approaches to social interaction suggests positive benefits to Conlisk's solution.[16] Hewes (1977) provided a more detailed analysis of these benefits.

A second alternative open to social interaction researchers can be found in Conlisk's (1976) recent contributions in the field of interactive Markov chains. While much work remains to be done in this area, present results suggest that the assumption of social interaction may be integrated into Markov chainlike models which retain enough of the standard Markov chain's tractability so that analytic results are possible. Conlisk's work should prove to be of interest for theorists concerned with models of social interaction.

Another major problem in Markov chain analysis concerns the way in which state categories are handled in subsequent data analysis. Coding schemes often include categories with too few observations to be useful, or include multiple categories which all index the same kind of behavior. Under such conditions a researcher may be tempted to collapse across categories. While this procedure usually has much to recommend it, special care must be taken in Markov chain analysis. The reason for this necessary caution rests in a property of Markov chains called "lumpability."

Kemeny and Snell (1960) demonstrated that if a process can be described by a Markov chain, collapsing (or expanding) the number of categories ("lumping") does not necessarily yield a new process also characterized by Markovian properties. This means, for instance, that the predictions of the original and "lumped" process would not necessarily be similar. It also suggests that if a process were "lumped" for some theoretical or practical reason, the statistical tests of the assumptions of the original process would not necessarily apply to the "lumped" process. These tests should be performed again on the "lumped" model [see Hawes & Foley (1973) for an example of a study which apparently suffers from this problem].

Kememy and Snell (1960, pp. 123–140) have described a necessary and sufficient condition for "lumpability" as well as special conditions for "weak lumpability," which is lumpability that holds only for certain, specified initial

---

[16]In reality, Conlisk's solution is a bit more complex than the one presented in the discussion of double interacts. Conlisk's solution assumes that the state of every member of a group at any moment of time might influence the state of any member of the group at the next moment of time (assuming that this is a first-order process). For instance, if there are two individuals (A and B) and two states (i and j), then Conlisk's full model would describe the state of the whole system in terms of the four possible combinations (2^2) of individuals and states: (A_i, B_i), (A_i, B_j), (A_j, B_i), (A_j, B_j). Thus, whereas a conventional Markov chain would define a transition matrix in terms of the transitions from state to state, i.e., a two by two matrix with transition from i to i, i to j, etc., the Conlisk model would represent this system with a four by four transition matrix, transitions occurring from (A_i, B_i) to (A_i, B_i), from (A_i, B_i) to (A_i, B_j), etc. This obviously leads to a much more complicated system when the number of states and/or the number of individuals is large. Hewes (1977) indicates how one might go about reducing this complexity to more manageable levels.

probability vectors. Researchers who plan on changing the state space of their category system should consult this source before proceeding.

5. SUMMARY OF TESTING ASSUMPTIONS

We have come to the end of our discussion of testing and modifying the assumptions of Markov chain models. It should be clear that these models provide a useful basis for evolving more comprehensive models of communication behavior. In discussing the assumptions of the simple Markov chain, I have tried to emphasize that detection of violations of assumptions, far from being a tragedy, might well lead one to adopt a more realistic view of the phenomenon being studies. Further, I have tried to underscore the necessity of an explanatory orientation when employing stochastic models. Too often the predictive or descriptive power of Markov chains has been taken as a substitute for explanation. Markov chains and their derivatives *can* provide an explanatory framework for communication phenomenon. Simple concern for *what* is being modeled and *why* it would have Markovian properties should enhance the theoretical import of stochastic models in communication research.

IV. WHERE DO WE GO FROM HERE?

Sections I and II focused on those philosophical, mathematical, and theoretical issues which, perhaps, we should have addressed with the introduction of stochastic modeling to the field of communication. Hopefully, these sections have at least opened these issues for more thorough investigation. I now hesitantly assume the role of oracle. My purpose in taking on this role is to answer the question, "Where do we go from here?" I believe I see certain issues emerging as central to the use of stochastic processes in communication research.

First among these issues is *the need for greater conceptual clarity in the application of stochastic models*. Present applications tend to wholeheartedly and uncritically adopt a set of mathematical formalisms without assessing the degree to which those formalisms might potentially distort the phenomenon they are supposed to represent. For instance, it is unclear that the discrete-state assumption (that all events may be parsed into a set of mutually exclusive and exhaustive categories) has ever been justified empirically or logically in any of the Markov chain research in communication. Further, the way in which those categories are defined (by the interactant, the observer, or both) remains a hotly debated issue (Grossberg & O'Keefe, 1975; Hewes, 1975b; Delia & Grossberg, 1977). Finally, the nature of time in these stochastic models must be addressed. Do we consider time to be continuous or discrete? Is time to be defined in terms of the occurrence of events or by the clock? Is a serial flow of time an accurate way of representing communication or will "embedding" of different types of communication invalidate

Markov representations of interaction, as it has Markov representations of linguistic phenomena? The answers to these conceptual questions will determine the form and function of stochastic models in future applications. The answers to these questions cannot, and I believe will not, left in the lurch as they have been in the past.

Along with the need for conceptual clarity stands *the need for theoretical grounding of stochastic models*. I have previously noted that in much of the present Markov-based research it is unclear why the phenomenon being investigated should manifest Markovian properties. Instead, much of this early research has been based on the notion that theory will somehow *emerge* from data filtered through these models (cf. Hawes & Foley, 1973, 1976).

It has become clear from the last 30 years of debate in the philosophy of science that the theoretical stance of observer, whether implicit or explicit, will strongly influence the perception of the phenomenon being observed (e.g., Hanson, 1961; Kuhn, 1970; Feyerabend, 1970). As Chomsky (1957, pp. 18–25; 1956) has correctly observed, Markov chain models contain highly directive assumptions concerning the nature of the phenomena to which they are applied. A more reasonable approach to the application of stochastic models is to impose, at the outset, a clear theoretical framework which *explicitly* incorporates Markovian assumptions into the theory (as opposed to the methodology) and which provides some explanation for the presence of these assumptions in a theory about the particular phenomenon being studied. For example, mathematical psychologists have been able to at least partially justify the discrete-state nature of learning and the use of first-order processes in their models (Levine & Burke, 1972; Greeno, 1974). Similarily, Hewes and Evans-Hewes (1974) were able to provide some justification for a Markov chain model of attitude change by appealing to a partial analogy between attitude change and learning processes. Justifications of this sort are sorely needed in other areas of communication research.

Before closing the discussion of theoretical grounding of stochastic models, one more point needs to be made. A virtually forgotten function of the theoretical endeavor in communication research is the a priori specification of parameter values. At the very best some ex post facto explanation is attempted (cf. Hawes & Foley, 1973), but even these attempts tend to be circular, creating an explanation with no criteria for verification beyond the very data from which they were constructed. If stochastic models are to serve some other purpose than summaries of data, a priori predictions of their parameter values must become a goal to future research (Hewes, 1977).

Clearly the conceptual clarity and theoretical grounding of stochastic models will require *increased methodological sophistication*. While the areas requiring methodological improvement must and should flow from the specific content problems under study, I believe that certain areas of advance are sufficiently general to warrant comment. For instance, we must become increasingly aware of biasing effects of unreliability (autocorrelated or not) on time-series stochastic models. All forms of time-series analysis face this problem (Hibbs, 1974). Fortunately, Coleman (1964b) has made some advances in this area which can be incorporated into our literature. A second problem involves the requirement of panel data in Markov chain analysis, a requirement particularly burdensome for survey researchers. Preliminary work on this problem has been undertaken; the general tack has been to develop methods for employing cross-sectional, sequential data (see Hewes, 1978c for a summary). These techniques would greatly expand the applicability of stochastic models. A third focus of communication research attention should be semi-Markov models. A semi-Markov chain is a process whose successive state occupancies are governed by the transition probabilities of a Markov process, but whose *stay* in any state is determined by a separate probabilistic mechanism (Howard, 1971; Singer & Spilerman, 1974) These models can be used to resolve a number of problems which relate to "temporal heterogeneity," that is, heterogeneity which results because individuals move through the same transition sequences but at different rates. For example, "temporal heterogeneity" may well explain the confusing results obtained in identifying "phases" in the small group problem-solving (Fisher, 1970; Hawes & Foley, 1973; Hewes, 1977).

In closing, let me reiterate what I consider to be the key points in this chapter. First, I am convinced that stochastic process models must not be considered to be "second class citizens" when compared to their deterministic cousins. Many applications clearly justify a stochastic approach over a deterministic one. The reverse is also true; therefore, it should be the nature of the problem, not fondly held assumptions, which dictates the choice of a class of models. Second, discrete-state representations should not be denigrated when compared to interval or ratio measures. No absolute judgment of the value of measurement levels can be made external to the phenomenon being studied. Third, violation of stochastic model assumptions should be looked on as a source of information, not as a source of irritation. After all, it is the *deviation* from known regularities which is the key to the advancement of knowledge (Toulmin, 1953). Fourth, and finally, stochastic models should not be imposed on a phenomenon; they should be adapted to it. The explanatory power of stochastic models is lost unless *explicit* reasons can be given a priori for the use of a stochastic model in a particular application. This is not to say that those reasons will remain unrevised. They may well be changed, but they still need to be posited in advance.

If these four prescriptions are kept in mind, stochastic modeling in communication will be materially improved. Even as reticent an oracle as I will risk such a prediction.

References

Acock, A. C., and Martin, J. D. The undermeasurement controversy: Should ordinal data be treated as interval? *Sociology and Social Research*, 1974, **58**, 427–433.
Anderson, T. W. Probability models for analyzing time changes in attitudes. In P. F. Lazarsfeld

(Ed.), *Mathematical thinking in the social sciences*. Glencoe, Illinois: Free Press, 1954. Pp. 17–66.

Anderson, T. W. *The statistical analysis of time series*. New York: Wiley, 1971.

Anderson, T. W., and Goodman, L. A. Statistical inferences about Markov chains. *Annals of Mathematical Statistics*, 1957, **23**, 89–110.

Arundale, R. *Sampling intervals and the study of change over time in communication*. Paper presented to the Information Systems Division of I.C.A., Portland, 1976.

Bailey, N. T. J. *The mathematical theory of infectious diseases and its applications*. New York: Hafner, 1975.

Baird, J. E. Jr. *Interaction analysis in small group communication research: A critical summary*. Paper presented to the Central States Speech Association Convention, Detroit, Michigan, 1977.

Bales, R. F. *Interaction process analysis*. Cambridge, Massachusetts: Addison-Wesley, 1950.

Bartholemew, D. *Stochastic models for social processes*. New York: Wiley, 1967.

Binder, A., Wolin, B. R., and Terebinski, S. J. Leadership in small groups: A mathematical approach. *Journal of Experimental Psychology*, 1965, **69**, 126–134.

Bower, G. H. Application of a model to paired-associate learning. *Psychometrika*, 1961, **26**, 255–280.

Box, G. E. P. The use and abuse of regression analysis. *Technometrics*, 1966, **9**, 625–629.

Box, G. E. P., and Jenkins, G. M. *Time series analysis*. San Francisco, California: Holden-Day, 1970.

Bunge, M. *Philosophy of physics*. Dordrecht, Holland: Reidel, 1973.

Cappella, J. N. Modeling interpersonal communication systems as a pair of machines coupled through feedback. In G. R. Miller (Ed.), *Explorations in interpersonal communication*. Beverly Hills, California: Sage, 1976.

Cattel, R. Principles of experimental design and analysis in relation to theory building. In R. Cattell (Ed.), *Handbook of multivariate experimental psychology*. Chicago, Illinois: Rand-McNally, 1966.

Chatfield, C. Statistical inference regarding Markov models. *Applied Statistics*, 1973, **22**, 16.

Chomsky, N. *Syntactic structures*. The Hague, Holland: Mouton, 1957.

Christ, C. *Econometric models and methods*. New York, Wiley, 1966.

Coleman, J. S. *Introduction to mathematical sociology*. New York: Free Press, 1964. (a)

Coleman, J. S. *Models of change and response uncertainty*. Englewood Cliffs, New Jersey: Prentice-Hall, 1964. (b)

Coleman, J. S. *The mathematics of collective action*. Chicago, Illinois: Aldine, 1973.

Conlisk, J. Interactive Markov chains. *Journal of Mathematical Sociology*, 1976, **4**, 157–185.

Cushman, D. P. *Alternative theoretical bases for the study of human communication: The rules perspective*. Paper presented at S.C.A., Houston, Texas, 1975.

Cushman, D. P. and McPhee, R. (Ed.), *Message–attitude–behavior relationship*. New York: Academic Press, 1980.

Delia, J. G., and Grossberg, L. Interpretation and evidence. *Western Journal of Speech Communication*, 1977, **4**, 32–42.

Derman, D., Glaser, L., and Olkin, I. *A guide to probability theory and application*. New York: Holt, 1973.

Diesing, P. *Patterns of discovery in the social sciences*. Chicago, Illinois: Aldine-Atherton, 1971.

Ellis, D. G., and Fisher, B. A. Phases of conflict in small group development: A Markov analysis. *Human Communication Research*, 1975, **1**, 195–210.

Festinger, L. Social psychology and group processes. *Annual Review of Psychology*, 1955, **6**, 187–216.

Feyerabend, P. K. Against method. In M. Radner and S. Winokur (Eds.), *Minnesota studies in the philosophy of science*. Minneapolis, Minnesota: Univ. of Minnesota Press, 1970.

Fisher, B. A. Decision emergence: Phases in group decision-making. *Speech Monographs*, 1970, **37**, 53–66.

Fisher, B. A., and Hawes, L. An interact system model: Generating a grounded theory of small groups. *Quarterly Journal of Speech*, 1971, **57**, 444–453.

Folger, J. P., and Puck, S. E. *Coding relational communication: A question approach.* Presented to the Interpersonal Communication Division of I.C.A., Portland, Oregon, 1976.

Gergen, K. J., and Marlowe, D. *Personality and social behavior.* Reading, Massachusetts: Addison-Wesley, 1970.

Ginsberg, R. B. Incorporating causal structure and exogenous information with probabilistic models: With special reference to choice, gravity, migration and Markov chains. *Journal of Mathematical Sociology*, 1972, **2**, 83–104.

Gordon, T., and Deleo, H. C. *Structural variation in "Galileo" space: Effects of varying the criterion pair in MDS.* Paper presented to the Information Systems Division of I.C.A., Portland, 1976.

Gouran, D. S. *Communication structure and the small group: Unanswered questions and new directions.* Paper presented to the Central States Speech Association Convention, Detroit, Michigan, 1977.

Greeno, J. G. Representation of learning as discrete transition in a finite state space. In D. H. Krantz, R. C. Atkinson, R. D. Luce, and P. Suppes (Eds.), *Contemporary developments in mathematical psychology*, (Vol. 1). San Francisco, California: Freeman, 1974.

Greeno, J. G. and Scandura, J. M. All-or-nothing transfer based on verbally mediated concepts. *Journal of Mathematical Psychology*, 1966, **3**, 388–411.

Grossberg, L., and O'Keefe, D. J. Presumptions, conceptual foundations, and communication theory: On Hawes' approach to communication. *Quarterly Journal of Speech*, 1975, **61**, 195–208.

Hanson, N. R. Is there a logic of scientific discovery? In H. Feigl and G. Maxwell (Eds.), *Current issues in the philosophy of science.* New York: Holt, 1961.

Hawes, L. C., and Foley, J. M. A Markov analysis of interview communication. *Speech Monographs*, 1973, **40**, 208–219.

Hawes, L. C. and Foley, J. M. Group decisioning: Testing a finite stochastic model. In G. R. Miller (Ed.), *Explorations in interpresonal communication.* Beverly Hills, California: Sage, 1976.

Hayes, D. P., Meltzer, L., and Wolf, G. Substantive conclusions are dependent upon techniques of measurement. *Behavioral Science*, 1970, **15**, 265–268.

Heine, R. T. *Quantitive analysis of multivial free recall learning.* Michigan Mathematical Psychology Program Report MMPP 70–12. Ann Arbor: The University of Michigan, 1970.

Hewes, D. E. *A stochastic model of the relationship between attitudes and behaviors.* Paper presented to the Information Systems Divison of I.C.A., Chicago, Illinois, 1975. (a)

Hewes, D. E. Finite stochastic modeling of communication processes: An introduction and some basic readings. *Human Communication Research*, 1975, **1**, 271–283. (b)

Hewes, D. E. *The sequential analysis of social interaction: What do we know and when should we stop knowing it?* Paper presented to the Speech Communication Association Convention, Washington, D.C., 1977.

Hewes, D. E. The "levels of measurement" problem in communication research: A review, critique, and partial solution. *Communication Research*, 1978 **5**, 87–127. (a)

Hewes, D. E. Interpersonal communication theory and research: A metamethodological overview. In B. Ruben (Ed.), *Communication Yearbook II.* New Brunswick, New Jersey: Transaction, 1978. (b)

Hewes, D. E. Process models for sequential, cross-sectional survey data. *Communication Research*, 1978, **5**, 455–482. (c)

Hewes, D. E. An axiomatized stochastic process theory of the relationships among messages, mediating variable and behaviors. In D.P. Cushman (Ed.), *Message–attitude–behavior relationship.* New York, Academic Press, 1980.

Hewes, D. E., Brazil, A. J., and Evans, D. E. A comparative test of two stochastic process models of messages, mediating variables, and behavioral expectations. In B. D. Ruben (Ed.),

Communication Yearbook I. New Brunswick, New Jersey: Transaction, 1977.

Hewes, D. E., and Evans-Hewes, D. *Toward a Markov chain theory of attitude change.* Debut paper presented to the Interpersonal and Small Group Communication Division of S.C.A., Chicago, Illinois, 1974.

Hempel, C. G. *Philosophy of natural science.* Englewood Cliffs, New Jersey: Prentice-Hall, 1966.

Hempel, C. G. and Oppenheim, P. Studies in the logic of explanation. *Philosophy of Science*, 1948, **15**, 135–175.

Hibbs, D. A. Problems of statistical estimation and causal inference in time-series regression models. In H. L. Costner (Ed.), *Sociological methodology* 1973–74. San Francisco: California: Josey-Bass, 1974.

Hovland, C., Lumsdaine, A., and Sheffield, F. The effects of presenting "one side" versus "both sides" in changing opinions on a controversial subject. In C. Hovland *et al.* (Eds.), *Experiments in mass communication.* Princeton, New Jersey: Princeton Univ. Press, 1949.

Howard, R. *Dynamic probabilistic systems*, Vol. 2. New York: Wiley, 1971.

Kemeny, J., and Snell, J. *Finite Markov chains.* Princeton, New Jersey: Van Nostrand-Reinhold, 1960.

Kibler, R., and Barker, L. (Eds.) *Conceptual frontiers in speech-communication.* New York: Speech Association of America, 1969.

Krivonos, P. D., and Knapp, M. L. Initiating communication: What do you say when you say hello? *Cental States Speech Journal*, 1975, **27**, 115–125.

Kuhn, T. S. *The structure of scientific revolutions*, 2nd ed. Chicago, Illinois: Univ. of Chicago Press, 1970.

Kullback, S., Kupperman, M., and Ku, H. Tests for contingency tables and Markov chains. *Technonetrics*, 1962, **4**, 573–608.

Lasswell, H. D. The structure and function of communications in society. *In* L. Bryson (Ed.), *The communication of ideas.* New York: Harper & Row, 1948.

Laplace, P. S. *A philosophical essay on probabilities* (translation by F. W. Truscott and F. L. Emory; orig. 1796). New York: Dover, 1951.

Lee, T. C., Judge, G. G., and Zellner, A. *Estimating the parameters of the Markov probability model from aggregated time series data.* Amsterdam, Netherlands: North-Holland, 1970.

Leik, R. K., and Meker, B. F. *Mathematical sociology.* Englewood Cliffs, New Jersey: Prentice Hall, 1975.

Lenzen, V. F. *Procedures of empirical science.* Chicago, Illinois: University of Chicago Press, 1938.

Levine, G., and Burke, C. *Mathematical model techniques for learning theories.* New York: Academic Press, 1972.

Lewis, D. K. *Convention.* Cambridge, Massachusetts: Harvard Univ. Press, 1969.

Lyman, S. M., and Scott, M. B. *A sociology of the absurb.* Palisades, California: Goodyear Publ., 1970.

Madansky, A. Least squares estimation in finite Markov processes. *Psychometrika*, 1959, **24**, 137–144.

Massy, W. F., Montgomery, D. B., and Morrison, D. G. *Stochastic models of buying behavior.* Cambridge, Massachusetts: MIT Press, 1970.

McClelland, P. *Causal explanation and model building in history, economics and the new economic history.* Ithaca, New York: Cornell Univ. Press, 1975.

McGuire, W. J. Persuasion, resistance, and attitude change. In I. des. Pool and W. Schramm (Eds.), *Handbook of communication.* Chicago, Illinois: Rand-McNally, 1973.

Miller, G. A. Finite Markov processes in psychology. *Psychometrika*, 1952, **17**, 149–167.

Mischel, T. Personal constructs, rules, and the logic of clinical activity. *Psychological Review*, 1964, **71**, 180–192.

Mischel, W. *Personality and assessment.* New York: Wiley, 1968.

Morrison, D. G., Massy, W. F., and Silverman, F. The effects of nonhomogeneous populations on Markov steady-state probabilities. *Journal of the American Statistical Association*, 1971, **66**, 268–274.

Natale, M. A Markovian model of adult gaze behavior. *Journal of Psycholinguistic Research*, **5**, 1976.

O'Keefe, B. J. *Interaction analysis and the analysis of interaction: Some methodological considerations*. Paper presented to the Central States Speech Association Convention, Detroit, Michigan, 1977.

Rescher, N. *Scientific explanation*. New York: Free Press, 1970.

Rogers, L. E., and Farace, R. V. Relational communication analysis: New measurement procedures. *Human Communication Research*, 1975, **1**, 222–239.

Schweder, R. A. How relevant is an individual difference theory of personality? *Journal of Personality*, 1975, **43**, 455–483.

Seibold, D. In D. P. Cushman (Ed.), *Explorations in the message, attitude, behavior relationship* (title approximate). East Lansing, Michigan: Michigan State Univ. Press, 1977.

Shaw, M. E., and P. R. Costanzo. *Theories of social psychology*. New York: McGraw-Hill, 1970.

Simon, A., and Agazarian, Y. *Sequential analysis of verbal interaction*. Philadelphia, Pennsylvania: Research for Better Schools, 1967.

Singer, B., and Spilerman, S. Social mobility models for heterogeneous populations. In H. L. Costner (Ed.), *Sociological methodology* 1973-74. San Francisco, California: Jossey-Bass, 1974.

Spilerman, S. The analysis of mobility preocesses by the introduction of independent variables into a Markov chain. *American Sociological Review*, 1972, **37**, 277–294. (a)

Spilerman, S. Extensions of the mover-stayer model. *American Journal of Sociology*, 1972, **78**, 599–627. (b)

Suppes, P., and Atkinson, R. C. *Markov learning models for multiperson interactions*. Stanford, California: Stanford Univ. Press, 1960.

Theios, J. Formalization of Spence's dual-process model for eyelid conditioning. In A. H. Black and W. F. Prokasy (Eds.), *Classical conditioning II: Current theory and research*. New York: Appleton, 1972.

Toulmin, S. *The philosophy of science*. London: Hutchinson, 1953.

Von Wright, G. *Explanation and understanding*. Ithaca, New York: Cornell Univ. Press, 1971.

Weick, K. E. *The social psychology of organizing*. Reading, Massachusetts: Addison-Wesley, 1969.

Wilson, T. Critique of ordinal variables. *Social Forces*, 1971, **49**, 433–444.

Woelfel, J. *Sociology and science*. Unpublished manuscript, 1970. (Available from Joseph Woelfel, Department of Communication, Michigan State Univ., East Lansing Michigan.)

Chapter 14

TIME-SERIES ANALYSIS MODELS FOR COMMUNICATION RESEARCH

DENNIS K. DAVIS

JAE-WON LEE
Department of Communication
Cleveland State University
Cleveland, Ohio

I. INTRODUCTION

The objective of time-series analysis (TSA) is to reach conclusions about the way variables change over time. Results of TSA may clarify theories about processes which may underlie the changes in variables observed over time. In this case, the observed variables serve as indicators of change in the

Copyright © 1980 by Academic Press, Inc.
All rights of reproduction in any form reserved.
ISBN 0-12-504450-X

underlying processes. TSA results can also be used to predict future values of the observed variables, or to provide the basis for controlling future changes. Prediction and control have been the most common applications of TSA models, but recent developments make TSA more useful for model construction and testing.

Most mathematical models used by social researchers can treat changes in variables over time. However, these models can incorporate only a few time periods for analysis and are limited in their ability to specify the functional form of the time dependence shown by the variable.

This chapter introduces communication researchers to the important categories of TSA models. We shall begin by discussing the historical development of TSA and illustrating its potential usefulness in communication research. Then we shall discuss two basic TSA models: the autoregression model (AR) and the moving average model (MA). We focus on two types of models based on stochastic processes: models developed by Box and Jenkins (1976) and spectrum analysis models. We provide an example comparing dynamic structural equation models, Box and Jenkins models, and spectrum analysis models for the analysis of bivariate relationships over time. Data collection constraints of TSA models are described, and some final comments are made about the potential of TSA models for communication research.

II. TIME-SERIES ANALYSIS: OVERVIEW AND APPLICATION TO COMMUNICATION RESEARCH

A. Overview of Time-Series Methods

Time-series analysis assumes that the processes which underlie observed phenomena can be understood, or at least predicted, by analyzing over time observations of certain variables. Observed variation is decomposed statistically into *pattern* and *random* components. Potentially useful inductions are identified when "hidden" patterns are detected from over time observations. TSA is especially useful when inferences are to be made from observations that can easily be gathered over time.

TSA can also be used to detect the impact of interventions (Hibbs, 1977). When used for this purpose, TSA provides an objective means of assessing the important parameters of a time-series process before, and then after, an intervention (such as a policy change) has been made. For example, Hibbs determined that unemployment in England was best explained by a model which had very different parameter estimates depending upon which government was in power when the observations were made. The pattern components of the time series were quite different depending on whether the Labor or Conservative party was in power. This application of TSA has potential for assessing the effects of mass media campaigns, the impact of the adoption of innovations, change in employee job satisfaction, etc.

B. Time-Series Analysis and Ordinary Regression

The main advantage of TSA over other techniques for assessing effects in experiments or quasi-experiments is its ability to work with dependent variables which show over time autocorrelation (i.e., successive values in the time series are correlated). Another advantage is its ability to analyze bivariate relationships which change as time passes. Ordinary least squares procedures will produce unbiased estimates of regression coefficients, but statistically inflated significance levels (i.e., the variance of the coefficients will be biased) if positive autocorrelation is present in a static model. Finally, TSA is useful when the amount of time required for an independent variable to effect a dependent variable (causal lag) is unknown, or may be changing. If enough observations are made, it may be possible to determine the length of time between changes in independent variables and changes in dependent variables.

Textbooks on communication devote much space to theories which speculate on the role of communication variables in various social and social psychological processes. But nearly all of our tests of these theories are based on cross-sectional data. Whenever cross-sectional data are analyzed by regression analyses, the causal inferences which are made can only be *assumed* to hold true in the future. For this assumption to be true, the process which underlies our observations must be at *equilibrium*. This means that the assumed causal relationships between variables are stable over an extended time period. Thus, cross-sectional analyses clearly require us to focus our research on processes which should be at equilibrium. One consequence of this requirement may be the high priority which we assign to locating time-invariant causal relationships involving communication variables. Our search for such "laws" is based on an assumption that we can find important processes, which remain at equilibrium, and then detect the unchanging causal relationships which are inherent in such processes.

TSA by contrast examines data gathered over time, though it is possible to combine cross-sectional and time-series analyses. Further, TSA requires only that the series be stationary, or be made stationary, for analysis to proceed.

C. Communication Phenomena from a Time-Series Point of View

Studies of the effects of televised violence appear to suffer from the constraint on equilibrium analyses previously noted. The ultimate objective of such studies has been to identify a time-invariant causal relationship linking level of viewing and aggressive behavior. When such a relationship could not be found, we sought to specify contingent conditions under which an invariant relationship might hold. Our own theories of the nature of communication should have warned us of the difficulty of isolating such relationships. An alternative approach is to conceptualize televised violence as significantly changing over time the social psychological processes that enable a child to orient to the world. These processes may pass through distinctly different stages as children develop, so exposure to violence on TV may be strongly related to aggression at one stage in the time series but unrelated at another stage.

Our traditional methods of conceptualizing and analyzing communication research problems make it difficult to cope with fluctuating relationships. We may conclude that such relationships are so complex that they cannot be objectively understood. In frustration, researchers may conclude that viewing of television violence has no effect because they cannot find a time-invariant relationship. We suggest that this type of complexity may be inherent in many of the phenomena which should be of interest to communication researchers. An exciting aspect of communication is its potential for inducing change—for altering existing states by temporarily disrupting the equilibrium of a process which moves the process to a new level (see Davis, 1977, for an extended discussion of this point). Further, we need to detect whether communication behavior alters relationships which are already undergoing changes as a normal function of growth. To do this we require methods to isolate the pattern components in dependent variables. Then we can determine whether any of these components is causally related to communication variables. Children may engage in increasing aggression over time as they seek to control the world around them. If we study whether viewing TV violence encourages abnormally high levels of aggressive behavior, we may first need to remove the pattern component which is associated with normal growth and changes in aggression levels.

We have suggested that TSA might stimulate more useful communication research. It is important to note some limitations of TSA that constrain this usefulness, as well as its overall explanatory power. Hibbs (1977, p. 172) argues that most TSA models provide good estimates of how dependent variables respond to independent variables, but provide no insight into the "causal structure underlying transmission of exogenous impulses through a dynamic system of independent social, economic or political relationships." TSA provides only very indirect tests of process theories like those which we have discussed. Such low explanatory power contrasts with the high explanatory power of structural equation models (SEM). Multivariate regression analysis can assess the relative causal influence of a large set of independent variables upon multiple dependent variables. Because SEM provide such an attractive alternative to TSA models, it is important to contrast the two types of models and consider more closely the strengths and weaknesses of SEM.

III. ELEMENTARY TIME-SERIES ANALYSIS MODELS

A basic understanding of the principles of TSA can be gained by examining two elementary TSA models, an autoregressive model and a moving average model. Our presentation is intended to provide an intuitive under-standing of these models.

Autoregressive models (AR) and moving average models (MA) have been used extensively by economists. They provide the basis for making predic-tions involving such diverse variables as consumer demand, market share, prices, project cash flow, and personnel turnover (Wheelwright & Makridakis, 1973, p. 2). These models provide an easy, inexpensive means of using information about past variation of variables to predict future variation. The models share some assumptions about past variation and differ in others. They share the notion that past variation can be conceived as having two components: a stable pattern and randomness (Wheelwright & Makridakis, 1973, p. 20); that is,

$$\text{observed over time variation} = \text{stable pattern} + \text{randomness} \quad (1)$$

The two components of variation are combined in any single observation of a value of a variable. Separation of the two components is made very difficult because while the pattern is stable over relatively long term time periods, it can show sharp fluctuations in any particular time period. It is only by making assumptions about the manner in which these two components are fluctuating that it is possible to separate them. The stable pattern can be assumed to have a specific form which is characterized by a constant mean and stable variation around this mean. The random component can be assumed to have a mean of zero and show stable variation around this mean. When combined, the two components should have a constant mean which is referred to as the "level" of the process and stable variation around this mean. Processes which have constant means and exhibit stable variation around these means are said to be *stationary*. Thus, when AR or MA models are applied to time-series data, the series must be assumed to be the empirical *realization* of an underlying stationary process. At first glance, this assump-tion would appear to be a serious limitation. Many time series of interest to communication researchers contain over time trends which would make the assumption of a constant mean impossible (for example, the data may exhibit a linear or quadratic trend). Fortunately, time-series data can frequently be transformed so that it is rendered stationary.

A. Autoregressive Models

The key assumption made by autoregressive models is that the best basis for predicting future observations can be found by *weighting* a small number of previous observations, supplemented by a random component. Communi-cation researchers are familiar with regression models in which previous values of independent variables are used to predict values of a dependent variable. In elementary AR models previous values of the dependent variable itself are used to predict future values. AR models contain regression weights which are calculated using a least squares procedure (Mendenhall & Rainmuth, 1971, p. 403). The "order" of an AR model is determined by the number of observations which are weighted to obtain an estimate of the value of the pattern component. The order is designed by the term p.

Let us assume we observe a single variable over time, and consider its values as indicating the realization of a stationary process. Suppose we consider the value of an observed variable at time t (X_t) as the result of the level of the process (u), a weighted function of values of our observations, and a prior contemporaneous random shock (a_t). Our general model looks like

$$X_t = U + \phi_1 X_{t-1} + \phi_2 X_{t-2} + \cdots + \phi_p X_{t-p} + a_t \qquad (2)$$

where ϕ_i are the weights for ith prior observed value, and p the number of prior time periods to be involved in the model. The value of p is the *order* of the autoregressive model. The model is called autoregressive because X_t is regressed on its own previous values. The values of the regression coefficients in the AR model indicate how dependent future values are on previous values. The size of the ϕs indicate how much randomness is present. Mendenhall and Reinmuth (1971, p. 403) point out that an autoregressive model will be useful only "if a high correlation exists between the values of a random process at constant intervals of time." Tukey (personal correspondence), however, has demonstrated that useful predictive models can be obtained in some cases, even with small individual autocorrelations.[1]

B. Moving Average Models

Again let us assume that we observe the values of a single variable over time, and consider these values as indicating the realization of a stationary process. In some circumstances, the value of our observed variable at time t (X_t) may be considered the result of the level of the process (u) and a weighted function of current and prior random "shocks." Our general model

---

[1]Professor Tukey has indicated the following: If $y_t = \frac{1}{3}(y_{t-1} + y_{t-10} + y_{t-100}) + \varepsilon_t$, where $\text{var}(\varepsilon_t) = 1$ and the εs are uncorrelated, then

$$\text{var}\{y_t\} = 2.5, \qquad \max \text{cor}\{y_t, y_{t-a}\} = .375, \qquad \text{Max } r_a = .15,$$

$$\text{cov}\left\{y_t, \tfrac{1}{3}(y_{t-1} + y_{t-10} + y_{t-100})\right\} = 1.125$$

$$\text{var}\left\{\tfrac{1}{3}(y_{t-1} + y_{t-10} + y_{t-100})\right\} = 2.5 - 1 = 1.5$$

so that correlation of y_t on $y_{t-1} + y_{t-10} + y_{t-100}$ is $= 1.125/[(2.5)(1.5)]^{1/2} = .61$. Certainly you would not feel that a model with prediction $-r = .61$ was not useful just because individual autocorrelations were only $\leq .15$.

then looks like

$$X_t = u + E_t \tag{3}$$

$$E_t = a_t + \theta_1 a_{t-1} + \cdots + \theta_q a_{t-q} \tag{4}$$

where E_t is total random component at time t, θ_i the weight for random shock at time i, a_i the random shocks at time i, and q the number of previous time periods to be included in the model. The value of q is the *order* of the moving average model. We should note that E_t, the total random component, will correlate with itself over time; this is autocorrelation (or serial correlation). This autocorrelation is due to the fact that each E_t is a function of current and past values of the random shocks; if E_t and $E_{t\prime}$ are both partly a function of a given random shock (say a_{t-1}, e.g.), then, in general, E_t and $E_{t\prime}$ must have a nonzero correlation. For this reason the total common term E_t, while consisting of truly random components, is itself not truly random. The a_ts do not correlate over time, while the E_ts exhibit some structure of autocorrelation. This structure depends on the order of the moving average model (see Section V.A). If we consider the variability in our observation to be purely a function of random shocks, our model is a moving average model. If we consider the variability in our observation to be a nontrivial function (i.e., the case in which not all ϕs are equal to zero) of its own prior values and a single, contemporaneous random shock, our model is autoregressive.

The choice of q can be arbitrary, based on experience with similar series in the past. However, as we will discuss later, Box and Jenkins propose more formal criteria for selecting the order of the MA. When business economists first applied MA models to the analysis of time series they based their choice of q on whatever value of q produced the best set of *predictions* of future values of the time series. Questions about the "validity" of a particular MA model for other similar series were not raised. Such a pragmatic criterion was found to pose problems. Occasionally one value of q was found to be best for making short term predictions while another value of q was best for long term predictions.

This discussion has revealed a serious limitation of TSA models which will be found to hold true even for the more complex models which we will consider later. The usefulness of any particular model can often be questioned because it reveals only one of many possible pattern components which could have been "hidden" by one of many conceivable random components. The assumptions made by the researcher about the form of the pattern and random components may determine the form of the pattern and random components which are found. When these assumptions are based on a theory, the chosen TSA model will estimate the pattern and random components but it cannot directly evaluate the validity of the theory. Validity can be assessed only indirectly by checking the correctness of the predictions of future time-series values. TSA models are not well suited to testing the explanations behind a given time series. Their strength lies in their ability to generate potentially useful theories. Gubbay (1973, p. 10) has discussed this situation. He points out that "for the test of fit for stochastic models themselves we are often at a loss, and it may seem impossible to make a choice between rival models or parameters because of our lack of firmly grounded statistical tests which grow out of the model . . . ."

IV. REGRESSION ANALYSIS OF TIME-SERIES DATA

Before considering more sophisticated analysis procedures for time-series data let us briefly consider the analysis of time-series data with more familiar regression procedures. The primary method used to analyze over time relationships at present in communication research is ordinary least squares methods, especially multiple regression, analysis of variance, and structural equation techniques (for the exactly identified recursive case with uncorrelated errors of prediction). Least squares procedures provide unbiased estimates of regression coefficients for time series (autocorrelated data), at least under certain conditions.

Let us suppose that we have a series of observations over time for two variables X, the predictor, and Y, the criterion. Let us suppose further that we have one observation unit over N time periods so that the problems of heterogeneity and cross-sectional autocorrelation are not present. The more general case of K observation units over N time periods is treated in Kmenta (1971, pp. 508–517).

Regressing Y on X under the assumption of no causal lag proceeds according to the model

$$Y_i = \alpha + \beta X_i + \varepsilon_i \tag{5}$$

under the usual regression assumptions (see Chapter 2; Kmenta, 1971, p. 202). The assumption of no autocorrelation causes particular problems with time-series data. In general, time series exhibit some form of autocorrelation thus rendering ordinary least squares estimates of variances of B statistically deflated. Econometricians have been successful in extending its usefulness by finding alternate estimation procedures (other than ordinary least squares) which provide unbiased estimates when the stochastic disturbance process has different forms. Hibbs (1974) describes in some detail an estimation procedure which provides unbiased estimates when the underlying stochastic disturbance process can best be assumed to be a first-order autoregressive process and thus violates the assumption of no autocorrelation. He points out that if ordinary least squares is used as the estimation method when the stochastic disturbance is a first-order autoregressive process, researchers will tend to overestimate the significance of causal relationships. Effects will tend to be found significant which are spurious artifacts of the autocorrelation. Thus multiple regression (and more general econometric procedures) may be adapted to handle time-series data at least when the causal lag interval is known.

Hibbs (1977, p. 174) has suggested that TSA and SEM approaches may be converging as more attention is given to understanding and incorporating stochastic disturbance processes in SEM while TSA models are developed which seek to incorporate more explanatory variables. Thus, it would be misleading to suggest that TSA and SEM approaches are incompatible and competing techniques. The best approach would be one which could combine the advantages of both (see also Simonton, 1977).

V. THE BOX AND JENKINS APPROACH TO TIME-SERIES ANALYSIS

Box and Jenkins (1976) have developed an approach to TSA which allows them to fit and evaluate the usefulness of a set of stationary stochastic models. These models have potential for predicting future values of a time series and for controlling the underlying process of a time series. We have provided a very abbreviated discussion of the Box and Jenkins strategy as applied to univariate time series. For a more extended but still elementary discussion of this strategy see Wheelwright and Makridakis (1973, pp. 123–143). Box and Jenkins (1976) provide a (necessarily) complex explanation of the practical details of their approach.

The Box and Jenkins approach can be viewed as an attempt to make the application of already commonly used time-series models more objective and powerful. They have devised a procedure for choosing which MA or AR models should be used to represent a time series. In our initial discussion of MA and AR models we noted that this represented an important limitation. Previously, the only basis for choice was a pragmatic criterion—one chose the model that provided the best predictions. Box and Jenkins devised a multistep iterative procedure for model selection and evaluation.

Box and Jenkins describe a different way of viewing MA and AR models. They regard these models as "linear filter models." They argue that the values of a time series can be viewed as the output from a linear filter. The input to the filter is a "white noise" process, a completely random process which has a normal probability density function with a mean of zero and stable variance.

Linear filters transform the white noise input into the observed time-series output. By specifying the parameters of the linear filter the researcher is able to describe the pattern of variability of the time series. The general form of a univariate Box and Jenkins model is (Box & Jenkins, 1976, p. 9):

$$Z_t = \mu + a_t + \psi_1 a_{t-1} + \psi_2 a_{t-2} + \cdots \tag{6}$$

where Z is the estimate of values of time series, a the random disturbance values, μ the parameter which indicates the level of the process, ψ_i the weights, and t the subscript indicating time period. In Eq. (6), Box and Jenkins view the values of the time series as a weighted linear function of previous random disturbances, not as a weighted function of previous observations. This is a general moving average model of the type previously presented.

A. Use of Autocorrelation and Partial Autocorrelation Functions

Box and Jenkins use two descriptive statistics as a basis for model selection: the autocorrelation function and the partial autocorrelation function. These two statistics provide insight into the form of the stochastic disturbance processes present. We will first describe how these two functions are calculated and then illustrate their use in model selection.

The autocorrelation function is used to indicate the number of time periods over which a significant amount of correlation exists between values of the *same* variable. The distance between time points in a time series is referred to as a lag. An autocorrelation function can indicate if a nonzero covariance relationship exists between observations separated by one or more lags. To calculate the autocorrelation function, a set of lagged variables must be constructed from the time series. The first variable in this set is the original time series. The second variable is a duplicate of the first variable except that its first value is the same as the second value in the original time series, its second value is the same as the third value in the original series, and so on. This second variable is referred to as a lagged variable with a lag of one time period. The third variable in the set is again a duplicate of the original time series except that the first value of this variable is the same as the third value in the original time series, the second value is the same as the fourth value, and so on. Each of these constructed variables will contain one less value because the original time series will lack information about the value of observations occurring after the series ends. At some point the constructed lagged variables will contain so few values that they cannot be used. Box and Jenkins recommend that the number of observations in the time series be divided by four to determine how many lagged variables should be created (see Wheelwright & Makridakis, 1973, p. 127, for a more detailed explanation of how sets of lagged variables are created).

Intercorrelation of all of the variables in the lagged variable set generates an $N \times N$ matrix (where N is the number of variables in the set). All of the nonredundant information in this matrix is contained in the major diagonal of the transpose of this matrix. Each of the correlation coefficients in this diagonal indicate the tendency for there to be a relationship between values separated by an increasing number of lags. Box and Jenkins describe a test which can be used to ascertain the statistical significance of the autocorrelations. This test uses an estimate of the variance of the estimated autocorrelations of a stationary normal process which was first determined by Bartlett.

Using this variance estimate, one can calculate the large lag standard error. To apply this test of significance the original time series must contain more than 50 time points (Box & Jenkins, 1976, pp. 34–35).

The other descriptive statistical function which Box and Jenkins use is the partial autocorrelation function (Box & Jenkins, 1976, pp. 64–67). This statistic is calculated using the same set of lagged variables created to calculate the autocorrelation function. The dependent variable in the equation is the unlagged time series. A standard error estimate derived from work by Quenouille (1949) is used to assess the significance of the partial autocorrelation coefficients obtained in this way.

Box and Jenkins demonstrate that the size of the various autocorrelations and partial autocorrelations provide insight into the stochastic disturbance processes which underlie a time series (assuming that this underlying process is stationary and has a normal pdf). If the underlying process is an AR process of order p, then the autocorrelation coefficients for small lags will be large and significant but will gradually become smaller for larger lags. The partial autocorrelations will be large and significant for small lags including the coefficient for p lags. All partial autocorrelations for lags greater than p will be insignificant. In such a case the partial autocorrelation function is said to be cut off sharply at p. If the underlying process is an MA process of order q, then the autocorrelation coefficients for lags of q or less will be significant but all coefficients for lags greater than q will be insignificant. In this case the autocorrelation function is said to cut off at q. For MA processes, the partial autocorrelations will be significant for small lags and gradually become insignificant as coefficients for larger lags are considered. In this case the partial autocorrelation function is said to tail off.

Box and Jenkins also discuss a category of mixed models which include both moving average and autoregressive disturbance processes. The models are labeled ARMA models. Both the partial autocorrelation coefficients and the autocorrelation coefficients will gradually become insignificant (tail off) as coefficients with larger lags are considered. Table I summarizes the rules for choosing stochastic disturbance models.

The general ARMA model, which includes both AR and MA terms (see Box & Jenkins, 1976, p. 74) is usually written

$$Z_t = \phi_1 Z_{t-1} + \phi_2 Z_{t-2} + \cdots + \phi_p Z_{t-p}$$

$$- \theta_1 a_{t-1} - \theta_2 a_{t-2} - \cdots - \theta_q a_{t-q} + a_t \tag{7}$$

where Z is the value of deviation of observation from process mean, a the value of random disturbance, ϕ the autoregressive weights, θ the moving average weights, t the subscript indicating time period, p the subscript indicating the order of the AR process, and q the subscript indicating the order of the MA process.

TABLE I

TSA Model Choices Based on the Autocorrelations and
Partial Autocorrelations

Partial autocorrelations	Autocorrelations	
	Cut off at lag q	Tail off
Cut off at lag p	Unknown	Autoregressive model of order p
Tail off	Moving average model of order q	Mixed MA and AR model of order p, q

B. Integrated Autoregressive Moving Average Models (ARIMA)

Box and Jenkins also define three additional models which are variants of the MA, AR, and ARMA models we have already considered. The models considered thus far are not appropriate when there is evidence that the disturbance process is nonstationary. Evidence of nonstationarity is provided by the autocorrelation coefficients. If the coefficients for larger lags remain significant (i.e., fail to cut off or tail off) then the disturbance process is likely to be nonstationary. One method described by Box and Jenkins for removing the nonstationary trend from the data is to "difference" the time series. It may be difficult to remove a trend if no information exists which can explain what type of trend may be present. Differencing the series provides a means of making the series stationary without any knowledge of the trend which is present.

First-differencing of a time series consists of subtracting from each value in the series the value which immediately precedes it. To second-difference a series, a first-differenced series is again differenced. Krull and Paulson (1977) note that first-differencing of a time series will eliminate a linear trend and second-differencing will eliminate a quadratic trend. Higher-order trends can be eliminated by further differencing.

When an MA model is fitted to a differenced series, it is referred to as an IMA model. When an ARMA model is fitted to a differenced series it is referred to as an ARIMA model. It is worth noting the obvious point that when one differences a time series, the resultant series has a very different form than the original series. A dominant trend in the data has been removed. If knowledge of this trend is of importance, then the ARIMA model will not be suitable as a complete model because it will only provide insight into the residual variation (combined with a model of trend, however, it may be quite adequate). Thus, while differencing enables Box and Jenkins to extend their models and apply them to a greater variety of time series, it may not aid in the solution of some research problems. (The researcher must also be wary of the unreliability of difference scores.)

VI. AN APPLICATION OF THE BOX AND JENKINS APPROACH

We produced six time series by obtaining weekly information on the amount of television advertising sold and the capitalization value (stock price multiplied by total outstanding shares) of the three television networks. This information was readily available from *Broadcasting* magazine. Data for 160 weeks from April 1974 to May 1977 were used. Figures 1 and 2 depict the time series. Our preliminary reason for analyzing this particular data set was pragmatic; we wanted to demonstrate the application of TSA models using a readily available time series. The data do have some inherent interest however. Much speculation exists as to whether advertising sales influence stock prices. The two variables are significantly correlated but such correlations may be spurious.

The chief purpose of utilizing TSA models is to gain insight into a time series when conventional SEM are unlikely to yield useful results. Conventional models should not be useful for three reasons. First, television advertising sales results are not released until two to three weeks after the week in which they take place. It is reasonable to expect a causal lag of at least two weeks to separate changes in ad sales from changes in capitalization value but the exact size of this lag cannot be predetermined. Second, capitalization values and advertising sales values are highly autocorrelated. The assumption of nonautocorrelated error terms is likely to be violated if a conventional regression model is used to estimate the relationship between sales and

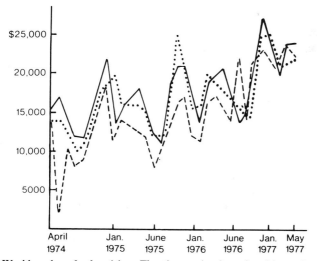

FIG. 1. Weekly sales of advertising. The time series for advertising sales for the three television networks is shown. Every fifth time point in each series has been graphed. ---, ABC; —, CBS; ..., NBC.

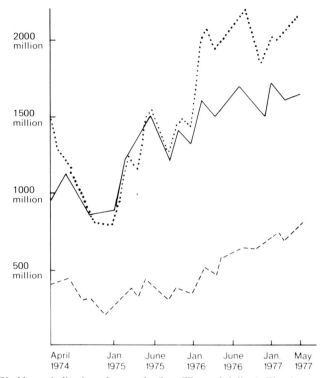

FIG. 2.   Weekly capitalization of networks (in millions of dollars). The time-series data for capitalization of the three networks is shown. Every fifth time point in each series has been graphed. – – –, ABC; —, CBS; . . . , NBC.

capitalization. Third, both advertising sales and capitalization value can be expected to be directly affected by overall business conditions.

Assuming that our model is first-order autoregressive and static, we began our analysis using the ordinary least squares regression program in the "Statistical Analysis Series" package of programs to estimate the standardized regression coefficients for the bivariate relationships for each network. For ABC we obtained a beta weight of .54 when sales were used to predict capitalization, for CBS we obtained a beta weight of .29, and for NBC we obtained a beta weight of .29. Each of these weights was judged to be statistically significant at the .0001 level. However, the Durbin–Watson test (Kmenta, 1971, pp. 294–296) for autoregressive error terms detected significant autocorrelation in the residuals for each network. Even if we could have safely assumed instantaneous causation, the presence of such autocorrelation of error terms implies that the naively calculated significance level is too extreme.

We then applied the Box and Jenkins strategy to analyze each of the time series individually to assess the form of the stochastic disturbance process which might underlie each series. Table II reports the results of this analysis.

TABLE II

AUTOCORRELATIONS (AC) AND PARTIAL AUTOCORRELATIONS (PAC) FOR ADVERTISING SALES AND CAPITALIZATION DATA FOR THE THREE MAJOR TELEVISION NETWORKS

| Causal | ABC | | | | CBS | | | | NBC | | | |
| | Sales | | Capital | | Sales | | Capital | | Sales | | Capital | |
lag	AC	PAC	AC	PAC	AC	PAC	AC	PAC	AC	PAC	AC	PAC
1	.75	—	.97	—	.67	—	.97	—	.71	—	.97	—
2	.69	.28	.94	.02	.61	.30	.95	.03	.67	.34	.96	.18
3	.63	.10	.92	.07	.59	.20	.92	.07	.58	.06	.94	.07
4	.59	.08	.90	.03	.51	.03	.90	.06	.52	.02	.93	− .08
5	.48^a	− .11	.88	− .06	.40^a	− .12	.88	.05	.42^a	− .07	.91	− .02
6	.44	.00	.86	.00	.32	− .09	.86	− .04	.37	− .01	.89	− .03
7	.41	.07	.84	.00	.25	− .05	.83	.01	.30	− .04	.87	− .04
8	.40	.06	.82	.03	.20	− .01	.81	− .04	.24	− .02	.85	− .01
9	.36	.02	.80	.00	.13	− .02	.79^a	.06	.17	− .05	.83	− .02
10	.32	− .04	.78^a	− .02	.06	− .05	.77	.01	.09	− .12	.81^a	− .01
11	.31	.01	.75	− .08	.02	− .03	.76	.05	.04	− .03	.79	− .04
12	.28	− .01	.73	.01	− .04	− .06	.75	.03	.00	.00	.77	− .01
13	.24	− .02	.71	.02	− .04	.06	.73	.00	− .03	.02	.76	.04
14	.23	.04	.69	.00	− .07	.01	.71	− .18	− .02	.10	.74	.04
15	.27	.16	.68	.07	− .06	.05	.69	− .03	− .05	− .01	.72	.01
16	.30	.13	.66	− .05	− .01	.12	.67	− .03	.07	.28	.71	− .06
17	.32	.06	.64	− .05	.03	.10	.64	− .03	.07	.04	.69	− .06
18	.31	− .06	.62	− .05	.04	.03	.62	− .03	.06	− .09	.66	− .09
19	.27	− .14	.59	− .04	.07	− .91	.60	.00	.08	− .02	.65	.07
20	.27	.01	.56	− .10	.09	− .02	.58	.03	.09	− .04	.63	− .03

^{a}Correlations for larger lags are insignificant at the .01 level.

A first-order autoregressive model appears to be likely to provide an appropriate model for the stochastic disturbances underlying each of the time series. In each case, the autocorrelation coefficients decrease in size as the size of the lag associated with each coefficient increases but the partial autocorrelations tend to cut off after the first coefficient. The coefficients for the three networks show other striking similarities. All of the autocorrelation coefficients tend to become insignificant at the .01 level for similar size lags. All autocorrelations for ad sales are insignificant when the lag is greater than 5. Coefficients for capitalization are insignificant for lags greater than 10. One anomaly in the partial autocorrelations for ad sales is the tendency for coefficients of lags 15, 16, or 17 to be substantially larger than neighboring coefficients. This is evidence of a seasonal cycle having a period of about four months. Such a cycle is not surprising in the sales data. Ad sales tend to peak during the fall and hold fairly strong through the winter and into the spring. They reach their lowest levels during the summer months. The relatively small size of the partial autocorrelations suggests that this cycle is not particularly regular. It does represent a source of nonstationary variation. If this were judged to be a significant source of variation, an effort would need to be made to model this cycle. In the next section, we will discuss how spectrum analysis might enable us to do this.

A Box and Jenkins analysis of the network time series suggests that a first-order autoregressive stochastic process can be used to model the error terms in both advertising sales and capitalization. Our objective is to try to establish whether a causal relationship exists between sales and capitalization. We have two sets of models available to us which can be used to assess this causal relationship. Box and Jenkins have proposed a set of bivariate models which they have labeled transfer function models. These transfer function models appear to us to be most useful when an appropriate SEM model is not available.

In the present case a SEM model is available to estimate causal relationships when first-order autoregressive stochastic disturbances are present. The model is one which has been described by Kmenta (1971, pp. 508–514). It is one of many generalized least squares regression models which have been developed for application when stochastic disturbances are known to violate the assumptions of the simple linear regression model. This model has been developed to provide useful estimates of the strength of the relationship between variables when first-order autoregressive disturbances are present. The model permits pooling of data for several units of analysis. In our case, we have three units of analysis—the three television networks. Each of the 160 time points in our time series is regarded as a cross-section of the two variables for each of the three networks. Data from the 160 cross-sections is pooled to obtain an overall estimate of the strength of relationships. Below we have presented the equation for this model. However, we have not included any discussion of the way in which the model is able to handle stochastic disturbances. Readers interested in applying this model should refer to Kmenta.

$$Y_{it} = \alpha + BX_{it} + \varepsilon_{it}$$

where Y is the estimate of the dependent variable, B the regression weight, X the observation of the independent variable, α the stochastic disturbance, i the subscript referring to unit of analysis, t the subscript referring to time period, and ε the intercept. The key to making this model useful for the analysis of this data set is the development of procedures for estimating B which are unbiased in the presence of cross-sectional correlation and first-order autoregression. Kmenta provides a detailed explanation of these estimation procedures.

We were able to fit this model to our data using a computer program available in the most recently released version of the "Statistical Analysis Series." An initial problem in this analysis was the differences in the means of the six series. In particular, the ABC capitalization mean was much lower than the NBC mean. We removed this difference by subtracting the mean value of each series from every value in that series, thus creating series of deviations. We used these mean deviations in our analysis. One problem which we could not resolve was deciding an appropriate causal lag for the relationship. We have pointed out that instantaneous causation is unlikely because sales figures are not publicly released until two to three weeks after the week in which they occur. Stock buyers may not respond to favorable or unfavorable sales figures for several weeks while waiting to see if a trend is being established. The model we used does not permit us to use lagged variables in our analysis. Consequently, we chose to assess causal lag by making ten different data analyses using the pooled cross-section time-series model. In each analysis, we increased the lag between sales and capitalization by one time period (week). The results of these ten analyses are reported in Table III. The table reports the Bs for each analysis, the intercept and the three stochastic disturbance estimates (one for each unit of analysis). A t-test of statistical significance was made for each of the Bs. Significant Bs were found for lags of 1 week and 5 weeks ($P < .05$). An almost significant B was found for a lag of 7 weeks. The model with a lag of 5 weeks appears to be the most plausible. It is encouraging to find small Bs for lags of 2, 3, and 4 weeks. These results do not permit us to reach definitive conclusions about the relationship between sales and capitalization. No estimate of the amount of

TABLE III

PARAMETER ESTIMATES FOR TIME-SERIES STRUCTURAL EQUATIONS MODELS[a]
ADVERTISING SALES USED TO PREDICT NETWORK CAPITALIZATION

Causal lag (weeks)	Intercept	B	1 (ABC)	2 (CBS)	3 (NBC)
1	4.67	1.34[b]	.83	.94	.86
2	4.05	.68	.80	.93	.87
3	− .23	.50	.81	.92	.86
4	− .67	.91	.82	.92	.95
5	− .82	1.55[b]	.80	.92	.86
6	−2.87	.05	.81	.92	.86
7	−2.02	1.44	.82	.92	.86
8	−2.41	.59	.81	.92	.86
9	−3.47	.80	.82	.91	.86
10	−3.24	.36	.82	.92	.86

[a]This table reports the results of 10 separate analyses. In each succeeding analysis the lag between the independent variable (advertising sales) and the dependent variable (capitalization) is increased by 1 time period (week).

[b]These unstandardized regression weights are significant at the .05 level when a t-test of statistical significance is used. Note, however, that since the probability of 2 or more out of 10 significant at 5% by pure chance is at least 8.7%, even the two cases individually significant at .05 have to be treated with caution.

variance in capitalization which can be explained by sales is possible. However, the results do strongly suggest that even after autoregressive disturbances are taken into account a significant causal relationship does exist between sales and capitalization.

VII. SPECTRUM ANALYSIS

Another set of TSA models exists which may be useful in modeling certain types of weakly stationary processes. These models are most obviously appropriate when *regular* cycles are present in a time series. In such cases it may be possible to model at least one of the pattern components in a time series using a sinusoidal wave model. We will briefly descirbe how such wave models can be used to examine the variation present in a time series. It should be noted that the strategy used in applying spectrum analysis is similar to that employed in most other forms of TSA. In the case of spectrum analysis, one searches for the best model for representing the pattern components in a time series by fitting a large number of sinusoidal constituents to the time series. If regular cycles are present in the data they can often be "discovered" by the spectrum analysis approach.

The formal mathematical term for a sinusoidal wave model is a sinusoidal function. Several parameters of sinusoidal functions require definition. Figure 3 provides a graphic representation of these parameters. In this graph a sine wave has been represented. The height and depth of this wave (A) are the amplitude of the wave. The wave is one cycle long. Two scales are used to refer to the wave, a time scale and a radian scale. By combining the two scales it is possible to create a measure which enables this wave to be compared to other waves. The wave completes a cycle in 6.28 units of time. One can divide the radian measurement by the time measurement to obtain the frequency of the wave model. In this case the frequency is $2\pi/T = 2\pi/6.28 = 1$. A final parameter is the phase of a wave model. In Fig. 3, the wave has a phase of zero because it "up-crosses" (goes through zero from negative to positive) at zero time.

As with models representing linear functions, sinusoidal wave models can be either deterministric or stochastic. A deterministic model is expected to provide an exact representation of known fluctuations in dependent variables and yield precise predictions of future values. Bloomfield (1976, p. 2) provides such a model:

$$X_t = R \cos(\omega t + \phi) \tag{8}$$

where X_t is the tth data value, R the amplitude, ϕ the phase, and ω the frequency.

He suggests that this model would provide an exact fit to measurements of the position of the sun. These positions would be found to have a cycle 365.25 days long. After measuring all of the positions of the sun on each day of 1

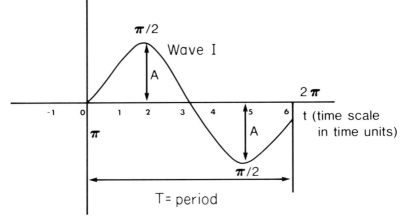

FIG. 3.

year, it would be possible to predict the sun's position in the following year with great accuracy.

A simple stochastic wave model would have the following expression (Bloomfield, p. 9):

$$X_t = \mu + R\cos(\omega t + \phi) + \varepsilon_t \tag{9}$$

where μ is an added constant and ε_t the $t$the residual. Bloomfield uses this model to represent the observed magnitude of a variable star on 600 successive nights. He demonstrates a least squares method of fitting a wave model to this data set. When one wave is fitted to the data set, a relatively large, autocorrelated (nonrandomly distributed) set of residuals is found. When a second wave model is fitted to these residuals, the final residuals are randomly distributed. Bloomfield used this example to illustrate one of the most classical applications of wave models in time-series analysis, the search for "hidden periodicities." In any time-series data set several waves may be superimposed upon each other. As a result, the attribute being measured may appear to be quite unstable over time. Yet, when each of the superimposed waves is taken out (the data set is said to be decomposed into its constituent parts), the individual waves may be found to be quite stable. Discovery of hidden regularities in a data set may provide a means of understanding what initially appears to be a very unstable attribute. Of course, finding such hidden stability does not explain why the stability exists but once such regular fluctuation has been found in an important attribute, theories can be constructed to explain it.

Professor Tukey (personal correspondence) has pointed out that more recent applications of spectrum analysis, especially to earth science (e.g., Tukey, 1966; Baith, 1974), do not involve the existence of spectral periods. Rather, they involve the relative concentration of contribution to total variance in one region of the spectrum as compared to another. Applications of this sort usually invole substantial amounts of data and are based on a more searching inquiry of how different sinusoidal waves are altered as they (a) pass through the earth, ocean, or atmosphere, (b) pass through measuring devices, and (c) pass through computations. (As a result, the degree to which different sinusoidal waves interact with one another can be understood, and this understanding used to guide analysis and interpretation.) Space is not available here to expand upon these important topics.

A. Use of Fast Fourier Transforms in Spectrum Analysis

Spectrum analysis represents a logical extension of the search for hidden periodicities which we discussed earlier. Just as light can be analyzed by identifying the waves which make it up and determining the frequencies at which those waves are oscillating, so it is possible to separate out the different frequencies which add up to form the observations in a time-series data set. While light can be physically decomposed into its constituent parts, the spectral analysis of time-series data must be done mathematically. Historically, several methods have been used to decompose time-series data. Most were cumbersome or provided inadequate estimates of constituent frequencies. In 1965, Cooley and Tukey proposed an algorithm (a related algorithm was independently discovered by Gordon Saude) which greatly simplified the computation of one of the more cumbersome methods—the calculation of the discrete Fourier transforms. This algorithm makes possible the rapid calculation of all of the discrete Fourier transforms for a data set and is known as the fast Fourier transform (Bloomfield, 1976, p. 61). Some understanding of the Fourier frequencies is necessary to appreciate the rationale for calculating all of the Fourier transforms. These frequencies serve to define waves which have the property of being orthogonal to each other. Any set of time-series data can be transformed into a linear combination of waves, one of each of the Fourier frequencies. Such a simultaneous fit of a set of orthogonal waves provides us, because of orthogonality, with the results of separate successive fits of the individual sinusoids to the data set. Those frequencies which have the best fit to the data will tend to have an amplitude greater than would be found by chance. Thus, in the simplest cases, by locating the models having significant amplitudes, it is possible to detect those which provide a useful explanation for the data set. When no special periods exist in a data set, a large number of frequencies may be found to have amplitudes of modest size. (For a detailed, mathematical explanation of the strategy for using Fourier transforms, see Bloomfield, 1976, pp. 42–60). A visual means of evaluating a set of Fourier transforms is known as the periodogram. This consists of a graphic display, typically on a logarithmic scale, of each of the amplitudes associated with each Fourier frequency.

The ordinate in a periodogram is scaled in terms of a function of the amplitude of each wave model tested. The formula for this function is:

$$I_{(\omega j)} = (N/2\pi)R_j^2 \tag{10}$$

where ωj is the frequency of each unique, orthogonal wave model, N the number of observations, and R_j the amplitude associated with the jth frequency model. The periodogram provides an easy means of assessing the amount of fluctuation accounted for by each frequency. When the periodogram is relatively flat or has a large number of amplitudes of equal though modest size, the data set contains little worth describing in frequency terms. If only a few amplitudes are large, these are the waves which provide a basis for formulating a useful explanation of the data. One of the most practical applications of spectrum analysis has been to assess whether or not seasonal (or other periodic fluctuations) have been removed from an important indicator by suitable adjustments in it. For example, spectrum analysis can be used to assess whether a seasonal adjustment in unemployment figures has successfully removed such variation. If so, the amplitudes at frequencies of one-/year, two/years, three/years, four/years, etc., will either be negligibly small (excellent adjustment) or no larger than amplitudes at neighboring frequencies (bearable adjustment). Similarly, residuals obtained from fitting other time-series models to a data set can be examined to determine whether the fitted models account for all frequency-describable variation in the data.

Every set of Fourier transforms will contain two results for each of half as many frequencies as there are observations in the data set. Thus, the greater the number of observations, the larger the number of discrete frequencies which could be examined.

It is important to note that significant disagreement exists among statisticians over the potential usefulness of spectrum analysis for social science research. This disagreement stems in part from differing views concerning the nature of social phenomena. One view is that social variables are so unstable over time that no regular periods can be found. Proponents of this view argue that spectrum analysis could produce misleading results. Periods might be "discovered" which are simply artifacts of the methodology. Substantive explanations might be created for these false periods leading to the construction of useless theories. Box and Jenkins (1976, pp. 39–40) maintain that many time series of interest to social scientists "are characterized by random changes in frequency, amplitude and phase." For this type of series the sample spectrum fluctuates widely and is not capable of any meaningful interpretation. This view is supported somewhat by the history of periodogram analysis. Early applications of periodograms, especially in economics, produced misleading results. Analyses based on periodograms were viewed with great skepticism. Thus, it is important to exercise caution in interpreting the results of a spectrum analysis. Periodicity must be carefully examined to determine whether or not it is artifactual.

An application of spectrum analysis which has not been criticized is its use in determining whether a variable contains no stable variation. While the presence of significant peaks in a periodogram at certain frequencies does not establish the usefulness of certain frequencies in explaining variation, the absence of both such peaks and any other detectable structure is strong evidence that a variable contains little variation usefully described in frequency terms.

In sum, spectrum analysis can potentially be put to three major uses: (1) as a means of discovering "hidden periodicities" in a time series, (2) as a means of checking for the presence of certain specific oscillatory trends in the data, and (3) as a means of checking if a time series is completely stationary.

B. Spectrum Analyses of the Television Network Data

Spectrum analysis of the three capitalization series showed one dominant frequency with a cycle of 160 weeks, the length of the entire series. No other significant wave models were found except for frequencies harmonic with this dominant frequency. It is likely that the significant amplitudes of these frequencies are simply artifacts of the crude spectrum analysis method that was used. (When a periodic function is not sinusoidal, its representation in terms of sinusoidal waves will require sinusoids of one or more—often several or many—harmonic frequencies as well as a sinusoid of the fundamental frequency.)

We attempted to ascertain whether the dominant frequency was simply an indication of a linear trend in the data. To do this we fitted a linear regression model to the data using time as the independent variable. Examination of the residuals of this regression analysis found the same dominant 160-week cycle. For a spectrum analysis to reveal anything more about these series, it would be necessary to reduce the impact of the 160-week component on the data. (The use of an appropriate data window should help in this regard.)

Spectrum analysis of the weekly sales data also found a large contribution from a 160-week cycle. However, this contribution was not as strong as that found in the capitalization series. A second strong frequency was found which had a cycle of 52 weeks. Several frequencies harmonic with this frequency also had significant amplitudes. These frequencies had periods of 26, 17, and 8.5 weeks. We noted earlier that our examination of the partial autocorrelations found some evidence of weak nonstationarity at about 17 weeks. Thus, the 17-week frequency found by spectrum analysis is particularly interesting. (The partial autocorrelation analysis was not extended far enough to examine 26- or 52-week periods.) Further research may be warranted to study the seasonal variation in the data. However, as Professor Tukey has pointed out (personal communication) the potential difficulties arising from the effects of general business conditions are also serious, so that further analysis should allow for this also. One simple approach he suggested would be to go over to "market shares" and "value shares" as illustrated by

$$\text{CBS market share} = \frac{\text{CBS sales}}{(\text{NBC sales}) + (\text{ABC sales}) + (\text{CBS sales})}$$

$$\text{CBS value share} = \frac{\text{CBS value}}{(\text{NBC value}) + (\text{ABC value}) + (\text{CBS value})}$$

a revision of variables which would tend to greatly reduce both the effects of general economic considerations and the effects of season.

VIII. CONCLUSIONS FROM THE DATA ANALYSES

Our analyses suggest that there is sufficient evidence of causal relationship between advertising sales and capitalization to warrent further investigation. But even granting the existence of such a relationship, it does not appear to account for much of the covariation present. The presence of a highly significiant autoregressive disturbance process suggests that certain un-measured factors influence both variables.

We have also noted the limitations of the data analysis methods which we used. In particular, the bivariate relationships went unanalyzed. We eventually chose to estimate the causal relationship using a SEM even though this model could not give us direct insight into the length of the causal lag present. We were able to use the Box and Jenkins approach to determine whether we could satisfy the most important assumptions of the SEM we used. As TSA methods are developed examination of bivariate relationships should become easier. Spectrum analysis would appear to be most suited to those time series in which regular cycles are present. Such cycles introduce weak nonstationarity into a time series making it difficult to meet the assumptions of other TSA models (notably the Box and Jenkins models) or SEM. In our data we found some evidence of a 17-week cycle in the advertising sales series. Removal of this cycle might improve our ability to predict capitalization value. This example illustrates the potential usefulness of spectrum analysis when there is reason to expect that seasonal cycles are present. Spectral analysis can assess the strength of these cycles and help determine whether they should be removed.

IX. DATA COLLECTION STRATEGIES
AND TIME-SERIES ANALYSIS

Our description of TSA should serve to emphasize the importance of data collection strategies. It is quite conceivable that different strategies could produce quite different results even though the variables being measured were the same and the data collection instruments similar. TSA methods were pioneered by researchers working with very different data sets than those normally used by communication researchers. The key difference is that early TSA was frequently based on many observations of a single unit of analysis. In some cases, this was because only one unit of analysis was of concern (e.g., the electromagnetic signal transmission of a particular radio station). Usually, it was easy and inexpensive to make the many observations required for such TSA, or the observations were already available as social statistics collected and reported by government agencies.

Communication researchers usually work with samples of large populations or with large groups that are considered to be representative. Such samples or groups are often observed at only one time period. Occasionally, when a researcher has sufficient financing it is possible to collect data from samples or groups several times. Such panel data represents a small step toward the collection of time-series data. The application of TSA to communication research will clearly require new data collection strategies. Panels will need to be extended over longer time periods with observations made at more frequent intervals.

Other disciplines have developed approaches which permit them to collect data which are ideally suited to TSA. One such approach is to try to conceptualize variables which can be regarded as important indicators of underlying processes. Economists have pioneered in the development of sets of economic indicators which they use to assess the development of very complex unobservable processes. The usefulness of these indicators in making predictions about the processes is constantly evaluated and indicators whose usefulness is in doubt can be discarded or given little weight. An elaborate TSA of such indicators may be successful in providing insight into the processes. If a key variable in the economic environment is manipulated, the impact of this manipulation upon the underlying processes may be inferred by observing the way in which indicator variables change. If no significant changes take place, the manipulation can be assumed to have had no effect.

Such a strategy would appear to be useful for communication research. If indicator variables existed for the decision making process which voters use to choose candidates in an election, then we could assess the extent to which manipulation of communication variables affects such a process. Let us say that we could establish that voters normally have very low knowledge of candidates' issue stands but very extensive knowledge of personal attributes. This might indicate that normally voter decisions depend heavily on "images" rather than "issues." If some communication variables were manipulated (for example, if debates between the candidate took place), then we could assess whether voters then know more about issues. Such evidence might indicate that the underlying decision making process has been disturbed and moved to a new state of equilibrium in which information about issues has assumed a new importance. Similar strategies might be used to study a wide variety of communication phenomena.

X. CONCLUSIONS

Our consideration of TSA has introduced some of the techniques which are presently being developed. We have shown how each of these techniques is based on a strategy for decomposing an observed time series into stable pattern components and random disturbances. In sophisticated, statistically based TSA strategies, time series are conceptualized as realizations of stationary or weakly stationary stochastic processes. As the joint probability density functions of a large number of such stochastic processes are determined, it will be possible to assess the likelihood that a particular time series is actually a realization of a specific stochastic process. If there is a strong probability that a time series could be a realization of a specific process, then the process may serve as a useful model of the time series. Sophisticated TSA strategies provide a procedure for selecting an appropriate stochastic process as a model for a time series and then for making estimates of the variance components present if the model is a valid representation. These estimates of the variance components may provide useful insights into the underlying processes which generated the time series.

Our enthusiasm for the TSA models was tempered by their relatively low explanatory power and the difficulty of applying them to data sets normally collected by communication researchers. Most existing TSA models can analyze only one or two variables. SEM offers an approach to studying causal relationships which can yield direct explanations of the causal mechanisms which may be generating a set of observations (see Cappella, Chapter 3). But SEM are also limited; their chief limitation is the difficulty in dealing with autocorrelated random disturbances. A second limitation is their insensitivity to changes in structural relationships which may take place over time. It is essential that researchers be familiar with the strengths and weaknesses of both TSA and SEM. Research strategies which integrate both types of models would appear to be most likely to produce useful results.

Very little research has been done using TSA models in communication research. However two recent studies (Krull & Paulson, 1978; Krull & Husson, 1977) provide innovative and potentially useful applications of Box and Jenkins models and spectrum analysis models to communications problems. For readers interested in more examples of how these models can be used to solve communication research problems, these two papers provide excellent discussions. The Krull and Paulson article provides an overview of TSA which may clarify points that we chose not to discuss in depth.

Communication researchers need to be more concerned about developing conceptualizations of the way in which they expect processes to change in response to communication variables. As TSA methods are perfected and as SEM are developed which have broader applications, it will become possible to empirically evaluate such process changes. Significant changes in indicator variables could be detected and analyzed. A most important function of communication is its ability to preserve or disturb equilibrium in social processes. We require models which allow us to empirically assess whether the equilibrium of specific processes has been disturbed or preserved by communication variables. It is our hope that this discussion of existing TSA models and strategies will encourage the development and evaluation of innovative and more useful communication theories.

ACKNOWLEDGMENTS

The authors wish to express their appreciation to Professors John Tukey, Edward Fink, Joseph Cappella, Peter Monge, and Richard V. Farace for helpful comments and suggestions for revision of earlier drafts of this chapter. The usual responsibility for authorship remains with us.

References

Baith, M. *Spectral analysis in geophysics* (Developments in solid earth geophysics). Amsterdam: Elsevier, 1974.

Bloomfield, P. *Fourier analysis of time series: An introduction.* New York: Wiley, 1976.

Box, G. E. P., and Jenkins, G. M. *Time series analysis: Forecasting and control.* San Francisco, California: Holden-Day, 1976.

Davis, D. K. Assessing the role of mass communication in social processes. *Communication Research,* 1977, **4**, 23–34.

Fishman, G. S. *Spectral methods in econometrics.* Cambridge, Massachusetts: Harvard Univ. Press, 1969.

Fox, K. A. *Intermediate economic statistics.* New York: Wiley, 1968.

Gubbay, J. Introduction: Stochastic models for sociology. In P. Halmos (Ed.), *Stochastic processes in sociology. The sociological review monograph 19.* Keele: Keele Univ., 1973.

Heise, D. *Causal analysis.* New York: Wiley, 1975.

Hibbs, D. A., Jr. Problems of statistical estimation and causal inference in time-series regression models. In H. L. Costner (Ed.), *Sociological methodology 1973-1974.* San Francisco, California: Jossey-Bass, 1974.

Hibbs, D. A., Jr. On analyzing the effects of policy interventions. In D. Heise (Ed.), *Sociological methodology 1977.* San Francisco, California: Josey-Bass, 1977.

Jenkins, G. M., and Watts, D. G. *Spectral analysis and its application.* San Francisco, California: Holden-Day, 1968.

Kmenta, J. *Elements of econometrics.* New York: Macmillan, 1971.

Krull, R., and Husson, W. G. *Children's attention to the television screen: A time series analysis.* Unpublished paper presented to the Association for Education in Journalism, 1977.

Krull, R., and Paulson, A. S. Time series analysis in communication research. In P. Hirsch, P. Miller & F. G. Kline (Ed.), *Strategies for communication research.* Beverly Hills, California: Sage, 1978.

Koopmans, L. H. *The spectral analysis of time series.* New York: Academic Press, 1974.

Lee, T. C., Judge, G. G., and Zellner, A. *Estimating the parameters of the Markov probability model from aggregate time series data.* Amsterdam: North Holland Publ., 1970.

Leik, R. K., and Meeker, B. F. *Mathematical sociology.* Englewood Cliffs, New Jersey: Prentice-Hall, 1975.

Malinvaud, E. *Statistical methods of econometrics.* Chicago, Illinois: Rand McNally, 1966.

Mandenhall, W., and Rainmuth, J. E. *Statistics for management and economics.* Belmont, California: Duxbury Press, 1971.

Nelson, C. R. *Applied time series analysis for managerial forecasting.* San Francisco, California: Holden-Day, 1973.

Paisley, M. B., and Paisley, W. *'Axiomatizing' non-experimental causal inference, or, finding a horse to put before the cart.* Unpublished paper, Institute for Communication Research, Stanford University, Stanford, California, 1973.

Simonton, D. K. Cross-sectional time-series experiments: Some suggested statistical analyses. *Psychological Bulletin,* 1977, **84(3)**, 489–502.

Tintner, G., and Sengupta, J. K. *Stochastic economics.* New York: Academic Press, 1972.

Tukey, J. W. Uses of numerical spectrum analysis in geophysics. *Bulletin of the International Institute of Statistics,* 1966, **41**, 267–295.

Wheelwright, S. C., and Makridakis, S. *Forecasting methods for management.* New York: Wiley, 1973.

Wiener, N. *Time series.* Cambridge, Massachusetts: MIT Press, 1949.

Chapter 15

SIMULATION

WILLIAM D. RICHARDS, JR.
Department of Communication
Simon Fraser University
Burnaby, British Columbia
Canada

I. INTRODUCTION

The chapters in this book describe multivariate techniques that are used in the analysis of situations encountered in the process of communication research. Analysis is the process associated with the analytic method, a particular epistemological approach to understanding the universe. A careful examination of the analytic method will be useful here to provide a context for the topic of this chapter.

> Analysis is an attempt to understand a complexity by examining its constituent parts. The parts being simpler, they are supposedly more amenable to understanding. The idea of analysis, then, is to understand the working of the parts . . . . The implied hope is that it is possible to 'build up' the understanding of a complexity by 'superimposing' the workings of the various parts [Rappaport and Horvath, 1968, p. 87].

[The relations between the parts] ... are determined one by one. These separate determinations are made possible by the method of controlled experiment. In order to bring out some causal relation free of disturbance by other factors, we deliberately try to hold constant all those factors suspected of having some influence. Thus the basic assumption underlying the empirical study of physical phenomena is that we can eliminate all disturbing phenomena and study the relation of interest alone. Next, by establishing several pairs of such relations, we can (we assume) combine them into a more general causality law, that is, an equation in which all the contributing factors appear as variables. This is called the *analytic* method. It has been phenomenally successful in the physical sciences [Rappaport, 1968, p. xiv].

The process as described proceeds in two fairly separate stages. First the whole "complexity" is *decomposed*. That is, it is broken down into parts and the relations between the parts are examined one at a time (in isolation from one another and from any "disturbing phenomena"). Second, an understanding of the whole is *synthesized* by "combining" or "superimposing" the partial descriptions. While the entire process includes both a "separation into parts" (decomposition) and a "reconstruction of the whole" (synthesis), most of the research methods discussed in textbooks are used mainly in the first step—the determination of relations between the parts. Methods used in the second stage have been given much less attention.

An example of the methods used in the decomposition stage is analysis of variance.[1] Structural equation modeling would exemplify the methods used mainly in the second stage. This chapter is about simulation techniques—a collection of methods that are used mainly in the reconstruction part of analysis.

Multivariate methods, including the ones described in other chapters of this book, move in a direction away from the classical two-variable model. Although these techniques may deal with several variables having fairly complex interrelationships, many of them are primarily useful in the decomposition stage of the analysis process as just described. The focus is still on the determination of the relationships between individual variables. The fact that this is done in the context of the entire set of relationships, however, makes multivariate techniques especially valuable as tools to be used in the study of complex situations, even though they do not transcend the gap from descriptions of relationships between variables to descriptions of the behavior of the systems characterized by the original variables. The investigator who uses only decompositional methods may thus be left wondering "how to put Humpty together again."

The problem is that in decomposition, things are "taken apart." The very act of describing a system in terms of discrete variables takes it apart. In the

---

[1]It should be noted that the synthesis or reconstruction phase may be included implicitly in many cases in which it is not explicitly recognized. The investigator who interprets a correlation matrix, for example, is "superimposing the workings of the various parts." Multivariate methods that examine interaction effects of several variables perform synthetic functions even while they may be used in order to examine the pairwise relations between variables.

system there are no variables or dimensions. These are created by the analyst to satisfy the requirements of the method, which are reinforced by the linear sequential nature of verbal language. While a complex system will simultaneously exhibit a variety of characteristics[2] which owe part of their nature to the fact that they coexist and interact, the Western mind is trained in methods of description that require a linear sequential form of exposition. A first step in describing a complex system is to decompose it—to isolate and name discrete "aspects" or "characteristics"—to create (more correctly, choose) variables.

What is required then is a way of going back from the separated parts to the intact whole—a method for "superimposing the workings of the ... parts." The addition of a reconstructive synthetic step to the analytic process can undo some of the damage done in decomposition; it is clearly necessary if an understanding of the system is to be obtained.

It is my position that simulation methods are uniquely suited to scientifically meet the need for synthesis. The rest of this presentation will expand on the argument previously outlined, showing both what the simulation process is and how it provides an answer to the problem created by the first steps in the analytic process.

II. MODELS AND EXPLANATION

A. Models

A popular definition of model, first proposed by Deutsch (1952, p. 357) and later modified by Hanneman (1970, p. 10), says that "a model is a structure of symbols and rules for relating those symbols, isomorphic with a set of points (data or theoretic) in an existing structure or process." In other words, a model is a representation of a structure or process, where some aspects of the original system are replaced by symbols and rules relating those symbols. The symbols and rules must (ideally) be isomorphic with the aspects of the system which they represent in the model (Hanneman, 1970, p. 26). According to Brodbeck (1959, p. 374), the condition of isomorphism requires: (a) there be a one-to-one correspondence between the elements of the model and the system being modeled and (b) the model behave according to the same causal laws or logical rules as the original system. In other words, there must be both a structural correspondence and a functional correspondence.

Because of the isomorphism, Kaplan says, a model of a system is useful in the study of the system: "[When] ... system A is a model of system B ... the

---

[2]The word "characteristics" is already too discrete. It implies separate and distinct qualities that can be observed, while, in reality, there may be only a "continuous field" of patterning. The observer decides (consciously or unconsciously) which parts of the pattern are significant and calls them "aspects," "characteristics," "properties," etc. See Brown (1969) for a better discussion of this problem.

study of A is useful for the understanding of B without regard to any direct or indirect causal connection between A and B" [1964, p. 263]. It is this fact that makes models useful.

The requirement of strict isomorphism—that there be a one-to-one mapping—is relaxed in almost all cases where the model is not identical to the original. It is replaced instead with a requirement of *homomorphism*. Whereas isomorphism requires a one-to-one relation, homomorphism accepts a many-to-one mapping. Thus, there could be many different models of a single object-system, as long as (a) each element of the original is represented in the model, and (b) the relations and operations among the elements in the original system are present also among the elements in the model (Bunge, 1973, p. 115).

A model thus has, at least in part, the same form as the system it represents. When the conditions for homomorphism are satisfied, there will be identities in terms of the structural aspects of the form of the two systems and in terms of the processual (dynamic) aspects. In other words, there will be formal identities of both structure and process.

Because the model is a representation of the form of the system, it is possible to formulate new descriptions of the original system, based on the appropriate observations made on the model and its behavior under different conditions. This is especially useful when differences that cannot be observed in the system because of practical, economic, or other reasons are readily observed in the model.

At this point a tentative, very loose definition of the term "simulation" can be put forth: Simulation is a process in which a dynamic model (i.e., one in which the flow of time is somehow represented as an internal process) of a system is constructed and studied in order to gain a better understanding of the original system. Barton (1970) says that "Simulation is simply the dynamic execution or manipulation of a model of an object system for some purpose [p. 6] . . . . Simulation models are dynamic models and always involve change in the state of the model through time" [p. 29].

It should be noted that *simulation* is distinguished from *emulation*. To "emulate" is to "give the appearance of." Where the main concern in simulation models is to give an accurate representation of the *internal* processes and structure of a system, the goal of emulation is to give an accurate representation of the *external* aspects of the original. Simulations, if they are accurate, will emulate; the converse cannot be said of emulation. To illustrate the distinction more clearly, consider a machine designed to play chess. The main concern of the designer is to construct a machine that plays a good game—hopefully, good enough so that human opponents are beaten. Let us say that the designer was only concerned with producing a winning machine. In other words, the correspondence between the way a human player decides which moves to make and the way the machine decides is irrelevant. Such a machine would be said to emulate a chess player. On the other hand, the machine could be constructed to follow principles used by human chess players. This type of machine would be a simulation. Obviously, the distinction breaks down in some cases. Nonetheless, it is an important one, as will be seen in later sections.

B. Multivariate Analysis (MVA) and Complexity

Early analytic methods were limited to situations involving two variables. One would be the independent variable and the other would be the dependent variable. The relationship would be a strictly one-way, sequential, cause-and-effect situation. Clearly the use of these methods in more complex situations would be problematic. Modern multivariate methods overcome this limitation to an extent. The incorporation of multiple variables is one step taken by the methods presented in this collection. A further step is taken by those methods that allow variables to behave as both "independent" and "dependent" in the same model. The information that can be obtained using sophisticated MVA techniques is clearly more useful in the construction of models than information obtained by the older two-variable methods.

There are still, however, problems not solved by present multivariate methods. One is encountered, for example, when there are multiple levels of analysis, as when formal (or informal) organizations are studied in terms of the behavior at the level of the work group as well as at the level of the individual person. The challenge here is to relate phenomena at each level to phenomena at other levels. This might be seen as a problem of aggregation. There are some good treatments of aggregation in the literature (i.e., Hannan, 1971), but we are not really interested in aggregates of *independent* individuals. We are faced instead with a much more complex problem: systems of *interdependent* interacting (communicating) individuals, where the behavior of individuals is altered both because it takes place and is interpreted in the context provided by the others in the group. Furthermore, we have the behavior of the higher levels in the system to contend with. Gerard (1968) argues that

> ... the class [of individuals] is, of course, a kind of individual; and the more the members of the class interact—even to the extent of developing into differentiated subclasses—rather than coexist, the more does the superordinate group become a true individual rather than a collection of ordinate individuals [p. 53].

At higher levels of analysis, then, we have entirely new variables—the ones associated with what have been called the "emergent properties" of the system.

> When the observer shifts his attention from one level of organization to the next, he expects to find obedience to all of the laws of the levels below. But upper levels of organization require specification of the *arrangement* of the lower units, which in turn generates richness and the basis of new and unexpected principles [Wilson, 1977, p. 137, italics added].

These emergent properties have their origins in the interactions among the individuals making up the system. A system of independent individuals is simply the sum of the individuals. Since the members of such a "system" are not altered by being members, there are no emergent properties observed. A system of interdependent individuals, on the other hand, includes not only the individuals, but also the relationships among them. Furthermore, the individuals are changed by being in the system. Since the patterns of interaction are included, it is possible to speak of the behavior of the system in terms of the interactions of the members. In a communication network, for example, it is possible to speak of the extent to which the network as a whole exhibits structural differentiation. This is an example of an emergent property that does not even make sense for either isolated individuals or sets of independent individuals.

An additional point that must be considered here is that statistical analysis involves the lumping of individuals into clusters where they are treated en masse, as groups of "typical" elements. This is appropriate for the examination of groups of independent individuals, taken out of the context of patterns of ongoing relationships. It is not appropriate for the analysis of sets of interacting individuals. For example, statistical analysis is useful in the study of randomly sampled subsets of large populations, where the assumptions of equal chance of inclusion and independence of elements are made. While statements can be made about subsets of such samples, they will be statements about the individuals in the subsets, rather than statements about the subsets themselves, taken as units in their own right. In the study of the communication networks in a bank, for example, the interrelationships among the individuals are important. There are no "typical" individuals in such a set, because each individual person occupies a unique position in the overall system. It is possible, here, to speak of the properties of groups of individuals or of the system as a whole. Such statements will be truly statements about the groups or about the system as a whole and not statements about the individual people in them. Statistical methods by themselves are not sufficient for this task.[3] They cannot adequately deal with emergent phenomena in organized systems.

It has been stated that emergent properties have their origins in the interactions among the individuals making up the system. Unfortunately for us, there is generally no straightforward relation between variables at one level of analysis and the emergent variables at other levels (Nagel, 1961, pp. 366–397). The best statistical methods can do is identify variance patterns, such as correlations, which may exist between such variables at different levels. While there may very well be relations of this sort, their identification does little to explain the causal or logical mechanisms linking the phenomena

---

[3]See Chapter 12 for a discussion of methods that examine topological, as well as statistical, relationships.

observed at different levels.[4] This is partly due to the types of relationships that may exist in the system being examined: Characteristics may be observed at one level that are very difficult to express in terms that make sense at other levels of analysis. Furthermore, very subtle behaviors may be caused by apparently simple combinations of well-understood entities (see Purcell, 1968, pp. 39–44). For example, the organization of communication networks in a bank may be such that, under certain combinations of customer demands, employee illness, fluctuations in foreign exchange rates, and the behavior of investors at the stock exchanges, a crisis in monetary flows may develop. It may also be the case that no existing models of the banking system will predict the problems encountered, perhaps because they fail to recognize the timing of the various disturbances of the system. Although the higher-level phenomena (i.e., the monetary-flow crisis) may be statistically related to lower level occurrences (i.e., my decision to place an order to sell my shares of Detroit Edison stock when the price reaches $22\frac{1}{2}$), the elucidation of the underlying processes may be exceedingly difficult. I have argued elsewhere (Richards, 1976, pp. 43–71) that one source of the difficulty is due to the complexity of the relation between the observer and the system being observed/described, especially in the case of multiple-level systems, as the processes of observation and description "interact" with the relations between the different levels in the system.

What methods can trace the links from one level to another? The decomposition stage of analysis can tell *that* a relationship is present, *that* it accounts for so much variance, or *that* it goes in one direction or another. However, it cannot tell *how* a set of variables at one level "combine" to give a new set at a different level. This limitation springs from the way "variables" are formulated. The description of a system in terms of "variables" requires that certain aspects of the system be singled out for incorporation as variables. Other aspects are ignored. The system is decomposed into discrete variables.

Two conditions are necessary if an explanation of the whole system is to be synthesized from the description resulting from the decomposition. First, the set of variables chosen to describe the system or its parts must incorporate the appropriate aspects of both. There are no straightforward procedures for this selection process. Second, the relationships between and among the variables must be represented in such a way that the context for each variable and relationship is reconstructed in the model. Without the synthetic step, in which the decomposed system is reconstructed, the investigator is left with a knowledge of parts, but not with an understanding of how they work in

[4]Even though some multivariate techniques (such as the causal modeling methods described in Chapter 5) may identify causal relations, I would argue that the kind of explanation being offered is closer to that of a "what explanation" rather than that of a "how" or "why" explanation. See Monge (1973, pp. 6–7) and Section II.C of this chapter for a better description of types of explanations and some implications of the different types.

concert, in the context of the intact system. When decomposition is combined with synthesis, it becomes possible to explain *how* variables at one level relate to those at other levels. I will elaborate on the way in which decomposition is combined with reconstruction after I have expanded the conceptual basis for this approach.

C. Explanation

At this point it will be useful to clarify a term that has been used without the benefit of a proper introduction: explanation. There are many different kinds of explanation. One is so widely used by researchers in our field that I feel it is necessary to note that it is not the kind of explanation I have in mind when I use the term here. Kerlinger (1964, p. 12) says that "scientific explanation boils down to specifying the exact relations between one class of empirical events and another under certain conditions." And later, "all the scientist has to work with is variance" [Kerlinger and Pedhauzer, 1973, p. 3]. He seems to imply that when we have determined how much of the variance in a dependent variable is accounted for by the independent variable(s), that we have "explained" the phenomena. I would say that we have *described* the external aspects of the phenomena, or that we have explained *that* the phenomenon occurs. In his discussion of types of explanation, Monge (1973, pp. 6–7) called this type of explanation a "what explanation." He said that "what explanations can be scientifically useful for classifying phenomena, but they do little to advance our understanding of [them]." With a what explanation, we may not have explained *how* the phenomenon works, although we may have provided a better understanding of what *did* happen.

My notion of an explanation includes a specification of the causal and/or logical relations involved in the phenomenon, including the relations between whatever variables may be of interest. For me, an explanation tells *how* or *why*, as well as *that*. According to Monge, *why* explanations differ from *what* explanations in that, whereas a *what* explanation is an explanation in that it removes uncertainty about the phenomenon by classifying and categorizing it with other phenomena, it does not explain why the phenomenon is classified the way it is. The "why" of *why* explanations is based upon the logic of a set of propositions, which, together with a universal generalization that is assumed to be true in all cases at all times (i.e., a covering law), forms the theory that allows us to go beyond the mere description of *what* explanation.

It is important to note, however, that the universal generalization upon which this type of explanation is based may be difficult to obtain. For this reason (together with other considerations), Monge suggests that a slightly different kind of explanation be used instead. He proposes what he calls a *system* explanation which begins with a set of variables together with rules which define the relations among them. Such a specification is said to explain, according to Monge (1973), "when: (1) the formal calculus [i.e. the specification of variables and the relationships among them] entails expectations, (2) the terms of the calculus are loaded with empirical referents (by rules of correspondence), and (3) isomorphism is established between the logical system and empirical reality" [p. 10].

The type of explanation I mean to use in this chapter is closer to a systems explanation than to either of the other two. An explanation is a description that is sufficiently complete in its specification of elements, variables, and functional relationships (including assumed causal laws or logical relations such as rules) that it could be expressed in the form of a model. Recall the criteria for a model: homomorphism of both structure and function—not only will the model behave in the same way as the original (i.e., not only does it emulate the original), but it will do so because its processes are governed by the same formal laws, or because the same logical relations are in effect (i.e., it also simulates the original). Thus, we have explained a system when we have simulated it.

III. MODELS AND SIMULATION

It was stated earlier that "the relation between a model and the system it represents is one of homomorphism." This identification specifies the necessary conditions for a model. It does not tell how a model is constructed or what its characteristics are. In this section I will expand the concept of model and formally introduce the *simulation*, a particular kind of model.

A. Homomorphism Revisited

A model is required to be homomorphic with the system it represents. This means it will have the same formal structure and be governed by the same formal laws or logical relations. But how is a model *different* from that which it represents? Obviously a model must be different, for if it were not, there would be no point in using one.

The differences between a model and that which it represents lie in: (a) the way in which the form of the original is manifested (the *substitution*) and (b) the degree to which the form of the original is expressed by the form of the model (the *simplification*).

Let us take these differences one at a time.

1. THE MANIFESTATION OF THE FORM (THE SUBSTITUTION)

The requirement of homomorphism states that there will be *formal* identities of structure and dynamic process. It does not require *physical* identities. This means that the model can incorporate *substitutions* of any kind for the corresponding components in the original system, as long as the formal identities are there. For example, I may use a network of pipes with fluid flowing through them as a model of a communication network where messages "flow" through the "channels" which correspond to the pipes.[5] Setting up the model would include the establishment of structural and functional similarities. For instance, the network of pipes would be made topologically congruent with the network of communication relations. Reservoirs with valves might be set up to represent people in the network. Leaks in the reservoirs would correspond to information loss through forgetting. Additional liquid sources and leaks would alter the flows from one reservoir to another to simulate the effects of noise in communication networks. Other relationships would be established in such a way as to create a sufficiently accurate mapping of structures and functions.

Some assumptions upon which the model is based would include: (a) Communication channels (pipes) are limited in the amount of information (water) they can carry in a given amount of time. (b) Certain kinds of communication channels (pipes) can carry more or less information (water) than other kinds. (c) There are fundamental similarities in what happens when a communication system is overloaded and what happens when a hydraulic system is overloaded. (d) Some configurations of communication channels (pipes) will result in more/less efficient transmission and processing for the whole system. Because of the structural and functional similarities, a network of pipes with fluids flowing can be used as a model of a communication network.

Alternatively, I might use a network of electrical parts in an analog computer or a system of (nonlinear and/or partial) differential equations or a series of FORTRAN instructions. As long as there is a formal identity of both structure and process, i.e., as long as there is a specifiable relation between components in the model and components in the system, as well as a correspondence between the laws or logical relationships governing dynamic behavior in the two systems, we can use the substitution as a model of the original system.

We can use *anything* for the substitution, as long as there is the formal identity of homomorphism. In the social sciences, two kinds of substitutions are seen more often than others. The first uses *individual persons* to replace larger groups of people. These models are often called "games." The second kind uses *computers*. These models are usually called "simulations." Although the term "simulation" is often used to mean any kind of dynamic or operating model, I use it here to mean *those models which substitute computers and computer programs for other kinds of systems*. Here the particular program establishes the formal identities of both structure and process.

---

[5]The use of this example should not be interpreted as suggesting that this particular substitution is valid. It is used merely as an illustration of the kinds of models that *could* be used in the study of communication.

2. The Degree to Which the Form of the System Is Expressed by the Form of the Model (The Simplification)

Models may vary in the extent to which they mirror the detail of the systems they represent. Obviously, when individual persons are substituted in games for nations or other groups of people, the model will be much simpler than the real system. The same is true of computer simulations. What happens here is a "smoothing out" of the fine differences so that the formal identities between the model and the original system are present over a range sufficient to allow description of any desired fineness to be formulated from an analysis of the model's behavior. In digital terms, this means that enough levels must be incorporated in the model to account for behavior down to the lowest level of analysis that may be desired. This approach makes the concept of homomorphism one of degree—the formal identities may be stronger or weaker, as more or less of the finer aspects of both structure and process are included in the model.

B. More on Models

Earlier sections examined the logical form of models; a few comments on some other characteristics of models are now appropriate. First, models are by their very nature synthetic rather than decompositional, holistic rather than pointillistic. The focus is on sets of relationships, taken together, rather than on individual variable pairs, taken in isolation from "disturbing" phenomena. Simulation models are synthetic—they combine previously isolated relationships into unified wholes. In this process information about the consequences of the interactions of the relationships is made readily available, where it was previously obscured by the decomposition of the original. The information associated with the interactions of the parts of the system, it will be recalled, is information associated with the emergent properties of the higher levels of analysis in the system. Perhaps an example will help to illustrate this process.

SIMORG (Richards and Monge, 1973) is a model of the social interaction process. Built into the simulation are several statements about the relations between a number of variables that are concerned with the perception of the attitudes of other people, the accuracy of these perceptions, the effects of previous histories of interaction, and so on. Some of these relationships are stated in verbal form here:

(1) The more two people interact, the more accurate each person's judgments of the other's attitudes will be.

(2) Perceptions of the attitudes of other people will be systematically distorted, so that (a) when the actual difference is less than a certain amount, the attitudes will be perceived to be more similar than they really are; (b)

when the actual difference is greater than a certain amount, the attitudes will be perceived to be more different than they really are. The difference below or above which distortion takes place defines what is known in the literature as a "latitude of acceptance."

(3)   There is, for each person, an optimum level of interaction, so that either more or less frequent interaction with others is an undesirable condition.

(4)   The discrepancy between a person's optimum level of interaction and the same person's actual level of interaction is inversely related to the person's latitude of acceptance. Thus, a person who experiences a period with very low frequencies of interaction will widen his/her latitude of acceptance. The opposite happens with very high levels of interaction.

(5)   There is a direct positive relationship between the perceived similarity of another person and the desirability of interacting with that person. The strength of this relationship is influenced by the discrepancy between the actual and the optimum levels of interaction for the actor.

(6)   The more successful interactions a pair of individuals share, the greater the chances of further successful interactions, assuming everything else remains constant.

These relationships were all drawn from empirical studies reported in the literature. Most of these studies were simple examinations of two-variable pairs. It is important to note that in no case are any statements made about such phenomena as group stability or differentiation. In other words, all the data used to construct the model were from the individual level of analysis. The entire set of these statements is the result of a fairly extensive decomposition of the social interaction processes that might be observed in groups of individuals who share a good deal of their time with one another. The combination into a single simulation model is a synthesis—a reconstruction of the decomposed system.

Because of the way the simulation was constructed, it became possible to make statements about the behavior of the whole system of interacting individuals. With the simulation, it was possible to examine such phenomena as group stability and differentiation, even though these variables were not explicitly entered into the model. These variables are the consequences of the interaction of the elements which were brought together in the model. These variables are the emergent characteristics of the system. This example indicates how the use of simulation models can make available information that is not explicitly contained in the parts of the model.

A second point about simulation models that is illustrated by the example is that they are capable of representing very complex relationships between the variables. In SIMORG, for example, the likelihood of successful interaction for a given pair of individuals depends on them both deciding that they want to interact. But first, each person evaluates the other. The memory of past interactions together with perceived attitudinal differences or similarities and the discrepancy between the actual and optimal levels of interaction all go together in complex ways to influence an individual's choice. Not only are the evaluations dependent on the characteristics of the individuals, they are also influenced by previous interactions. Even though only a few of the relationships that are included in the model have been mentioned here, it is easy to see that a statistical or mathematical expression of the set of relationships would be at best very difficult to work with. Relationships such as these are not difficult to incorporate in simulation models. Part of the reason is that logical relationships, even ones involving symbolic transformations, are easily handled by the language structures used in computer programs.

Finally, because they are dynamic, working representations, simulation models incorporate the flow of time into their structure. The fact that time is explicitly included as a variable in simulation models makes them especially useful when we are interested in, for example, the effects of modifications of the way in which various events are sequenced. Some simulation models can be run backwards as well as forwards, making it possible to "extrapolate" to initial conditions so that the past, as well as the future, can be "predicted."

The fact that the investigator has control over the flow of time means that the model can be run over and over again. This is useful in two different kinds of situations. In the first, a series of runs may be used as a sample. In this way it is possible to construct distributions and to make comparisons with known populations. In the second, repeated runs may have slight variations in one or more variable. This allows the investigator to simulate the effects of an isolated change while holding everything else constant. In the real world it is usually impossible to hold "everything else" constant.

IV. SIMULATING

At this point we turn to some more practical issues. In the first part of this section I will discuss the steps involved in the creation of models. Included here will be a brief discussion of some of the problems frequently encountered in this process. The second part takes the model and turns it into a computerized simulation. Most of this part centers around limitations and restrictions imposed by the form of computers and computer languages. I have also included in this section a quick review of some of the power that computers bring to the modeling situation. The final part focuses on the testing and validation of simulations.

A. Creating the Model

Although it is quite easy to say that the creation of a model means "the establishment of homomorphism," It is more difficult to say just how this is done. In the cases in which all the needed information is on hand, a model can be set up by specifications of the components of the model and of the relationships among the components. This implies, of course, that the information that is needed is not only available, but properly organized. In reality, no investigator will be faced with such an unusual situation. It is much more likely that the available information is only partially complete, that it is inaccurate, and that it is not clearly organized. It is this kind of situation to which the rest of the comments in this section apply.

The first step is the definition of the goals of the investigation. If these are not clearly laid out, it will be difficult if not impossible to proceed with the construction and validation of the model, since many decision criteria depend on the goals of the analysis. The general nature of the substitutions and simplifications should also be made explicit at this point, as these will influence later steps in the process.

After the context has been set, a set of components which will correspond to the components in the real world system may be specified. Great care must be taken in this step because the specific choices made here will influence all parts of the model. For example, the choice of units—the way the system is "punctuated"—will determine which levels will be included and which will be excluded from consideration and where the boundaries between units and levels will be drawn.[6] It should also be kept in mind that the choice of units will determine, to an extent, which dynamic behaviors and processes will need to be represented and which can be ignored. It may very well be the case that information is available only for some kinds of units and some of the dynamic processes they may be involved in. Better to start with a set of units for which information is available than to attempt to use a set that will require too many unfounded assumptions to be made.

In the case of the SIMORG simulation, individual people were chosen as the units of analysis. Although it is known that human information processing, which includes general social interaction behavior, is the product of the interaction of large numbers of neurons, about which a great deal is known, it was felt that not enough was known about the relation between neural behavior and human behavior to require or justify the inclusion of the former into the model. Similarly, since the aim of SIMORG was to combine a number of empirical findings at the level of the individual to see if they would be sufficient to explain some aspects of higher-level social behavior, any information concerned with larger groups of people was left out. The basic unit of analysis, then, was the individual person.

Included in the specification of units must be a stipulation of any internal structure which is thought to influence the behavior of the units. For example, in the SIMORG model, it was appropriate to include such factors as attitudinal structures and past histories of interaction as well as some personality

[6]See Wilden (1972), Bateson (1972), and Watslawick, Beavin, and Jackson (1967) for better discussions of the concept of system punctuation and some of its implications.

characteristics, such as preferred or optimum amount of interaction, sensitivity to deviations from the norm, and resistance to change. In general, the more complete and accurate the specification of units, the more trust the final model will warrant as more of the dynamics governing the behavior of the units is explicitly built into the model, rather than being implicitly suggested by the way the model is used.

The second step in the creation of the model is the specification of the relations between the components and the laws or rules governing these relations. The amount of effort that must be expended here will be inversely proportional to the amount that went into the specification of any internal aspects of the components felt to influence their dynamic behavior. If the components were specified in great detail, major substantive additions will not be necessary at this point. On the other hand, if the components were just "sketched in," it will be necessary to supply much of the information that was left out of the earlier specification. This is so because vague specifications leave much freedom in the way units may interact with one another. More complete and explicit specifications constrain this freedom, thereby limiting —in the most extreme case, determining—the dynamics of the relationships between units.

The statement that more complete specifications of the characteristics of components constrains the behavior of the components stems from the perhaps obvious fact that the characteristics of units and the kinds of relationships into which the units may enter are closely related. This same kind of interdependence will be seen between variables and the relationships among them. In a sense, variables are defined by the kinds of relationships they are found in. Since a variable is defined by each relationship it enters, and since consistency in the definition of variables is necessary if the model is to be valid, it is important to make sure that the definitions implied by the relationships are themselves consistent.

In SIMORG, this second level of specification included a detailing of the processes by which individual characteristics were brought to bear on the interaction process per se. Here, for example, it was necessary to specify the way in which the past history of interaction would interact with attitudinal differences and the state of the individual to result in a decision to attempt to interact or to avoid interaction. The state of the individual was conceptualized as the general level of satisfaction with the "way things were going" and operationalized as the discrepancy between the preferred and actual levels of interaction.

One final point needs to be made at this time. *Models created for the purpose of computer simulation must be complete and explicit.* There can be no logical gaps or holes in the reasoning from one point to another. Vagueness and ambiguity are not acceptable. It was already stated that the use of terms and concepts must be consistent throughout the model. Anything that is to be included in the model must be clearly and completely explicated, as must its relation to the rest of the model. The requirements for completeness, consistency, clarity, and explicitness are made necessary by the fact that the model is to be computerized. Although these qualities are certainly desired in any model, they are absolutely essential for computerized models. This is due to the nature of computers—they do precisely, literally what they are told. No more or less. The only way to avoid serious problems is to be completely, consistently, clearly explicit about the model.

Immediately there arises a problem: what to do about "knowledge gaps"—small segments in the model for which there is no data available. In an informal verbal model such gaps are easily skimmed over. This will not do for a computerized model. Here, the gaps must be somehow plugged. If possible, more research can be done in order to obtain the missing data. If not, it will be necessary to do the next best thing—use an educated guess. What would the prevailing theory suggest? What would make sense? What would be a "reasonable value"?

Sometimes the inputs to and outputs from a process will be known, but not the intervening mechanisms. In this case the "black box" is used. The black box is simply a set of rules that produces the correct outputs when given the inputs. It is realized that the rules have no necessary correspondence to what really happens. Black boxes are thus descriptions, rather than models. The important thing is to close the gap between the input and the output.

In both of the cases just mentioned, assumptions are being made. The validity of the model is thrown into doubt. As soon as possible, the stopgap measures should be replaced with information based on empirical research. If the simulation is based mainly on theory, rather than on data, a new assumption is temporarily added to the rest of the theory. Its fit with the more established parts of the model will determine whether or not it is plausible. If it produces realistic results, it may be incorporated into the body of the theory.

A second problem is encountered more often than wide open gaps in knowledge: specificity lapses. Most social science research results in statements like "the more X, the more Y." Only rarely is the amount of change in X linked with the amount of change in Y. This introduces some uncertainty in the form of vagueness to the model. The computer, however, must be told by how much to increase Y. The model must specify this quantity. When specific knowledge is not available, it may be necessary to try a value that seems reasonable. An alternative is to build probabilistic relations into the model. A specification of the amount of variance accounted for by a relation can be translated into a computerized model with relative ease. This may be a more attractive alternative than "picking a reasonable value." At any rate, a careful examination must be made of the role in the model of any variable for which specific values must be chosen when there is insufficient information. Sensitivity analysis (described in a later section) is a useful approach to take here. When the model is found to be sensitive to small changes in one of these variables, more effort should be spent in trying to empirically determine values for the model. When large variations have little or no effect on the model, less doubt is raised by the inclusion of these kinds of variables.

To summarize, a model which is used for a computer simulation must have these characteristics:

(a)   It must

(1)   specify the units in the model which replace the units in the original system;
(2)   specify any internal structural characteristics of those units which influence the behavior of the units as they interact with other units;
(3)   specify the functional laws or rules which govern the behavior of the units, whether or not the behavior is a result of interactions with other units;
(4)   specify the relationships through which any dynamic change in one part of the model leads to changes in other parts of the model.

(b)   Furthermore, these specifications must be complete, consistent, clear, and explicit; with no logical gaps, ambiguities, or unintentional uncertainties.

B. Turning the Model into a Simulation: Computerization

1. ABOUT COMPUTERS

There are two types of computers: analog and digital. Analog computers are essentially electrical networks (they may also be hydraulic or mechanical), which may be altered so as to represent any process that can be expressed as a series of flows and rates. In an analog computer, processing is parallel and simultaneous. Thus, there can be both multiple inputs and multiple operations, all taking place concurrently throughout the network. This has obvious implications for the simulation of complex situations involving multiple parallel processes. A digital computer, on the other hand, has two basic components—memory and a processor. Memory is composed of strings of *bits* ("bit" is a contraction of Binary digit). Each bit may take on either one of two values—1 or 0: on or off, true or false. Processing on a digital computer is strictly sequential. The processor executes instructions one at a time. Therefore, only one discrete operation can be performed at any particular time.

The two types of computers may be compared along several dimensions:

(a)   *Representation of quantities.*   The analog machine uses continuously variable voltages whereas the digital computer uses strings of discrete bits.

(b)   *Type of processing.*   Digital machines have central processing units (CPUs) which operate sequentially on one instruction at a time, while in analog computers the whole network is the "processor." Processing is thus parallel, simultaneous, and continuous, since "values" are not restricted to the discrete 0 or 1 of the bit.

(c) *Memory*. Digital computers often have very large memories and can thus store massive amounts of information. Analog computers do not have discrete memories. Instead, information is "stored" in the network in the voltage potentials.

Analog computers are thus well suited to represent situations involving quantities that may be related to one another through networks of simultaneous relationships, while digital computers can handle sequential logical structures and manipulate enormous amounts of symbolic information.

Clearly there are certain advantages unique to each type of computer. It is possible, however, to get the best of both worlds by combining two machines into a hybrid digital–analog system. Since analog computers are extremely difficult to use for most social science applications, and since hybrid systems are both limited in accessibility and difficult to program, most social science simulations are done on digital computers, which are fast, powerful, easily accessible, and relatively easy to program. For this reason, the rest of my comments are limited to simulations using digital computers.

2. REPRESENTATION OF TIME

Most simulation work is done with digital computers, which, as has been explained, are sequential, one-step-at-a-time information processors. Since most communication research involves continuous processes which proceed concurrently, there are problems of a fundamental sort. One solution is to chop up the flow of time into tiny increments. At the end of each increment a new description of the state of the system is calculated by applying the dynamic relations specified in the model to the previous state description. By making the time intervals very short, it is possible to simulate continuous processes in such a way that jumps from one cycle to the next are not problematic.

This technique of slicing time can be used to simulate processes involving any number of simultaneous behaviors. With this approach it does not matter how much work has to be done between time increments, because all the action is frozen. It is a lot like stopping a motion picture projector on a single frame, in order to go out to the kitchen to make a sandwich, without missing any of the action. When the projector is turned back on, everything picks up where it was interrupted. The movie is not influenced. This strategy can also be used to advantage in simulations to take measurements without disturbing the processes being simulated.

The process of advancing time in uniform steps works well when the level of dynamic activity throughout the model is fairly consistent over time. In some cases, however, there may be periods of activity separated by long periods in which there are no important changes. For these types of simulations, time may be advanced from one event to the next, bypassing the periods of relative dormancy in between. In any case, the basic interval is called a *cycle*, whether it is a time increment of standard length or the interval from one discrete event to the next.

In models of hierarchically organized processes, the method of advancing time may vary from one level of description in the model to the next. For example, in a simulation of social interaction processes, the basic cycle may be defined in terms of discrete events, where the event is an interaction. At this level of description, everything that happens between interactions is ignored. Time is advanced directly from the end of one interaction to the beginning of the next. Within each interaction, however, time may be advanced in standard increments which may correspond, say, to minutes or fractions of hours. Of course this model is a simplification: It assumes that the important action takes place during the interaction itself and that people do not change when they are not interacting. It does, however, illustrate the use of different methods of representing the passage of time in a single hierarchical model.[7]

3. PROBABILISTIC RELATIONS

Most processes that social scientists are interested in are thought of as being probabilistic rather than deterministic. That is, while there are very few situations in which a particular event will always occur when certain conditions are met, there are many cases in which the meeting of the conditions is often or usually followed by the occurrence of the event. In many instances it may be possible to specify the probability of a given event in terms of a function of a clearly defined set of variables. The accuracy of such probabilistic relational statements will, of course, depend on the quality of the data that was used in the analysis of the original system, as well as on the nature of the relationship itself. The use of advanced multivariate techniques will often allow fairly precise stochastic descriptions to be made.

While it is somewhat more difficult to model probabilistic relations than deterministic ones, the necessary procedures are fairly straightforward. They depend on the fact that it is possible to write a subroutine that will generate a series of apparently random numbers. These subroutines are called pseudo-random number generators or simply random number generators (RNG). While there are many methods for obtaining apparently random sequences of numbers, the most satisfactory of these is the multiplicative congruential method.[8] With this technique, it is possible to obtain very long sequences of pseudo-random numbers with uniform rectangular distributions over specified ranges. A most useful RNG is a subroutine using the multiplicative congruence method which returns numbers distributed over the range from zero to one.

[7]See Shannon (1975, pp. 109–113) and Lave (1967) for more detailed discussion of methods of representing time in simulation models.

[8]Besides Mize and Cox (1968) and Mihram (1972), see also Uspensky and Heaslet (1939) for more detailed descriptions of the generation and use of random variates.

There are several methods for using RNGs to generate sequences of random variates (Mize and Cox, 1968, pp. 63–69; also Mihram, 1972). Some are based on cumulative probability curves, others on various kinds of algebraic statements of relationships, and still others on indexing or look-up tables. The specific choice that is used will be determined by the kinds of relationships that are being modeled. With the appropriate choice of functions or look-up table values, it is possible to produce variates having any desired distributional characteristics. A sequence of particular values constitutes a sample drawn from a population whose parameters have been determined by the modeler. Obviously, this is useful when one is simulating a system according to a model based on analyses of statistical properties of the original system. A series of runs of a simulation model may be used to determine the characteristics of the distributions determined by the complex interaction of many probabilistic processes in a way that might not otherwise be possible. Furthermore, this characterization may be made as precise as limitations of computer time allow, even though a direct mathematical computation may be impossible.

4. Accurately Modeling Distributions and Functional Relationships

A variety of methods may be used during the construction of the model to ensure its validity as an accurate representation of the situation being modeled. This section describes very briefly the general procedures the analyst might follow in using some of these methods.

a. Distributions   There are two basic approaches that may be taken in the description of various types of probability distributions in simulation models. In the first, the investigator selects a number of different kinds of distributions, such as normal, Poisson, binomial, gamma, etc., and compares them with the distribution that is to be modeled. To make the task easier, a rough visual comparison may be carried out to eliminate the theoretical distributions that are obviously unsuitable. A visual comparison can be done if the original data are plotted so that the shape of the distribution can be easily seen. Then, using information about the data, such as the mean, the variance, the skewness, and the kurtosis, the parameters which specify one distribution from each family of curves may be selected. At this point a number of statistical tests may be used in order to assess how well the observed data are described by the particular theoretical distributions. The chi-square test, for example, may be used to compare a set of expected (theoretical) frequencies with a set of observed frequencies. When there is no significant difference, i.e., when the data could have come from the theoretical distribution, the fit is said to be good. When the fit is good, the theoretical distribution can be used in the model to represent the phenomenon empirically described by the data. Space limitations prevent further discussion of this process here. The interested reader is referred to Bartee (1966) for a more extended discussion.

The second approach to the modeling of probability distributions is to use a packaged computer program that does the matching and testing for the modeler. One such program compares a set of observations against each of ten different theoretical distributions and evaluates the goodness of fit for each comparison with five different statistical tests (Phillips, 1972).

b. Functional relations In almost all simulations it is necessary to model situations in which two or more variables are functionally related in some manner. In the SIMORG model described earlier, for example, an individual's latitude of acceptance was inversely related to the discrepancy between that person's preferred level of interaction and the actual amount. The procedures that may be used in the modeling of functional relationships such as this one are similar to the ones used in the modeling of distributions. First, the data will be plotted. This allows the form of the relationship to be seen and compared to a number of types of theoretical relationships.

There are a wide variety of types of relationships that could be used in simulation models. Besides the family of straightforward nth degree curves (i.e., of the form $Y = a_0 + a_1X + a_2X^2 + a_3X^3 + \cdots$) there are many others to choose from. For example, sigmoid curves are often used to describe diffusion situations, whether it is the diffusion of an innovation, such as 2, 4 D weed spray, or the spread of knowledge about the assassination of President Kennedy. Logarithmic curves are used to describe the information explosion in its many forms, and various kinds of sinusoidal curves are used in the description of periodic behaviors, such as biorhythms.

Once the general form of the curve is selected, it is necessary to determine the coefficients of the best-fitting curve of that type. Usually the "fit" of a curve is measured with some form of least squares analysis. The mathematical procedure that performs this operation is regression analysis. Correlation coefficients are used to determine how much of the variation in the original data is accounted for or explained by the regression equation. The general procedures described here can be extended to complex situations involving large numbers of variables or discontinuous relationships.[9]

5. TESTING AND VALIDATING THE SIMULATION

The next stage in the construction of a simulation will be one of testing and validation. Obviously the investigator will want to try out the simulation to see if it works and, further, to see if it is a valid model. The first test is straightforward: Put the program on the computer and let it run. Gross errors will be immediately evident, as will subtle errors which cause grossly abnormal behavior. The location and correction of these errors is largely a task that concerns the computer programmer.

[9]Several multivariate techniques are described in this book; e.g., Chapters 2 and 5. See also Bartee (1966) for a more complete description of these procedures.

The issue of validity is more complex. For our purposes there are two distinct types of validity. The first has to do with the match between structures and process in the real-world system and those in the model. This is an issue of internal homomorphism. The second type of validity has to do with the match between the behavior of the real-world system and that of the simulation. This is an issue of external homomorphism. Another way of explaining the difference is to say that the second type of validity, external validity, is all that is necessary in an emulation type of model. Both types are important in simulations.

a. Internal validity (homomorphism)   A simulation is internally valid to the extent to which it accurately represents both structures and processes of the system being modeled. Is there a correspondence between components in the simulation and components in the original? Are the formal laws or rules governing dynamic behavior the same? Using the SIMORG model as an illustration, we might ask whether or not real people go through all the bother of perceptual distortion and systematic evaluation of other people before they attempt to interact with them. If we discover that there is no relation between what the model says about how people decide who to talk to and the way it is done by real people, we would have discovered that the model used in SIMORG is internally invalid.

Several goodness-of-fit procedures for testing theoretical distributions and functional relations were described earlier. Careful attention to the appropriate use of these methods during the construction of the model will result in a model that is at least partly internally valid. In a sense, then, the use of these procedures during the construction of the model is a validation process. It is not important that the validation is done concurrently with the construction rather than afterwards; what is important is that the end result is a model in which the alledged homomorphisms are, in fact, valid homomorphisms.

There is a problem here, however. Although a model of a functional relation that is valid during the construction of a model will continue to be valid after the model has been completed unless conditions in the world have changed in the meantime, a simulation that is constructed from several valid parts may easily be invalid in the whole. This is due to two kinds of problems. First, there may be missing parts. Relationships and variables may have been left out of the model. The problem is not with what is in the model; rather, it is with what is not in the model. Second, the interactions among the parts may be causing difficulties. The interactions among the parts can only be seen and tested in the whole. Therefore, these cannot be tested or validated until the whole set of parts is assembled into a single unit. This is the type of internal validity that will be tested after the model has been completed.

It may be useful to distinguish between two other aspects of internal validity. One is qualitative, in that it refers to the types of relationships or processes that are included in the model as representations of corresponding hypothesized relationships or processes in the original. The other is quantitative, in that it refers to the accuracy with which relationships or processes are represented. This distinction may prove to be very useful in the actual conceptualization of the simulation, even though it may be difficult to tell whether an improper functional relationship has been included or correct relationships have been represented inaccurately.

A different approach to the testing for internal validity involves the comparison of sensitivities of the real world system with those of the model. The process of *sensitivity testing* examines the relations between individual variables and the rest of the model. It may be contrasted with goodness-of-fit tests, which focus more closely on individual relationships. The process in sensitivity testing is to vary some parameter in the real system which has a corresponding parameter in the model. The reaction of the two systems is compared. Agreement is evidence of validity. In some cases it will not be possible to perform the manipulations that would be needed to compare the behavior of the model to that of the original. In these cases the behavior of the model is examined as the questionable parameter is varied over its range. If relatively large variations of the parameter have only small effects on the model's behavior, it is possible to proceed with confidence, knowing that the situation may be hopeless, but not serious. When even small variations in the parameter lead to large effects on the model, there is more cause for a renewed investigation of the role of the parameter in the real system. In this case, the parameter in question will be identified as one of central importance.

It is clear that a complete sensitivity analysis for every parameter in even a moderately complex model may be extremely time consuming, as each parameter should be tested over its entire range for all combinations of all of the other parameters. A more realistic approach is to examine the questionable parameters under all conditions that are likely to be seen. This will result in a substantial reduction of the amount of effort that must be expended, as many combinations or conditions will not be expected to obtain under normal circumstances. Unfortunately it is precisely the unusual conditions that may be of most interest.[10]

It is not possible to conclusively test the internal validity of a simulation. Validity testing is very much like theory testing (in a sense, it *is* theory testing). A theory can fail to be shown to be false; it cannot be shown to be true. Similarly while a model can be shown to be invalid, it cannot be shown to be valid. There is thus no straightforward, unambiguous test for overall internal validity. Even if it seems like this would be a serious problem, there

---

[10]See Shannon (1975, pp. 218–237) for a more complete discussion of the general process of validation. The discussion there presents a much wider variety of statistical techniques than there is room to include here. See also Naylor and Finger (1967), Schrank and Holt (1967), and Van Horn (1971).

are some consolations. First, although it may not be possible to prove, once and for all time, that a particular model is valid, the amount of confidence that may be placed in the model may be very high if the model has been examined under a wide range of conditions and not found to be invalid. Second, it may be sufficient for the model to produce results that match those of the real world under a limited range of conditions. This requirement is much easier to meet than complete internal validity. Finally, the issue of validity might not be an important one if the heuristic uses of the simulation are highly valued.

   b. External validity   A simulation is externally valid to the extent to which the behavior of the model matches the behavior of the original system. A successful "black box" type of simulation may behave in such a way that it is indistinguishable from the real system. It is not necessary, however, for the internal structures and processes of the two systems to be similar in any way. Thus, a simulation may be externally valid, even though there is no internal correspondence. Such a simulation—one that is only valid externally—would be useful in predicting the behavior of the real system; it does not, however, explain that behavior.

   It can be said that internal validity is sufficient for external validity, although it is not necessary. Similarly, external validity is necessary for internal validity. Therefore, while there is no way of testing to see if a simulation is internally valid, any model that is found to be lacking in external validity (i.e. fails to match the real system's behavior) will also be deficient internally. The same techniques that are used to test internal validity are used to test external validity. The major exception is that, while internal validity testing is concerned mainly with the parts of the model, external testing examines the performance of the model as a whole.

V. THE USES OF SIMULATION

   Why simulate? Why go through the complicated process of building a simulation that can never be shown to be completely valid? Besides the reasons already hinted at—to gain the kind of knowledge that can only be gained by synthesis—there are other, more practical reasons. In Section A below there is a brief discussion of some general ways in which the investigator is benefited by using simulations. Section B will describe different uses for simulations and simulation approaches. [See Koopman and Berger (1965) for an expanded discussion.]

A. General Benefits

1. ECONOMY

   Many systems are simply too large and expensive to study directly. For example, it is obviously cheaper to study the effects of contemplated changes on a model of a switching network for a telephone system than to make the modifications on the system itself and then study the effects to see if they were beneficial. If a new freeway is being planned to cut across the center of a city, a simulation of the resulting changes in patterns of traffic flow might reveal some unanticipated results, like extra congestion at access points. These problems could cost millions of dollars to remedy, if they were discovered after changes had been made in the real freeway system, rather than in a computerized simulation. In other words, unanticipated and costly results can be avoided by a "trial run" of the planned changes on a simulation.

The same kinds of benefits are realized when the system being simulated is one that can only be manipulated or observed at great cost. Experiments which could not be done on the real system for this reason can often be done on a simulation model at much more reasonable expense assuming, of course, that a validated simulation model is available. One case in which this is especially evident is when the costs are due to long periods of time that are necessary for the natural processes to occur. A simulation may "run through" in a few minutes a process that would normally take years to go to completion, thus allowing the process to be examined quickly and easily, and several times if necessary.

2. VISIBILITY

The use of a simulation, according to Raser (1969, p. 16), frequently increases the visibility of the phenomenon under study in two ways. First, the simulated phenomenon may be physically more accessible and thus more readily observed. In a simulation, all aspects of the process are open to observation and measurement, usually without the typical problems of disruption caused by the measurement process. An example of this kind of benefit is seen in the simulations of potential "world scenarios" that the Club of Rome projected from several alternative decisions regarding population and resources.[11] They altered several key parameters in their model to simulate alternative policy decisions. The effects of these different decisions were then projected for varying lengths of time into the future. After each run the simulation would be restarted, with a different set of assumptions. In this way the investigators were able to study the relation between sets of policy decisions and world conditions several years into the future. Clearly, this kind of experimentation could never be done in the real world, since it is never possible to go back and change a decision to see what would have happened had things been different. Thus, the simulation made the system more visible and accessible for investigation.

[11]See Meadows, Meadows, Randors, and Behrens (1972). Note that Meadows' work has come under severe attack from a number of sources and places. The issue here, however, is not the validity of the Meadows et al. model, but rather the illustration of the concept of the "visibility" of simulation models.

Besides making a phenomenon more accessible, the use of a simulation makes the process of measurement less disruptive to the operation of the system than it normally is in the real world. In the SIMORG model, for example, the value of every variable at every point of time in the course of a "run" is easily recorded by the computer. Even if people could assess their states on the corresponding dimensions with sufficient accuracy, the repeated interruptions that would be necessary to get approximations of continuous records would surely interact with the ongoing processes. The situation is therefore one in which the people can be left alone to behave as they normally would, in which case measurement is not done; or the activity can be measured, in which case the processes are altered, and the measured system is different from the unmeasured one. Measurements in the simulated system are not disruptive to the system; they require no interference with ongoing processes. Simulated systems are thus more visible than their real world counterparts.

3. CONTROL

A third reason for using simulations is the greatly increased control over all aspects of the system that is provided by the abstraction and substitution that are done when translating from real to model systems. The investigator is free to repeatedly run the simulation, varying parameters each time. Additional influences may be introduced in the middle of a run. Parameters may be varied systematically or randomly, allowing either controlled experiments or sampling experiments to be done.

There are thus two kinds of benefits from the control provided by the simulation approach: The ability to systematically vary selected aspects of the model, thus allowing questions like "What if X had happened?" to be asked; and the ability to run the simulation over and over again, reproducing the conditions as accurately as desired, thus allowing the derivation of probabilistic statements when the outcome of any single run is uncertain. The world models of the Club of Rome took advantage of both of these strategies.

4. PRECISION AND COMPLEXITY

Theories in the social sciences tend to be complex, incorporating many interrelated variables. Even when the relations between pairs of variables are known to a high degree of precision it is difficult or impossible to determine the effects of the interaction of the entire set of variables, even when the individual relationships can be expressed as mathematical equations. This difficulty is compounded by the fact that, besides the large numbers of variables, there may be variables of different types, from different levels of analysis, or at different levels of abstraction.[12] Furthermore, relationships

[12]See Pattee (1973, pp. 71–108) for a better discussion of the problems of the relationships between hierarchical levels in complex systems.

between variables may be deterministic or probabilistic, linear or nonlinear, continuous or discrete, constant or changing over time.

These factors all combine to produce a situation in which it is virtually impossible for the analyst to study the entire set of variables and relationships in any meaningful way without the aid of some kind of model to keep track of the huge amounts of information needed to maintain the precision that is required for conclusions to be drawn regarding the behavior of the whole system. In a verbal model it is easy to omit details and gloss over points that should be recognized as important aspects of the model. Words are vague or ambiguous; their meanings shift and change as they are used in varying contexts. The language of verbal descriptions is simply not precise enough to ensure the consistent maintenance of distinctions and levels in a situation as complex as this.

The language of mathematical description, in contrast, is sufficiently precise and consistent. However, complex mathematical descriptions are very difficult to work with. It seems that the cost of precision is meaning, for the language of mathematical signs and expressions is a very abstract one. Thus, systems of equations become "opaque"—only highly trained mathematicians can see through the equations to the relationships they express. Where verbal descriptions make it difficult to be precise about complex situations, mathematical description makes it easy to be precisely wrong. Errors here will be as difficult to correct as logical errors due to imprecision in the other situation. Perhaps most important is the difficulty of solving complex systems of equations: There are no precise mathematical techniques for working with the complex sets of equations that would be needed to express many of the theories we might be interested in.

The simulation approach incorporates the best aspects of the two methods of description at the same time it avoids many of their problems. The level of description is roughly midway between the ease of verbal language and the abstract precision of the algebraic language of math. High level computer languages look a lot more like natural language than like mathematical language. They express logical relations, in addition to algebraic ones, and yet they allow the precision of description that is difficult to attain with natural language.

The simulation approach thus begins with a level of description that is more appropriate for the social scientist than either verbal or mathematical descriptions. Since it is a dynamic working approach to modeling, the simulation approach makes the drawing of conclusions regarding the behavior of the whole system much easier than the verbal approach (which is not precise enough) or the mathematical approach (whose descriptions are often opaque and intractable). The simulation approach can handle more complex systems, having both more variables and relationships and more types of variables and relationships, than can the mathematical approach. It can do so with more precision and accuracy than can the verbal approach.

The simulation approach thus seems an ideal one for the problems of complexity and precision in the explanation of human communication. As Verba (1964) says,

> A simulation is a model of a system. Other models . . . may attempt to represent a system through verbal means, mathematical means, or pictorial means. Like simulations, they involve the abstraction of certain aspects of the system one is studying and an attempt to replicate these aspects by other means, such as words or mathematical symbols. But the simulation model differs in that it is an *operating* model. Once the variables that have been selected are given values within the simulation and the relations among the variables are specified, the model is allowed to operate. It may operate through the interaction of people who play roles within the mode or it may operate on a computer . . . the computer program represents the premises of the model. Its operation produces the implications [p. 491].

B. Specific Applications

1. THEORY DEVELOPMENT

Computer simulation requires completeness, consistency, clarity, and explicitness in the specification of models. It follows almost automatically that the reformulation of a verbal model in the format required for simulation will force the analyst to add these qualities to the model if they are not already there. Since verbal thinking and description do not demand the discipline required for a simulation it is likely that any verbal model will benefit from this reformulation, even if the actual simulation is not constructed. Indeed, it has been suggested that one of the best tests of the adequacy of a statement of theory is to attempt to cast it in the form of a simulation. Any faults in the original statement will quickly be made evident in the process. It is likely that many "theories" will be found so deficient that they will be abandoned in the face of requirements of specificity, completeness, clarity, and consistency.

But there are other ways in which simulation helps in the development of theory. HOMUNCULUS, a simulation of interpersonal relations designed by Gullahorn and Gullahorn (1963), illustrates one way in which simulations can be used to both reveal contradictions among the parts of a theoretical body and areas in which the parts overlap, and help the researcher see possibilities for integrating larger bodies of theory. Because the simulation process involves the reconstruction of a system that has been decomposed in the process of trying to understand its complexities, it can reveal the implications of putting the parts back together again. This was pointed out earlier in the discussion of emergent properties.

2. HEURISTIC USES

Because simulations are dynamic expressions of theory, they make dynamic behaviors implied by the theory visible and accessible for investigation. Because these behaviors may be only indirectly implied by the theory, or because they may be implied in subtle and complex ways, they may be unexpected when they are first observed. The discovery of these kinds of behavior may suggest new areas of research that might have gone unnoticed without the aid of the simulation.

In a similar way, the careful study of the responses of the simulation to varying conditions or to minor modifications may suggest areas that are likely to be fruitful for further investigation, as well as areas that are not likely to lead to new findings. In this way, both theory and research may be guided in more efficient directions.

3. SIMULATION AS A LABORATORY

Although much valid and important communication research has been done in very simple situations that are easily and inexpensively replicated, many research questions involve larger numbers of people across longer periods of time. Because of the greater expense involved with this type of research, only those fortunate enough to be directly involved with one of these studies can take advantage of the research opportunities they offer. One of these opportunities is especially useful for students who are learning about research methods. It is not sufficient to read about studies that have been done; it is necessary also to be directly involved in the whole process, from hypothesis formulation to the interpretation of results. This is where the opportunity to participate in actual ongoing research is valuable. By providing a "laboratory" in which research methods may be practiced, simulations expand the range of types of research to which students may be exposed.

Simulations have three qualities which make them useful as laboratories: economy, control, and visibility. With a computer simulation, it is sometimes possible for students to run experiments that would be prohibitively expensive to carry out in the real world. If multiple control groups are needed, the simulation can simply be run repeatedly with the appropriate parameter settings. Conditions may be consistently and precisely varied in a simulation, and measurement is both precise and unobtrusive, although the kinds of measurements that may be made are likely to be limited to a rather small range of possibilities. A major shortcoming of simulation laboratories is that they are too well behaved in comparison to real research conditions. They do as they are told; they do not ask questions or try to please the experimenter; and they do not interact with external conditions such as the weather or football games. To an extent, these shortcomings put real limits on the amount of confidence that should be placed in simulation models.

4. PREDICTING WITH SIMULATIONS

Validated simulations can be used to predict what would happen in the real system under a variety of conditions. It was suggested earlier that this could be useful for the planning and development of any type of large-scale system or an intervention into an ongoing process in such a system. This will only be the case, however, when the system can be validly simulated. In many cases it may be more expensive to construct and test a simulation than to carry out the changes in the real system and take the consequences. Nonetheless, there are many situations in which simulation methods are the only way the impact of some types of intervention may be assessed ahead of time.

It should be pointed out that there will always be an element of risk involved in accepting the predictions of a simulation—the model might be totally or partly invalid. For this reason more stringent criteria will be required for a simulation used to predict when the consequences of error would be serious. Besides other tests, for example, a simulation may be run in such a way that it is used to predict present conditions from previous historical ones. If the predictions are accurate, confidence is increased. It must be kept in mind that conditions in the world change in subtle and unexpected ways, and a simulation that was valid yesterday may be useless tomorrow. For this reason, extrapolations into the distant future merit less confidence than extrapolations into the near future. Even when a particular model has been carefully and extensively tested, it would be foolish to place blind trust in its predictions. Human behavior is simply too complex to be precisely modeled; given our current state of (mis)understanding, we simply do not have enough information to construct accurate representations that will work in all (or even most) situations.

VI. CONCLUSION

A discussion on when to simulate and when to use other methods is probably not necessary at this point. The requirements of simulation models have been stated several times in the presentation of the approach. Some of the benefits and some of the drawbacks have been indicated. The simulation approach is unique in both the power it brings and the cost that it extracts.

In trying to gain an understanding of human systems we are usually struck by the dense complexity of the behavior we are trying to explain. In the face of such complexity we try to simplify. We do this by trying to break the complexity down into its component parts. This is called decomposition. In order to go from an understanding of isolated parts, methods are needed which reconstruct the whole we started with. Simulation is offered as a reconstructive technique that is unique in its ability to portray the dynamic consequences of the recombination of the decomposed parts of the system. This knowledge is not obtained without cost. The simulator does not have a set of clear straightforward techniques to use. The assumptions built into a simulation model are difficult to trace. There is no set of rules, which, if followed, promise valid, useful results. Indeed, simulations can not be conclusively shown to be valid.

The demands placed on the researcher who is trying to develop a computer simulation of some aspect of human behavior are severe. The approach requires a thorough accurate description that is not easily supplied, given the nature of the object of investigation. Human communication processes are complex because they involve people, who are inconsistent at best and downright confusing most of the rest of the time. Communication processes are made even more complex by the fact that they involve many ill-defined, vague coding systems that depend on the context for meaning as much as they depend on the messages and symbols being exchanged by the participants.

From the right kinds of data, however, the simulator can draw meaning that others cannot. This is because simulations, being dynamic expressions of theory, make visible the dynamic behaviors hidden in more static forms of expression. "The simulation model differs in that it is an operating model" [Verba, 1964, p. 491]. Because they are operating models, and because they allow the implications of the combinations of the parts of a theory to be played out in a dynamic manner, simulation models help to make the emergent characteristics accessible to researchers in a unique way. This is probably the most important contribution to knowledge offered by the method.

References

Bartee, E. M. *Statistical methods in engineering experiments.* Columbus, Ohio: Merrill Publ., 1966.

Barton, R. F. *A primer on simulation and gaming.* Englewood Cliffs, New Jersey, Prentice-Hall: 1970.

Bateson, G. *Steps to an ecology of mind.* New York: Ballantine, 1972.

Blalock, H. E. (Ed.) *Causal models in the social sciences.* Chicago, Illinois: Aldine, 1971.

Borko, H. *Computer applications in the behavioral sciences.* Englewood Cliffs, New Jersey: Prentice-Hall, 1962.

Brown, G. S. *Laws of form.* London: Allen & Unwin, 1969.

Brodbeck, M. Models, meaning, and theories. In L. GROSS (Ed.), *Symposium on sociological theory.* New York: Harper, 1959. Pp. 373–403.

Buchler, I. R. (Ed.) *Applications of the theory of games in the behavioral sciences.* Univ. of Texas, final technical report, ONR GRANT NONR (G)-00042-66, December 1966.

Bunge, M. Analogy, simulation, representation. *General Systems* (1970), **15**, 27–34.

Cohen, K. J., and Rhenman, E. The role of management games in education and research. *Management Science*, 1961, **7**, 131–166.

Conway, R. W., Johnson, B. M., and Maxwell, W. L. Some problems of digital systems simulation. *Management Science*, 1959, **6**.

Deutsch, K. W. On communication models in the social sciences. *Public Opinion Quarterly*, 1952, **16**, 356–380.

Dixon, W. J., and Massey, E. J. *Introduction to statistical analysis.* New York: McGraw-Hill, 1957.

Emshoff, J. P., and Sisson, R. L. *Design and use of computer simulation models.* New York: MacMillan, 1970.

Evans, G. W., Wallce, G. F., and Sutherland, C. L. *Using digital computers.* Englewood Cliffs, New Jersey: Prentice-Hall, 1967.

Gerard, H. Units and concepts of biology. In W. Buckley (Ed.), *Modern systems research for the behavioral scientist.* Chicago, Illinois: Adline, 1968.

Goldhamer, H., and Spencer, H. Some observations on political gaming. *World Politics*, 1959, **12**, 71–73.

Gullahorn, J. T., and Gullahorn, J. E. A computer model of elementary social behavior. *Behavioral Science* (1963), **8**, 354–362.

Hannan, M. T. Problems of aggregation. In H. M. Blalock, (ed.), *Causal models in the social sciences*. Chicago, Illinois: Aldine: Pp. 473–508, 1971.

Hanneman, G. J. *Models and mathematical models in communication research: An introduction.* Unpublished manuscript, mimeo, Michigan State Univ., Department of Communication, 1970.

Hermann, C. F. Validation problems in games and simulations with special reference to models of international politics. *Behavioral Science*, (1967), **12**, 216–231.

Higman, B. *A comparative study of programming languages*. New York: American Elsevier, 1967.

Howrey, P., and Kelejian, H. H. Simulation versus analytical solutions. In T. H. Naylor (Ed.), *The design of computer simulation experiments*. Durham, North Carolina: Duke Univ. Press, 1969.

Kaplan, A. *The conduct of inquiry*. San Francisco, California: Chandler, 1964.

Kerlinger, F. N. *Foundations of behavioral research*. New York: Holt, 1964.

Kerlinger, F. N., and Pedhauzer, E. J. *Multiple regression in behavioral research*. New York: Holt, 1978.

Kiviat, P. J. Digital computer simulation: computer programming languages. Rand Report RM-5993-PR, January 1969.

Koopman, B. O., and Berger, H. N. Use and misuse of simulation. Presented at Nato conference on the role of digital simulation, Hamburg, Germany, September 1965.

Lave, R. E. Jr. Timekeeping for simulation. *The Journal of Industrial Engineering*, (1967), **17**.

Meadows, D. H., Meadows, D. L., Randers, J., and Behrens, W. W. *The limits to growth*. A report for the Club of Rome's project on the predicament of Mankind. New York: Universe Books, 1972.

Mihram, G. A. *Simulation: statistical foundations and methodology*. New York: Academic Press, 1972.

Mitroff, I. I. Fundamental issues in the simulation of human behavior: A case in the strategy of behavioral science. *Management Science*, (1969), **15**.

Mize, J., and Cox, J. G. *Essentials of simulation*. Englewood Cliffs, New Jersey: Prentice-Hall, 1968.

Monge, P. R. Theory construction in the study of communication. *Journal of Communication*, (1973), **23**, 5–16.

Nagel, E. *The structure of science*. New York: Harcourt, Brace, 1961.

Naylor, T. H. *et al. Computer simulation techniques*. New York: Wiley, 1968.

Naylor, T. H. and Finger, J. M. Verification of computer simulation models. *Management Science*, (1967), **14**.

Pattee, H. H. *Hierarchy theory*. New York: Braziller, 1973.

Phillips, D. T. *Applied goodness of fit testing*. O. R. Monograph Series, No. 1, AIIE-OR-72-1, American Institute of Industrial Engineers, Atlanta, Georgia, 1972.

Purcell, E. Parts and wholes in physics. In W. Buckley, (Ed.), *Modern systems theory for the behavioral scientist*. Chicago, Illinois: Aldine, 1968.

Quade, E. S. An extended concept of model. In J. R. Lawrence (Ed.), *Proceedings of the 5th international O. R. conference*. London: Tavistock Publ., 1970.

Rappaport, A. Foreword, In W. Buckley, (Ed.), *Modern systems research for the behavioral scientist*. Chicago, Illinois: Aldine, 1968. Pp. xiii–xxii.

Rappaport, A., and Horvath, A. Thoughts on organization theory. In W. Buckley, (Ed.), *Modern systems research for the behavioral scientist*. Chicago, Illinois: Aldine, 1959. Pp. 71–75.

Raser, J. R. *Simulation and society*. Boston, Massachusetts: Allyn and Bacon.

Richards, W. D. *A coherent systems methodology for the analysis of human communication systems*. Pitt Report, No. 25, Institute for Communication Research, Stanford Univ., 1976.

Richards, W. D., and Monge, P. R. *A computer simulation of human communication.* A paper presented to the Information Systems Division of the International Communication Association, Montreal, Canada, 1973.

Schrank, W. E., and Holt, C. C. Critique of: Verification of computer simulation models, *Management Science,* 1967, **14,** No. 2.

Shannon, R. E. *Systems simulation: The art and science.* Englewood Cliffs, New Jersey: Prentice-Hall.

Simon, H. The organization of complex systems. In Pattee (Ed.), *Hierarchy theory.* New York: Braziller, 1973.

Specht, R. D. *War games,* P. 1041. Santa Monica, California: Rand Corporation, March 1957. Pp. 7–10.

Spinelli, D. N. Occam, a content addressable memory model for the brain. In K. H. Pribam, and D. Broadbent, (Eds.), *The biology of memory.* New York: Academic Press, 1970. Pp. 293–306.

Thomas, C. J. *The genesis and practice of operational gaming. Proceedings of the first International Conference on Operations Research,* Baltimore, Maryland: Operations Research Society of America, 1957.

Upensky, J. V., and Heaslet, M. A., *Elementary number theory.* New York: McGraw-Hill, 1939.

Van Horn, R. L. Validation of simulation results. *Management Science,* 1971 **17,** No. 5.

Verba, S. Simulation, reality, and theory in international relations. *World Politics,* 1964, **16,** No. 3, 491.

Watslawick, P., Beavin, J., and Jackson, D. *The pragmatics of human communication.* New York: Norton, 1967.

Weiner, M. G. An introduction to war games. Santa Monica, California: Rand Corporation, 1959. Pp. 1773.

Wilden, A. *System and structure.* London: Tavistock, 1972.

Wilson, E. D. Biology and the social sciences. *Daedalus, Journal of the American Academy of Arts and Sciences.* Fall 1977, 127–140.

Chapter 16

METHODOLOGICAL COMMENTS FOCUSED ON OPPORTUNITIES

JOHN W. TUKEY

Department of Statistics
Princeton University
Princeton, New Jersey

Bell Laboratories
Murray Hill, New Jersey

MULTIVARIATE TECHNIQUES
IN HUMAN COMMUNICATION RESEARCH

I. INTRODUCTION

The comments that follow are intended to show opportunities—most of them not at all confined to the data analytic problems of communication science—for improving (i) the attitudes and understandings that have to underlie the sorts of analysis discussed in this book; (ii) the ways in which the varied problems of multiplicity are faced; and (iii) opportunities for the use of newer techniques, so far not widely enough recognized. While there may be occasional comments relating to specific points in earlier chapters, these specifics are usually most important as illustrations of the general points to which they relate.

II. ESSENTIAL SUPPORTS

Many readers will know that I am deeply devoted to the analysis of data; because I like to do it, because I like to improve it, because I judge its consequences important.

Given the brief space of a chapter, however, I must focus on the difficulties, on the needs for change, on the opportunities to do better. To do this is intended to support and propagate data analysis—*not* at all to denigrate or devalue it. Most, perhaps all, of the kinds of warnings or encouragements that follow apply to aspects of single-response data analysis as well as to aspects of multiple-response data analysis. Since this is in a book on multiple-response analysis, however, my cautionary examples will involve multiple responses, but cannot thereby be taken as criticizing the simultaneous examination of multiple responses.

All is not quite sweetness and light, however. I have no doubt that single-response analyses have been more carefully thought through, that single-response analyses are misused *and* misleadingly reported at least somewhat less frequently. Recognizing these facts should *not* drive us away from multiple-response analysis. It should, however, cause us to think much harder about what we are doing—in single-response situations as well as multiple-response ones. It should cause us to look harder for more appropriate techniques—in single-response situations as well as multiple-response ones. It should, in particular, cause us to be more careful in separating exploratory processes from confirmatory ones—in single-response situations as well as multiple-response ones.

The gathering of knowledge is, in practice, fairly clearly divided into exploratory and confirmatory phases. Often, confirmation requires a new unexplored set of data. Often, data gathered for confirmation deserves exploration also. In the paradigm of quantitative detective work, exploration involves finding as many clues as you can, whether or not they point to the right criminal. And confirmation corresponds to the trial, whose aim (as the Scotch verdict "not proven" shows so eloquently) is to decide whether the desired degree of proof has been attained. (In actual legal proceedings there is likely to be but one body of evidence, but an important fraction of it is often gathered after a likely culprit has been identified.)

Exploration, then, responds to: What appears to be going on?—confirmation to: Do we have firm evidence that such-and-such is happening (has happened)?

Exploration has been rather neglected; confirmation has been rather sanctified. Neither action is justifiable.

A. Exploration versus Confirmation

There seem to be two reasons for today's (and yesterday's) overemphasis on confirmation:

(1) as a group, and as textbook writers, statisticians have concentrated on confirmation, on sticking as close as possible to mathematical proof.

(2) investigators have sought the utopian goal of having their results sanctified, hopefully beyond further inquiry, by mathematics or statistics.

The time is long past, if it ever was, when such attitudes were truly profitable to those engaged in enlarging our knowledge and understanding.

We need to take seriously such essential points as (a) *both* exploration and confirmation are important, (b) exploration comes *first*, (c) any given study can, and usually should, combine *both*. For more on exploration see the opening pages of Tukey (1977). For more about the dangers of sanctification see Tukey (1969).

We have spent few lines on this topic, mainly because there are reasonable references. Its relative importance is far greater than its brevity of treatment might suggest.

B. Significance versus Measurement

Statisticians must also bear a large share of the responsibility for the widespread idea, all too often a fallacy, that it is enough to show significance—that enough precision to make the use of the term "measurement" reasonable is not needed, or not worth the effort. To an ex-chemist like myself, presence or absence is hardly "measurement." The uncertainty in something appropriately called a "measurement" should at most be a reasonable part of the apparent value.

There are situations where the expense—in effort, time, or money—of learning very much about something is unbearably large. These situations should be regarded as unfortunate, rather than usual. If the question is important, we ought to think hard about how to reach measurement (not bare "significance") with bearable cost.

This question is not confined to any one class of subject matter areas. For an engineering example, for instance, see Tukey (1977a).

In the social science fields, one approach that has not been explored nearly enough is that of cooperative data collection and separate analysis of individual aspects. This would allow considerable sharing of data collection costs, often the bar to measurement.

C. Looking Hard at Data

It is not easy to look at data—yet it is almost always important. Looking here means just what is says—there are to be pictures. If naive pictures will do, so much the better. If sophisticated pictures are needed, we should use them. The needed paradigm is one of little to very much arithmetic, followed by careful, imaginative graphical/pictorial display.

We will need ever more diverse kinds of display. All of us ought to plan to invent new kinds of display, hoping that a small percentage of those we try will prove worthwhile.

The highest art, both in itself and in graphical display, is finding the unexpected. Done properly, pictures [only a few kinds of which are graphs in the elementary sense; see, e.g., Tukey (1972)] offer us the greatest hope of doing just this.

D. Assumptions?

When methodologies are unwisely—and falsely—regarded as routes to sanctification and certain truth, it is natural to refer to their "assumptions." After all, certainty is hard to reach, even with firm foundations. But with the "assumption" that methodology, especially quantitative methodology, will give certainty, almost always *false*, any inferences we draw from that "assumption" are equally almost sure to be false.

In practice, *methodologies* have *no assumptions* and deliver *no certainties*.

One has to take this statement as a *whole*. So long as one does *not* ask for certainties one can be carefully imprecise about assumptions. There are, of course, situations where a given methodology works very well, and others where it fails dismally. Sometimes we believe we know which is which. Sometimes, more often when our knowledge comes from experience (or perhaps insight into how the methodology's "wheels go round") than when it comes from theorems, we are right in our belief. We will do well, so long as we do not seek certainties, to be casual about "the assumptions" when the technique will work very well, but to be firm about them when the technique would fail dismally. Doing this is, of course, not easy.

If, on the other hand, we *are* striving for certainty, whether or not it is available, we shall have to come much closer to demanding that "the assumptions" hold. This may seem easier, but is not usually safer.

Quantitative methodologies are often, perhaps usually, developed with a particular "leading situation" in mind. (The term should remind us of "leading cases" in law.) Their performance in such a situation—or class of situations—may have little to do with their practical usefulness, since the differences between leading situations and practical arenas are often large, if not catastrophic.

If all we know about our methodologies is their leading situation behavior, we are truly ill informed. Let us turn to a couple of specifics. In Chapter 14, we once could have read: "Spectrum analysis is only good for analyzing such stationary processes." This is a faithful representation of what is conveyed by many textbooks. It is also very misleading. "Stationarity" is part of the assumptions of the leading situation within which spectrum analysis was first developed and within which it is usually introduced. Yet many of the greatest triumphs of spectrum analysis have only been possible because what was being analyzed was *not* stationary. One example is the detection and explication of ocean waves a millimeter high and a kilometer apart, coming from 10,000 miles away. [See Munk and Snodgrass (1951); discussed by Tukey (1965) and more broadly investigated by Munk, Miller, Snodgrass, and Barber, (1963).]

In Chapter 6, Section III.A, we are told that "A third assumption of discriminant analysis is that the populations from which the K groups are sampled are discrete, and that they exhaust the criterion of interest." Here I am less familiar with the textbook literature, but I suspect such words and ideas are all too common. Yet in some of the areas where multiple discriminant functions (specifically stepwise multiple discriminant functions) have proved most useful, their use is frequently that of contrasting a high group with a low group.

I repeat "methodologies have no assumptions!"

1. CHECKING ASSUMPTIONS?

Why then do we find so much about "checking the assumptions" particularly from relatively clear thinking authors? I suspect that much talk about "checking the assumptions" is really being used as an excuse for "looking to see what is happening." Looking is very desirable, let us applaud it wherever we can find it. But let us not cover it up in a way likely to be misleading to the innocent.

2. OMNICOMPETENCE!

The most dangerous assumptions are almost always implicit. One that deserves our most careful attention is the implicit assumption of omnicompetence. Many writers on quantitative methodology make this assumption. They say, or imply, that if the reader only knows exactly what was done to go from "data" to "results," he or she will have no difficulty in understanding what the results mean. This is so often *not so* that we should all be wiser if we acted as if it were never so.

How then are we to explain which aspects of the data are illuminated by the numbers that come out of our calculation?

In a relatively pleasant and very utopian world, some kind of formal mathematics should suffice to answer such questions. Our world is not like that. In my experience, we are lucky if formal mathematics tells us about the broad outlines of when a methodology functions best and how well it functions. How then are we to proceed?

There are four major routes to such understanding:

(1) experience with synthetic examples, often under such labels as simulation, experimental sampling, and Monte Carlo;

(2) experience with actual examples, which often needs to be extensive to be helpful;

(3) such mathematical results as can be found;

(4) analogies with what we know—or believe we understand—about other methodologies in which relatively similar processes go on.

We dare not neglect any one of them.

Turning back to specifics and Chapter 12, Section V, where we may read: "while such [simulation] studies are valuable, the most useful contrasts among network analysis procedures should derive from the mathematical formulations of their operation." If this be true, we are fortunate. If, however, the study of network analysis procedures behaves like the study of robust/resistant procedures of estimation, we will not be that fortunate. In early 1977 I asked a temporary colleague, adept in the mathematics of robustness, which three theoretical results about robustness, published in the last three years, had important implications for practice. I did not receive his list for some time. By contrast, Zachary Rattner's simulations, as part of a recent Princeton Senior Thesis (Rattner, 1977), have had significant implications for practice.

When we can have them, then, mathematical results often (but far from always) give the most broadly useful bases for understanding methodologies, but if we restricted ourselves to only that route, we would be in the methodological dark ages.

E. Scales and Quality of Measurement

Thinking carefully about fundamentals is not easy. When well done, the result is impressive. As a result, the "conclusions" reached may be taken seriously.

Measurement in classical physical science was thought through by Norman Robert Campbell (1920, reprinted as 1957; 1928). The results were impressive —rightly so within the field he covered—a physics where errors and fluctuations were to be made steadily smaller and smaller and could almost always be so made, a physics which had seen great revolutions in theory and understanding as a result of measuring "another decimal place." (Classical physicists of the 1890s had stated publicly their discouragement that there was nothing left for physics but to measure another decimal place or two.)

Campbell believed that the only measurement that mattered was in the style of physics (and that the Gaussian distribution was unrealistic for measurements by being too *long* tailed, that there was a finite upper limit beyond which errors of measurement would never go).

The role of protector of social science measurement from such unfortunate attack was taken by S. S. Stevens, who emphasized the distinctions between such types of scales as ratio, interval, and ordinal. In inevitable reaction to Campbell's doubts, Stevens stressed the formal importance of such distinctions, and, together with other workers, emphasized the inappropriateness of apparently interval-based statistical techniques for ordinal data, etc.

This was a historically unfounded overreaction. Actual scales of physical measurement are only approximately interval scales. While many have an underlying *conceptual* interval scale, based on conceptual operations, all differ from this in some decimal place, often a not very distant one. Before the gas laws, when temperatures were based on liquid-in-glass thermometers, somewhat mutually inconsistent for different liquids and somewhat less so for different glasses, the measurement of temperature was overtly only approximately on an interval scale. Would that be a reason not to use a t-test to compare two groups of such temperatures, say for two centuries at Edinburgh and Aberdeen? No sensible person would object for such a reason.

A similar answer applies today when we have measures on a well-defined scale which we hope comes somewhere near being an interval scale. Not to use t-tests because it is not exactly an interval scale will usually be sheer nonsense.

How have we painted ourselves into a corner on such matters? Mainly, I would argue, because of sanctification. If our p-values or confidence intervals are to be sacred, they must be exact. (Since nothing is exactly Gaussian of distribution, such exactness would never occur for exact interval scaling, either.) In the practical world, we would like to know that looking at y, $\sqrt{y}$, or $\log y$, for instance, would not change p-values too much. (Unpublished work of David Brown is both relevant and encouraging here.)

We have a difficult task, for we must:

(1) pay a reasonable amount of attention to ratio versus interval versus ordinal.

(2) expect to work with approximately ratio or approximately interval scales if we are lucky.

(3) expect that the scale on which the observations are recorded is perhaps infrequently the scale on which they are most usefully analyzed or thought about (these two usually coincide).

(4) plan to learn from data, often from a larger body of data than that we are analyzing, how to re-express the recorded numbers for analysis and cogitation.

(5) plan to use a methodology for which interval-scaled data is the leading case for wide varieties of approximately (or even crudely) interval-scaled data. It is fine if we can learn how much difference exact-versus-approximate makes, but in the meantime we will ordinarily do best not wait for such information.

Uncertainty is judged by some to be the spice of life. It will be long before the choices of data analysis are bland and tasteless by such a standard.

F. Some Specifics

Let us turn to some specifics related to these points. In Chapter 11, Section X, there is emphasis of the importance of failures of the triangle inequality of separation. Two considerations are important in that context: just noticeable differences (j.n.d.) and re-expression.

Fluctuations of attention and judgment aside, the fact that psychologists so frequently write about j.n.d.'s implies that "A similar to B, B similar to C, and A *not* similar to C" is not only logically necessary (if we bisect each *not* similar part, we will sooner or later reach such a situation) but frequently occurring in practice. Any attempt we make to rely upon, or test the applicability of the triangle inequality, must allow for this fact.

Such relatively microscopic issues aside, we need to return to S. S. Stevens. Another of his major thrusts was against Weber-Fechner and toward the comparison of sizes across modalities (as in comparison of strength of electric shocks with numerousness of dots, etc.). The latter led to the use of such words as "prothetic continua" and an emphasis on power-law relations between amounts of different modalities judged equivalent (electric voltage and count of dots, for instance).

In his later years, Stevens paid increasing attention to the observation that power-law interrelation of raw values is equivalent to linear dependence of logarithms. The evolutionary argument that most changes we meet occur in the logarithms, so that such linear dependence is what we ought to expect was probably not brought to his attention forcefully enough.

The present writer would feel that using, for example,

$$(\text{verbal report of apparent separation})^p$$

for some well-chosen $p \neq 1$ was just as plausible a basis for hoped for triangle inequalities as would have been its use for $p = 1$. Accordingly, he would probably have explored a variety of ps before accepting "imaginary dimensions." (He would not exclude the latter.)

For another example, one where reasonableness finally overcomes consistency, turn to Chapter 9, Section V, where fixing the maximum at one and the minimum at zero is derided as "inapplicable to nominal metric variables, and if applied to ordinal data, it would assume interval characteristics that are not there" while fixing the variance at unity, presumably again by a linear transformation, is blessed as "one that I prefer." The earlier castigation must be taken as overemphatic for even quite crude approximations to an interval scale. The latter approval can almost certainly be justified for any degree of crudity that would reasonably permit the first kind of normalization. Notice carefully that we are not objecting to the quoted author's choice. On balance, the variance standardization is likely to be the better choice. But the reason cannot be compatibility or incompatibility with a less than interval scale. (There are other and better reasons.) And neither would be satisfactory if we were very, very far from an interval scale.

G. Details of Re-expression

There is, ordinarily, no guarantee that the form in which numbers reach us is that best fitted for the use that concerns us (at some specific moment). Cubical boxes could, for instance, be described in any of the following ways: length of side, length of longest diagonal, surface area, value, or number per cubic yard, when closely packed. Each of us, if we think hard enough, can imagine combinations of situation and purpose in which any one of these five is more useful than any one of the other four.

We receive data expressed in one way, whose choice may be quite accidental so far as our current purpose goes. We will use them best when they are expressed in a way suitable for that purpose. To do this, we are likely to need to change their expression—to re-express them.

In re-expressing, we ought to expect to look to data—possibly identical to ours, preferably similar to it, frequently only analogous to it, sometimes only just what has been used variously—as the basis for the choices that we make. This has several consequences:

(1) We cannot choose at an empty writing table in an empty study with an empty mind (to do so would be an extreme form of the tabula rasa fallacy).

(2) The more data that is closely relevant, the more detailed a choice we can use.

(3) We ought to expect, unless some one or several has beaten us to it (both in fact and in print) to try at least two or three alternatives and see how well they perform, at least on (a) our data, or (b) the largest easily available collection of data.

(4) We feel free to be semirigid with little data (or with data insensitive to our choice of expression); but more and more flexible as our data tells us more.

Specifics again offer some examples. In Chapter 12, Section IV.B, Eq. (1), where it is appropriate to reverse direction, we need not try only

$$d_{ij} = 1/s_{ij}$$

(properly mopped up at the limiting cases). We could also try

$$d_{ij} = 1/(c + s_{ij})$$

for various values of c, or

$$d_{ij} = 1/(c + s_{ij})^p$$

for various values of c and $p > 0$.

In Chapter 9, at the end of Section V, where the use of Yule's association coefficient

$$s_{ij} = (ad - bc)/(ad + bc)$$

is mentioned, we could also consider the use of the fflog, given as

$$s_{ij} = \tfrac{1}{2}\log_e(ad/bc)$$

or equivalently as

$$\log_e \sqrt{a} - \log_e \sqrt{b} - \log_e \sqrt{c} + \log_e \sqrt{d}$$

(see Tukey, 1977a, pp. 515ff., for further discussion).

While the fflog is exactly a function of this association coefficient, and vice versa, experience in other fields suggests that the fflog is likely to work rather better.

Again, in Chapter 6, Section III.A, where we are told about the investigations of Lachenbrach, Sneering, and Revo on transformed variables, the immediate question is: "If we had asked the simulated data sets whether and how their variables asked to be re-expressed, and if we had followed the data's suggestions—how then would conventional discriminant analysis have worked?"

Two rules of thumb deserve emphasis:

(1) Never expect the expression in which the data were observed to be the wise choice for its analysis. (Be grateful if it is.)

(2)   Never expect any corpus of data to be large enough to tell us how that corpus is best analyzed. (But do all you can, whether by classical methods or the use of new and unpublished methods, such as guided re-expression, to ask your corpus to tell you as much as it is able about how it ought to be analyzed.)

Developers of methodology have not really completed their task until they tell us all, not only how to try the methodology, but also how to look and see whether we ought to make any of a variety of adjustments in how we applied the methodology to our data. By this standard, few methodologies are nearly completed, though we are doing fairly well with some. (In most cases, we will also have to choose one class of purposes out of several before we can begin to ask about indicated variations in the style or details of the methodology's application to our data.)

H. Coordinates

Statistics and data analysis make considerable use, particularly when judged by word counts, of the ideas of n-dimensional geometry. But many of the most important concepts, most important for these applications, are left fuzzy or incorrectly understood. We are now going to try to correct a few of these. Unless the key concepts are straight, we can hardly expect to understand either the machinery or the results it produces. Indeed, we may not be able to even use the machinery blindly but correctly.

I. The Nature of a Coordinate

Consider an ordinary plot, such as we might make on graph paper. The graph paper gives us a fairly good feeling of what either one of its two coordinates is, namely:

(1)   a family of noncrossing curves in the plane (in the simplest case, parallel lines), or a family of noncrossing surfaces in a three-dimensional space (in the simplest case, the slats of a venetian blind, a stack of parallel planes), or a family of noncrossing hypersurfaces in a higher-dimensional space (in the simplest case, a stack of parallel hyperplanes);

(2)   a way of assigning numbers to these level curves, level surfaces, or level hypersurfaces.

In the graph paper case, (1) is a family of parallel lines, and (2) is the assignment of values to those lines.

Re-expression of a single quantity, as when x becomes $\sqrt{x}$ or $\log x$ or e^x, does not change the stack of curves, surfaces, or hypersurfaces. It is natural to say we have not changed the underlying variable, only the way it is expressed.

The ordinary graph, in which the somewhat confusing grid has been removed, leaving only the coordinate axes (hopefully with arrowheads, labels, and scales), does very little to remind us of what the coordinates are like. We owe it to ourselves to internalize the proper idea of a coordinate sufficiently firmly for such slight hints to bring it clearly to our attention.

Three reasons—one each of parsimony, pictorial clarity, and dodgeability —seem largely responsible for our liking such a weak hint and for our trying to escape with it, namely:

(1)   when we ourselves draw, either on blackboard or paper, something about a coordinate, we try to avoid the *effort* of drawing *many* lines or curves;

(2)   when we make a graphical picture, to have all the graph paper's lines in view would *hinder* us in seeing the important parts of the picture;

(3)   by adopting the tradition that an arrow (perhaps a coordinate axis, ending in an arrowhead) corresponds to the stack of lines perpendicular to it, we can often *dodge* the heavy labor and pictorial confusion of putting in many parallel lines.

These considerations are not going to change. Most blackboard and printed page plots are going to continue to use arrows, but we can—and, for many purposes must—change our mental state, recognizing that

an arrow is not a coordinate

If we don't, we will be in trouble.

A simple example, drawn from the cities of the United States, may help us. Consider the rough map shown in Fig. 1, and begin by forgetting Duluth and San Diego. Does the arrow from New Orleans to Seattle, two cities easily recognized as different in meaningful ways, tell us about a coordinate? Not really.

The proof is clear when we ask whether Duluth—or San Diego—is supposed to be like Denver, or Seattle, or New Orleans. If the coordinate we want is East–West, with North–South (vertical) level lines, Duluth is like New Orleans in the aspect that concerns us. If it is North–South, with East–West (horizontal) level lines, Duluth is like Seattle. If it is Northwest–Southeast, with Northeast–Southwest level lines, Duluth is like Denver. If it is Northeast–Southwest, with Northwest–Southeast level lines, Duluth is like no other one of the listed cities in the aspect that concerns us. Just giving the arrow from New Orleans to Seattle, even though they happen to be the most different cities in the aspect that concerns us, does not at all identify that aspect.

A coordinate is a numerical description of an aspect. To describe an aspect it is much more important to say what is alike than what is different. Is

Fig. 1

Denver like Phoenix or Las Vegas? Either of these is consistent with New Orleans being very different from Seattle, but the ways in which Denver is like Las Vegas are very different from the ways in which Denver is like Phoenix.

Specifically, locating "objects" along a line, as discussed in Chapter 11, Section II, is not a satisfactory way to identify an attribute (to define a coordinate). Similarly, line segments joining semantic opposites (e.g., good–bad, see Chapter 11, Section IV) can*not* be taken as defining an attribute.

J. Orthogonality Is Often a Trap

We are so used to having our graph paper line systems cross one another at right angles, that we tend to believe that this is natural, essential, and automatic, In fact it is none of these three. Except for making *simple* pictures easier to represent, orthogonality is, in my experience, a snare and a delusion.

We need to recognize clearly that there are two different kinds of vectors, closely interrelated. In the language of today's mathematicians we usually deal with dual vector spaces.

If one kind of vector is being represented as arrows, the other will be represented by venetian blinds (each by a stack of parallel lines). And we can always find a representation where the two kinds exchange roles: the arrows becoming venetian blinds, and vice versa.

In a discriminant function

$$\hat{b}_1 X_1 + \hat{b}_2 X_2 + \cdots + \hat{b}_k X_k$$

for instance, $(\hat{b}_1, \hat{b}_2, \ldots, \hat{b}_k)$ is one instance of one kind of vector, and $(X_1, X_2, \ldots, X_k)$ is one instance of the other.

Let us take $k = 2$ for perspicuity. In a picture where each data point (X_1, X_2) is shown by an arrow, each discriminant function $(\hat{b}_1, \hat{b}_2)$ is represented by a stack of lines, along each of which the discriminant function, $\hat{b}_1 X_1 + \hat{b}_2 X_2$, takes a common value. In a picture where each discriminant function, specified by its coefficients $(\hat{b}_1, \hat{b}_2)$, is an arrow (less often plotted, but sometimes very important), each data point (X_1, X_2) is represented by a stack of lines, along each of which (which now means for all discriminant functions that lie on that line) the value of the (varying) discriminant function at the (constant) data point is constant. (If we need to consider linear combinations of discriminant functions, we need a picture of this latter kind!)

Again we have not taken the space that the importance of a useful and proper view of coordinates would deserve. We urge the reader to reread this section frequently, and to make many pictures, both in general and relevant to his/her own data and uses of methodology.

K. Causation

Each of us, rightly, seeks to establish causation. Would that it were easy. But it is not.

If we know causation then we can predict the effect of changes. But if all we know is today's associations, we need not be able to predict the effects of changes correctly. If "children" range from 1 to 15 years of age, then it is almost a truism that taller children speak better French. But who would expect mechanical stretching on a rack, or confinement to a dark, silenced prison cell for ten years (with good nutrition and antibiotics) to appreciably improve the speaking of French? All of us believe that we are aware of such difficulties of association not meaning causation, but I fear even the most careful of us slip a little from time to time.

An author who considered that the possible consequence of high levels of attention to violence on television might be learning aggressive action would deserve some credit for inserting "may" in all sentences of conclusion. But ought we not to have asked, or demanded, that such an author go further and suggest the opposite alternative, that those naturally happy with aggressive actions may therefore give high levels of attention to violence on television. Why not? What sort of stereotypic view of child development would be responsible for the dissymmetry? One in which genetically or early-baby-hood-upbringing caused tendencies are absent? One in which physical aggression is absent from the natural man, and its occurrence just ought to have an easily removable cause?

If causation could be established statistically, how much easier would our world be to live in—and how much easier would it be to make the right policy decisions. But that would not be our world.

The trustworthy establishment of causality comes, so far as I can discover, only by a combination of (1) the establishment of association, and (2) the elimination of any possibility that the association comes from (a) backwards causation or (b) common causation by other variables. The soundest basis for (2) is randomized experiment. [Precedence in time can eliminate (a), we observation that the more of the opponent's fighters came up, the smaller the dispersion of the bombers' bombing pattern—both turned out to be caused by clear weather.] Most instances where we think causation is well established are still open to question—and some fraction of them will blow up in our face. (As when a procedure for making "neurotic rats" won an AAAS thousand dollar prize and was found to be merely the first case of audiogenic seizure.)

L. Trustworthiness

What has been said so far, particularly that "methodologies have no assumptions," that "sanctification" is a dangerous intellectual "dead end" (implied by reference), and that "causation is very difficult to establish," might lead the reader to feel that I doubt the intrinsic trustworthiness of almost any kind of data analysis. In this he would be right. Conversely, however, there are many instances where I have a firm faith in the extrinsic trustworthiness of specific data analysis methodologies in specific kinds of situations. Experience has taught us many situation–technique combinations that offer us good results. The a priori has sometimes suggested things that work well—and sometimes those that work unbearably poorly. Even so theory-centered a methodologist as Fisher (1946) has pointed out how essential it may be to try out techniques on real data, writing: "Such theoretical writing must at present be regarded as of a purely academic character, unless and until the methods proposed are found, by objective tests, to be appropriate to real bodies of data."

Until we have learned by experience that the results of data analysis are to be trusted, we will do better to take each of them with a grain of salt of appropriate size (very large for some, very small for others). This need not be too painful a realization if we recall the message of physical science that one person's careful work is not enough, that repeatability over people, time, and space is the criterion for embeddability into the wall of science.

M. Validation and Vindication

In Chapter 9, Section X (Krippendorff), there is a carefully reasoned discussion under this heading. I shall discuss certain aspects to contrast my own basic views with his.

I find it almost impossible to imagine a situation where *validation*, as he carefully describes it, could properly be applied to a formal clustering. He says (Section X), "For example, if the resulting clusters from cliques or other social forms of organization, then knowledge about the way such social groupings emerge is indispensible in the validation of the procedure," and again (Section X) "validation asks whether the way in which information is processed within the clustering procedure is consistent with the way such information would be processed in the real world", and yet again (Section X) "But a better way of rendering such results plausible is to get into the very procedure that produced them and to show that the procedure is, at least ideally, a homomorphic representation of the processes known to explain the phenomena under consideration." I am forced by these words to believe that Krippendorff is actually asking, in particular, that clustering of data gathered at a single time should be homomorphic to those processes extending over time that brought the system in question to the state in which it was observed. It seems to me certain that this is just impossible.

I need now to carefully make clear what I am *not* saying. I am *not* denying the usefulness of clustering procedures. I am merely making clear that, to me at least, their results, like those of other data analytic procedures, are more or less strong suggestions, never sanctified infinitely trustworthy conclusions.

Neither am I deriding Krippendorff's insights into the relationships between the nature of the clustering problem and the more suitable types of clustering procedure. Quite the contrary, had I to do some clustering, whether for myself or for a client, I would expect to read Krippendorff's clustering chapter again very carefully, for his insights bear the earmarks of much careful thought and considerable experience.

What I am saying is that *validation* of data analysis methodology, in the sense used by Krippendorff after Feigl, is *not* something whose existence I believe possible. Trying to reach it with an expectation of success can be very dangerous, either because we think we have succeeded or because we think we have failed. Trying to *approach* it may be very much worthwhile, offering very useful guidance about how to conduct ourselves.

N. Need Clustering Be Trustworthy?

Clustering regarded as an end in itself seems to me to be almost inevitably dangerous. The work of Day (1969) shows how apparently bimodal random samples from a highly multivariate Gaussian distribution are likely to be.

Clustering regarded as a tentative step on which other tentative steps can be built, or as a practical convenience (as in exposition), seems to me quite a different matter. I am glad to consider it a plausible tool.

Consider a long narrow island, more or less uniformly populated, and a need to divide the island into religious congregations, school districts, water districts, or voting precincts. Chopping up the island into compact pieces is likely to be quite useful, without any regard for the "reality" of the chosen boundaries. While this is an extreme case of clustering for convenience (and not as a reflection of any deep truth) I believe most useful instances of clustering are nearer this extreme than they are to the extreme which, if it existed, would permit validation.

I would not go along with Krippendorff's words (Chapter 9, Section X): "All users of clustering techniques should be expected to make at least some effort at validation when publishing their results," but I would be glad to support: All users of clustering techniques should be expected to make at least some effort (a) to explain why they chose the methods used and (b) to make as clear as is reasonable the tentative character of clustering results in general and the degree to which this applies to those they describe. I applaud Krippendorff's emphasis on the Lance and Williams example of the dependence of dendrogram on β, and I stress that β can never be chosen wholly from an arm chair. (The results for some data set or sets must be compared with some external reference; even if only with our own misguided anticipation of how the world should behave.) The same will, of course, apply to other choices in clustering.

III. CURRENT PROBLEMS

We now turn away from the attitudes and basic insights that have to support our data analysis and toward the techniques now in use, and the relatively general problems that plague them. Most of these problems seem to be associated in one way or another, with questions of multiplicity.

A. Dependence in SSTs

Just as airports have problems with one kind of SSTs (supersonic transports) so too do data analysts have problems with another kind of SST (simultaneous significance tests). Most of the latter problems can, however, be dealt with.

An obvious heresy that has long been accepted as gospel is this: If a set of quantities are statistically independent under ideal conditions, it is all right to test them statistically in parallel, but if they are statistically dependent under ideal conditions, we ought not to test them all. One reason why this is an obvious heresy is that something being exactly true under ideal conditions can never (well almost never!) be a sound basis for practice.

What are the facts? Let us consider two instances, in each of which the same set of particular significance procedures, each with its fallibilities and strengths, are being made. In one instance the significance tests are mutually independent in the *probability* sense of that word, in the other they are mutually dependent in that sense, while in both they are *logically* independent, in the sense that the significance–nonsignificance of any one need not imply that of any other. (The many meanings of "independence" has made both that word—and the related concepts—unduly treacherous.)

Let us ask first about the average number of false significances if the situations are repeated again and again. The number of false significances contributed by a specified significance test is either zero or one, the value of the corresponding indicator function. The total number, in a given repetition, is just the value of the sum of these indicator functions. The average total number is just the *average* of the *sum* of these indicator functions.

But an *average* of a *sum* and the *sum* of the *averages* are always equal. So the average total number of false significances is just the sum, over all the significance tests, of the average number of false significances on a given test —and thus is the sum of the probabilities of false significances on each test. If the two instances are indeed equivalent, except for the mutual dependence in a probability sense of the significance tests, then the average number of false significances will be exactly the same in the two instances.

Moreover, there is one case in which we can calculate this average number easily. If all the null hypotheses are true—a situation we might refer to as the *null null* hypothesis, then the average number of false significances will be exactly the

sum of the levels at which the tests are made

If all k tests are made at $p\%$ level, then, on the null null hypothesis, the average number of false significances will be $kp\%$. If a young psychologist tries 250 utterly useless tests to distinguish two groups, on the average he will find $(25)(5\%) = 1250\% = 12.5$ tests significant at 5%, and $(250)(1\%) = 250\% = 2.5$ significant at 1%!

B. Continuing with the Question

So far we have found no basis for preferring either the dependent or independent situations. How can we look farther?

The parable of the young psychologist reminds us that it is both natural and appropriate for any one of us to look hardest at the apparently most significant test. So perhaps we ought to ask, instead of about average number, about the chance of at least one false significance. What will dependence do to us here?

Two kinds of dependence are possible, and would have opposite effects if they really occurred. There might be pairs of significance tests such that the significance of one made that of another less likely. This is far from common unless the tests are logically related (as when we ask, separately, both whether a given statistic—a single number—is too high and whether it is too low). The common sort of dependence in the probability sense is a tendency, more or less strong, for pairs of significance tests to both be significant or both not to be together.

What will this last do to our total number of significances? Clearly it will make it more variable. But the average is unaffected. Thus we will be surprised if the number of zero values does not go up when we shift from independence to dependence. But zero false significances is just the chance of making no error. Probabilistic dependence, of the usual kind, thus increases our chance of making no error. Should we object to that?

Why should any rational person, then, object to probabilistic dependence among SSTs (among simultaneous significance tests)? The average number of errors is unaffected; the chance of at least one error is decreased.

While I shall be glad to receive suggestions of other explanations, my own reflections suggest only the following explanation. More or less consciously, those who decry dependence have recognized that, especially when there are many SSTs, one cannot trust results merely because they are individually significant. If the young psychologist had returned with 11 of his 250 psychological tests significant at 5%, two of which were significant at 1%, should we feel anything but as negative result? After all, pure chance delivers averages of 12.5 and 2.5! Perhaps subconsciously, or semiconsciously, those who decry dependence might be prepared to think about the number of false significances and try to keep this from getting too large by chance so that cases where there are many significant results can be given an overall significance.

If the tests are independent in the probability sense, and for convenience all to be conducted at the same p level, and the null null hypothesis holds, then the number of apparent significances will be binomial and we can take as a satisfactorily approximate test (for small $p\%$, which is all that concerns us) the result of referring

$$\sqrt{2 + 4(\# \text{ observed significant})} - \sqrt{1 + 4(kp\%)}$$

to a unit Gaussian (often miscalled normal) distribution, If there is probability dependence, this kind of overall test, sometimes called "binomial pooling" or "second-order significance" or "the higher criticism," will almost surely be unduly loose (there will be too many large values in a null situation)—and therefore dangerous.

If my analysis is correct, the reasons for decrying dependence depend upon giving up attention to individual significance tests where many are simultaneous, and looking instead, for instance, at a comparison of the number observed to be significant with the number expected by pure chance. The effects of being explicit about such a change of base (from a quite untenable position) are so very much larger than the effects of dependence after the change, that I, for one,

(1)   would be so happy with the change of base as not to be too deeply concerned with the question of "dependence or not," and

(2)   would tell my friends and clients that, if they had grown in wisdom to the point where a change in base was a recognized need, there was another sort of new base that appears to be even better.

C. Error Rates per What Have You

We know that the average number of false significances is $kp\%$ whatever the dependence–independence situation. If we want this to be 5%, then we need only take $p\% = 5\%/k$ or if we want it to be 20%, we need only take $p\% = 20\%/k$ and so on.

The only difficulty that is likely to arise is a narrowly practical one: Can we find appropriate critical values for our tests? If our young psychologist is using t-tests, he can surely find critical values for a $5\%/250 = 0.02\%$ tail area of Student's t. If he had taken 387 tests, however, he could find it difficult to find $5\%/387 = 0.0129\%$ points. For the simplest tests this difficulty is well on its way to elimination (e.g., Dayton & Schafer, 1973). In general, since we rarely know whether an overall 5% or an overall 20% error rate is needed, even rougher approximations to the actual value of

$$(\text{overall }\%) / (\text{number of parallel tests})$$

will serve us well enough.

D. Error Rates Batchwise

Partly from historical reasons, and partly because of the very human motivation to find something significant if you possibly can, there has been—and presumably will continue to be—a lot of interest in replacing, for a batch of significance tests, the

$$\text{error rate per batch} = \frac{\text{\# of false significances in any batch}}{\text{\# of batches}}$$

by a rate that is slightly smaller, namely,

$$\text{error rate batchwise} = \frac{\text{\# of batches with} \geq 1 \text{ false significance}}{\text{\# of batches}}$$

and then holding only the latter rate to, say, 5%.

This does allow one to find a few more batches to contain significances. In most situations, however, the change is not as great as one might expect. Not only do we have, for example (where CV stands for the critical value with which comparison is to be made),

CV at 5% per batch $\geq$ CV at 5% batchwise $\geq \geq$ CV at 20% per batch

and

CV at 1% per batch $\geq$ CV at 1% batchwise $\geq \geq$ CV at 4% per batch

but the batchwise CVs are much nearer the left-hand bounds in these inequalities.

When we also know that "per batch" critical values are unaffected by probabilistic dependence among the SSTs while "batchwise" critical values can be affected (though not, as these inequalities show, very greatly), it seems natural and wise to take the following positions:

(1) In our general thinking, focus on "per batch" error rates.

(2) Where "batchwise" critical values are available, and where a little thought about the possible extent of probabilistic dependence leaves us no more than moderately concerned, feel free to use the "batchwise" critical values.

(3) Otherwise, use "per batch" critical values, or reasonable approximations thereto, with a light heart and a clear conscience.

E. Parsimony—and the Cost of Multiplicity

If our young psychologist could have sorted out the 20 best tests, and taken 20 instead of 250 into the field, his or her chances to come back with a per-batch-significant result would have been greatly enhanced. Testing many possibilities always degrades the sensitivity with which we test the few. We owe it to ourselves to be wisely and effectively selective in advance if we are to use parsimony to improve our results.

F. Useful Power

The *mathematical* power of a significance test is defined as the probability of significance (at some specified "distance" from the null hypothesis). Churchill Eisenhart has defined the *practical* power of a significance test as the *product* of the mathematical power *and* the probability that the procedure will be applied (Tukey, 1954; Hinchen, 1969).

Let us define the *useful* power of a significance test as the *product* of the mathematical power *and* the probability that, if we meet a significant result, we can satisfactorily interpret the meaning of that result. (The definition of *practically useful* power can be left to the reader.)

The message of this definition is clear—loss of parsimony by including comparisons or significance tests whose results are likely to be hard, or even impossible, to interpret is *sheer waste*.

There are many instances where this principle needs to be recognized in practice. One extreme arises when we deal with the simplest multiple comparison problem. Here, use of F-tests dilutes our testing of the simple comparisons we can all understand with testing all the other contrasts (linear combinations whose coefficients sum to zero) among the things to be compared, most of which are very hard to interpret. The other extreme, probably not yet reached, presumably lies in some very complicated multivariate analysis. (We will come to an intermediate case in the following.) We need to keep the ideas and understandings related to "useful power" in our minds at all times.

In any conventional ANOVA (analysis of variance) or MANOVA (multiple-response analysis of variance) this principle often applies *more than once*. We have to face not only:

(1) the multiplicity of comparisons in a given line of the analysis (comparisons among treatments in a main-effect line, comparisons among interactions otherwise), but also

(2) the multiplicity of different lines (which, for example, in a complete 6-way ANOVA includes 6 main effects, 15 2-factor interactions, 20 3-factor interactions, 15 4-factor interactions and one lone 5-factor interaction; $2^6 - 1 = 63$ lines in all).

And in multiple response problems also

(3) the multiplicity of aspects of the response, each corresponding to a particular linear combination of the elementary responses.

In each case we need to seek useful power by concentrating our attention where it will do the most good.

In occurrences of (1) we can, and almost always should, focus on the simple comparisons by taking the studentized range, q, as the key statistic (instead of F). (In the exceptional cases we will want to move only a small part of the way toward F.) To do this does not mean giving up looking at more general contrasts. We still have a confidence statement for any contrast (provided the error term for simple comparisons is still the correct error term for this contrast) by combining the simultaneous confidence statements for individual comparisons offered us by the q-procedure.

In an occurrence of (2) of any real complexity we can, and almost always should, consider how we ought to share out the total error rate we are willing to accept among the various lines. (I have never seen an at all complicated analysis where all the various lines deserved equal error rate.) Since this is hardly the place for an extensive discussion, we shall confine ourselves with a reference to the most classical proposal, the use of "nomination" as practiced at East Malling (Pearce, 1953, 1976).

In occurrences of (3), we have an equal need to focus our attention on those linear combinations of elementary responses that are most likely to be interpretable (more anon in Sections 31–35).

G. Joint Dependence

Neither the English language or our usual education prepares us to deal with the complexities of joint dependence. One clear proof of this is the unfortunate frequency with which investigators insist that there must be a way to say "what fraction" of some desirable or undesirable effect comes from each of a number of causes.

When you ask such an unwarranted simplicist (if this is the right word for an optimist about the world having to be simple) what fraction of the cause of a gunshot came from loading the gun and what fraction from pulling the trigger, he or she will ordinarily be logical enough to admit that the question has no general answer. But the ability to deal with the black and white case, at least if pushed, is no guarantee of ability to deal with the dark gray and light gray cases.

The two situations shown in Fig. 2 are only two of many that arise with only two sets of variables. To the left we see situations where neither variable(s) A or variable(s) B account(s) for much of the observed response by itself, but both together do very well. Conversely, on the right, we see a situation where either variable(s) A or variable(s) B will do very well, yet combining them does very little better than either one alone.

The point is *not* that these are the two common instances. Rather we are pointing out that different instances can be very different and that there is no substitute for each of us looking at our own cases in enough detail to recognize what is going on.

Figure 3 shows how we can accommodate three sets of variables in such a picture without difficulty—and four sets with some difficulty and loss of perspicuity.

In addition to making such plots with an SS (sum of squares) or r^2 (squared correlation) scale, we may sometimes find it illuminating to use a z scale, where

$$z = \ln[(1 + r)/(1 - r)]$$

which reminds us more effectively how far beyond $r = .9$ is $r = .99$, and how far beyond that is $r = .999$.

To be able to even *try* to talk, in even the simplest cases, about "fractions of variability" due to specific sources of variability implies attention to a

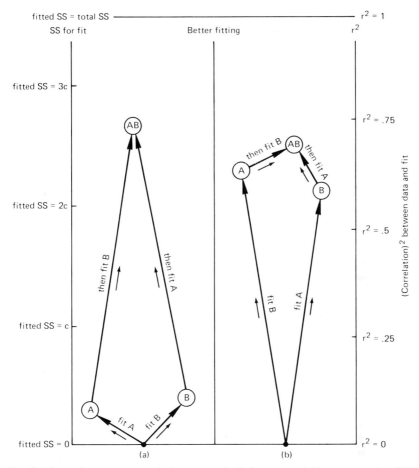

FIG. 2. Alternative patterns of relative success in fitting two variables (or sets of variables) as measured either by the amount of the total sum of squares accounted for by the fit or by the fraction of the total sum of squares so accounted for (this is, of course, r^2). (Horizontal positions purely schematic; vertical position numeric, on either of two scales.) (a) Fitting one or both of A and B; (b) fitting one or both of A and B.

specific population or other specific situation. In a world in which all guns are reloaded the moment they are fired, the relative importance of pulling the trigger is inevitably enhanced. In a world in which everyone, noticing a gun, pulls the trigger, the relative importance of loading the gun is enhanced. Any attempt to fractionate joint dependence must be *relative* to a situation—in the simplest cases relative to a population. This is a crucial point; all of us need to internalize it carefully.

Once we have done this, we can, if we wish, recognize the difference between the two sides of exhibit 1 as measured by interrelationship, at least in the simple case where there is but one variable A and one variable B. If we

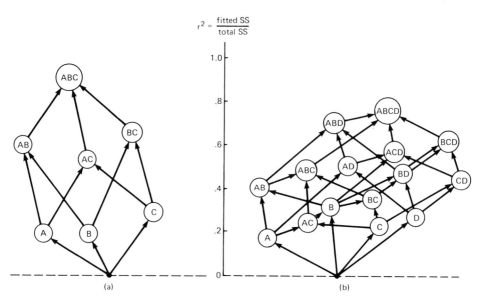

FIG. 3. Instances of degree of success in fitting by using one or more of three and four variables (compare with Fig. 2). (Horizontal position purely schematic; vertical position numeric.) (a) Fitting one or more of A, B, and C; (b) fitting one or more of A, B, C, and D.

change the signs of these xs, if needed, to make the dependence of y on each positive, the left-hand side of exhibit 1 corresponds to a large negative interrelationship between x_A and x_B, while the right-hand side corresponds to a large positive interrelationship between them.

H. Where Interdependence Cannot Be Forgotten

There are many variations on a regression theme where (1) we calculate estimates of a number of coefficients, and (2) it is conventional to calculate—and even to use—estimates of the variances of these estimates. Regrettably, we do not calculate estimates of the *covariances* among such estimates nearly as often as we should. (We ought to calculate these covariances, at least roughly, in every such case! In saying this, I include "all the covariances have been shown to be small" as a rough calculation.)

Like the sporting maxim "you can't tell the players without a scorecard," we ought to repeat to ourselves: "You can't evaluate multiple regression coefficients, beta-weights, discriminant coefficients, canonical variate coefficients, and the like" without having (and using, if only roughly) indications of their covariances as well as of their variances.

I. Roots and Factors

Many multiple-response problems end up with roots and/or factors. These often share a common danger—overvaluing "firstness", "secondness" and the like.

The exact nature of the linear combination associated with the "largest root" is rarely either important or meaningful, at least in situations where two or more roots are large enough to deserve serious attention.

What is important is something quite other than "firstness" and "second-ness"; rather it is: (1) How many roots are small? (2) What linear subspace is shared by the linear combinations associated with the roots that are not small? There are somewhat diverse reasons for these statements. First, ordinary random sampling not only causes changes in the estimated sizes of roots, it also causes changes, often larger, in the linear combinations associated with such roots. Second, if we turn our attention to a different population (perhaps only in a adjacent county) we have neither theoretical nor empirical reasons to believe that either roots or corresponding linear combinations will prove to be even moderately stable. (The hope for stability of the number of large dimensions, and even for stability of the subspace they span is much greater.)

The useful procedure is that of condensation.

Indeed, it may be in "dust bowl empiricist factor analysis" (cf. Chapter 8, Section II) that one of the great virtues of simple structure (á la Thurstone) is that it covers up any distinction between "first factor" and "second factor" and the like.

Even the subspace (generated by linear combinations associated with not-small factors) is subject to sampling fluctuation. Accordingly, we ought not feel bound to stick to exactly the subspace estimated from the data, particularly if there is a nearby subspace that is easier to describe and easier to think about.

Accordingly we ought to be prepared to modify the linear combinations arising in any of the procedures listed about, first tentatively, and then, after assessing the quality of approximation, usually definitively. The sorts of modification to be considered are all those that ease understanding of and/or thinking about the resulting linear combinations, such as: using only simple coefficients, dropping coefficients (replacing by zero) when this seems justi-fied, or equalizing coefficients, when justifiable. To live, for example, with a discriminant function whose coefficients are complicated and unperspicuous, when there are nearby discriminant functions that are simple and understand-able, can only be scored as a major error.

J. Significance and Reality

A classical mistake, propagated by too many books on statistics, is a confusion, too often deliberate, between what is significant and what is real. The extent to which this must be a logical fallacy is pointed out by the fact that some equate "truth" to "significance at 5%" and others to "significance at 1%." Both cannot be right, and it takes little thought to see that neither can be.

A prominent place where this mistake is made is in using significance to decide which "model" is to be used to analyze a batch of data. The general principle is still that "only rarely, if ever, does a body of data tell us enough to fix the details of its own analysis!" Consider an investigator who has collected data on weight, height, and age on a small group of children and who has calculated the variances and covariances of the logarithms of weight, height, and age, finding the simple numbers given in Table I. We find $r_{12.3} = .652$ and $r_{13.2} = .378$. If there were 4 to 28 children, and if we adhere to a "truth $\equiv$ significance at 5%" rationale, the conclusion is that we should use

$$x_1 = b_{12} \cdot x_2 + \text{constant}$$

which gives here the estimate

$$\log \text{weight} = (1.00)(\log \text{height}) + \text{constant}$$

An investigator who believes it well established that both height and age matter would fit

$$x_1 = b_{12.3}x_2 + b_{13.2}x_3 + \text{constant}'$$

which gives here the estimate

$$\log \text{weight} = (.61)(\log \text{height}) + (.50)(\log \text{age}) + \text{constant}$$

While there may be grounds for useful discussion as to which analysis is better for a specific purpose, there is no doubt at all that the significance test on $b_{13.2}$ (or equivalently on $r_{13.2}$) at a prechosen level, while it may contribute to the answer, does not settle it.

Notice, also the substantial difference in the coefficient of log height—1.00 or .61—depending on which choice is made. A procedure of the form (1) initial fitting of many coefficients, (2) deletion of those not significant (at what level?), and (3) refitting of the remainder (e.g. Chapter 5) involves many more subtleties than may first appear. In particular (see Mosteller and Tukey, 1977, Chapter 13, for greater generality) just because b_{12} and $b_{12.3}$ both multiply log weight, it does *not* follow that they have the same meaning. In fact, they have quite distinct meanings.

TABLE I

	Variance	Covariances	
x_1 = log weight	.09		
		.07	
x_2 = log height	.07		.07
		.06	
x_3 = log age	.08		

K. Regression and Analysis of Variance

The rise of computing power has changed the relative costs of number-crunching and program writing to the point where it seems sensible to do a significant fraction of our analysis-of-variance-like computations by regression. In doing this we must notice that regression, as conventionally formulated, has a place for only a single error term. As a consequence, when two or more error terms play a role in what is fitted (and not just in how mean squares are interpreted), the regression approach is likely not to be equivalent to the analysis-of-variance approach.

This occurs when (a) because of unbalance or (b) once robust/resistant methods are used in fitting, two error terms are involved in guiding any part of the fit, as, for example, in a situation where, under (a) or (b), both "interaction" and "within cell" variations contribute to the error of what is being assessed. Cases where we wish to allow for differences in error variability "by stripes" (e.g., "by rows" or "by columns") may call for doing separate regressions for separate parts of the data.

L. Nonorthogonal Analysis?

The preceding remarks (Chapter 5, Section IV) about the lack of need for orthogonality or balance in analysis-of-variance-like designs and the foolishness (no weaker word is acceptable) of throwing data away to attain balance deserve to be stressed and repeated. Fortunately, however, the importance of these points does not mean that we must always rush to a nonorthogonal analysis when our data is only mildly unbalanced.

In the transposed example just offered (Chapter 5, Section V), the numbers of cases in each cell were 7, 10, 11, 16. Simple (equally investigated) combinations of cell means, *if σ^2 were applicable within every cell*, would lead to

$$\frac{1}{16}\left(\frac{\sigma^2}{7} + \frac{\sigma^2}{10} + \frac{\sigma^2}{11} + \frac{\sigma^2}{16}\right) = .02477\sigma^2$$

while optimum weighting would give

$$\frac{1}{(44)^2}\left(7^2\frac{\sigma^2}{7} + 10^2\frac{\sigma^2}{10} + 11^2\frac{\sigma^2}{11} + 16^2\frac{\sigma^2}{16}\right) = \frac{44\sigma^2}{(44)^2} = \frac{\sigma^2}{44} = .02273\sigma^2$$

showing that equal weight is 91.7% efficient. This calculation is somewhat too simple to apply directly to the whole of the analysis of variance, but can be trusted to give a good general idea of the loss in efficiency, here about 8%, of making an analysis in terms of cell means, taking account of the varying cell sizes only in the calculation of an appropriate error term and appropriate formulas for average mean squares.

The simplicity of the analysis in terms of (equally treated) cell means offers important dividends of various sorts, including results easier to understand, as well as to calculate. (These become more important when "Method 2" or

"Method 3" is used.) My own advice would be to *include* such an equal-treat-ment-of-cell-means analysis, at least as an alternate, so long as the sort of calculation made above gave a rough efficiency of at least 75%, and to *consider omitting* the nonorthogonal analysis if the rough efficiency exceeded 90% (or, for conservatives perhaps, 95%). Thus I would be willing to do only the equal-treatment-of-cell-menas analysis in the example just considered (Chapter 5, Section V).

Finally, if we have made both an equally-treated-means-of-cells and an unbalanced analysis, we ought to compare their results very carefully, looking for any aspect in which they differ more than trivially. (Bear carefully in mind in such comparisons that two analysis, one of which is *significant* because $p = 4\%$ while the other is *not significant* because $p = 6\%$ do differ *only trivially*.)

The message here is simple: *do not* fear unbalance, *do not* throw data away to reach balance, *do not* bother with an unbalanced analysis unless it's needed, *do not* omit an equally-treated-means-of-cells analysis unless it is very poor, *do* compare the two analyses carefully if two are made.

IV. OPPORTUNITIES

We are ready to turn to a few opportunities that now beckon those who either want to do new things, or to do old things better.

A. Robust/Resistant Procedures

We are now in the midst of a rapid retooling—a retooling that promises to extend to essentially all the techniques used in analyzing data. Initially we were very happy to have very high (preferably 100%) efficiency in only one situation—samples from a pure Gaussian distribution. Some call this the *over-utopian* situation. Later we went "nonparametric" and asked only for 5% to mean 5% in each of a very wide variety of situations, asking nothing explicit in the way of efficiency. Today we are trying to be reasonable (rather than puristic) and ask first for high efficiency in each of a rather wide variety of situations. An estimate which does this is called robust of efficiency. After reaching this behavior for the estimate, we go on to ask that, in significance or confidence, "5%" is either close to, or less than, 5% in a similarly wide variety of situations.

Consider the special case of location, where $y_1, y_2, \ldots, y_n$ are independent estimates of the same parameter. Were the ys a sample from a Gaussian distribution, it is classical that (1) we should pay equal attention to the values of each y and (2) we do this best with an arithmetic mean. If, instead, the ys are a sample from a stretched-tail distribution (tails increasingly more ex-tended relative to the shoulders than for the Gaussian), it is easy to show that the more extreme the y, the less attention it should be given.

If, in two situations, the appropriate weight for a small fraction of the observations is very different, it is easy to show that the most reasonable compromises give those values close to the smaller weight. Thus, if we are to obtain good performance in both the Gaussian and the stretched-tail situations we must reduce the weight on the more exotic values.

One way to do this is with a biweight estimate (also called a bisquare estimate). The process begins with an estimate of spread, S, often the median average deviation from the median (in more complicated cases, S may be the median absolute residual), and with a convenient constant, c, often between 4 and 9. For any y_i, we can define an "exoticness"

$$u_i = (y_i - \dot{y})/cS$$

where $\dot{y}$ is the *median*. (In more complicated situations, the role of $\dot{y}$ is played by $\hat{y}_i$, the fitted value corresponding to y_i.) We then define a weight by

$$w_i = \begin{cases} (1 - u_i^2)^2, & \text{for} \quad u_i^2 \leqslant 1, \\ 0, & \text{else} \end{cases}$$

and use these weights to define the biweight estimate

$$y_{bi} = \Sigma w_i y_i / \Sigma w_i$$

With a careful choice of c we can obtain better than 91% efficiency for any of the following (almost equally unrealistic) situations: (1) 20 observations from Gau(μ, σ^2), (2) 19 observations from Gau(μ, σ^2) and one from Gau($\mu, 100\sigma^2$), or (3) 20 observations from a slash distribution, where Gau(μ, σ^2) symbolizes a Gaussian distribution with average μ and variance σ^2, and the prototype form of the slash distribution (like a Cauchy distribution in the tails, but less unrealistically peaked in the center) is the distribution of the ratio of independent quantities, numerator from Gau($0, \sigma^2$) and denominator from a rectangular distribution uniform on [0, A].

Since most realistic situations are not as extreme as these three, it is reasonable to expect better than 91% efficiency in any realistic situation where $y_1, y_2, \ldots, y_n$ are all estimates of the same thing.

Multiple regression by similar techniques works quite well. There are almost equally good robust/resistant measures of spread. For the location case there is a good significance/confidence procedure. [See Mosteller and Tukey (1977, Chapter 10) for further details.]

If such techniques are fully available for what you plan to do, *at least* use them as alternatives.

In multivariate work, at least consider the use of such techniques for all summarization of batches.

Change may be uncomfortable, but here it is inevitable.

The development of robust/resistant techniques tends to be verbally concerned with protection in the face of stretched-tail distributions, but the situations most often used as touchstones of performance involve both stretched-tail distributions and nonconstant variability (neither of which can necessarily be reduced by even the most adroit re-expression). The extent to which concern with further kinds of nonutopianness (e.g., granularity of values, stability of covariances or correlations) will become commonplaces of robust/resistant methodology is as yet uncertain.

B. The Jackknife

One recurring problem is the interesting quantity that we know how to calculate from data but we do not know any explicit way in which to assess its variability, to make significance or confidence calculations. In such a situation, we ought to be glad to be offered a method of wide general applicability for doing confidence or significance, even if the method is approximate. The best such method so far available is the jackknife, a leave-out-one technique adapted to the use of Student's t.

We sketch only the outlines of the technique here, referring the reader wishing more details to Mosteller and Tukey (1977, Chapters 7 and 8).

The basic idea is to divide the data into r more or less equivalent pieces, and then to obtain the result of calculating the quantity once for all the data; r times for all but one piece of the data, each piece being left out in turn. Writing y_{all} for the result of using all the data, and $y_{(i)}$ for the result of using all but the ith piece, we proceed to define pseudovalues by

$$y_{*i} = ry_{all} - (r-1)y_{(i)}$$

which lead to

$$y_* = \frac{1}{r}\sum_1 y_{*i}, \qquad s^2_* = \frac{1}{r(r-1)}\sum(y_{*i} - y_*)^2$$

and to treatment of

$$\frac{y_* - \text{contemplated value}}{s_*}$$

as distributed as Student's t, possibly with reduced degrees of freedom.

Jackknife technique is very widely applicable, but is more effective when we are careful with the choices which are usually offered, such as how y is expressed.

C. Better than MANOVA

We have already emphasized the need to gain useful power. Techniques like the conventional MANOVA, multiresponse analysis of variance, that look at *all* linear combinations of the elementary responses are doing their best to avoid useful power. What might we consider using to replace conventional MANOVA?

We do not have, so far as I know, a field-tested technique to replace MANOVA. So the best we can do, today, is to make a somewhat tentative suggestion. For all its tentative character, however, the writer would not hesitate to recommend its use, instead of MANOVA, to a client.

The main points of the suggested approach are these:

(A)   Only individual (elementary) responses and very simple composites, if found significantly nonnull, will be simply interpreted.

(B)   Therefore, we should construct a small number of very simple composites (linear combinations of elementary response), say q in number, to go with the p elementary responses.

(C)   Then we can proceed to analyze all $p + q$ individually, in a univariate way, using $5\%/(p + q)$ for each when 5% overall is appropriate [and $1\%/(p + q)$ for each when 1% overall is appropriate].

(D)   Whatever we can find we can interpret directly, so all our power will be useful power. (And our overall error rates will be no larger than they are claimed to be.)

(E)   I assert that doing this will give us more useful power than using MANOVA could. (And I hope someone will be interested enough to try things out comparatively on real data.)

The only aspect of all these points that requires even a little careful attention is the selection of composites. So let us turn to this.

The following seem to be the main points:

(B1)   We could calculate principal components, but they are not likely to be simply interpretable. So let us not.

(B2)   Much the same could be said about "dust bowl empiricists factor analysis" (see Chapter 8, Section II). So we will not use this either. (And, since we are not likely to have chosen elementary responses that fit neatly into clusters, we do not plan to use factor analysis in the mode of Hunter (see Chapter 8).

(B3)   As a first step, let us multiply each response by a very simple number, so chosen as to make the variances of the modified response reasonably near one another. (Plausible choices of simple numbers would be, for instance, any number of the form 1, 2, or 5 times a power of 10 and for another, any number from ... $\frac{1}{8}, \frac{1}{4}, \frac{1}{2}$, 1, 2, 4, 8, ... Either might serve us well, although we might possibly want to select our simple multiplier from a sequence somewhat less coarse.) We will try to use 1 as a multiplier as often as we dare.

(B4)   Having chosen a simple scale for each response, we will now confine ourselves to: using coefficient values of either $+1$, or 0, or -1; including each response (with a nonzero coefficient) in *at most* one composite.

These are the main points, although again we will need to go somewhat further in detail.

The requirements (a) that no response be included in more than one composite and (b) that any composite include at least two responses combine to ensure that we will never receive more than $p/2$ composites, and often many fewer. Thus $p + q$ will satisfy $p + q \leqslant \frac{3}{2}p$ and will often be much closer to p. We will have given up little parsimony to include composites, and we may reasonably hope that, where a composite will help us say more than the individual responses permit us to say, we will be able to make good use of our composites.

D. Guidance in Selecting the Composites

Our remaining task is to pick out the $+1$ or -1 coefficients and the elementary responses to be included in each of our few composites. A wide variety of procedures might serve us here. It is not easy to judge which of these will do what we want to do.

And what is it that we want to do? What are our few composites to do that the elementary responses could not do for us? A fair amount of thought will convince us that the situation we need most to deal with is one where all pairs among a certain number of elementary responses (possibly some with signs changed) are all reasonably substantially negatively correlated, with the result that the corresponding linear combination with positive coefficients is less (possibly much less) variable than we would expect if we knew only the variances of the components.

Two negatively correlated responses have a cigar-shaped distribution, running NW and SE, which we can think of as falling in a square box. If we are to cut off nearly as much nearly empty space with two parallel lines as we can, these lines need to be roughly parallel to the cigar. They will then correspond to relatively extreme values of a linear combination with positive coefficients of the two negatively correlated responses.

If we have three responses, all mutually negatively correlated, the distribution will be pancake shaped, the most effective pair of planes will be roughly perpendicular to the all-positive body diagonal, thus being the level planes of a positive linear combination of the three negatively correlated responses.

Those who want a more algebraic approach may wish to argue as follows: We have two responses. The composite that will help us more is the composite that is less correlated with the individual responses. If the variances and covariance are v_1 and v_2, and $c < 0$, respectively, then the variances of the simple composites, and their covariances with the two component responses, which we will denote as y and z, respectively, are as follows:

$$
\begin{array}{c|l}
y + z & v_1 + v_2 + 2c \\
& \qquad\qquad v_1 + c \\
y & \quad v_1 \qquad\qquad\qquad v_2 + c \\
& \qquad\qquad c \qquad\qquad\qquad v_1 - v_2 \\
z & \quad v_2 \qquad\qquad v_1 - c \\
& \qquad\qquad -v_2 + c \\
y - z & v_1 + v_2 - 2c
\end{array}
$$

where, to the right of the vertical bar, we have first a column of variances, then a column of covariances between vertically adjacent variables (e.g., y and z, or z and $y - z$), then a column of covariances between vertically next-to-adjacent variables (i.e., for $y + z$ and z, followed by for y and $y - z$) and last the covariance between the vertically most separated variables, namely, $y + z$ and $y - z$. (The two prominent diagonal directions in this display correspond to rows and columns in a more conventional square array.)

Continuing, the squared correlations with the coordinates are, for $y + z$,

$$(v_1 + c)^2/v_1(v_1 + v_2 + 2c) \qquad \text{and} \qquad (v_2 + c)^2/v_2(v_1 + v_2 + 2c)$$

and for $y - z$,

$$(v_1 - c)^2/v_1(v_1 + v_2 - 2c) \qquad \text{and} \qquad (v_2 - c)^2/v_1(v_1 + v_2 - 2c)$$

It is now easy to show that, if $c < 0$, each squared correlation for $y + z$ is smaller than the corresponding squared correlation for $y - z$ (unless $v_1 v_2 - c^2 = 0$, when y and z are perfectly correlated). Thus we do better to use $y + z$ as the composite.

E. A Specific Suggestion

Let us then use this guidance to propose an algorithm for selecting the composites, namely:

(B4A) Consider the within (= error) correlation matrix and modify its off-diagonal entries as follows (we assume that $+0$ can be distinguished from -0, either by eye or by computer): any correlation > 0 and less than its standard error is replaced by "$+0$"; any correlation < 0 and less in magnitude than its standard error is replaced by "-0."

(B4B) Select the highest correlation that (a) was not modified in (B4A) and (b) has not been used in earlier composites. Choose the two corresponding responses to begin the definition of the (next) composite. Change the sign of one response (temporarily) to make the correlation between the two selected responses < 0. Call these two responses, temporarily, the core of the (new) composite being built.

(B4C) Identify all additional responses that have correlations of the same sign with the two responses in the core. Change the sign of each such additional response if necessary to make correlations < 0.

(B4D) Arrange these selected (and possibly sign-changed) additional responses in decreasing order of the smaller magnitude of the two correlations with the initially chosen responses.

(B4E) Add these additional responses to the core one at a time, in the order just specified, skipping over any one for which the correlations with all previously included in the core (including the two initially chosen) fail to be < 0 in five-sixths of all cases.

(B4F) Ask now whether any of the remaining responses have a correlation of the same sign with at least five-sixths of the responses now in the core. If necessary, change their signs so that those $\geqslant$ five-sixths are < 0.

(B4G) Arrange these newly selected variables in order of decreasing median |correlation|. Add them, one at a time, to the core, skipping any one that does not meet the $\frac{5}{6}$ rule.

(B4H) Repeat (B4F) and (B4G) until there are no new additions.

(B4I) Convert the core thus obtained into a composite, by assigning coefficient $+1$ to each response in the core whose sign was *not* changed during the construction of the core, and coefficient -1 to each response in the core whose sign *was* changed.

(B4J) Return to (B4B), unless all unmodified correlations involve responses that have already been included in a composite.

There are many details of this suggested procedure that are open to modification. It will take experience to learn how it works and how to tune it to work better.

F. An Alternate Approach

Another way to choose linear combinations to be given special attention is to start with the variance–covariance matrix for error, and construct an orthogonal set of linear combinations. Then, taking these as new coordinates, we can select a convenient set of further linear combinations of them as the q to be used.

For an example, let us turn to the example drawn by Bochner and Fitzpatrick (1978) from Woodward and Overall (1975). The variance–covariance matrix for error (original variables) can be calculated to be (including Sum $= D + Pd + Sc$ for immediate convenience) as in the Initial panel of Table II.

Let us choose

$$K = \text{Sum} = D + Pd + Sc$$

TABLE II

SOME LINEAR COMBINATIONS AND VARIANCE–COVARIANCES IN EXAMPLE

	Linear combination	Variance	Covariances		
Initial	D	.6416			
			.2005		
	Pd	.5561		.4236	
			.5503		1.26570
	Sc	1.2638		1.30690	
			2.23770		
	$K = $ Sum	4.8103			
First modifications	K	4.8103			
			− .0000		
	$L = Pd - .27169K$	.2010		+ .0000	
			− .1434		.0000
	$M = D - .26312K$	.3086		.0000	
			.0000		
	$N = M + .71323L$	.2063			

	Linear combinations	Coefficients of			Variance	Covariances
		Bd	D	Sc		
Orthonormal Linear Combinations	$A = K/\sqrt{4.8103}$	.4560	.4560	.4560	1	
						0
	$B = L/\sqrt{.2010}$	1.6244	− .6060	− .6060	1	0
						0
	$C = N/\sqrt{.1063}$	2.0489	1.4176	− .1527	1	
and their Octahedral Combinations	$A + B + C$	4.1293	1.2676	− .3027		
	$A + B - C$	.0315	− 1.5676	.0027		
	$A - B + C$	.8805	2.4796	.9093		
	$-A + B + C$	3.2173	.3556	− 1.2146		

as one of our new orthogonal coordinates. It is easy to modify Pd (to L) and D (to M) so as to make their covariances with sum zero. If we choose to keep L as another new coordinate, it is easy to modify M (to N) so as to make its covariance with L zero (while keeping its covariance with K zero). The calculations are shown under First modifications in Table II.

For convenience, and as a further step that we might take, the next panel brings K, L, and N to unit length, as measured according to the error matrix. This means that A, B, C have variances and covariances in "error" shown to the right of this panel.

Now if A, B, C are the coordinates whose ± 1 values define the faces of the unit cube, the faces of the corresponding octahedra are specified by

$$A + B - C = \pm d, \qquad A - B + C = \pm d, \qquad -A + B + C = \pm d$$

for each value of d (each size of octahedron) we wish to consider. Thus if we wish to replace the 3 coordinates by 4 symmetrical linear combinations it is natural to take the 4 thus obtained, whose coefficients, as linear combinations of the original variables, are given in the last lines of Table II.

If we had wanted 6, we could have taken the 6 linear combinations giving the 12 faces of the dodecahedron; if 10, the 10 linear combinations giving the 20 faces of the icosahedron. And there would be no reason not to take these in any combination, giving a choice among

$q = 3$	(*new coordinates*)
$q = 4$	(*octahedron*)
$q = 6$	(*dodecahedron*)
$q = 7 = 3 + 4$	(*coordinates + octahedron*)
$q = 10$	$\left\{ \begin{array}{l} (\textit{icosahedron}) \\ (\textit{octahedron + dodecahedron}) \end{array} \right\} \begin{array}{l} \textit{can be} \\ \textit{equivalent} \end{array}$
$q = 13 = 3 + 10$	
$q = 14 = 4 + 10$	
$q = 16 = 6 + 10$	
$q = 17 = 3 + 4 + 10$	

Any geometrically ingenious reader can invent further, more-or-less symmetric (in error matrix terms) patterns if someone has an itch to use some other value of q.

The situation for more than three responses is not quite as geometrically neat, but once one has new coordinates brought to unit variance there are many things that can be done.

In fact, the only objection to this approach seems to be the extreme variety of possibilities—and the danger that complaints about "cooking the data" might arise. There is need for an algorithm that starts with, say, the correlation matrix among the elementary responses and proceeds in a specified way based upon this matrix. Before proposing a specific algorithm, we should obtain more experience with such alternatives, and with what values of q are reasonably selected for general use with a particular value of p.

G. Simple Linear Combinations

If we take the discussion of useful power as seriously as it should be taken, then the arithmetically complex coefficients of the last section are not very acceptable. Convenient multiples of the linear combination of Table II are as in the upper part of Table III. Simple linear combinations—linear combinations expressed by simple coefficients—corresponding to these are as in the lower part of that table. Even though these coefficients have, in some views, been drastically simplified, it will be hard enough to give clear subject matter interpretation to significance/confidence results for most of them. Again, we might prefer to begin in a slightly different way, perhaps by standardizing the responses (here bringing them to unit variance "in error") and then looking

TABLE III

LINEAR COMBINATIONS CLOSE TO MULTIPLES OF THOSE OF TABLE II

	Linear combinations	Coefficient of		
		Pd	D	Sc
Rescaled	$K = A\sqrt{4.8103}$	1.	1.	1.
Linear	$B/.6060$	2.68	−1.	−1.
Combinations	(3 times same)	(8.04)	(−3.)	#(−3)
	$C/.1527$	13.42	9.28	−1.
	$(A + B + C)/.3027$	13.64	4.18	−1.
	$-(A + B - C)/.0315$	−1.	+49.76	−.08
	$(A - B + C/.8805$	1.	2.82	1.03
	$(-A + B + C)/.3556$	9.02	1.	−3.41
Simple		1.	1.	1.
Approximations		8.	−3.	−3.
		13.	9.	−1.
		14.	4.	−1.
		0.	1.	0.
		1.	3.	1.
		9.	1.	−3.

for linear combinations with simple coefficients in the standardized variables.

If we had chosen to work with equally treated means of cells, we would, of course, pool the error matrices for the four cells somewhat differently.

Again recrimination will be minimized if a completely specified algorithm can be adopted.

It is a curious sidelight on the state of our technology—and of where our operational values seem to lie—that the only objectively positive feature of MANOVA that the writer recognizes is that it is a completely specified algorithm. Surely we can agree on other procedures that are better.

H. Spectrum Analysis—Should We Try It?

Methods for analyzing time series that involve or are related to spectrum analysis: can be very powerful, work well when the structure of the data is really appropriate, otherwise are rarely worth the effort. My own experience with applications to the social and behavioral sciences runs about as follows:

(1) a great reluctance to try until I had a collaborator who I was sure understood the subject matter issues,

(2) cooperative work with Milton Friedman (at the CASBS in 1957–1958) on some monetary series, where the main result was a clear and convincing indication that the adjustments for the rotation of the weeks within the months was inadequate,

(3) a chance to be involved in Robert P. Abelson's Princeton Ph.D. thesis, where he successfully used spectrum analysis to study the time intervals

between successive dottings, when a subject was asked to dot repeatedly as often as he could, and

(4)   a bystander's view of the use of such techniques in studying seasonal adjustment of economic series.

The result of all this has been quite firm convictions that: there are sociobehavioral situations where such techniques are useful, they are not common, and one should not waste time trying such techniques unless the circumstances are reasonably plausibly adapted to their use.

How then are we to judge plausibility? At the minimum, we require repeated behavior which could occur (absence of a response can be an occurrence of behavior) at each of a reasonably long sequence of times or situations, and which was observed at each of an at least moderately long sequence. We also require each of these times or situations to be related to the preceding one in a reasonably stable way.

My own advice to communication scientists would be to wait until such a situation arose, one where, in addition, there was a meaningful question which it seemed spectrum analysis, or related techniques, might illuminate.

I. Spectrum Analysis—Some Fundamentals

Some, when they think of spectrum analysis, think of loosely defined waves. The mean temperature of a place, measured week by week for a few years, though irregular, will repeat in its broad aspects. It would be wrong, however, to regard such a "wave of the seasons" as representing what a spectrum "blip" at 1 cycle/year should mean. For, at most places, such a "wave of the seasons" would not be sinusoidal.

One might represent it fairly well as a sum of a small number of sinusoidal constituents—one at 1 cycle/year, one at 2 cycles/year, one at 3 cycles/year, and so on. Thus the corresponding spectrum would have significant contributions at all these frequencies.

The emphasis on sinusoids is not accidental, nor is it easily removable.

The importance of sinusoids lies in their relation to systems which have a time function as input and another time function as output, and which, further, obey simple conditions for superposition and time-origin-shift. More specifically, if $K(t)$ is the output when $k(t)$ is the input, and if $J(t)$ is the output where $j(t)$ is the input, then these conditions become (1) $J(t) + K(t)$ is the output when $j(t) + k(t)$ is the input, and (2) $K(t + h)$ is the output when $k(t + h)$ is the input. If these conditions hold, whatever reasonable inputs are taken for $j(t)$ and $k(t)$, then if follows mathematically that if $a \cos \omega t + b \sin \omega t$ is the input, then, for some c and d, $c \cos \omega t + d \sin \omega t$ is the output, with the same ω. Using the superposition condition again we learn that sines/cosines of two or more different frequencies pass through such a process without any tendency to interaction with one another (without any tendency toward what the hi-fi specialist would call intermodulation distortion). It is this that distinguishes sines and cosines from other waves; it is this that makes spectrum analyses valuable—valuable in those areas of science and technology where things do satisfy superposition and time-origin-shift conditions. (In those areas, spectrum analysis can be very powerful.)

V. CLOSE

A. A View from Afar

The week before the writers of this book gathered at Asilomar, I was in England, where drives from London to Sheffield and return left plenty of opportunity to ask some statisticians that I trusted what they thought were the useful parts of "multivariate analysis." It may be interesting to report the high spots here.

First, frequency of use in their practice, where statements varied from 1 problem in 50 to 1 problem in 200.

Second, the recall of an aphorism: "problems we don't understand, we call multivariate."

Third, a list of techniques regarded as fruitful, namely:

(1) discriminant functions, including multiple-group discriminant functions,
(2) "canonical analysis" as a display of same,
(3) dimension reduction, as, for instance, via principal components,
(4) canonical regression (use of principal or canonical components as carriers, often in a stepwise situation),
(5) Andrews plots (see, e.g., Gnanadesikan, 1977, pp. 207–217), and
(6) clustering and congregation.

It is interesting to speculate why the subjects of substantial chapters above were not included by these skilled and active consultants. (The absence of structural modeling topics, however, reflects only a verbal habit, I am sure, according to which such techniques are often *not* defined as multiresponse.)

Three 1977 books can, I hope, be commended to all readers: Gnanadesikan (1977) (multivariate data analysis), Mosteller and Tukey (1977) (regression), and Tukey (1977) (exploratory data analysis).

B. And So . . .

I shall close by saying that reading Gnanadesikan (1977) and participating in the session at Asilomar has caused me to try to assemble and depict a taxonomy of multiresponse-analysis building blocks, both available and needed. Space for its inclusion here was obviously not available.

ACKNOWLEDGMENT

This chapter was prepared in part in connection with research at Princeton University supported by the Office of Naval Research.

References

Campbell, N. R. *Physics, the elements*. London and New York: Cambridge Univ. Press, 1920.

Campbell, N. R. *An account of the principles of measurement and calculation*. London: Longmans, Green, 1928.

Campbell, N. R. *Foundation of science: The philosophy of theory and experiment*. New York: Dover, 1975 (reprint of Campbell, 1920).

Day, N. E. Estimating the components of a mixture of normal distributions. *Biometrika*, 1969, **56**, 463–474 (especially Figure 1 on p. 470).

Dayton, C. M., and Schafer, W. D. Extended tables of t and chi-square for Bonferroni tests with unequal error allocation, *Journal of the American Statistical Association*, 1973, **68**, 78–83.

Feigl, H. Validation and Vindication: An Analysis of the Nature and Limits of Ethical Alignments. In W. Sellers and J. Hospers (Eds.), *Readings in Ethical Theory*. New York: Appleton, 1952.

Fisher, R. A. Tests of significance applied to Haldane's data on partial linkage. *Annals of Eugenics*, 1946, **7**, 87–104 (*Collected Papers of R. A. Fisher, Adelaide* **3**: 496–513).

Gnanadesikan, R. *Methods for statistical data analysis of multivariate observations*. New York: Wiley, 1977.

Hinchen, J. D. *Practical statistics for chemical research*. London: Methuen, 1969, especially p. vi.

Mosteller, F., and Tukey, J. W. *Data analysis and regression: A second course in statistics*. Reading, Massachusetts: Addison-Wesley, 1977.

Munk, W. H., and Snodgrass, F. Measurements of southern swell at Guadeluped Island. *Deep-Sea Research*, 1951, **4**, 272–286.

Munk, W. H. Miller, G. E., Snodgrass, F. E., and Barber, W. F. Directional recording of swell from distant storms, *Philosophical Transactions of the Royal Society of London Series A*, 1963, **256**, 505–589.

Pearce, S. C. *Field experimentation with fruit trees and other perennial plants being technical communication No. 23, Commonwealth bureau of Horticulture and Plant Crops*. East Malling, Farnham Royal (Slough). Commonwealth Agricultural Bureau, 1953 (1976, revised ed.).

Rattner, Z. *A Monte Carlo study: jackknife width estimation of robust statistics*. Unpublished Senior Thesis, Princeton Univ., 1977.

Tukey, J. W. Unsolved problems of experimental statistics. *Journal of the American Statistical Association*, 1954, **49**, 706–731. Especially Pp. 725–726.

Tukey, J. W. Uses of numerical spectrum analysis in geophysics. *Bulletin of the International Institute of Statistics*, 1966, **41**, 267–295.

Tukey, J. W. Analyzing data: sanctification or detective work. *American Psychologist*, 1969, **24**, 83–91.

Tukey, J. W. Some graphic and semigraphic displays. In T. A. Bancroft (Ed.), *Statistical papers in honor of George W. Snedecor*. Iowa State Univ. Press: Ames Iowa, 1972. Pp. 293–316.

Tukey, J. W. *Exploratory data analysis*. Reading, Massachusetts: Addison-Wesley, 1977. (a)

Tukey, J. W. A re-examination, from statistical and some measurement viewpoints of the corrosion measurement on the Widow's Creek #5 Boiler. To appear as an appendix of a TVA report to EPA, 1977. (b)

Chapter 17

AN OVERVIEW OF SIX WIDELY DISTRIBUTED STATISTICAL PACKAGES

KOOK CHING HUBER

Client Services Department
Information Sciences Division
Blue Cross and Blue Shield of Indiana
Indianapolis, Indiana

I. INTRODUCTION

Since the introduction of high-speed digital computers in the 1950s and the development of the first statistical software package by the UCLA biomedical computing group for medical research in the early 1960s (Dixon, 1967), social scientists have increasingly relied on the computer for data analysis and statistical computation. The decade following the appearance of BMD (Biomedical Computing Programs) has witnessed the phenomenal growth of

MULTIVARIATE TECHNIQUES
IN HUMAN COMMUNICATION RESEARCH

literally thousands of "canned" programs. Needless to say, this chapter cannot review all of the available software packages for multivariate analysis but can only point readers to some of the programs which will prove especially useful for the multivariate techniques discussed in this book.

The packages to be discussed here are: BMD (Biomedical Computer Programs, Dixon, 1973), BMDP Series (Dixon, 1975), Statistical Packages for the Social Sciences (SPSS, Nie, Hull, Jenkins, Steinbrenner, & Brent, 1975), ESP (Econometric Software Package, Cooper & Curtis, 1976), OSIRIS III, (Organized Set of Integrated Routines for Investigation with Statistics, Inter-University Consortium for Political Research, 1973), and Statistical Analysis System (SAS, Barr, Goodnight, Sall, & Helwig, 1976). These packages have been chosen because they represent some of the most widely distributed software systems and because most readers are likely to have access to them in their own university computer centers. Moreover, consideration of the historical development of these packages provides a better understanding of the unique features of each package which complement the others in meeting the needs of a variety of research activities. The present chapter will include a brief description of the six software systems mentioned and information on the use of these programs for the multivariate statistical techniques discussed elsewhere in this book.

II. DESCRIPTION OF PACKAGES

A. Biomedical Computer Program—BMD and BMDP

The BMD series occupies a special place in the history of the development of statistical packages for the social scientist. The oldest statistical software package, the BMD series has served as a model as well as a testing ground for improving subsequent packages since its first appearance in 1961 (Dixon, 1967, 1973). The package is essentially a collection of individual programs without a common "housekeeping" module. Control card format is quite rigid and entries must appear in prespecified columns. Many of its programs demand that the input data be sorted and prearranged in a specific order. But for all its restrictions, the package has the most thoroughly debugged programs. In its V-series programs it still offers the best collection of powerful programs for a variety of models within the analysis of variance and covariance techniques.

The middle of the 1960s marked the beginning of an accelerated usage of computers for statistical data analyses. The users demanded a well-designed, integrated, and language-oriented package. In 1968, the UCLA biomedical computing group rewrote many of the BMD programs, incorporated newly available statistical techniques and computing algorithms, and moved from a fixed format to a free format language control. The result is the BMDP series (Dixon, 1975). This new series offers greater capabilities for data edit and screening, case grouping and selection, and missing data specification. Although several programs from the original series have not been replaced, the users are assured of the continuous development of the system and can look forward to the eventual inclusion of new programs.

Both series were originally written for IBM 360/370 computers, but have been adapted to non-IBM machines. The P-series is available for CDC CYBER, Honeywell 600/6000, Univac Series 70/90 and 1108, Xerox Sigma 7, PDP-11, and DEC-10.

B. Statistical Package for the Social Sciences—SPSS

The Statistical Package for the Social Sciences or SPSS (Nie *et al.*, 1975) is among the most widely distributed packages for statistical analyses. Unlike the BMD series, SPSS was developed to meet the specific needs of social science data analyses. It was especially designed to accommodate the greater demands of social scientists in data handling and file editing. SPSS is an integrated system in which all statistical procedures are under control of one supervisory program and can be accessed in any order within a given program setup. The output from one procedure can be easily saved for input to another procedure (though not within the same program setup). The control-card language is a simplified, quasi-natural language consisting of self-explanatory key words such as MISSING VALUES, REGRESSION, INPUT MEDIUM, etc. The SPSS User's Manual is more than an instructional aid for using the system. It also contains a general discussion of various statistical techniques in easy-to-understand, nonmathematical terms including, as well, illustrations of how the statistics may be used and examples of program setups.

Although SPSS includes a good selection of descriptive and inferential statistics, it still lacks many of the multivariate techniques discussed in this book such as MDS, cluster analysis, time-series analysis, and simultaneous equations (see Table I). However, it should surprise no one that these techniques will be included in the system in the future. Users can keep abreast of new developments in the system by subscribing to the free newsletter occasionally published by SPSS, Inc., of Chicago. SPSS was originally developed for IBM 360/370 computers; however, 23 conversions for machines other than IBM are now available (*SPSS Newsletter*, No. 12, June, 1977).

C. Econometric Software Package—ESP[1]

The Econometric Software Package, ESP (Cooper & Curtis, 1976) is a system designed for the statistical analyses of time-series data and other general computational procedures in econometric research. Unlike the other

[1]ESP is a greatly revised and extended version of an earlier program, TSP (Time Series Processor).

TABLE I

Multivariate techniques	BMD (1973)	BMDP (1975)	SPSS (1975)	ESP (1973)	OSIRIS (1973)	SAS (1976)	Others
(1) Canonical analysis	BMD09M	BMDP6M	CANCORR				LISREL III[a]
(2) Cluster analysis		BMDP1M BMDP2M BMDP3M			CLUSTER4 HICLSTR	CLUSTER	
(3) Discriminant (analysis)	BMD04M	BMDP7M	DISCRIMINANT			DISCRIM NEIGHBOR	
(4) Factor analysis	BMD01M	BMDP4M	FACTOR	PRIN	FACTAN	FACTOR SCORE	LISREL III[a] COFAMM EFAP
(5) Multivariate analysis	BMD12V		(MANOVA)[b]		MANOVA	GLM	
(6) Multidimensional scaling analysis					MDSCAL		GALILEO MULTISCALE
(7) Multiple regression	BMD01R BMD02R BMD03R	BMDP1R BMDP2R	REGRESSION	OLSQ	REGRESSN	GLM NLIN STEPWISE SYSREG	LISREL III[a]
(8) Simultaneous equations				Z3SLS INST			
(9) Smallest space analysis							MINSSA GUTTMAN- LINGOES SSA

[a]LISREL III is an extremely versatile program and can be set up to perform various multivariate analyses.
[b]MANOVA will be available in the SPSS system in the early part of 1979. For more information on the program, see *SPSS Newsletter, No. 15, July, 1978.*

packages discussed in this chapter, ESP is designed on a computer programming language model instead of a quasi-natural language model. Program statements such as GOTO label, PRINT, and PUNCH are part of the vocabulary of the system.

ESP contains many valuable multivariate techniques which are now used chiefly in economics research, such as regression analyses with serially correlated errors, random coefficient regression (Swamy, 1970), three-stage least squares regression (Zellner & Theil, 1962), and Box–Jenkins time-series analysis (Box & Jenkins, 1972). As social scientists move toward a more interdisciplinary approach to quantitative research of the kind suggested in this book, they will find ESP attractive as a tool to expand their repertory of research techniques. ESP is available only for IBM 360/370 computers.

D. Organized Set of Integrated Routines for Investigation with Statistics—OSIRIS

While packages such as SPSS allow users to perform extensive data transformations, they require that input data files be complete, properly sorted, and merged with no duplication or absence of needed records. Researchers who collect their own research data know that producing a properly match-merged data set consumes much of their time. Such researchers, especially those with a large volume of data, often have to rely on computer programmers to write special utility programs to perform such tasks. To assist the researcher in this particular data management need, OSIRIS developed, as an integral part of its package, an extensive capacity to organize, edit, and correct input data as well as to sort, merge, and copy data files. Table I shows other multivariate techniques in OSIRIS which are not found in other packages discussed in this book. OSIRIS is available for IBM 360/370 computers. Non-IBM versions have been developed, however, for CDC, UNIVAC, and DEC-IV computers. For further information, the reader should contact the Institute for Social Research at the University of Michigan in Ann Arbor.

E. Statistical Analysis System—SAS

An experienced statistical software user and methodologist in social research will find the Statistical Analysis System or SAS (Barr, Goodnight, Sall, & Helwig, 1976) a welcome addition to his collection of research tools, not only for his analytical work but for his experiments in developing specialized methodology. SAS, developed in North Carolina State University, is designed on a computer language model. Its PL/I-like statements together with the 26 matrix operators and 48 matrix functions offer researchers who enjoy programming exciting possibilities. Using its versatile least squares procedures, users can produce a wide variety of linear and nonlinear regression analyses, analyses of variances and covariances, and multivariate analyses of variance.

A beginning "cookbook" user of statistics may find the specification of models and hypotheses testing a bit demanding. But learning to set up these parameters will bring insight into the understanding of statistics being used. SAS runs on IBM 360/370 computers. For further information, contact SAS Institutes, Inc., of Raleigh, North Carolina.

III. SPECIFIC PROGRAMS FOR MULTIVARIATE STATISTICS

Table I serves as a quick locater of some specific programs or procedures in the six packages which perform many of the multivariate analyses discussed in this book. Also included in the table are programs discussed elsewhere in this volume but not treated in this chapter. An example is the collection of programs for Guttmann–Lingoes smallest space analysis discussed by Norton in Chapter 10. These and similar programs have been included because a particular technique was discussed in the book for which none of the six packages has a program [for instance, LISREL III by Joreskog and Sorbom (1976) which allows for analysis of a structural equations model with both errors in equations and errors in observed variables as discussed by Fink in Chapter 4].

In the following sections, a brief description of these programs will be given. Such information is not intended to replace the user's manuals for the packages but only to serve as a guide in locating programs designed to meet a particular research need. The reader will still have to consult the relevant manual for the proper control card setup and for detailed documentation of the programs.

A. Canonical Analysis

BMDP6M, the P-series version of BMD09M, has the additional output of eigenvalues associated with each pair of canonical variables, of correlations of variables with canonical variables, and of bivariate plots for original and canonical variables. CANCORR in SPSS is the most versatile of the programs containing all of the features of BMDP6M plus canonical correlation coefficients and canonical scores for each subject. It also includes two interesting and useful options which allow the continuation of computation if either variable set is linearly dependent and if a matrix is not positive definite. In the former case, the program excludes the guilty variable from the correlation matrix and in the latter case the program sets the coefficients for some of the variables at zero, ensuring that only a consistent set of variables remains.

B. Cluster Analysis

BMDP1M clusters similar variables according to the measure of association and the amalgamation rule specified by the user. The measures can be correlation, covariance, angle, or the Euclidean distances between variables. The rules for amalgamation can be minimum, maximum, or the average distance or similarity. BMDP2M clusters cases according to the distances between them which can be either the pth root of the sum of the pth powers of differences (when $p = 2$, this is the Euclidean distance) or according to the chi-square or phi-square statistic. BMDP3M simultaneously clusters cases and variables. Input for these programs can be either data or distance matrix.

Both the CLUSTER and HICLUSTER programs of OSIRIS III require the input of a matrix of correlations or a matrix of other similarity data. The clustering units may be subjects or variables. For interval data, CLUSTER groups units according to the highest average correlation with other units already in the cluster; for ordinal data, the program adds the variable which has the highest minimum correlation to the current cluster. The procedure used in HICLUSTER is based on an algorithm by Johnson (1967).

CLUSTER of SAS is similar to the HICLUSTER program of OSIRIS III and uses Johnson's algorithm on hierarchical cluster analysis (1967). It accepts raw input data and computes its own Euclidean distance matrix.

C. Discriminant Analysis

BMDP7M combines into one program the different types of discriminant analysis performed in BMD04M (discriminant analysis for two groups), BMD05M (discriminant analysis for several groups), and BMD07M (stepwise discriminant analysis). Several portions of this program were also adapted by the DISCRIMINANT program of SPSS. Both direct and stepwise selection of variables into the discriminant functions are available in DISCRIMINANT.

Criteria for the selection of a variable can be specified from these five options: (1) to minimize Wilks's lambda; (2) to maximize the Mahalonobis distance between two groups; (3) to maximize the smallest F ratio between pairs of groups; (4) to contribute the largest increase in Rao's V; and (5) to minimize R between pairs of groups, where $R = 1/(1 + (D_{ij}/4)$ and D_{ij} is the Mahalonobis distance. Among many of its fine output features is a matrix consisting of F ratios for each pair of groups which can be used to test for the equality of pairs of centroids, the Box's M and its associated F-test (Cooley & Lohnes, 1971) for equality of groups covariance matrices, and the probability of membership in each category of the dependent variables and the predicted variable.

DISCRIM of SAS develops its classification criterion based on a measure of generalized square distance. A special feature of this program is its capability of storing the calibration information as a special SAS data set and applying it as a classification criterion to a data set other than the one for which it was developed. NEIGHBOR program of SAS performs nearest neighbor discriminant analysis (Cover & Hart, 1967).

D. Factor Analysis

FACTOR in SPSS is the most versatile of the programs among the six packages for factor analysis. Methods of factoring in BMD01M, BMD08M, PRIN, and FACTAN are limited to principal component and principal factor analyses. BMDP4M is the only program among the packages discussed which provides a maximum likelihood solution of extracting the initial factor; when a singular correlation matrix is encountered the rank and a list of redundant variables is reported. This feature provides a valuable tool for detecting multicollinearity among variables. FACTOR in SPSS covers all of the other methods found in these programs. The user has the option of specifying one of the five following methods of factoring: principal factoring with iteration, Rao's canonical factoring, alpha factoring, and image factoring (Nie, *et al.*, 1976). Among the five methods of rotation offered by SPSS, the user can select he following: the orthogonal varimax, the orthogonal quartimax, the orthogonal equimax, oblique rotation, or no rotation. Among the various and useful statistics output are: communalities, proportion of total and common variance, factor score coefficients, and plots of rotated factors. Many users may also find it desirable to have the program produce factor loadings as well.

FCOMP in OSIRIS III can be used to assess the comparability of two matrices which may represent either factor structures of variables gathered at different time periods, or factor structures drawn from two populations or measured by two scaling methods.

FACTOR of SAS is similar to that of SPSS. It offers the same factoring methods except Rao's canonical factoring method. Instead, it allows users to input a factor pattern when an investigation on a different rotation for an already computed factor matrix is desired.

EFAP offers four methods for exploratory factor analysis, which are: (1) factor analysis by Joreskog's method (Joreskog, 1963); (2) unweighted least squares (Harman, 1967); (3) generalized least squares method (Joreskog & Goldberger, 1972); (4) the maximum likelihood method by Joreskog (1967). COFAMM may be used to analyze data from one group of individuals or from several independent groups by confirmatory factor analysis or covariance structure analysis (Joreskog, 1969, 1970). Unlike the other widely distributed software packages, inexperienced users may find the specifications of program control cards quite formidable. They will, therefore, find Carol Stein's "A Simple User's Guide to LISREL" a welcome relief (Stein, 1976).

E. Multivariate Analysis of Variance and Covariance

MANOVA of OSIRIS III performs both univariate and multivariate analysis of variance and covariance, using a general linear hypothesis model. It was adapted from the MANOVA program by Hall and Cramer (1965) and uses a hierarchical regression approach. Through specifications of the contrast matrices, the user has available a variety of designs for analysis such as the crossed and/or nested design or the ordinary factorial design. A design matrix specifying treatment classification and interaction is then constructed by the program using Krondecker products from these matrices. Up to 8 factors and up to 19 dependent variables can be used. Output statistics include means for each cell, intercorrelations among the normal equation coefficients, the error correlation matrix, and statements of regression analysis of N covariates and others. For a univariate analysis the program also prints a single conventional ANOVA table adjusted for covariates, if any. For a multivariate analysis, it prints the F ratio for the likelihood ratio criterion with the degrees of freedom, canonical variances of the principal components of the hypothesis, contrast components scores for estimated effects, cumulative Bartlett's chi-square-test on the roots, and univariate F ratios for each variable.

F. Multidimensional Scaling Analysis

MDSCAL of OSIRIS III is a nonmetric multidimensional scaling program designed for the analysis of similarities. The method of analysis was developed by Shepard (1962) and Kruskal (1964a, b). Input to the program should be a matrix of similarities. The user may specify an initial configuration or let the program internally create one. The program will then start with this configuration and iterate over successive trial configurations to improve the stress coefficient. This coefficient is a "goodness-of-fit" measure. The program output documents the history of the computation.

GALILEO is a program developed by Woelfel and others for metric multidimensional scaling utilizing paired distance judgement data (see Chapter 11). For further information on the program, contact Joseph Woelfel, Department of Communications, Michigan State University.

MULTISCALE is a set of four programs for metric multidimensional scaling written by James Ramsey using the principle of maximum likelihood (Ramsey, 1977). The four distance models used in the programs are: (a) simple Euclidean straight-line distances; (b) simple Euclidean distances with power transformations estimated for each subject; (c) Euclidean distances with individualized weighting of dimensions and power transformations; (d) simple Euclidean distances with power transformations, but with judgmental precisions varying from stimulus to stimulus. The user's manual offers a good nonmathematical introduction to multidimensional scaling methodology. MULTISCALE is distributed by the International Educational Services of Chicago.

G. Multiple Regression Analysis

Programs for multiple regression analysis are generally among the first programs developed in any statistical package. The two programs, BMDP1R and BMDP2R, in the BMDP series are improved versions of BMD01R,

BMD02R, and BMD03R in the original BMD series. REGRESSION in SPSS, REGRESSN in OSIRIS III and BMDP2R are comparable in terms of the computational algorithm used and the available statistical output, although REGRESSN does not produce plots of residuals against the predicted values. All three programs provide an option for regression in a stepwise manner. While REGRESSION in SPSS does not allow for the removal of a variable once it is entered in the regression, users of REGRESSN and BMDP2R can specify a critical value to which the partial F value for each variable in the regression at each step is compared. The variable whose partial F ratio falls below this critical value is removed from the model. The Durbin–Watson statistic used to detect the first-order correlation among the residuals can be requested in REGRESSION of SPSS. BMDP2R outputs the normal probability plot and the detrended normal probability plot of residuals which provides a visual aid for the examination of residuals.

SAS offers a wide variety of regression techniques. GLM is among the most versatile programs. It uses the principle of least squares to fit a fixed-effects linear model to virtually any type of data. It allows the specification of any degree of interactions and nested effects. Together with the sum of squares associated with each hypothesis tested, the user may request the form of the estimable function employed in the test. GLM enters a multivariate mode when more than one dependent variable is specified in the model. The Hotelling–Lawley trace, Pillai's trace, Wilks's criterion, and Roy's maximum criterion statistics are printed with approximate test statistics. NLIN of SAS produces least squares or weighted least squares estimates of coefficients of a nonlinear model. Three iterative methods are used to estimate the coefficients: a modified Gauss–Newton method (Hartley, 1961); the Marquardt method (Marquardt, 1963); or the gradient or steepest-descent method (Bard, 1970).

H. Structural Equation Models

The estimation of parameters in structural equation models can be found in several programs. Methods of estimation are described by the underlying assumptions of the model. ESP provides a variety of methods. For a diagonally recursive system of equations, OLSQ (Ordinary Least Squares, which is the commonly used multiple regression analysis) carries out a two-stage least squares estimation. Estimates from this method are in general not asymptotically efficient though consistent because this method disregards the correlation of the disturbances across equations. Such deficiency can be overcome by using Z3SLS (Zellner Three-Stage Least Squares), a procedure which involves a straightforward application of Aitkens' generalized estimation. Among the programs which provide estimations of parameters in a structural equations system, LISREL III (estimation of LInear Structural RELations by maximum likelihood methods) can be considered to be one of the most powerful and generalized programs. LISREL III was developed and programmed by Karl E. Joreskog and Dag Sarbom of the University of Upsala, and is now distributed by National Education Resources, Inc., of Chicago. The LISREL program is especially designed for estimating parameters in models which allow for both errors in equations (residuals, disturbances) and errors in the observed variables (error of measurement). The program is difficult to use, and the users may find the official user's manual (Joreskog & Sorbom, 1976) quite overwhelming. Carol Stein of Michigan State University has written a simplified user's guide which will surely help the first time user (Stein, 1976).

SYSREG of SAS offers a variety of methods in estimating coefficients of a structural equation model. They are (a) ordinary least squares (OLS); (b) two-stage least squares (2SLS); (c) limited information maximum likelihood (LIML); (d) three-stage least squares (3SLS); and (e) "seemingly unrelated" regression.

I. Smallest Space Analysis

MINISSA, a nonmetric scaling program belonging to SRCLIB (Survey Research Center Library) sponsored by the Survey Research Center Computer Support Group of the University of Michigan, is compatible with OSIRIS. The input is a matrix of similarity or dissimilarity coefficients; the output is a geometric representation of the matrix in m dimensions. The program constructs a configuration of points in space using information about the order relations among coefficients.

IV. CONCLUSION

It is hoped that this chapter has given readers a brief overview of some of the packages available to them and will serve as a quick locater for programs which may be utilized for the multivariate techniques discussed in this book. Readers should be aware that continual changes are being made in these programs, so they should consult their computing centers for the latest developments.

References

Bard, Y. Comparison of gradient methods for the solution of nonlinear parameter estimation problems. *SIAM Journal of Numerical Analysis*, 1970, **7**, No. 1, 157–186.

Barr, A. J., Goodnight, J. H., Sall, J. R., and Helwig, J. T. SAS: Statistical Analysis System. Raleigh, North Carolina: SAS Institute Inc., 1976.

Box, G. E. P., and Jenkins, G. M. *Time series analysis*. San Francisco, California: Holden-Day, 1972.

Cover, T. M., and Hart, P. E. Nearest neighbor pattern classification. *IEEE Transactions on Information Theory*, 1967, **IT-13** (1), 21–27.

Cooley, W. W., and Lohnes, P. R. *Multivariate data analysis*. New York: Wiley, 1971.

Cooper, J. P., and Curtis, G. A. *ESP: econometric software package*. Chicago, Illinois: Graduate School of Business, Univ. of Chicago, 1976.

Dixon, W. J. (Ed.) *BMD biomedical computer programs*. Los Angeles, California: UCLA, 1967.

Dixon, W. J. (Ed.) *BMD biomedical computer programs*. Los Angeles, California: UCLA, 1973.

Dixon, W. J. (Ed.) *BMDP biomedical computer programs*. Los Angeles, California: UCLA, 1975.

Hall, C. E., and Cramer, E. M. *A general purpose program to compute multivariate analysis of variance on an IBM 7090 computer*, 2nd ed. George Washington University Biometric Laboratory, 1965 (now out of print).

Harman, H. H. *Modern factor analysis*. 2nd ed. Chicago, Illinois: University of Chicago, 1967.

Hartley, H. O. The modified Gauss-Newton method for the fitting on nonlinear regression functions by least square. *Technometrics*, 1961, **3**, No. 2, 269–280.

Inter-University Consortium for Political Research. OSIRIS III. University of Michigan, 1973.

Johnson, S. C. Hierarchical clustering schemes. *Psychometrika*, 1967, **32**, 241–254.

Joreskog, K. G. *Statistical estimation in factor analysis*. Stockholm: Almqvist and Wiksell, 1963.

Joreskog, K. G. Some contributions to maximum likelihood factor analysis. *Psychometrika*, 1967, **32**, 443–482.

Joreskog, K. G. A general approach to confirmatory maximum likelihood factor analysis. *Psychometrika*, 1969, **34**, 183–202.

Joreskog, K. G. A general method for analysis of covariance structures. *Biometrika*, 1970, **57**, 239–251.

Joreskog, K. G., and Goldberger, A. S. Factor analysis by generalized least squares. *Psychometrika*, 1972, **37**, 243–260.

Joreskog, G. D., and Sorbom, D. *LISREL III: estimation of linear structural equation systems by maximum likelihood methods*. Chicago, Illinois: National Educational Resources, 1976.

Kruskal, J. B. Multidimensional scaling: a numerical method. *Psychometrika*, 1964, **29**, 1–27. (a)

Kruskal, J. B. Multidimensional scaling by optimizing goodness of fit to a nonmetric hypothesis. *Psychometrika*, 1964, **29**, 115–129. (b)

Marquardt, D. W. An algorithm for least squares estimation of nonlinear parameters. *Journal of Society of Industrial Applications of Mathematics*, 1963, **11**, No. 2, 431–441.

Nie, N. H., Hull, G. H., Jenkins, J. G., Steinbrenner, K., and Brent, D. H. *SPSS: Statistical package for the social sciences*. New York: McGraw-Hill, 1975.

Ramsey, J. O. Maximum likelihood estimation in multidimensional scaling. *Psychometrika*, 1977, **42**, 241–266.

Shepard, R. N. The analysis of proximities: multidimensional scaling with an unknown distance function. I, II. *Psychometrika*, 1962, **27**, 125–140, 219–246.

Stein, C. A simple user's guide to LISREL. Department of Communications, Michigan State Univ., 1976.

Swamy, P. A. V. B. Efficient inference in a random coefficient regression model. *Econometrica*, 1970, **38**, 311–323.

Zellner, A., and Theil, H. Three-stage least squares: simultaneous estimation of simultaneous equations. *Econometrica*, 1962, **30**, 54–78.

INDEX